The Living God

The Living God

READINGS IN CHRISTIAN THEOLOGY

MILLARD J. ERICKSON, EDITOR

BAKER BOOK HOUSE
Grand Rapids, Michigan

TO MY FIRST-BORN DAUGHTER

KATHI

ISBN: 0-8010-3305-5

Fifth printing, February 1983

Copyright © 1973
Baker Book House Company

Printed in the United States of America

Preface

Necessity, it is said, is the mother of invention. In the case of this volume, this is certainly true. Over a period of several years of teaching introductory theology courses, my conviction deepened that the students ought to be exposed to the major issues of theology, and to a variety of theological perspectives. In the first years, this was handled through assigned readings in representative books placed on reserve. Later, with larger classes, it became apparent that there would be value in a common core of materials gathered into a single volume, which the students could read and discuss together. The present book is a result of that concern. It is intended to acquaint the student with a variety of theological literature in three areas often discussed in the early part of a basic course in Christian theology. It should assist the student, under the guidance of the instructor, in formulating his own position in interaction with these statements. It should also serve as a refresher and reference volume for ministers whose theology was studied sometime previously. The brief introductions are provided to place the readings in their contexts, not to substitute for their reading and interpretation.

A number of persons have helped to bring this work into being. My students in systematic theology at Bethel Theological Seminary during the fall quarters of 1970 and 1971 evaluated materials from which the present collection was chosen. I also sought the counsel of colleagues in theology in sister institutions, and several responded with constructive suggestions. Of particular helpfulness were comments from Professors Ralph Powell of North American Baptist Seminary, Gordon Lewis of Conservative Baptist Theological Seminary, and Kenneth Kantzer of Trinity Evangelical Divinity School. My own dean, Dr. Gordon Johnson, encouraged me to carry through this project, and helped make possible a pilot run with the materials. Mrs. Eileen Voth and Miss Kathy Lang typed the copy. My wife, Virginia, was of immense encouragement to me to persist in the task in the face of the numerous obstacles which were encountered. I appreciate the help of each one who in one way or another contributed to this undertaking. Its shortcomings are my responsibility alone.

I also wish to acknowledge the cooperation of the following who have granted permission to reprint copyrighted materials: James Nisbet, *The Authority of the Bible;* Harper and Row, *A Theology of the*

Living Church; The Society for Promoting Christian Knowledge, *Kerygma and Myth;* University of Chicago Press, *Systematic Theology;* Westminster Press, *New Directions in Theology Today,* Vol. I, *The Case for a New Reformation Theology,* and *Honest to God;* Garnstone Press, *Natural Theology;* T. & T. Clark, "The Attributes of God in the Light of Process-Thought"; Holt, Rinehart and Winston, *Basic Christian Doctrines;* Judson Press, *The Christian Religion in its Doctrinal Expression;* Presbyterian and Reformed Publishing Company, *The Defense of the Faith; Christianity Today,* "The Meaning of Religious Language," "Criteria of Biblical Inerrancy," and "The Reality and Identity of God"; Wm. B. Eerdmans Publishing Co., *Special Revelation and the Word of God, The Pattern of Religious Authority, Systematic Theology, The Providence of God,* and *Revelation and Inspiration;* Muhlenberg Press, *The Moment Before God;* Dr. Charles W. Lowry, *The Trinity and Christian Devotion;* Dr. Dewey Beegle, *The Inspiration of Scripture;* Dr. Merrill Tenney, *The Word for This Century.*

MILLARD J. ERICKSON

Arden Hills, Minnesota
September, 1972

The Authors

Charles Hodge was professor of didactic theology and New Testament exegesis at Princeton Theological Seminary from 1822 until his death in 1878. The selection reprinted here is from his magnum opus, *Systematic Theology* (1871-73).

Edgar Y. Mullins served as professor of theology and as president of Southern Baptist Theological Seminary during the first quarter of the twentieth century. *The Christian Religion in its Doctrinal Expression* was published in 1917.

L. Harold DeWolf, after many years at Boston University School of Theology, became professor of systematic theology and dean of Wesley Theological Seminary, Washington, D.C. He published *A Theology of the Living Church* in 1953.

William Hordern is president of Lutheran Theological Seminary, Saskatoon, Canada. He formerly taught at Garrett Theological Seminary. His *Case for a New Reformation Theology* was one of a trilogy published by Westminster Press in 1959. He is editor of the series, *New Directions in Theology Today,* and the author of the introductory volume, published in 1966.

Cornelius Van Til is professor emeritus of apologetics at Westminster Theological Seminary, where he taught for over forty years. *The Defense of the Faith* was first published in 1955.

Paul Tillich spent the major portion of his teaching career at Union Theological Seminary, New York, as professor of systematic theology. *Systematic Theology,* volume I, was published in 1951.

Rudolf Bultmann's teaching was done in New Testament at the University of Marburg, Germany. In 1941 his essay, "The New Testament and Mythology," served to define the method of demythologization.

Jerry Gill, professor of philosophy, Florida Presbyterian College, published "The Meaning of Religious Language" in *Christianity Today,* January, 1965.

Thomas Aquinas's writings cast the shape of Roman Catholic theology for many centuries. His teaching career was spent at the University of Paris. He worked on the *Summa Theologica* from 1265 until his death in 1274.

Karl Barth is widely regarded as the father of neo-orthodoxy. He taught at the Universities of Gottingen, Bonn, and Basel. His "No!", a rejoinder to Emil Brunner, first appeared in German in 1934.

John Calvin was the great theological systematizer of the Swiss Reformation. The first edition of his *Institutes of the Christian Religion* was written in 1536. The final edition, from which this selection is taken, appeared in 1559.

Kenneth Kantzer is dean and professor of Biblical and systematic theology at Trinity Evangelical Divinity School, Deerfield, Illinois. His essay on the authority of the Bible was part of a volume issued on the centennial of Wheaton College (Illinois), in 1960.

Bernard Ramm is professor of systematic theology and Christian apologetics, The American Baptist Seminary of the West, Covina, California. He authored *The Pattern of Religious Authority* in 1957 and *Special Revelation and the Word of God* in 1961.

Benjamin B. Warfield was professor of didactic and polemic theology at Princeton Theological Seminary. "The Biblical Idea of Inspiration" was written for *The International Standard Bible Encyclopedia* in 1915. "The Real Problem of Inspiration" is from *The Presbyterian and Reformed Review,* 1893.

James Orr served as professor of apologetics and theology in Glasgow College of the United Free Church of Scotland. *Revelation and Inspiration* was first published in 1910.

Charles H. Dodd taught New Testament at a number of schools, most notably Oxford and Cambridge. *The Authority of the Bible* was written in 1928.

Dewey Beegle is professor of Old Testament at Wesley Theological Seminary, Washington, D.C. *The Inspiration of Scripture* came from his pen in 1963.

Everett F. Harrison was one of the charter faculty members of Fuller Theological Seminary and is now senior professor of New Testament there. The article "Criteria of Biblical Inerrancy" appeared in *Christianity Today,* January, 1957.

John A. T. Robinson is bishop of Woolwich, England. His widely read *Honest to God* appeared in 1963.

Louis Berkhof was professor of dogmatic theology and president of Calvin Theological Seminary. He authored *Systematic Theology* in 1938.

Borden P. Bowne developed the philosophy of personalism during his years as professor of philosophy at Boston University. He wrote *The Immanence of God* in 1905.

Martin Heinecken was professor of systematic theology at Lutheran Theological Seminary, Philadelphia. *The Moment Before God* (1956) is an interpretation of the thought of the Danish theologian-philosopher Soren Kierkegaard (1813-1855).

Norman Pittenger, for many years professor of apologetics, General Theological Seminary, New York, is now lecturer in divinity, Cambridge University, England. A leading advocate of process thought, his article appeared in *The Expository Times* in October, 1969.

Carl F. H. Henry, after several years as editor-in-chief of *Christianity Today,* is visiting professor of theology at Eastern Baptist Theological Seminary. His two-part analysis of process thought in *Christianity Today,* March, 1969, is reprinted here.

Charles Lowry, formerly director of the Foundation for Religious Action, Washington, D.C., is minister of the Village Chapel, Pinehurst, North Carolina. *The Trinity and Christian Devotion* is dated 1946.

St. Augustine, one of the great formulators of Christian theology, was bishop of Hippo, North Africa. Among his many works was *The Trinity* (probably begun about 400 and completed about 416).

Samuel Wakefield, a nineteenth century Arminian theologian, wrote his *Complete System of Christian Theology* in 1869.

Harold Kuhn is professor of philosophy of religion at Asbury Seminary. His article, "Creation," first appeared in *Christianity Today* in May, 1961, and was later reprinted in *Basic Christian Doctrines.*

G. C. Berkouwer, a leading continental conservative theologian, is professor of systematic theology at the Free University, Amsterdam. One of a series of *Studies in Dogmatics, The Providence of God* appeared in 1952.

Contents

Part One

What Theology Is

Editor's Introduction

Theology means many different things to many different persons. Basic to most definitions, however, is the idea that the task of theology is to state, in some intelligible and orderly fashion, the doctrines of Christianity. The precise tactics and objectives of theology will vary from one period to another, and among theologians at a given time. Because theology does not function in a vacuum, it is essential that the mood of a particular time be understood, in constructing a theology.

The study of theological method can be pursued in either of two ways: didactic and formally, or inductively and indirectly. In a didactic approach, a theologian states or describes his methodology, explaining his philosophy or theory of theological method, and his procedures. An inductive approach, on the other hand, would not concern itself with what theologians *say* about how they do theology, but rather with how they *do* it. In this anthology, both techniques are employed. This first section contains selections from theologians expounding their theological methodology. The later units supply us with actual samples of theological work.

We turn to three articles attempting to characterize the method of systematic theology. Charles Hodge represents a classical orthodox position as a member of the Princeton Seminary nineteenth-century Reformed theology. Regarding the Bible as God's revelation in language to man, he considers theology an inductive endeavor. What nature is to the man of science, the Bible is to the theologian. It is his storehouse of facts, and the theologian's task to examine and compile those facts. In so doing, he makes certain assumptions, and follows definite methodological procedures. The Bible, and the Bible alone, is the source of theology, and the induction must be as complete as possible. The internal work of the Holy Spirit plays a vital role, as well. His work is not in the communication of new information, but rather in guiding the believer to the correct understanding of the source of his theology and the content of his faith.

Two significant issues of theological method have been addressed by Hodge, and need to be part of the agenda of any theology. The first is the source of the content of theology. For Hodge, this is restricted to the Bible. No other possible source really is considered. Further is the question of the treatment of the materials from which the content is drawn. Hodge's approach is not, in the modern sense of the term, critical. The task of the theologian is to understand and compile the Biblical material, not to evaluate it. Thus, in both of these dimensions, Hodge's method must be characterized as stressing the objective element. It is the content of the material, not the experience or the intellectual judgment of the theologian, that is the primary factor in theology. While the Holy Spirit has a part in the process, He does not contribute materially to the content of the message nor does He guide the theologian in evaluating what is correct and valid and what is not.

E. Y. Mullins, on the other hand, proposes an experiential approach. While the Bible is for him, as for Hodge, the prime source of doctrine, it is the Christian experience of these truths that affords the best understanding of them. This means that the study of God is not to be merely an abstract endeavor, but concerned with the relationship between God and man, as in the experience of redemption. Similarly, the apologetic for the deity of Christ would not merely be handled from the approach of historical proofs for the resurrection. It would include consideration of the effect of Christ's redeeming work in transforming man. In this respect Mullins's theology could be called more subjective than that of Hodge. What he seems to be seeking, however, is subjectivity without subjectivism.

L. Harold DeWolf brings yet another perspective to the discussion. DeWolf stands in the general tradition known as liberalism, although he would have to be considered a "reconstructed liberal," or a "neo-liberal." He emphasizes the role of reason in the theologizing process. He has been especially critical of neo-orthodoxy's "revolt against reason," as an early book of his was entitled. He differs from the other two men whose writings appear here, in several important respects. The first is the scope of the sources to be treated. In addition to the Bible, he intends to consult the history of Christianity, and relevant data drawn from other disciplines such as philosophy, psychology, sociology, and physics.

DeWolf also lays greater stress than do either Hodge or Mullins upon the critical role of the theologian in evaluating the traditions, rather than merely reporting them. Truth for Hodge is what the Bible asserts, and the theologian simply has to "mine it" from the Bible. For DeWolf, however, the Bible is a mixture of truth and human error. The truth must be sifted from the error, and the theologian is the one who carries the responsibility for this task of weighing the various elements in the traditions, and identifying them. This search for truth, he insists, must be pursued with dispassionate objectivity. Prejudice, sentiment, and tradition must not be allowed to impede the search for truth.

In one respect, this makes DeWolf's method more subjective than that of Mullins and even more so that of Hodge. The subject of theology (the theologian) does not simply accept the data; he scrutinizes and evaluates it. Yet, there is another sense in which the method of De-Wolf has to be characterized as objective, particularly when contrasted with Mullins's. The reason which DeWolf commends is a rather objective reason. Inward experience of doctrines plays a relatively minor role, and neither intuition nor some experiential witness of the Holy Spirit come in for any major consideration.

Another difficulty is found in the obvious change in the cultural situation from Biblical times until the present. This gap between the way people think now and the mind set of Biblical persons means that completely literal repetition of the Biblical language and concepts will probably result in some misunderstanding or at least incomplete understanding by the hearer. Since the church presumably has something to say to the world, it is faced with the problem of how best to say it.

This is the question that William Hordern poses in the selection from *New Directions in Theology Today:* the place of dialogue between Christian theology and the world. Hordern is fully conscious of the problem which the church has with the seeming irrelevance of its language. Those who hear the message do not regard it as true, or if they do, fail to see why this should have any significance for them, or worse yet, do not even understand what Christians are talking about. If this is indeed the case, contends Hordern, the church must enter into dialogue with the world. It must listen to the world and learn how it thinks, in order to speak effectively to it. If this is not done, there will be only monologue.

As he surveys the theological scene, Hordern notes two different types of attempts at dialogue with the world. The first group, which he terms "transformers," feels that the world has changed so radically and qualitatively that modern man can accept the Christian message only if it is radically altered. The transformer is willing to abandon or alter significant essentials of the faith if necessary, in order to communicate the message.

The other trend is signified by the translators." They believe that the essential content of the Christian message is to be retained, but that it may be necessary to find new ways of expressing this truth. The translators hold that to be of any value and effect, the church's message must tell the world something more than the world is telling itself. Translators recognize that even when the non-Christian fully understands the Christian message, acceptance of the matter is quite another matter and that there is a natural obstacle to faith—there are elements of the gospel message which are inherently repulsive to the nonbeliever. To eliminate these in order to remove the offense of the gospel would be to change the very nature of Christianity.

Not all theologians would fit within this translator-transformer schematism, however. Many who would accept the designation of fundamentalist would reject either of these approaches, because they seem to assume an ability of the natural or non-Christian man to comprehend and judge spiritual truth. Rather, what must be done is to simply declare, "Thus saith the Lord." No man can make the message intelligible or acceptable to the non-Christian. This must be accomplished by the Holy Spirit.

Although not a fundamentalist in the classical usage of that term, Cornelius Van Til represents this relatively nondialogical approach to the presentation of the message. A conservative theologian of strongly Calvinistic orientation, Van Til holds that man apart from Christ is basically sinful, and that the very core of this sinfulness is his autonomy: he regards himself as the standard and judge of truth. To present the Christian message to him as if he is capable of understanding and deciding upon its truth is to belie the message itself, which affirms his total depravity. What must rather be done is to tell him that he must make a total reversal of his life and thinking. He must accept the truth of what God has said about him. Only then can he really understand what Christianity is saying. From a very different perspective, that of neo-orthodoxy, Karl Barth has said some quite similar things. There is no "point of contact" in man for the reception of the message. It is only when God chooses to make the words become the Word of God that there is any reception of the gospel. "Dialogue" is hardly the word for these approaches to the world.

Although in actual practice Paul Tillich transforms the message, he lays down in the selection included here, a sort of blueprint for translating. The task of the theologian is twofold. He must make a philosophical analysis of the "situation" of the world. This is an existential expression in various cultural forms of the questions being asked by a given culture. It supplies the questions to which the theologian then correlates the answers derived from the pole of theological authority. This method of correlation is to characterize all of the doctrines which the theologian discusses. While the theological authority supplies the content, the analysis of the "existential situation" governs the form of expression which the message takes. He is critical of the liberal theology, which attempted to gain both form and content, question and answer, from the analysis. He also eschews the fundamentalist, who regards both the content and the form as fixed once and for all by the theological authority, which for the fundamentalist would be the Bible.

Rudolf Bultmann appears to qualify as one of Hordern's "transformers," although he seemingly disavows that nomenclature. He claims he is not giving a new meaning to the Christian message, but getting back to the true meaning and giving new expression to it. Yet, in so doing, he maintains that there is much in the New Testament that is mythological and untenable for today. What we must see, he argues, is that the New Testament is not attempting to give an objective account of history, or a theory of cosmology. Rather, it is a message of existential self-understanding. Many commentators have felt, however, that Bultmann has not merely given a new statement to the old message, but has actually stated a fundamentally different message.

The final problem discussed in this section is religious language. The earlier essay by Hordern pointed up the severity of this issue. Through the influence of the movement known as "logical positivism," the issue came into prominence. Logical positivism made it apparent that the meaning of religious language could not be demonstrated in the cognitive fashion of scientific language. This led to focus upon two problems, one more theoretical and the other more practical in character. The former was: Does religious language have meaning, and particularly does it have cognitive status? The latter was: Just how is the meaning of the religious language to be communicated? Some theologians have argued that the nature of religious language is unique. It is not a subdivision of some other type of language, such as the language of history or science. Others see at least an analogy for the religious usage of language in other forms of language use.

Jerry Gill describes the issue of religious language against the background of the fundamental problems raised by the logical positivists and those who followed in their tradition. He regards the challenge as still pertinent. There are, Gill observes, three types of responses to the challenge:

1. Those who accept the validity of the positivist critique, and who maintain that religious language is significant, but not cognitively (i.e., dealing with issues of what may be true or false). Rather, its meaning is emotional, ethical, or existential.

2. Those who argue for the cognitive meaning of religious language, but without claiming that it has empirical reference. They would challenge the contention that cognitive meaning is restricted to the empirical.

3. Those who would agree that cognitive meaning is dependent upon empirical reference, and who claim that religious language fulfills this criterion. They attempt to illustrate and demonstrate this empirical import of religious language.

Gill analyzes briefly some examples of each of these responses. He himself favors the third approach.

And so, we have been brought back to the point of beginning. The thelogian must ascertain from whence he derives the content of his message, how he goes about formulating it, how he understands what he means by it, and how he makes it meaningful to others. This is the foundation upon which the rest of the theological enterprise is built.

The Method and Material
of Theology

1

Charles Hodge

Systematic Theology: The Method

The Inductive Method

It is so called because it agrees in everything essential with the inductive method as applied to the natural sciences.

First, The man of science comes to the study of nature with certain assumptions. (1) He assumes the trustworthiness of his sense perceptions. Unless he can rely upon the well-authenticated testimony of his senses, he is deprived of all means of prosecuting his investigations. The facts of nature reveal themselves to our faculties of sense, and can be known in no other way. (2) He must also assume the trustworthiness of his mental operations. He must take for granted that he can perceive, compare, combine, remember, and infer; and that he can safely rely upon these mental faculties in their legitimate exercise. (3) He must also rely on the certainty of those truths which are not learned from experience, but which are given in the constitution of our nature. That every effect must have a cause; that the same cause under like circumstances, will produce like effects; that a cause is not

From Charles Hodge, *Systematic Theology*. Grand Rapids: Wm. B. Eerdmans Publishing Company, 1952.

a mere uniform antecedent, but that which contains within itself the reason why the effect occurs.

Second, The student of nature having this ground on which to stand, and these tools wherewith to work, proceeds to perceive, gather, and combine his facts. These he does not pretend to manufacture, nor presume to modify. He must take them as they are. He is only careful to be sure that they are real, and that he has them all, or, at least all that are necessary to justify any inference which he may draw from them, or any theory which he may build upon them.

Third, From facts thus ascertained and classified, he deduces the laws by which they are determined. That a heavy body falls to the ground is a familiar fact. Observation shows that it is not an isolated fact; but that all matter tends toward all other matter; that this tendency or attraction is in proportion to the quantity of matter; and its intensity decreases in proportion to the square of the distance of the attracting bodies. As all this is found to be universally and constantly the case within the field of observation, the mind is forced to conclude that there is some reason for it; in other words, that it is a law of nature which may be relied upon beyond the limits of actual observation. As this law has always operated in the past, the man of science is sure that it will operate in the future. It is in this way the vast body of modern science has been built up, and the laws which determine the motions of the heavenly bodies; the chemical changes constantly going on around us; the structure, growth, and propagation of plants and animals, have, to a greater or less extent, been ascertained and established. It is to be observed that these laws or general principles are not derived from the mind, and attributed to external objects, but derived or deduced from the objects and impressed upon the mind.

A. *The Inductive Method as Applied to Theology*

The Bible is to the theologian what nature is to the man of science. It is his store-house of facts; and his method of ascertaining what the Bible teaches, is the same as that which the natural philosopher adopts to ascertain what nature teaches. In the first place, he comes to his task with all the assumptions above mentioned. He must assume the validity of those laws of belief which God has impressed upon our nature. In these laws are included some which have no direct application to the natural sciences. Such, for example, as the essential distinction between right and wrong; that nothing contrary to virtue can be enjoined by God; that it cannot be right to do evil that good may come; that sin deserves punishment, and other similar first truths, which God has implanted in the constitution of all moral beings, and which no objective revelation can possibly contradict. These first principles, however, are not to be arbitrarily assumed. No man has a right to lay down his own opinions, however firmly held, and call them "first truths of reason," and make them the source or test of Christian doctrines. Nothing can rightfully be included under the category of first truths, or laws of belief, which cannot stand the tests of universality and necessity, to which many add self-evidence. But self-evidence is included in universality and necessity, in so far, that nothing which is not self-evident can be universally believed, and what is self-evident forces itself on the mind of every intelligent creature.

Facts to Be Collected

In the second place, the duty of the Christian theologian is to ascertain, collect, and combine all the facts which God has revealed concerning Himself and our relation to Him. These facts are all in the Bible. This is true, because everything revealed in nature, and in the constitution of man concerning God and our relation to Him, is contained and authenticated in Scripture. It is in this sense that "the Bible, and the Bible alone, is the religion of Protestants." It may be admitted that the truths which the theologian has to reduce to a science, or, to speak more humbly, which he has to arrange and harmonize, are revealed partly in the external works of God, partly in the constitution of our nature, and partly in the religious experience of believers; yet lest we should err in our inferences from the works of God, we have a clearer revelation of all that nature reveals, in his Word; and lest we should misinterpret our own consciousness and the laws of our nature, everything that can be legitimately learned from that source will be found recognized and authenticated in the Scriptures; and lest we should attribute to the teaching of the Spirit the operations of our own natural affections, we find in the Bible the norm and standard of all genuine religious experience. The Scriptures teach not only the truth, but what are the effects of the truth on the heart and conscience, when applied with saving power by the Holy Ghost.

The Theologian to Be Guided by the Same Rules as the Man of Science

In the third place, the theologian must be guided by the same rules in the collection of facts, as govern the man of science.

1. This collection must be made with diligence and care. It is not an easy work. There is in every department of investigation great liability to error. Almost all false theories in science and false doctrines in theology are due in a great degree to mistakes as to matters of fact. A distinguished naturalist said he repeated an experiment a thousand times before he felt authorized to announce the result to the scientific world as an established fact.

2. This collection of facts must not only be carefully conducted,

but also comprehensive, and if possible, exhaustive. An imperfect induction of facts led men for ages to believe that the sun moved round the earth, and that the earth was an extended plain. In theology a partial induction of particulars has led to like serious errors. It is a fact that the Scriptures attribute omniscience to Christ. From this it was inferred that He could not have had a finite intelligence, but that the Logos was clothed in Him with a human body with its animal life. But it is also a Scriptural fact that ignorance and intellectual progress, as well as omniscience, are ascribed to our Lord. Both facts, therefore, must be included in our doctrine of his person. We must admit that He had a human, as well as a divine intelligence. It is a fact that everything that can be predicated of a sinless man, is in the Bible, predicated of Christ; and it is also a fact that everything that it predicated of God is predicated of our Lord; hence it has been inferred that there were two Christs,—two persons,—the one human, the other divine, and that they dwelt together very much as the Spirit dwells in the believer; or, as evil spirits dwelt in demoniacs. But this theory overlooked the numerous facts which prove the individual personality of Christ. It was the same person who said, "I thirst;" who said, "Before Abraham was I am." The Scriptures teach that Christ's death was designed to reveal the love of God, and to secure the reformation of men. Hence Socinus denied that his death was an expiation for sin, or satisfaction of justice. The latter fact, however, is as clearly revealed as the former; and therefore both must be taken into account in our statement of the doctrine concerning the design of Christ's death.

Necessity of a Complete Induction

Illustrations without end might be given of the necessity of a comprehensive induction of facts to justify our doctrinal conclusions. These facts must not be willfully denied or carelessly overlooked, or unfairly appreciated. We must be honest here, as the true student of nature is honest in his induction. Even scientific men are sometimes led to suppress or to pervert facts which militate against their favorite theories; but the temptation to this form of dishonesty is far less in their case, than in that of the theologian. The truths of religion are far more important than those of natural science. They come home to the heart and conscience. They may alarm the fears or threaten the hopes of men, so that they are under strong temptation to overlook or pervert them. If, however, we really desire to know what God has revealed we must be conscientiously diligent and faithful in collecting the facts which He has made known, and in giving them their due weight. If a geologist should find in a deposit of early date implements of human workmanship, he is not allowed to say they are natural productions. He must either revise his conclusion as to the age of the deposit, or carry back to an earlier period the existence of man. There is no help for it. Science cannot make facts; it must take them as they are. In like manner, if the Bible asserts that Christ's death was a satisfaction to justice, the theologian is not allowed to merge justice into benevolence in order to suit his theory of the atonement. If the Scriptures teach that men are born in sin, we cannot change the nature of sin, and make it a tendency to evil and not really sin, in order to get rid of difficulty. If it be a Scriptural fact that the soul exists in a state of conscious activity between death and the resurrection, we must not deny this fact or reduce this conscious activity to zero, because our anthropology teaches that the soul has no individuality and no activity without a body. We must take the facts of the Bible as they are, and construct our system so as to embrace them all in their integrity.

Principles to Be Deduced from Facts

In the fourth place, in theology as in natural science, principles are derived from facts, and not impressed upon them. The properties of matter, the laws of motion, of magnetism, of light, etc., are not framed by the mind. They are not laws of thought. They are deductions from facts. The investigator sees, or ascertains by observation, what are the laws which determine material phenomena; he does not invent those laws. His speculations on matters of science unless sustained by facts, are worthless. It is no less unscientific for the theologian to asume a theory as to the nature of virtue, of sin, of liberty, or moral obligation, and then explain the facts of Scripture in accordance with his theories. His only proper course is to derive his theory of virtue, of sin, of liberty, of obligation, from the facts of the Bible. He should remember that his business is not to set forth his system of truth (that is of no account), but to ascertain and exhibit what is God's system, which is a matter of the greatest moment. If he cannot believe what the facts of the Bible assume to be true, let him say so. Let the sacred writers have their doctrine, while he has his own. To this ground a large class of modern exegetes and theologians, after a long struggle, have actually come. They give what they regard as the doctrines of the Old Testament; then those of the Evangelists; then those of the Apostles; and then their own. This is fair. So long, however, as the binding authority of Scripture is acknowledged, the temptation is very strong to press the facts of the Bible into accordance with our preconceived theories. If a man be persuaded that certainty in acting is inconsistent with liberty of action; that a free agent can always act contrary to any amount of influence (not destructive of his liberty) brought to bear upon him, he will inevitably deny that the Scriptures teach the contrary, and thus be forced to explain away all facts which prove the absolute control of God over the will and volitions of men. If he hold that sinfulness can be predicated only of intelligent, voluntary action in contravention of law, he must deny that men are born in sin, let the Bible teach what it may. If he believes that ability limits obligation, he must believe independently of the Scriptures, or in opposition to them, it matters not which, that men are able to repent, believe, love God perfectly, to live without sin, at any, and all times, without the least assistance from the Spirit of God. If he deny that the innocent may justly suffer penal evil for the guilty, he must deny that Christ bore our sins. If he deny that the merit of one man can be the judicial ground of the pardon and salvation of other men, he must reject the Scriptural doctrine of justification. It is plain that complete havoc must be made of the whole system of revealed truth, unless we consent to derive our philosophy from the Bible, instead of explaining the Bible by our philosophy. If the Scriptures teach that sin is hereditary, we must adopt a theory of sin suited to that fact. If they teach that men cannot repent, believe, or do anything spiritually good, without the supernatural aid of the Holy Spirit, we must make our theory of moral obligation accord with that fact. If the Bible teaches that we bear the guilt of Adam's first sin, that Christ bore our guilt, and endured the penalty of the law in our stead, these are facts with which we must make our principles agree. It would be easy to show that in every department of theology,—in regard to the nature of God, his relation to the world, the plan of salvation, the person and work of Christ, the nature of sin, the operations of divine grace, men, instead of taking the facts of the Bible, and seeing what principles they imply, what philosophy underlies them, have adopted their philosophy independently of the Bible, to which the facts of the Bible are made to bend. This is utterly unphilosophical. It is the fundamental principle of all sciences, and of theology among the rest, that theory is to be determined by facts, and not facts by theory. As natural science was a chaos until the principle of induction was admitted and faithfully carried out, so theology is a jumble of human speculations, not worth a straw, when men refuse to apply the same principle to the study of the Word of God.

The Scriptures Contain All the Facts of Theology

This is perfectly consistent, on the one hand, with the admission of intuitive truths, both intellectual and moral, due to our constitution as rational and moral beings; and, on the other hand, with the controlling power over our beliefs exercised by the inward teachings of the Spirit, or, in other words, by our religious experience. And that for two reasons: First, All truth must be consistent. God cannot contradict himself. He cannot force us by the constitution of the nature which He has given us to believe one thing, and in his Word command us to believe the opposite. And, second, All the truths taught by the constitution of our nature or by religious experience, are recognized and authenticated in the Scriptures. This is a safeguard and a limit. We cannot assume this or that principle to be intuitively true, or this or that conclusion to be demonstrably certain, and make them a standard to which the Bible must conform. What is self-evidently true, must be proved to be so, and is always recognized in the Bible as true. Whole systems of theologies are founded upon intuitions, so called, and if every man is at liberty to exalt his own intuitions, as men are accustomed to call their strong convictions, we should have as many theologies in the world as there are thinkers. The same remark is applicable to religious experience. There is no form of conviction more intimate and irresistible than that which arises from the inward teaching of the Spirit. All saving faith rests on his testimony or demonstrations (I Cor. 2:4). Believers have an unction from the Holy One, and they know the truth, and that no lie (or false doctrine) is of the truth. This inward teaching produces a conviction which no sophistries can obscure, and no arguments can shake. It is founded on consciousness, and you might as well argue a man out of a belief of his existence, as out of confidence that what he is thus taught of God is true. Two things, however, are to be borne in mind. First, That this inward teaching or demonstration of the Spirit is confined to truths objectively revealed in the Scriptures. It is given, says the Apostle, in order that we may know things gratuitously given, i.e., revealed to us by God in his Word (I Cor. 2:10-16). It is not, therefore, a revelation of new truths, but an illumination of the mind, so that it apprehends the truth, excellence, and glory of things already revealed. And second, This experience is depicted in the Word of God. The Bible gives us not only the facts concerning God, and Christ, ourselves, and our relations to our Maker and Redeemer, but also records the legitimate effects of those truths on the minds of believers. So that we cannot appeal to our own feelings or inward experience, as a ground or guide, unless we can show that it agrees with the experience of holy men as recorded in the Scriptures.

The Teaching of the Spirit

Although the inward teaching of the Spirit, or religious experience, is no substitute for an external revelation, and is no part of the rule of faith, it is, nevertheless, an invaluable guide in determining what the rule of faith teaches. The distinguishing feature of Augustinianism as taught by Augustin himself, and by the purer theologians of the Latin Church throughout the Middle Ages, which was set forth by the Reformers, and especially by Calvin and the Geneva divines, is that the inward teaching of the Spirit is allowed its proper place in determining our theology. The question is not first and mainly, What is true to the understanding, but what is true to the renewed heart? The effort is not to make the assertions of the Bible harmonize with the speculative reason, but to subject our feeble reason to the mind of God as revealed in his Word, and by his Spirit in our inner life. It might be easy to lead men to the conclusion that they are responsible only for their voluntary acts, if the appeal is made solely to the understanding. But if the appeal be made to every man's, and especially to every Christian's inward experience, the opposite conclusion is reached. We are convinced of the sinfulness of states of mind as well as of voluntary acts, even when those states are not the effect of our own agency, and are not subject to the power of the will. We are conscious of being sold under sin; of being its slaves; of being possessed by it as a power or law, immanent, innate, and beyond our control. Such is the doctrine of the Bible, and such is the teaching of our religious consciousness when under the influence of the Spirit of God. The true method in theology requires that the facts of religious experience should be accepted as facts, and when duly authenticated by Scripture, be allowed to interpret the doctrinal statements of the Word of God. So legitimate and powerful is this inward teaching of the Spirit, that it is no uncommon thing to find men having two theologies,—one of the intellect, and another of the heart. The one may find expression in creeds and systems of divinity, the other in their prayers and hymns. It would be safe for a man to resolve to admit into his theology nothing which is not sustained by the devotional writings of true Christians of every denomination. It would be easy to construct from such writings, received and sanctioned by Romanists, Lutherans, Reformed, and Remonstrants, a system of Pauline or Augustinian theology, such as would satisfy any intelligent and devout Calvinist in the world.

The true method of theology, is, therefore, the inductive, which assumes that the Bible contains all the facts or truths which form the contents of theology, just as the facts of nature are the contents of the natural sciences. It is also assumed that the relation of these Biblical facts to each other, the principles involved in them, the laws which determine them, are in the facts themselves, and are to be deduced from them, just as the laws of nature are deduced from the facts of nature. In neither case are the principles derived from the mind and imposed upon the facts, but equally in both departments, the principles or laws are deduced from the facts and recognized by the mind.

2

Edgar Y. Mullins

Religion and Theology

Twofold Aim

The aim of this treatise is twofold: first, to set forth the contents of the Christian religion; and, secondly, to set forth the doctrines of the religion which arise out of it and which are necessary to explain its meaning.

The aim implies a necessary connection between religion and theology. Theology has often been defined as the science which treats of God. This definition is based on the derivation of the word from the Greek words meaning God (*Theos*) and reason (*logos*). But Christian theology is something more than the science which treats of God. It also includes in its field of investigation man's relations to God. The reason for this wider definition of Christian theology becomes clear when we consider the nature of Christianity. The Christian religion is not a theory or speculation about God. It is more than deductions from objective facts concerning his nature and attributes. These are not altogether excluded from Christian theology, but they are not its foundations nor the chief elements of its content. Pri-

From Edgar Y. Mullins, *The Christian Religion in its Doctrinal Expression*. Philadelphia: Judson Press, 1917. Used by permission.

marily religion is man's relations to the divine Being. It involves fellowship and obedience on man's part, and self-revelation on God's part. It is a form of experience and of life. It is an order of facts. Theology is the systematic and scientific explanation of this order of facts. Sometimes the term theology is used in a narrower sense, meaning the doctrine of God as distinguished from the doctrine of man, or the doctrine of sin or the doctrine of salvation, or other particular doctrines. This, however, is not in conflict with what has just been said as to the general use of the word. It has come to mean the whole range of doctrines regarding God in his relations to man.

This meaning appears in the use of the term in various departments of theology. When we speak of the theology of the Old Testament we mean the systematic exposition of the truths about God and his revelations to man arising out of the life and experience of God's people in the Old Testament history. New Testament theology means the corresponding truths given in the life and religion of the actors and writers of the New Testament. The Pauline or Johannine theology means the truths found in the writings of Paul or John. In general, biblical theology is the scientific exposition of the theology of the Bible unmixed with speculative or other elements drawn from physical nature or the human reason. But in every instance mentioned, theology covers all the relations between God and man. It is not limited to the doctrine of the divine nature or attributes. Systematic theology is the orderly and harmonious presentation of the truths of theology with a view to unity and completeness. Reason may supply certain elements in such presentation which would be inappropriate in a rigidly biblical method of treatment. Historical theology traces the stages in the development of doctrines through the Christian centuries, with a view to showing their inner connections from age to age.

Another method of dealing with the doctrines of the Christian religion is that which gives prominence to Christian experience. It is the method adopted in this work.

In principle the experiential way of dealing with Christian doctrine has been employed in every vital and living system which has been produced since New Testament times. But in most cases it has been implicit rather than explicit. Christian experience has been tacitly assumed. It is the principle which animates all the biblical writers of both the Old and New Testaments. It is the source of power in the writings of an Augustine, a Clement, a Schleiermacher. All theology must be vitalized by experience before it can become a real force for the regeneration of men.

But when we speak of making experience explicit in expounding the doctrines of Christianity, we are by no means adopting that as the sole criterion of truth. He would be a very unwise man who should attempt to deduce all Christian doctrine from his own subjective experience. As we shall soon see, Christianity is a historical religion. Jesus Christ is its sole founder and supreme authority as the revealer of God. The Scriptures are our only source of authoritative information about Christ and his earthly career. These are fundamental to any correct understanding of our religion.

When, therefore, we speak of making Christian experience explicit as a principle in theological statement, we are simply seeking to understand Christianity first of all as a religion. We certainly cannot know the meaning of the religion until we know what the religion is. There are ways of handling Christian doctrine which lead away from the truth. A theologian may adopt some abstract logical or philosophical principle and construct a system having but slight connection with the New Testament. To avoid this error the best recourse is the religion of the New Testament itself.

It will be noted, then, that the clear recognition in doctrinal discussion of the experience of Christians does not render theology less biblical, or less systematic, or less historical. The Bible is the greatest of all books of religious experience. The theology of its great writers is all, in a sense, the expression of their experience under the guidance of God's Holy Spirit. Paul's conversion was a formative influence in all his doctrinal teachings.

Again, our treatment is none the less systematic because it is experiential. We may be more cautious in drawing logical and philosophical inferences from doctrines revealed and known in experience. But this does not at all hinder a systematic arrangement and exposition of doctrine.

So also while the limits of space and method of treatment forbid any general review of the history of doctrine, the entire treatment of theology here represented implies the historical background and the whole course of doctrinal development through the Christian centuries.

We may now sum up in a general way the factors which must be taken into account if we are to understand the Christian religion and the doctrinal teachings which arise out of it.

First of all, we must recognize Jesus Christ as the historical revelation of God to men. What he is in himself, and what he means for our faith, are truths which must await development at a later stage of this book. But Christianity is bound up indissolubly with the facts of the historical Jesus.

Secondly, we must assign to their proper place the Scriptures of the New Testament as the indispensable source of our knowledge of the historical Jesus and his work for our salvation.

In the third place, we must recognize the place and work of the Holy Spirit in the hearts of men. He continues the work of Christ. It is through him that we are led to accept Christ. It is in and through him that the meaning of the Christian facts is brought home to us.

Fourthly, we must seek to define and understand the spiritual experiences of Christians as subject to the operation of God's Spirit revealing Christ to them. The history of doctrine will aid in this, but we must make also a direct study of experience itself.

Now it is in the combination and union of all these factors, and not in any one or two of them taken by themselves, that we find what we seek when we undertake a systematic study of the Christian religion and its theology. We may specify some of the advantages of this method of study in the following statements:

1. It enables us to avoid a false intellectualism in theology. It keeps theology properly anchored to facts and their meaning. It requires little discernment to see that systematic theologies which are chiefly concerned with the logical or philosophical relations between truths in a unified order, may easily overlook vital interests of the spiritual life. The Scriptures rarely present truth in this way. They never present it apart from the vital needs of the soul. The sense of proportion in the emphasis upon truth may be easily lost in our admiration for the harmony and beauty of a systematic arrangement. A single doctrine or conception, such as the sovereignty of God, or election, or human freedom, may be given a dominating position and all other truths modified to make them conform. Theological controversy may lead to one-sided systems. Thus Calvinism and Arminianism have sometimes taken on extreme forms and have led to unfortunate results. Other issues, more common in modern times, produce the same reactions to extreme forms of statement.

Now when the interests of life and experience are made explicit, many errors of this kind are avoided. So also a restraint is felt thus which prevents too great license in speculative and metaphysical deductions from biblical truths. We cannot have theology without metaphysics, but our metaphysics should arise out of the data supplied by the Scriptures and understood through our living experience of God in Christ.

2. The method also affords the necessary fact basis for the scientific presentation of the truths of Christian theology. The finest thing in the modern scientific spirit is its demand for facts and its painstaking and conscientious interpretation of facts. The desire to know reality as it is in itself and not as we wish it to be, combined with the patient effort to express exactly its meaning, is of the essence of the scientific spirit. Now this motive and aim are most welcome to those who would study the Christian religion and who would express its meaning in a system of theology.

It is clear, upon reflection, that all the factors named are essential to such a thoroughgoing study of the Christian religion. If we study the historical Jesus apart from the other factors mentioned, we never get beyond a problem of history. If we devote ourselves solely to the study of the Scriptures by means of the most approved critical and scientific methods, we never rise above the issues involved in literary and historical criticism, or at best in questions of exegesis. In neither case do we rise to the level of religion itself. Again, if we grow weary of historical and exegetical study and devote ourselves to the work of the Holy Spirit in our hearts, to the exclusion of the other factors, we do indeed come to the study of religion. But under these conditions it is not and cannot be the Christian religion in its fulness and power. We cannot dispense with Christ, and we are indissolubly bound to the Scriptures in any attempt to understand that religious experience we call Christian.

Two fundamental questions arise at the outset in any adequate study of the Christian religion. One relates to Jesus Christ. Who is Jesus, and what is he to men? The other relates to our experience of God's redeeming power in the soul. What is the relation of Jesus Christ to that experience? Those questions inevitably lead back to the question of the New Testament, the historical source of our information about Christ. They also lead back to the work of God's Spirit in our hearts. Hence we conclude that all four of the factors named are essential to a scientific study of the Christian religion.

In the light of these statements we see how defective are some efforts which are called scientific, to express the meaning of Christianity. Numerous attempts have been made to set forth "the essence of Christianity." It is not our purpose here to dwell upon these at length. But usually they are efforts to extract from the Gospel records some small remainder of what is held to be the religion of the New Testament by Christians generally, and cast away the other elements as worthless. Of course it is always open to any one to raise the question whether the original gospel has been perverted. But too often efforts of this kind fail to take account of all the elements in the problem. Christianity cannot be reduced to a simple problem of historical criticism. The facts involved have a much wider range. Again, Christianity cannot be construed under the guidance of some previously formed world-view of philosophy of the universe. We must begin with the facts in their totality and reckon with them. This is simply another way of saying that we must adopt the scientific method of dealing with the question.

3. Again, the method gives the best apologetic foundation for a system of theology. The term apologetics is perhaps not the most appropriate one for designating the scientific defense of the Christian religion against attack. But it has come into general use for this purpose and is well enough understood. Apologetics is, of course, a distinct department of theology, and calls for discussion of some problems which cannot be treated in systematic theology. And yet the latter requires a sound apologetic foundation in order to maintain itself among other sciences. The method adopted in this work affords the strongest apologetic foundation for theology because it emphasizes the facts of history and of experience. A comparison with some

of the older apologetic defenses will show this. We name a few of these:

(1) The proof of God's existence from the phenomena of the universe has long been a favorite method. It possesses, no doubt, elements of great strength. But along with these there are elements of weakness. Logical deduction from physical phenomena lends itself to many theories of the universe. Each of them claims to be most in accord with the facts. There results always an unstable equilibrium of theories. None of them satisfies fully. Immanuel Kant held that we cannot know what is behind the phenomena. We can only know reality in its manifestations. And so long as we are limited to deductive reasoning from data objective to the mind itself there is much truth in his view. That which arises is a high degree of probability rather than knowledge in the strict sense, when we reason deductively to prove God's existence. But for the Christian who recognizes the reality and meaning of his experience of God in Christ a new kind of knowledge of God arises. The "proofs" are transferred from the world without to the world within. Thus direct knowledge of God arises.

(2) Again, the proof of Christianity from miracles has always been questioned by many of the devotees of physical science. Christians have rightly replied that the objections were not well founded. But here again the proof resides in the realm of a remote history. Debate continues indefinitely because preference or preconception determines the view adopted. It is most probable that Christians themselves are not convinced entirely by the logical demonstration based on the reliability of the New Testament witnesses. Unconsciously they have been influenced by their own experience of a supernatural power working in them and redeeming them. It is easy to believe the New Testament miracles if the same power is known as a personal and vital experience. If then we make clear and explicit what that experience is, and combine it with the witness of the well-supported historical records, we have a much more powerful argument from miracles.

(3) The deity of Christ has been employed as a means of establishing the truth of Christianity. A powerful argument is constructed from the witness of Jesus to himself, from the impression he made on others, from his resurrection, from his place and power in Christian history, and in other ways. But when to these considerations we add the facts as to Christ's redeeming power in men, we have greatly increased the strength of the appeal to his divinity.

The above will suffice to show the nature of the apologetic foundation which is laid for theology when the redemptive experience of God in Christ is made explicit and clear as an essential factor in the interpretation of Christianity. This does not by any means imply that we are henceforth done with history or logical proofs, or any of the ordinary processes by which the mind works out its conclusions. It only implies that from the center of a well-founded history, as interpreted in the light of a divinely inwrought experience, we may properly estimate the value of all the proofs. The Christian religion as a power in the soul, redeeming and transforming it, is its own best evidence.

4. The method adopted has a further advantage in that it enables us to show the reality, the autonomy, and freedom of the Christian religion. These are great demands which the modern world makes upon religion. A scientific age has given rise to a passionate demand for the real in the study of all subjects. Make-believes and shams of all kinds are subject to the most rigid scrutiny and criticism. Nothing can long remain secure which cannot endure the fierce heat and light of ruthless investigation. The religion of Christ welcomes this. It is the glory of Christ that he made the spiritual universe real to men. He brought God home to their souls. Those who know God in Christ find in him the supreme reality.

The religion of Christ is autonomous. This means that it has its resources in itself. The Christian has the guidance of God's Spirit when in humility he seeks it. He acquires a relation to and knowledge of the Bible which is for him most convincing and conclusive. He has the witness in himself. His faith performs for him a service, secures for him a power, brings to him a blessedness and a peace which he finds in no other way. The conflict between flesh and spirit, between the visible and invisible, between the temporal and eternal order, is reconciled and overcome in Christ. He does not value other forms of human activity less than he did before, but rather more. But he sees that religion is the supreme value of life, the supreme function of the soul. In it all else, art, science, education, philosophy, are transformed into new forms of development and of ministry. But he also sees that they all find their completion and fulfilment in religion itself.

The religion of Christ is free. It is not subject to the rule of any form of human culture alien to itself. It is in conflict with no legitimate activity of man. Each great department of life has its special method, its great underlying principle. Physical science works with the principle of causality. Philosophy employs that of rationality. Religion deals with personality. God and man in relations of mutual love and service are the great realities with which it deals. There is no conflict between any of these, as we shall see. It arises only when one of these spheres undertakes to rule the other.

As autonomous and free, and as dealing with the greatest of all realities, the Christian religion in every age of the world comes to redeem men. They accept it under the conditions of their own age, confronted by their own difficulties and problems. Hence arises the need for restating its doctrines in terms of the living experience of each generation. Human creeds are valuable as such expressions. But they do not serve all the ends of doctrine. We must ever return to the Scriptures for new inspiration. We must ever ask anew the questions as to Christ and his relations to the needs of each generation. He does not change. His religion is the same in all ages. But our difficulties and problems are shaped anew by the forms of life which ever change about us. Hence we must revitalize our faith by deepening our communion with God and witnessing to his power in us.

5. The experiential method of dealing with Christian truth helps in defining the nature of the authority of the Bible. The Bible, against tradition and against the authority of the papal system, was one of the watchwords of the Reformation. Protestantism has from the beginning made the Bible the authoritative source of the knowledge of the gospel of Christ. Opponents have urged objections to the biblical authority on various grounds. It has been objected that the Bible is not infallible and hence cannot be an authority. The existence of textual errors, scientific, or historical deviations from exact truth, discrepancies of various kinds, proves that the Bible cannot be accepted as an infallible guide in religion, so it was argued. Christian apologists used to expend great energy and pains in answering all of these charges. Finally they came to see that the objector demanded more than faith required. We are not bound to prove in a way which compels assent that the Bible is the supreme authority for Christian faith. Such proof would not produce faith at all. It could only produce intellectual assent. The Christian's acceptance of the Bible arises in another way. It comes to him in "demonstration of the Spirit and of power." It is the life in him which answers to the life the Scriptures reveal which convinces him. So that the Bible is not for him an authority on all subjects, but in religion it is final and authoritative. At this stage the objector took a further step and urged that no authority which is external to the soul can be accepted. Truth must be assimilated and understood, not imposed by authority of any kind, whether pope or church or Bible. The Christian then framed his reply on the basis of his own inner experience. He urged that the very essence of the redemption he knows in Christ is inwardly assimilated truth and actual knowledge of the great spiritual realities. He proceeded to define and expound the truth thus inwardly known and assimilated. But then the objector gave the argument another turn entirely. He charged that the alleged knowledge of the Christian was merely inward and subjective. It was lacking in objective reality, and hence was unreliable. Of course these objections contradict each other. . . .

Now the Christian rises above and overcomes both forms of the objection by insisting that it is in the union and combination of the objective source and the subjective experience that certainty and assurance are found. He is no less interested in objective reality than his opponent. He is no less interested in inward assimilation of truth. But he finds both in the religion of Christ. He finds Jesus Christ to be for him the supreme revelation of God's redeeming grace. He finds the Scriptures the authoritative source of his knowledge of that revelation. And then he finds in his own soul that working of God's grace which enables him to know Christ and to understand the Scriptures. Thus the objective and subjective elements find a unity and harmony which is entirely satisfying.

Now if the opposite method is pursued and either the Bible or experience is taken alone, no such finality is possible. If the Bible is considered in an intellectual way merely, apart from the experience of God's redeeming grace in Christ, then again we have a recurrence of the old debate on grounds of history and criticism. Theories are then framed according to mental prepossessions, and unity of view is impossible. Again, if experience is taken apart from the history, the old charge of subjectivism at once recurs. Hence, for the Christian there is no finally convincing and satisfying view except in the combination of the two elements. For the opponent of the Christian view this also makes the strongest appeal. There is an inward reality which corresponds to objective facts of history. God's approach to man in and through Christ finds its reaction in man's response. Faith completes the union, and the life of God flows into the life of man and transforms it.

3

L. Harold DeWolf

The Task of Theology

In the midst of the world's tyranny, oppression and fear a wonderful story once began and spread like wildfire from village to village and from nation to nation. Those who told it called it "the good news" and they were so full of its wonder and gladness that even the sternest commands and harshest punishments of emperors could not stop the telling of it. So revolutionary was their message and its power that guardians of the old order said to one another, "They are turning the world upside down." So they were. By the influence of their faith slaves were freed, cruel oppressors were brought down from their thrones, the poor were assisted, the ill were healed, little children were made to laugh and sing as never before and the timid were enabled to face death with triumphant serenity and even with fierce joy.

One striking result of all this great new power in the world was that those who experienced it in their lives invariably banded themselves together in loyal, intimate fellowship. So strong were the ties

From pp. 17-22 in *A Theology of the Living Church* by L. Harold De-Wolf (2nd revised edition). Copyright © 1953, 1960, 1968 by Harper & Row Publishers, Inc. Reprinted by permission of Harper & Row Publishers, Inc.

which the believers of the story felt for one another that their comradeship broke over all the barriers of age, sex, class and nation. They formed a single body, sensitive in every part to the weakness and strength, the sorrow and joy of every other. "The church" they called it, while even their cynical persecutors exclaimed in wonder, "See how these Christians love one another!"

Even after the passage of many centuries, today millions of human beings, both learned and ignorant, rich and poor, put their trust in the ancient story. To these people, who call themselves Christians, the story and the life of the church which has risen from the faith in that story give the clue to solving both the deepest problems of the philosophers and the most stubborn practical difficulties of men and nations.

The theoretical questions and the problems of conduct take new forms in every age. Hence in every age the meaning of the Christian faith must be re-examined in relation to the changing thought and experience of mankind. Such a task of interpretation and testing has been performed wherever men have loved truth and have taken the Christian faith seriously enough to think it worth examining. This work includes both the theoretical task of systematic statement, critical evaluation and rational defense and the practical task of translating the meanings of the faith into personal and corporate commitment and appropriate action. The theoretical work is Systematic Theology.

Systematic Theology is the critical discipline devoted to discovering, expounding and defending the more important truths implied in the experience of the Christian community.

A. A Critical Task

Especially would many writers object to speaking of theology as critical. The traditional definitions often describe it as a "science,"[1] but do not mean to suggest by this that its content is subject to independent critical judgment. The content has been widely regarded as given "once and for all" in ancient revelation, or as having developed in the life of the church in such a way that it would now be presumptuous or impious for the theologian to propose changes in its doctrinal substance. Therefore, it is supposed, the theologian's task is to expound, systematize and defend[2] the traditional doctrine, but not to add, subtract or criticize.

Even the thinkers who have exercised a large measure of critical originality and have not hesitated to reject ancient doctrines when new evidence showed them to be untenable, have nevertheless shown a marked reluctance to avow a critical purpose in defining their subject. Thus, such vigorous and independent thinkers as William Adams Brown and Albert C. Knudson define Christian theology in terms hardly suggesting such critical treatment as they actually give to the subject.[3]

Actually all theology is critical, whether avowedly and rationally so or not. This is attested by the wide disagreement among theologians, even among the Roman Catholic writers and among the most conservative Protestants, by their denunciations of opposing views and by the historical origination of doctrines in theological writings, even of such conservative defenders of tradition as Augustine, Aquinas, Luther, Calvin and Karl Barth. Each writer uses some set of standards for judgment. These standards differ greatly and often they are hidden, but they are invariably present. No theologian accepts every doctrine which has been taught as revealed. Much has been added to the body of Christian teaching by the original thought of theological writers.

Theology is critical. There are distinct advantages in stating this fact in the definition and keeping it steadily in mind throughout the investigation.

By this means our study can be prevented from being confused with a mere description of traditions without regard to their truth. History of doctrine is an important discipline but taken alone it is not of much help to the person seeking a system of truth by which to live. The history of Christian thought sets forth ideas far too promiscuous and mutually contradictory to qualify for indiscriminate acceptance.

Again, by openly professing the critical nature of theology its students may do something to bring to it more respect from people who are not accustomed to believing everything they hear. Much of theological writing shows little sustained, orderly effort to distinguish between truth and falsehood. Hence it does not commend itself to thoughtful minds sincerely eager to find truth and avoid error. It therefore behooves the theological writer who intends to "test everything; hold fast what is good,"[4] to say so clearly from the beginning of his work.

Finally, a critical intention candidly avowed at the start may be expected to promote clarity of purpose and directness of approach. These are values not to be despised. Surely truth is more likely to be discovered and effectively taught when sought with clear purpose and set forth with candid directness than when treated with obscurity and pious evasion.

B. The Discipline of Theology

Theology has often been known as a science and even as "queen of the sciences."[5] This is quite proper if the meaning is not misunderstood. The writer has no scruples against it. However, in the formal definition, to avoid the narrowing connotation which modern usage has often attached to the word "science," theology has been called a "critical discipline," instead. The necessity of its being critical has been briefly set forth. It must be emphasized also that it is a discipline.

A curious notion of our proudly scientific age is that in the most important matters "one man's opinion is as good as another's." Yet this age has produced appalling evidence that some views of men and nations lead to almost incredible chaos and desolation. Some opinions are not so good as others. Indeed, some are monstrously false. In matters of ethics, metaphysics and theology, as well as in matters of chemistry and biology, only that man who pays the price of learning the relevant data, mastering the needed critical procedures and persisting in the loyal quest of truth earns the right to have his opinions seriously regarded.

Theology has the reputation of being difficult. In part this reputation is a result of bad writing by some theologians. On the other hand, it must not be expected that a critical study of weighty problems which have most occupied many great minds, ancient and modern, can be effectively pursued without the paying of a price. The effort required is, in the main, of three kinds.

First, there is the intellectual effort of learning a wide range of relevant facts, following with sympathetic understanding some of the various, opposing interpretations of the facts, patiently evaluating the worth of these arguments and drawing appropriate conclusions.

Second, there is the moral and spiritual task of living the kind of life in which the relevant data are to be found. The data of religion can be no more effectively evaluated without entering into the disciplines of prayer and self-denial than the evidence of astronomy can be properly evaluated without giving attention to the instruments, charts and tables by which celestial observations and computations are made and recorded. Christian theology, well expounded, should be reasonably *intelligible* to an educated and diligent student who is not a Christian. But many of its evidences are not likely to seem *convincing* to him unless some Christian who witnesses to their truth has become for him an authority in such matters. Even then the evidence will take on new significance when he commits himself to "the Way" and shares the experience of the Christian community.

There are really minimal and maximal requirements in this matter. At the least, the student must disarm himself of hostility and defensive prejudice so that his mind will be open. Religious ideas, like other ideas having to do with deeply personal experiences and relationships, must be entertained with at least tentative sympathy in order to be understood. It seems fair to ask of every reader a self-disciplined exercise of this receptive and imaginative open-mindedness. It is not fair to expect a person not committed to the Christian faith to make an all-embracing, momentous and decisive commitment to it without reason. But it can be added that those who have, by an open-minded reception and evaluation of the evidence, found reason to meet the maximum requirements of faith and have given themselves in unstinted devotion, have discovered then a wealth of evidence previously unknown to them.

Finally, this pursuit requires the discipline of dispassionate objectivity in which prejudices are discounted and the love of truth overmatches every opposing motive. If any believer is afraid to subject his belief to this kind of single-minded truth-seeking, his fear betrays the fact that he has already ceased to accept it as true. What he calls his belief is his desire or his public profession, but it is no longer his belief when he dares not to search with all his powers for the fullest truth concerning it. This is why Tennyson was right in saying,

> There lives more faith in honest doubt,
> Believe me, than in half the creeds.[6]

C. The Scope of Christian Theology

All specialized studies, if pressed persistently enough, bring the student into some consideration of problems and data lying outside their distinctive fields. Thus the serious botanist, astronomer and physicist all find themselves confronting problems in chemistry, mathematics and logic and no thorough sociologist can avoid questions of psychology, economics and ethics. But this fact of the overlapping and interpenetration of the various subjects does not make botany identical with chemistry nor sociology with economics. To this general rule, theology is no exception.

Christian systematic theology unavoidably and properly is in mutual interdependence with various other disciplines. But the distinctive, central area of its specialization is the experience of the Christian community. To be sure, much experience of Christians is like the experience of everyone else, just as many characteristics of living plants are like those of all other physical objects. But just as the botanist concentrates his attention on those problems and data of living plants which are peculiarly characteristic of them, so the Christian theologian devotes his thought primarily to the problems and data which are peculiarly relevant to the Christian community.

His data embrace the Bible, the history of Christianity—including external events, recorded personal experiences and past theological writings—and the present religious experience of himself and others. His problems are those which most concern the Christian community. He will not be disturbed when he finds these problems leading him into areas shared with philosophy, psychology, sociology and physics, nor will he fail to employ important relevant data from the other disciplines. On the other hand, he will make his best contribution to the whole field of knowledge as well as to his chosen area if he persistently concentrates attention on the problems and experiences belonging peculiarly to his special province.

From what has been said it will be obvious that systematic theology is most immediately dependent on the following related disciplines: Biblical studies, church history, history of doctrine, psychology of religion and sociology of religion. No less intimate is its relation to philosophy of religion. Philosophy of religion is a critical search for truth in all the religions of the world. It deals especially with problems and data which occur in all religions, or at least in several. Systematic theology is a more specialized study of that particular religion known as Christianity. Each of these two studies is of great aid to the other.

One part of the definition may seem particularly vague, namely, the phrase "the experience of the Christian community."[7] A really precise explanation of the Christian community would necessarily presuppose a great amount of theological labor already done. Not the easiest problem of our subject will be the refining of that very concept near the end of the present volume. However, it can be pointed out that in the definition it is used very broadly. It is an ecumenical or catholic concept. It refers not merely to "good" or "orthodox" Christians, much less to members of some particular denomination, Catholic or Protestant. Until such time as good reason for limitation may appear, it includes the experience of all persons who are bound together with other persons in the profession of a religious faith which they or others call Christian. This does not mean that all who are called Christians are so, much less that the experiences of all professed Christians are of equal theological value. It is only insisted that the distinction between true and false Christians or between more and less significant experiences, will need to come forth as a *result* of critical study, not as a *presupposition* to it.

Finally, something must be said about the meaning of the word "implied." In the definition, reference is made to "the more important truths implied in the experience of the Christian community." It might be supposed that all the beliefs and practices of Christians were to be taken at face value as premises from which conclusions might be drawn. This would, of course, constitute a denial of the intention to make this study critical. In the history of the church and of theology many doctrines have been tried out theoretically and practically. This testing has produced much evidence against many of them as well as data of a more favorable character. The negative implications will be relevant to our study as well as the positive evidences. People called Christians have given many horrible examples of beliefs and practices which ought not to be embraced, as well as other examples of ennobling truth in thought and life. We should profit by both kinds of experience.

D. The Problem of Method

The method to be relied upon for the gaining of truth is an important problem for the systematic theologian. Particularly, the relations between reason, revelation and faith must undergo careful study. . . .

Notes

[1]So Thomas Aquinas, many times in Part I of the *Summa Theologica.* Cf. A. H. Strong, and William B. Pope.

[2]Karl Barth is one who insists that it must not be defended. All his polemical writings are a kind of defense, nevertheless. See his *Credo,* pp. 185-86.

[3]See Brown, *Christian Theology in Outline,* pp. 3,4, and Knudson, *The Doctrine of God,* p. 19.

[4]I Thess. 5:21.

[5]Cf. the able argument for the treatment of theology as a science in Alan Richardson, *Christian Apologetics.*

[6]*In Memoriam,* 96:3.

[7]Cf. Charles C. Morrison's statement that the theology of the early church "was the church's explanation of its own existence." *What is Christianity?* (New York: Harper & Brothers, 1940), p. 179.

Theological Dialogue

4

William Hordern

Theology in Dialogue

Behind the loss of intellectuals and the failure of the church to inspire its members to Christian action, many see a failure of Christian language. The church speaks a tongue that no longer communicates. Thus secular authors, whose interests are close to those of Christian theology, often fail to see through the theological language to the common concerns. Even church members have failed to see any connection between the pious language they hear on Sunday and the practical affairs they face the rest of the week.

If its language seems irrelevant, the church must enter into dialogue with the world; it must listen to the world and learn, so that it can speak relevantly to it. A pioneer in dialogue was Paul Tillich. At the very center of his theology, he put his method of correlation. Theology must operate, he said, by correlating its answers to the questions that man actually asks.[2] We can almost say that, for Tillich, theology does not *enter* into dialogue with the world, it *is* dialogue with the word. Similarly, Rudolf Bultmann's program of demythologization can be seen as an effort at dialogue. The strange language

From *New Directions in Theology Today*, Volume I, *Introduction*, by William Hordern. The Westminster Press. Copyright © MCMLXVI, W. L. Jenkins. Used by permission.

of Biblical myth is to be interpreted through the thought forms of modern man as found in Heidegger's existential analysis.

From the beginning, the ways of dialogue raised questions. To be relevant to modern man, Tillich spoke of God as "the Ground of Being." Perhaps this is relevant, for even the atheist must confess that there is some ground for his being. But, in attempting to be relevant, has theology been cut loose from its moorings in historical Christianity? Can we identify the Ground of Being with the God and Father of Jesus Christ? When I was dealing with Tillich in one of my courses, a student came to class early and wrote on the blackboard, "The ground of being is dirt." His semifacetious remark found serious support as both philosophers and theologians discussed whether Tillich was an atheist. In our discussion of the demythologization debate, we saw that many critics charge that Bultmann has lost much of the essence of Christian faith. Furthermore, we found that some of his left-wing followers have advocated an abandonment of the kerygma itself. As we look back, it appears that, whether they succeeded or not, it was the intention of both Tillich and Bultmann to preserve and make relevant the essentials of Christian faith. Today, however, there are many theologians who openly abandon this intention.

When we examine the contemporary concern with dialogue, we find two major trends that threaten to split theology more decisively than any of the former theological debates of this century. Both trends recognize the need for dialogue with the world and both are attempting to engage in it. One trend, however, is working on the assumption that the changes in the modern world have resulted in a qualitative transformation of man and his thinking. As a result, theologians in this trend believe that modern man can accept the Christian message only if it is changed drastically. The second trend includes theologians who admit that we live in a fast-changing world and that we must strive to translate the faith for modern men. But they do not agree that the essentials of the faith must be changed or abandoned.

Because the distinction between these trends has only recently begun to come to light, and because those within each of the trends do not agree completely with each other, we do not have any established terms with which to describe the trends. The first trend is widely referred to as "radical" or "left wing" theology. Presumably this makes the second trend conservative or middle-of-the-road. But this is not a useful terminology. From the point of view of traditional Christian faith, the first trend is radical, while the second is more conservative. But, from the point of view of the main currents of thought today, it is the first group that identifies itself with the *status quo,* and it is the second group that brings a radical criticism of the modern world. For the sake of convenience, we shall refer to those who follow the first trend as "transformers," and to those who follow the second trend as "translators." Although many in the first trend speak of what they are doing as "translating," and many in the second speak of themselves as "transforming" the message of the church, our usage of the terms has some merit. To transform something normally implies a drastic change. A translation, however, implies that although we are speaking in a different language, we are still saying the same thing.

The battle lines between these two groups are not yet hard and fast. There are a number of men who are on the border lines and might be put into either camp. For example, in his *Honest to God,* Bishop Robinson sounded like a transformer. He said that he could understand those who urge that we should give up speaking of God for a generation.[3] Statements about God, he affirmed, are really statements about the "ultimacy" of personal relationships.[4] He called for a new morality[5] and a new way to pray.[6] But in his more recent book, *The New Reformation?* Robinson sounds like a translator. He denies that he wishes to reduce Christianity to humanism.[7] He affirms that even "after his death" God "is disturbingly alive."[8] To clarify the nature of the two groups we shall choose representatives who clearly represent the division.

The "God is dead" theologians represent the transformers. It hardly needs to be argued that if we present the Christian faith without God, we have transformed the nature of its message. Thomas Altizer has expressed the point clearly. The "contemporary theologian," he tells us, "knows that he is not a Christian in any sense that could be drawn from the creeds and confessions of the historic church."[9] For the God is dead theology, a change has come over the world, so that it is no longer possible to believe in God. As William Hamilton says: "And this is an experience that is not peculiar to a neurotic few, nor is it private or inward. Death of God is a public event in our history, we are saying."[10]

Van Buren claims that modern "secular" man cannot understand language about God. Thus, when Bonhoeffer or Ebeling seek to speak of God in a "worldly" way, he charges that they are evading the real problem because they are still trying to speak about God, and that is what modern man cannot understand. "The empiricist in us finds the heart of the difficulty not in what is said about God, but in the very talking about God at all. We do not know 'what' God is, and we cannot understand how the word 'God' is being used."[11]

If God is dead, what is left that is Christian? The "God is dead" theologians believe that modern man can have loyalty to the man, Jesus, and they claim that their commitment to Jesus means that they are still within the Christian framework. Of course, the Jesus that modern man can accept is not the unique son of God or the risen Lord. He was a man like us in all ways except that he was "a man for others," one who lived in service to his fellowmen. As such, Jesus retains his power to win men.

As Christians we do not look for a god to come to our aid, but we do seek to find Jesus where he may be found today. Hamilton says: "Jesus may be concealed in the world, in the neighbor, in this struggle for justice, in that struggle for beauty, clarity, order. Jesus is in the world as masked and the work of the Christian is to strip off the masks of the world to find him."[12] If a critic says that such a theology has become no more than ethics, van Buren has a ready answer. "In a secular age, what would that 'more' be?"[13] He affirms that alchemy was "reduced" to chemistry and astrology to astronomy. In the same way he believes that the time has come to "reduce" theology to ethics. Theology, freed of its metaphysical bondage, can turn its attention to the human, the historical, and the empirical.

The "God is dead" theology tries to distinguish itself from more familiar forms of atheism and thus justify its claim to be theological and Christian. Altizer has continued to speak of the "sacred," although he cannot speak of God. Often using mystical language, he encourages us to find the sacred in and through the profane. Van Buren attempts to show that his secular meaning of the gospel gets to the heart of what the Bible and the historic creeds were really trying to say. Hamilton at one time said that the "God is dead" theologian is still waiting for God, although, in personal conversation, he has indicated that he no longer holds this position.

The real heart of the "God is dead" theology, however, seems to be a call to accept the modern world and all that it means. Altizer tells us that "a theologian who cannot affirm his own destiny—the actual moment of time in which he exists—has ceased to be Christian."[14] As a result, "we know that Christ is present in the concrete actuality of our history or he is not truly present at all." Van Buren is ready to concede that secularism is neither a better nor a worse mode of thought than that of ancient times. But, with an almost fatalistic attitude, he goes on to affirm that it is the only way of thought man can understand today.[15]

Hamilton describes this acceptance of the modern world in terms of Luther's movement from the cloister to the world. Furthermore, he does not mean what so many theologians mean when they speak of going to the world. They speak of going to pessimistic writers like Kafka or Beckett to get illustrations for their doctrines of sin. But Hamilton, in a startling passage, affirms that he does not go to the world of these "modern" writers, he goes into the world they reject— "the world of technology, power, money, sex, culture, race, poverty, and the city."[16] Hamilton's position is based upon an optimism about man and his abilities. In developments like the civil rights movement, man is standing up to solve his own problems, and he who would find Christ today must join such efforts.

In distinguishing two trends within the concept of theology in dialogue, we have chosen the "God is dead" school to represent those who advocate transformation of the gospel. This does not mean that all who fit into this trend have abandoned belief in God. Some have transformed Christianity by removing from it belief in the resurrection of Christ or belief that Christ is necessary to salvation. There are two qualifying marks of the transformer. First, he insists that, to be relevant today, theology must not just change how it speaks by finding new ways to present its message, it must change the message itself. Secondly, his criterion for this change is not found in some "purer" form of Christianity such as the Bible or tradition, his criterion is what "modern man" can accept.

As we turn to discuss those whom we have called translators, it must be kept in mind that we are not speaking of a clearly defined school of thought. We are looking at a trend that is beginning to take shape in modern theology. Recent debates have restructured our theological division, so that, among those who fit into the translating trend, we find representatives of the new conservatism, of liberalism, and of neo-orthodoxy. There are two characteristics that define the translator. First, he takes as seriously as the transformer the need to enter into dialogue with the modern world and to express Christian faith in terms that speak to modern men. Secondly, he repudiates the claim of the transformer that such dialogue calls for a radical revision in Christian faith. The translator learns from his dialogue with the world *how* he must speak today, but he does not look to the modern world to find *what* he must say. Translators do not agree among themselves on all theological issues, but they agree that their differences cannot be settled by asking what modern man can accept. Modern man cannot be the ultimate authority for what Christians may believe.

Translators are convinced that theology is relevant only when it is able to tell the world something that the world is not already telling itself. As the translators see it, this is a point where the transformers fail. Thus Helmut Gollwitzer, in a review of Robinson's *Honest to God,* says that though Robinson "wishes to make the Christian proclamation worth noticing for men today, he is in danger of making it superfluous instead—and this because he largely reduces it to what a man even without revelation, without considering the phenomenon of Jesus Christ, without listening to the proclamation about him, can say to himself."[17]

Gollwitzer expands this theme in his criticism of certain existentialist theologians. He charges that, in their desire to be relevant, they have transformed the Christian faith. In the Bible, faith is a *new* possibility because it is a dependence upon the Lord who has made himself known. God's act in Christ has opened a new relationship for man. However, Gollwitzer argues, when the attempt is made to pour Christianity into existentialist molds, faith becomes nothing more than an understanding of existence that men can have without Christianity.[18] The translators thus fear that the transformers have not produced a dialogue with the world. Their theology is a monologue in which the modern world speaks to itself.

When the translators make the claim that theology must say something to the world that it is not saying to itself, they raise the question of the truth of Christianity. And here we note a strange tendency among almost all the transformers. They seldom raise the question of truth. As Langdon Gilkey says, they have tended to confuse psychological pressures with logical necessities.[19] No doubt the secular atmosphere of the modern age discourages belief in many aspects of Christianity, but it does not follow from this that the modern world is logically correct.

In recent years a number of books have appeared to argue that, despite changes in the world, the truth of Christian faith can be defended. A new form of apologetics is beginning to appear. The old apologetics hoped that it could begin with evidence that was available to any man, and by an argument that would be obvious to all rational men, it hoped to demonstrate the truth of at least parts of the Christian faith. The classic proofs of God are examples of this form of apologetic. Most of the theologians who accept the contemporary dialogue with the world are convinced that this traditional form of apologetic is no longer effective. We live in an age when the primary differences between men are not in the matter of their conclusions but in the premises from which they begin to reason. We cannot settle our differences by going to the evidence, for what divides us is a question of what constitutes evidence. Thus David Jenkins says that the real problem for belief in God today is a question of epistemology. Many today have a concept of "knowledge" which, by definition, makes knowledge of God impossible.[20]

The new apologetic thus cannot hope to begin simply where man now stands; it must question his very standing place. It must approach him by honestly confessing that it speaks from faith. It must strive to show that the world and life make more sense if we start from Christian premises than if we start from atheistic ones. Typical of such apologetics are the books *The Christian Belief in God* by Daniel Jenkins, and *The Existence of God as Confessed by Faith,* by Helmut Gollwitzer. Although Jenkins and Gollwitzer differ at several points, they agree that Christian faith must affirm the reality of God's existence and that the Christian can make a persuasive case for belief in God from a standpoint of faith.

The theologians of translation deny the transformers' claim that the change in the world and its thought have made it necessary to abandon the basic affirmations of Christian faith. Daniel Jenkins points out at considerable length that it is false to assume that once, in the times of our forefathers, it was easy to have "simple faith," but that things have changed so that it is now impossible. In fact, all of the objections to Christian faith that are made today were made at its very beginning. For all the changes in man and his thought, there are no new arguments against Christian faith.[21]

The philosopher Paul Holmer develops a similar theme. When transformers would have us abandon belief in God because metaphysical schemes are out of favor today with the intellectuals, Holmer replies that there is no evidence that Christian faith was easier in times of flourishing metaphysical thought. "The depiction of faith in past ages is deceptive: it sustains the illusion that once theology was indubitable, compelling and immediately relevant to all intelligent people, whereas today it is dubious, optional at best, and pertinent only to people who already believe on other than intellectual bases." But, Holmer argues, in all ages Christian faith has called for "courage to believe in a God who redeems, and judges, cares and creates." Christian faith does not depend upon some special technique developed by intellectuals; it is a matter of common sense. "All of us, as a matter of common sense, come to believe in people, the world and perhaps God. We have no special proof for existence, only very ordinary ways to come to the confidences by which we live." Thus it appears to Holmer that the difficulties faced by Christian faith today are quite similar to those always faced and the reasons for believing are as powerful as they ever were.[22]

The question of the degree to which the world has changed also raises the question of who is the "modern man" that is met so frequently in all the discussions of dialogue. The transformers have disagreed among themselves as to who modern man is. Van Buren says, "One wonders where the left-wing existentialist theologians have found their 'modern man.'" In place of the existentialist modern man, van Buren finds the prototype of modern man in the Anglo-Saxon analytical philosopher.

In the light of the failure of the transformers to agree among themselves about modern man, it is not surprising that the translators have pressed this issue. Langdon Gilkey agrees that van Buren has a point against the existentialists, but he goes on to ask where van Buren finds his modern man. Van Buren says that modern man cannot understand language about God, but he remains confident that modern man will find that Jesus and his teachings are relevant to his life. Gilkey objects, "For surely contemporary modern man, committed to the self-oriented values of modern society, would find the self-surrendering, altruistic 'perspective' and 'freedom' of this ancient martyr as strange, as unintelligible, and as offensive as are the old 'myths' in which this story is ordinarily phrased."[23]

Gilkey's comment points to a crucial difference between the translators and the transformers. The transformers seem confident that modern man will accept and live the ideals of Christ when they are freed from "mythical" and "metaphysical" frameworks. As Paul Holmer says, they create the impression "that the whole world would like to become Christian if only the theologians would become modern."[24] But the translators remained convinced that there is a scandal to the Christian faith as it meets us in Christ. Man does not naturally want to be a "man for others," nor does he want to batter down the doors to enter the Kingdom of Heaven. Thus the translators insist that man still needs grace from beyond himself if he is to follow Christ. The Christian ethic cannot live without its theological foundations.

This debate reveals a serious problem for theology that is committed to dialogue. Such theology must ask who is the modern man to which it hopes to speak. But perhaps instead we should speak of modern men rather than of modern man. Never has there been a time when it was more difficult to put one's finger on the essence of the age. There is no world view that is dominant today. This is why theology in our time often reads like the autobiography of the theologian. Those who say that God is dead are describing how they have come to feel about God, and often those who answer them do so by saying that they feel differently. This hardly solves any questions.

Ours is an age of strange contrasts. Twentieth-century man buys the latest model automobile and then places a plastic icon of Jesus on the dashboard to protect him from accidents. A man walks in outer space and returns to describe the good luck charms that he took with him. Theologians say that our age has matured beyond religion, but a drug is discovered that induces religious experiences and a thriving cult grows up to practice religion out of a test tube. Perhaps theology is called to many dialogues with many men. Theologians have been far too hasty in supposing that a Heidegger or a Flew spoke for modern man. Translators thus agree that if we transform the faith so that we make it relevant to one modern group of men, we shall immediately make it irrelevant to most other modern groups.

Another question raised by the translators is whether "modern man" however we define him, is so impressive that we must transform Christian faith to suit him. Is modern man still the old-fashioned sinner dressed up in a space suit? Are the unbelievers of today, like the unbelievers of Paul's days, "blinded by the god of this passing age"? (II Cor. 4:4, NEB)

This point is pressed home by the new conservatives. In an editorial, *Christianity Today* argues that those who would change the Christian message have asked the wrong question and thus come up with the wrong answer. They have asked how they can transform Christianity to enlist modern man and they have come up with the answer, "Restructure the Gospel! rather than *Regenerate the sin-*

ner!"[25] But the conservatives are not alone. Even Erik Routley, who agrees with much of Robinson's *Honest to God,* reminds us that " 'the world' is still a sad and unreconciled world."[26]

Karl Barth likewise challenges us to ask whether it is the Christian gospel or modern man who is irrelevant. Barth suggests that our problem is not with a world come of age but with "a world which *regards* itself as of age (and proves daily that it is precisely not that)."[27] In such a situation, Barth says that it is dangerous to approach modern man "with some sort of gibberish, which, for the moment, is modern," because what we have to say both to other men and to ourselves "is a strange piece of news." The important thing is to see that it is "the *great* piece of news." To translators it appears that the gospels of the transformers have lost all greatness. They are acceptable to modern man precisely because they do not challenge him deeply. Such "radical theology" turns out to be nothing more than a slightly theological expression of what is heard on all sides today.

There is a final critique which the translators might make of the transformers. Most of the transformers have shown a strange reluctance to enter into dialogue with modern believers. Certainly it can be granted that theology must be open to dialogue with the world of unbelief and it must listen to the "cultured despisers" of religion. Nonetheless, we must ask if there is not a serious weakness in the transformers' assumption that all traditional believers are excluded by definition, from the glorious circle of "modern men." One would have thought that there should be much to learn from those men living in the modern age who have struggled through to an honest and living grasp of the Christian tradition.

An interesting sidelight is thrown on the "God is dead" theology in a statement by Altizer that is quoted with approval by Hamilton. Altizer says that "contemporary theology must be alienated from the Church . . . [and] the theologian must exist outside the Church." Hamilton concludes, "The theologian does not and cannot go to church; he is not interested; he is alienated."[28] Is there a parable here? Does this say that God will seem to be dead to the man who tries to live his life outside of dialogue within the fellowship of those who know and are committed to God through Christ?

Today's theology is committed to the way of dialogue. It has no alternative if it is to be relevant in the fast-changing age. As we look back over the chapters of this book, it is evident that the problems of dialogue are implicit in all the themes that we have discussed. Demythologization and the discussion of history are themes that arise from dialogue with the world. The new conservatives are seeking dialogue with their world and a way to translate without transforming the gospel. The revival of the doctrine of sanctification seeks to speak to the world through actions as well as through words.

Worldly or secularized Christianity is by its very nature involved in dialogue with the world in which it finds itself.

It is too early to forecast what the results of the contemporary dialogue will be. Already it is apparent that theologians who are most concerned about dialogue are more prone to speak than to listen. Having heard a little from someone that appeals to them, they crown him as "Mr. Modern Man" and then speak only to him. Perhaps theology has for too long been the monopoly of seminaries and, to a lesser degree, of college departments of religion. The dialogue needs to be extended so that it involves laymen, believing and unbelieving. We also need more contributions from the parish clergymen. Too often they have been intimidated into thinking that they can make no theological contributions, but they are often more likely to know what modern men are really thinking than are their brothers in the academic world.

In a serious theological dialogue many things may happen. It could be that the church will be revealed to be irrelevant and outdated. It could be that modern man will be exposed as irrelevant and in desperate need of salvation. More likely it will appear that there is fault upon both the side of the church and the unbeliever today. At this point we can expect that the church will try to gloss over its own shortcomings by blaming its failures on the hardness of men's hearts. Where that happens we need the persistent voices of the transformers. They will always appear strange and annoying in the life of the church, but they can serve as a needed goad to spur the church toward continuing reformation. At the same time, the dialogue will tempt many to cast their lot with the god of this passing age. Where that happens, we need the persistent voices of those who, while ready to translate the faith for the modern times, are not prepared "to practice cunning or to tamper with God's word" (II Cor. 4:2).

Notes

[2] Paul Tillich, *Systematic Theology* (The University of Chicago Press, 1951), Vol. I, pp. 59-66.

[3] John A. T. Robinson, *Honest to God* (The Westminster Press, 1963), pp. 7-8.

[4] *Ibid.*, p. 50.

[5] *Ibid.*, Ch. 6.

[6] *Ibid.*, pp. 92 ff.

[7] John A. T. Robinson, *The New Reformation?* (The Westminster Press, 1965), p. 50.

[8] *Ibid.*, p. 115.

[9]Thomas J. J. Altizer, "Creative Negation in Theology," *The Christian Century*, Vol. LXXXII, No. 27 (July 7, 1965), p. 865.

[10]William Hamilton, *loc. cit.*, p. 45.

[11]Van Buren, *op.cit.*, p. 84.

[12]Hamilton, *loc.cit.*, p. 46.

[13]Van Buren, *op.cit.*, p. 198.

[14]Altizer, *op.cit.*, p. 866.

[15]Van Buren, *op.cit.*, pp. 193-200.

[16]Hamilton, *loc.cit.*, p. 38.

[17]Gollwitzer, *op.cit.*, p. 251.

[18]*Ibid.*, pp. 62-64.

[19]L. Gilkey, *How the Church Can Minister to the World Without Losing Itself*, p. 54 (footnote).

[20]David Jenkins, "Whither the Doctrine of God Now?" in *New Theology*, ed. by M. E. Marty and D. G. Peerman (The Macmillan Company, 1965), pp. 66 ff. See also, David Jenkins, *A Guide to the Debate About God* (The Westminster Press, 1966).

[21]Daniel Jenkins, *The Christian Belief in God* (The Westminster Press, 1963), pp. 128 ff.

[22]See P. L. Holmer, "Contra the New Theologies," *The Christian Century*, Vol. LXXXII, No. 11 (March 17, 1965), p. 330.

[23]L. Gilkey, "A New Linguistic Madness," in Marty and Peerman, *New Theology*, No. 2, p. 44.

[24]Holmer, *loc.cit.*, p. 331.

[25]*Christianity Today*, Vol. IX, No. 21 (July 16, 1965), p. 1075.

[26]E. Routley, *The Man for Others* (Oxford University Press, 1964), p. 87.

[27]Karl Barth, *The Humanity of God* (John Knox Press, 1960), pp. 58-59.

[28]William Hamilton, "Tomorrow's Theologian, Thursday's Child," in *Theology Today*, Vol. XX, No. 4 (Jan. 1964), p. 490.

5

Cornelius Van Til

The Reformed Position

The fully Biblical conception of the point of contact, it ought now to be clear, is the only one that can escape the dilemma of absolute ignorance or absolute omniscience.

The one great defect of the Roman Catholic and the Arminian view is, as noted, that it ascribes ultimacy or self-sufficiency to the mind of man. Romanism and Arminianism do this in their views of man as stated in their works on systematic theology. It is consistent for them, therefore, not to challenge the assumption of ultimacy as this is made by the non-believer. But Reformed theology, as worked out by Calvin and his recent exponents such as Hodge, Warfield, Kuyper and Bavinck, holds that man's mind is derivative. As such it is naturally in contact with God's revelation. It is surrounded by nothing but revelation. It is itself inherently revelational. It cannot naturally be conscious of itself without being conscious of its creatureliness. For man self-consciousness presupposes God-consciousness. Calvin speaks of this as man's inescapable sense of deity.

For Adam in paradise God-consciousness could not come in at the end of a syllogistic process of reasoning. God-consciousness was

From Cornelius Van Til, *The Defense of the Faith*. Philadelphia: Presbyterian and Reformed Publishing Company, 1963. Used by permission.

for him the presupposition of the significance of his reasoning on anything.

To the doctrine of creation must be added the conception of the covenant. Man was created as a historical being. God placed upon him from the outset of history the responsibility and task of reinterpreting the counsel of God as expressed in creation to himself individually and collectively. Man's creature-consciousness may therefore be more particularly signalized as covenant-consciousness. But the revelation of the covenant to man in paradise was supernaturally mediated. This was naturally the case inasmuch as it pertained to man's historical task. Thus, the sense of obedience or disobedience was immediately involved in Adam's consciousness of himself. Covenant consciousness envelops creature-consciousness. In paradise Adam knew that as a creature of God it was natural and proper that he should keep the covenant that God had made with him. In this way it appears that man's proper self-consciousness depended, even in paradise, upon his being in contact with both supernatural and natural revelation. God's natural revelation was within man as well as about him. Man's very constitution as a rational and moral being is itself revelational to man as the ethically responsible reactor to revelation. And natural revelation is itself incomplete. It needed from the outset to be supplemented with supernatural revelation about man's future. Thus the very idea of supernatural revelation is correlatively embodied in the idea of man's proper self-consciousness.

It is in this way that man may be said to be by his original constitution in contact with the truth while yet not in possession of all the truth. Man is not in Plato's cave. He is not in the anomalous position of having eyes with which to see while yet he dwells in darkness. He has not, as was the case with the cave-dwellers of Plato, some mere capacity for the truth that might never come to fruition. Man had originally not merely a capacity for receiving the truth; he was in actual possession of the truth. The world of truth was not found in some realm far distant from him; it was right before him. That which spoke to his senses no less than that which spoke to his intellect was the voice of God. Even when he closed his eyes upon the external world his internal sense would manifest God to him in his own constitution. The *matter* of his experience was in no sense in need of a mere *form* with which he might organize the raw material. On the contrary the *matter* of his experience was lit up through and through. Yet it was lit up for him by the voluntary activity of God whose counsel made things to be what they are. Man could not be aware of himself without also being aware of objects about him and without also being aware of his responsibility to manage himself and all things for the glory of God. Man's consciousness of objects and of self was not static. It was consciousness in *time*. Moreover, consciousness of objects and of self in time meant consciousness of *history* in relationship to the plan of God back of history. Man's first sense of self-awareness implied the awareness of the presence of God as the one for whom he had a great task to accomplish.

It is only when we begin our approach to the question of the point of contact by thus analyzing the situation as it obtained in paradise before the fall of man that we can attain to a true conception of the natural man and his capacities with respect to the truth. The apostle Paul speaks of the natural man as actually possessing the knowledge of God (Rom. 1:19-21). The greatness of his sin lies precisely in the fact that "when they knew God, they glorified him not as God." No man can escape knowing God. It is indelibly involved in his awareness of anything whatsoever. Man *ought,* therefore, as Calvin puts it, to recognize God. There is no excuse for him if he does not. The reason for his failure to recognize God lies exclusively in him. It is due to his willful transgression of the very law of his being.

Neither Romanism nor Protestant evangelicalism can do full justice to this teaching of Paul. In effect both of them fail to surround man exclusively with God's revelation. Not holding to the counsel of God as all-controlling they cannot teach that man's self-awareness always pre-supposes awareness of God. According to both Rome and evangelicalism man may have some measure of awareness of objects about him and of himself in relation to them without being aware at the same time of his responsibility to manipulate both of them in relation to God. Thus man's consciousness of objects, of self, of time and of history are not from the outset brought into an exclusive relationship of dependence upon God. *Hinc illae lacrimae!*

Of course, when we thus stress Paul's teaching that all men do not have a mere capacity for but are in actual possession of the knowledge of God, we have at once to add Paul's further instruction to the effect that all men, due to the sin within them, always and in all relationships seek to "suppress" this knowledge of God (Rom. 1:18, ASV). The natural man is such a one as constantly throws water on a fire he cannot quench. He has yielded to the temptation of Satan, and has become his bondservant. When Satan tempted Adam and Eve in paradise he sought to make them believe that man's self-consciousness was ultimate rather than derivative and God-dependent. He argued, as it were, that it was of the nature of self-consciousness to make itself the final reference point of all predication. He argued, as it were, that God had no control over all that might come forth in the process of time. That is to say, he argued, in effect, that as any form of self-consciousness must assume its own ultimacy, so it must also admit its own limitation in the fact that much that happens is under no control at all. Thus Satan argued, as it were, that man's consciousness of time and of time's products in history, is, if intelligible at all, intelligible in some measure independently of God.

Romanism and Evangelicalism, however, do not attribute this assumption of autonomy or ultimacy on the part of man as due to sin. They hold that man should quite properly think of himself and of his relation to objects in time in this way. Hence they do injustice to Paul's teaching with respect to the effect of sin on the interpretative activity of man. As they virtually deny that originally man not merely had a capacity for the truth but was in actual possession of the truth, so also they virtually deny that the natural man suppresses the truth.

It is not to be wondered at that neither Romanism nor Evangelicalism are little interested in challenging the "philosophers" when these, as Calvin says, interpret man's consciousness without being aware of the tremendous difference in man's attitude toward the truth before and after the fall. Accordingly they do not distinguish carefully between the natural man's own conception of himself and the Biblical conception of him. Yet for the question of the point of contact this is all-important. If we make our appeal to the natural man without being aware of this distinction we virtually admit that the natural man's estimate of himself is correct. We may, to be sure, even then, maintain that he is in need of information. We may even admit that he is morally corrupt. But the one thing which, on this basis, we cannot admit, is that his claim to be able to interpret at least some area of experience in a way that is essentially correct, is mistaken. We cannot then challenge his most basic epistemological assumption to the effect that his self-consciousness and time-consciousness are self-explanatory. We cannot challenge his right to interpret all his experience in exclusively immanentistic categories. And on this everything hinges. For if we first allow the legitimacy of the natural man's assumption of himself as the ultimate reference point in interpretation in any dimension we cannot deny his right to interpret Christianity itself in naturalistic terms.

The point of contact for the gospel, then, must be sought within the natural man. Deep down in his mind every man knows that he is the creature of God and responsible to God. Every man, at bottom, knows that he is a covenant-breaker. But every man acts and talks as though this were not so. It is the one point that cannot bear mentioning in his presence. A man may have internal cancer. Yet it may be the one point he will not have one speak of in his presence. He will grant that he is not feeling well. He will accept any sort of medication so long as it does not pretend to be given in answer to a cancer diagnosis. Will a good doctor cater to him on this matter? Certainly not. He will tell his patient that he has promise of life, but promise of life on one condition, that is, of an immediate internal operation. So it is with the sinner. He is alive but alive as a covenant-breaker.

But his own interpretative activity with respect to all things proceeds on the assumption that such is not the case. Romanism and evangelicalism, by failing to appeal exclusively to that which is within man but is also suppressed by every man, virtually allow the legitimacy of the natural man's view of himself. They do not seek to explode the last stronghold to which the natural man always flees and where he always makes his final stand. They cut off the weeds at the surface but do not dig up the roots of these weeds, for fear that crops will not grow.

The truly Biblical view, on the other hand, applies atomic power and flame-throwers to the very presupposition of the natural man's ideas with respect to himself. It does not fear to lose a point of contact by uprooting the weeds rather than by cutting them off at the very surface. It is assured of a point of contact in the fact that every man is made in the image of God and has impressed upon him the law of God. In that fact alone he may rest secure with respect to the point of contact problem.[1] For that fact makes men always accessible to God. That fact assures us that every man, to be a man at all, must already be in contact with the truth. He is so much in contact with the truth that much of his energy is spent in the vain effort to hide this fact from himself. His efforts to hide this fact from himself are bound to be self-frustrative.

Only by thus finding the point of contact in man's sense of deity that lies underneath his own conception of self-consciousness as ultimate can we be both true to Scripture and effective in reasoning with the natural man.

Notes

[1]Here, as throughout this chapter, the argument is not that we should start our analysis of the knowledge of the natural man from the notion of an "absolute ethical antithesis" but from the sense of deity in the way that Calvin does.

6

Paul Tillich

Introduction to Systematic Theology

The Rational Character of Systematic Theology

The questions of the source, the medium, and the norm of systematic theology are related to its concrete-historical foundation. But systematic theology is not a historical discipline (as Schleiermacher wrongly asserted);[14] it is a constructive task. It does not tell us what people have thought the Christian message to be in the past; rather it tries to give us an interpretation of the Christian message which is relevant to the present situation. This raises the question, "To what extent does systematic theology have a rational character?" Certainly reason must be used constructively in building a theological system. Nevertheless, there have been and still are many doubts and controversies concerning the role of reason in systematic theology.

The first problem is an adequate definition of "rational" in the present context. Providing such a definition would, however, involve an extensive discussion of reason in its various structures and functions. Since such a discussion is impossible in this Introduction, we must make the following anticipatory statements. There is a kind of

From Paul Tillich, *Systematic Theology*, Vol. 1. Chicago: The University of Chicago Press, 1951 Copyright © 1951 by The University of Chicago. Used by permission.

cognition implied in faith which is qualitatively different from the cognition involved in the technical, scholarly work of the theologian. It has a completely existential, self-determining, and self-surrendering character and belongs to the faith of even the intellectually most primitive believer. Whoever participates in the New Being participates also in its truth. The theologian, in addition is supposed not only to participate in the New Being but also to express its truth in a methodical way. We shall call the organ with which we receive the contents of faith "self-transcending," or ecstatic, reason, and we shall call the organ of the theological scholar "technical," or formal, reason. In both cases reason is not a source of theology. It does not produce its contents. Ecstatic reason is reason grasped by an ultimate concern. Reason is overpowered, invaded, shaken by the ultimate concern. Reason does not produce an object of ultimate concern by logical procedures, as a mistaken theology tried to do in its "arguments for the existence of God." The contents of faith grasp reason. Nor does the technical or formal reason of the theologian produce its content, as has been shown in the discussion of his sources and his medium.

But the situation is not so simple as it would be if the act of reception were merely a formal act without any influence on what is received. This is not the case. Content and form, giving and receiving, have a more dialectical relationship than the words seem to connote. At this point a difficulty arises. The difficulty is obvious in the formulation of the theological norm. This formulation is a matter of personal and communal religious experience and, at the same time, a matter of the methodological judgment of the theologian. It is simultaneously received by ecstatic reason and conceived through technical reason. Traditional and neo-orthodox theologies do not differ at this point. The ambiguity cannot be avoided so long as there is theology, and it is one of the factors which make theology a "questionable" enterprise. The problem could be solved only if man's formal reason were in complete harmony with his ecstatic reason, if man were living in a complete theonomy, that is, in the fulness of the Kingdom of God. One of the basic Christian truths to which theology must witness is that theology itself, like every human activity, is subject to the contradictions of man's existential situation.

Although the problem of the rational character of systematic theology finally must remain unsolved, some directing principles can be stated.

The first principle determining the rational character of systematic theology is a semantic one. There are words which are used in philosophical, scientific, and popular language. If the theologian uses these words, he often can assume that the content indicates the realm of discourse within which the term stands. But this is not always the case. There are terms which for centuries have been adopted by theology, although, at the same time, they have retained religious, philosophical, and other meanings. In this situation the theologian must apply *semantic rationality*. The glory of scholasticism was that it had become a semantic clearing-house for theology as well as for philosophy. And it is almost always a shortcoming and sometimes the shame of modern theology that its concepts remain unclarified and ambiguous. It may be added, however, that the chaotic state of the philosophical and the scientific terminologies makes this situation more or less inevitable.

The principle of semantic rationality must not be confused with the attempt to construct a pan-mathematical formalism. In the realm of spiritual life words cannot be reduced to mathematical signs, nor can sentences be reduced to mathematical equations. The power of words denoting spiritual realities lies in their connotations. The removal of these connotations leaves dead bones which have no meaning in any realm. In such instances the logical positivists are right in rejecting them. When theology employs a term like "Spirit," connotations are present which point to philosophical and psychological concepts of spirit, to the magic world view in which breath and spirit are identical, to the mystic-ascetic experience of Spirit in opposition to matter or flesh, to the religious experience of the divine power grasping the human mind. The principle of semantic rationality does not demand that these connotations should be excluded but the main emphasis should be elaborated by relating it to the connotations. Thus "Spirit," for example, must be related to "spirit" (with a lower case *s*); the primitive magic sense must be excluded, the mystical connotations must be discussed in relation to the personalistic connotations, etc.

Another example is the term "New Being." Being carries connotations of a metaphysical and logical character; it has mystical implications when used in relation to God as being-itself. "New" in connection with "Being" has connotations of creativity, regeneration, eschatology. These elements of meaning always are present when a term like "New Being" appears. The principle of semantic rationality involves the demand that all connotations of a word should consciously be related to each other and centered around a controlling meaning. If the word "history" is used, the different levels of the scientific meaning of history are more in the foreground than in the two preceding examples. But the specific modern emphasis on history as progressive, the specific prophetic emphasis on God as acting through history, and the specific Christian emphasis on the historical character of revelation are united with the scientific meanings whenever history is discussed in a theological context. These examples illustrate the immense importance of the principle of semantic rationality for the systematic theologian. They also suggest how difficult it is to apply this principle—a difficulty which is rooted in the fact that every significant theological term cuts through several levels of meaning and that all of them contribute to the theological meaning.

The semantic situation makes it evident that the language of the theologian cannot be a sacred or revealed language. He cannot restrict himself to the biblical terminology or to the language of classical theology. He could not avoid philosophical concepts even if he used only biblical words; and even less could he avoid them if he used only the word of the Reformers. Therefore, he should use philosophical and scientific terms whenever he deems them helpful for his task of explaining the contents of the Christian faith. The two things he must watch in doing so are semantic clarity and existential purity. He must avoid conceptual ambiguity and a possible distortion of the Christian message by the intrusion of anti-Christian ideas in the cloak of a philosophical, scientific, or poetic terminology.

The second principle determining the rational character of theology is *logical rationality*. This principle refers first of all to the structures which determine any meaningful discourse and which are formulated in the discipline of logic. Theology is as dependent on formal logic as any other science. This must be maintained against both philosophical and theological protests.

The philosophical protest against the all-controlling position of formal logic has been made in the name of dialectical thinking. In dialectics yes and no, affirmation and negation, demand each other. But in formal logic they exclude each other. However, there is no real conflict between dialectics and formal logic. Dialectics follows the movement of thought or the movement of reality through yes and no, but it describes it in logically correct terms. The same concept always is used in the same sense; and, if the meaning of the concept changes, the dialectician describes in a logically correct way the intrinsic necessity which drives the old into the new. Formal logic is not contradicted when Hegel describes the identity of being and nonbeing by showing the absolute emptiness of pure being in reflective thought. Nor is formal logic contradicted when, in the dogma of the Trinity, the divine life is described as a trinity within a unity. The doctrine of the Trinity does not affirm the logical nonsense that three is one and one is three; it describes in dialectical terms the inner movement of the divine life as an eternal separation from itself and return to itself. Theology is not expected to accept a senseless combination of words, that is, genuine logical contradictions. Dialectical thinking is not in conflict with the structure of thinking. It transforms the static ontology behind the logical system of Aristotle and his followers into a dynamic ontology, largely under the influence of voluntaristic and historical motives rooted in the Christian interpretation of existence. This change in ontology opens new vistas for the task of logic in describing and interpreting the structure of thought. It posits in a new way the question of the relation of the structure of thought to the structure of being.

Theological dialectics does not violate the principle of logical rationality. The same is true of the paradoxical statements in religion and theology. When Paul points to his situation as an apostle and to that of Christians generally in a series of *paradoxa* (II Corinthians), he does not intend to say something illogical; he intends to give the adequate, understandable, and therefore logical expression of the infinite tensions of Christian existence. When he speaks about the paradox of the justification of the sinner (in Luther's formula, *simul peccator et iustus*), and when John speaks about the Logos becoming flesh (later expressed in the *paradoxa* of the creed of Chalcedon), neither of them wishes to indulge in logical contradictions.[15] They want to express the conviction that God's acting transcends all possible human expectations and all necessary human preparations. It transcends, but it does not destroy, finite reason; for God acts through the Logos which is the transcendent and transcending source of the *logos* structure of thought and being. God does not annihilate the expression of his own Logos. The term "paradox" should be defined carefully, and paradoxical language should be used with discrimination. Paradoxical means "against the opinion," namely, the opinion of finite reason. Paradox points to the fact that in God's acting finite reason is superseded but not annihilated; it expresses this fact in terms which are not logically contradictory but which are supposed to point beyond the realm in which finite reason is applicable. This is indicated by the ecstatic state in which all biblical and classical theological *paradoxa* appear. The confusion begins when these *paradoxa* are brought down to the level of genuine logical contradictions and people are asked to sacrifice reason in order to accept senseless combinations of words as divine wisdom. But Christianity does not demand such intellectual "good works" from anyone, just as it does not ask artificial "works" of practical asceticism. There is, in the last analysis, only *one* genuine paradox in the Christian message—the appearance of that which conquers existence under the conditions of existence. Incarnation, redemption, justification, etc., are implied in this paradoxical event. It is not a logical contradiction which makes it a paradox but the fact that it transcends all human expectations and possibilities. It breaks into the context of experience or reality, but it cannot be derived from it. The acceptance of this paradox is not the acceptance of the absurd, but it is the state of being grasped by the power of that which breaks into our experience from above it. Paradox in religion and theology does not conflict with the principle of logical rationality. Paradox has its logical place.

The third principle determining the rational character of systematic theology is the principle of *methodological rationality*. It implies that theology follows a method, that is, a definite way of deriving and stating its propositions. The character of this method is dependent on many non-rational factors (see chap. i), but, once it has been established, it must be carried through rationally and consistently. The final expression of consistency in applying methodological rationality is the theological system. If the title "Systematic Theology" has any justification, the systematic theologian should not be afraid of the system. It is the function of the systematic form to guarantee the consistency of cognitive assertions in all realms of methodological knowledge. In this sense some of the most passionate foes of the system are most systematic in the totality of their utterances. And it often happens that those who attack the systematic form are very impatient when they discover an inconsistency in someone else's thought. On the other hand, it is easy to discover gaps in the most balanced system, because life continuously breaks through the systematic shell. One could say that in each system an experienced fragment of life and vision is drawn out constructively even to cover areas where life and vision are missing. And, conversely, one could say that in each fragment a system is implied which is not yet explicated. Hegel's imposing system was built on his early fragmentary paragraphs on the dialectics of life, including the dialectics of religion and the state. The "blood" of his system, as well as its immense historical consequences, were rooted in this fragmentary vision of existence. The lines he later drew with the help of his logical tools soon became obsolete. Nietzsche's many fragments seem to be permanently contradictory. But in all of them a system is implicit, the demonic strength of which has become manifest in the twentieth century. A fragment is an implicit system; a system is an explicit fragment.

The systematic form frequently has been attacked from three points of view. The first attack is based on a confusion between "system" and "deductive system." The history of science, philosophy, and theology shows that a deductive system has very rarely even been attempted except in the field of mathematics. Spinoza made the attempt in his *Ethics,* which he elaborated *more geometrico;* it was envisaged, though not executed, by Leibniz when he suggested a *mathesis universalis* which would describe the cosmos in mathematical terms. Classical physicists, having reached their principles inductively, tried to be deductively systematic, but again in mathematical terms. With the exception of Raimundus Lullus, theology never has attempted to construct a deductive system of Christian truth. Because of the existential character of the Christian truth, such an attempt would have been a contradiction in terms. A system is a totality made up of consistent, but not of deduced, assertions.

The second criticism of the system is that it seems to close the doors to further research. Behind this feeling lies the violent reaction of science since the second half of the nineteenth century against the Romantic philosophy of nature. This reaction has now spent its power and should determine neither our attitude to the scientific achievements of the philosophy of nature (for instance, in the doc-

trine of man and the psychology of the unconscious) nor our attitude to the systematic form in all realms of cognition. It is a historical fact that the great systems have stimulated research at least as
much as they have inhibited it. The system gives meaning to a whole
of factual or rational statements, showing their implications and consequences. Out of such a total view, and out of the difficulties involved
in carrying it through, new questions arise. The balance sheet of positive and negative consequences of "the system" for empirical research
is at least equal.

The third reason for enmity against the system is largely emotional.
It seems like a prison in which the creativity of spiritual life is
stifled. Acceptance of a system seems to imply that "adventures in
ideas" are prohibited. History shows that this is not the case. The
great schools of Greek philosophy produced many creative pupils who
remained in the school, accepted the system on which it was based,
and, at the same time, transformed the ideas of the founder. The
same was true of the theological schools of the nineteenth century.
The history of human thought has been, and still is, identical with the
history of the great systems.

The distinction between three terms may conclude the discussion
of the systematic character of systematic theology and of its methodological rationality. System stands between *summa* and essay. The
summa deals explicitly with *all actual* and many potential problems.
The essay deals explicitly with *one actual* problem. The system deals
with a group of *actual* problems which demand a solution in a special
situation. In the Middle Ages the *summa* was predominant, though
by no means exclusively so. At the beginning of the modern period
the essay became predominant, although the systematic trend never
ceased to exist. Today a need for systematic form has arisen in view
of the chaos of our spiritual life and the impossibility of creating a
summa.

The Method of Correlation

The principle of methodological rationality implies that, like all
scientific approaches to reality, systematic theology follows a method.
A method is a tool, literally a way around, which must be adequate
to its subject matter. Whether or not a method is adequate cannot
be decided a priori; it is continually being decided in the cognitive
process itself. Method and system determine each other. Therefore,
no method can claim to be adequate for every subject. Methodological
imperialism is as dangerous as political imperialism; like the latter,
it breaks down when the independent elements of reality revolt against
it. A method is not an "indifferent net" in which reality is caught,
but the method is an element of the reality itself. In at least one
respect the description of a method is a description of a decisive
aspect of the object to which it is applied. The cognitive relation

itself, quite apart from any special act of cognition, reveals something about the object, as well as about the subject, in the relation. The cognitive relation in physics reveals the mathematical character of objects in space (and time). The cognitive relation in biology reveals the structure (Gestalt) and spontaneous character of objects in space and time. The cognitive relation in historiography reveals the individual and value-related character of objects in time (and space). The cognitive relation in theology reveals the existential and transcending character of the ground of objects in time and space. Therefore, no method can be developed without a prior knowledge of the object to which it is applied. For systematic theology this means that its method is derived from a prior knowledge of the system which is to be built by the method.

Systematic theology uses the method of correlation. It has always done so, sometimes more, sometimes less, consciously, and must do so consciously and outspokenly, especially if the apologetic point of view is to prevail. The method of correlation explains the contents of the Christian faith through existential questions and theological answers in mutual interdependence.

The term "correlation" may be used in three ways. It can designate the correspondence of different series of data, as in statistical charts; it can designate the logical interdependence of concepts, as in polar relations; and it can designate the real interdependence of things or events in structural wholes. If the term is used in theology all three meanings have important applications. There is a correlation in the sense of correspondence between religious symbols and that which is symbolized by them. There is a correlation in the logical sense between concepts denoting the human and those denoting the divine. There is a correlation in the factual sense between man's ultimate concern and that about which he is ultimately concerned. The first meaning of correlation refers to the central problem of religious knowledge. . . . The second meaning of correlation determines the statements about God and the world; for example, the correlation of the infinite and the finite. . . . The third meaning of correlation qualifies the divine-human reationship within religious experience.[16] The third use of correlative thinking in theology has evoked the protest of theologians such as Karl Barth, who are afraid that any kind of divine-human correlation makes God partly dependent on man. But although God in his abysmal nature[17] is in no way dependent on man, God in his self-manifestation to man is dependent on the way man receives his manifestation. This is true even if the doctrine of predestination, namely, that this way is foreordained by God and entirely independent of human freedom, is maintained. The divine-human relation, and therefore God as well as man within this relation, changes with the stages of the history of revelation and with the stages of every personal development. There is a mutual interdependence between "God for us" and "we for God." God's wrath and God's grace are not contrasts in the "heart" of God (Luther), in the depth of his being; but they are contrasts in the divine-human relationship. The divine-human reation is a correlation. The "divine-human encounter" (Emil Brunner) means something real for both sides. It is an actual correlation, in the third sense of the term.

The divine-human relationship is a correlation also in its cognitive side. Symbolically speaking, God answers man's questions, and under the impact of God's answers man asks them. Theology formulates the questions implied in human existence, and theology formulates the answers in divine self-manifestation under the guidance of the questions implied in human existence. This is a circle which drives man to a point where question and answer are not separated. This point, however, is not a moment in time. It belongs to man's essential being, to the unity of his finitude with the infinity in which he was created . . . and from which he is separated. . . . A symptom of both the essential unity and the existential separation of finite man from his infinity is his ability to ask about the infinite to which he belongs: the fact that he must ask about it indicates that he is separated from it.

The answers implied in the event of revelation are meaningful only in so far as they are in correlation with questions concerning the whole of our existence, with existential questions. Only those who have experienced the shock of transitoriness, the anxiety in which they are aware of their finitude, the threat of nonbeing, can understand what the notion of God means. Only those who have experienced the tragic ambiguities of our historical existence and have totally questioned the meaning of existence can understand what the symbol of the Kingdom of God means. Revelation answers questions which have been asked and always will be asked because they are "we ourselves." Man is the question he asks about himself, before any question has been formulated. It is, therefore, not surprising that the basic questions were formulated very early in the history of mankind. Every analysis of the mythological material shows this.[18] Nor is it surprising that the same questions appear in early childhood, as every observation of children shows. Being human means asking the questions of one's own being and living under the impact of the answers given to this question. And, conversely, being human means receiving answers to the questions of one's own being and asking questions under the impact of the answers.

In using the method of correlation, systematic theology proceeds in the following way: it makes an analysis of the human situation out of which the existential questions arise, and it demonstrates that the symbols used in the Christian message are the answers to these questions. The analysis of the human situation is done in terms which today are called "existential." Such analyses are much older than existentialism; they are, indeed, as old as man's thinking about himself, and they have been expressed in various kinds of conceptualization since the beginning of philosophy. Whenever man has looked at his world, he has found himself in it as a part of it. But he also has realized that he is a stranger in the world of objects, unable to penetrate it beyond a certain level of scientific analysis. And then he has become aware of the fact that he himself is the door to the deeper levels of reality, that in his own existence he has the only possible approach to existence itself.[19] This does not mean that man is more approachable than other objects as material for scientific research. The opposite is the case! It does mean that the immediate experience of one's own existing reveals something of the nature of existence generally. Whoever has penetrated into the nature of his own finitude can find the traces of finitude in everything that exists. And he can ask the question implied in his finitude as the question implied in finitude universally. In doing so, he does not formulate a doctrine of man; he expresses a doctrine of existence as experienced in him as man. When Calvin in the opening sentences of the *Institutes* correlates our knowledge of God with our knowledge of man, he does not speak of the doctrine of man as such and of the doctrine of God as such. He speaks of man's misery, which gives the existential basis for his understanding of God's glory, and of God's glory, which gives the essential basis for man's understanding of his misery. Man as existing, representing existence generally and asking the question implied in his existence, is one side of the cognitive correlation to which Calvin points, the other side being the divine majesty. In the initial sentences of his theological system Calvin expresses the essence of the method of correlation.[20]

The analysis of the human situation employs materials made available by man's creative self-interpretation in all realms of culture. Philosophy contributes, but so do poetry, drama, the novel, therapeutic psychology, and sociology. The theologian organizes these materials in relation to the answer given by the Christian message. In the light of this message he may make an analysis of existence which is more penetrating than that of most philosophers. Nevertheless, it remains a philosophical analysis. The analysis of existence, including the development of the questions implicit in existence, is a philosophical task, even if it is performed by a theologian, and even if the theologian is a reformer like Calvin. The difference between the philosopher who is not a theologian and the theologian who works as a philosopher in analyzing human existence is only that the former tries to give an analysis which will be part of a broader philosophical work, while the latter tries to correlate the material of his analysis with the theological concepts he derives from the Christian faith. This does not make the philosophical work of the theologian heteronomous. As a theologian he does not tell himself what is philosophically true. As a philosopher he does not tell himself what is theologically true. But he cannot help seeing human existence and existence generally in such a way that the Christian symbols appear meaningful and understandable to him. His eyes are partially focused by his ultimate concern, which is true of every philosopher. Nevertheless, his act of seeing is autonomous, for it is determined only by the object as it is given in his experience. If he sees something he did not expect to see in the light of his theological answer, he holds fast to what he has seen and reformulates the theological answer. He is certain that nothing he sees can change the substance of his answer, because this substance is the *logos* of being, manifest in Jesus as the Christ. If this were not his presupposition, he would have to sacrifice either his philosophical honesty or his theological concern.

The Christian message provides the answers to the questions implied in human existence. These answers are contained in the revelatory events on which Christianity is based and are taken by systematic theology *from* the sources, *through* the medium, *under* the norm. Their content cannot be derived from the questions, that is, from an analysis of human existence. They are "spoken" *to* human existence from beyond it. Otherwise they would not be answers, for the question is human existence itself. But the relation is more involved than this, since it is correlation. There is a mutual dependence between question and answer. In respect to content the Christian answers are dependent on the revelatory events in which they appear; in respect to form they are dependent on the structure of the questions which they answer. God is the answer to the question implied in human finitude. This answer cannot be derived from the analysis of existence. However, if the notion of God appears in systematic theology in correlation with the threat of nonbeing which is implied in existence, God must be called the infinite power of being which resists the threat of nonbeing. In classical theology this is being-itself. If anxiety is defined as the awareness of being finite, God must be called the infinite ground of courage. In classical theology this is universal providence. If the notion of the Kingdom of God appears in correlation with the riddle of our historical existence, it must be called the meaning, fulfilment, and unity of history. In this way an interpretation of the traditional symbols of Christianity is achieved which preserves the power of these symbols and which opens them to the questions elaborated by our present analysis of human existence.

The method of correlation replaces three inadequate methods of relating the contents of the Christian faith to man's spiritual existence. The first method can be called supranaturalistic, in that it takes the Christian message to be a sum of revealed truths which have fallen into the human situation like strange bodies from a strange world. No mediation to the human situation is possible. These truths themselves create a new situation before they can be received. Man must become something else than human in order to receive divinity. In terms of the classical heresies one could say that the supranaturalistic method has docetic-monophysitic traits, especially in its valuation of the Bible as a book of supranatural "oracles" in which human receptivity is completely overlooked. But man cannot receive answers to questions he never has asked. Furthermore, man has asked and is asking in his very existence and in every one of his spiritual creations questions which Christianity answers.

The second method to be rejected can be called "naturalistic" or "humanistic." It derives the Christian message from man's natural state. It develops its answer out of human existence, unaware that human existence itself *is* the question. Much of liberal theology in the last two centuries was "humanistic" in this sense. It identified man's existential with his essential state, overlooking the break between them which is reflected in the universal human condition of self-estrangement and self-contradiction. Theologically this meant that the contents of the Christian faith were explained as creations of man's religious self-realization in the progressive process of religious history. Questions and answers were put on the same level of human creativity. Everything was said by man, nothing to man. But revelation is "spoken" to man, not by man to himself.

The third method to be rejected can be called "dualistic," inasmuch as it builds a supranatural structure on a natural substructure. This method, more than others, is aware of the problem which the method of correlation tries to meet. It realizes that, in spite of the infinite gap between man's spirit and God's spirit, there must be a positive relation between them. It tries to express this relation by positing a body of theological truth which man can reach through his own efforts or, in terms of a self-contradictory expression, through "natural revelation." The so-called arguments for "the existence of God," which itself is another self-contradictory term, are the most important section of natural theology. These arguments are true . . . in so far as they analyze human finitude and the question involved in it. They are false in so far as they derive an answer from the form of the question. This mixture of truth and falsehood in natural theology explains why there always have been great philosophers and theologians who have attacked natural theology, especially the arguments for the existence of God, and why others equally great have defended it. The method of correlation solves this historical and systematic riddle by resolving natural theology into the analysis of existence and by resolving supranatural theology into the answers given to the questions implied in existence.

The Theological System

The structure of the theological system follows from the method of correlation. The method of correlation requires that every part of the system should include one section in which the question is developed by an analysis of human existence and existence generally, and one section in which the theological answer is given on the basis of the sources, the medium, and the norm of systematic theology. This division must be maintained. It is the backbone of the structure of the present system.

One could think of a section which mediates between the two main sections by interpreting historical, sociological, and psychological materials in the light of both the existential questions and the theological answers.[21] Since these materials from the sources of systematic theology are used not as they appear in their historical, sociological, or psychological setting but in terms of their significance for the systematic solution, they belong to the theological answer and do not constitute a section of their own.

In each of the five parts of the system which are derived from the structure of existence in correlation with the structure of the Christian message, the two sections are correlated in the following ways. In so far as man's existence has the character of self-contradiction or estrangement, a double consideration is demanded, one side dealing with man as he essentially is (and ought to be) and the other dealing with what he is in his self-estranged existence (and should not be). These correspond to the Christian distinction between the realm of creation and the realm of salvation. Therefore, one part of the system must give an analysis of man's essential nature (in unity with the essential nature of everything that has being), and of the question implied in man's finitude and finitude generally; and it must give the answer which is God. This part, therefore, is called "Being and God." A second part of the system must give an analysis of man's existential self-estrangement (in unity with the self-destructive aspects of existence generally) and the question implied in this situation; and it must give the answer which is the Christ. This part, therefore, is called "Existence and Christ." A third part is based on the fact that the essential as well as the existential characteristics are abstractions and that in reality they appear in the complex and dynamic unity which is called "life." The power of essential being is ambiguously present in all existential distortions. Life, that is, being in its actuality, displays such a character in all its processes. Therefore, this part of the system must give an analysis of man as living (in unity with life generally) and of the question implied in the ambiguities of life; and it must give the answer which is the Spirit. This part, therefore, is called "Life and the Spirit." These three parts represent the main body of systematic theology. They embrace the Christian answers to the questions of existence. But for practical reasons it is necessary to "split off" some of the material from each part and combine it to form an epistemological part. This part of the system must give an analysis of man's rationality, especially his cognitive rationality (in unity with the rational structure of reality as a whole), and of the questions implied in the finitude, the self-estrangement, and the ambiguities of reason; and it must give the answer which is Revelation. This part, therefore, is called "Reason and Revelation."

Finally, life has a dimension which is called "history." And it is helpful to separate the material dealing with the historical aspect of life from the part dealing with life generally. This corresponds to the fact that the symbol "Kingdom of God" is independent of the trinitarian structure which determines the central parts. This part of the system must give an analysis of man's historical existence (in unity with the nature of the historical generally) and of the questions implied in the ambiguities of history; and it must give an answer which is the Kingdom of God. This part is called "History and the Kingdom of God."

It would be most advantageous to begin with "Being and God," because this part outlines the basic structure of being and gives the answer to the questions implied in this structure—an answer which determines all other answers—for theology is first of all doctrine of God. But several considerations make it necessary to begin with the epistemological part, "Reason and Revelation." First, every theologian is asked, "On what do you base your assertions; what criteria, what verification, do you have?" This necessitates an epistemological answer from the very start. Second, the concept of reason (and Reason) must be clarified before statements can be made in which there is the assumption that reason transcends itself. Third, the doctrine of revelation must be dealt with at the very beginning, because revelation is presupposed in all parts of the system as the ultimate source of the contents of the Christian faith. For these reasons, "Reason and Revelation" must open the system, just as for obvious reasons "History and the Kingdom of God" must close it. One cannot avoid the fact that in each part elements of the other parts are anticipated or repeated. In a way each part contains the whole from a different perspective, for the present system is by no means deductive. The very fact that in each part the question is developed anew makes any possible continuity of deduction impossible. Revelation is not given as a system. But revelation is not inconsistent either. The systematic theologian, therefore, can interpret that which transcends all possible systems, the self-manifestation of the divine mystery, in a systematic form.

Notes

[14]*Kurtze Darstellung des theologischen Studiums zum Gebrauche fur Vorlesungen* (2d ed., 1830).

[15]It is the mistake of Brunner in *The Mediator* that he makes the offense of logical rationality the criterion of Christian truth. This "offense" is neither that of Kierkegaard nor that of the New Testament.

[16]Luther: "As you believe him so you have him."

[17]Calvin: "In his essence."

[18]Cf. H. Gunkel, *The Legends of Genesis* (Chicago: Open Court Publishing Co., 1901).

[19]Cf. Augustine's doctrine of truth dwelling in the soul and transcending it at the same time; the mystical identification of the ground of being with the ground of self; the use of psychological categories for ontological purposes in Paracelsus, Bohme, Schelling, and in the "philosophy of life" from Schopenhauer to Bergson; Heidegger's notion of "Dasein" (being there) as the form of human existence and the entrance to ontology.

[20]"The knowledge of ourselves is not only an incitement to seek after God, but likewise a considerable assistance towards finding him. On the other hand, it is plain that no man can arrive at the true knowledge of himself, without having first contemplated the divine character, and then descended to the consideration of his own" (John Calvin, *Institutes,* I, 48).

[21]In former outlines, especially in the "Propositions" prepared for my lectures, such a section always was inserted.

7

Rudolf Bultmann

New Testament and Theology

THE TASK OF DEMYTHOLOGIZING THE NEW TESTAMENT PROCLAMATION

The Problem

1. The Mythical View of the World and the Mythical Event of Redemption

The cosmology of the New Testament is essentially mythical in character. The world is viewed as a three-storied structure, with the earth in the centre, the heaven above, and the underworld beneath. Heaven is the abode of God and of celestial beings—the angels. The underworld is hell, the place of torment. Even the earth is more than the scene of natural, everyday events, of the trivial round and common task. It is the scene of the supernatural activity of God and his angels on the one hand, and of Satan and his daemons on the other. These supernatural forces intervene in the course of nature and in all that men think and will and do. Miracles are by no means rare.

From Rudolf Bultmann, "New Testament and Mythology." *Kerygma and Myth,* Vol. I, ed. Hans Barsch. New York: Harper and Row, 1961. Reprinted by permission of Harper & Row, Publishers, Inc.

Man is not in control of his own life. Evil spirits may take possession of him. Satan may inspire him with evil thoughts. Alternatively, God may inspire his thought and guide his purposes. He may grant him heavenly visions. He may allow him to hear his word of succour or demand. He may give him the supernatural power of his Spirit. History does not follow a smooth unbroken course; it is set in motion and controlled by these supernatural powers. This aeon is held in bondage by Satan, sin, and death (for "powers" is precisely what they are), and hastens towards its end. That end will come very soon, and will take the form of a cosmic catastrophe. It will be inaugurated by the "woes" of the last time. Then the Judge will come from heaven, the dead will rise, the last judgment will take place, and men will enter into eternal salvation or damnation.

This then is the mythical view of the world which the New Testament presupposes when it presents the event of redemption which is the subject of its preaching. It proclaims in the language of mythology that the last time has now come. "In the fulness of time" God sent forth His Son, a pre-existent divine Being, who appears on earth as a man.[1] He dies the death of a sinner[2] on the cross and makes atonement for the sins of men.[3] His resurrection marks the beginning of the cosmic catastrophe. Death, the consequence of Adam's sin, is abolished,[4] and the daemonic forces are deprived of their power.[5] The risen Christ is exalted to the right hand of God in heaven[6] and made "Lord" and "King."[7] He will come again on the clouds of heaven to complete the work of redemption, and the resurrection and judgment of men will follow.[8] Sin, suffering, and death will then be finally abolished.[9] All this is to happen very soon; indeed, St. Paul thinks that he himself will live to see it.[10]

All who belong to Christ's Church and are joined to the Lord by Baptism and the Eucharist are certain of resurrection to salvation,[11] unless they forfeit it by unworthy behaviour. Christian believers already enjoy the first instalment of salvation, for the Spirit[12] is at work within them, bearing witness to their adoption as sons of God,[13] and guaranteeing their final resurrection.[14]

2. The Mythological View of the World Obsolete

All this is the language of mythology, and the origin of the various themes can be easily traced in the contemporary mythology of Jewish Apocalyptic and in the redemption myths of Gnosticism. To this extent *the kerygma is incredible to modern man, for he is convinced that the mythical view of the world is obsolete.* We are therefore bound to ask whether, when we preach the Gospel to-day, we expect our converts to accept not only the Gospel message, but also the mythical view of the world in which it is set. If not, does the New Testament embody a truth which is quite independent of its mythical setting? If it does, theology must undertake the task of stripping the kerygma from its mythical framework, of "demythologizing" it.

Can Christian preaching expect modern man *to accept the mythical view of the world as true?* To do so would be both senseless and impossible. It would be senseless, because there is nothing specifically Christian in the mythical view of the world as such. It is simply the cosmology of a pre-scientific age. Again, it would be impossible, because no man can adopt a view of the world by his own volition— it is already determined for him by his place in history. Of course such a view is not absolutely unalterable, and the individual may even contribute to its change. But he can do so only when he is faced by a new set of facts so compelling as to make his previous view of the world untenable. He has then no alternative but to modify his view of the world or produce a new one. The discoveries of Copernicus and the atomic theory are instances of this, and so was romanticism, with its discovery that the human subject is richer and more complex than enlightenment or idealism had allowed, and nationalism, with its new realization of the importance of history and the tradition of peoples.

It may equally well happen that truths which a shallow enlightenment had failed to perceive are later rediscovered in ancient myths. Theologians are perfectly justified in asking whether this is not exactly what has happened with the New Testament. At the same time it is impossible to revive an obsolete view of the world by a mere fiat, and certainly not a mythical view. For all our thinking to-day is shaped irrevocably by modern science. A blind acceptance of the New Testament mythology would be arbitrary, and to press for its acceptance as an article of faith would be to reduce faith to works. Wilhelm Herrmann pointed this out, and one would have thought that his demonstration was conclusive. It would involve a sacrifice of the intellect which could have only one result—a curious form of schizophrenia and insincerity. It would mean accepting a view of the world in our faith and religion which we should deny in our everyday life. Modern thought as we have inherited it brings with it criticism of *the New Testament view of the world.*

Man's knowledge and mastery of the world have advanced to such an extent through science and technology that it is no longer possible for anyone seriously to hold the New Testament view of the world—in fact, there is no one who does. What meaning, for instance, can we attach to such phrases in the creed as "descended into hell" or "ascended into heaven"? We no longer believe in the three-storied universe which the creeds take for granted. The only honest way of reciting the creeds is to strip the mythological framework from the truth they enshrine—that is, assuming that they contain any truth at all, which is just the question that theology has to ask. No one who is old enough to think for himself supposes that God lives in a local heaven. There is no longer any heaven in the traditional sense of the word. The same applies to hell in the sense of a mythical underworld beneath our feet. And if this is so, the story of Christ's descent into hell and of his Ascension into heaven is done with. We can no longer look for the return of the Son of Man on the clouds of heaven or hope that the faithful will meet him in the air (I Thess. 4:15 ff.). Now that the forces and the laws of nature have been discovered, we can no longer believe in *spirits, whether good or evil.* We know that the stars are physical bodies whose motions are controlled by the laws of the universe, and not daemonic beings which enslave mankind to their service. Any influence they may have over human life must be explicable in terms of the ordinary laws of nature; it cannot in any way be attributed to their malevolence. Sickness and the cure of disease are likewise attributable to natural causation; they are not the result of daemonic activity or of evil spells.[15] The *miracles of the New Testament* have ceased to be miraculous, and to defend their historicity by recourse to nervous disorders or hypnotic effects only serves to underline the fact. And if we are still left with certain physiological and psychological phenomena which we can only assign to mysterious and enigmatic causes, we are still assigning them to causes, and thus far are trying to make them scientifically intelligible. Even occultism pretends to be a science.

It is impossible to use electric light and the wireless and to avail ourselves of modern medical and surgical discoveries, and at the same time to believe in the New Testament world of spirits and miracles.[16] We may think we can manage it in our own lives, but to expect others to do so is to make the Christian faith unintelligible and unacceptable to the modern world.

The mythical eschatology is untenable for the simple reason that the parousia of Christ never took place as the New Testament expected. History did not come to an end, and, as every schoolboy knows, it will continue to run its course. Even if we believe that the world as we know it will come to an end in time, we expect the end to take the form of a natural catastrophe, not of a mythical event such as the New Testament expects. And if we explain the parousia in terms of modern scientific theory, we are applying criticism to the New Testament, albeit unconsciously.

But natural science is not the only challenge which the mythology of the New Testament has to face. There is the still more serious challenge presented by *modern man's understanding of himself.*

Modern man is confronted by a curious dilemma. He may regard himself as pure nature, or as pure spirit. In the latter case he distinguishes the essential part of his being from nature. In either case, however, *man is essentially a unity.* He bears the sole responsibility for his own feeling, thinking, and willing.[17] He is not, as the New Testament regards him, the victim of a strange dichotomy which exposes him to be the interference of powers outside himself. If his exterior behaviour and his interior condition are in perfect harmony, it is something he has achieved himself, and if other people think their interior unity is torn asunder by daemonic or divine interference, he calls it schizophrenia.

Although biology and psychology recognize that man is a highly dependent being, that does not mean that he has been handed over to powers outside of and distinct from himself. This dependence is inseparable from human nature, and he needs only to understand it in order to recover his self-mastery and organize his life on a rational basis. If he regards himself as spirit, he knows that he is permanently conditioned by the physical, bodily part of his being, but he distinguishes his true self from it, and knows that he is independent and responsible for his mastery over nature.

In either case he finds *what the New Testament has to say about the "Spirit" (pneuma) and the sacraments utterly strange and incomprehensible.* Biological man cannot see how a supernatural entity like the *pneuma* can penetrate within the close texture of his natural powers and set to work within him. Nor can the idealist understand how a *pneuma* working like a natural power can touch and influence his mind and spirit. Conscious as he is of his own moral responsibility, he cannot conceive how baptism in water can convey a mysterious something which is henceforth the agent of all his decisions and actions. He cannot see how physical food can convey spiritual strength, and how the unworthy receiving of the Eucharist can result in physical sickness and death (I Cor. 11:30). The only possible explanation is that it is due to suggestion. He cannot understand how anyone can be baptized for the dead (I Cor. 15:29).

We need not examine in detail the various forms of modern *Weltanschauung,* whether idealist or naturalist. For the only criticism of the New Testament which is theologically relevant is that which arises *necessarily* out of the situation of modern man. The biological *Weltanschauung* does not, for instance, arise necessarily out of the contemporary situation. We are still free to adopt it or not as we choose. The only relevant question for the theologian is the basic assumption on which the adoption of a biological as of every other *Weltanschauung* rests, and that assumption is the view of the world which has been moulded by modern science and the modern conception of human nature as a self-subsistent unity immune from the interference of supernatural powers.

Again, the biblical doctrine that *death is the punishment of sin* is equally abhorrent to naturalism and idealism, since they both regard death as a simple and necessary process of nature. To the naturalist death is no problem at all, and to the idealist it is a problem for that very reason, for so far from arising out of man's essential spiritual being it actually destroys it. The idealist is faced with a paradox. On the one hand man is a spiritual being, and therefore essentially different from plants and animals, and on the other hand he is the prisoner of nature, whose birth, life, and death are just the same as those of the animals. Death may present him with a problem, but he cannot see how it can be a punishment for sin. Human beings are subject to death even before they have committed any sin. And to attribute human mortality to the fall of Adam is sheer nonsense, for guilt implies personal responsibility, and the idea of original sin as an inherited infection is sub-ethical, irrational, and absurd.

The same objections apply to *the doctrine of the atonement*. How can the guilt of one man be expiated by the death of another who is sinless—if indeed one may speak of a sinless man at all? What primitive notions of guilt and righteousness does this imply? And what primitive idea of God? The rationale of sacrifice in general may of course throw some light on the theory of the atonement, but even so, what a primitive mythology it is, that a divine Being should become incarnate, and atone for the sins of men through his own blood! Or again, one might adopt an analogy from the law courts, and explain the death of Christ as a transaction between God and man through which God's claims on man were satisfied. But that would make sin a juridical matter; it would be no more than an external transgression of a commandment, and it would make nonsense of all our ethical standards. Moreover, if the Christ who died such a death was the pre-existent Son of God, what could death mean for him? Obviously very little, if he knew that he would rise again in three days!

The *resurrection of Jesus* is just as difficult for modern man, if it means an event whereby a living supernatural power is released which can henceforth be appropriated through the sacraments. To the biologist such language is meaningless, for he does not regard death as a problem at all. The idealist would not object to the idea of a life immune from death, but he could not believe that such a life is made available by the resuscitation of a dead person. If that is the way God makes life available for man, his action is inextricably involved in a nature miracle. Such a notion he finds incomprehensible, for he can see God at work only in the reality of his personal life and in his transformation. But quite apart from the incredibility of such a miracle, he cannot see how an event like this could be the act of God, or how it could affect his own life.

Gnostic influence suggests that this Christ, who died and rose again, was not a mere human being but a God-man. His death and resurrection were not isolated facts which concerned him alone, but a cosmic event in which we are all involved.[18] It is only with effort that modern man can think himself back into such an intellectual atmosphere, and even then he could never accept it himself, because it regards man's essential being as nature and redemption as a process of nature. And as for the pre-existence of Christ, with its corollary of man's translation into a celestial realm of light, and the clothing of the human personality in heavenly robes and a spiritual body —all this is not only irrational but utterly meaningless. Why should salvation take this particular form? Why should this be the fulfilment of human life and the realization of man's true being?

The Task Before Us

1. Not Selection or Subtraction

Does this drastic criticism of the New Testament mythology mean the complete elimination of the kerygma?

Whatever else may be true, we cannot save the kerygma by selecting some of its features and subtracting others, and thus reduce the amount of mythology in it. For instance, it is impossible to dismiss St. Paul's teaching about the unworthy reception of Holy Communion or about baptism for the dead, and yet cling to the belief that physical eating and drinking can have a spiritual effect. If we accept *one* idea, we must accept everything which the New Testament has to say about Baptism and Holy Communion, and it is just this one idea which we cannot accept.

It may of course be argued that some features of the New Testament mythology are given greater prominence than others: not all of them appear with the same regularity in the various books. There is for example only one occurrence of the legends of the Virgin birth and the Ascension; St. Paul and St. John appear to be totally unaware of them. But, even if we take them to be later accretions, it does not affect the mythical character of the event of redemption as a whole. And if we once start subtracting from the kerygma, where are we to draw the line? The mythical view of the world must be accepted or rejected in its entirety.

At this point absolute clarity and ruthless honesty are essential both for the academic theologian and for the parish priest. It is a duty they owe to themselves, to the Church they serve, and to those whom they seek to win for the Church. They must make it quite clear what their hearers are expected to accept and what they are not. At all costs the preacher must not leave his people in the dark about what he secretly eliminates, nor must he be in the dark about it himself. In Karl Barth's book *The Resurrection of the Dead* the cosmic eschatology in the sense of "chronologically final history" is eliminated in favour of what he intends to be a non-mythological "ultimate history." He is able to delude himself into thinking that this is exegesis of St. Paul and of the New Testament generally only because he gets rid of everything mythological in I Corinthians by subjecting it to an interpretation which does violence to its meaning. But that is an impossible procedure.

If the truth of the New Testament proclamation is to be preserved, the only way is to demythologize it. But our motive in so doing must not be to make the New Testament relevant to the modern world at all costs. The question is simply whether the New Testament message consists exclusively of mythology, or whether it actually demands the elimination of myth if it is to be understood as it is meant to be. This question is forced upon us from two sides. First there is the nature of myth in general, and then there is the New Testament itself.

2. The Nature of Myth

The real purpose of myth is not to present an objective picture of the world as it is, but to express man's understanding of himself in the world in which he lives. Myth should be interpreted not cosmologically, but anthropologically, or better still, existentially.[19] Myth speaks of the power or the powers which man supposes he experiences as the ground and limit of his world and of his own activity and suffering. He describes these powers in terms derived from the visible world, with its tangible objects and forces, and from human life, with its feelings, motives, and potentialities. He may, for instance, explain the origin of the world by speaking of a world egg or a world tree. Similarly he may account for the present state and order of the world by speaking of a primeval war between the gods. He speaks of the other world in terms of this world, and of the gods in terms derived from human life.[20]

Myth is an expression of man's conviction that the origin and purpose of the world in which he lives are to be sought not within it but beyond it—that is, beyond the realm of known and tangible reality—and that this realm is perpetually dominated and menaced by those mysterious powers which are its source and limit. Myth is also an expression of man's awareness that he is not lord of his own being. It expresses his sense of dependence not only within the visible world, but more especially on those forces which hold sway beyond the confines of the known. Finally, myth expresses man's belief that in this state of dependence he can be delivered from the forces within the visible world.

Thus myth contains elements which demand its own criticism—namely its imagery with its apparent claim to objective validity. The real purpose of myth is to speak of a transcendent power which controls the world and man, but that purpose is impeded and obscured by the terms in which it is expressed.

Hence the importance of the New Testament mythology lies not in its imagery but in the understanding of existence which it enshrines. The real question is whether this understanding of existence is true.

Faith claims that it is, and faith ought not to be tied down to the imagery of New Testament mythology.

3. The New Testament Itself

The New Testament itself invites this kind of criticism. Not only are there rough edges in its mythology, but some of its features are actually contradictory. For example, the death of Christ is sometimes a sacrifice and sometimes a cosmic event. Sometimes his person is interpreted as the Messiah and sometimes as the Second Adam. The kenosis of the pre-existent Son (Phil. 2:6 ff.) is incompatible with the miracle narratives as proofs of his messianic claims. The Virgin birth is inconsistent with the assertion of his pre-existence. The doctrine of the Creation is incompatible with the conception of the "rulers of this world" (I Cor. 2.6 ff.), the "god of this world" (II Cor. 4:4) and the "elements of this world" *stoicheia tou kosmou* (Gal. 4:3). It is impossible to square the belief that the law was given by God with the theory that it comes from the angels (Gal. 3:19 f.).

But the principal demand for the criticism of mythology comes from a curious contradiction which runs right through the New Testament. Sometimes we are told that human life is determined by cosmic forces, at others we are challenged to a decision. Side by side with the Pauline indicative stands the Pauline imperative. In short, man is sometimes regarded as a cosmic being, sometimes as an independent "I" for whom decision is a matter of life or death. Incidentally, this explains why so many sayings in the New Testament speak directly to modern man's condition while others remain enigmatic and obscure. Finally, attempts at demythologization are sometimes made even within the New Testament itself. But more will be said on this point later.

4. Previous Attempts at Demythologizing

How then is the mythology of the New Testament to be re-interpreted? This is not the first time that theologians have approached this task. Indeed, all we have said so far might have been said in much the same way thirty or forty years ago, and it is a sign of the bankruptcy of contemporary theology that it has been necessary to go all over the same ground again. The reason for this is not far to seek. The liberal theologians of the last century were working on the wrong lines. They threw away not only the mythology but also the kerygma itsef. Were they right? Is that the treatment the New Testament itself required? That is the question we must face today. The last twenty years have witnessed a movement away from criticism and a return to a naive acceptance of the kerygma. The danger both for theological scholarship and for the Church is that this uncritical resuscitation of the New Testament mythology may make the Gospel message unintelligible to the modern world. We cannot dismiss the critical labours of earlier generations without further ado. We must take them up and put them to constructive use. Failure to do so will mean that the old battles between orthodoxy and liberalism will have to be fought out all over again, that is assuming that there will be any Church or any theologians to fight them at all! Perhaps we may put it schematically like this: whereas the older liberals used criticism to *eliminate* the mythology of the New Testament, our task to-day is to use criticism to *interpret* it. Of course it may still be necessary to eliminate mythology here and there. But the criterion adopted must be taken not from modern thought, but from the understanding of human existence which the New Testament itself enshrines.[21]

To begin with, let us review some of these earlier attempts at de-mythologizing. We need only mention briefly the allegorical interpretation of the New Testament which has dogged the Church throughout its history. This method spiritualizes the mythical events so that they become symbols of processes going on in the soul. This is certainly the most comfortable way of avoiding the critical question. The literal meaning is allowed to stand and is dispensed with only for the individual believer, who can escape into the realm of the soul.

It was characteristic of the older liberal theologians that they regarded mythology as relative and temporary. Hence they thought they could safely eliminate it altogether, and retain only the broad, basic principles of religion and ethics. They distinguished between what they took to be the essence of religion and the temporary garb which it assumed. Listen to what Harnack has to say about the essence of Jesus' preaching of the Kingdom of God and its coming: "The kingdom has a triple meaning. Firstly, it is something supernatural, a gift from above, not a product of ordinary life. Secondly, it is a purely religious blessing, the inner link with the living God; thirdly, it is the most important experience that a man can have, that on which everything else depends; it permeates and dominates his whole existence, because sin is forgiven and misery banished." Note how completely the mythology is eliminated: "The kingdom of God comes by coming to the individual, by entering into his *soul* and laying hold of it."[22]

It will be noticed how Harnack reduces the kerygma to a few basic principles of religion and ethics. Unfortunately this means that the *kerygma has ceased to be kerygma:* it is no longer the proclamation of the decisive act of God in Christ. For the liberals the great truths of religion and ethics are timeless and eternal, though it is only within human history that they are realized, and only in concrete historical processes that they are given clear expression. But the apprehension and acceptance of these principles does not depend on the knowledge and acceptance of the age in which they first took shape, or of the historical persons who first discovered them. We are all capable of verifying them in our own experience at whatever period we happen to live. History may be of academic interest, but never of paramount importance for religion.

But the New Testament speaks of an *event* through which God has wrought man's redemption. For it, Jesus is not primarily the teacher, who certainly had extremely important things to say and will always be honoured for saying them, but whose person in the last analysis is immaterial for those who have assimilated his teaching. On the contrary, his person is just what the New Testament proclaims as the decisive event of redemption. It speaks of this person in mythological terms, but does this mean that we can reject the kerygma altogether on the ground that it is nothing more than mythology? That is the question.

Next came the History of Religions school. Its representatives were the first to discover the extent to which the New Testament is permeated by mythology. The importance of the New Testament they saw, lay not in its teaching about religion and ethics but in its actual religion and piety; in comparison with that all the dogma it contains, and therefore all the mythological imagery with its apparent objectivity, was of secondary importance or completely negligible. The essence of the New Testament lay in the religious life it portrayed; its high-watermark was the experience of mystical union with Christ, in whom God took symbolic form.

These critics grasped one important truth. Christian faith is not the same as religious idealism; the Christian life does not consist in developing the individual personality, in the improvement of society, or in making the world a better place. The Christian life means a turning away from the world, a detachment from it. But the critics of the History of Religions school failed to see that in the New Testament this detachment is essentially eschatological and not mystical. Religion for them was an expression of the human yearning to rise above the world and transcend it: it was the discovery of a supramundane sphere where the soul could detach itself from all earthly care and find its rest. Hence the supreme manifestation of religion was to be found not in personal ethics or in social idealism but in the cultus regarded as an end in itself. This was just the kind of religious life portrayed in the New Testament, not only as a model and pattern, but as a challenge and inspiration. The New Testament was thus the abiding source of power which enabled man to realize the true life of religion, and Christ was the eternal symbol of the cultus of the Christian Church.[23] It will be noticed how the Church is here defined exclusively as a worshipping community, and this represents a great advance on the older liberalism. This school rediscovered the Church as a *religious* institution. For the idealist there was really no place for the Church at all. But did they succeed in recovering the meaning of the Ecclesia in the full, New Testament sense of the word? For in the New Testament the Ecclesia is invariably a phenomenon of salvation history and eschatology.

Moreover, if the History of Religions school is right, the kerygma has once more ceased to be kerygma. Like the liberals, they are silent about a decisive act of God in Christ proclaimed as the event of redemption. So we are still left with the question whether this event and the person of Jesus, both of which are described in the New Testament in mythological terms, are nothing more than mythology. Can the kerygma be interpreted apart from mythology? Can we recover the truth of the kerygma for men who do not think in mythological terms without forfeiting its character as kerygma?

5. An Existentialist Interpretation the Only Solution

The theological work which such an interpretation involves can be sketched only in the broadest outline and with only a few examples. We must avoid the impression that this is a light and easy task, as if all we have to do is to discover the right formula and finish the job on the spot. It is much more formidable than that. It cannot be done single-handed. It will tax the time and strength of a whole theological generation.

The mythology of the New Testament is in essence that of Jewish apocalyptic and the Gnostic redemption myths. A common feature of them both is their basic dualism, according to which the present world and its human inhabitants are under the control of daemonic, satanic powers, and stand in need of redemption. Man cannot achieve this redemption by his own efforts; it must come as a gift through a divine intervention. Both types of mythology speak of such an intervention: Jewish apocalyptic of an imminent world crisis in which this present aeon will be brought to an end and the new aeon ushered in by the coming of the Messiah, and Gnosticism of a Son of God sent down from the realm of light, entering into this world in the guise of a man, and by his fate and teaching delivering the elect and opening up the way for their return to their heavenly home.

The meaning of these two types of mythology lies once more not in their imagery with its apparent objectivity but in the understanding of human existence which both are trying to express. In other words, they need to be interpreted existentially. A good example of such treatment is to be found in Hans Jonas's book on Gnosticism.[24]

Our task is to produce an existentialist interpretation of the dualistic mythology of the New Testament along similar lines. When, for instance, we read of daemonic powers ruling the world and holding mankind in bondage, does the understanding of human existence which underlies such language offer a solution to the riddle of human life which will be acceptable even to the non-mythological mind of to-day? Of course we must not take this to imply that the New Testament presents us with an anthropology like that which modern science can give us. It cannot be proved by logic or demonstrated by an appeal to factual evidence. Scientific anthropologies always take for granted a definite understanding of existence, which is invariably the consequence of a deliberate decision of the scientist, whether he makes it consciously or not. And that is why we have to discover whether the New Testament offers man an understanding of himself which will challenge him to a genuine existential decision.

DEMYTHOLOGIZING IN OUTLINE

A. The Christian Interpretation of Being

The Event of Jesus Christ

Anyone who asserts that to speak of an act of God at all is mythological language is bound to regard the idea of an act of God in Christ as a myth. But let us ignore this question for a moment. Even Kamlah thinks it philosophically justifiable to use "the mythological language of an act of God" (p. 353). The issue for the moment is whether that particular event in which the New Testament sees the act of God and the revelation of his love—that is, the event of Jesus Christ—is essentially a mythical event.

a. The Demythologizing of the Event of Jesus Christ

Now it is beyond question that the New Testament presents the event of Jesus Christ in mythical terms. The problem is whether that is the only possible presentation. Or does the New Testament itself demand a restatement of the event of Jesus Christ in non-mythological terms? Now, it is clear from the outset that the event of Christ is of a wholly different order from the cult-myths of Greek or Hellenistic religion. Jesus Christ is certainly presented as the Son of God, a pre-existent divine being, and therefore to that extent a mythical figure. But he is also a concrete figure of history—Jesus of Nazareth. His life is more than a mythical event; it is a human life which ended in the tragedy of crucifixion. We have here a unique combination of history and myth. The New Testament claims that this Jesus of history, whose father and mother were well known to his contemporaries (John 6:42) is at the same time the pre-existent Son of God, and side by side with the historical event of the crucifixion it sets the definitely non-historical event of the resurrection. This combination of myth and history presents a number of difficulties, as can be seen from certain inconsistencies in the New Testament material. The doctrine of Christ's pre-existence as given by St. Paul and St. John is difficult to reconcile with the legend of the Virgin birth in St. Matthew and St. Luke. On the one hand we hear that "he emptied himself, taking the form of a servant, being made in the likeness of men: and

being found in fashion as a man . . ." (Phil. 2:7), and on the other
hand we have the gospel portraits of a Jesus who manifests his divinity in his miracles, omniscience, and mysterious elusiveness, and
the similar description of him in Acts as "Jesus of Nazareth, a man
approved of God unto you by mighty works and wonders and signs"
(Acts 2:22). On the one hand we have the resurrection as the exaltation of Jesus from the cross or grave, and on the other the legends
of the empty tomb and the ascension.

We are compelled to ask whether all this mythological language is
not simply an attempt to express the meaning of the historical figure
of Jesus and the events of his life; in other words, significance of
these as a figure and event of salvation. If that be so, we can dispense with the objective form in which they are cast.

It is easy enough to deal with the doctrine of Christ's pre-existence
and the legend of the Virgin birth in this way. They are clearly attempts to explain the meaning of the Person of Jesus for faith. The
facts which historical criticism can verify cannot exhaust, indeed they
cannot adequately indicate, all that Jesus means to me. How he
actually originated matters little, indeed we can appreciate his significance only when we cease to worry about such questions. Our interest in the events of his life, and above all in the cross, is more
than an academic concern with the history of the past. We can see
meaning in them only when we ask what God is trying to say to
each one of us through them. Again, the figure of Jesus cannot be
understood simply from his inner-worldly context. In mythological
language, this means that he stems from eternity, his origin is not a
human and natural one.

We shall not, however, pursue the examination of the particular
incidents of his life any further. In the end the crux of the matter
lies in the cross and resurrection.

b. The Cross

Is the cross, understood as the event of redemption, exclusively
mythical in character, or can it retain its value for salvation without
forfeiting its character as history?

It certainly has a mythical character as far as its objective setting
is concerned. The Jesus who was crucified was the pre-existent, incarnate Son of God, and as such he was without sin. He is the victim
whose blood atones for our sins. He bears vicariously the sin of the
world, and by enduring the punishment for sin on our behalf he de-
livers us from death. This mythological interpretation is a mixture
of sacrificial and juridical analogies, which have ceased to be tenable
for us to-day. And in any case they fail to do justice to what the
New Testament is trying to say. For the most they can convey is that
the cross effects the forgiveness of all the past and future sins of man,
in the sense that the punishment they deserved has been remitted. But

the New Testament means more than this. The cross releases men not only from the guilt, but also from the power of sin. That is why, when the author of Colossians says "He [God] . . . having forgiven us all our trespasses, having blotted out the bond written in ordinances that was against us, which was contrary to us; and he hath taken it out of the way, nailing it to the cross" he hastens to add: "having put off from himself the principalities and powers, he made a show of them openly, triumphing over them in it" (Col. 2:13-15).

The historical event of the cross acquires cosmic dimensions. And by speaking of the cross as a cosmic happening its significance as a historical happening is made clear in accordance with the remarkable way of thinking in which historical events and connections are presented in cosmic terms, and so its full significance is brought into sharper relief. For if we see in the cross the judgement of the world and the defeat of the rulers of this world (I Cor. 2:6 ff.), the cross becomes the judgement of ourselves as fallen creatures enslaved to the powers of the "world."

By giving up Jesus to be crucified, God has set up the cross for us. To believe in the cross of Christ does not mean to concern ourselves with a mythical process wrought outside of us and our world, with an objective event turned by God to our advantage, but rather to make the cross of Christ our own, to undergo crucifixion with him. The cross in its redemptive aspect is not an isolated incident which befell a mythical personage, but an event whose meaning has "cosmic" importance. Its decisive, revolutionary significance is brought out by the eschatological framework in which it is set. In other words, the cross is not just an event of the past which can be contemplated, but is the eschatological event in and beyond time, in so far as it (understood in its significance, that is, for faith) is an ever-present reality.

The cross becomes a present reality first of all in the sacraments. In Baptism men and women are baptized into Christ's death (Rom. 6:3) and crucified with him (Rom. 6:6). At every celebration of the Lord's Supper the death of Christ is proclaimed (I Cor. 11:26). The communicants thereby partake of his crucified body and his blood outpoured (I Cor. 10:16). Again, the cross of Christ is an ever-present reality in the everyday life of the Christians. "They that are of Christ Jesus have crucified the flesh with the passions and the lusts thereof" (Gal. 5:24). That is why St. Paul can speak of "the cross of our Lord Jesus Christ, through which the world hath been crucified unto me, and I unto the world" (Gal. 6:14). That is why he seeks to know "the fellowship of his sufferings," as one who is "conformed to his death" (Phil. 3:10).

The crucifying of the affections and lusts includes the overcoming of our natural dread of suffering and the perfection of our detachment from the world. Hence the willing acceptance of sufferings in which death is already at work in man means: "always bearing about in our body the dying of Jesus" and "always being delivered unto death for Jesus' sake" (II Cor. 4:10 f.).

Thus the cross and passion are ever-present realities. How little they are confined to the events of the first Good Friday is amply illustrated by the words which a disciple of St. Paul puts into his master's mouth: "Now I rejoice in my sufferings for your sake, and fill up on my part that which is lacking of the afflictions of Christ in my flesh for his body's sake, which is the Church" (Col. 1:24).

In its redemptive aspect the Cross of Christ is no mere mythical event, but a historic (*geschichtlich*) fact originating in the historical (*historisch*) event which is the crucifixion of Jesus. The abiding significance of the cross is that it is the judgement of the world, the judgement and the deliverance of man. So far as this is so, Christ is crucified "for us," not in the sense of any theory of sacrifice or satisfaction. This interpretation of the cross as a permanent fact rather than a mythological event does far more justice to the redemptive significance of the event of the past than any of the traditional interpretations. In the last resort mythological language is only a medium for conveying the significance of the historical (*historisch*) event. The historical (*historisch*) event of the cross has, in the significance peculiar to it, created a new historic (*geschichtlich*) situation. The preaching of the cross as the event of redemption challenges all who hear it to appropriate this significance for themselves, to be willing to be crucified with Christ.

But, it will be asked, is this significance to be discerned in the actual event of past history? Can it, so to speak, be read off from that event? Or does the cross bear this significance because it is the cross of *Christ?* In other words, must we first be convinced of the significance of Christ and believe in him in order to discern the real meaning of the cross? If we are to perceive the real meaning of the cross, must we understand it as the cross of Jesus as a figure of past history? Must we go back to the Jesus of history?

As far as the first preachers of the gospel are concerned this will certainly be the case. For them the cross was the cross of him with whom they had lived in personal intercourse. The cross was an experience of their own lives. It presented them with a question and it disclosed to them its meaning. But for us this personal connection cannot be reproduced. For us the cross cannot disclose its own meaning: it is an event of the past. We can never recover it as an event in our own lives. All we know of it is derived from historical report. But the New Testament does not proclaim Jesus Christ in this way. The meaning of the cross is not disclosed from the life of Jesus as a figure of past history, a life which needs to be reproduced by historical research. On the contrary, Jesus is not proclaimed merely as the crucified; he is also risen from the dead. The cross and the resurrection form an inseparable unity.

c. The Resurrection

But what of the resurrection? It is not a mythical event pure and simple? Obviously it is not an event of past history with a self-evident meaning. Can the resurrection narratives and every other mention of the resurrection in the New Testament be understood simply as an attempt to convey the meaning of the cross? Does the New Testament, in asserting that Jesus is risen from the dead, mean that his death is not just an ordinary human death, but the judgement and salvation of the world, depriving death of its power? Does it not express this truth in the affirmation that the Crucified was not holden of death, but rose from the dead?

Yes indeed: the cross and the resurrection form a single, indivisible cosmic event. "He was delivered up for our trespasses, and was raised for our justification" (Rom. 4:25). The cross is not an isolated event, as though it were the end of Jesus, which needed the resurrection subsequently to reverse it. When he suffered death, Jesus was already the Son of God, and his death by itself was the victory over the power of death. St. John brings this out most clearly by describing the passion of Jesus as the "hour" in which he is glorified, and by the double meaning he gives to the phrase "lifted up," applying it both to the cross and to Christ's exaltation into glory.

Cross and resurrection form a single, indivisible cosmic event which brings judgement to the world and opens up for men the possibility of authentic life. But if that be so, the resurrection cannot be a miraculous proof capable of demonstration and sufficient to convince the sceptic that the cross really has the cosmic and eschatological significance ascribed to it.

Yet it cannot be denied that the resurrection of Jesus is often used in the New Testament as a miraculous proof. Take for instance Acts 17:31. Here we are actually told that God substantiated the claims of Christ by raising him from the dead. Then again the resurrection narratives: both the legend of the empty tomb and the appearances insist on the physical reality of the risen body of the Lord (see especially Luke 24:39-43). But these are most certainly later embellishments of the primitive tradition. St. Paul knows nothing about them. There is however one passage where St. Paul tries to prove the miracle of the resurrection by adducing a list of eye-witnesses (I Cor. 15:3-8). But this is a dangerous procedure, as Karl Barth has involuntarily shown. Barth seeks to explain away the real meaning of I Cor. 15 by contending that the list of eye-witnesses was put in not to prove the fact of the resurrection, but to prove that the preaching of the apostle was, like the preaching of the first Christians, the preaching of Jesus as the risen Lord. The eye-witnesses therefore guarantee St. Paul's preaching, not the fact of the resurrection. An historical fact which involves a resurrection from the dead is utterly inconceivable!

Yes, indeed: the resurrection of Jesus cannot be a miraculous proof by which the sceptic might be compelled to believe in Christ. The difficulty is not simply the incredibility of a mythical event like the resuscitation of a dead person—for that is what the resurrection means, as is shown by the fact that the risen Lord is apprehended by the physical senses. Nor is it merely the impossibility of establishing the objective historicity of the resurrection no matter how many witnesses are cited, as though once it was established it might be believed beyond all question and faith might have its unimpeachable guarantee. No; the real difficulty is that the resurrection is itself an article of faith, and you cannot establish one article of faith by invoking another. You cannot prove the redemptive efficacy of the cross by invoking the resurrection. For the resurrection is an article of faith because it is far more than the resuscitation of a corpse—it is the eschatological event. And so it cannot be a miraculous proof. For, quite apart from its credibility, the bare miracle tells us nothing about the eschatological fact of the destruction of death. Moreover, such a miracle is not otherwise unknown to mythology.

It is however abundantly clear that the New Testament is interested in the resurrection of Christ simply and solely because it is the eschatological event *par excellence*. By it Christ abolished death and brought life and immortality to light (II Tim. 1:10). This explains why St. Paul borrows Gnostic language to clarify the meaning of the resurrection. As in the death of Jesus all have died (II Cor. 5:14 f.), so through his resurrection all have been raised from the dead, though naturally this event is spread over a long period of time (I Cor. 15:21 f.). But St. Paul does not only say: "In Christ shall all be made alive"; he can also speak of rising again with Christ in the present tense, just as he speaks of our dying with him. Through the sacrament of baptism Christians participate not only in the death of Christ but also in his resurrection. It is not simply that we *shall* walk with him in newness of life and be united with him in his resurrection (Rom. 6:4 f.); we are doing so already here and now. "Even so reckon ye yourselves to be dead indeed unto sin, but alive unto God in Jesus Christ" (Rom. 6:11).

Once again, in everyday life the Christians participate not only in the death of Christ but also in his resurrection. In this resurrection-life they enjoy a freedom, albeit a struggling freedom, from sin (Rom. 6:11 ff.). They are able to "cast off the works of darkness," so that the approaching day when the darkness shall vanish is already experienced here and now. "Let us walk honestly as in the day" (Rom. 13:12 f.): "we are not of the night, nor of the darkness . . . Let us, since we are of the day, be sober . . ." (I Thess. 5:5-8). St. Paul seeks to share not only the sufferings of Christ but also "the power of his resurrection" (Phil. 3:10). So he bears about in his body the dying of Jesus, "that the life also of Jesus may be manifested in our body" (II Cor. 4:10 f.). Similarly, when the Corinthians demand a proof of his apostolic authority, he solemnly warns them: "Christ is not weak, but is powerful in you: for he was crucified in weakness, yet he liveth in the power of God. For we also are weak in him, but we shall live with him through the power of God toward you" (II Cor. 13:3 f.).

In this way the resurrection is not a mythological event adduced in order to prove the saving efficacy of the cross, but an article of faith just as much as the meaning of the cross itself. Indeed, *faith in the resurrection is really the same thing as faith in the saving efficacy of the cross,* faith in the cross as the cross of Christ. Hence you cannot first believe in Christ and then in the strength of that faith believe in the cross. To believe in Christ means to believe in the cross as the cross of Christ. The saving efficacy of the cross is not derived from the fact that it is the cross of Christ: it is the cross of Christ because it has this saving efficacy. Without that efficacy it is the tragic end of a great man.

We are back again at the old question. How do we come to believe in the cross as the cross of Christ and as the eschatological event *par excellence?* How do we come to believe in the saving efficacy of the cross?

There is only one answer. This is the way in which the cross is proclaimed. It is always proclaimed together with the resurrection. Christ meets us in the preaching as one crucified and risen. He meets us in the word of preaching and nowhere else. The faith of Easter is just this—faith in the word of preaching.

It would be wrong at this point to raise again the problem of how this preaching arose historically, as though that could vindicate its truth. That would be to tie our faith in the word of God to the results of historical research. The word of preaching confronts us as the word of God. It is not for us to question its credentials. It is we who are questioned, we who are asked whether we will believe the word or reject it. But in answering this question, in accepting the word of preaching as the word of God and the death and resurrection of Christ as the eschatological event, we are given an opportunity of understanding ourselves. Faith and unbelief are never blind, arbitrary decisions. They offer us the alternative between accepting or rejecting that which alone can illuminate our understanding of ourselves.

The real Easter faith is faith in the word of preaching which brings illumination. If the event of Easter Day is in any sense an historical event additional to the event of the cross, it is nothing else than the rise of faith in the risen Lord, since it was this faith which led to the apostolic preaching. The resurrection itself is not an event of past history. All that historical criticism can establish is the fact that the first disciples came to believe in the resurrection. The historian can perhaps to some extent account for that faith from the personal intimacy which the disciples had enjoyed with Jesus during his earthly life, and so reduce the resurrection appearances to a series of subjective visions. But the historical problem is not of interest to Christian belief in the resurrection. For the historical event of the rise of the Easter faith means for us what it meant for the first disciples—namely, the self-attestation of the risen Lord, the act of God in which the redemptive event of the cross is completed.[25]

We cannot buttress our own faith in the resurrection by that of the first disciples and so eliminate the element of risk which faith in the resurrection always involves. For the first disciples' faith in the resurrection is itself part and parcel of the eschatological event which is the article of faith.

In other words, the apostolic preaching which originated in the event of Easter Day is itself a part of the eschatological event of redemption. The death of Christ, which is both the judgement and the salvation of the world, inaugurates the "ministry of reconciliation" or "word of reconciliation" (II Cor. 5:18 f.). This word supplements the cross and makes its saving efficacy intelligible by demanding faith and confronting men with the question whether they are willing to understand themselves as men who are crucified and risen with Christ. Through the word of preaching the cross and the resurrection are made present: the eschatological "now" is here, and the promise of Isa. 49:8 is fulfilled: "Behold, now is the acceptable time; behold, now is the day of salvation" (II Cor. 6:2). That is why the apostolic preaching brings judgement. For some the apostle is "a savour from death unto death" and for others a "savour from life unto life" (II Cor. 2:16). St. Paul is the agent through whom the resurrection life becomes effective in the faithful (II Cor. 4:12). The promise of Jesus in the Fourth Gospel is eminently applicable to the preaching in which he is proclaimed: "Verily I say unto you, He that heareth my words and believeth on him that sent me, hath eternal life, and cometh not unto judgement, but hath passed out of death into life. . . . The hour cometh and now is, when the dead shall hear the voice of the Son of God; and they that hear shall live" (John 5:24 f.). In the word of preaching and there alone we meet the risen Lord. "So belief cometh of hearing, and hearing by the word of Christ" (Rom. 10:17).

Like the word itself and the apostle who proclaims it, so the Church where the preaching of the word is continued and where the believers or "saints" (i.e., those who have been transferred to eschatological existence) are gathered is part of the eschatological event. The word "Church" is an eschatological term, while its designation as the Body of Christ emphasizes its cosmic significance. For the Church is not just a phenomenon of secular history, it is phenomenon of significant history, in the sense that it realizes itself in history.

Conclusion

We have now outlined a programme for the demythologizing of the New Testament. Are there still any surviving traces of mythology? There certainly are for those who regard all language about an act of God or of a decisive, eschatological event as mythological. But this is not mythology in the traditional sense, not the kind of mythology which has become antiquated with the decay of the mythical world view. For the redemption of which we have spoken is not a miraculous supernatural event, but an historical event wrought out in time and space. We are convinced that this restatement does better justice to the real meaning of the New Testament and to the paradox of the kerygma. For the kerygma maintains that the eschatological emissary of God is a concrete figure of a particular historical past, that his eschatological activity was wrought out in a human fate, and that therefore it is an event whose eschatological character does not admit of a secular proof. Here we have the paradox of Phil. 2:7: "He emptied himself;" of II Cor. 8:9: ". . . though he was rich, yet for your sakes he became poor;" of Rom. 8:3: "God, sending his Son in the likeness of sinful flesh;" of I Tim. 3:16: "He was manifested in the flesh;" and above all of the classic formula of John 1:14: "The Word became flesh."

The agent of God's presence and activity, the mediator of his reconciliation of the world unto himself, is a real figure of history. Similarly the word of God is not some mysterious oracle, but a sober, factual account of a human life, of Jesus of Nazareth, possessing saving efficacy for man. Of course the kerygma may be regarded as part of the story of man's spiritual evolution and used as a basis for a tenable *Weltanschauung*. Yet this proclamation claims to be the eschatological word of God.

The apostles who proclaim the word may be regarded merely as figures of past history, and the Church as a sociological and historical phenomenon, part of the history of man's spiritual evolution. Yet both are eschatological phenomena and eschatological events.

All these assertions are an offense which will not be removed by philosophical discussion, but only by faith and obedience. All these are phenomena subject to historical, sociological, and psychological observation, yet for faith they are all of them eschatological phenomena. It is precisely its immunity from proof which secures the Christian proclamation against the charge of being mythological. The transcendence of God is not as in myth reduced to immanence. Instead, we have the paradox of a transcendent God present and active in history: "The Word became flesh."

Notes

[1]Gal. 4:4; Phil. 2:6 ff.; II Cor. 8:9; John 1:14, etc.

[2]II Cor. 5:21; Rom. 8:3.

[3]Rom. 3:23-26; 4:25; 8:3; II Cor. 5:14, 19; John 1:29; I John 2:2, etc.

[4]I Cor. 15:21 f.; Rom. 5:12 ff.

[5]I Cor. 2:6; Col. 2:15; Rev. 12:7 ff., etc.

[6]Acts 1:6 f.; 2:33; Rom. 8:34, etc.

[7]Phil. 2:9-11; I Cor. 15:25.

[8]I Cor. 15:23 f., 50 ff., etc.

[9]Rev. 21:4, etc.

[10]I Thess. 4:15 ff.; I Cor. 15:51 f.; cf. Mark 9:1.

[11]Rom. 5:12 ff.; I Cor. 15:21 ff., 44b ff.

[12]Rom. 8: 23; II Cor. 1:22; 5:5.

[13]Rom. 8:15; Gal. 4:6.

[14]Rom. 8:11.

[15]It may of course be argued that there are people alive to-day whose confidence in the traditional scientific view of the world has been shaken, and others who are primitive enough to qualify for an age of mythical thought. And there are also many varieties of superstition. But when belief in spirits and miracles has degenerated into superstition, it has become something entirely different from what it was when it was genuine faith. The various impressions and speculations which influence credulous people here and there are of little importance, nor does it matter to what extent cheap slogans have spread an atmosphere inimical to science. What matters is the world view which men imbibe from their environment, and it is science which determines that view of the world through the school, the press, the wireless, the cinema, and all the other fruits of technical progress.

[16]Cp. the observations of Paul Schutz on the decay of mythical religion in the East through the introduction of modern hygiene and medicine.

[17]Cp. Gerhardt Kruger, *Einsicht und Leidenschaft, Das Wesen des platonischen Denkens*, Frankfort, 1939, p. 11 f.

[18]Rom. 5:12 ff.; I Cor. 15:21 ff., 44b.

[19]Cp. Gerhardt Kruger, *Einsicht und Leidenschaft*, esp. p. 17 f., 56 f.

[20]Myth is here used in the sense popularized by the "History of Religions" school. Mythology is the use of imagery, to express the other worldly in terms of this world and the divine in terms of human life, the other side in terms of this side. For instance, divine transcendence is

expressed as spatial distance. It is a mode of expression which makes it easy to understand the cultus as an action in which material means are used to convey immaterial power. Myth is not used in that modern sense, according to which it is practically equivalent to ideology.

[21] As an illustration of this critical re-interpretation of myth cf. Hans Jonas, *Augustin und das paulinische Freiheitsproblem*, 1930, pp. 66-76.

[22] *What is Christianity?* Williams and Norgate, 1904, pp. 63-4 and 57.

[23] Cp. e.g. Troeltsch, *Die Bedeutung der Geschichtlichkeit Jesu für den Glauben*, Tubingen, 1911.

[24] *Gnosis und spatantiker Geist, I. Die mythologische Gnosis*, 1934.

[25] This and the following paragraphs are also intended as an answer to the doubts and suspicions which Paul Althaus has raised against me in *Die Wahrheit des kirchlichen Osterglaubens*, 1941, p. 90 ff. Cp. also my discussion of Emanuel Hirsch's "Die Auferstehungsgeschichten und der christliche Glaube," 1940, in *Theol. Lit.-Ztg.*, 1940, pp. 242-6.

Theological Language

8

Jerry H. Gill

The Meaning
of Religious Language

Traditionally the relation between philosophy and religion has been one either of identity, as in the early Middle Ages, or of hostility, as in the Age of Reason. In the eighteenth and nineteenth centuries this hostility focused on the question whether the claims of religion were true, and the task of the Christian philosopher was to show that the assertions of religious language were indeed true.

Within the last thirty years the situation has been transformed by the rise of the philosophical movement known as "logical empiricism." In light of the vast and profound influence of this movement, the philosophical world can now be said to hurl a completely different challenge at those who make religious assertions. Religious language is no longer given the privilege of being classified as *false*; it is now classified as *meaningless*. The relation between philosophy and religion is no longer one of positive hostility; the former simply *ignores* the latter as *"non-sense."*

At first religious thinkers were at a loss as to how to respond to such a challenge, except to deny it. Within the last ten years, however,

Copyright 1965, *Christianity Today*. Used by permission.

a large number of scholars, particularly in Britain, have attempted to meet the challenge head-on. Much of the impetus for this response has come from the writings and influence of Ludwig Wittgenstein's later philosophy, which is known today as "ordinary language philosophy," or "linguistic analysis." The meeting of the challenge hurled by logical empiricism is fast becoming the focal point of much of contemporary philosophy and theology, as is shown by the many articles and books on the subject. For example, a large part of the religion section of the July 10, 1964, issue of *Time* magazine was devoted to this.

The challenge that logical empiricism presents to those who use religious language can be stated in a variety of ways. The following syllogistic statement of this challenge serves to distinguish the various responses quite clearly, and so it is especially appropriate for the purposes of this study.

1. All cognitively meaningful language is either definitional or empirical in nature;

2. no religious language is either definitional or empirical in nature;

3. no religious language is cognitively meaningful language.

Three things about this syllogism should be noted at the outset. First, this is the core of the challenge as it is presented by A. J. Ayer in *Language, Truth and Logic* (New York: Dover Publications, Inc., 1946). Although many logical empiricists, including Ayer himself, have offered helpful modifications of their original, somewhat dogmatic position, there has been no attempt to retract the essence of this argument as it applies to religious language.

Second, the term "cognitively meaningful language" is used to refer to those statements that admit to true and false judgments. Cognitive meaning is thus to be sharply distinguished from emotional or existential meaning, which is better termed "significance." This is not to say that cognitively meaningful statements are void of emotional significance, but it is to say that the nature of each is quite distinct. The statement, "It is raining," can have both cognitive meaning and emotional significance; but the fact that the former is susceptible to true and false judgments while the latter is not makes it clear that the two can and need to be differentiated.

Third, this syllogism is obviously valid. This eliminates the possibility of maintaining that the premises are true but that the conclusion is false.

Three main approaches have arisen in response to this challenge, aside from those that accept its conclusion and thereby dismiss religious language as non-sense. This latter view will not be discussed, since according to it nothing remains to be said.

Some thinkers, by training and vocation usually more philosophical than theological, respond to the foregoing argument by accepting the truth of both of the premises and of the conclusion as well. These thinkers differ, however, from those who go on to say that religious language is nonsensical. They maintain that even though religious language is not cognitively meaningful, it is very significant from an emotional, ethical, or existential point of view. That is to say, once we get straight about the true nature of religious language, the challenge of logical empiricism is no longer devastating to the use of such language.

Belief: A Matter of Perspective

Two very prominent British philosophers have expressed this point of view, namely R. M. Hare and R. B. Braithwaite. Hare develops his view of religious belief as an unverifiable and unfalsifiable interpretation of one's experience in his contribution to *New Essays in Philosophical Theology* (ed. by Antony Flew and Alasdair McIntyre, London: SCM Press, 1955, pp. 99-103). He suggests that religious beliefs are really principles of interpretation, or frames of reference, by means of which one interprets his experience. As such, religious beliefs are not subject to true and false judgments because they simply do not assert any state of affairs. Hare calls such beliefs "bliks" and likens them to the perspective of a paranoid who is convinced that all Oxford dons are out to do him in. Thus there is no factual disagreement between the two statements "God exists" and "God does not exist." The real difference is one of perspective—like the difference between optimism and pessimism.

> Suppose we believe that everything that happened, happened by pure chance. This would not of course be an assertion; for it is compatible with anything happening or not happening, and so, incidentally, is its contradictory. But if we had this belief, we would not be able to explain or predict or plan anything. Thus, although we should not be asserting anything different from those of a more normal belief, there would be a great difference between us; and this is the sort of difference that there is between those who really believe in God and those who really disbelieve in him [*New Essays in Philosophical Theology*, pp. 101, 102].

It is clear that if religious beliefs are viewed as bliks, then the language in which these beliefs are expressed is neither empirical nor definitional in nature. Thus Hare accepts the argument of logical empiricism but endeavors to redefine the nature and function of religous beliefs and language.

R. B. Braithwaite also redefines the nature of religious language by likening it to the language of morals and commendations. When a person expresses a religious statement, he is not asserting a fact but indicating a commitment to, and commendation of, a certain attitude or source of action. In his own words:

A religious assertion, for me, is the assertion of an intention to carry out a certain behavior policy, subsumable under a sufficiently general principle to be a moral one, together with the implicit or explicit statement, but not the assertion of certain stories [*An Empiricist View of the Nature of Religious Belief*, Cambridge: Cambridge University Press, 1955, p. 32].

In other words, Braithwaite, like Hare, concurs with the argument of logical empiricism that religious language is not cognitively meaningful, but he does not think that this renders religious language ethically meaningless.

By way of criticism, at least three things can be said about this approach. First, it is simply not in harmony with the way religious language is used. Most religious people would object if you told them that their religious beliefs are neither true nor false. Second, it leaves unanswered the question as to how one chooses between right and wrong bliks, and/or ethical commitments. Third, there is a strong possibility that the teachings of Christ were meant as assertions about human experience that could be confirmed or disconfirmed. But more about this later.

Other thinkers are not prepared to accept the argument offered by logical empiricism. These, by training and vocation usually more theological than philosophical, respond to the challenge by accepting the truth of the minor premise (2), while rejecting the truth of the major premise (1). The main contention of those taking this approach is that cognitive meaning cannot be confined to the logical and empirical realms. Here it is maintained that religious truth, along with other forms of metaphysical truth, is a form of cognition that has a unique nature. Since such truth is embodied in religious language, religious language may be cognitively meaningful even though it is neither logical nor empirical in nature.

Revelation and Mystery

One of the best-known exponents of the point of view that rejects the first premise is Michael Foster (*Mystery and Philosophy*, London: SCM Press, 1957). Foster identifies revelation, and thus the religious language that expresses revelation, with mystery. He objects to the logical empiricists' demand for clarity in our talk about experience. Thus he would conclude that revelation can be cognitively meaningful, that is, subject to the judgment "true," without being reducible to either logical or empirical language. Foster says:

Revelation is of mystery, but mystery revealed is not eliminated, but remains mysterious. It remains an object of wonder, which is dispelled when mystery is eliminated. There is no method by which revelation can be commanded: "it is" (in the Bible) "not a thing to be procured from God by any technique." That is to say, it is not subject to human mastery ["Contemporary British Philosophy and Christian Belief," *The Christian Scholar*, Fall, 1960, p. 194].

Although the first sentence raises many other questions, there can be no question that Foster rejects the major premise of the logical empiricist argument.

Willem Zuurdeeg also refuses to accept the statement that all cognitively meaningful statements are either logical or empirical in nature (*An Analytical Philosophy of Religion*, Nashville: Abingdon, 1961). He maintains that religious truth, and thus religious language, is unique in that it is not limited to propositional assertions. Moreover, it cannot be analyzed or justified. Nevertheless, Zuurdeeg wants to maintain that such statements are still meaningful and true.

> I must protest vehemently against the notion that language of Christian faith consists of propositions which can be analyzed by means of logic. If it does not make sense to a philosopher to attempt a logical analysis of persons, how much sense will it make to a theologian to try to do so with the Lord God? Exactly in the way that man is man-who-speaks, so God is God-who-speaks. Can we offer a logical analysis of the Creator of Heaven and Earth? Shall we discard the doctrine of the Trinity simply because the language in which it is expressed is logically inconsistent ["Implications of Analytical Philosophy for Theology," *The Journal of Bible and Religion*, July, 1961, p. 209].

Despite the fact that the approach represented here by Foster and Zuurdeeg argues on the side of angels, there are several reasons for rejecting it as inadequate. First, it runs the risk of rendering religious language so distinct from all other language that it becomes irrelevant. Second, no extra-logical criteria are offered by means of which one can even decipher the content of religious statements, let alone distinguish between those that are meaningful and those that are not. Third, there is no contesting the fact that reality and experience cannot be completely re-presented in language, but this obvious fact should not be used to license sloppy talk. Fourth, as John Locke clearly saw, whether or not revelation is true is not the real problem; rather, the problem is which statements are to be taken as revelation. The best way to honor revelation and mystery is to apply rigid standards so as to be able to distinguish non-sense and falsehood from meaning and truth.

Relevance and Truth-Value

Another way of responding to the argument of logical empiricism is to accept the major premise (1), while rejecting the minor premise (2), and there are those thinkers who have taken up the responsibility of constructing such an approach. The main drive of this approach is to be found in the attempt to relate religious language to experience and thereby to establish it as cognitively meaningful. Thus, it might be called a form of Christian empiricism. The thesis of this approach is that religious language very often fulfills empirical functions and is, therefore, at those times cognitively meaningful. The main burden of such an approach is to specify the exact situations in which religious language can be said to be empirical.

One of the most interesting presentations of the cognitive status of religious language is to be found in the writings of John Hick of Princeton Theological Seminary (*Faith and Knowledge*, Ithaca: Cornell University Press, 1957; "Theology and Verification," *Theology Today*, April, 1960; and *Philosophy of Religion*, Englewood Cliffs: Prentice-Hall, 1963). Hick maintains that statements that make predictions about experiences taking place after death are open to verification (or at least confirmation). Such verification is termed "eschatological" by Hick, and firmly establishes the cognitive meaningfulness of this type of statement. Space will not permit a full analysis of Hick's views at this juncture. It is sufficient to note that they are explained and presented by one who is fully aware of the challenge of logical empiricism and who endeavors to learn from its insights. Concerning the claim that there will be experiences after death, Hick says:

> The logical peculiarity of the claim is that it is open to confirmation but not to refutation. There can be conclusive evidence for it if it be true, but there cannot be conclusive evidence against it if it be untrue. For if we survive bodily death we shall (presumably) know that we have survived it, but if we do not survive death we shall not know that we have not survived it. The verification situation is thus asymmetrical. However, the religious doctrine at least is open to verification and is accordingly meaningful. Its eschatological prediction assures its status as an assertion [*Faith and Knowledge*, p. 150].

Another recent explication of the empirical nature of religious language is found in John Hutchison's *Language and Faith* (Philadelphia: Westminster, 1963). Hutchison maintains that since religion is to be understood primarily as a means of comprehensive life orientation, the language of religion is to be understood as the expression and description of various orientations to life. He contends that, like poetry, religious language is very often intended to communicate certain feelings, values, facts, and interpretations of human experience.

It should be clear that such theories or interpretations of life are subject to true and false judgments in the same sense that broad theories about the physical universe are—namely, in terms of confirmation and fruitlessness. In chapter five of his book, Hutchison uses the term "adequacy" to designate the standard by means of which life-orientational theories are to be evaluated. This adequacy implies, in addition to rational consistency and coherence, the standards of sufficient reason, simplicity, empiricism, and critical rigor (*Language and Faith*, pp. 129 ff.).

Other writers suggest that much of religious language functions as an empirical-theoretic model. A helpful development of religious language in terms of models can be found in the writings of Frederick Ferré (*Language, Logic and God*, New York: Harper & Row, 1961; and "Mapping the Logic of Models in Science and Theology," *The Christian Scholar*, Spring, 1963). He outlines the functions of theological models in the following way:

> Theological speech projects a model of immense responsive significance, drawn from "the facts," as the key to its conceptual synthesis. This model, for theism, is made up of the "spiritual" characteristics of personality: will, purpose, wisdom, love, and the like. For Christianity, more specifically, the conceptual model consists in the creative, self-giving, personal love of Jesus Christ. In this model is found the only literal meaning which these terms, like "creative," "personal," and "love," can have in the Christian vocabulary. All the concepts of the Christian are organized and synthesized in relation to this model. The efforts of systematic theology are bent to explicating the consistency and coherence of the synthesis built on this model of "God" as key concept. Christian preaching is devoted to pointing out the applicability of this conceptual synthesis to common experiences of life. And Christian apologetics struggles to show that the synthesis organized around this model is adequate to the unforced interpretation of all experience, including suffering and evil [*Language, Logic and God*, p. 164].

Ferré goes on to point out that since the language, thoughts, and actions that are based on a given conceptual model can be evaluated in terms of their coherence and adequacy in dealing with experience, it is possible to speak of one model as being more appropriate, or more fruitful, than others (*ibid.*, p. 165). This sort of evaluation implies cognitive meaning, since although the criteria and results of such evaluation are difficult to determine, the models are, in theory, confirmable or disconfirmable.

The Disclosure-Commitment Concept

The one writer who perhaps has done more than any other to develop an explication of the complex elements involved in this experiential use of religious language is Ian T. Ramsey of Oriel College, Oxford (*Religious Language*, New York: Macmillan, 1957; and "Contemporary Empiricism," *The Christian Scholar*, Fall, 1960). Ramsey develops the concept of "discernment" or "disclosure" to describe the nature of the situations that provide the experimental basis for religious language. He maintains that a religious disclosure gives rise to a "commitment" to what is disclosed, and that this disclosure-commitment situation in turn gives rise to what we have termed experiential-religious language. It is maintained that such disclosure-commitment situations are anchored in experience and in this sense can be said to be empirical.

One group of examples Ramsey uses to illustrate what he terms "discernment" or "disclosure" is composed of situations in which, because of a unique set of personal experiences, the significance is always greater than what can be expressed in terms of physical description alone. In a way he is saying that because of the facts of highly personal experience, seemingly ordinary, public situations are "seen," or discerned, in a new light. In other words, one's personal, mental experience often acts as a catalyst, or a category, which fills a situation with more significance than just a description of the objective facts would provide. Thus such situations are more than empirical in the narrow or sensory sense of that word, but are still empirical (experiential) in the broad sense.

Ramsey maintains that the experiential-religious language that arises out of religious experiences in both similar to and different from ordinary language. It is different in that it is not about objects, and thus follows a logic that is a bit "odd" at key points, e.g., in the use of the term "God." Such talk is similar, however, to that type of ordinary language which pertains to personal experience. Thus Ramsey maintains that the term "God" is no more odd than the term "I" as employed in such personal talk as, for instance, the discussion of one's motives.

> So our conclusion is that for the religious man "God" is a key word, an irreducible posit, an ultimate of explanation expressive of the kind of *commitment* he professes. It is to be talked about in terms of the object-language over which it presides, but only when this object-language is qualified; in which case this qualified object-language becomes also currency for that odd discernment with which religious *commitment*, when it is not bigotry or fanaticism, will necessarily be associated.
>
> Meanwhile, as a corollary, we can note that to understand religious language or theology we must first evoke the odd kind of situation to which I have given various parallels above. This is plainly a *sine qua non* for any religious apologetic.
>
> At the same time we must train ourselves to have a nose for odd language, for "logical impropriety," and it is possible to do this by concerning ourselves with other examples of odd language which may not in the first instance be religious [*Religious Language*, p. 47].

The main point that Ramsey makes, in good Wittgensteinian fashion, is that just the fact that talk which arises from personal, religious discernment is odd with respect to the language of physics, is no reason to conclude that it does not have an adequate logic that is similar to other forms of ordinary language. Thus this experiential-religious language can be cognitive to the extent that (1) it is anchored in experience and (2) it has an established use by means of which appropriate and inappropriate talk can be distinguished.

A Qualified-Model

In discussing the attempts to describe God, Ramsey develops the concept of a "qualified-model" to explain the logic of such phrases as "infinitely good" and "first cause." In such phrases the terms "good" and "cause" are models in the sense that they are taken from experience, while the terms "infinite" and "first" are qualifiers that indicate the logical oddness of this particular use of the model terms. Thus to say that God is "infinitely good" is to say that he is similar to the moral quality of goodness we experience in everyday life, and that his goodness has a different quality than human goodness.

Now it would seem that this analysis suggests a way of dealing with religious language that conforms both to the way religious language is used and to the criteria of legitimate theoretic language. To talk of God as a "heavenly father" or "divine creator" is to speak analogically and hypothetically. That is, one is endeavoring to suggest a qualified similarity between a concrete aspect of past and present experience, and future experience. This qualified similarity must be taken as a tentative hypothesis, or conceptual model, which may be confirmed or disconfirmed on the basis of its fruitfulness in enabling a person (and perhaps a society) to appreciate, understand, and predict experience. (Ramsey suggests the concept of "empirical fit" as a criterion of confirmation in his new book, *Models and Mystery* [New York: Oxford, 1964].) Obviously, if such models tend to be disconfirmed, then they should be withdrawn, and vice versa. In any case, they have an experiential, albeit a theoretic, nature, and thus it can be said that they involve cognitive meaning.

This, then, is a sketch of the challenge and main responses concerning the meaning of religious language. Obviously, this writer is more impressed with the third, or empirical, response to the challenge because it preserves both the relevance and the truth-value of religious assertions. The other two responses are weak at these two points. All of the responses, however, are only in their beginning stages, and a great deal of work remains to be done. Further explorations may reveal more fruitful approaches.

Part Two

How God Is Known

Editor's Introduction

Less general than the preceding considerations, yet basic to all of the rest of theology, is the issue of the source of knowledge of God. Where and how do we find God? What persons, institutions, or documents are to be accepted as affording acquaintance with God, what He is like and what He does? What are the criteria by which we recognize the sources of the knowledge of God? What are the limits of this knowledge? What are the methods of investigation of the sources?

Christian theology has usually affirmed that God is known to man as and where He makes Himself known to man. Because man is limited and God presumably is superior to him in many ways, God must take the initiative in establishing the relationship. This self-manifestation is termed revelation.

A first question concerns the extent of this revelation. Is the possibility of knowing God limited to a certain national group, or those who belong to a particular religion, or who have access to a certain set of religious literature? Or can all men, everywhere and at all times, know something about God, just by virtue of being human?

A number of classic responses have been given to this question, from the medieval period to the titanic divergence between Karl Barth and Emil Brunner in the 1930s. One position which has commanded a large following, particularly in the Roman Catholic Church, is known as "natural theology." This maintains that there is a knowledge of God to be found in nature, history, and in the human personality, which is objectively present and accessible to anyone who will take the trouble to observe and reflect upon it. This is consequently termed a "general revelation." Further, this view assumes that man's ability to perceive spiritual truth has not been seriously affected by the presence of sin in his life and personality. Consequently, any rational man, willing to examine the evidence, should be able to arrive at the truth of certain of the doctrines of the Christian faith, particularly the assertion that God exists. Certain classic "proofs" for the existence of God have emerged, and Thomas's versions of them are stated here. Not all natural theologians would regard the conclusions as following by such direct logical deductions as Thomas employs. Rather, they see these conclusions as the best explanation of the whole sweep of evidence. This form of natural theology was found in certain varieties of religious liberalism, as well as some more conservative theologies. It is still represented by men like L. Harold DeWolf.

There is both strength and weakness to natural theology. The strength is that the Christian in approaching the non-Christian need not fall back upon an authoritarianism of quoting his own religion's sacred book. Rather, he can appeal to seemingly neutral evidence, which all men may behold. The weakness comes in the apparent lack of efficacy of the method. Some very intelligent and presumably open-minded men look at the data and simply do not recognize the presence of God. Some have proposed that the arguments are actually invalid. Even when the arguments are regarded as successful, question is raised whether this is really the Christian God. There is a considerable difference between Aristotle's prime mover and the Biblical Good Shepherd.

Other Christian theologians therefore reject the natural theology approach. While those outside of Christianity may center their criticism of natural theology upon its philosophical shortcomings, these thinkers criticize it theologically. Man as sinner is not as able to recognize spiritual truth as God intended him to be. Although the existence of God should be self-evident, the natural man looks at the data and fails to see God.

One of the most vociferous denunciations of natural theology has come from Karl Barth. Barth insisted that all revelation of God is centered upon Christ. Because he sees all knowledge of God as redemptive in character, if there were other channels of revelation besides Christ there would also be the possibility of at least partial salvation outside of Christ. The principle of salvation by grace alone would be compromised. Man would be regarded as capable of contributing something to his own salvation. Facing Biblical passages such as the nature psalms and Romans 1:18-23, Barth observes that they were written by believers. The psalmist did not see the presence and activity of God in nature because it was objectively there. Rather, he was acquainted with God through the special revelation, and he *projected* this prior knowledge upon nature. Thus, not only is natural theology rejected, but general revelation is even regarded as invalid.

A somewhat mediating position is found in the statement of John Calvin. He emphasizes the positive fact of the reality of revelation in nature. There is a genuine revelation of God for all men. Yet man in his sinfulness distorts this. He does see, but only dimly, like a person with poor eyesight, who can only make out a word here and there. The perception is genuine but fragmentary. The Scriptures, however, are depicted by Calvin in his famous analogy of the spectacles. Just as spectacles correct faulty vision, enabling the person to see clearly, so the Scriptures enable man to see clearly and to recognize the reality of God in nature. While it is not possible to construct a full-fledged natural theology, general revelation is objectively present.

The question of general revelation may seem like an abstruse theological problem, unrelated to practical issues of ministering the gospel of Jesus Christ. Rather, it has some basic implications for the strategy of the Christian church in its action. One's conclusion upon the nature, extent, and efficacy of general revelation will go a long way toward determining his answer to such questions as the following:

1. Are there any intellectual considerations which can be appealed to in persuading the non-Christian of the truth of Christianity?

2. Are there any points where the non-Christian is still in contact with the truth of the Christian message, and thus is sensitive to that message? To what facet of man's experience, if any, can one try to build a bridge for the Christian message, by such devices as analogy?

3. Is there any possibility that the non-Christian can from his examination of "natural sources" discern anything of God's commands to him, and thus do genuinely good and moral acts?

4. Is there any possibility that on the basis of such natural light as he may have, a man who has not heard the distinctly Christian mes-

sage contained in the Bible, may nonetheless respond properly in faith
to God, and thus enter into fellowship with him?

Beyond this comes the question of special revelation. Has God
made Himself known in certain unique and more intensive ways,
which are not necessarily available to all? In the mainstream of
Protestant Christianity this has particularly been identified in some
way with the Bible. In Catholicism, it has generally been the Bible
plus the unwritten tradition of the apostles, found especially in the
teaching or ruling authority of the church.

One of the answers has identified the Bible as actually *being* a
special revelation from God to man. God has spoken, He has genuinely comunicated Himself to man, in order to bring man into the
proper relationship with Himself as a person. This He has done through
His acts in history, and especially through the coming of Christ in
the God-man form.

According to Kenneth Kantzer, God has not merely acted; He has
also spoken. Rather than giving us a divine pantomime in history, He
has given us a divine interpretation of those acts. He has revealed
truth about Himself, which has been preserved in written form in
the Bible. Thus, the words of the Bible are objective truths which
God wanted man to know.

William Hordern speaks for a movement which has been known
popularly as neo-orthodoxy, or as he prefers to call it, new reformation theology. The emphasis here is upon the process of revelation,
rather than on its product. Revelation is not the communication of
truths about God; it is the personal presence of God Himself. The
Bible is not the Word of God, or revelation. It is the medium through
which God may choose to encounter man. It is the witness of the
Biblical writers that God's revelation has come to them, and the
promise that it will occur again. The propositions of the Bible and
of theology are not revelation in and of themselves. Rather, they are
pointers to the revelation, and when God chooses to make them so,
they are in that moment, the Word of God.

Again the divergence of positions may seem relatively slight initially
but becomes greater as the implications are extended. If revelation is
personal encounter rather than information, then the Christian (or
would-be Christian) is called upon, not to accept these teachings in
some literal sense, or these commands to be carried out as the very
directive of God. He is rather called upon to expose himself to these
witnesses, in the anticipation that God will also meet with him and
on the basis of that meeting he then believes and acts. If on the other
hand, revelation includes actual truths, one can say of these, "This is
what God says to man." It should be noted that Kantzer is insistent
that it is not *either* propositions *or* personal encounter; it is *both/and*.
Bernard Ramm's article discusses the manner of the revelation as involving a condescension. The revelation comes through earthly forms

or modes, so that it may make contact with man. Kantzer would say that these are merely mediums through which revelation occurs.

For the conservative, who maintains that the Bible is the Word of God, a further issue is crucial. It is one thing to say that when men observed the acts of God in Biblical times, as the Exodus and the works of Jesus, they were seeing the activity of God, objectively present in history. Coupled with this is the assertion that the messages of Jesus, of Paul, and others were the truths which God wanted man to know. Those events are not recurring, however. In what sense do we have today what came to those men two thousand and more years ago? If the Word of God is not a repeated event but rather a permanent fact, there must be some preservation of the revelation. Without such, its efficacy would be limited to the immediate recipients. This act of God in preserving the revelation in written form is termed the inspiration of the Scriptures. It is the doctrine that the Spirit of God worked supernaturally upon the writers of Scripture in such a way that what they wrote can be properly termed the Word of God. But what is the nature of this divine guidance?

Two somewhat different approaches are presented by Benjamin B. Warfield and James Orr. Warfield gives primary attention to the Bible's testimony to its own inspiration, while Orr assigns priority to the facts (or phenomena, as they are often called) which illustrate the *nature* of inspiration, as seen in the book itself. Neither man ignores the other factor, but it is a matter of relative emphasis.

Warfield consequently examines in some detail the pertinent texts in which the Bible seems to teach something about the nature of its own inspiration. He concludes that the Biblical authors regarded the words of Scripture in its entirety as being the Words of God. This extends to such details as the tense of a verb, or the number of a noun, in Jesus' usage. While he considers the Bible thoroughly God's book, yet he is insistent that thereby no violence is done to the nature of the Biblical authors as men.

Orr, while examining some of the teachings of the Bible regarding its own inspiration, spends more time on a scrutiny of the actual types of material that inspiration has produced. He points out the freedom of literary style employed by the Scripture writers. They used existing historical materials in the production of their writings. He sees a somewhat freer activity of inspiration and resulting writings. He does not find an inerrancy of the Biblical record down to the minutest details, and does not consider the reality of authoritative revelation to depend upon such inerrancy, although he notes the remarkable accuracy and dependability of the Biblical record. In the final analysis, the proof of the inspiration of the Bible is to be found in its life-giving quality: what happens in the experience of the person who believes.

The question of authority mentioned briefly in the beginning of this essay comes in for explicit treatment in the two articles by Ramm and C. H. Dodd. In the latter part of the Reformation and in post-Reformation Protestantism, two polar views developed in terms of objectivism and subjectivism. Some of the more extreme Anabaptists emphasized a direct speaking of the Holy Spirit to the person. Later Lutheran orthodoxy tended to rely solely upon the Bible, which became a rather coldly objective book.

Ramm, however, insists upon a combination of factors, or a *pattern* of authority. Ultimately, authority in religious matters belongs to God alone. By giving us the Bible as His Word, however, He has in effect delegated authority. While the Bible is objectively God's Word, it is also essential that there be the subjective application of this by the Holy Spirit, the inward speaking or testimony of the Spirit to the truth of Scripture.

Dodd speaks from a more liberal stance. The authority of the Bible is not primarily the result of some intrinsic quality which it possesses. Rather it is authoritative instrumentally: as it affects the lives of men, and to the degree that it does so.

For the conservative, the issue of Biblical inspiration also raises the question of inerrancy of the Bible. If the Scriptures are fully inspired by God, must they not be completely truthful as a result? We have already noted the tendency of different theologians to construct their theory of inspiration predominantly from either the perspective of the Biblical teachings about inspiration or the nature of Scripture itself. This is carried over into the question of inerrancy.

Warfield argues primarily from the Biblical doctrine. He maintains that the apostles and Jesus held a view of inspiration which was such that it must be completely free from error. This is taught as clearly and firmly as are their views of the person and work of Christ, salvation, or any other doctrine. We accept their view of the Bible and its inspiration for the same reasons that we accept their doctrines in these other areas: the whole set of historical, philosophical, and psychological evidences that they are dependable teachers of doctrine. This evidence is so strong that any problems raised by the phenomena of Scripture are only difficulties, not real obstacles.

Dewey Beegle comes to the problem from the opposite direction. He believes that the nature of inspiration and specifically the question of inerrancy must be decided inductively. Accordingly, he produces numerous problem passages. He observes three possible resolutions of the difficulty: (1) The Bible teaches inerrancy and these are genuine errors; therefore its claim is false; (2) The Bible teaches inerrancy and these accordingly are not real errors; (3) The Bible does not teach its own inerrancy; therefore these can be accepted as errors.

While Warfield tended to rest his case primarily upon the doctrinal basis, many who hold his position have maintained that the difficulties such as those raised by Beegle can be accounted for without postulating the presence of error, and have offered harmonizations of the data. Everett Harrison's brief article concludes this section with an attempt to define criteria for evaluating the questions of inerrancy. He suggests certain spurious criteria which have sometimes been employed both by those who accept and those who reject the concept. When properly understood in their cultural settings, the writings which comprise the Bible can be appropriately described as fully truthful and free from all error.

General Revelation

9

Thomas Aquinas

The Existence of God

Three questions are asked concerning the existence of God.
1. Whether it is self-evident that God exists. 2. Whether the existence of God can be demonstrated. 3. Whether God exists.

Article One

Whether It Is Self-Evident That God Exists

We proceed to the first article thus:

1. It seems to be self-evident that God exists: Things are said to be self-evident when the knowledge of them is naturally in us, as is obviously the case with first principles. Now the Damascene says that "the knowledge that God exists is naturally inborn in all men" (1 *De Fid. Orth.* 1, 3). It is therefore self-evident that God exists.

2. Again, as the philosopher says of the first principles of demonstration, whatever is known as soon as the terms are known is self-evident (1 *Post. An.*, ch. 2). Thus we know that any whole is greater than its part as soon as we know what a whole is, and what a part

From Thomas Aquinas, *Summa Theologica,* Book I. *The Library of Christian Classics,* Vol. XI. Trans. and ed. by A. M. Fairweather. The Westminster Press. Copyright © MCMLIV, W. L. Jenkins. Used by permission.

is. Now when it is understood what the term "God" signifies, it is at once understood that God exists. For the term "God" means that than which nothing greater can be signified, and that which exists in reality is greater than that which exists only in the intellect. Hence since "God" exists in the intellect as soon as the term is understood, it follows that God exists also in reality. It· is therefore self-evident that God exists.

3. Again, it is self-evident that truth exists. For truth exists if anything at all is true, and if anyone denies that truth exists, he concedes that it is true that it does not exist, since if truth does not exist it is then true that it does not exist. Now God is truth itself, according to John 14:6: "I am the way, and the truth, and the life." It is therefore self-evident that God exists.

On the other hand: no one can conceive the opposite of what is self-evident, as the philosopher explains in dealing with the first principles of demonstration (4 *Metaph.*, text 9; 1 *Post. An.*, texts 5 and ult.). Now the opposite of "God exists" can be conceived, according to Ps. 53:1: "The fool hath said in his heart, There is no God." It follows that it is not self-evident that God exists.

I answer: there are two ways in which a thing may be self-evident. It may be self-evident in itself, but not self-evident to us. It may also be self-evident both in itself and to us. A proposition is self-evident when its predicate is contained in the meaning of its subject. For example, the proposition "man is an animal" is self-evident because "animal" is contained in the meaning of "man." Hence if the predicate and the subject are known to everyone, the proposition will be self-evident to everyone. This is obviously the case with regard to the first principles of demonstration, whose terms are universals known to everyone, such as being and not-being, whole, part, and the like. But when there are some to whom the predicate and the subject are unknown, the proposition will not be self-evident to them, however self-evident it may be in itself. Thus Boethius says (*Lib. de Hebd.*—Whether All Existence is Good): "it happens that some universal concepts of mind are self-evident only to the wise, e.g., that the incorporeal is not in space." I say, then, that this proposition "God exists" is self-evident in itself, since its predicate is the same with its subject. For God is his existence, as we shall show in Q. 3., Art 4. But since we do not know what God is, it is not self-evident to us, but must be proved by means of what is better known to us though less well known to nature, i.e., by means of the effects of God.

On the first point: the knowledge that God exists is inborn in us in a general and somewhat confused manner. For God is the final beatitude of man, and a man desires beatitude naturally, and is also naturally aware of what he desires. But this is not absolute knowledge that God exists, any more than to know that someone is coming is to know that Peter is coming, even though it should actually be Peter who comes. Many indeed think that riches are man's perfect good, and constitute his beatitude. Others think that pleasures are his perfect good, and others again something else.

On the second point: he who hears the term "God" may not understand it to mean that than which nothing greater can be conceived, since some have believed that God is a body. But given that one understands the term to mean this, it does not follow that he understands that that which the term signifies exists in the nature of things, but only that it exists in the intellect. Neither can it be argued that God exists in reality, unless it is granted that that than which nothing greater can be conceived exists in reality, which is not granted by those who suppose that God does not exist.

On the third point: it is self-evident that truth in general exists. But it is not self-evident to us that the first truth exists.

Article Two

Whether God's Existence Can Be Demonstrated

We proceed to the second article thus:

1. It seems that God's existence cannot be demonstrated. God's existence is an article of faith. But matters of faith cannot be demonstrated, since demonstration makes a thing to be known, whereas the apostle makes it clear that faith is of things not seen (Heb., ch. 11). It follows that God's existence cannot be demonstrated.

2. Again the medium of demonstration is the essence. But as the Damascene says (1 *De. Fid. Orth.* 4), we cannot know what God is, but only what he is not. It follows that we cannot demonstrate that God exists.

3. Again, God's existence could be demonstrated only from his effects. But his effects are not proportionate to God himself, since God is infinite while they are finite, and the finite is not proportionate to the infinite. Now a cause cannot be demonstrated from an effect which is not proportionate to itself. It follows that God's existence cannot be demonstrated.

On the other hand: the apostle says in Rom. 1:20: "the invisible things of him . . . are clearly seen, being understood by the things that are made." Now this is possible only if God's existence can be demonstrated from the things that are made. For the first thing that is understood about anything is its existence.

I answer: there are two kinds of demonstration. There is demonstration through the cause, or, as we say, "from grounds," which argues from what comes first in nature. There is also demonstration by means of effects, or "proof by means of appearances," which argues from what comes first for ourselves. Now when an effect is more apparent to us than its cause, we reach a knowledge of the

cause through its effect. Even though the effect should be better
known to us, we can demonstrate from any effect that its cause
exists, because effects always depend on some cause, and a cause
must exist if its effect exists. We can demonstrate God's existence
in this way, from his effects which are known to us, even though
we do not know his essence.

On the first point: the existence of God, and similar things which
can be known by natural reason as Rom., ch. 1, affirms, are not
articles of faith, but preambles to the articles. Faith presupposes
natural knowledge as grace presupposes nature, and as perfection
presupposes what can be perfected. There is no reason, however,
why what is in itself demonstrable and knowable should not be accepted in faith by one who cannot understand the demonstration
of it.

On the second point: when a cause is demonstrated by means
of its effect, we are bound to use the effect in place of a definition
of the cause in proving the existence of the cause. This is especially
the case with regard to God. For in proving that something exists,
we are bound to accept the meaning of the name as the medium of
demonstration, instead of the essence, since the question of what a
thing is must follow the question of its existence. Since the names
applied to God are derived from his effects, as we shall show in
Q. 13, Art. 1, we may use the name "God" as the medium in demon-
strating God's existence from his effect.

On the third point: effects which are not proportionate to their
cause do not give us perfect knowledge of their cause. Nevertheless,
it can be clearly demonstrated from any effect whatever that its
cause exists, as we have said. In this way we can prove God's existence from his effects, even though we cannot know his essence
perfectly by means of them.

Article Three

Whether God Exists

We proceed to the third article thus:

1. It seems that God does not exist. If one of two contraries
were to be infinite, the other would be wholly excluded. Now the
name "God" means that he is infinite good. There would therefore
be no evil if God were to exist. But there is evil in the world. It
follows that God does not exist.

2. Again, what can be explained by comparatively few principles
is not the consequence of a greater number of principles. Now if we
suppose that God does not exist, it appears that we can still account
for all that we see in the world by other principles, attributing all
natural things to nature as their principle, and all that is purposive
to human reason or will. There is therefore no need to suppose that
God exists.

On the other hand, in Exod. 3:14 God says in person: "I AM THAT I AM."

I answer: God's existence can be proved in five ways. The first and clearest proof is the argument from motion. It is certain, and in accordance with sense experience, that some things in this world are moved. Now everything that is moved is moved by something else, since nothing is moved unless it is potentially that to which it is moved, whereas that which moves is actual. To move is nothing other than to bring something from potentiality to actuality, and a thing can be brought from potentiality to actuality only by something which is actual. Thus a fire, which is actually hot, makes wood, which is potentially hot, to be actually hot, so moving and altering it. Now it is impossible for the same thing to be both actual and potential in the same respect, although it may be so in different respects. What is actually hot cannot at the same time be potentially hot, although it is potentially cold. It is therefore impossible that, in the same respect and in the same way, anything should be both mover and moved, or that it should move itself. Whatever is moved must therefore be moved by something else. If, then, that by which it is moved is itself moved, this also must be moved by something else, and this in turn by something else again. But this cannot go on forever, since there would then be no first mover, and consequently no other mover, because secondary movers cannot move unless moved by a first mover, as a staff cannot move unless it is moved by the hand. We are therefore bound to arrive at a first mover which is not moved by anything, and all men understand that this is God.

The second way is from the nature of an efficient cause. We find that there is a sequence of efficient causes in sensible things. But we do not find that anything is the efficient cause of itself. Nor is this possible, for the thing would then be prior to itself, which is impossible. But neither can the sequence of efficient causes be infinite, for in every sequence the first efficient cause is the cause of an intermediate cause, and an intermediate cause is the cause of the ultimate cause, whether the intermediate causes be many, or only one. Now if a cause is removed, its effect is removed. Hence if there were no first efficient cause, there would be no ultimate cause, and no intermediate cause. But if the regress of efficient causes were infinite, there would be no first efficient cause. There would consequently be no ultimate effect, and no intermediate causes. But this is plainly false. We are therefore bound to suppose that there is a first efficient cause. And all men call this God.

The third way is from the nature of possibility and necessity. There are some things which may either exist or not exist, since some things come to be and pass away, and may therefore be or not be. Now it is impossible that all of these should exist at all times, because there is at least some time when that which may possibly not exist does not exist. Hence if all things were such that they might not exist, at some time or other there would be nothing. But if this were true there would be nothing existing now, since what does not exist cannot begin to exist, unless through something which does exist. If there had been nothing existing it would have been impossible for anything to begin to exist, and there would now be nothing at all. But this is plainly false, and hence not all existence is merely possible. Something in things must be necessary. Now everything which is necessary either derives its necessity from elsewhere, or does not. But we cannot go on to infinity with necessary things which have a cause of their necessity, any more than with efficient causes, as we proved. We are therefore bound to suppose something necessary in itself, which does not owe its necessity to anything else, but which is the cause of the necessity of other things. And all men call this God.

The fourth way is from the degrees that occur in things, which are found to be more and less good, true, noble and so on. Things are said to be more and less because they approximate in different degrees to that which is greatest. A thing is the more hot the more it approximates to that which is hottest. There is therefore something which is the truest, the best, and the noblest, and which is consequently the greatest in being, since that which has the greatest truth is also greatest in being, as is said in 2 *Metaph.*, text 4. Now that which most thoroughly possesses the nature of any genus is the cause of all that the genus contains. Thus fire, which is most perfectly hot, is the cause of all hot things, as is said in the same passage. There is therefore something which is the cause of the being of all things that are, as well as of their goodness and their every perfection. This we call God.

The fifth way is from the governance of things. We see how some things, like natural bodies, work for an end even though they have no knowledge. The fact that they nearly always operate in the same way, and so as to achieve the maximum good, makes this obvious, and shows that they attain their end by design, not by chance. Now things which have no knowledge tend towards an end only through the agency of something which knows and also understands, as an arrow through an archer. There is therefore an intelligent being by whom all natural things are directed to their end. This we call God.

On the first point: as Augustine says (*Enchirid.* II): "since God is supremely good, he would not allow any evil thing to exist in his works, were he not able by his omnipotence and goodness to bring good out of evil." God's infinite goodness is such that he permits evil things to exist, and brings good out of them.

On the second point: everything that can be attributed to nature must depend on God as its first cause, since nature works for a predetermined end through the direction of a higher agent. Similarly, whatever is due to purpose must depend on a cause higher than the reason or will of man, since these are subject to change and defect. Anything which is changeable and subject to defect must depend on some first principle which is immovable and necessary in itself, as we have shown.

10

Karl Barth

No!

Brunner next asserts that the world is "somehow recognisable" to man as the creation of God, that "men somehow know the will of God." "The creation of the world is at the same time revelation, self-communication of God." And the possibility of recognising it as such is adversely affected but not destroyed by sin. It is not enough to give such knowledge of God as will bring salvation. Moreover, the revelation of God in nature can be known "in all its magnitude" only by him "whose eyes have been opened by Christ." But it is "somehow" recognisable—though but distortedly and dimly —even by those of whom this cannot be said. The idea that revelation is "recognisable" dominates the beginning of that section. But Brunner also says that surprisingly enough "sin makes man blind for what is visibly set before our eyes." This makes it not quite clear whether Brunner does not wish to speak of a purely formal possibility of knowing God through his creation, which is not actualised. But I think that I understand Brunner rightly when I assume that the affection of the eyes, of which he speaks, is, according to his opinion, very acute, but not to the extent of resulting in total blind-

From Karl Barth, "No!", *Natural Theology* (with Emil Brunner). London: Geoffrey Bles, 1946. Used by permission of Garnstone Press.

ness. Hence real knowledge of God through creation does take place without revelation, though only "somehow" and "not in all its magnitude." I think this interpretation is correct. If it is not, I cannot think what Brunner's exposition of the matter intends to convey. Therefore in view of what was said above about the total loss of the "material" *imago,* one is tempted to think that when in this context Brunner speaks of "God" and his "revelation" he means one of those creatures of man's philosophical phantasy, one of those principalities and powers of the world of ideas and demons, which most certainly do exist and which reveal themselves and are known to us quite concretely. For if man "can do nothing of himself for his salvation," they alone can be the objects of his *de facto* knowledge of God through nature! But what Brunner says and means is different. What would be the significance of the assertion of such a knowledge of "God" for his thesis concerning man's capacity for revelation? It would mean that the God revealed, in nature is not known to, but rather is very much hidden from, man. What would then become of the *theologica naturalis?* All that would be left would be a systematic exposition of the history of religion, philosophy and culture, without any theological claims or value. No, when he speaks of the God who can be and is "somehow" known through creation, Brunner does unfortunately mean the one true God, the triune creator of heaven and earth, who justifies us through Christ and sanctifies us through the Holy Spirit. It is he who is *de facto* known by all men without Christ, without the Holy Spirit, though knowledge of him is distorted and dimmed and darkened by sin, though he is "misrepresented" and "turned into idols." There are two kinds of revelation, both revealing the one true God. This is to be affirmed once and for all (on the basis of Scripture!). Only after that may it be asked "how the two revelations, that in creation and that in Jesus Christ, are related." But if that is Brunner's opinion, shall we be able to understand him otherwise than "somehow" distortedly, dimly and darkly? Is it his opinion that idolatry is but a somewhat imperfect preparatory stage of the service of the true God? Is the function of the revelation of God merely that of leading us from one step to the next within the all-embracing reality of divine revelation? Moreover, how can Brunner maintain that a real knowledge of the true God, however imperfect it may be (and what knowledge of God is not imperfect?) does not bring salvation? And if we really do know the true God from his creation without Christ and without the Holy Spirit—if this is so, how can it be said that the *imago* is materially "entirely lost," that in matters of the proclamation of the Church Scripture is the only norm, and that man can do nothing towards his salvation? Shall we not have to ascribe to him the ability to prepare himself for the knowledge of God in Christ at least negatively? Shall we not have to do what

Roman Catholic theology has always done and ascribe to him a *potentia oboedientialis* which he possesses from creation and retains in spite of sin? Has not Brunner added to man's "capacity for revelation," to what we have been assured is purely "formal," something very material: man's practically proved ability to know God, imperfectly it may be, but nevertheless really and therefore surely not without relevance to salvation? Perhaps he can swim a little, after all? If he has really done this, we are happy to know now more clearly what he means by "capacity for revelation." But how can Brunner wish to do this? The echo of his audible confession of the Reformers' doctrines of original sin, justification and the Scriptures is still sounding in our ears! Then he does *not* want to do it? But if not, then what *does* he want to do? No, after all, we still remain rather unhappy.

Next, Brunner asserts a special "preserving grace," i.e. the preserving and helping presence which God does not deny even to the fallen and estranged creature. We could easily understand this if Brunner meant to say that it is due to grace that after the fall man and his world exist at all or do not exist in a much worse state of disruption than is actually the case. Creation is the work of the truly free, truly undeserved grace of the one true God, both as an act and in its continuance. All very well, we can say. But by what right and in what sense does Brunner speak of another special (or rather "general") grace which as it were precedes the grace of Jesus Christ? If this were not so (but as Brunner wishes to obtain a separate *theologia naturalis* it *has* to be so), one could come to an understanding with Brunner. We could agree that the grace of Jesus Christ includes the patience with which God again and again gives us time for repentance and for the practice of perseverance, the patience by which he upholds and preserves man and his world, not for his own sake but for the sake of Christ, for the sake of the Church, for the sake of the elect children of God. We have time, because Christ ever intercedes for us before the judgment-seat of God. How can the preservation of man's existence and of the room given him for it be understood as the work of the one true God unless one means thereby that man is preserved through Christ for Christ, for repentance, for faith, for obedience, for the preservation of the Church? How can it be understood unless baptism is taken into account? How can one speak of these things unless the one revelation of Christ in the Old and New Testaments is taken into account? And how can one carry the severance of creation and reconciliation into the Bible? Does not the Bible relate all that Brunner calls a special "preserving grace" to prophecy and fulfilment, to law and gospel, to the covenant and the Messiah, to Israel and to the Church, to the children of God and their future redemption? Where did Brunner read of another abstract preserving grace? But since he insists on it we must go on to ask how far his "preserving grace" is grace at all. We are ever and again allowed to exist under various conditions which at least moderate the worst abuses. Does that deserve to be called "grace"? Taken by itself it might just as well be our condemnation to a kind of antechamber of hell! If it is anything else—as indeed it is—then not on account of our preservation as such! We must go on to ask: Can we really know that our preservation as such, e.g. "what we derive from our people and their history," is a special grace of the one true God? Does this not mean that the principle *sola scriptura* which Brunner accepts, most inopportunely blocks an important source of knowledge? Does it not mean that the Church cannot possibly have her basis and her justification, her law and her possibility, purely and solely in divine revelation? Does it not mean—am I dreaming?—that the poor "German Christians" may have been treated most unfairly? We must go on to ask: are not both the preservation of our existence as such and its conditions—Brunner mentions, e.g., the State—so much bound up with our own human possibilities that it cannot be said of this "grace" that man can of himself do nothing towards it? Brunner himself declares: "Consequently human activity comes within the purview of divine grace—not of redeeming but of preserving grace. All activity of man, which the creator uses to preserve his creation amid the corruptions of sin, belongs to this type of activity within preserving grace." Human activity which the creator uses to carry out the work of his grace? This concept is intelligible on the basis of the Augustinian idea of the indirect identity of human and divine activity or of the Thomist idea of the cooperation of the divine *causa materialis* with a human *causa instrumentalis*. It might be favourably understood if Brunner were speaking of the one justifying and sanctifying grace of Jesus Christ. For in that case also human activity "comes within the purview of divine grace." But that is not what Brunner wants. He wishes to speak of a special "preserving grace"! Has he not by so doing included in his doctrine an entire sphere (one which is, as it were, preparatory to revelation in the proper sense) in which the Reformers' principle of *sola gratia* cannot possibly be taken seriously? If there really is such a sphere of preparation, will this leave the understanding of revelation proper unaffected? Once Brunner has started to deal in abstractions such as these, will he be able to refrain from joining the Romanists, enthusiasts and pietists of all times in teaching also a special grace of life, a special grace of realisation, etc., for which God "uses" man no less than in the sphere of preparation? And where is all this going to lead us?

Brunner's fourth assertion is partly an exposition of the third. It treats separately of the "ordinances," the "constant factors of historical and social life . . . without which no communal life is conceivable, which could in any way be termed human." But among them he wishes to ascribe to matrimony as an "ordinance of creation" a "higher dignity" than to the State which is a mere "ordinance of preservation" relative to sin. Of the "ordinances of creation" it is said that "through the preserving grace of God they are *known* also to natural man as ordinances that are necessary and somehow holy and are by him *respected* as such." Of matrimony in particular it is said that "it is realised to some extent by men who are ignorant of the God revealed in Christ." The believer understands these ordinances of creation "better" than the unbeliever; he even understands them "rightly" and "perfectly." Nevertheless even the believer "cannot but allow his instinct and his reason to function with regard to these ordinances, just as in the arts." What can one say to that? No doubt there are such things as moral and sociological axioms which seem to underlie the various customs, laws and usages of different peoples, and seem to appear in them with some regularity. And there certainly seems to be some connection between these axioms and the instinct and reason which both believers and unbelievers have indeed every reason to allow to function in the life of the community. But what are these axioms? Or who—among us, who are "sinners through and through"!—decides what they are? If we consulted instinct and reason, what might or might not be called matrimony? Do instinct and reason really tell us what is the form of matrimony, which would then have to be acknowledged and proclaimed as a divine ordinance of creation? If we were chiefly concerned with the clarity and certainty of knowledge, would not the physical, biological and chemical "laws of nature" or certain axioms of mathematics have a much greater claim to being called ordinances of creation than those historico-social constants? And who or what raises these constants to the level of commandments, of binding and authoritative demands, which, as divine ordinances, they would obviously have to be? Instinct and reason? And what yardstick have we for measuring these sociological "ordinances of creation," arranging them in a little hierarchy and ascribing to one a greater, to the other a lesser, "dignity"? Do we as "believers" sit in the councils of God? Are we able to decide such a question? On the basis of instinct and reason one man may proclaim one thing to be an "ordinance of creation," another thing—according to the liberal, conservative or revolutionary inclinations of each. Can such a claim be anything other than the rebellious establishment of some very private *Weltanschauung* as a kind of papacy? Do theologians do well in taking part in one of these rebellions and in giving their blessing to them by proclaiming them to be divinely necessary? But let us assume for the moment that Brunner is right and that we possess some criterion for establishing here and there divine "ordinances of creation" on the basis of instinct and reason. What are we then to think of Brunner's assertion that these ordinances of creation are not only known but also respected and "to some extent realised" by men who do not know the God revealed in Christ? Of what Christian, however faithful, can it be said that he "to some extent realised" the ordinances of God? Is he not "a sinner through and through"—who would be lost if the law were not realised—but not merely "to some extent" but completely, finally and sufficiently for us all!—in Christ? If man can realise the law "to some extent" without Christ, how much more must "capacity for revelation" mean than merely the formal fact of man being human, i.e. a responsible and rational subject! Where, where has the distinction of the formal and the material *imago* got to? It is now purely arbitrary to continue to say that only holy Scripture may be the standard of the Church's message, that man can do nothing for his salvation, that it takes place *sola gratia,* that the Church must be free from all national and political restrictions! If man is from the start, and without the revelation and grace of Christ even "to some extent" on such good terms with God, if he can swim enough to help his deliverer by making a few good strokes—if all this is so, why are we suddenly so exclusive?

11

John Calvin

The Knowledge of God Conspicuous in the Creation and Continual Government of the World

1. Since the perfection of blessedness consists in the knowledge of God, he has been pleased, in order that none might be excluded from the means of obtaining felicity, not only to deposit in our minds that seed of religion of which we have already spoken, but so to manifest his perfections in the whole structure of the universe, and daily place himself in our view, that we cannot open our eyes without being compelled to behold him. His essence, indeed, is incomprehensible, utterly transcending all human thought; but on each of his works his glory is engraven in characters so bright, so distinct, and so illustrious, that none, however dull and illiterate, can plead ignorance as their excuse. Hence, with perfect truth, the Psalmist exclaims, "He covereth himself with light as with a garment" (Ps. 104:2); as if he had said that God for the first time was arrayed in visible attire when, in the creation of the world, he displayed those glorious banners, on which, to whatever side we

From John Calvin, *Institutes of the Christian Religion*. London: James Clark and Co., 1953.

turn, we behold his perfections visibly portrayed. In the same place, the Psalmist aptly compares the expanded heavens to his royal tent, and says, "He layeth the beams of his chambers in the waters, maketh the clouds his chariot, and walketh upon the wings of the wind," sending forth the winds and lightnings as his swift messengers. And because the glory of his power and wisdom is more refulgent in the firmament, it is frequently designated as his palace. And, first, wherever you turn your eyes, there is no portion of the world, however minute, that does not exhibit at least some sparks of beauty; while it is impossible to contemplate the vast and beautiful fabric as it extends around without being overwhelmed by the immense weight of glory. Hence, the author of the Epistle to the Hebrews elegantly describes the visible worlds as images of the invisible (Heb. 11:3), the elegant structure of the world serving us as a kind of mirror, in which we may behold God, though otherwise invisible. For the same reason, the Psalmist attributes language to celestial objects, a language which all nations understand (Ps. 19:1); the manifestation of the Godhead being too clear to escape the notice of any people, however obtuse. The apostle Paul, stating this still more clearly, says, "That which may be known of God is manifest in them, for God hath showed it unto them. For the invisible things of him from the creation of the world are clearly seen, being understood by the things that are made, even his eternal power and Godhead" (Rom. 1:20).

2. In attestation of his wondrous wisdom, both the heavens and the earth present us with innumerable proofs, not only those more recondite proofs which astronomy, medicine, and all the natural sciences, are designed to illustrate, but proofs which force themselves on the notice of the most illiterate peasant, who cannot open his eyes without beholding them. It is true, indeed, that those who are more or less intimately acquainted with those liberal studies are thereby assisted and enabled to obtain a deeper insight into the secret workings of divine wisdom. No man, however, though he be ignorant of these, is incapacitated for discerning such proofs of creative wisdom as may well cause him to break forth in admiration of the Creator. To investigate the motions of the heavenly bodies, to determine their positions, measure their distances, and ascertain their properties, demands skill, and a more careful examination; and where these are so employed, as the providence of God is thereby more fully unfolded, so it is reasonable to suppose that the mind takes a loftier flight, and obtains brighter views of his glory.[1] Still, none who have the use of their eyes can be ignorant of the divine skill manifested so conspicuously in the endless variety, yet distinct and well-ordered array, of the heavenly host; and, therefore, it is plain that the Lord has furnished every man with abundant proofs of his wisdom. The same is true in regard to the structure

of the human frame. To determine the connection of its parts, its symmetry and beauty, with the skill of a Galen (Lib. De Usu Partium), requires singular acuteness; and yet all men acknowledge that the human body bears on its face such proofs of ingenious contrivance as are sufficient to proclaim the admirable wisdom of its Maker.

3. Hence certain of the philosophers[2] have not improperly called man a *microcosm (miniature world),* as being a rare specimen of divine power, wisdom, and goodness, and containing within himself wonders sufficient to occupy our minds, if we are willing so to employ them. Paul, accordingly, after reminding the Athenians that they "might feel after God and find him," immediately adds, that "he is not far from every one of us" (Acts 17:27); every man having within himself undoubted evidence of the heavenly grace by which he lives, and moves, and has his being. But if, in order to apprehend God, it is unnecessary to go farther than ourselves, what excuse can there be for the sloth of any man who will not take the trouble of descending into himself that he may find Him? For the same reason, too, David, after briefly celebrating the wonderful name and glory of God, as everywhere displayed, immediately exclaims, "What is man, that thou are mindful of him?" and again, "Out of the mouths of babes and sucklings thou has ordained strength" (Ps. 8:2, 4). Thus he declares not only that the human race are a bright mirror of the Creator's works, but that infants hanging on their mothers' breasts have tongues eloquent enough to proclaim his glory without the aid of other orators. Accordingly, he hesitates not to bring them forward as fully instructed to refute the madness of those who, from devilish pride, would fain extinguish the name of God. Hence, too, the passage which Paul quotes from Aratus, "We are his offspring" (Acts 17:28), the excellent gifts with which he has endued us attesting that he is our Father. In the same way, also, from natural instinct, and, as it were, at the dictation of experience, heathen poets call him the father of men. No one, indeed, will voluntarily and willingly devote himself to the service of God unless he has previously tasted his paternal love, and been thereby allured to love and reverence Him.

4. But herein appears the shameful ingratitude of men. Though they have in their own persons a factory where innumerable operations of God are carried on, and a magazine stored with treasures of inestimable value—instead of bursting forth in his praise, as they are bound to do, they, on the contrary, are the more inflated and swelled with pride. They feel how wonderfully God is working in them, and their own experience tells them of the vast variety of gifts which they owe to his liberality. Whether they will or not, they cannot but know that these are proofs of his Godhead, and yet they inwardly suppress them. They have no occasion to go farther than

themselves, provided they do not, by appropriating as their own that which has been given them from heaven, put out the light intended to exhibit God clearly to their minds. At this day, however, the earth sustains on her bosom many monster minds—minds which are not afraid to employ the seed of Deity deposited in human nature as a means of suppressing the name of God. Can anything be more detestable than this madness in man, who, finding God a hundred times both in his body and his soul, makes his excellence in this respect a pretext for denying that there is a God? He will not say that chance has made him differ from the brutes that perish; but, substituting nature as the architect of the universe, he suppresses the name of God. The swift motions of the soul, its noble faculties and rare endowments, bespeak the agency of God in a manner which would make the suppression of it impossible, did not the Epicureans, like so many Cyclops, use it as a vantage-ground, from which to wage more audacious war with God. Are so many treasures of heavenly wisdom employed in the guidance of such a worm as man, and shall the whole universe be denied the same privilege? To hold that there are organs in the soul corresponding to each of its faculties, is so far from obscuring the glory of God, that it rather illustrates it. Let Epicurus tell what concourse of atoms, cooking meat and drink, can form one portion into refuse and another portion into blood, and make all the members separately perform their office as carefully as if they were so many souls acting with common consent in the superintendence of one body.

5. But my business at present is not with that stye: I wish rather to deal with those who, led away by absurd subtleties, are inclined, by giving an indirect turn to the frigid doctrine of Aristotle, to employ it for the purpose both of disproving the immortality of the soul and robbing God of his rights. Under the pretext that the faculties of the soul are organised, they chain it to the body as if it were incapable of a separate existence, while they endeavor as much as in them lies, by pronouncing eulogiums on nature, to suppress the name of God. But there is no ground for maintaining that the powers of the soul are confined to the performance of bodily functions. What has the body to do with your measuring the heavens, counting the number of the stars, ascertaining their magnitudes, their relative distances, the rate at which they move, and the orbits which they describe? I deny not that Astronomy has its use; all I mean to show is, that these lofty investigations are not conducted by organised symmetry, but by the faculties of the soul itself apart altogether from the body. The single example I have given will suggest many others to the reader. The swift and versatile movements of the soul in glancing from heaven to earth, connecting the future with the past, retaining the remembrance of former years, nay, forming creations of its own—its skill, moreover, in making astonishing

discoveries, and inventing so many wonderful arts, are sure indications of the agency of God in man. What shall we say of its activity when the body is asleep, its many revolving thoughts, its many useful suggestions, its many solid arguments, nay, its presentiment of things yet to come? What shall we say but that man bears about with him a stamp of immortality which can never be effaced? But how is it possible for man to be divine and yet not acknowledge his Creator? Shall we, by means of a power of judging implanted in our breast, distinguish between justice and injustice, and yet there be no judge in heaven? Shall some remains of intelligence continue with us in sleep, and yet no God keep watch in heaven? Shall we be deemed the inventors of so many arts and useful properties that God may be defrauded of his praise, though experience tells us plainly enough, that whatever we possess is dispensed to us in unequal measures by another hand? The talk of certain persons concerning a secret inspiration quickening the whole world, is not only silly, but altogether profane. Such persons are delighted with the following celebrated passage of Virgil:[3]

> Know, first, that heaven and earth's compacted frame,
> And flowing waters, and the starry flame,
> And both the radiant lights, one common soul
> Inspires and feeds—and animates the whole.
> This active mind, infused through all the space,
> Unites and mingles with the mighty mass:
> Hence, men and beasts the breath of life obtain,
> And birds of air, and monsters of the main.
> Th' ethereal vigour is in all the same,
> And every soul is filled with equal flame.[4]

The meaning of all this is, that the world, which was made to display the glory of God, is its own creator. For the same poet has in another place,[5] adopted a view common to both Greeks and Latins:

> Hence to the bee some sages have assigned
> A portion of the God, and heavenly mind;
> For God goes forth, and spreads throughout the whole,
> Heaven, earth, and sea, the universal soul;
> Each, at its birth, from him all beings share,
> Both man and brute, the breath of vital air;
> To him return, and, loosed from earthly chain,
> Fly whence they sprang, and rest in God again
> Spurn at the grave, and, fearless of decay,
> Dwell in high heaven, and star th' ethereal way.[6]

Here we see how far that jejune speculation, of a universal mind animating and invigorating the world, is fitted to beget and foster piety in our minds. We have a still clearer proof of this in the profane verses which the licentious Lucretius has written as a deduction from the same principle.[7] The plain object is to form an unsubstantial deity, and thereby banish the true God whom we ought to fear and worship. I admit, indeed, that the expression, "Nature is God," may be piously used, if dictated by a pious mind; but as it is inaccurate and harsh (Nature being more properly the order which has been established by God), in matters which are so very important, and in regard to which special reverence is due, it does harm to confound the Deity with the inferior operations of his hands.

6. Let each of us, therefore, in contemplating his own nature, remember that there is one God who governs all natures, and, in governing, wishes us to have respect to himself, to make him the object of our faith, worship, and adoration. Nothing, indeed, can be more preposterous than to enjoy those noble endowments which bespeak the divine presence within us, and to neglect him who, of his own good pleasure, bestows them upon us. In regard to his power, how glorious the manifestations by which he urges us to the contemplation of himself; unless, indeed, we pretend not to know whose energy it is that by a word sustains the boundless fabric of the universe—at one time making heaven reverberate with thunder, sending forth the scorching lightning, and setting the whole atmosphere in a blaze; at another, causing the raging tempests to blow, and forthwith, in one moment, when it so pleases him, making a perfect calm; keeping the sea, which seems constantly threatening the earth with devastation, suspended as it were in air; at one time, lashing it into fury by the impetuosity of the winds; at another, appeasing its rage, and stilling all its waves. Here we might refer to those glowing descriptions of divine power, as illustrated by natural events, which occur throughout Scripture; but more especially in the book of Job and the prophecies of Isaiah. These, however, I purposely omit, because a better opportunity of introducing them will be found when I come to treat of the Scriptural account of the creation. (*Infra,* chap. xiv. s. 1, 2, 20, *sq.*) I only wish to observe here, that this method of investigating the divine perfections, by tracing the lineaments of his countenance as shadowed forth in the firmament and on the earth is common both to those within and to those without the pale of the Church. From the power of God we are naturally led to consider his eternity, since that from which all other things derive their origin must necessarily be self-existent and eternal. Moreover, if it be asked what cause induced him to create all things at first, and now inclines him to preserve them, we shall find that there could be no other cause than his own goodness. But if this is the only cause, nothing more should be required to draw forth our love towards him; every creature, as the Psalm-

ist reminds us, participating in his mercy. "His tender mercies are over all his works" (Ps. 145:9).

7. In the second class of God's works, namely, those which are above the ordinary course of nature, the evidence of his perfections are in every respect equally clear. For in conducting the affairs of men, he so arranges the course of his providence, as daily to declare, by the clearest manifestations, that though all are in innumerable ways the partakers of his bounty, the righteous are the special objects of his favour, the wicked and profane the special objects of his severity. It is impossible to doubt his punishment of crimes; while at the same time he, in no unequivocal manner, declares that he is the protector, and even the avenger of innocence, by shedding blessings on the good, helping their necessities, soothing and solacing their griefs, relieving their sufferings, and in all ways providing for their safety. And though he often permits the guilty to exult for a time with impunity, and the innocent to be driven to and fro in adversity, nay, even to be wickedly and iniquitously oppressed, this ought not to produce any uncertainty as to the uniform justice of all his procedure. Nay, an opposite inference should be drawn. When any one crime calls forth visible manifestations of his anger, it must be because he hates all crimes; and, on the other hand, his leaving many crimes unpunished, only proves that there is a judgment in reserve, when the punishment now delayed shall be inflicted. In like manner, how richly does he supply us with the means of contemplating his mercy, when, as frequently happens, he continues to visit miserable sinners with unwearied kindness, until he subdues their depravity, and woos them back with more than a parent's fondness?

8. To this purpose the Psalmist (Ps. 107), mentioning how God, in a wondrous manner, often brings sudden and unexpected succour to the miserable when almost on the brink of despair, whether in protecting them when they stray in deserts, and at length leading them back to the right path, or supplying them with food when famishing for want, or delivering them when captive from iron fetters and foul dungeons, or conducting them safe into harbour after shipwreck, or bringing them back from the gates of death by curing their diseases, or, after burning up the fields with heat and drought, fertilising them with the river of his grace, or exalting the meanest of the people, and casting down the mighty from their lofty seats:—the Psalmist, after bringing forward examples of this description, infers that those things which men call fortuitous events, are so many proofs of divine providence, and more especially of paternal clemency, furnishing ground of joy to the righteous, and at the same time stopping the mouths of the ungodly. But as the greater part of mankind, enslaved by error, walk blindfold in this glorious theatre, he exclaims that it is a rare and singular wisdom

to meditate carefully on these works of God, which many, who seem most sharp-sighted in other respects, behold without profit. It is indeed true, that the brightest manifestation of divine glory finds not one genuine spectator among a hundred. Still, neither his power nor his wisdom is shrouded in darkness. His power is strikingly displayed when the rage of the wicked, to all appearances irresistible, is crushed in a single moment; their arrogance subdued, their strongest bulwarks overthrown, their armour dashed to pieces, their strength broken, their schemes defeated without an effort, and audacity which sets itself above the heavens is precipitated to the lowest depths of the earth. On the other hand, the poor are raised up out of the dust, and the needy lifted out of the dunghill (Ps. 113:7), the oppressed and afflicted are rescued in extremity, the despairing animated with hope, the unarmed defeat the armed, the few the many, the weak the strong. The excellence of the divine wisdom is manifested in distributing everything in due season, confounding the wisdom of the world, and taking the wise in their own craftiness (I Cor. 3:19); in short, conducting all things in perfect accordance with reason.

9. We see there is no need of a long and laborious train of argument in order to obtain proofs which illustrate and assert the Divine Majesty. The few which we have merely touched show them to be so immediately within our reach in every quarter, that we can trace them with the eye, or point to them with the finger. And here we must observe again . . . , that the knowledge of God which we are invited to cultivate is not that which, resting satisfied with empty speculation, only flutters in the brain, but a knowledge which will prove substantial and fruitful wherever it is duly perceived, and rooted in the heart. The Lord is manifested by his perfections. When we feel their power within us, and are conscious of their benefits, the knowledge must impress us much more vividly than if we merely imagined a God whose presence we never felt. Hence it is obvious that, in seeking God, the most direct path and the fittest method is, not to attempt with presumptuous curiosity to pry into his essence, which is rather to be adored than minutely discussed, but to contemplate him in his works, by which he draws near, becomes familiar, and in a manner communicates himself to us. To this the Apostle referred when he said that we need not go far in search of him (Acts 17:27), because, by the continual working of his power he dwells in every one of us. Accordingly, David (Ps. 145), after acknowledging that his greatness is unsearchable, proceeds to enumerate his works, declaring that his greatness will thereby be unfolded. It therefore becomes us also diligently to prosecute that investigation of God which so enraptures the soul with admiration as, at the same time, to make an efficacious impression on it. And, as Augustine expresses it (in Ps. 144), since we are unable to comprehend Him, and are, as it were,

overpowered by his greatness, our proper course is to contemplate his works, and so refresh ourselves with his goodness.

10. By the knowledge thus acquired, we ought not only to be stimulated to worship God, but also aroused and elevated to the hope of future life. For, observing that the manifestations which the Lord gives both of his mercy and severity are only begun and incomplete, we ought to infer that these are doubtless only a prelude to higher manifestations, of which the full display is reserved for another state. Conversely, when we see the righteous brought into affliction by the ungodly, assailed with injuries, overwhelmed with calumnies, and lacerated by insult and contumely, while, on the contrary, the wicked flourish, prosper, acquire ease and honour, and all these with impunity, we ought forthwith to infer, that there will be a future life in which iniquity shall receive its punishment and righteousness its reward. Moreover, when we observe that the Lord often lays his chastening rod on the righteous, we may the more surely conclude, that far less will the unrighteous ultimately escape the scourges of his anger. There is a well-known passage in Augustine (De Civitat. Dei, lib. i. c. 8), "Were all sin now visited with open punishment, it might be thought that nothing was reserved for the final judgment; and, on the other hand, were no sin now openly punished, it might be supposed there was no divine providence." It must be acknowledged, therefore, that in each of the works of God, and more especially in the whole of them taken together, the divine perfections are delineated as in a picture, and the whole human race thereby invited and allured to acquire the knowledge of God, and, in consequence of this knowledge true and complete felicity. Moreover, while his perfections are thus most vividly displayed, the only means of ascertaining their practical operation and tendency is to descend into ourselves, and consider how it is that the Lord there manifests his wisdom, power, and energy,—how he there displays his justice, goodness, and mercy. For although David (Ps. 92:6) justly complains of the extreme infatuation of the ungodly in not pondering the deep counsels of God, as exhibited in the government of the human race, what he elsewhere says (Ps. 40) is most true, that the wonders of the divine wisdom in this respect are more in number than the hairs of our head. But I leave this topic at present as it will be more fully considered afterwards in its own place. . . .

11. Bright, however, as is the manifestation which God gives both of himself and his immortal kingdom in the mirror of his works, so great is our stupidity, so dull are we in regard to these bright manifestations, that we derive no benefit from them. For in regard to the fabric and admirable arrangement of the universe, how few of us are there who, in lifting our eyes to the heavens, or looking abroad on the various regions of the earth, ever think of the Creator? Do we not rather overlook Him, and sluggishly content our-

selves with a view of his works? And then in regard to supernatural events, though these are occurring every day, how few are there who ascribe them to the ruling providence of God—how many who imagine that they are casual results produced by the blind evolutions of the wheel of chance? Even when, under the guidance and direction of these events, we are in a manner forced to the contemplation of God (a circumstance which all must occasionally experience) and are thus led to form some impressions of Deity, we immediately fly off to carnal dreams and depraved fictions, and so by our vanity corrupt heavenly truth. This far, indeed, we differ from each other, in that every one appropriates to himself some peculiar error; but we are all alike in this, that we substitute monstrous fictions for the one living and true God—a disease not confined to obtuse and vulgar minds, but affecting the noblest, and those who, in other respects, are singularly acute. How lavishly in this respect have the whole body of philosophers, betrayed their stupidity and want of sense? To say nothing of the others whose absurdities are of a still grosser description, how completely does Plato, the soberest and most religious of them all, lose himself in his round globe?[8] What must be the case with the rest, when the leaders, who ought to have set them an example, commit such blunders, and labour under such hallucinations? In like manner, while the government of the world places the doctrine of providence beyond dispute, the practical result is the same as if it were believed that all things were carried hither and thither at the caprice of chance; so prone are we to vanity and error. I am still referring to the most distinguished of the philosophers, and not to the common herd, whose madness in profaning the truth of God exceeds all bounds.

12. Hence that immense flood of error with which the whole world is overflowed. Every individual mind being a kind of labyrinth, is it not wonderful, not only that each nation has adopted a variety of fiction, but that almost every man has had his own god? To the darkness of ignorance have been added presumption and wantonness, and hence there is scarcely an individual to be found without some idol or phantom as a substitute for Deity. Like water gushing forth from a large and copious spring, immense crowds of gods have issued from the human mind, every man giving himself full license, and devising some peculiar form of divinity, to meet his own views. It is unnecessary here to attempt a catalogue of the superstitions with which the world was overspread. The thing were endless; and the corruptions themselves, though not a word should be said, furnish abundant evidence of the blindness of the human mind. I say nothing of the rude and illiterate vulgar; but among the philosophers[9] who attempted, by reason and learning, to pierce the heavens, what shameful disagreement! The higher any one was endued with genius, and the more he was polished

by science and art, the more specious was the colouring which he gave to his opinions. All these, however, if examined more closely, will be found to be vain show. The Stoics plumed themselves on their acuteness, when they said[10] that the various names of God might be extracted from all the parts of nature, and yet that his unity was not thereby divided; as if we were not already too prone to vanity, and had no need of being presented with an endless multiplicity of gods, to lead us further and more grossly into error. The mystic theology of the Egyptians shows how sedulously they laboured to be thought rational on this subject.[11] And, perhaps, at the first glance, some show of probability might deceive the simple and unwary; but never did any mortal devise a scheme by which religion was not foully corrupted. This endless variety and confusion emboldened the Epicureans, and other gross despisers of piety, to cut off all sense of God. For when they saw that the wisest contradicted each other, they hesitated not to infer from their dissensions, and from the frivolous and absurd doctrines of each, that men foolishly, and to no purpose, brought torment upon themselves by searching for a God, there being none: and they thought this inference safe, because it was better at once to deny God altogether than to feign uncertain gods, and thereafter engage in quarrels without end. They, indeed, argue absurdly, or rather weave a cloak for their impiety out of human ignorance; though ignorance surely cannot derogate from the prerogatives of God. But since all confess that there is no topic on which such difference exists, both among learned and unlearned, the proper inference is, that the human mind, which thus errs in inquiring after God, is dull and blind in heavenly mysteries. Some praise the answer of Simonides, who being asked by King Hiero what God was, asked a day to consider. When the king next day repeated the question, he asked two days; and after repeatedly doubling the number of days, at length replied, "The longer I consider, the darker the subject appears."[12] He, no doubt, wisely suspended his opinion, when he did not see clearly: still his answer shows, that if men are only naturally taught, instead of having any distinct, solid, or certain knowledge, they fasten only on contradictory principles, and, in consequence, worship an unknown God.

13. Hence we must hold, that whatsoever adulterates pure religion (and this must be the case with all who cling to their own views), make a departure from the one God. No doubt, they will allege that they have a different intention; but it is of little consequence what they intend or persuade themselves to believe, since the Holy Spirit pronounces all to be apostates who, in the blindness of their minds, substitute demons in the place of God. For this reason Paul declares that the Ephesians were "without God" (Eph. 2:12), until they had learned from the gospel what it is to worship the true God. Nor

must this be restricted to one people only, since, in another place, he declares in general, that all men "became vain in their imaginations," after the majesty of the Creator was manifested to them in the structure of the world. Accordingly, in order to make way for the only true God, he condemns all the gods celebrated among the Gentiles as lying and false, leaving no Deity anywhere but in Mount Zion, where the special knowledge of God was professed (Hab. 2:18, 20). Among the Gentiles in the time of Christ, the Samaritans undoubtedly made the nearest approach to true piety; yet we hear from his own mouth that they worshipped they knew not what (John 4:22); whence it follows that they were deluded by vain errors. In short, though all did not give way to gross vice, or rush headlong into open idolatry, there was no pure and authentic religion founded merely on common belief. A few individuals may not have gone all insane lengths with the vulgar; still Paul's declaration remains true, that the wisdom of God was not apprehended by the princes of this world (I Cor. 2:8). But if the most distinguished wandered in darkness, what shall we say of the refuse? No wonder, therefore, that all worship of man's device is repudiated by the Holy Spirit as degenerate. Any opinion which man can form in heavenly mysteries, though it may not beget a long rain of errors, is still the parent of error. And though nothing worse should happen, even this is no light sin—to worship an unknown God at random. Of this sin, however, we hear from our Saviour's own mouth (John 4:22), that all are guilty who have not been taught out of the law who the God is whom they ought to worship. Nay, even Socrates in Xenophon (lib. i. Memorabilia) lauds the response of Apollo enjoining every man to worship the gods according to the rites of his country, and the particular practice of his own city. But what right have mortals thus to decide of their own authority in a matter which is far above the world; or who can so acquiesce in the will of his forefathers, or the decrees of the people, as unhesitatingly to receive a god at their hands? Every one will adhere to his own judgment sooner than submit to the dictation of others. Since, therefore, in regulating the worship of God, the custom of a city, or the consent of antiquity, is a too feeble and fragile bond of piety: it remains that God himself must bear witness to himself from heaven.

14. In vain for us, therefore, does Creation exhibit so many bright lamps lighted up to show forth the glory of its Author. Though they beam upon us from every quarter, they are altogether insufficient of themselves to lead us into the right path. Some sparks, undoubtedly, they do throw out; but these are quenched before they can give forth a brighter effulgence. Wherefore, the apostle, in the very place where he says that the worlds are images of invisible things, adds that it is *by faith* we understand that they were framed by the word of God (Heb. 11:3); thereby intimating that the invis-

ible Godhead is indeed represented by such displays, but that we have no eyes to perceive it until they are enlightened through faith by internal revelation from God. When Paul says that that which may be known of God is manifested by the creation of the world, he does not mean such a manifestation as may be comprehended by the wit of man (Rom. 1:19); on the contrary, he shows that it has no further effect than to render us inexcusable (Acts 17:27). And though he says, elsewhere, that we have not far to seek for God, inasmuch as he dwells within us, he shows, in another passage, to what extent this nearness to God is availing. God, says he, "in times past, suffered all nations to walk in their own ways. Nevertheless, he left not himself without witness, in that he did good, and gave us rain from heaven, and fruitful seasons, filling our hearts with food and gladness" (Acts 14:16, 17). But though God is not left without a witness, while, with numberless varied acts of kindness, he woos men to the knowledge of himself, yet they cease not to follow their own ways, in other words, deadly errors.

15. But though we are deficient in natural powers which might enable us to rise to a pure and clear knowledge of God, still, as the dulness which prevents us is within, there is no room for excuse. We cannot plead ignorance, without being at the same time convicted by our own consciences both of sloth and ingratitude. It were, indeed, a strange defence for man to pretend that he has no ears to hear the truth, while dumb creatures have voices loud enough to declare it; to allege that he is unable to see that which creatures without eyes demonstrate; to excuse himself on the ground of weakness of mind, while all creatures without reason are able to teach. Wherefore, when we wander and go astray, we are justly shut out from every species of excuse, because all things point to the right path. But while man must bear the guilt of corrupting the seed of divine knowledge so wondrously deposited in his mind, and preventing it from bearing good and genuine fruit, it is still most true that we are not sufficiently instructed by that bare and simple, but magnificent testimony which the creatures bear to the glory of their Creator. For no sooner do we, from a survey of the world, obtain some slight knowledge of Deity, than we pass by the true God, and set up in his stead the dream and phantom of our own brain, drawing away the praise of justice, wisdom, and goodness from the fountain-head, and transferring it to some other quarter. Moreover, by the erroneous estimate we form, we either so obscure or pervert his daily works, as at once to rob them of their glory, and the author of them of his just praise.

THE NEED OF SCRIPTURE, AS A GUIDE AND TEACHER, IN COMING TO GOD AS A CREATOR

1. Therefore, though the effulgence which is presented to every

eye, both in the heavens and on the earth, leaves the ingratitude of man without excuse, since God, in order to bring the whole human race under the same condemnation, holds forth to all, without exception, a mirror of his Deity in his works, another and better help must be given to guide us properly to God as a Creator. Not in vain, therefore, has he added the light of his Word in order that he might make himself known unto salvation, and bestowed the privilege on those whom he was pleased to bring into nearer and more familiar relation to himself. For, seeing how the minds of men were carried to and fro, and found no certain resting-place, he chose the Jews for a peculiar people, and then hedged them in that they might not, like others, go astray. And not in vain does he, by the same means, retain us in his knowledge, since but for this, even those who, in comparison of others, seem to stand strong, would quickly fall away. For as the aged, or those whose sight is defective, when any book, however fair, is set before them, though they perceive that there is something written, are scarcely able to make out two consecutive words, but, when aided by glasses, begin to read distinctly, so Scripture, gathering together the impressions of Deity, which, till then, lay confused in their minds, dissipates the darkness, and shows us the true God clearly. God therefore bestows a gift of singular value, when, for the instruction of the Church, he employs not dumb teachers merely, but opens his own sacred mouth; when he not only proclaims that some God must be worshipped, but at the same time declares that He is the God to whom worship is due; when he not only teaches his elect to have respect to God, but manifests himself as the God to whom this respect should be paid.

The course which God followed towards his Church from the very first, was to supplement these common proofs by the addition of his Word, as a surer and more direct means of discovering himself. And there can be no doubt that it was by this help, Adam, Noah, Abraham, and the other patriarchs, attained to that familiar knowledge which, in a manner, distinguished them from unbelievers. I am not now speaking of the peculiar doctrines of faith by which they were elevated to the hope of eternal blessedness. It was necessary, in passing from death unto life, that they should know God, not only as a Creator, but as a Redeemer also; and both kinds of knowledge they certainly did obtain from the Word. In point of order, however, the knowledge first given was that which made them acquainted with the God by whom the world was made and is governed. To this first knowledge was afterwards added the more intimate knowledge which alone quickens dead souls, and by which God is known, not only as the Creator of the world, and the sole author and disposer of all events, but also as a Redeemer, in the person of the Mediator. But as the fall and the corruption of nature have not yet been considered, I now postpone the consideration of the remedy (for which, see Book

II. c. vi., etc.). Let the reader then remember, that I am not now treating of the covenant by which God adopted the children of Abraham, or of that branch of doctrine by which, as founded in Christ, believers have, properly speaking, been in all ages separated from the profane heathen. I am only showing that it is necessary to apply to Scripture, in order to learn the sure marks which distinguish God, as the Creator of the world, from the whole herd of fictitious gods. We shall afterward, in due course, consider the work of Redemption. In the mean time, though we shall adduce many passages from the New Testament, and some also from the Law and the Prophets, in which express mention is made of Christ, the only object will be to show that God, the Maker of the world, is manifested to us in Scripture, and his true character expounded, so as to save us from wandering up and down, as in a labyrinth, in search of some doubtful deity.

Notes

[1]Augustinus: *Astrologia magnum religiosis argumentum, tormentumque curiosis.*

[2]See Aristot. *Hist. Anim.* lib. i. c. 17; Macrob. in Somn. Scip. lib. ii. c. 12; Boeth. De Definitione.

[3]*Æneid*, vi. 724 sq. See Calvin on Acts xvii. 28. Manil. lib. i. Astron.

[4]Dryden's *Virgil, Æneid*, Book vi. 1. 980-990.

[5]Georgic iv. 220. Plat. in *Tim. Arist.* lib. i. *De Animo.* See also Metaph. lib. 1. Diere. Trismegr. in Pimandro.

[6]Dryden's *Virgil*, Book iv. 1. 262.

[7]He maintains, in the beginning of the First Book, that nothing is produced of nothing, but that all things are formed out of certain primitive materials. He also perverts the ordinary course of generation into an argument against the existence of God. In the Fifth Book, however, he admits that the world was born and will die.

[8]Plato in Timaeos. See also Cic. De Nat. Deorum, lib. i; Plut. De Philos Placitis, lib. i.

[9]Cicero: Qui deos esse dixerunt tanta sunt in varietate ac dissensione, ut eorum molestum sit enumerare sententias.—Cicero, De Nat. Deorum, lib. i. and ii. Lactant Inst. Div. lib. i & c.

[10] Seneca, De Benef., lib. iv. c. 7, et Natural. Quaest, lib. i. in Praef., et lib. ii, c 45.

[11]Plutarch. lib. De Iside et Osiride.

[12]Cicero, De Nat. Deor. lib. i.

Special Revelation

12

Kenneth S. Kantzer

The Authority of the Bible

In a famous essay on revelation Archbishop William Temple strikes the keynote for theological thinking in our day. He writes, "The dominant problem of contemporary religious thought is the problem of revelation. Is there such a thing at all? If there is, what is its mode and form? Is it discoverable in all existing things or only in some? If in some, then in which? And by what principles are these selected as its vehicle? Where is it found? Or believed to be found? What is its authority?"[1]

This contemporary debate about revelation is no tempest in a teapot. It reflects two things. First it attests once again that the topic "revelation" is of fundamental significance for human existence. Long before Christians carried the gospel to the ancient world, men agonized about the meaning of life. It is sadly true that man has not always assented gracefully to the right answers to his questions—even when they have been forthcoming. Desperate minds, nonetheless, have searched after God in the hope that they might find him (Acts 17). No man has found true peace of mind or heart until he has been able to answer the questions, How can I know God? How am I to under-

From *The Word for This Century*, ed. Merrill E. Tenney. Copyright © 1960 Oxford University Press, Inc. Used by permission.

stand myself? What is my proper relationship to God? These are the very questions which revelation seeks to answer. No small wonder is it then that modern man cannot ignore this crucial topic.[2]

The current debate over revelation reflects also the theological bankruptcy of the mid-twentieth century. Orthodoxy has lost its grip upon the minds of men. Modernism has finally spent its strength; and at least in the form in which it has previously exhibited itself, it is no longer a live option. To the present moment no alternative has proved capable of capturing and holding the allegiance of modern man. Hearts and minds therefore are empty, and men are without direction or meaning for life. As C. J. Jung puts it, "Side by side with the decline of religious life, the neuroses grow noticeably more frequent. Everywhere the mental state of European men shows an alarming lack of balance. We are living undoubtedly in a period of the greatest restlessness, nervous tension, confusion and disorientation of outlook. . . . Everyone of them has the feeling that our modern religious truths have somehow or other grown empty."[3]

The American theologian Nels Ferré documents this personal crisis in the religious life of one of his own students: "One of the ablest and most thoughtful students in my seminar recently expressed his problem thus: 'If I simply accept faith and then reason out what follows from there, I cannot feel sure of myself. How do I know that I am not just rationalizing? If, however, I insist on justifying my faith by reason, it seems to me that I have no faith. In one case I am arbitrary and have nothing to say to all the people who start from another faith and refuse to examine it. In the other case I have no hope and driving power for a world like this!' "[4]

The predicament of the student is that of many thinking people throughout the world. Anyone who has lost his faith in the authority of the Bible must inevitably ask, What is truth? What shall I believe? How can I know whether this doctrine or the opposite doctrine is true? A deep pall of skepticism hangs threateningly over the heads of all who do not possess the authority of divine revelation.[5]

The surging tide of debate about revelation, therefore, proves not only that the topic of revelation is of perennial and crucial significance to mankind; it also proves that modern man, in particular, having strayed from the revelation that was his in the past, is today lost, without God and without hope in the world.

This double significance of the contemporary debate over revelation calls imperatively for evangelical Christians to speak forth boldly and earnestly upon the issues of today. Men are confused and willing to listen. They are restless and searching for answers to their desperate questions. They are determined to find an answer—some answer—any answer.

Seeking to resolve these uncertainties, Christians down through the centuries have pointed to the Bible. The Bible alone, they testify, points unerringly to Jesus Christ as Saviour. The Bible alone is the infallible rule of faith and practice. It alone can speak with the authority of the omniscient God Himself. It alone can tell man what he ought to believe, and what he ought to do. And in it alone can man find full assurance for his faith so that he dares affirm, "I know what I believe."

Long ago St. Augustine (c. A.D. 400), searching desperately for truth to lighten the gloom of ancient skepticism, turned to the Scriptures and found in them peace of mind and heart. Of this book he exclaimed, "As to all other writings . . . I do not accept their teaching as true on the mere ground of the opinion being held by them; but . . . these canonical writings . . . are free from error."[6]

The testimony of Augustine is the testimony of the united voice of the ancient church. From Irenaeus to Billy Graham the orthodox Christian faith has stood unequivocally for the divine inspiration and inerrant authority of Scripture. The forthright claim of Gaussen, made over a hundred years ago, has never been successfully challenged: "With the single exception of Theodore of Mopsuestia (c. A.D. 400), that philosophical divine whose numerous writings were condemned for their Nestorianism in the fifth ecumenical council . . . it has been found impossible to produce in the long course of the first eight centuries of Christianity a single doctor who had disowned the plenary inspiration of the Scriptures, unless it be in the bosom of the most violent heresies."[7]

Luther took his place in the main stream of historic Christianity when he declared, "Holy Scriptures cannot err."[8] Calvin was no less explicit in his reference to the Bible as the "pure word of God," and as the "infallible rule of His holy truth."[9] This same conviction as to the authority of the Bible found its expression in all the great creeds of classical Protestantism.[10]

It has been echoed and re-echoed in the time-honored question of the ordination ceremony: "Do you believe the Scriptures of the Old and New Testaments to be the Word of God, the only infallible rule of faith and practice?"

Beginning in the eighteenth century, however, this doctrine has come under increasing attack. Although few cared to put the matter so bluntly, most modern theologians agreed in essence with Hendrick Van Loon when he wrote, "The Old Testament was a national Jewish scrapbook. It contained stories and legends and genealogies and love poems and songs, classified and arranged and re-classified and rearranged without any regard for chronological order or literary perfection."[11]

Such a view of the origin of the Bible is, of course, utterly incompatible with the traditional doctrine of its divine inspiration and authority. In his *Outline of Biblical Theology*, Millar Burrows accurately summarizes the typical modern viewpoint: "The Bible is full of things which to an intelligent educated person of today are either quite incredible, or at best highly questionable. From the account of creation in the first chapter of Genesis to the description of the heavenly city in the closing chapters of Revelation, statements abound that even the most tortuous interpretations cannot reconcile with the modern scientific conception of the universe . . . The protracted struggle of theology to defend the inerrancy of the Bible against the findings of astronomy, geology and biology has been a series of retreats ending in a defeat which has led all wise theologians to move to a better position."[12]

On the positive side, modern thinkers tended to regard the Bible as a more or less historical account (rather less than more) of the development of religious life in a particular nation with a genius for God. For them the Bible was the story of men who attained a successful religious experience and in their writings passed on their best insights to posterity. The apex of this development was to be found in Jesus Christ, the greatest genius of them all. To Him they would accord even the honorific titles: "Saviour" (because He has helped us the most) and "Lord" (because He is the best authority). During the nineteenth century such views of the inspiration and authority of the Bible gradually spread throughout the nominal Christian church both in Europe and in America. By the first third of the twentieth century these views had become almost universally accepted in the leading theological schools on both continents.

Suddenly, however, at the zenith of its influence the whole structure of modern theology fell apart. Although its leaders sincerely attempted to remain within the structure of Christian tradition, it became increasingly obvious as time went by that Modernism had made a radical break with all that was essential to earlier Protestant faith. Emil Brunner only echoed the substance of fundamentalist apologetic when he declared, "[Anyone] possessed of a reasonably correct knowledge of Christianity, will have little difficulty in proving that the modernist teaches, under the label of Christianity, a religion that has nothing in common with Christianity except a few words, and that those words cover concepts which are irreconcilable with the content of Christian faith."[13]

The most obvious predicament of Modernism was its lack of authority. In the time-honored custom of preaching, a Bible which had become a mere scrapbook of Jewish devotional material could do well enough in a pinch as a source book for sermon texts, but such a Bible was totally unfitted for proclamation in ancient prophetic style, "Thus saith the Lord."

Karl Barth relates how in the early days of his ministry he gradually became disillusioned with the milk-toast "good advice," which was all he had to offer his parishioners. Faced with the realities of war, he discovered to his consternation that he possessed only a frothy palaver of superficial guesses. As he mounted the pulpit Sunday mornings to deliver his sermons, the table of the law slipped between his fingers. He stood before his people a mere man pleading a man's wisdom which even he only half believed.[14]

As the religious bankruptcy of Modernism became more and more obvious, disillusioned leaders began to look back with nostalgia upon historic Protestantism with its strong note of authority and its comforting gospel for sinners. "Our grandfathers, after all, were right," Barth declares, "when they struggled so desperately for the truth that there is revelation in the Bible and our fathers were right when they guarded warily against being drawn out upon the shaky scaffolding of religious self-expression. We live in a sick old world which cries out from its soul out of deep need, 'Heal me, O Lord, and I will be healed.' And for all men whoever and whatever and wherever they may be, there is a longing for exactly this which is within the Bible."[15]

In the last few decades a new theological movement has appeared upon the horizon and indeed has conquered the field. The "strange new world within the Bible" first discovered by Karl Barth back in 1916 is now no longer either new or strange, but has made for itself a large place in the sun. Neo-orthodoxy has superseded Modernism as the dominant theology in mid-twentieth century and with it has come an entirely new view of the Bible—yet not new, so its enthusiasts assert, but the old view rediscovered—the view of the Bible set forth in the classical Protestantism of the reformers.

This return to the authority of the Bible is by no means to be misconstrued as a return to the fundamentalist view. The Neo-orthodox revolt against the liberal reduction of the Bible to a mere human word of religious advice is at the same time accompanied by severe criticism of traditional orthodoxy.

Brunner asserts bluntly, "The orthodox doctrine of verbal inspiration has been finally destroyed. It is clear that there is no connection between it and scientific research and honesty. We are forced to make a decision for or against this view."[16] He further explains his own departure from Fundamentalism by adding, "I myself am an adherent of a rather radical school of Biblical criticism which for example, does not accept the Gospel of John as an historical source and finds much to be objected to in many parts of the synoptic gospels . . . the theology of the apostles is not an absolute entity but is presented in a series of different types of doctrines which differ considerably from one another."[17]

Karl Barth, usually less belligerent against Fundamentalism than Brunner, makes the same point clear. "Where the Bible is held up as a collection of authoritative documents and witnesses, its human element must be denied or overlooked. The human features of the Bible must then become a shame, and man is called upon for a sacrifice of the intellect."[18] The orthodox view is not only ruled out on grounds of our modern scientific knowledge, but it is not even the view which the Bible presents of itself. "It is," declares Barth, "a noteworthy contradiction that those who wish to raise the Bible to this height are in fact not true to the Bible. The Bible itself claims something quite different for itself." Therefore the orthodox who seem to hold such a high view of the complete truth and inspiration of the Bible, are in reality setting themselves against the teaching of the Bible. Any truly Biblical theologian, Barth therefore insists, must repudiate the orthodox position just because he *is* Biblical.[18]

The fundamental objection of the Neo-orthodox against traditional orthodoxy is their conviction that Christ, not the Bible, is the proper object of religious faith. Fundamentalists, they say, reverse this order, thereby erecting the Bible into an idol. For them belief in the Bible comes first; and because they believe the Bible, they also profess to believe in Christ. On the contrary, the right basis for belief, so the Neo-orthodox affirm, is Christ first. And then to the degree that the Bible witnesses to the living Christ, they accept the Bible. In his *Christian Doctrine of God* Brunner seeks to put the Biblical writings in their proper place. "That means," he explains, "that their witness can never be the basis and object of faith, but only a means of faith. We do not believe in Jesus Christ because we first of all believe in the story and teaching of the apostles, but by means of the testimony of their narrative we believe as they do and in a similar state of freedom. Faith in Jesus Christ is not based upon a previous faith in the Bible, but it is based solely upon the witness of the Holy Spirit." Protestant orthodoxy, therefore, which professes so glibly to be the guardian of the true faith, has in reality turned aside to an idolatrous form of Christianity.[19]

In their view of the authority of Holy Scripture, the Neo-orthodox are united in their opposition to Modernism and Fundamentalism, but the same cannot be said of their positive attempts to construct a new view of the Bible. They are, nonetheless, in remarkable agreement upon the main outlines of their understanding of the inspiration of the Bible and of the nature of its authority. One of the basic and most tenaciously held convictions of the Neo-orthodox theologians is that revelation can never be a body of truth or set of propositions. It is always an act or event in which God discloses His person. In an authoritative article in Kittel's *Theologisches Wörterbuch,* the German scholar Albrecht Oepke writes, "Revelation is not the communication of rational knowledge and not the stimulation of numinous [a sense of God] . . . feelings. In itself, however, revelation is neither of these things, but is quite essentially a transaction of Yahweh—an unveiling of His essential hiddenness—His offering of Himself in mutual fellowship."[20]

Emil Brunner defends the same viewpoint: "In the time of the apostles as in that of the Old Testament prophets, divine revelation always meant the whole of the divine activity for the salvation of the world. Divine revelation is not a book or a doctrine. Revelation is God Himself in His self-manifestation within history. Revelation is something that happens."[21]

In accordance with this deep-seated conviction that revelation is the personal activity of God and never an interpretation of truth, the Neo-orthodox rule out the Bible as a revelation from God. The Bible, rather, is a record of revelation. It tells the story of what God has done in history to reveal Himself. It relates the testimonies of men to whom God has revealed Himself in the past. The Bible represents a human attempt to understand and to bear witness to the revelatory works of God.

As a human record of revelation, the Bible can by no means be infallible. Barth declares, "The prophets and apostles even as such, even in their office, even in their function as witnesses, even in the action of writing down their testimonies were really historically, and therefore in their deeds, sinful, and in their spoken and written word capable of error and actually erring men like us all."[22]

The Bible, however, is not *merely* a book which contains the Word of God. It also in God's sovereignty becomes the instrument through which men experience a contemporary revelation of God in their own souls. Just as He spoke to the Biblical witnesses long ago, so today God's Spirit works upon the hearts and minds of men to speak to them from the pages of Scripture. By this act of divine inspiration the Bible here and now becomes the contemporary, living Word of God, calling men into fellowship with Himself.

The Neo-orthodox view of Scripture is thus best understood by an analogy with a sermon. A sermon is obviously a human production, which may contain errors. The pastor may miss the date in his literary reference to Caesar's crossing of the Rubicon. He may, in fact, display deplorable mistakes in exegesis. He may fall into grievous doctrinal errors. In spite of blunders, even a pulpit tyro may deliver a useful sermon, which may lead man to Jesus Christ and the revelation of God.

Indirectly, the sermon may even be called the Word of God. We do not mean that every word of the sermon is composed of words given by God, but notwithstanding literary flaws and doctrinal errors here and there, the sermon sets forth the gospel of Jesus Christ clearly enough so that men may hear it, understand it, receive it, and be saved. So Barth recognizes the Bible to be the Word of God. "That sinful and erring men as such spoke the Word of God, that is the miracle of which we speak when we say the Bible is God's word."[23]

The analogy between a sermon and the Bible as conceived by the Neo-orthodox can be carried one step farther. A man frequently hears a sermon only with his ears, but does nothing about it; for to him it does not actually unveil Jesus Christ as a Saviour. Then suddenly the message of the sermon strikes home. Jesus Christ is unveiled to him. The impotent human word spoken by the preacher is no longer impotent, but becomes in truth God's word to him. So the Bible becomes God's word when God actually speaks to man in and through the words of the Bible. And as He speaks it, this Bible is God's word.[24]

For the Neo-orthodox, finally, this erring human Bible, which may become God's word, is also the ultimate authority for man's religious life. The extent of Biblical authority is conceived in radically different ways by various Neo-orthodox thinkers. Some find the authority of the Bible only in its inmost message and then disagree as to what that message really is. For Rudolph Bultmann and Reinhold Niebuhr it is the message of the absolute self-giving love of God for man, the sinner. This absolute love is set forth in the Biblical "myth" of Christ's atoning death. Here, mythologically speaking, God takes to Himself the sin of man and so forgives man freely.[25]

For Emil Brunner, on the other hand, the authority of the Bible centers about what it tells of the Christ, the God-man. Unfortunately Brunner never defines precisely what he thinks are the limits of Biblical authority; and, accordingly, his dependence upon it varies greatly from one passage of his writings to another.[26]

For Karl Barth, the most conservative Neo-orthodox thinker, the Bible is the standard of all right teaching and all right thinking about God. The Bible, no doubt, contains errors; but those errors do not negate Biblical authority. If God condescends to speak to men in and through fallible words, Barth queries, why should any man be so proud that he is unwilling to hear what God has to say? Is man more fastidious than God? "In spite of apparent human defects," Barth declares forcibly, "God now speaks what this text speaks." And he adds, "Everything which is here to be said can be put together in the sentence: 'The faith in the inspiration of the Bible stands or falls with this, that the concrete life of the church and members of the church is a life ruled by the exegesis of the Bible.' "[27] The Bible taken as a whole, therefore, is the authority for the church, the final court of appeal in faith and practice.

As a result of this new trend in contemporary theology, an atmosphere of uncertainty and indecision has been created within the ranks of evangelical Christianity. Battle lines have become exceedingly confused. Not precise definitions, but rather foggy and misleading generalizations are the fashion of our day. Theological discussions are often carried on under conditions of exceedingly low intellectual and spiritual visibility. In the confusion and heat of the battle, some evangelicals have fearfully suggested that we must reconstruct the whole of the evangelical position with respect to the Bible and its inspiration and authority. Others, equally fearful, have sought to harden the clichés of a past generation in its battle against Modernism and they refuse to examine their inherited convictions in the light of contemporary thinking. Sad to say, these men sometimes think that it is more important to be against Barth than for Biblical truth.

A true and living orthodoxy must never become static. If we are to remain faithful to the orthodox faith of our fathers, we dare not merely repeat our fathers' answers to opponents of a generation ago. A living orthodoxy, rather, must rethink for its own generation the doctrines of revelation and inspiration. It must be prepared to fight on the battle lines as they are drawn today, and must appropriate the truth of God as it has been given. Certainly no Christian need ever fear the honest search for truth in humble dependence upon the illumination of the Holy Spirit.

In his re-examination of Biblical authority in the light of contemporary debate, however, the evangelical Christian is not like a rudderless ship floating aimlessly upon a boundless sea, driven and tossed by every passing wind. He is bound by the same hard core of revelational facts which have determined orthodox thinking in the past. By no means does he consider these facts to be an infringement upon his freedom to think realistically, constructively, and honestly. A tough-minded, even literal, adherence to every least fact provided by the data of revelation is the only possible foundation for clear and effective thinking about God and man's relationship to God. To rethink, therefore, is not necessarily to throw overboard the orthodox view of Biblical authority; rather, it is to constitute it a true and living *orthodoxy* (straight thinking and teaching).

In the light of the contemporary debate about revelation and authority the Biblical position may be outlined in the following points:

1. The ultimate object of all Biblical revelation is God as a person.

All revelation has God for its object. The Bible does not present man with a set of universal truths like the propositions of Euclid in geometry. It does not set forth in formal fashion the arguments and counter-arguments of a theological textbook. No creedal formulations —certainly not the fundamental doctrines of the older liberal theology, such as the universal fatherhood of God, the universal brotherhood of man, and the supremacy of love—are the focus of Biblical revelation.

The ultimate goal of revelation is not so much to make man wise as it is to bring him into a direct encounter with God as a person, and to evoke from him a response of love and obedience to God. The Apostle Paul sets forth the goal of all revelation: "That I may be personally acquainted with him" (Phil. 3:10).[28]

2. Biblical revelation is by divine acts.

Biblical revelation is the unfolding of the gracious acts of God in behalf of sinful man. From the skin of a slain animal with which God sought to cover the shame of our first parents, to the vision of the heavenly city in Revelation 22, the long course of Biblical history is the story of what God has done for His people—the righteous acts of Jehovah (Micah 6:5 ARV).

3. Biblical revelation culminates in Jesus Christ.

In the "fulness of time" came Jesus Christ (Gal. 4:4). "God . . . hath . . . spoken unto us by His Son" (Heb. 1:1). The supreme act by which God reveals Himself is by His incarnation. God became man, lived as man, died for man, and rose again from the dead. Indeed, the story of these events is good *news*—news about something which happened in the land of Palestine during the reigns of Augustus and Tiberius Caesar. It is news of what Christ did on Calvary (I Cor. 15:1-4). There God performed His mightiest act by giving Himself for the redemption of lost humanity (Luke 20:9 ff.).

The Bible preserves an important distinction between Christ as redeemer and Christ as revealer. In both of these roles Jesus Christ is supreme. As redeemer, however, Christ is not merely supreme over all other modes of redemption. His uniqueness is absolute. Like Christ, the prophets also spoke; but the prophets did not redeem. As revealer, Christ's uniqueness lies in the completeness and finality of His revelation. Others beside Him spoke the Word of God; but He was, in truth, *God speaking.*[29]

4. Biblical revelation is also divine interpretation of meaning.

That God reveals Himself as a person and that He does so by His acts does not preclude the fact that God also reveals truth about Himself. According to the Scriptures, man is responsible for knowing who God is (Deut. 6:4; Matt. 16:13), and what is His will (Lev. 20:7), and what are His plans and goals (Mark 16:15). These truths man must know in order rightly and effectively to know the person of God and to enter into obedient fellowship with Him. Our Lord spoke with luminous insight into the needs of the human heart when He declared, "the truth shall make you free" (John 8:32).

To those outside the framework of strict orthodoxy, few see this more clearly than does Edwin Lewis. "Revelation," Lewis argues, "means that God is categorically affirmed and that He bears a certain character and that He is working for certain ends; and what these ends are, likewise, is included in the revelation. God utters His Word, but the meaning of what is uttered is still to be conveyed and this is the work of the Holy Spirit. Revelation brings a disclosure of truth which would otherwise have remained at best only a speculation."[30]

According to the teaching of Scripture, therefore, God reveals to man truths or propositions about Himself and His will, about ourselves and our needs, and about His provision and care and promise of grace. Thus in First Corinthians 2:9-12 and 16 we read:

> Eye hath not seen, nor ear heard, neither have entered into the heart of man the things which God hath prepared for them that love him. (10) But God hath revealed them unto us by his spirit: for the spirit searcheth all things, yea the deep things of God. (11) For what man knoweth the things of a man save the spirit of man which is in him? Even so the things of God knoweth no man, but the Spirit of God. (12) Now we have received, not the spirit of the world, but the spirit which is of God; that we might know the things that are freely given to us of God. (16) For who hath known the mind of the Lord, that he might instruct Him? But we have the mind of Christ.

The flow of Paul's thought is inescapable. God has certain plans for those who love Him. These plans are, of course, quite unknown and undiscoverable by man. Just as man can know what is in his own mind, however, so the Spirit of God knows fully the truth lying within the divine mind, and out of love and grace chooses to convey this otherwise inaccessible truth to the minds of men. The process whereby this communication of divine truth takes place is specifically labeled as revelation.

Other New Testament passages bear out the same idea. Matthew 11:22 gives us revealed truth regarding God's future judgment. Unto the Jews, declares the Apostle Paul, "were committed the oracles of God" (Rom. 3:2). In the third chapter of Ephesians the same apostle refers to the revealed truth that Jews and Gentiles are to be one body. In Matthew 16:17 the revealed truth is that Jesus Christ is the Son of God, and in Luke 2:26 the revelation (*chrematidzo*) brings to Simeon truth as to his own destiny.[31]

In the Old Testament we find a similar pattern of thought. In the third chapter of First Samuel the writer ascribes to God a revelation of the truth about Samuel's call. The Old Testament prophets often claimed that God had revealed to them secrets (Amos 3:7; Dan. 2). Special propositional communications from God are frequently labeled as revealed truths (Isa. 22:14; Dan. 2:29, 30; II Sam. 7:27).

The hesitation of Neo-orthodox thinkers to accept the unequivocal claims of Scripture in support of revelation in and through a divinely given interpretation of meaning is indeed strange, coming from those who pride themselves upon their "Biblical theology." The God of most contemporary theologians can act but does not speak. Prophetic testimony becomes no longer "the more sure word of prophecy" given forth with divine authority (II Peter 1:19-21). It is reduced to mere private interpretation stemming from the will of man. Human insight thus replaces divine truth.

The God of the Bible is very different from this concept. He is the God who acts! He is also the God who speaks to His servants. "The Biblical writers," so C. H. Dodd reminds us, "were not philosophers constructing a speculative theory from their observation of events. What they said was 'Thus saith the Lord'; and they firmly believed that God spoke to men. The interpretation of history which they offered was not invented by process of thought; it was the meaning which they experienced in the events when their minds were open to God as well as open to the impact of outward facts. Thus the prophetic interpretation of history and the impetus and direction which that gave to subsequent history were alike the Word of God to men."[32]

An inductive study of the Scriptures, therefore, leads inevitably to the conclusion that Biblical revelation includes divine revelation of truth. The all but unanimous view of contemporary theologians that Biblical revelation is personal and through acts, but never propositional, simply will not bear the test of exegesis. It is true that God reveals Himself as a person; and it is true that He does so through acts. But it is also true that God gives specific revelation of truth to His prophets and apostles. He is a living, acting, speaking person who enters into social intercourse and fellowship with man and who gives to men a revelation, His own divine interpretation of the meaning of things.

5. This revelation is brought to men by the Bible.

The redemptive acts of God together with the divine interpretation of these mighty acts were recorded in the writings of the apostles and prophets. The Bible thus becomes the means through which revelations given directly to prophets in Old Testament history and to apostles in New Testament history are made available for the needy sinner of every succeeding generation. In this sense is to be found the element of truth contained in the oft-repeated phrase, "The Bible contains the Word of God."

The central message of both Testaments is, of course, Jesus Christ. In the Old Testament is to be found the preparatory revelation. Our Lord Himself declared that the Scriptures testify of Him (John 5:39). He rebuked those who did not find Him in the Old Testament for their failure to understand the sacred text (Luke 24:25).

In perfect harmony with the claims of Christ as to the central message of the Old Testament, the apostle John revealed the purpose of his gospel. "These are written that ye might believe that Jesus is the Christ, the Son of God, and that believing ye might have life through his name" (John 20:31).

The primary purpose of the whole Bible, therefore, is that man may come to know Jesus Christ, the living Word of God. It is a book which tells about Him and which brings to men of every age the revelation which God has given as to the meaning of Jesus Christ for lost sinners.

6. Revelation must be subjectively appropriated.

The objective side of the divine work of revelation needs to be supplemented by an internal subjective work of the Spirit of God. in the language of the classroom, and therefore does not preserve this work by the term *illumination*. The Bible, of course, does not speak in the language of the classroom, and therefore does not preserve this nice distinction between revelation (Old Testament, *galah;* New Testament, *apokalupto*) and illumination.

In I Samuel 3:7, for example, we read: "Now Samuel did not yet know the Lord. Neither was the Word of the Lord yet revealed unto him." From the context we learn that God had already spoken, but Samuel had not yet perceived that Word as from God. In one sense the word was uncovered objectively but in another sense it was not yet subjectively uncovered for Samuel himself.

Both of these concepts, subjective revelation and objective revelation or illumination, are introduced without being named specifically in the classic passage, I Corinthians 2. God gave a revelation to His chosen apostle. In this case the revelation is not merely a divine act, but an act to convey truth from the mind of God to the apostle. With divine sanction and authority this revealed truth is in turn conveyed by the apostle to others. The natural man, however, whose mind is darkened by sin, cannot receive as true the message which God revealed. He needs the illumination of the Holy Spirit so that he can really see what is there available for him. In short, from the Biblical point of view, man needs subjective illumination so that what has been objectively revealed in the past and brought to him objectively through the inspiration of the prophets may become subjectively revealed to him personally.

The cliché, "The Bible *becomes* the Word of God," thus has a significant element of truth in it. The Biblical message came from God whether men receive it as such or whether they do not, but now and again the Spirit of God takes the words of the Bible and makes them subjectively the Word of God to individual men. Instead of the dead letter of the law, the Bible thereby becomes the living voice of the Spirit in the heart of men. It becomes God's contemporary message, spanning in an instant the millennia between the prophet of old and the man of today.[33]

7. The authority of the Bible is known by revelation.

Once it is granted that the Bible *contains* the Word of God, it immediately becomes important to ascertain what this divine word found in the Bible has to say about the place of the Bible in the life of the believer. If, for example, the Bible provides for us a reliable record of the revelation of Jesus Christ as God incarnate, then it is obvious that we cannot stop at this point. Once we are committed to the Lordship of Jesus Christ, we must immediately accept also the authority of the Bible; for we discover that our Lord Himself accepted its authority and taught His followers to do likewise. To admit that Jesus is Lord, but to reject His instruction as to the authority of the Bible is, to put the matter bluntly, little more than pious self-deception.

In similar fashion, if we accept the claims of the apostles and prophets for the divine origin and authority of their message, we must accordingly receive their conclusions with respect to the authority of the Bible when that constitutes part of their message. To acknowledge the claims of the Biblical writers that they are transmitting to us not their own word but the Word of God, and then to ignore what that Word has to say about the authority of their own writings, is illogical.

Modern thinkers have resorted to all sorts of desperate expedients in order to circumvent this simple conclusion. It is, so some suggest, an argument in a circle: Major premise: Whatever the Bible teaches is true; Minor premise: The Bible teaches that it is true; Conclusion: Therefore, the Bible must be true.[34] If the basis for belief in the deity of Christ and for belief in the doctrinal authority of the prophets and apostles depended first upon our prior belief in the verbal inspiration of the Bible or in its inerrant authority, then the charge of a circular argument could stand. Such, however, is not the case.

Belief in the deity of Christ rests in part upon the whole sum of historical, logical, and experiential evidences that validate to men the truth of Christian faith. These evidences, moreover, are brought home to the human heart and mind as God creates in His elect a certainty of the truth of Christ through the witness of His Holy Spirit working immediately and directly upon the human mind.

Likewise the authority of the apostles and prophets rests upon their relationship to Jesus Christ and upon the trustworthiness of their testimony concerning the divine origin of their message. Since, therefore, our confidence in Christ and in the validity of the revelation contained in the Scriptures rests not upon our belief in the divine inspiration of these writings but upon objective evidences and, especially, upon the internal testimony of the Holy Spirit, the charge of arguing in a circle cannot stand.

Other opponents of Biblical authority, with more show of logic, argue that the Scriptures may contain revelation but also contain what is merely human speculation. The teachings of the Bible about its own authority fall into the latter category of the human element rather than that derived from divine revelation. Such an argument, however, does not apply to the testimony of Christ. If Jesus Christ is the divine Lord, then insofar as the gospel writers accurately record His words, we are bound to receive all that He taught and commanded us to receive. Anything less than this is to do despite to Him as Lord of our lives.

The Bible is so full and deep in its teaching on the authority of Scripture that all who argue this way are placed in an impossible dilemma. Either the Biblical writers are utterly untrustworthy in their claims that they have received authority to teach from God; or, if their claims are valid at all, they are certainly true at this point. There is no other question on which the apostolic writers are in such clear agreement or on which they speak with more freedom or assurance than upon the doctrine of the authority of the Scriptures.[35]

The Biblical teaching as to the completeness of its authority is so obvious that to discuss it here may seem superfluous. In His sermon on the mount (Matt. 5:17-19) our Lord declared, "One jot or one tittle shall in no wise pass from the law." He rebuked His disciples for not believing "all that the prophets had spoken" (Luke 24:25). In controversy with the Jews (John 10:35) He argued, "Scripture cannot be broken [dissolved or discarded]." On one occasion He introduced an isolated passage of the Old Testament with the formula "God says" (Matt. 19:5). In the thought and teaching of our Lord the law of Moses is explicitly labeled the "Word of God" (Mark 7:6 ff).

Just at this point is to be found the Achilles' heel of the Neo-orthodox. By appealing from the written Scripture to a voice of the Spirit they are in effect setting themselves above the Bible. They put the Bible into a sieve and receive from it only what sifts through. The sieves used may vary greatly. One who uses a sieve with large holes receives much of the Bible. Another uses such a fine sieve that practically nothing of Scripture filters through to him.

Karl Barth thus seems inconsistent when he decries the rejection of Biblical authority evidenced by American left-wing Neo-orthodox theologians. They "theologize on their own account," charges Barth, "that is to say, without asking on what Biblical grounds one puts forward this or that professedly Christian view. They would quote the Bible according to choice, according as it appeared to them to strengthen their own view and without feeling any need to ask whether the words quoted really have in their context the meaning attributed to them." The Bible, in short, is for them no true authority; and Barth adds that "to this irresponsible attitude toward the Bible" he is "irrevocably opposed."[37] To this testimony of Barth we can only reply, *"Et tu, Brute!"*

In similar fashion a liberal critic of Reinhold Niebuhr declares, "Niebuhr claims to base his faith on the Bible and calls it Biblical faith, but a careful examination shows that he corrects the Bible according to his own convictions. According to Niebuhr many of the truths of the Bible are presented in the form of myths, but myths are defective, he admits, and even Jesus and Paul were deceived by them. When Niebuhr corrects the errors of the Biblical authorities, I think Niebuhr points out that Niebuhr's faith is determined by himself and not by the Bible. Niebuhr may be right and the Bible wrong, but I should like to hear what Jesus and Paul had to say in their own defense before pronouncing Niebuhr right and Jesus and Paul mistaken about the Christian faith."[38]

When, on the contrary, Billy Graham stands up to preach, he declares: "The Bible says . . ." By this twentieth-century equivalent of the apostolic, "It is written," he clearly intends that what the Bible says is not merely his opinion, or that of a first-century sage, but it is the truth of God coming with the authority of God Himself. This unshakable conviction that in the Bible God has spoken and, therefore, that the Bible message possesses divine authority, transforms the Christian evangelist from a purveyor of good advice into a divinely commissioned ambassador of Jesus Christ.

8. The authority of the Bible is derived from its divine inspiration.

Referring to the Old Testament, the Apostle Paul declares, "All Scripture [is] given by inspiration," literally "breathed out" or given forth by God. In this divine giving of the Scripture Paul finds the explanation for the fact that it is "profitable for doctrine, for reproof, for correction, for instruction in righteousness: that the man of God may be throughly furnished" (II Tim. 3:16, 17).

The Apostle Peter likewise explains why Scripture is a "more sure word of prophecy" by basing its authority on its origin. The prophets of old did not give their personal interpretation of the events which they describe, but rather they were moved by the Holy Ghost so that what they said derived ultimately from God (II Peter 1:19-21). The Apostle does not teach that the Bible was dictated by God but rather that it was produced by the prophets through a divine energizing and enabling, the precise nature of which is not described, but the effect of which was to constitute the prophetic writings God's divinely authoritative message to men.

Karl Barth strongly objects to this understanding of the nature of Biblical inspiration. He refers to it as a "denial of the humanity" of Scripture demanding of us a "sacrifice of the intellect."[39] Our Lord and His apostles, however, did not envisage any such drastic antinomy between a human authorship and a divine control and production of Scripture. The human qualities in Scripture are properly recognized, but in and through the human authors of Scripture God's guiding hand produced the writings He wished in order to convey His thoughts to men. It is this "divine plus" of which the apostles speak when they refer to the inspiration of the Bible by God and seek in this inspiration to explain the true authority of Scripture.

This view of the inspiration and authority of the Bible is quite obviously what is traditionally known as verbal inspiration. Unfortunately the term has been misunderstood. It means the work of the Holy Spirit by which, without setting aside the personality and literary talents of its human authors, He guided the writers of Scripture so that the words of the Bible in its entirety unfold His divinely written Word to men and therefore teach the truth without error.[40]

The method by which this inspiration was accomplished is, of course, scarcely referred to in Scripture and is certainly not discussed at length. The *fact* of the inspiration of Scripture by God and *its consequent authority* are of vital importance to the Scriptural writers. The mechanics of inspiration are left unexplained. To argue that a divine inspiration must necessarily negate the freedom and humanity of the Biblical writers is scarcely possible for one who pretends to be a Christian. Whatever may be said for or against a rational solution of this problem, it ought to be abundantly clear that no theist who believes in God's providential control of the universe can possibly use this objection against the inspiration of the Bible. The God of Romans 8:28, who works all things together for good, including the sinful acts of wicked men, could certainly have worked through the will and personality of His prophets to secure the divine Word which He wished to convey through them.

9. The Bible must be rightly interpreted.

A Biblical view of inspiration does not rule out either historical or textual criticism. Rather it demands legitimate application of these studies to a proper understanding of the Bible. In the science of higher criticism, for example, the Christian scholar investigates the origin, authorship, genuineness, date, and authenticity of the various books of the Bible. It is an obvious fact that one who concludes that the book of Deuteronomy was a sixth-century fraud foisted upon a superstitious king by pious forgers can scarcely hold to the inspiration and divine authority of that book. The Biblical view does not rule out higher criticism, but it does rule out certain conclusions to which many higher critics have come; namely, all those conclusions contradicting anything taught in the original words of Scripture or assuming that only a human author, not God, is responsible for the words of Scripture.

By the scientific use of the correct principles of lower criticism, likewise, the reverent scholar is able in most instances to ascertain the original text of Scripture. In the introduction to their Greek New Testament, Westcott and Hort declare that except for differences in spelling and trivial variations having no effect on the teaching of the passage, the words of our present text about which there can be any reasonable doubt form hardly more than a thousandth part of the whole.[41]

The correct text thus secured serves as a reliable basis for exegetical study, and its faithful interpretation provides man with the very Word of God. Only by holding a completely authoritative original can one have confidence that he has the truth of God which comes to him with divine authority. Were it not for the doctrine of the infallible authority of the original manuscripts, one could never be sure, even after he had finished the task of textual criticism, that he had anything more than a mere man's opinion as to what is the truth.

Unfortunately the Bible frequently suffers much from misinterpretation. To hold to the complete authority of the Bible does not by any means commit one to say that God approved of all unethical practices mentioned in the Bible; nor does it mean that every statement quoted in Scripture is true, for in Psalm 14 we find the words, "There is no God." The author of Scripture obviously does not endorse this blasphemy, but correctly ascribes it to the fool. Inspiration does not guarantee that Scripture gives us specific technical data in current scientific vocabulary. Scripture speaks, rather, in the language of the common man of two or more millennia ago, but what it speaks it speaks truthfully, whether it deals with ethics or with the natural world of science.

The question at issue is always: What is really the teaching of Scripture? No doubt some very foolish things have been said at this point. The King James Bible has been made to substantiate all sorts of strange scientific theories. No doubt those who point back to an infallible original have sometimes placed an almost magical interpretation upon the Scripture so as to transform it from a book of faith and practice into a scientific textbook suitable for a course in biology. This is to misinterpret the message of the Bible, and to make it say what it does not intend to say at all.

Adequate Biblical interpretation, moreover, does not preclude the use of figurative, allegorical, and symbolical language. It does not guarantee that two Biblical writers describing the same event may not avail themselves of very different, and to a superficial reader, discrepant words. It does mean that the words of Scripture are studied faithfully in their total context in order to discover the thought which God seeks to communicate to the minds of men. He who would learn of God is not to seek to go behind the Scripture in his interpretation of it. He is not to seek some message of God suggested to him upon the basis of the Scripture. He is to go to the Scripture, place himself under its lordship, and seek to discover exactly what it teaches. When he has discovered what Scripture teaches, precisely this is the message of God for him, which comes to him with all the authority of God Himself and calls forth from man an existential response of obedience or of disobedience to the Word of God.

10. The fact of Biblical authority is the foundation for a valid theology.

Once more the question comes back to the basic issue: What think ye of Christ? And to this question we must add also: What shall we do about the prophetic and apostolic claim to authority?

This decision of history flows from an inner logic deep within the structure of Christian faith. Some short-sighted individuals may inquire, "Why not accept the inner essence of Christianity, its gospel of Christ, but reject the troublesome doctrine of the complete authority of Scripture?" How can this be done? The truth of Christianity and the authority of the Bible stand or fall together. Recent scholarship, radical as well as conservative, has tended more and more to agree that Jesus, the man of history, believed unequivocally in the ordinary view of the inspiration and authority of the Scripture held by the Jewish people of His day. Even more unanimous is the conclusion that the apostolic writers were in essential agreement with their Jewish opponents in accepting the complete authority of the Old Testament.[42]

To accept Christ as Lord and to submit to His teaching regarding the complete authority of Scripture is consistent. Again, to acknowledge the validity of apostolic claims to authority and to receive their teaching as to the complete authority of Scripture is also consistent. To accept Christ's Lordship and the authority of His apostles and prophets and at the same time to reject their unequivocal teaching regarding the inspiration and authority of Scripture is not consistent. This inner logic explains the crucial place assumed in church history by the doctrine of Biblical authority.

This issue, it must be added, does not merely concern some single, though important doctrine of Christianity. At stake is the whole orthodox method of building theology. Throughout history the standard of doctrine for all evangelical churches was the Bible. The Bible was the only infallible rule of faith and practice. In its creeds the Church professed a system of doctrine taught in the Bible. The teaching of Scripture was the foundation of orthodox theology.

Modernism rejected that foundation. It sought to build its doctrine first upon a red-letter New Testament, upon the teaching of Jesus alone, later upon Christian experience, and finally upon the unaided human intellect. Biblical truth was to be judged at the bar of human reason. Those parts of Scripture were to be accepted that could be established according to the canons of the science of history, or according to the principles of comparative religious psychology, or according to the systematic coherence of Biblical truths within the framework of some system of human philosophy.

The Neo-orthodox seek to bridge the gap between Modernism and orthodoxy. They seek a foundation ultimately in a mystical intuition which, however, is closely associated with the Bible. The Bible in their thought becomes an authority *in part*. This, however, is to set another foundation for Christian doctrine just as much as did the Modernists of a generation ago. If the Neo-orthodox are successful, then the Christian Church will have to build a new theology upon a new basis, and that new basis is not the teaching of the Bible.

Here lies the crucial difference between the most conservative of the Neo-orthodox and every true evangelical. Genuine evangelical theology is based upon the teaching of the whole Bible received as the authoritative written Word of God. Its theology rests solidly upon the holy Scriptures, for they and they alone are not only able to make us wise unto salvation but are also possessed of God-given authority and are profitable for doctrine. Not a jot or tittle of Scripture can be set aside as void by any true follower of Jesus Christ.

Notes

[1] William Temple, "Revelation" (John Baillie and Hugh Martin, *Revelation*, ed.) (New York: Macmillan, 1927), p. 83.

[2] Material for this paragraph as well as for certain other parts of this essay originally formed part of the Griffith-Thomas Lectures printed in *Bibliotheca Sacra,* April 1958 to January 1959. Permission to use this material was given by the editor.

[3] *Modern Man in Search of a Soul* (New York: Harcourt, Brace & Co., 1935), pp. 264 ff.

[4] *Faith and Reason* (New York: Harper & Bros., 1946), pp. ix and x.

[5] It is no accident that all three great periods of speculative philosophy, ancient, medieval, and modern, though beginning with brave asseverations as to the meaning of existence, have fizzled out on a dismal note of skepticism.

[6] "Letter to Jerome," *The Confessions and Letters of St. Augustine* ("A Select Library of the Nicene and Post-Nicene Fathers of the Christian Church," Vol. LXXXII, Sec. 3; Buffalo: The Christian Literature Company, 1886-89), p. 350.

[7]L. Gaussen, *The Inspiration of the Holy Scriptures* (Chicago: Moody Press, 1940), pp. 139-40.

[8]"Vom Missbrauch der Messe" in *Dr. Martin Luthers polemische deutsche Schriften,* ed. Johann Konrad Armischer (Erlangen: Carl Heyder, 1833), xxviii, p. 35.

[9]*Institutes of the Christian Religion,* trans. Henry Beveridge (Edinburgh: Calvin Translation Society, 1845), III, 166; II, 402; *Commentaries on the Epistle of Paul to the Hebrews,* trans. John Owen (Edinburgh: Calvin Translation Society, 1855), p. xxi.

[10]For the Lutheran position, see the Augsburg Confession, Article XXVIII; for the Calvinistic, see the Canons of the Synod of Dort, Articles IV and V, and the Westminster Confession, Article XIV:2; for the Anglican, see the Thirty-nine Articles, Section XX; and for the Baptist (Northern Churches), see the New Hampshire Confession, Article I. All of these are available in Philip Schaff, *Creeds of Christendom* (New York: Harper & Bros., 1919), Vol. III.

[11]*Story of the Bible* (London: Vision Press, Ltd., 1952), p. 277.

[12]*An Outline of Biblical Theology* (Philadelphia: Westminster Press, 1946), pp. 9, 44.

[13]*The Theology of Crisis* (New York: Charles Scribner's Sons, 1929), p. 9.

[14]"The Author's Preface to the English Translation," *The Epistle to the Romans* (London: Oxford University Press, 1933), p. v.

[15]*The Word of God and the Word of Man,* trans. Douglas Hort (Grand Rapids, Mich.: Zondervan, 1935), pp. 44, 50.

[16]*The Mediator* (New York: Macmillan, 1942), p. 185.

[17]*The Theology of Crisis,* p. 41. Cf. also *Christian Doctrine of God* (London: Lutterworth, 1949), p. 12.

[18]*Das Christliche Verständnis der Offenbarung* (München: Chr. Kaiser, 1948), p. 29.

[19]Pp. 3, 34. See also Karl Barth, *Kirchliche Dogmatik* (4 vols. Zurich: Evangelischer Verlag, 1932), Vol. III, Part I, p. 25.

[20]"Kalupto," *Theologisches Wörterbuch* (Stuttgart: Von W. Kahlhammer, 1938), *in loco.*

[21]*Revelation and Reason* (Philadelphia: Westminster, 1946), p. 8.

[22]*Kirchliche Dogmatik,* I, p. 587.

[23]Ibid. p. 587.

[24]Ibid. p. 594.

[25]See Reinhold Niebuhr, *Beyond Tragedy: Essays on the Christian In-*

terpretation of History (New York: Charles Scribner's Sons, 1937), p. 23; and Hans Werner Bartsch (ed.), *Kerygma and Myth: A Theological Debate,* trans. Reginald H. Fuller (London: S.P.C.K., 1953).

[26]Paul Jewett documents this same criticism of Emil Brunner in his monograph *Emil Brunner's Doctrine of Scripture* (London: J. Clarke, 1954), pp. 168-72.

[27]*Kirchliche Dogmatik,* Vol. I, Part II, pp. 592, 595.

[28]See also Galatians 1:16, "to reveal his son." The final condemnation of the heathen is not that they are ignorant but that they are unthankful and do not worship God (Romans 1:18 ff.).

[29]Biblically this may be stated in the following manner. With respect to Jesus Christ as redeemer, "There is none other name under heaven given among men whereby ye must be saved" (Acts 4:12). "But now once in the end of the world hath he appeared to put away sin by the sacrifice of himself" (Hebrews 9:26). The role of prophet, however, Jesus Christ shared with others. "A prophet shall the Lord your God raise up unto you of your brethren like unto me . . . his Son Jesus" (Acts 3:22 and 26). Though He was not the only one to act as prophet, He was a unique prophet, for He not only revealed God in a unique way ("Never man spake like this man," John 7:46); He, unlike all other prophets, *is* the revealed One ("He who hath builded the house hath more honor than the house," Hebrews 3:1-6).

[30]*The Philosophy of Revelation* (3rd ed.; New York: Harper & Bros. 1940), p. 256.

[31]Of the New Testament examples which he specifically cites as in one class or the other, Bauer lists six usages of *apokalupto* as referring to revelation of ideas as true and nine instances in which the object is a person. With the noun form, *apokalupsis,* four take a truth as the object; and five, a person. Walter Bauer, *A Greek-English Lexicon of the New Testament,* trans. Wm. F. Arndt and F. Wilbur Gingrich (Chicago: University of Chicago Press, 1957), *in loco.*

[32]*The Bible Today* (Cambridge: The University Press, 1948), p. 51.

[33]This aspect of Bibliology was discussed by the older theologians under the head of "The Means of Grace." Because it was thus separated from the discussion of the inspiration and authority of the Bible and was generally tucked away in the remote sections of the last volume of their dogmatic systems, most contemporary theologians assume wrongly that the older dogmaticians had no doctrine of a present work of the Spirit in and through the written Word of Scripture. See Charles Hodge, *Systematic Theology,* 3 vols. (New York: Scribner, Armstrong & Co., 1873), III, pp. 466-84.

[34]Harold de Wolf, Review of *Inspiration and Authority of the Bible* by Benjamin B. Warfield, *Journal of Bible and Religion,* XVII, No. 4 (October 1949), 273.

[35]Professor Henry Joel Cadbury once remarked that the evidence for Jesus' view of the authority of the Old Testament was far more conclusive than that for Jesus' view of His own Messiahship.

[36]See, for example, Hugh Mackintosh, *Is Christ Infallible and the Bible True?* (Edinburgh: T. & T. Clark, 1901); J. W. Wenham, *Our Lord's View of the Old Testament* (London: Tyndale Press, 1953); B. B. Warfield, *The Inspiration and Authority of the Bible* (Philadelphia: Presbyterian and Reformed Pub. Co., 1948); and R. Laird Harris, *Inspiration and Canonicity of the Bible* (Grand Rapids, Mich.: Zondervan, 1957).

[37]*Time*, January 10, 1949, pp. 61-2.

[38]Henry Nelson Wieman, "A Religious Naturalist Looks at Reinhold Niebuhr" in *Reinhold Niebuhr: His Religious, Social, and Political Thought*. Edited by Charles W. Kegley and Robert W. Bretall (New York: Macmillan, 1956), pp. 339-40.

[39]*Das Christliche Verständnis Offenbarung*, p. 19.

[40]*The Wheaton Position on Inspiration*, Bible Department of Wheaton College. (Multilith material)

[41]Brooke Foss Westcott and Fenton John Anthony Hort, *The New Testament in the Original Greek* (New York: Harper & Bros., 1882), p. 87. See also Frederick E. Kenyon, *Texts of the Greek Bible* (London: Duckworth, 1949), p. 252.

[42]Cf. Emil Brunner, *Christian Doctrine of God*, p. 107; and John Knox, *Jesus: Lord and Christ* (New York: Harper, 1958).

13

William Hordern

The Nature of Revelation

Closely related to the questions of faith and reason is the question of revelation. How is God made known to man? Twentieth-century theology has been deeply concerned with this question, and it may well be that its greatest contributions to posterity will be made in this area. The question was posed by the intellectual developments of the last two centuries. Christianity, a religion based upon the faith that God was revealed through history, found its Scriptures subjected to radical historical criticism. In an age geared to scientific and rational thought, the Christian faith would be an insult to intelligence if it asked that certain truths be accepted without undergoing the normal means of verification.

Revelation was a basic issue in the fundamentalist-modernist controversy. Fundamentalism denied the relevance of a historical criticism of the Scriptures; it insisted that the Bible contained an inerrant message from God. Liberalism insisted that honesty forced us to admit that the Bible was a fallible book, with internal contradictions and statements that had been proved wrong by science and

From *The Case for a New Reformation Theology,* by William Hordern. The Westminster Press. © W. L. Jenkins MCMLIX. Used by permission.

historical research. Fundamentalism preserved the Christian faith in revelation but did it in such a manner that it led to open conflict with science and scholarship. Liberalism accepted science and historical criticism, but it was often embarrassed to explain in what sense the Bible was a necessary source of knowledge about God.

Basically the liberals tried to find a subjective refuge from the threats to the faith. Following Schleiermacher's emphasis upon religious experience and Ritschl's emphasis upon moral experience or value judgments, liberals found the vindication of their faith within their own experience. Instead of faith resting upon miraculously verified events of the past, it rested upon what happens within a man's heart here and now. Such a refuge from the threats of historical criticism is tempting, and we find both Bultmann and Tillich still exploring this possibility.

It is doubtful, however, if the Christian faith can take this way out. This method always runs the danger of wishful thinking—what objective check is there to man's inner feelings? Furthermore, the Christian faith claims that God became man. If he did, we cannot escape from the fact that God put himself fully into our human midst. As no legion of angels swept out of the skies to save Jesus from the cross, neither can a legion of mystical angels save the record of his life from being subjected to historical criticism. If we take seriously the faith that God revealed himself through a historical person, we cannot long comfort ourselves with the idea that our faith can live no matter what history says about this person.[1]

Where liberalism tended toward subjectivity, fundamentalism strived after pure objectivity. God's revelation, it affirmed, is objectively present in the words of the Bible, attested by divine miracle. But whereas liberalism left a question about objective criteria, fundamentalism left a problem of the subjective. What has this historical record of long ago to do with me here and now? Does not the living God have a Word to speak to the twentieth century or has he spoken and fallen into silence?

In this situation a new reformation theology must strive to preserve the Reformation's faith in the objectivity of revelation given through the Scriptures. And it must do justice to the subjective facts of revelation; the objective revelation must be witnessed to by the Holy Spirit, as the Reformers affirmed. To meet the present century this Reformation faith must be expressed in the light of the new situation that we face because of the development of historical criticism and modern thought in general.

Revelation means an unveiling, the making known of that which was formerly unknown. As a result, it is not uncommon to hear any new knowledge called revelation. Nature, we are told, reveals its secrets to the scientist. In fact, liberalism with its immanent view of God often argued that there is no basic difference between the revelation of God and the revelation of knowledge about nature. But the term "revelation," as I would define it, can be used of scientific knowledge only in a metaphorical sense because it implies activity on the part of a revealer. We do not normally think of nature taking the initiative to make itself known. Nature just is, and man may or may not discover its secrets; it depends upon man. If God simply waits until man, on his own initiative, discovers whatever clues to his nature God may have dropped when he created the universe, then we can use the term "revelation" in theology only inexactly.

The term "revelation" implies a view that God is, in some sense at least, personal. John Baillie says: "For the revelation of which the Bible speaks is always such as has place within a personal relationship. It is not the revelation of an object to a subject, but a revelation from subject to subject, a revelation of mind to mind."[2] It is the prerogative of a person to reveal himself. We take the initiative in revealing more of ourselves to some people than to others. Thus we speak of "revealing circumstances," incidents in which a person through his behavior or words reveals himself and his nature with particular clarity. Of course finite human persons often reveal themselves inadvertently; they let slip a word, or thoughtlessly perform an act that drops the veil from their character. But if God is truly the Lord, we cannot suppose that he reveals himself except where he wills it. If there is revelation of God, it can be only because God took the initiative to make himself known to man.

Revelation is a personal act of disclosing that which is otherwise unknown. But the great question is, What does God reveal? For many centuries it was taken for granted that what God reveals is information that can be put into rational propositions like any other knowledge. In fact, it has not been unusual for persons holding this view to argue that some of the information revealed by God is such that man could have discovered it for himself, but God, in his goodness, revealed it so that the wise would have no advantage over the ignorant.

Where revelation is believed to be items of information in the form of propositions, the proper response to it is humble belief. Consequently, wherever this view has been held, faith usually has come to mean belief (*credentia*). If God reveals information, we almost have to accept the view that the revelation is infallible. As the fundamentalist says, if you deny any statements in the Bible, you are calling God a liar. In fundamentalism and conservatism this view is carried to its conclusion by insisting that although the Bible is not a book of science, nonetheless any statements that it makes in this area are preserved from error.[3]

A cogent argument for informational revelation is made by the

Roman Catholic theologian, Victor White. He admits that faith is more than assent to propositions, but he insists that it does not follow that we can dispose of verbal teachings. The revelation of Christ must be communicated to me if I am to live it, and it must be communicated accurately. It is not enough for my salvation that Christ lived and died, but I must know this fact and I must know who Christ was and is. Furthermore, I cannot do the will of God unless I know his will, and I cannot receive his grace unless I know where he has chosen to give it to me. Thus White says:

> Words, spoken or written, are still indispensable to *convey* the Word, the Christ-fact, to us. He himself, while still living and working amongst us, *speaks;* speaks human words to convey divine truths about himself and his Kingdom: the truths about our own selves and the way whereby we are to receive his salvation.[1]

The disciples, continues White, were called to tell others what they had received; they were to take Jesus' place when he was gone and to speak with his authority. But the disciples had no authority to teach whatever they wanted; they were to teach the gospel that they had received. Therefore, they had to teach with infallibility. They were not given verbal dictation, but they were so assisted by God that they were incapable of error in their apostolic function. Thus the Bible was infallibly inspired, but the need for infallibility did not end there, as was shown by the rise of heretics who misinterpreted the Bible. Consequently, the church has inherited the apostle's authority in order that it may interpret the Scriptures accurately.

This is a strong rational argument. If we grant the premise that God has imparted to man certain information that is necessary for salvation, the rest follows with stunning logic. Obviously, such important information cannot be at the mercy of the vicissitudes that haunt normal pieces of information. Protestant fundamentalism or conservatism is made to seem incomplete. Even if the Bible is inerrant, how can we know which of the conflicting interpretations of the Bible is correct? Does each reader of the Bible become a pope who can interpret it infallibly? The Roman Catholic seems to have an unanswerable point when he insists that if an infallible revelation is necessary at all, there must be a continuing infallibility.

It is no wonder that such an argument has persuaded many through the centuries. The strongest answer to it is to challenge its basic premise—that what God reveals is information, and this we shall do later. But here we might note that for all of its strength, the argument runs into serious problems.

First of all, it tends to lead to idolatry of the Bible and/or the church. A man's relationship to the church's teaching or his stand on the Bible becomes the acid test. Instead of asking whether he has faith in God, he is asked if he accepts the teachings of the church or of the Bible. The church and the Bible are beyond all possible criticism; they are absolutes in and of themselves. Instead of pointing to the absoluteness of God, they now share his absoluteness.

Secondly, although the view always claims to be the preserver of the unity and the catholicity of the church, it inevitably leads to division. From an early time the church lacked true catholicity. The more authoritatively the church taught, the less true unity it had. This is evident in the rise of Montanists, Donatists, Albigensians, Waldensians, and the rest. For a time the grim hand of political authoritarianism could give a false vision of unity, but beneath lay the rebellion that broke loose as soon as there was freedom to do so. Similarly, fundamentalism has divided and subdivided. And there is good reason why this is so. If you believe that you possess the infallible information necessary for salvation, it is difficult to have fellowship with any man who denies the least jot or tittle of what you proclaim.

The doctrine of infallible propositional revelation has become more and more difficult to hold in the face of modern knowledge. This is the view that has been involved in the science-religion debates of recent centuries. It has presented an unenlightened critique of the findings of Biblical scholarship. It is significant that conservatism has retreated to the point where it admits that no manuscript of the Bible that we now possess is inerrant. Only the original manuscripts, now lost, were without error. Since that time copyists have made mistakes, so that no existing manuscript is perfect. But, it is affirmed, God has kept this process under control, so that there has been no error in any doctrine necessary for man's salvation.[5] This concession, however, obviously leads to the subjective influences that the conservative has tried to avoid. How do we decide what is necessary for salvation and hence free from error?

One of the gravest problems of the concept of inerrant propositional revelation is in the question of what it means. Man always has a tendency to take a magical view of words as if they had some kind of power and being in their own right. But words and propositions have only one purpose—to communicate from one person to another by pointing to a reality beyond themselves. Thus I cannot sit on "chair": it is simply the symbol that I use in communication with others to point to the object upon which I can sit. A proposition is a tool; it has a task to perform, and to perform its task it must be spoken and it must be received.

When a proposition is spoken, however, it is affected by the hearer. No matter how carefully we choose our words, they run the continual risk of being interpreted differently from what we intended. If we think of propositions independently of their environment and not engaged in doing what propositions are meant to do, then we might refer to them as inerrant. That is, they are absolutely correct words to refer to the objects desired by the speaker, even though no one has understood them. But if we think of propositions acting as propositions are meant to act, what does it mean to call them inerrant? The fact that they may have issued from the speaker "infallibly" is irrelevant unless they come into the understanding of the hearer meaning precisely what the speaker meant by them. In short, to call a proposition inerrant, and to mean anything serious about reality in the statement, we must mean that it is not only spoken to express infallibly what the speaker wants to say, we must also say that it is impossible to hear it otherwise than as the speaker intended it to be heard.

But no defender of inerrant propositional revelation has pretended that all hearers of the propositions understood them perfectly. The Bible is understood differently by different people. And Roman Catholicism does not solve this dilemma by its claim that the church must interpret the Bible infallibly. It only shifts the problem from the Bible to the church. It is impossible to claim that everyone who has heard the church's infallible declaration of doctrine has found the same meaning in it. Not only do those outside the church fail to see the meaning, but even within Catholicism there are wide differences of opinion as to the meaning of the declared doctrines and, worse still, debates as to what has been declared doctrine and is hence infallible.

In short, I find serious confusion in the very concept of an inerrantly revealed proposition. If anyone, for any reason, fails to understand what God desired to have understood in the proposition, then it can be called inerrant only in a strained and unreal sense. It has not performed inerrantly what it was meant to perform. Earlier we mentioned that fundamentalism tried to give an objective defense against Biblical criticism, but now we can see why this is not enough. An objective revelation is not inerrant until it is inerrantly received. The subjective receiver of revelation is an indispensable link in the chain. As Kierkegaard put it, there is no truth until there is truth to me. If there is to be inerrant revelation of propositions, the hearer would have to be as inerrant as the speaker. If man is not infallible, and seldom have Roman Catholics or fundamentalists claimed infallibility for the hearer, then it may be emotionally comforting to claim that God spoke without error, but it is meaningless to us men who are fallible hearers, for we can never know infallibly that we understand correctly the infallible revelation.

The practical problems involved are well illustrated by the long debate between science and Genesis. For example, Genesis says that God created the world in six days (Gen. 1:1 to 2:3). This seems to be a simple enough statement; it means that in a period of one hundred and forty-four hours God completed creation. And so Christians interpreted it for centuries. When science first began to show that the events of Genesis must have taken longer than this interpretation implied, fundamentalists rejected the idea. But scientific evidence became more and more convincing. Then fundamentalists decide that a "day" in Genesis did not mean twenty-four hours but a period of indefinite time. Similarly, the Genesis story seems to teach that God created each separate species and again most Christians so understood it. But when the evolutionary theory became too much to resist, the conservatives found that God created "kinds," not species, and the evolution may have occurred within these kinds.[6]

Finally, Carl Henry, summarizing the agonizing of the conservatives over Genesis and science, suggests that although science must not be permitted to fix the content of revelation, "it is welcomed as a negative check against false exegesis."[7] In other words, Genesis is an inerrant picture of creation, but the Christian cannot know what it means until the "assured results" of science come in. This means that the doctrine of Scriptural inerrancy has become a purely emotive reaction to the Bible; it can give no practical knowledge since we must await science to see if our exegesis is correct. Worse still, it would seem that the words of the Bible can be stretched to mean anything that, in view of science, they "should" mean.

Such dilemmas might have been avoided if Protestants had remembered the emphasis of the Reformers that the Holy Spirit must illuminate the heart of the reader if he is to hear the Word of God in the Scriptures. Thus Calvin says that, "if we were inclined to argue the point," there are certain arguments that we could bring forward to indicate that God is speaking in Scripture. But Calvin hastens to say that "yet it is acting a preposterous part, to endeavor to produce sound faith in the Scripture by disputations." Men, he tells us, cannot have Christian faith if they are persuaded by arguments, even arguments from Scripture. "The testimony of the Spirit is superior to all reason. For as God alone is a sufficient witness of himself in his own word, so also the word will never gain credit in the hearts of men, till it be confirmed by the internal testimony of the Spirit."[8] Furthermore, when Calvin begins his chapter on "Rational Proofs to Establish the Belief of the Scripture," he opens it with the warning that all such arguments are vain without something more than such arguments. And he concludes it by again affirming that, without the Holy Spirit's witness, belief in the Scriptures will be in vain.[9] This is equally clear in the thought of Luther who always affirmed that in Scripture, it is only God himself, who can tell us that this is God speaking.

If the Word of God is heard only where and when the Holy

Spirit illuminates the receiver of revelation, then it is not crucial whether or not the propositions involved are inerrant. In fact, we may insist that the man who reads them without the guidance of the Holy Spirit cannot hear what God intended to say through them and so for him they cannot be inerrant. But, just as God became man and revealed himself through the limited human person of Jesus, so the Holy Spirit can speak to us through these human and finite words.

We have seen difficulties in the view of an infallible revelation of propositions. These difficulties are not likely to persuade the believer in such revelation to give up his belief, but they are sufficient to make the concept impossible for many persons in our age. Many find that intellectual integrity will not allow them to accept propositions that strain their credulity just because some authority tells them that they must accept them. But the strongest argument against this view is the showing of an alternative.

Faced with the dilemmas and the problems that we have seen, and rediscovering the views of the Reformers, modern theologians have presented a new understanding of the nature of revelation. This view has been most adequately summarized by saying that what God reveals is not propositions or information—what God reveals is God. In revelation we do not receive a doctrine or some esoteric piece of information that man's wisdom could not have discovered. In revelation we are brought into a living relationship with the person of God. God's Word never consists of black marks on the pages of a book called the Bible; God's Word is the living Word which he speaks through the Bible and to which man must respond by saying yes or no.

This view has been developed through many creative thinkers. Soren Kierkegaard, Martin Buber, Karl Barth, Emil Brunner, Richard Niebuhr, William Temple, and others have made their particular contributions. Although the view is in many ways a twentieth-century development, it can, in all fairness, be claimed that it is true to the Biblical view and to the view of the Reformers.

Central to this viewpoint is the recognition that there is a basic difference between the way in which we know things and the way in which we know persons. No doubt the distinction between "I-it" and "I-thou" relationships has been overemphasized by some thinkers, but the distinction is necessary. To know things I need I.Q. and training; to know persons I need to be a self; I need moral character. I know things by observing them, experimenting with them, and I seek to know them in order that I may be able to manipulate them. But to know a person I must enter into fellowship and communion with him; there has to be give and take. Of course my relationship with another person may be an I-it relation; I may think of him and treat him as a thing. When that happens, although I may gain extensive information about him, I do not know him as a person. We can know *about* things and, in impersonal relations with persons, we know *about* persons. But we can only *know* persons.

The importance of this for theology has been pointed up by Buber, who has shown that there is no analogy between knowing the Biblical God and knowing things, but there is a real analogy between knowing God and knowing persons. One of the services that analytic philosophy renders to theology is to help us see that so long as we try to speak about God as we speak about things, we end up in speaking nonsense.[10] John Wisdom, in a lecture, pointed out that the question, Is there a God? is in no sense like the question, Are there cookies in the jar in the cupboard? The Biblical God never appears as a thing or an object to be studied. Theology has little to learn from philosophy's discussion of how we know things. But there is much to be learned from the problem of how we know "other minds."

In our relationship with the God of revelation, we are not called into an I-it relation with the First Cause; rather, we are called into a personal relation with the Father of Jesus Christ. Jesus did not say, "Blessed are the brilliant: for they shall logically prove God's existence"; he said, "Blessed are the pure in heart: for they shall see God" (Matt. 5:8). In personal relations the purity of one's heart is a vital factor in knowing. That is, love, moral integrity, imagination, empathy, are needed to know a person as they are not needed to know a thing. When God's revelation comes to us, it does not come as propositions to subdue the mind; it comes as a challenge to the "heart," it appeals to the whole man. The faith to which it calls us is not the submissive believing of propositions but the commitment of the self in trust to the God who is encountered. The view of propositional revelation distorts this by directing our attention to an I-it relation with a book, a church, or a creed.

Theology and creeds are man-made devices to point to the fact of God's revelation of himself. As Barth puts it, they are witnesses to revelation. They are useful to the degree that they can point beyond themselves to God, but we should never commit the idolatry of mistaking them for revelation. God reveals himself in order that, through fellowship with him, man's life might be renewed, redeemed, saved. But propositions cannot do this; they can only point to it.

Even in our relationships with other persons, we find that propositions are grossly inadequate to express the reality that we know. This is why we turn to poetry, to symbolic actions, and to anecdotes to express what we know about the uniqueness of the other person. A police description of a young girl might be scientifically accurate, but her mother and her lover would agree that it failed to do justice to her reality. How much less can we expect propositions to do justice to the reality of God's person! Most Christians would agree that John's proposition, "God is love" (I John 4:8), is an excellent description of God as revealed in Scripture. But we cannot consider it infallible. To many a hearer it will convey the wrong impression, because the word "love" today has many connotations that cannot be applied to God. To know what love means in this context we have to point to the acts of God in revelation—to his choosing of the Jews, to Jesus' relationships with little children, to the woman taken in adultery, and to the Pharisees. Finally, and above all, we must see its meaning in Jesus' death and in the Bible's interpretation of the meaning of that death.

There is another way of approaching the problem. In collecting new items of knowledge, the collector of knowledge does not normally change. He increases his volume of knowledge, but he remains essentially what he was before. Knowledge may broaden a man, but his center can remain stationary. But the whole point of knowing God is that it changes the man, the center of his life is shifted. It may or may not add new information to a man's store of knowledge. Referring back to our discussion of the faith-reason problem, revelation occurs when a man's perspective or frame of reference is changed. "I was blind, but now I see," he cries; the face of Christ appears in place of the landscape.

Many persons saw Jesus when he lived; they saw his acts and heard his words, but they found in him no revelation of God. Pilate's experience was broadened through his contact with Jesus; he had a new set of anecdotes to tell at the drinking parties in Rome, but Pilate heard no revelation, no Word of God. At first the disciples were in the same situation as Pilate. They were deeply impressed by Jesus as a man, so impressed that they sacrificed much to follow him. But one day, faced by the challenge of Jesus' question about who men said he was, Peter confessed, "Thou art the Christ, the Son of the living God" (Matt. 16:16). And Jesus tells him that flesh and blood have not revealed this to him, but God himself. This incident might well form the text for the position we are defending. The believer in propositional revelation is trying to find revelation in the equivalent of "flesh and blood," that is, in the words of Scripture or the church. But revelation is revelation only when it is made known by God himself, that is, through the Holy Spirit.

Peter is the rock upon which the church is founded, not because he was the first pope, but because every Christian must come to revelation as Peter came. Like Peter, we must first see the man, Jesus. Here is the objective side of revelation; this is the givenness of God's action. But God is hidden as well as revealed in Jesus; many had seen Jesus without hearing the Word of God. As God awakened the response of faith in Peter's heart, so he must awaken it in each Christian's heart.

We do not see Jesus in the flesh, as did Peter; we must read about him in the Bible. This is why the Bible is the indispensable medium of God's revelation; it alone records the events through which God was revealed. In the Bible we read the witness of the Biblical writers that through this Jesus of Nazareth God's revelation came to them. In the Old Testament we find the preparation for this revelation, and in the New Testament we see it received and accepted. But we may read the Bible from cover to cover and never hear the Word of God. On the other hand, at any moment God may use a word of the Bible to speak his Word to our hearts, and in that moment we can confess, with Peter, "Thou art the Christ." This, I believe, is what Luther had in mind when he called the Bible the crib that holds Christ. The Bible is the earthen vessel through which at any moment God may speak to man (II Cor. 4:7).

Barth and others have seen a parallel between the doctrine of Christ and the doctrine of revelation. The church has been forced to combat two heresies about Christ. One denies his divinity, and the other denies his humanity. Either claim would destroy the Christian faith. Both these heresies arose in the early church, and both have been persistent ever since. If the church has had difficulty in persuading unbelievers that Christ is divine, it has had almost equal difficulty in persuading believers that he is truly human. Of course, ever since the early creeds were established, most Christians have paid lip service to the humanity of Jesus, but in thought and speech there has often been an implicit denial of true humanity. It is significant that the full implications of the church's belief about Christ did not appear until after heresies had arisen, that is, until explicit positions were put forward that were recognized as destructive of the faith.

I suggested earlier that the twentieth century's chief contribution to theology might be in its analysis of revelation. In fact, I believe that it may be doing for the Bible and revelation what the first six centuries did for Christology. And it can do this, not because the men of our century are wiser than men in earlier centuries, but because, as the early centuries had to face the twin Christological heresies, so our century has had to face opposing heresies about the Bible.

The rise of Biblical criticism brought to the fore two sharply opposed positions. On the one hand, there were many liberals who could no longer find revelation in any meaningful sense in the Bible. It was an impressive book of human wisdom but not essentially different from other human writings. It represented a particularly fruitful search by man for knowledge of God and moral values. Immediately this position was opposed by fundamentalism and conservatism. Whereas some of the liberals saw the Bible as a purely human book, just as some had seen Jesus as simply a human being, the conservatives followed a path similar to that of the Docetists and denied the true humanity of the Bible. It is true that conservatives have been most careful to insist that they do see a human element in the Bible.

They do not want to argue that the Biblical writers were only dicta-phones transcribing God's words. But, as many pay lip service to the humanity of Jesus and then deny it in practice, so the conservative position often denies in effect the true humanity of the Biblical writings. God so overwhelmed the humanity of the writers that the normal tendency to err was erased.[11] And what the conservatives do for the Bible the Catholic position does for the church.

The new reformation position arose in this century in answer to these two viewpoints. Against all who would deny divine revelation in the Bible, the twentieth century has rediscovered the Word of God speaking through the Bible. In the Bible we find recorded the unique events, the mighty acts, through which God revealed himself to man, and we meet the witness of the writers to whom God spoke through these events. The Bible is not man's noble search for God; it is God's gracious search for man. But, thanks to the higher criticism of the Bible, we can no longer ignore the completely human element that entered into its writing. Whatever may be the ultimate fate of current views in Biblical criticism, we cannot lose sight of the fact that the Bible is a human book, arising in human situations, and written by human men with all the frailties of finiteness.

Barth has a way sometimes of overstating his case, but these words of his are a healthy antidote to the claims of an infallible propositional revelation:

> Every time we turn the Word of God into an infallible Biblical word of man or the Biblical word of man into an infallible Word of God we resist that which we ought never to resist, i.e., the truth of the miracle that here fallible men speak the Word of God in fallible human words—and we therefore resist the sovereignty of grace, in which God himself became man in Christ, to glorify himself in his humanity. . . . To the bold postulate that if their word is to be the Word of God they must be inerrant in every word, we oppose the even bolder assertion, that according to the Scriptural witness about man, which applies to them too, they can be at fault in any word, and have been at fault in every word, and yet according to the same Scriptural witness, being justified and sanctified by grace alone, they have still spoken the Word of God in their fallible and erring human word.[12]

As a result, Barth finds conservatism (and the same would apply to Catholicism) guilty of trying to possess God. Man in his sinful insecurity longs to control God. He refuses to trust God and God alone for his salvation. Instead, he claims that in the Biblical words or in his creeds he holds the very words of God himself. This is a refusal to confess that God is truly Lord and sovereign even over the Bible and revelation.[13] We can never possess God; grace alone freely gave the Bible and grace alone can cause it to be revelation to man.

The claim has been made that this view of revelation is more true to the Bible itself than the claim that revelation comes as propositional information. We do not have the space to deal adequately with this subject, but there have been a number of excellent defenses of this thesis.[14] Here we can only summarize a few points made in greater detail by other writers.

First, it is significant that the Bible is primarily a book of history. Brunner points out that it contains nothing remotely resembling a catechism or a system of doctrines.[15] There is no other sacred Scripture that provides us with such reliable and extensive historical data. John Baillie says that the Christian faith is truly "good news" because it is not a summary of eternal truths, but a report of concrete events—the things that God has done. But what is revealed through events and actions is the person of the actor. Of course, propositions must be made about the events, but such propositions point beyond themselves to the reality of what is revealed through the events.

The Biblical faith says, "I know whom I have believed" (II Tim. 1:12), not *"what* I have believed." But, as Brunner points out, the church was early overcome with an intellectualism that perverted this understanding. It switched from the personal I-thou to an impersonal I-it understanding of revelation. It changed from what Brunner calls "truth as encounter" to "truth as idea." "The church turned the revelation of the Son into the revelation of an eternal truth 'about the Son.' "[16]

Brunner, of course, recognizes as clearly as White, the Catholic, that we need doctrines and propositions to communicate the faith. Even Peter's confession, "Thou art the Christ," was a proposition. But the point is that for the believer in propositional revelation, the proposition *is* revelation, for Brunner it *point*s to revelation. For the former, the proposition is beyond dispute; it must be accepted. But for Brunner, the proposition must always be kept under criticism by revelation itself. We must ask of the proposition, "Does it point to Christ?" If it does, we keep it; if not, we seek for another proposition that will do so more adequately.

The proposition, "Thou art the Christ," was the proposition that came naturally to Peter, the Jew, as he tried to express the revelation that had occurred to him in the presence of Jesus. The Christ, or Messiah, was the highest concept that a Jew had to apply to Jesus. As a witness to revelation it was necessary, but it was not inerrant, for when Peter drew the natural meaning of that time from the proposition and affirmed that Jesus should not die, Jesus rebuked him harshly (Matt. 16:21-23). Far from being an infallible statement, even to the man who spoke it, the statement had an ambiguous meaning. It is significant that the later Biblical writers seldom described Jesus as the Messiah, or Christ. Even in the New Testament the term "Christ" became a name rather than a title for Jesus.

Instead, Jesus was called the Lord, the Logos (Word), the Savior, the Redeemer, the Only-begotten Son, and so on.

Sometimes these various terms to describe Jesus have been used as evidence that there are many Christologies in the New Testament. But it is my belief that such an interpretation misses the vital point. All these terms are propositions or words used to point to the revelation experienced in Christ. No one of them was adequate for the simple reason that each was a category used before Christ came, but when he came, he was unique, he belonged to no prior category. Peter quite rightly took the highest category that he knew to describe Jesus, but immediately he has shown how inadequate this category was to express the new revelation. And so other categories were tried, and each, in its own way, was an adequate pointer to the revelation, and yet each fell short. Not one could be claimed as an inerrant expression of the revelation, for any of them could be used to mean the wrong thing.[17]

And this is the problem of all creeds. They are necessary because man has to try to point to the revelation that has found him. But creeds and propositions can never be final; they must change with changing times. The church must always agonize over purity of doctrine, for doctrines are indispensable to point to Christ. If our doctrine is inadequate, it will point wrongly or dimly so that men do not see revelation. But no doctrine can be so pure that it may be placed above criticism.

Brunner says that Catholics have dogmas, Protestants have confessions of faith. Dogma is "that which one must believe"; the man who does not is excommunicated, cut off from the means of salvation. Unfortunately Protestants often have fallen into this viewpoint, but it is opposed to the genius of Protestantism. A Protestant does not believe in a doctrine; he believes in Christ. And so Luther said, "The one doctrine which I have supremely at heart, is that of faith in Christ, from whom, through whom, and unto whom all my theological thinking flows back and forth day and night."[18] Any doctrine is a confession of faith that points to Christ; it has no other purpose or value. For the Protestant the Bible and doctrine are like telescopes; they are made to look through, not to look at.

We can illustrate our position by referring to Christ. Whatever else Christians may or may not agree upon, they do agree that the fullness of God's revelation is found in him. But how is revelation found in Christ? Many have extolled Jesus as a spiritual pioneer who discovered the great spiritual truths upon which Christianity is built. This view was found in liberalism, although many liberals found it inadequate. But the problem is that Jesus was not so original a teacher as this implies. Most of Jesus' teachings find their parallels in other religions, certainly in pre-Christian Judaism.

But there is an even greater difficulty in the view of Jesus as a teacher. Brunner, building on Kierkegaard, has pointed out that Jesus fails to fulfill the essential function of a teacher. The true teacher does not point to himself; he points to the truth. He is most happy when he has made himself unnecessary, and his pupil goes forward to find the truth for himself. But if we look to the New Testament, we find that Jesus deliberately made himself indispensable; he did not point beyond himself to the truth, but he pointed to himself as "the way, the truth, and the life" (John 14:6). Jesus tells his disciples that they will be persecuted, not for his teachings, but for his "name's sake" (Mark 13:13). A man's very status before God will depend upon his relationship to Christ. "Whosoever therefore shall confess me before men, him will I confess also before my Father which is in heaven" (Matt. 10:32). The illustrations could be multiplied to show that Jesus put himself at the center of his message.

Faced with the problem that Jesus presents himself as more than a teacher, the radical liberal often retreated to the claim that Jesus was unique because he not only taught but also lived his teachings. Although others may have taught the same things, Jesus alone lived them. Jesus is therefore important because we do not know of what man is capable until we see manhood fulfilled in Jesus. We cannot reject this view completely because Paul taught in his doctrine of the second Adam that Christ reveals what man was meant to be (Rom. 5:12-21). But precisely when we understand this, we find that we need more than a teacher and an example in Jesus, for if the perfect Christ is man as man was meant to be, we find ourselves unable to become what we were meant to be. We are sinners. And so Jesus does not simply present himself as an ideal; he calls men to himself where they may be remade by God.

Now this amazing teaching is precisely what we might expect if our view of revelation is correct. We have asserted that what the Bible reveals is the person of God. God acts, and in the Bible God inspired prophets to interpret his acts, and through this comes the revelation of God's nature, will, and person. But finally a person can be revealed fully and completely only by himself appearing. The subjects may see the acts of their king, and they may hear his messages sent through his heralds; but before they can truly know him, he must himself appear in their midst and speak with them. Therefore, if the kind of revelation to which the Bible bears witness is to be fulfilled, God himself must appear. And in Christ, the Christian believes, this mystery of mysteries has occurred. If information could have saved man, the prophets would have sufficed. But salvation requires personal communion with the Savior.

Jesus Christ is thus revelation for us, not as teacher, although we must not forget that he was a teacher, nor as example, although he was that too. Jesus becomes revelation through his whole life and person, and in them the eyes of faith see God. "God was in Christ, reconciling the world unto himself" (II Cor. 5:19).

We can also approach the Biblical view of revelation through an analysis of the Biblical view of faith. We pointed out that if revelation is the revelation of infallible propositions, then the proper response would be to bow in submission and believe the infallible truths. Faith would thus be belief (*credentia*). In fact, it is not unusual to find defenders of this position arguing that the more unbelievable the doctrine, the greater the merit for believing it. But if we turn to the Bible, we find that saving faith does not primarily mean belief.

There are many passages on faith with which we might deal. I shall refer to the sixth chapter of Romans. Here, as elsewhere, Paul makes it clear that man is not saved by submitting his reason to divinely revealed propositions; he is saved by a faith-relationship with Christ. Shall we continue to sin so that grace can abound? asks Paul, and he answers with a resounding NO. How can we continue in sin if we have really *died* with Christ and if we now live in him alone? Where we were the slaves of sin, we have become the servants of Christ. It is quite clear that for Paul faith is not primarily a belief at all; it is a relationship with God through Christ, a relationship that remolds the whole of life.

On the other hand, if we turn to James's epistle, where salvation by faith is criticized, it is clear that James is not denying the faith that Paul is affirming. The faith that James asserts cannot save is belief in doctrine. Thus he says, "Thou believest that there is one God; thou doest well: the devils also believe, and tremble" (James 2:19). We know that in the later writings of the New Testament, the concept of faith as belief was already beginning to form. In James we find an attack upon such a concept. But James is not in opposition to Paul. The belief that a devil can have is not the faith through which Paul found that he was a new man in Christ.

Again we admit that every act of faith in the Pauline sense will include, at least implicitly, certain beliefs. John Baillie says, "When I trust somebody . . . I am manifestly at the same time believing certain things about him to be true, yet I may find it very difficult to say exactly what these things are—I may even flounder helplessly in the attempt to assign the reasons for my trust."[19] And so the propositions believed in saving faith may be so implicit that the believer is at a loss to express them. The purpose of theology is to clarify the propositions involved in faith, but we must never mistake belief in the propositions for the faith. There may be faith with only implicit belief; there may be explicit belief without faith.

In the Bible we find continually the theme that we are to have faith in God. Barth says that if we are true to the Bible, we must meet the surprising fact that the Bible never points to itself but always to God. Conservatism runs the danger of losing this Biblical insight.

Subtly it calls us to put faith in the Bible, the inerrant book, while Catholicism calls us to faith in the church.

The appeal to the authority of the church or Bible has its difficulties. If the unbeliever asks why he should accept the Bible as infallible, it is hard to give a reason. We may quote the Bible itself, but the verses are ambiguous and the argument is circular. Even if the quoted verses do say that the Bible is infallible (and I fail to see that they do), the man who doubts its infallibility will doubt the verses. We cannot use the miracles to persuade the unbeliever because he doubts the truth of all miracle stories. If we say that the Bible is an ancient book that has long inspired and guided men, and if we point to its high moral tone, its fine style, etc., the unbeliever quite rightly points out that the same can be said for the Bhagavad-Gita, the Analects of Confucius, and other sacred books.

But not only is the method ineffective; it is most destructive when it is successful. Brunner points out that it puts Christianity upside down. "It bases our faith-relation to Jesus Christ upon our faith in the apostles."[20] That is, *because* we believe the Bible or the church, we believe in Christ. But this is not Christian faith at all. We are not called to believe in Christ because the Bible or some apostle tells us to do so. We believe because God has convinced us just as God convinced Peter. The Christian ought not first to believe in the trustworthiness of apostle, church, or Bible. He first comes to faith in Christ, and through this he is led to a secondary belief in the words of the Bible, the apostle, or the church.

This viewpoint certainly has its justification in the teachings of Luther and Calvin. But I believe that it is unfortunate that the men who have rediscovered this in the present century have so widely ignored the witness of sectarian Christianity at this point. For it was the Reformation sects, with their deep suspicion of all human authorities, who often witnessed most clearly to the principle. We can point, for example, to George Fox. He wandered about the churches of his day seeking truth, but everywhere he went he found men pointing him to the authority of the church, or the Bible, or a creed. But Fox could find no peace there. And then one day, he recorded in his journal: "When all my hopes in . . . all men were gone, so that I had nothing outwardly to help me, nor could tell what to do, then, O then, I heard a voice which said, 'There is one, even Christ Jesus, that can speak to thy condition,' and when I heard it, my heart did leap for joy." Here we find the nature of Christian witness. What we have to confess is that Christ Jesus has spoken to our condition, that in him we have heard the Word of God. We can invite the unbeliever to look to Christ also. If he finds that Christ does speak to his condition, then he will believe in the Bible as the witness to the truth he has found. But if he does not find that Christ speaks to his condition, there is no way in which we can prove to him the truth of the Bible. Revelation is that which brings us to know God; it is God himself speaking to us. This is the truth, long obscured, that has been rediscovered in our time.

We began by saying that a new reformation theology has to have a view of revelation that does justice to the Reformation and to the modern situation. I believe that this is what the view we have outlined does. It emphasizes the objectivity of the revelation given by God and mediated to us through the Bible, and thus preserves the Reformers' emphasis upon the objectively given revelation in the Bible. It accepts wholeheartedly the findings of Biblical criticism. We are thankful that, having been shown the human and finite nature of the Bible, we are saved from an idolatry of the book. Finally, we do not have to insult the modern world's intelligence by calling it to submit its reason to authoritatively given propositions; we invite it instead to a "divine-human encounter" in which a new perspective is given from which one can behold the world.

Finally, when we see that the knowledge of God that the Christian claims is a person-to-person knowledge, it becomes evident that natural theology can contribute little to this knowledge. The natural theologian would gain knowledge about God by examining the world. But a scientific (or metaphysical) examination of the world will discover less about the person of the living God than the medical student can learn about the former personality of the cadaver he has been given to dissect. The student may draw some tentative conclusions about the character and person of his cadaver. From the remains he can deduce that this was a clean-living person who took care of himself and so on. But he can do this because there is a basis of comparison. He knows from past experience how other bodies have been affected by the character and life of the person. But when we try to gain a clue about God's person from the universe, we face the fact that we have only one universe—there is no other with which to compare it. Thus, for example, what the presence of evil in this world means about the character of the Creator we cannot say, since we have no way of knowing what another universe, constructed differently from ours, might be like. We may have great fun in second-guessing God in his creation, but we have only the wildest of speculation to go on. If the person and character of God are what we are trying to know, it must be God himself who reveals them to us. No one else has the information. "For what person knows a man's thoughts except the spirit of the man which is in him? So also no one comprehends the thoughts of God except the Spirit of God" (I Cor. 2:11, RSV).

Notes

[1]For a discussion of the significance of the history of Jesus, see Donald M. Baillie, *God Was in Christ,* Ch. II. Charles Scribner's Sons, 1948.

[2]John Baillie, *The Idea of Revelation in Recent Thought,* p. 24. Columbia University Press, 1956.

[3]See H. Lindsell and C. J. Woodbridge, *A Handbook of Christian Truth,* p. 26. Fleming H. Revell Company, 1953.

[4]Victor White, *God the Unknown,* p. 192. Harper & Brothers, 1956.

[5]See Edward John Carnell, *An Introduction to Christian Apologetics,* pp. 198-201. Wm. B. Eerdmans Publishing Co., 1948.

[6]*Ibid.,* pp. 236-242.

[7]Carl F. H. Henry, editor, *Contemporary Evangelical Thought,* p. 272. Channel Press, 1957.

[8]John Calvin, *Institutes of the Christian Religion,* tr. by John Allen, Bk. I. Ch. vii. Sec. 4. Presbyterian Board of Christian Education, n.d.

[9]*Ibid.,* I. viii.

[10]E.g., see I. M. Crombie, "The Possibility of Theological Statements," in Basil Mitchell, *op. cit.,* Ch. II.

[11]H. Lindsell and C. Woodbridge, *op. cit.,* pp. 25-26.

[12]K. Barth, *Church Dogmatics,* Vol. I, Pt. 2, pp. 529-530.

[13]*Ibid.,* p. 513.

[14]See J. Baillie, *op. cit.,* Ch. IV; Emil Brunner, *Revelation and Reason,* tr. by Olive Wyon, Chs. 2-13. The Westminster Press, 1946; K. Barth, *Church Dogmatics,* Vol. I, Pt. 2, Ch. iii; Bernhard Anderson, *Rediscovering the Bible,* Chs. 1 and 2. Association Press, 1951.

[15]E. Brunner, *Revelation and Reason,* p. 149.

[16]*Ibid.*

[17]See F. C. Grant, *An Introduction to New Testament Thought,* Ch. 9. Abingdon Press, 1950.

[18]Martin Luther, *Commentary on Epistle to the Galatians,* p. 16. Fleming H. Revell Company, n.d.

[19]J. Baillie, *op. cit.,* p. 92.

[20]E. Brunner, *Revelation and Reason,* p. 168.

14

Bernard Ramm

Special Revelation
and the Word of God

Special Revelation as Cosmic and Anthropic

The knowledge of God is that indispensable structuring of the spiritual order given in grace to man so that he may know how to "move about." This is not intellectualism in religion, for its opposite is not "spirituality" but ignorance. Persons enter into fellowship with each other only as they authentically know each other. Thus throughout the Scriptures the reality of the spiritual life is predicated upon the knowledge of God. There is a massive witness to this assertion in the one hundred and seventy-six verses of Psalm 119!

The knowledge of God in Scripture is never an end in itself but is the necessary instrument for the worship of God, fellowship with God, and the service of God. All man's motions towards God are to be directed by the knowledge of God. It is this profound insight into biblical truth which led Calvin to speak of faith in one of its aspects as the knowledge of God (III, ii). For example, he wrote that "we

From Bernard Ramm, *Special Revelation and the Word of God*, Grand Rapids: Wm. B. Eerdmans Publishing Company, 1961. Used by permission.

certainly cannot directly tend towards (Christ) except under the guidance of the gospel" (III, ii, 6)—i.e., the knowledge of God in the gospel.

One of the important aspects of Romans 1:18-32 is that it shows the interconnectedness of the knowledge of God, the worship of God, and human righteousness or sinfulness. Sin disrupts man's communion with God. But it also leads to a corruption of the knowledge of God which leads to false notions of God, climaxing in idolatry. When sin starts tearing the fabric of the divine communion it does not cease its work until the knowledge of God is corrupted within the creature and he changes the glory of God to that of some earthly creature, and worships and serves the idol and not the Creator. *As soon as sin corrupts the human heart general revelation is helpless to make amends.* As Vos puts it, "Nature cannot unlock the door of redemption."[1] Or in Calvin's words, "For as an eye, either dimmed by age or weakened by another cause, sees nothing distinctly without the aid of glasses, so (such is our imbecility) if Scripture does not direct our inquiries after God, we immediately turn vain in our imagination" (I, xiv, 1).

If there is to be a recovery of the knowledge of God it must then have its foundation in the action of God, an action of grace and redemption. Man's sickened condition does not compel God to speak, for as Kuyper properly notes, God moves *first* for his glory.[2] The potter-vessel relationship set out by Paul in Romans 9:20-21 is the God-man relationship of the entire Scriptural revelation. But out of God's love and mercy for man he does move!

Special revelation possesses the same contours as those of redemption. It commences in the grace and glory of God; it is a free and gracious movement towards man; and it terminates upon man in an authentic manner. Our particular concern is how the acting and speaking of God effectively terminates upon man.

To refer to an earlier matter, special revelation is special in that it comes to specific persons but not to humanity in general. It is special also in the second sense that it comes to resolve a particular difficulty: the loss of the knowledge of God through sin. *Special revelation, then, comes to particular men.*

It must also be observed that when revelation comes to a particular man he is living *in a concrete situation, and revelation meets him in his concrete situation.* The man who receives revelation lives in this country, not that; he lives in this decade, speaks this language, exists in this specific culture. Specific revelation comes to a man already characterized by a bundle of particularities.

To make authentic contact with such a man, special revelation must come in a *cosmic form* (to use Kuyper's term),[3] or a *sacramental* form (to use Barth's term),[4] or in an *anthropic* form. By *cosmic* Kuyper means that special revelation must truly enter our world and take the forms of our world in order to be comprehended by us. By *sacramental* Barth means that the elements of this world are called into the service of revelation to serve as signs of revelation. By *anthropic* we mean accommodated to man, his language, his culture, and his powers. This cosmic, sacramental, and anthropic character of revelation *is the form of the great condescension of God.*

On many different occasions Calvin speaks of this great condescension of God in which he bends down and, lowering himself, lisps that we might hear and understand him. Just as the Son of God emptied himself and lowered himself to our estate, so revelation comes to us in a humbled, lowered form that we might cradle it in our minds. This thought has been beautifully stated by Kuyper:

> Here, also, the parallel maintains itself between the incarnate and the written Logos. As in the Mediator the Divine nature weds itself to the human, and appears before us in *its* form and figure, so also the Divine factor of the Holy Scripture clothes itself in the garment of our form of thought and holds itself to our human reality . . . when, on Sinai, God with His own finger engraves in human words His law upon the tables of stone, and the revelation remains not absolutely transcendent, but makes use here, also, of the human as instrument. All the shadows and types bear the same mixed character. All of sacred history rests upon the same entwining of both factors. And even in miracles, the Divine factor remains never purely transcendent, but in order to reveal Himself, ever enters into human reality. Hence, in all parts of the rich scenery interpreted to you by the Word of God, it is ever the transcendent, Divine factor, which exhibits itself to your eye in a human form or in a human reality. . . . As the Logos has not appeared *in the form of glory,* but in the form of a servant, joining Himself to the reality of our nature, as this had come to be through the results of sin, so also, for the revelation of His Logos, God the Lord accepts *our* consciousness, our human life *as it is.* . . . The "spoken words," however much aglow with the Holy Ghost, remain bound to the limitation of our language, disturbed as it is by anomalies. As a product of writing, the Holy Scripture also bears on its forehead the mark of the form of a servant.[5]

The Anglican theologian, L. S. Thorton, has argued very persuasively in his trilogy, *The Form of a Servant,*[6] that the form and the spirit of the incarnation is the form and spirit of revelation and therefore of Sacred Scripture. Just as the truth that Jesus is Lord should not blind us to his hunger, his thirst, his temptation, and his death, so the divine character of Scripture should not be embarrassed by the marks of humanity and humiliation which it bears. Both the divine Saviour and the divine Scriptures bear *the form of a servant* even though both contain within themselves the divine glory.

Inasmuch as revelation has this cosmic, sacramental, and anthropic form, it is also thereby *a mediated revelation*. That is to say, it comes through *specific* cosmic or anthropic entities. The normal pattern for revelation is not the exaltation of the prophet to heaven, but the condescension of revelation to the prophet on earth. Revelation does not burst the bands of man's creaturely existence but it respects this creaturely existence. Revelation honors it, adjusts itself to it, and bending down to it *mediates itself by it to the consciousness of man.*

A metaphor which would express the mixed character of revelation without some inaccuracy is difficult to find. However, one such faltering metaphor would be laminated wood. The top layer is the truth of God, and the bottom layer is the *cosmic-mediated form,* yet both layers are glued together so firmly they virtually make one piece of wood.

A dream, for example, is one of the cosmic, anthropic modes of revelation. Dreams are common experiences of men. But because dreams are common experiences they are drawn into the complex of revelation. The dream bears the structure of laminated wood. On the top side it carries the divine truth; on the bottom side it is a typical human experience. Yet the revelation-bearing dream forms a unity we cannot divide up without destroying its reality. Or to put it another way. By means of the dream special revelation *comes within the human orbit in an authentic manner*. But it is special revelation coming into the human orbit so that the dream carries this as a precious cargo.

Therefore we are not confronted with the dream-in-itself, as if dreams themselves had revelation-bearing powers. Nor are we confronted with revelation-in-itself, as if revelation could reach our consciousness separate from any medium. The dream becomes revelation-bearing when God in his grace so sanctifies it and uses it to this purpose; and the word of God in special revelation truly comes to us when God chooses to send it to us by the use of some cosmic conductor.

Because revelation is cosmic-mediated in structure, it does enter our world and does truly make a difference. Something is here which cannot be accounted for by the sum total of all things human. Myths and tales as such do not make a difference, for they may be accounted for *within* the sum total of human things. Revelation, on the contrary, comes into our orbit by virtue of the divine action. When God sanctifies some medium as the instrument of revelation, and thus *causes* revelation to occur—for example, as we just mentioned in the dream —a genuine difference is made in the on-going of human history. Unless there is this cosmic-mediated contact, unless there is this difference made by the divine action, there would be no authentic knowledge of God. Revelation would possess no meaning, no substance, no reality. Religion would be in every instance but another human conceptual scheme.[7]

There is no loss of truth because revelation has this cosmic-mediated form.[8] Admittedly the *whole* divine truth is not given to man, and what is given is seen in a mirror dimly (I Cor. 13:12). But according to the same text, *we do see!* The partial knowledge of God given in cosmic-mediated revelation, partially understood by the believer, is nevertheless sufficient for God's purposes. The cosmic-mediated revelation does mediate the word of God. The cosmic form does not inhibit the knowledge of God from "getting through." By virtue of God's power and God's grace the medium does mediate and the intentions of God are accomplished.[9]

(i) The first character, then, of special revelation as the divine condescension is that it is *anthropic*. By anthropic we mean that it is *marked by human characteristics throughout*. It speaks of the supersensible world (II Cor. 4:18) in the terms and analogies of our sensible world. The knowledge of God is framed in the language, concepts, metaphors, and analogies of men. The backdrop of revelation is earth and not heaven, and even when man is given a vision of heaven it is according to earthly analogies and figures. The anthropic character of revelation speaks of God's stooping down and humbling his revelation so that it enters our world and takes the shape and form of the human race.[10]

Professor Wright has properly noted that the fundamental images of Scripture are drawn from human society and not from nature.[11] From human society come such divine appellations as Lord, King, Judge, Shepherd, Father, and Husband. Also from human society come so many of the images of salvation—a ransoming, a purchasing, a delivering, a shepherding, a leading, etc. Such lists can be greatly extended but this is not necessary, for the point is fairly obvious that such matters as these reveal the anthropic character of revelation.

The anthropic character of revelation becomes most apparent in *anthropomorphisms*. Revelation speaks of God in terms of man's bodily parts (e.g., the arm of the Lord, the eye of the Lord, etc.) of man's mental life (e.g., God thinks or repents), or of man's spiritual nature (e.g., when it speaks of God's soul loathing something). Upon this subject Calvin has written with his usual brilliance:

> The Anthropomorphites also, who dreamed of a corporeal God, because mouth, ears, eyes, hands, and feet are often ascribed to him in Scripture, are easily refuted. For who is so devoid of intellect as not to understand that God, in so speaking, lisps with us as nurses are wont to do with little children? Such modes of expression, therefore, do not so much express what kind of being God is, as accommodate the knowledge of him to our feebleness. In doing so, he must of course stoop far below his proper height. . . . What then is meant by the term repentance

[of God]? The very same that is meant by the other forms of expression, by which God is described to us humanly. Because our weakness cannot reach his height, any description which we receive of him must be lowered to our capacity in order to be intelligible. And the mode of lowering is to represent him not as he really is, but as we conceive of him. Though he is incapable of every feeling or perturbation, he declares that he is angry with the wicked. Wherefore, as when we hear that God is angry, we ought not to imagine that there is any emotion in him, but ought rather to consider the mode of speech accommodated to our sense (I, xiii, 1; I, xvii, 13).[12]

These Scriptural anthropomorphisms represent one of the means by which the divine revelation bends down and touches human consciousness. They make the knowledge of God "picturable," i.e., imaginable and therefore assimilable. And what man can imagine and assimilate he can repeat in sermon or writing. The anthropomorphic "pictures" are not man's struggle to imagine deity, but they are one of the means whereby God "pictures" himself to man.

Anthropomorphisms must not be treated as crude or impure forms of revelation. Usually back of the attitude which considers anthropomorphisms as crude media of revelation is the belief that abstractions are the purest form of communication.[13] The difference between the anthropic and the anthropomorphic is one of degree and not of kind. The anthropomorphic is the extension of the anthropic to the end of the line. On the other hand, the abstraction is not as abstract as we might think. There is much metaphor even in our abstractions. What is supposedly gained in precision in the abstraction is always at the price of rich imagery. "God's omniscience and omnipotence secure his providential care of my life" does not quite reproduce, "The Lord is my shepherd, I shall not want."

Another very important aspect of the anthropic character of cosmic-mediated revelation is that *it takes the form of human language.* The Jewish rabbis rightly said that the Lord of heaven speaks with the tongues of men. Whatever revelation has to say, it says it in some specific language of men. If it came to Isaiah, it came in the form of Hebrew; if it came to Daniel, it came in Aramaic; and if it came to Paul, it came in Greek.

Older generations attempted to give Hebrew and Greek special status among the languages of men because they were called into the service of divine revelation. But this is not defensible in terms of the science of linguistics nor of the structure of special revelation. The important point from the perspective of special revelation is *that human languages are called into its service!* A caution must be raised here against the exaltation of the Hebrew and Greek. If we exalt the Hebrew then we must be prepared to account for the Aramaic in Daniel and the Greek in the New Testament. If we exalt the

Greek we might imply that only those who know the sacred Greek have saving faith.

A language brings the culture of the speaker along with it. It is unrealistic to think that language can be separated from culture. The relationship at this point is intimate, for the language "structures" the speaker's environment and the speaker's environment is "reflected" in the language. Thus as special revelation uses the Hebrew, Aramaic, and Greek languages it reflects the culture of the speakers and writers. We can accordingly infer from the language of Scripture the manner in which the Hebrews structured their physical environment, their social environment, their inner mental "geography," and their bodily parts. We can gather, for example, how the Hebrews structured the heavens, the plants, and the animals from the characteristics of the creation account. We would tell this story somewhat differently today.

But the appearance of the Hebrew cultural structures in the body of revelation is no cause for concern, but a point of strength. The *anthropic* character of special revelation calls not only language into its service, but the structures which the language reflects. *Special revelation uses the structures as well as the languages.* For example, the majesty and glory of an earthly king is the point of departure for speaking of the King of glory (Ps. 24:7-10). The rising of the morning sun dissipating the darkness with the brilliance of its rays is a faithful picture of the glory of God shining upon Israel (Isa. 60:1-3). The relationship of an earthly father to an earthly son is the analogy of the relationship of God to the redeemed (Heb. 12:7-11).

Inasmuch as revelation is cosmic-mediated, in that it is anthropic, in that it does employ the languages of men and thereby catches up the elements of man's total environment into its structure, *it possesses the power of genuine assertibility.* One of the standard objections to revelation is that because it comes from God it is like a stone thrown over a wall. It can have no possible meaning for us. It would be like Martians attempting to understand a football game. But this is a very unhappy analogy. God *adapts* his revelation to this cosmos; he *mediates* it at our level; he *gives* it an anthropic character suitable to our language and mentality. It is therefore *assimilable* by us, and what we can assimilate we can *assert.*

(ii) A second feature of the divine condescension of special revelation, and somewhat an extension of its anthropic character, is that special revelation is *analogical in form.*

The Christian faith affirms that God is incomprehensible and that the essence of dogmatics is mystery.[14] It further asserts that how God is in himself is inaccessible to man.[15]

Parallel to these assertions it boasts that God is known in Judah (Ps. 76:1). The bridge from the incomprehensibility of God to the knowability of God is the analogy. *An analogy is that conceptual device whereby something in one universe of discourse is employed to explain, illustrate, or prove something in another universe of discourse.*

The concept of analogy has a long and complex history, being used in mathematics, philosophy, law, literature, and philology. In special revelation we are not concerned with analogy as a mode of argumentation (logic, law); nor as a form of theological inference (as in the debate over a natural theology); *but as a literary device.* The process of noting similarities of all kinds is instinctive in human speaking. It is accordingly a universal phenomenon in literature. In this comprehensive sense analogy pertains to all forms or modes of comparison, and thus includes similes, metaphors, parables, allegories, types, and symbols.[16] The attempt to structure analogy too carefully at this point would be a failure to recognize the flexible and fluid character of human speaking and the spontaneous action of forming analogies.

In special revelation there are two universes of discourse: the knowledge which God has of himself, and man's knowledge of himself and his environment. In special revelation God chooses that element in *our* universe of discourse which can serve to convey the truth in *his* universe of discourse. God alone knows his own mind; he knows that which corresponds best to his truth in our universe of discourse; and thus in special revelation he gives us *relevant analogies.*

The authenticity of these biblical analogies is that they are drawn by God himself. Once again, their structure is not that of a human projection into the divine reality; but of God's sacramental use of our universe of discourse. They are not instances of man struggling to formulate a spiritual order out of the materials of his own experience. The human mind, to be sure, can do this![17] And it cannot be denied that Scripture may use some of these products! But the validity of the analogy (or symbol, or concept) does not derive from man's ingenuity but from the action of God in special revelation. To speak perhaps too intellectualistically, the analogies of special revelation are the divine projections into our conceptual life.

There are four aspects of the analogical character of special revelation which need more detailed exploration: (a) The analogies of Scripture are drawn by God.[18] This we have already asserted, but it needs to be asserted from another perspective. The possibilities for analogy in our environment are virtually infinite. Which analogies will advance the knowledge of God man cannot know of himself. Butler could spike the arguments of the deists by arguing within a circle of accepted analogies. But only God truly knows which analogies are most apt, and therefore only he can select the proper ones for his purposes.

(b) The analogies called into the service of special revelation do reflect the truth of God. They are vehicles of human language which are adequate to the intentions of revelation. They are *ectypes* (copies) of an *archetype* (model). The ectype is not a perfect representation of the archetype, but an adequate representation. We must not argue for an unrealistic perfection of the language of Scripture any more than we should be boxed in by a linguistic agnosticism. Reflective theologians have not hesitated to point out the partial and limited knowledge which we have in special revelation by virtue of the limitation of language. Ridderbos has written that the Scriptures come to us "written in human languages, under the sentence of our curse of the confusion of tongues, and which are, for yet other reasons, imperfect vehicles for the transmission of human thoughts, and, *a fortiori,* of divine thoughts."[19]

Although partial and enigmatic, this analogical revelation is knowledge. The writer of the *Wisdom of Solomon* said: "For by the greatness and beauty of the creatures proportionably (*analogos*) the Maker of them is seen" (13:5). By virtue of the analogy, *God is seen and known.* From the standpoint of logic there is a sufficiently univocal element of truth in the analogy so that the truth of God is adequately communicated.

We do not know God in himself. We know him in a cosmic-mediated, anthropic, and analogical revelation. But we do know him! The assertions of special revelation *do assert.* They do refer to a Reality. Within their own universe of discourse, and in terms of their own special characteristics, they do possess warranted assertibility.

(c) The variety of analogies in Scripture is great, and our vision must not be restricted at this point. The Scriptures call into service a vast number of resemblances, parallelisms, similes, and metaphors as well as symbols and types. As can be expected from the nature of poetry, the poetic passages of Scripture are heavily laden with analogies. Speaking of analogies Lecerf calls them "these most gracious and profound modalities." That is exactly what they are: means, instruments, modalities, by which God makes himself and his will known to Israel and the Church.

(d) The product of analogical revelation is a revelation of the nature and intentions of God which men of this world may comprehend. Revelation in this form is conceivable and imaginable. The analogical character of revelation informs us that revelation does not approach us with such purity that it would escape our human minds, but it approaches with such concreteness and earthiness that we are not left pondering the meaning of abstract or mystical symbols.

(iii) The very specific manner in which revelation comes to us in its cosmic-mediated form is by *modalities* (forms, media, instruments). These modalities are a further part of the divine condescension in revelation. Dreams, visions, or theophanies make clear to us the very real and direct contact which special revelation makes. These modalities are not in every instance unique to Christianity. The authenticity of these modalities is not that they necessarily in themselves are revelation-bearing, but because God uses them. In the divine condescension God in mercy and grace uses these modalities in the service of special revelation. As Berkouwer[20] states, God's sovereignty overcomes the earthly weakness of these forms so that they mediate a dependable knowledge of God.

The modalities of special revelation are the nerves or wires which directly conduct special revelation. Certainly these modalities are employed in connection with a concurrent action of the Holy Spirit. Illumination and faith run concurrently with the modalities in the experience of the prophet. When Moses stood before the burning bush and saw this unusual spectacle, there was at the same time a working of the Holy Spirit in his heart. Moses did not engage in a soliloquy about desert hallucinations. As in all instances of revelation and inspiration there is the accompanying inward work of the Holy Spirit—an insight we owe to Calvin's exploration of the witness of the Holy Spirit as not only a feature of individual salvation but as accompanying the giving of special revelation. The Holy Spirit is operative in all those events which form the substance of Scripture as well as in the formation of the Scriptures themselves.

Coming directly to these modalities we shall note some of more obvious modalities of Scripture.[21] (a) *The lot.* Decision by lot was used extensively in antiquity. In Israel, however, the lot was not used in a magical context but in a spiritual one ("The lot is cast into the lap, but the decision is wholly from the Lord," Prov. 16:33). It was the expectation that not fate but the sovereign Lord would rule in the casting of the lot. When the lot is used in the New Testament to reveal the will of God, it is sanctified for this use by prayer (Acts 1:21-26). As lowly as man of the twentieth century might regard the lot, it did serve in its humble way in the course of special revelation.

(b) *The Urim and Thummim.* There is a great obscurity about these two stones. They were used to make the will of God known in Israel, but how they did this is not clear. They are classed with the typical modalities of revelation (dreams and prophets) in I Samuel 28:6. Rowley is of the opinion that "they were two flat stones, one side of which was the auspicious side and the other the inauspicious, so that if they both fell with the same side upward the answer was given, while if they revealed different sides there was no answer. Be that as it may, the sacred lot provided a mechanical means of finding out the will of God, though its possibility of no answer meant that it was recognized that man could not compel God to answer."[22]

(c) *Deep sleep.* In Job 4:13 and 33:15 an unusually deep sleep is the precursor to dreams and visions. Kuyper notes how this mode of revelation more than any other separates man from his normal manner of existence. It renders the dreamer completely passive. It is more a matter of the dreamer being caught up into the world of revelation than of that world being lowered to him.[23]

(d) *The dream.* James Orr thinks that the dream is the lowest modality of special revelation,[24] but even so it is a genuine modality. Dreams occur in the service of revelation from Genesis to Acts. The redeemed and the unredeemed (Pharaoh, Nebuchadnezzar) experience them. In the dream the human mind is the screen upon which the divine revelation is reflected. Because the dream is part of the anthropic and mediated revelation the dreamer dreams within the schemata of his own culture and its symbols. The special revelation does not deliver a man out of his historical and cultural connections. Thus Joseph's dreams are Palestinian, Pharaoh's Egyptian, and Daniel's Mesopotamian.

The use of the dream is unusual in that it involves the divine control of the complex structure of the human mind. On the psychological side the dreamer is passive and thus a very proper recipient of a divinely given revelation. But any study of the dream from a psychological or symbolical perspective is not germane to special revelation, for in special revelation this rather ordinary experience is caught up into an extraordinary service. As with many modalities of special revelation, man enters the modality normally from his side, yet because God enters it from his side, it immediately takes on a supernatural aspect. Because God does enter the dream-modality from his side, the dream is a dependable modality in the service of divine revelation and the knowledge of God.

(e) *The vision.* The vision is a combination of the pictorial and the oral. It may occur in a dream, in ecstasy, or in a normal state (Isaiah calls his entire ministry a vision, Isa. 1:1). The prophetic ecstasy is not a pantheistic or mystical experience, for it arises out of complete absorption in the word of God. This is expressed by the prophet's "having the hand of the Lord upon him"—a strong figure of speech, referring to the sovereign activity of God.

There is a major difference between the dream and the vision: in the dream the emphasis is on what is *seen,* but in the vision the emphasis is on what is *heard.* This is underscored in Psalm 89:19, "Of old thou didst speak in a vision." Thus in and through the vision there is given the authentic speaking of the Lord.

(f) *Theophanies.* Even more remarkable are these unique manifestations of the divine Presence. They may be visitations of God in human form to man, or the rapturing of man to a vision of God. Of the former type the angel of the Lord is most representative. The concept has been the subject of considerable discussion.[25] From the perspective of special revelation it is one of the most remarkable modalities by which God reveals himself to man. The distance between God and man present in all special revelation becomes shorter. The human form itself becomes a modality of the divine revelation, and by virtue of this modality more of the precious substance of special revelation is conveyed to man.

In contrast to the modality of the angel of the Lord is the rapturous vision of God. Moses sees a token of the glory of God while in the cleft of the rock (Exod. 33); Isaiah sees the Lord of hosts upon a throne (Isa. 6); Ezekiel sees a most unusual vision of God in which the glory of God appears in the likeness of a man (Ezek. 1); Daniel sees the Ancient of Days (Dan. 7); and John sees the Father on his throne (Rev. 4). In each of these instances there are many symbolic elements, and in each instance the prophet or apostle never quite sees God. But in the vision and its complex symbolism is conveyed some authentic representation of the living God.

Among those phenomena which accompany some of these visions of God are lightning, thunder, clouds, voices, and fire. Of these the fire and the cloud are most important. Both play a very special role in the biblical representation of the presence of God. Mediating between these phenomena and the visions of God is the concept of the glory of God. It appears in the Pentateuch as a gleaming fire which is inside the pillar of fire and cloud but can be localized within the tabernacle (later, the temple). From this it becomes the radiance or light which surrounds God as the sign of his majestic presence, and then in the bold symbolism of Ezekiel the glory of God is represented in human form (Ezek. 1:26, 28).

God also uses signs to indicate either his nearness or his speaking. The Shekinah glory was of course the most real and most fearful sign of Yahweh's presence. But the voice of God from heaven at our Lord's baptism is also such a sign. The coming of the Holy Spirit was signified by the sound of a rushing wind, tongues of fire, and speaking in tongues by the apostles.

(g) *Angels*. Angels play a very important role in the history of special revelation. The most impressive aspect of the biblical teaching about them is that they form the mighty, glorious court of God. Involved in the concept of glory is both weight and *number*. Thus the glory of a forest lies in the *number* of its trees, and the glory of a nation lies in the *number* of its soldiers. Part of the presentation of the glory of God in Scripture, then, is that he is surrounded by a *numberless* host of beings glorious in themselves. This in itself is rich in its revelation-bearing value. The angels help us to understand the glory, majesty, splendor, and beauty of God. Without them we would lack one of the most profound biblical modalities for expressing the transcendence and majesty of God.

On the other hand angels are messengers, and they play a large role in this capacity in the history of special revelation. Their activities as the heavenly messengers stretch from Genesis through the great cosmic delineations of the Book of Revelation. Certainly as far as special revelation is concerned, the most impressive role assigned to them is the mediation of the Mosaic law (Acts 7:39; Gal. 3:19).[26]

The Importance of the Modalities

The modalities of special revelation are absolutely crucial to the concept of special revelation. The incomprehensible God can be known only in mediated knowledge. Pantheism confesses as much when it interprets the cosmos as a body whose soul is God. Religious liberalism admits as much when it asserts that man is such an analogue of God that his religious experiences ("feeling" in Schleiermacher, "valuation" in Ritschl, and "filial piety" in Sabatier) form a principle in the knowledge of God. In a very direct way the major traditions of Christian theology have maintained the necessity of these modalities.

In the past one hundred years or more, however, theologians under the pressure of anti-supernaturalism have depreciated the biblical modalities for a more "spiritual" type of modality. More than one of these modalities has been written off as a piece of typical religious superstition which can be found in any number of non-Judaic and non-Christion religions. In reply to the depreciation of these modalities and in their defense the following may be said:

(i) The Scriptures strenuously protest against all false or spurious use of the true modalities. There is an intensity of opposition throughout the Old Testament to the *false prophet*,[27] and a constant New Testament warning against false apostles and false teachers.[28] The human side of the modalities can be imitated by men who do not have the Spirit of God, and this counterfeiting does occur in both the Old and New Testament periods. *Therefore Scripture is especially severe with counterfeits of the true modalities.* The Old Testament does not hesitate to bring the death penalty upon false prophets (Deut. 18:20), and Paul urges an anathema upon the perverters of the gospel of Jesus Christ who pose as the true apostles (Gal. 1:6-9).[29]

That there were false prophets, that they were to be challenged and exposed, and that they were to be dealt with very harshly is apparent from such Scriptures as Isaiah 9:15, Jeremiah 14:4, 23:14-27, Ezekiel 13:4-22, and Micah 2:11. In Deuteronomy 18:21 the test for a false prophet is discussed.[30] The uniform charge against the false prophet is that *he lies*—he says that he has the word of God and speaks with the authority of God but he does not have either the word or the authority.

That there would be false teachers, false prophets, and false Christs in the Christian Church is taught in such passages as Matthew 7:15, 24:24, I John 4:1, II Peter 2:1, and II Corinthians 11:13. What is said of false prophets and false apostles also applies to false dreamers (Deut. 13:1), false seers (Jer. 23:16—"Thus says the Lord of hosts: 'Do not listen to the words of the prophets who prophesy to you, filling you with vain hopes; they speak visions of their own minds, *not from the mouth of the Lord.*'" (italics are mine), and false workers of wonders. That the serpent of Moses overcame the serpents of the magicians, and that Paul overpowered the miracle-workers and soothsayers of his day (e.g., Acts 13:6 ff., 16:1 ff., and 19:11 ff.) are in strict keeping with the biblical witness that there shall be no counterfeiting of the divine modalities.

(ii) There are not only strictures against the spurious employment of true modalities, but there are also unusually strong judgments against *the wrong kind of modality.* From the perspective of special revelation these false modalities are exceptionally wicked as they move in the opposite direction of the true modalities. They represent either human pride or unrestrained human curiosity or rebellion against the word of God. They are illegitimate modes of attempting to penetrate the divine mystery.

Augury, witchcraft,[31] traffic with familiar spirits, wizardry, divination, astrology, sorcery, necromancy, exorcism, and enchantment are all false modalities and in many instances are punishable by death (cf. Lev. 19:11; 20:6, 27; Isa. 8:19; Deut. 18:10). Although such a penalty appears harsh to us it must be remembered that: (a) these false modalities represent a wicked prying action of man replacing and displacing the sure word of God; and (b) their presence in the formative period of divine revelation is infinitely more damaging than after revelation is finished and preserved in written form. Certainly the New Testament allows only spiritual warfare and the destruction of arguments and not men (II Cor. 10:4-5). The judgment a man deserves is uniformly turned over to God (Gal. 1:6) and the strongest anathema John calls upon the preachers of a false gospel is that they be denied hospitality (II John 10). The great unmasking and judgment upon the false apostles, false prophets, and antichrists takes place in the eschatological drama at the end of the age.

(iii) Many critical scholars looked upon these modalities as typical religious phenomena common to many religions and as not a necessary part of the real substance of Scripture. These modalities were replaced by a mode or modes of communication which were supposedly more spiritual and more enlightened.

Certainly if the living God is known to man, He is known by some kind of modality. The robust doctrine of creation by the word of God as found in Scripture prevents the Christian faith from accepting any form of pantheism in which the world is a revelation of God by being the body of God. The knowledge of God in creation can be recovered only by the modalities of special revelation because these modalities correspond to both the creaturehood and sinnerhood of man. Although creation is recorded upon the first page of Scripture, the writer—a redeemed Israelite!—knew Yahweh first as Redeemer. The call of Abraham by the grace of God and the great exodus deliverance formed the two pillars of the theology and piety of Israel. Having learned of Yahweh as Redeemer, Israel was enabled to rediscover him as Creator.[32]

The critical spirit in modern theology finds itself antipathetic to the strong supernaturalism implicit in the modalities. It either rejects them outright or engages in such psychological explanations of them as to empty them of any real power to communicate the word of God. Accordingly the prophets cease to be men of the word of God (who spoke the *dabar* of Yahweh under the authority [*Auftrag*] of Yahweh)[33] and became men with unusual insights into personal religion, into the ethical quality of acceptable worship, and into principles of social justice.

When the real force of these modalities is broken, however, the possibility of an authentic knowledge of God is also broken. One cannot but agree with Barth's often repeated thesis that when religious liberalism renounced any version of the historic doctrine of revelation, it had no real criterion left whereby it could differentiate the voice of God from the voice of man. In many instances it simply identified the finest religious insights of man with revelation, and the ethical convictions of a refined gentleman with the divine imperative.[34]

Notes

[1]*Biblical Theology*, p. 31.

[2]*Principles of Sacred Theology*, p. 258.

[3]Kuyper, *op. cit.*, p. 219.

[4]*Church Dogmatics*, II/1, pp. 52-55. Barth also uses the expression *Welthaftigkeit*.

[5]*Op. cit.*, pp. 478-479. Italics are his.

[6]Cf. particularly his work, *Revelation and the Modern World*.

[7]Religion without the data or control of revelation is but human projection-schemes of the divine reality. Metaphysical schemes are also forms of projection-systems. Idealism or materialism are projection-schemes based upon some analogy or metaphor of life and language. Much of the contemporary objection to Christianity is that scholars consider it too to be a projection-scheme. To them Christianity postulates religious realities (God, the soul, immortality) which are incapable of any kind of verification. But revelation is no such projection. Rather, it is projection in reverse. It is the projection of the will and mind of God *into* our cosmos. Revelation is the language of man in the service of God by virtue of God's projection of his truth into our cosmos. Revelation is not disguised religious philosophy or religious metaphysics. Thus revelation makes a difference in our cosmos because it is a divine projection. Of course, we use the word "projection" simply to make this one point. The total structure of revelation is too complex to be summed up by the one word "projection."

[8]It was Butler's *Analogy of Religion* which set forth the Christian revelation as a "Universal Scheme Partially Understood." We must not, accordingly, overstate the case for revelation. Special revelation is no full-orbed system. It has a piecemeal character (cf. the adverbs of Heb. 1:1). It is an *authentic* and *sufficient* revelation for the intentions of God.

[9]Berkouwer (*General Revelation, ad loc.*) criticizes the manner in which Barth relates the media of revelation to the revelation itself. Barth permits a real cleavage between the media and the word of God. According to Berkouwer God sovereignly uses the media so that they convey an adequate and trustworthy word of God.

[10]Kuyper, *The Work of the Holy Spirit,* p. 62.

[11]G. E. Wright, *God Who Acts,* pp. 48-49.

[12]Cf. James Lindsay, "Anthropomorphism," ISBE, I, 152-154.

[13]Cf. Barth, *Church Dogmatics,* II/1, p. 222. It is refreshing to see how recent Old Testament scholarship shows a better insight into the character of anthropomorphisms. Cf. G. A. F. Knight, *A Christian Theology of the Old Testament,* pp. 20 f., 268 ff.; Paul Heinisch, *Theology of the Old Testament,* pp. 57-59; Th. C. Vriezen, *An Outline of Old Testament Theology,* pp. 129 ff.; E. Jacob, *Theology of the Old Testament,* p. 39. L. Köhler, *Old Testament Theology,* pp. 22-25. Köhler writes: "One realizes at this point the function of the anthropomorphisms. . . . the purpose of anthropomorphisms is to make God accessible to man. They hold open the door for encounter and controversy between God's will and man's will. They represent God as person. They avoid the error of presenting God as a careless and soulless abstract Idea or a fixed Principle standing over against man like a strong silent battlement. God is Person. . . . Through the anthropomorphisms of the Old Testament God stands before man as the personal and living God, who meets him with will and with works, who directs His will and His words towards men and draws near to men. God is the living God (Jer. 10:10)" (pp. 24-25).

[14]Bavinck, *The Doctrine of God,* p. 13.

[15]Lecerf, *An Introduction to Reformed Dogmatics,* p. 154. Michael Foster's *Mystery and Philosophy* is one of the few books in the present discussions about the language of philosophy which properly assesses the feature of mystery in dogmatics.

[16]Cf. W. O. Johnson, *Analogy and the Problem of God's Personality,* Lecture II, "Anthropomorphisms: Outmoded or Inevitable?"

[17]Such activities of man have been sketched out brilliantly by Edwyn Bevan in his *Symbolism and Belief.*

[18]Cf. Bavinck, *op. cit.,* chap. iii. Barth, *Church Dogmatics,* II/1, pp. 240 ff. Abraham Wolf, "Analogy," EB, I, 866-867. G. M. Sauvage, "Analogy," *The Catholic Encyclopedia,* I, 449-450. James J. Fox, "Anthropomorphism," *The Catholic Encyclopedia,* I, 558-559. Lecerf, *op. cit.,* pp. 150-170. G. C. Joyce, "Analogy," HERE, I, 415-419. Morton Smith indicates that Occam was the first one to see the logical problem in drawing analogies of God. Cf. "Analogy," *Dictionary of Theology,* p. 40.

[19]Cited by Lecerf, *op. cit.,* p. 165.

[20]*General Revelation,* p. 297.

[21]Berkouwer says that these modalities cannot be schematized (*op. cit.,* p. 109) although this certainly has been tried. The modalities are discussed in detail by Kuyper, *Principles of Sacred Theology,* pp. 481 ff.; Oepke, *TWNT,* III, 573; James Orr, *Revelation and Inspiration,* pp. 79 ff.;

G. Vos, *Biblical Theology*, pp. 83 ff.; Warfield, *The Inspiration and Authority of the Bible*, pp. 83 ff.

[22]*The Faith of Israel*, p. 29.

[23]*Principles of Sacred Theology*, p. 489.

[24]*Op. cit.*, p. 79. Cf. also Rowley, *op. cit.*, pp. 31 f. Vriezen, *An Outline of Old Testament Theology*, pp. 243 ff.

[25]Cf. Köhler, *op. cit.*, pp. 122-123. Knight, *op. cit.*, pp. 78-83. Heinisch *op cit.*, pp. 104-106. Jacob, *op. cit.*, pp. 75-77. Vriezen, *op. cit.*, pp. 247 f.

[26]Barth's unexpected and exceptionally thorough defense of the biblical doctrine of angels will be found in *Kirchliche Dogmatik*, III/3, pp. 426 ff.

[27]Cf. TWNT, VI, 807-808.

[28]TWNT, I, 446.

[29]Behm makes it clear that the *anathema* is not merely churchly excommunication but a judgment of God (*der Richterzorn Gottes*). *TWNT*, I, 356.

[30]Orr notes four tests for a prophet: (i) he must have a known character as a man of God; (ii) his word must be supported by its own internal power; (iii) the coherence of the prophets' utterances with the organism of revelation (i.e., any *dabar* of the prophet must concur with the *debarim* of the law); and (iv) fulfillment of his word (*Revelation and Inspiration*, pp. 95-96).

[31]The article by T. W. Davies ("Witch, Witchcraft," ISBE, V, 3097-3098) corrects much popular misapprehension about witches and witchcraft. He states among other things that "since the ideas we attach to 'witch' and 'witchcraft' were unknown in Bible times, the words have no right place in our English Bible" (p. 3097).

[32]Barth is vexed with both Roman Catholicism and religious liberalism for being guilty of the same fault; namely, they both attempt to work from the presuppositions of general revelation and in so doing surrender the priority of special revelation. Cf. *Church Dogmatics*, I/1, pp. 68 f., 218 ff.; I/2, pp. 12, 208 f., 227, 252, 290.

[33]Cf. the strong words of Vriezen, *op. cit.*, p. 258.

[34]Religious liberalism redefined revelation as religious insight, and located the power of the Bible in its ability to inspire men of all generations to the same pious experiences. The words of Coleridge have had a wide influence in religious liberalism and reveal its inmost spirit: "the words of the Bible find me in greater depths of my being; and that whatever finds me brings with it an irresistible evidence of its having proceeded from the Holy Spirit." Cited by H. D. McDonald, *Ideas of Revelation*, p. 173. Revelation thus comes through religious insight. Oman's thesis in *Vision and Authority* is that vision is authority. In all

of this the magisterial word of God is excluded and Barth's accusation that at bottom religious liberalism's theology is but religious anthropology is difficult to rebut. Barth uses Feuerbach rather effectively against the liberals. On the other side, the modalities of special revelation are the biblically sanctioned channels whereby the knowledge of God does come to us and without them we know less of God, not more.

De Wold attempts to do some fence-patching by incorporating mighty acts of salvation into his system (*The Case for Theology in Liberal Perspective,* p. 86), and the unique event (p. 57) but without anything genuinely supernatural (p. 43). But one simply cannot have it both ways.

The Inspiration of the Bible

15

Benjamin B. Warfield

The Biblical Idea of Inspiration

The word "inspire" and its derivatives seem to have come into Middle English from the French, and have been employed from the first (early in the fourteenth century) in a considerable number of significations, physical and metaphorical, secular and religious. The derivatives have been multiplied and their applications extended during the procession of the years, until they have acquired a very wide and varied use. Underlying all their use, however, is the constant implication of an influence from without, producing in its object movements and effects beyond its native, or at least its ordinary powers. The noun "inspiration," although already in use in the fourteenth century, seems not to occur in any but a theological sense until late in the sixteenth century. The specifically theological sense of all these terms is governed, of course, by their usage in Latin theology; and this rests ultimately on their employment in the Latin Bible. In the Vulgate Latin Bible the verb *inspiro* (Gen. 2:7; Wisd. 15:11; Ecclus. 4:12; II Tim. 3:16; II Peter 1:21) and the noun *inspiratio* (II Sam. 22:16; Job 32:8; Ps. 17:16; Acts 17:25) both occur four or five times in somewhat diverse applications. In the development of a theological nomenclature,

From Benjamin B. Warfield, *The Inspiration and Authority of the Bible*, Philadelphia: Presbyterian and Reformed Publishing Co., 1964.

however, they have acquired (along with other less frequent applications) a technical sense with reference to the Biblical writers or the Biblical books. The Biblical books are called inspired as the Divinely determined products of inspired men; the Biblical writers are called inspired as breathed into by the Holy Spirit, so that the product of their activities transcends human powers and becomes Divinely authoritative. Inspiration is, therefore, usually defined as a supernatural influence exerted on the sacred writers by the Spirit of God, by virtue of which their writings are given Divine trustworthiness.

Meanwhile, for English-speaking men, these terms have virtually ceased to be Biblical terms. They naturally passed from the Latin Vulgate into the English versions made from it (most fully into the Rheims-Douay: Job 32:8; Wisd. 15:11; Ecclus. 4:12; II Tim. 3:16; II Peter 1:21). But in the development of the English Bible they have found ever-decreasing place. In the English versions of the Apocrypha (both Authorized Version and Revised Version) "inspired" is retained in Wisd. 15:11; but in the canonical books the nominal form alone occurs in the Authorized Version and that only twice: Job 32:8, "But there is a spirit in man: and the inspiration of the Almighty giveth them understanding"; and II Tim. 3:16, "All scripture is given by inspiration of God, and is profitable for doctrine, for reproof, for correction, for instruction in righteousness." The Revised Version removes the former of these instances, substituting "breath" for "inspiration"; and alters the latter so as to read: "Every scripture inspired of God is also profitable for teaching, for reproof, for correction, for instruction which is in righteousness," with a marginal alternative in the form of, "Every scripture is inspired of God and profitable," etc. The word "inspiration" thus disappears from the English Bible, and the word "inspired" is left in it only once, and then, let it be added, by a distinct and even misleading mistranslation.

For the Greek word in this passage . . . *theopneustos* . . . very distinctly does not mean "inspired of God." This phrase is rather the rendering of the Latin, *divinitus inspirata,* restored from the Wyclif ("Al Scripture of God ynspyrid is . . .") and Rhemish ("All Scripture inspired of God is . . .") versions of the Vulgate. The Greek word does not even mean, as the Authorized Version translates it, "given by inspiration of God," although that rendering (inherited from Tindale: "All Scripture given by inspiration of God is . . ." and its successors; cf. Geneva: "The whole Scripture is given by inspiration of God and is . . .") has at least to say for itself that it is a somewhat clumsy, perhaps, but not misleading, paraphrase of the Greek term in the theological language of the day. The Greek term has, however, nothing to say of *in*spiring or of *in*spiration: it speaks only of a "spiring" or "spiration." What it says of Scripture is, not that it is "breathed into by God" or is the product of the Divine "inbreathing" into its human authors, but that it is breathed out by God, "God-breathed," the product of the creative breath of

God. In a word, what is declared by this fundamental passage is simply that the Scriptures are a Divine product, without any indication of how God has operated in producing them. No term could have been chosen, however, which would have more emphatically asserted the Divine production of Scripture than that which is here employed. The "breath of God" is in Scripture just the symbol of His almighty power, the bearer of His creative word. "By the word of Jehovah," we read in the significant parallel of Ps. 33:6, "were the heavens made, and all the host of them by the breath of his mouth." And it is particularly where the operations of God are energetic that this term (whether . . . *ruah,* or . . . *neshamah*) is employed to designate them—God's breath is the irresistible outflow of His power. When Paul declares, then, that "every scripture," or "all scripture" is the product of the Divine breath, "is God-breathed," he asserts with as much energy as he could employ that Scripture is the product of a specifically Divine operation.

(1) II Tim. 3:16: In the passage in which Paul makes this energetic assertion of the Divine origin of Scripture he is engaged in explaining the greatness of the advantages which Timothy had enjoyed for learning the saving truth of God. He had had good teachers; and from his very infancy he had been, by his knowledge of the Scriptures, made wise unto salvation through faith in Jesus Christ. The expression, "sacred writings," here employed (ver. 15), is a technical one, not found elsewhere in the New Testament, it is true, but occurring currently in Philo and Josephus to designate the body of authoritative books which constituted the Jewish "Law." It appears here anarthrously because it is set in contrast with the oral teaching which Timothy had enjoyed, as something still better, he had not only had good instructors, but also always "an open Bible," as we should say, in his hand. To enhance yet further the great advantage of the possession of these Sacred Scriptures the apostle adds now a sentence throwing their nature strongly up to view. They are of Divine origin and therefore of the highest value for all holy purposes.

There is room for some difference of opinion as to the exact construction of this declaration. Shall we render "Every Scripture" or "All Scripture"? Shall we render "Every [or all] Scripture is God-breathed and [therefore] profitable," or "Every [or all] Scripture, being God-breathed, is as well profitable"? No doubt both questions are interesting, but for the main matter now engaging our attention they are both indifferent. Whether Paul, looking back at the Sacred Scriptures he had just mentioned, makes the assertion he is about to add, of them distributively, of all their parts, or collectively, of their entire mass, is of no moment: to say that every part of these Sacred Scriptures is God-breathed and to say that the whole of these Sacred Scriptures is God-breathed, is, for the main matter, all one. Nor is the difference great between saying that they are in all their parts, or in their whole extent, God-breathed and therefore profitable, and saying that they are in all their parts, or in their whole extent, because God-breathed as well as profitable. In both cases these Sacred Scriptures are declared to owe their value to their Divine origin; and in both cases this their Divine origin is energetically asserted of their entire fabric. On the whole, the preferable construction would seem to be, "Every Scripture, seeing that it is God-breathed, is as well profitable." In that case, what the apostle asserts is that the Sacred Scriptures, in their every several passage—for it is just "passage of Scripture" which "Scripture" in this distributive use of it signifies—is the product of the creative breath of God, and, because of this its Divine origination, is of supreme value for all holy purposes.

It is to be observed that the apostle does not stop here to tell us either what particular books enter into the collection which he calls Sacred Scriptures, or by what precise operations God has produced them. Neither of these subjects entered into the matter he had at the moment in hand. It was the value of the Scriptures, and the source of that value in their Divine origin, which he required at the moment to assert; and these things he asserts, leaving to other occasions any further facts concerning them which it might be well to emphasize. It is also to be observed that the apostle does not tell us here everything for which the Scriptures are made valuable by their Divine origination. He speaks simply to the point immediately in hand, and reminds Timothy of the value which these Scriptures, by virtue of their Divine origin, have for the "man of God." Their spiritual power, as God-breathed, is all that he had occasion here to advert to. Whatever other qualities may accrue to them from their Divine origin, he leaves to other occasions to speak of.

(2) II Peter 1:19-21: What Paul tells here about the Divine origin of the Scriptures is enforced and extended by a striking passage in II Peter (1:19-21). Peter is assuring his readers that what had been made known to them of "the power and coming of our Lord Jesus Christ" did not rest on "cunningly devised fables." He offers them the testimony of eyewitnesses of Christ's glory. And then he intimates that they have better testimony than even that of eyewitnesses. "We have," says he, "the prophetic word" (English versions, unhappily, "the word of prophecy") : and this, he says, is "more sure," and therefore should certainly be heeded. He refers, of course, to the Scriptures. Of what other "prophetic word" could he, over against the testimony of the eyewitnesses of Christ's "excellent glory" (Authorized Version) say that "we have" it, that is, it is in our hands? And he proceeds at once to speak of it plainly as "Scriptural prophecy." You do well, he says, to pay heed to the prophetic word, because we know this first, that "every prophecy of scripture. . . ." It admits of more question, however, whether by this phrase he means the whole of Scripture, designated according to its character, as prophetic that is, of Divine origin; or only that portion of Scripture which we discriminate as particularly

prophetic, the immediate revelations contained in Scripture. The former is the more likely view inasmuch as the entirety of Scripture is elsewhere conceived and spoken of as prophetic. In that case, what Peter has to say of this "every prophecy of scripture"—the exact equivalent, it will be observed, in this case of Paul's "every scripture" (II Tim. 3:16) —applies to the whole of Scripture in all its parts. What he says of it is that it does not come "of private interpretation"; that is, it is not the result of human investigation into the nature of things, the product of its writers' own thinking. This is as much as to say it is of Divine gift. Accordingly, he proceeds at once to make this plain in a supporting clause which contains both the negative and the positive declaration: "For no prophecy ever came [margin "was brought"] by the will of man, but it was as borne by the Holy Spirit that men spoke from God." In this singularly precise and pregnant statement there are several things which require to be carefully observed. There is, first of all, the emphatic denial that prophecy—that is to say, on the hypothesis upon which we are working, Scripture—owes its origin to human initiative: "No prophecy ever was brought—'came' as the word used in the English version text, with 'was brought' in Revised Version margin—by the will of man." Then, there is the equally emphatic assertion that its source lies in God: it was spoken by men, indeed, but the men who spoke it "spake from God." And a remarkable clause is here inserted, and thrown forward in the sentence that stress may fall on it, which tells us how it could be that men, in speaking, should speak not from themselves, but from God: it was "as borne"—it is the same word which was rendered "was brought" above, and might possibly be rendered "brought" here—"by the Holy Spirit" that they spoke. Speaking thus under the determining influence of the Holy Spirit, the things they spoke were not from themselves, but from God.

Here is as direct an assertion of the Divine origin of Scripture as that of II Tim. 3:16. But there is more here than a simple assertion of the Divine origin of Scripture. We are advanced somewhat in our understanding of how God has produced the Scriptures. It was through the instrumentality of men who "spake from him." More specifically, it was through an operation of the Holy Ghost on these men which is described as "bearing" them. The term here used is a very specific one. It is not to be confounded with guiding, or directing, or controlling, or even leading in the full sense of that word. It goes beyond all such terms, in assigning the effect produced specifically to the active agent. What is "borne" is taken up by the "bearer," and conveyed by the "bearer's" power, not its own, to the "bearer's" goal, not its own. The men who spoke from God are here declared, therefore, to have been taken up by the Holy Spirit and brought by His power to the goal of His choosing. The things which they spoke under this operation of the Spirit were therefore His things, not theirs. And that is the reason which is assigned why "the prophetic word" is so sure. Though spoken through the instrumentality of men, it is, by virtue of the fact that these men spoke "as borne by the Holy Spirit," an immediately Divine word. It will be observed that the proximate stress is laid here, not on the spiritual value of Scripture (though that, too, is seen in the background), but on the Divine trustworthiness of Scripture. Because this is the way every prophecy of Scripture "has been brought," it affords a more sure basis of confidence than even the testimony of human eyewitnesses. Of course, if we do not understand by "the prophetic word" here the entirety of Scripture described, according to its character, as revelation, but only that element in Scripture which we call specifically prophecy, then it is directly only of that element in Scripture that these great declarations are made. In any event, however, they are made of the prophetic element in Scripture as written, which was the only form in which the readers of this Epistle possessed it, and which is the thing specifically intimated in the phrase "every prophecy *of scripture.*" These great declarations are made, therefore, at least of large tracts of Scripture; and if the entirety of Scripture is intended by the phrase "the prophetic word," they are made of the whole of Scripture.

(3) John 10:34 f.: How far the supreme trustworthiness of Scripture, thus asserted, extends may be conveyed to us by a passage in one of Our Lord's discourses recorded by John (John 10:34-35). The Jews, offended by Jesus' "making himself God," were in the act to stone Him, when He defended Himself thus: "Is it not written in your law, I said, Ye are gods? If he called them gods, unto whom the word of God came (and the scripture cannot be broken), say ye of him, whom the Father sanctified [margin "consecrated"] and sent into the world, Thou blasphemest; because I said, I am the Son of God?" It may be thought that this defence is inadequate. It certainly is incomplete: Jesus made Himself God (John 10:33) in a far higher sense than that in which "Ye are gods" was said of those "unto whom the word of God came": He had just declared in unmistakable terms, "I and the Father are one." But it was quite sufficient for the immediate end in view—to repel the technical charge of blasphemy based on His making Himself God: it is not blasphemy to call one God in any sense in which he may fitly receive that designation; and certainly if it is not blasphemy to call such men as those spoken of in the passage of Scripture adduced gods, because of their official functions, it cannot be blasphemy to call Him God whom the Father consecrated and sent into the world. The point for us to note, however, is merely that Jesus' defence takes the form of an appeal to Scripture; and it is important to observe how He makes this appeal. In the first place, He adduces the Scriptures as law: "Is it not written in your law?" He demands. The passage of Scripture which He adduces is not written in that portion of Scripture which was more specifically called "the Law," that is to say, the Pentateuch; nor in any portion of Scripture

of formally legal contents. It is written in the Book of Psalms; and in a particular psalm which is as far as possible from presenting the external characteristics of legal enactment (Ps. 82:6). When Jesus adduces this passage, then, as written in the "law" of the Jews, He does it, not because it stands in this psalm, but because it is a part of Scripture at large. In other words, He here ascribes legal authority to the entirety of Scripture, in accordance with a conception common enough among the Jews (cf. John 12:34), and finding expression in the New Testament occasionally, both on the lips of Jesus Himself, and in the writings of the apostles. Thus, on a later occasion (John 15:25), Jesus declares that it is written in the "law" of the Jews, "They hated me without a cause," a clause found in Ps. 35:19. And Paul assigns passages both from the Psalms and from Isaiah to "the Law" (I Cor. 14:21; Rom. 3:19), and can write such a sentence as this (Gal. 4:21 f.): "Tell me, ye that desire to be under the law, do ye not hear the law? For it is written . . ." quoting from the narrative of Genesis. We have seen that the entirety of Scripture was conceived as "prophecy"; we now see that the entirety of Scripture was also conceived as "law": these three terms, the law, prophecy, Scripture, were indeed, materially, strict synonyms, as our present passage itself advises us, by varying the formula of adduction in contiguous verses from "law" to "scripture." And what is thus implied in the manner in which Scripture is adduced, is immediately afterward spoken out in the most explicit language, because it forms an essential element in Our Lord's defence. It might have been enough to say simply, "Is it not written in your law?" But Our Lord, determined to drive His appeal to Scripture home, sharpens the point to the utmost by adding with the highest emphasis: "and the scripture cannot be broken." This is the reason why it is worth while to appeal to what is "written in the law," because "the scripture cannot be broken." The word "broken" here is the common one for breaking the law, or the Sabbath, or the like (John 5:18; 7:23; Matt. 5:19), and the meaning of the declaration is that it is impossible for the Scripture to be annulled, its authority to be withstood, or denied. The movement of thought is to the effect that, because it is impossible for the Scripture—the term is perfectly general and witnesses to the unitary character of Scripture (it is all, for the purpose in hand, of a piece)—to be withstood, therefore this particular Scripture which is cited must be taken as of irrefragable authority. What we have here is, therefore, the strongest possible assertion of the indefectible authority of Scripture; precisely what is true of Scripture is that it "cannot be broken." Now, what is the particular thing in Scripture, for the confirmation of which the indefectible authority of Scripture is thus invoked? It is one of its most casual clauses—more than that, the very form of its expression in one of its most casual clauses. This means, of course, that in the Saviour's view the indefectible authority of Scripture attaches to the very form of expression of its most casual clauses. It belongs to Scripture through and through, down to its most minute particulars, that it is of indefectible authority.

It is sometimes suggested, it is true, that Our Lord's argument here is an *argumentum ad hominem,* and that His words, therefore, express not His own view of the authority of Scripture, but that of His Jewish opponents. It will scarcely be denied that there is a vein of satire running through Our Lord's defence: that the Jews so readily allowed that corrupt judges might properly be called "gods," but could not endure that He whom the Father had consecrated and sent into the world should call Himself Son of God, was a somewhat pungent fact to throw up into such a high light. But the argument from Scripture is not *ad hominem* but *e concessu;* Scripture was common ground with Jesus and His opponents. If proof were needed for so obvious a fact, it would be supplied by the circumstance that this is not an isolated but a representative passage. The conception of Scripture thrown up into such clear view here supplies the ground of all Jesus' appeals to Scripture, and of all the appeals of the New Testament writers as well. Everywhere, to Him and to them alike, an appeal to Scripture is an appeal to an indefectible authority whose determination is final; both He and they make their appeal indifferently to every part of Scripture, to every element in Scripture, to its most incidental clauses as well as to its most fundamental principles, and to the very form of its expression. This attitude toward Scripture as an authoritative document is, indeed, already intimated by their constant designation of it by the name of Scripture, the Scriptures, that is "the Document," by way of eminence; and by their customary citation of it with the simple formula, "It is written." What is written in this document admits so little of questioning that its authoritativeness required no asserting, but might safely be taken for granted. Both modes of expression belong to the constantly illustrated habitudes of Our Lord's speech. The first words He is recorded as uttering after His manifestation to Israel were an appeal to the unquestionable authority of Scripture; to Satan's temptations He opposed no other weapon than the final "It is written"! (Matt. 4:4, 7, 10; Luke 4:4, 8). And among the last words which He spoke to His disciples before He was received up was a rebuke to them for not understanding that all things "which are written in the law of Moses, and the prophets, and psalms" concerning Him—that is (ver. 45) in the entire "Scriptures"—"must needs be" (very emphatic) "fulfilled" (Luke 24:44). "Thus it is written," says He (ver. 46), as rendering all doubt absurd. For, as He had explained earlier upon the same day (Luke 24:25 ff.), it argues only that one is "foolish and slow at heart" if he does not "believe in" (if his faith does not rest securely on, as on a firm foundation) "all" (without limit of subject-matter here) "that the prophets" (explained in ver. 27 as equivalent to "all the scriptures") "have spoken."

The necessity of the fulfilment of all that is written in Scripture, which is so strongly asserted in these last instructions to His disciples, is frequently adverted to by Our Lord. He repeatedly explains of occurrences occasionally happening that they have come to pass "that the scripture might be fulfilled" (Mark 14:49; John 13:18; 17:12; cf. 12:14; Mark 9:12, 13). On the basis of Scriptural declarations, therefore, He announces with confidence that given events will certainly occur: "All ye shall be offended (literally "scandalized") in me this night: *for* it is written . . ." (Matt. 26:31; Mark 14:27; cf. Luke 20:17). Although holding at His command ample means of escape, He bows before on-coming calamities, for, He asks, how otherwise "should the scriptures be fulfilled, that thus it must be?" (Matt. 26:54). It is not merely the two disciples with whom He talked on the way to Emmaus (Luke 24:25) whom He rebukes for not trusting themselves more perfectly to the teaching of Scripture. "Ye search the scriptures," He says to the Jews, in the classical passage (John 5:39), "because ye think that in them ye have eternal life; and these are they which bear witness of me; and ye will not come to me, that ye may have life!" These words surely were spoken more in sorrow than in scorn: there is no blame implied either for searching the Scriptures or for thinking that eternal life is to be found in Scripture; approval rather. What the Jews are blamed for is that they read with a veil lying upon their hearts which He would fain take away (II Cor. 3:15 f.). "Ye search the scriptures"—that is right: and "even you" (emphatic) "think to have eternal life in them"—that is right, too. But "it is these very Scriptures" (very emphatic) "which are bearing witness" (continuous process) "of me; and" (here is the marvel!) "ye will not come to me and have life!"—that you may, that is, reach the very end you have so properly in view in searching the Scriptures. Their failure is due, not to the Scriptures but to themselves, who read the Scriptures to such little purpose.

Quite similarly Our Lord often finds occasion to express wonder at the little effect to which Scripture had been read, not because it had been looked into too curiously, but because it had not been looked into earnestly enough, with sufficiently simple and robust trust in its every declaration. "Have ye not read even this scripture?" He demands, as He adduces Ps. 118 to show that the rejection of the Messiah was already intimated in Scripture (Mark 12:10; Matt. 21:42 varies the expression to the equivalent: "Did ye never read in the scriptures?"). And when the indignant Jews came to Him complaining of the Hosannas with which the children in the Temple were acclaiming Him, and demanding, "Hearest thou what these are saying?" He met them (Matt. 21:16) merely with, "Yea: did ye never read, Out of the mouths of babes and sucklings thou hast perfected praise?" The underlying thought of these passages is spoken out when He intimates that the source of all error in Divine things is just ignorance of the Scriptures: "Ye do err," He declares to His questioners, on an important occasion, "not knowing the scriptures" (Matt. 22:29); or, as it is put, perhaps more forcibly, in interrogative form, in its parallel in another Gospel: "Is it not for this cause that ye err, that ye know not the scriptures?" (Mark 12:24). Clearly, he who rightly knows the Scriptures does not err. The confidence with which Jesus rested on Scripture, in its every declaration, is further illustrated in a passage like Matt. 19:4. Certain Pharisees had come to Him with a question on divorce and He met them thus: "Have ye not read, that he who made them from the beginning made them male and female, and said, For this cause shall a man leave his father and mother, and shall cleave to his wife; and the two shall become one flesh? . . . What therefore God hath joined together, let not man put asunder." The point to be noted is the explicit reference of Gen. 2:24 to God as its author: *"He who made them . . .* said"; "what therefore *God* hath joined together." Yet this passage does not give us a saying of God's recorded in Scripture, but just the word of Scripture itself, and can be treated as a declaration of God's only on the hypothesis that all Scripture is a declaration of God's. The parallel in Mark (10:5 ff.) just as truly, though not as explicitly, assigns the passage to God as its author, citing it as authoritative law and speaking of its enactment as an act of God's. And it is interesting to observe in passing that Paul, having occasion to quote the same passage (I Cor. 6:16), also explicitly quotes it as a Divine word: "For, The twain, saith he, shall become one flesh"—the "he" here, in accordance with a usage to be noted later, meaning just "God."

Thus clear is it that Jesus' occasional adduction of Scripture as an authoritative document rests on an ascription of it to God as its author. His testimony is that whatever stands written in Scripture is a word of God. Nor can we evacuate this testimony of its force on the plea that it represents Jesus only in the days of His flesh, when He may be supposed to have reflected merely the opinions of His day and generation. The view of the Scripture He announces was, no doubt, the view of His day and generation as well as His own view. But there is no reason to doubt that it was held by Him, not because it was the current view, but because, in His Divine-human knowledge, He knew it to be true; for, even in His humiliation, He is the faithful and true witness. And in any event we should bear in mind that this was the view of the resurrected as well as of the humiliated Christ. It was after He had suffered and had risen again in the power of His Divine life that He pronounced those foolish and slow of heart who do not believe all that stands written in all the Scriptures (Luke 24:25); and that He laid down the simple "Thus it is written" as the sufficient ground of confident belief (Luke 24:46). Nor can we explain away Jesus' testimony to the Divine trustworthiness of Scripture by interpreting it as not His own, but that of His followers, placed on His lips in their reports of His words. Not only is it too constant, minute, intimate and in part incidental, and therefore, as it were, hidden, to admit of this interpretation; but it so pervades all our channels of information concerning Jesus' teaching as to make it certain that it comes actually from Him. It belongs not only to the Jesus of our evangelical records but as well to the Jesus of the earlier sources which underlie our evangelical records, as anyone may assure himself by observing the instances in which Jesus adduces the Scriptures as Divinely authoritative that are recorded in more than one of the Gospels (e.g. "It is written," Matt. 4:4, 7, 10 [Luke 4:4, 8, 10]; Matt. 11:10 [Luke 7:27]; Matt. 21:13 [Luke 19:46; Mark 11:17]; Matt. 26:31 [Mark 14:21]; "the scripture" or "the scriptures," Matt. 19:4 [Mark 10:9]; Matt. 21:42 [Mark 12:10; Luke 20:17]; Matt. 22:29 [Mark 12:24; Luke 20:37]; Matt. 26:56 [Mark 14:49; Luke 24:44]). These passages alone would suffice to make clear to us the testimony of Jesus to Scripture as in all its parts and declarations Divinely authoritative.

The attempt to attribute the testimony of Jesus to His followers has in its favor only the undeniable fact that the testimony of the writers of the New Testament is to precisely the same effect as His. They, too, cursorily speak of Scripture by that pregnant name and adduce it with the simple "It is written," with the implication that whatever stands written in it is Divinely authoritative. As Jesus' official life begins with this "It is written" (Matt. 4:4), so the evangelical proclamation begins with an "Even as it is written" (Mark 1:2); and as Jesus sought the justification of His work in a solemn "Thus it is written, that the Christ should suffer, and rise again from the dead the third day" (Luke 24:46 ff.), so the apostles solemnly justified the Gospel which they preached, detail after detail, by appeal to the Scriptures, "That Christ died for our sins according to the scriptures" and "That he hath been raised on the third day according to the scriptures" (I Cor. 15:3, 4, cf. Acts 8:35; 17:3; 26:22; and also Rom. 1:17; 3:4, 10; 4:17; 11:26; 14:11; I Cor. 1:19; 2:9; 3:19; 15:45; Gal. 3:10, 13; 4:22, 27). Wherever they carried the gospel it was as a gospel resting on Scripture that they proclaimed it (Acts 17:2; 18:24, 28); and they encouraged themselves to test its truth by the Scriptures (Acts 17:11). The holiness of life they inculcated, they based on Scriptural requirement (I Peter 1:16), and they commended the royal law of love which they taught by Scriptural sanction (James 2:8). Every detail of duty was supported by them by an appeal to Scripture (Acts 23:5; Rom. 12:19). The circumstances of their lives and the events occasionally occurring about them are referred to Scripture for their significance (Rom. 2:26; 8:36; 9:33; 11:8; 15:9, 21; II Cor. 4:13). As Our Lord declared that whatever was written in Scripture must needs be fulfilled (Matt. 26:54; Luke 22:37; 24:44), so His followers explained one of the most startling facts which had occurred in their experience by pointing out that "it was needful that the scripture should be fulfilled, which the Holy Spirit spake before by the mouth of David" (Acts 1:16). Here the ground of this constant appeal to Scripture, so that it is enough that a thing "is contained in scripture" (I Peter 2:6) for it to be of indefectible authority, is plainly enough declared: Scripture must needs be fulfilled, for what is contained in it is the declaration of the Holy Ghost through the human author. What Scripture says, God says; and accordingly we read such remarkable declarations as these: "For the scripture saith unto Pharaoh, For this very purpose did I raise thee up" (Rom. 9:17); "And the scripture, foreseeing that God would justify the Gentiles by faith, preached the gospel beforehand unto Abraham, . . . In thee shall all the nations be blessed" (Gal. 3:8). These are not instances of simple personification of Scripture, which is itself a sufficiently remarkable usage (Mark 15:28; John 7:38, 42; 19:37; Rom. 4:3; 10:11; 11:2; Gal. 4:30; I Tim. 5:18; James 2:23; 4:5 f.), vocal with the conviction expressed by James (4:5) that Scripture cannot speak in vain. They indicate a certain confusion in current speech between "Scripture" and "God," the outgrowth of a deep-seated conviction that the word of Scripture is the word of God. It was not "Scripture" that spoke to Pharaoh, or gave his great promise to Abraham, but God. But "Scripture" and "God" lay so close together in the minds of the writers of the New Testament that they could naturally speak of "Scripture" doing what Scripture records God as doing. It was, however, even more natural to them to speak casually of God saying what the Scriptures say; and accordingly we meet with forms of speech such as these: "Wherefore, even as the Holy Spirit saith, To-day if ye shall hear his voice," etc. (Heb. 3:7, quoting Ps. 95:7); "Thou art God . . . who by the mouth of thy servant David hast said, Why did the heathen rage," etc. (Acts 4:25 Authorized Version, quoting Ps. 2:1); "He that raised him from the dead . . . hath spoken on this wise, I will give you . . . because he saith also in another (place) . . ." (Acts 13:34, quoting Isa. 55:3 and Ps. 16:10), and the like. The words put into God's mouth in each case are not words of God recorded in the Scriptures, but just Scripture words in themselves. When we take the two classes of passages together, in the one of which the Scriptures are spoken of as God, while in the other God is spoken of as if He were the Scriptures, we may perceive how close the identification of the two was in the minds of the writers of the New Testament.

This identification is strikingly observable in certain catenae of quotations, in which there are brought together a number of passages of Scripture closely connected with one another. The first chapter of the Epistle to the Hebrews supplies an example. We may begin with ver. 5: "For unto which of the angels said he"—the subject being necessarily "God"—"at any time, Thou art my Son, this day have I begotten thee?"—the citation being from Ps. 2:7 and very appropriate in the mouth of God—"and again, I will be to him a Father, and he shall be to me a Son?"—from II Sam. 7:14, again a declaration of God's own—"And when he again bringeth in the first-born into the world he saith, And let all the angels of God worship him"—from Deut. 32:43, Septuagint, or Ps. 97:7, in neither of which is God the speaker—"And of the angels he saith, Who maketh his angels winds, and his ministers a flame of fire"—from Ps. 104:4, where again God is not the speaker but is spoken of in the third person—"but of the Son he saith, Thy throne, O God, etc."— from Ps. 45:6, 7 where again God is not the speaker, but is addressed —"And thou, Lord, in the beginning, etc."—from Ps. 102:25-27, where again God is not the speaker but is addressed—"But of which of the angels hath he said at any time, Sit thou on my right hand?" etc.—from Ps. 110:1, in which God is the speaker. Here we have passages in which God is the speaker and passages in which God is not the speaker, but is addressed or spoken of, indiscriminately assigned to God, because they all have it in common that they are words of Scripture, and as words of Scripture are words of God. Similarly in Rom. 15:9 ff. we have a series of citations the first of which is introduced by "as it is written," and the next two by "again he saith," and "again," and the last by "and again, Isaiah saith," the first being from Ps. 18:49; the second from Deut. 32:43; the third from Ps. 117:1; and the last from Isa. 11:10. Only the last (the only one here assigned to the human author) is a word of God in the text of the Old Testament.

This view of the Scriptures as a compact mass of words of God occasioned the formation of a designation for them by which this their character was explicitly expressed. This designation is "the sacred oracles," "the oracles of God." It occurs with extraordinary frequency in Philo, who very commonly refers to Scripture as "the sacred oracles" and cites its several passages as each an "oracle." Sharing, as they do, Philo's conception of the Scriptures as, in all their parts, a word of God, the New Testament writers naturally also speak of them under this designation. The classical passage is Rom. 3:2 (cf. Heb. 5:12; Acts 7:38). Here Paul begins an enumeration of the advantages which belonged to the chosen people above other nations; and, after declaring these advantages to have been great and numerous, he places first among them all their possessions of the Scriptures: "What advantage then hath the Jew? or what is the profit of circumcision? Much every way: first of all, that they were intrusted with the oracles of God." That by "the oracles of God" here are meant just the Holy Scriptures in their entirety, conceived as a direct Divine revelation, and not any portions of them, or elements in them more especially thought of as revelatory, is perfectly clear from the wide contemporary use of this designation in this sense by Philo, and is put beyond question by the presence in the New Testament of habitudes of speech which rest on and grow out of the conception of Scripture embodied in this term. From the point of view of this designation, Scripture is thought of as the living voice of God speaking in all its parts directly to the reader; and, accordingly, it is cited by some such formula as "it is said," and this mode of citing Scripture duly occurs as an alternative to "it is written" (Luke 4:12, replacing "it is written" in Matt.; Heb. 3:15; cf. Rom. 4:18). It is due also to this point of view that Scripture is cited, not as what God of the Holy Spirit "said," but what He "says," the present tense emphasizing the living voice of God speaking in Scriptures to the individual soul (Heb. 3:7; Acts 13:35; Heb. 1:7, 8, 10; Rom. 15:10). And especially there is due to it the peculiar usage by which Scripture is cited by the simple "saith," without expressed subject, the subject being too well understood, when Scripture is adduced, to require stating; for who could be the speaker of the words of Scripture but God only (Rom. 15:10; I Cor. 6:16; II Cor. 6:2; Gal. 3:16; Eph. 4:8; 5:14)? The analogies of this pregnant subjectless "saith" are very widespread. It was with it that the ancient Pythagoreans and Platonists and the mediaeval Aristotelians adduced each their master's teaching; it was with it that, in certain circles, the judgments of Hadrian's great jurist Salvius Julianus were cited; African stylists were even accustomed to refer by it to Sallust, their great model. There is a tendency, cropping out occasionally, in the Old Testament, to omit the name of God as superfluous, when He, as the great logical subject always in mind, would be easily understood (cf. Job 20:23; 21:17; Ps. 114:2; Lam. 4:22). So, too, when the New Testament writers quoted Scripture there was no need to say whose word it was: that lay beyond question in every mind. This usage, accordingly, is a specially striking intimation of the vivid sense which the New Testament writers had of the Divine origin of the Scriptures, and means that in citing them they were acutely conscious that they were citing immediate words of God. How completely the Scriptures were to them just the word of God may be illustrated by a passage like Gal. 3:16: "He saith not, And to seeds, as of many; but as of one, And to thy seed, which is Christ." We have seen Our Lord hanging an argument on the very words of Scripture (John 10:34); elsewhere His reasoning depends on the particular tense (Matt. 22:32) or word (Matt. 22:43) used in Scripture. Here Paul's argument rests similarly on a grammatical form. No doubt it is the grammatical form of the word which God is recorded as having spoken to Abraham that is in question. But Paul knows what grammatical form God employed in speaking to Abraham only as the Scriptures have transmitted it to him; and, as we have seen, in citing the words of God and the words of Scripture he was not accustomed to make any distinction between them. It is probably the Scriptural word as a Scriptural word, therefore, which he has here in mind: though, of course, it is possible that what he here witnesses to is rather the detailed trustworthiness of the Scriptural record than its direct divinity—if we can separate two things which apparently were not separated in Paul's mind. This much we can at least say without straining, that the designation of Scripture as "scripture" and its citation by the formula, "It is written," attest primarily its indefectible authority; the designation of it as "oracles" and the adduction of it by the formula, "It says," attest primarily its immediate divinity. Its authority rests on its divinity and its divinity expresses itself in its trustworthiness; and the New Testament writers in all their use of it treat it as what they declare it to be—a God-breathed document, which, because God-breathed, as through and through trustworthy in all its assertions, authoritative in all its declarations, and down to its last particular, the very word of God, His "oracles."

That the Scriptures are throughout a Divine book, created by the Divine energy and speaking in their every part with Divine authority directly to the heart of the readers, is the fundamental fact concerning them which is witnessed by Christ and the sacred writers to whom we owe the New Testament. But the strength and constancy with which they bear witness to this primary fact do not prevent their recognizing by the side of it that the Scriptures have come into being by the agency of men. It would be inexact to say that they recognize a human element in Scripture: they do not parcel Scripture out, assigning portions of it, or elements in it, respectively to God and man. In their view the whole of Scripture in all its parts and in all its elements, down to the least minutiae, in form of expression as well as in substance of teaching, is from God; but the whole of it has been given by God through the instrumentality of men. There is, therefore, in their view, not, indeed, a human element or ingredient in Scripture, and much less human divisions or sections of Scripture, but a human side or aspect to Scripture; and they do not fail to give full recognition to this human side or aspect. In one of the primary passages which has already been before us, their conception is given, if somewhat broad and very succinct, yet clear expression. No "prophecy," Peter tells us (II Peter 1:21), "ever came by the will of man; *but as borne by the Holy Ghost,* men spake from God." Here the whole initiative is assigned to God, and such complete control of the human agents that the product is truly God's work. The men who speak in this "prophecy of scripture" speak not of themselves or out of themselves, but from "God": they speak only as they are "borne by the Holy Ghost." But it is they, after all, who speak. Scripture is the product of man, but only of man speaking from God and under such a control of the Holy Spirit as that in their speaking they are "borne" by Him. The conception obviously is that the Scriptures have been given by the instrumentality of men; and this conception finds repeated incidental expression throughout the New Testament. It is this conception, for example, which is expressed when Our Lord, quoting Ps. 110, declares of its words that "David himself said in the Holy Spirit" (Mark 12:36). There is a certain emphasis here on the words being David's own words, which is due to the requirements of the argument Our Lord was conducting, but which none the less sincerely represents Our Lord's conception of their origin. They are David's own words which we find in Ps. 110, therefore; but they are David's own word, spoken not of his own motion merely, but "in the Holy Spirit," that is to say—we could not better paraphrase it—"as borne by the Holy Spirit." In other words, they are "God-breathed" words and therefore authoritative in a sense above what any words of David, not spoken in the Holy Spirit, could possibly be. Generalizing the matter, we may say that the words of Scripture are conceived by Our Lord and the New Testament writers as the words of their human authors when speaking "in the Holy Spirit," that is to say, by His initiative and under His controlling direction. The conception finds even more precise expression, perhaps, in such a statement as we find—it is Peter who is speaking and it is again a psalm which is cited—in Acts 1:16, "The Holy Spirit spake by the mouth of David." Here the Holy Spirit is adduced, of course, as the real author of what is said (and hence Peter's certainty that what is said will be fulfilled); but David's mouth is expressly designated as the instrument (it is the instrumental preposition that is used) by means of which the Holy Spirit speaks the Scripture in question. He does not speak save through David's mouth. Accordingly, in Acts 4:25, "the Lord that made the heaven and earth," acting by His Holy Spirit, is declared to have spoken another psalm "through the mouth of . . . David," His "servant"; and in Matt. 13:35 still another psalm is adduced as "spoken through the prophet" (cf. Matt. 2:5). In the very act of energetically asserting the Divine origin of Scripture the human instrumentality through which it is given is constantly recognized. The New Testament writers have, therefore, no difficulty in assigning Scripture to its human authors, or in discovering in Scripture traits due to its human authorship. They freely quote it by such simple formulae as these: "Moses saith" (Rom. 10:19); "Moses said" (Matt. 22:24; Mark 7:10; Acts 3:22); "Moses writeth" (Rom. 10:5); "Moses wrote" (Mark 12:19; Luke 20:28); "Isaiah . . . saith" (Rom. 10:20); "Isaiah said" (John 12:39); "Isaiah crieth" (Rom. 9:27); "Isaiah hath said before" (Rom. 9:29); "said Isaiah the prophet" (John 1:23); "did Isaiah prophesy" (Mark 7:6; Matt. 15:7); "David saith" (Luke 20:42; Acts 2:25; Rom. 11:9); "David said" (Mark 12:36). It is to be noted that when thus Scripture is adduced by the names of its human authors, it is a matter of complete indifference whether the words adduced are comments of these authors or direct words of God recorded by them. As the plainest words of the human authors are assigned to God as their real author, so the most express words of God, repeated by the Scriptural writers, are cited by the names of these human writers (Matt. 15:7; Mark 7:6; Rom. 10:5, 19, 20; cf. Mark 7:10 from the Decalogue). To say that "Moses" or "David says," is evidently thus only a way of saying that "Scripture says," which is the same as to say that "God says." Such modes of citing Scripture, accordingly, carry us little beyond merely connecting the name, or perhaps we may say the individuality, of the several writers with the portions of Scripture given through each. How it was given through them is left meanwhile, if not without suggestion, yet without specific explanation. We seem safe only in inferring this much: that the gift of Scripture through its human authors took place by a process much more intimate than can be expressed by the term "dictation," and that it took place in a process in which the control of the Holy Spirit was too complete and pervasive to permit the human qualities of the secondary authors in any way to condition the purity of the product as the word of God. The Scriptures, in other words, are conceived by the writers of the New Testament as through and through God's book, in every part expressive of His mind, given through men after a fashion which does no violence to their nature as men, and constitutes the book also men's book as well as God's, in every part expressive of the mind of its human authors.

16

James Orr

Revelation and Inspiration

The proposition may be laid down, that, if a revelation has been given, it is natural and reasonable to expect that a record will be made or kept of the stages of that revelation, either by its immediate recipients, or by those who stand within the circle of the revelation, and are possessed in an eminent degree of its Spirit. While the necessity of such a record, if revelation is not altogether to fail of its object, cannot of itself prove the existence of a code of sacred writings, it creates a presumption of their existence, and powerfully supports the claim of a body of Scriptures professing to satisfy this requirement, and actually presenting qualities answering to their claim.

I. Preliminary Positions

A first point in the above proposition is, that, if a revelation has been given by God, it is reasonable to expect that provision will be made for *the preservation* of the knowledge of the revelation *in some permanent and authoritative form*. Otherwise the object in giving the revelation would be frustrated. The means of the transmission of

From James Orr, *Revelation and Inspiration,* Grand Rapids: Wm. B. Eerdmans Co., 1952. Used by permission.

knowledge may be oral, so long as oral tradition, combined with careful instruction,[1] can be depended on; or it may be partly oral and partly documentary; or it may be documentary from the beginning. It may not be possible now to trace all the links in this process of transmission; but the product may bear in itself evidence that the result intended has been surely accomplished.

Other points assumed in this proposition are that the record of His revelation which God gives will be made either (1) by the *original recipients* of the revelations (e.g., the prophets wrote their own books, Paul his own Epistles, John his own Gospel); or (2) by those who *stand within the circle* of the *revelation* (e.g., Mark and Luke belonged to the immediate apostolic circle); and (3) that those who produce the record *possess in an eminent degree the Spirit of the revelation,* and are fitted by insight and sympathy to produce the kind of record that is required for the purposes in view.

A yet more fundamental assumption underlying the proposition is, that there is, and has been from the beginning, *a Holy Spirit* in the community of believers who can and does confer these qualifications. The denial of the Holy Spirit in the community of God's people may fitly be described as *the primal heresy*—the heresy of all heresies— in the Christian Church. Scripture assumes as axiomatic a presence and work of the Spirit from its first page to its last.

II. Extension of the Idea of Revelation

When the question is raised of the relation of revelation to its record, it is first to be noted that *an important extension* must be made of the idea of revelation—an extension carrying us much beyond the scope of the previous discussion. This in several respects.

1. It is obvious that the word must here be taken as including, not only direct divine acts and communications, but *the whole divinely-guided history* of the people of Israel, and, in the New Testament, *the apostolic action* in the founding of the Church. Here again the principle of the co-operation of divine providence with revelation for the subserving of the ends of the latter finds application.[2] To providence must be entrusted the securing and preserving of such materials as are necessary for a proper presentation of the history. These materials need not be the work of inspired men, but may come through the ordinary channels of information—may consist of traditions, monuments, state records, genealogies, etc., as well as written narratives. Inspiration is seen in the use made of these materials, not in the providing of them.

2. A further step is taken when it is observed that revelation ("unveiling"), in this wider sense, must be held to include the *insight* given by the divine Spirit into the *meaning* of the history, through which holy men are enabled to write it for the instruction of all ages.[3]

It is analogous to, though, as befitted their special task, a higher degree of, that "Spirit of wisdom and revelation" in the knowledge of Christ which is bestowed on all Christians[4]—a form of the revelation of *illumination* applied to the laws and workings of God's providence in the accomplishing of the ends of His kingdom. The prophetic insight is of necessity much deeper than that of the ordinary believer, because it is *prophetic*—a special endowment of the Spirit of revelation for a special end.

3. It is, however, not simply the history of revelation on its *divine* side which is of spiritual interest, but the *human reception* also of that revelation, and the *actings of the human spirit* under its influence, and in response to it, which are to be taken into account. This also is a necessary part of the unfolding of the meaning of revelation. In other words, there is needed, in a book which is to be the record of divine revelation, not only the record of what may be called its *external* historical course, but the record of its *internal* history in the life and experience of souls that have grasped its meaning, and felt its power. What, for instance, would the record of revelation be in the Old Testament without the Book of Psalms?

It begins to be evident that a record of revelation in the broad sense includes a great deal more than the divine acts and communication, or even the history, with which we began. It includes psalms, songs, wisdom-teaching, Epistles,—records of human doubt, struggle, temptation, victory,—sections which unfold the *principles* of revelation, apply and enforce them, turn them into subjects of praise, deal with them reflectively as doctrine. All this, too, in a very important sense, is revelation. A very weighty conclusion follows. We began rightly by distinguishing between revelation and the record of revelation. There is an important truth in that distinction, for it marks the fact that there is an objective revelation in divine acts and words prior to any written record. But we have now found that the line between revelation and its record is becoming very thin, and that, in another true sense, *the record,* in the fulness of its contents, *is itself for us the revelation.* There are parts of the revelation—some of the prophetic discourses, e.g., or the Epistles—which never existed in any but written form. But the record as a whole is the revelation—God's complete word—for us. Its sufficiency is implied in the fact that beyond it we do not need to travel to find *God's whole will* for our salvation.

III. Inspiration—the Biblical Conception

We are thus brought to the particular consideration of the much-debated subject of *inspiration*—a subject in the treatment of which, all will allow, peculiar difficulties emerge.

Two methods present themselves in dealing with this subject.

1. We might analyse, as has often been done, the *testimony of Scripture* to its own inspiration, then proceed to inquire how far the facts agree with this testimony. Or—

2. We may begin with *the facts* which illustrate the *nature* of inspiration, as seen in the book itself, then endeavour to show how this agrees with the witness of Scripture to itself.

For the end at present in view the latter is the preferable course. It assumes nothing, and is not open to the objection of forcing the phenomena of Scripture into harmony with any preconceived theory. Still, some indication of the general view taken of inspiration by the Biblical writers cannot be wholly omitted. It may surprise those who have not looked into the subject with care to discover how strong, full, and pervasive, the testimony of Scripture to its own inspiration is. Meanwhile it may suffice to recall the summary which the apostle gives of the qualities imparted by inspiration to Scripture in what may be called the *classical* passage on the subject—that, viz., in II Tim. 3:15-17.

Comparing this passage as it stands in the Authorized Version with the form it has in the Revised Version, it will be observed that certain important changes are made in the latter.

1. In verse 15, the words "Holy Scriptures" are more correctly translated "sacred writings." The terms (*ta hiera grammata*) are different from those used in ver. 16, "every Scripture" (*pasa graphē*). The verse then reads: "That from a babe thou hast known the sacred writings which are able to make thee wise unto salvation through faith which is in Christ Jesus."

2. Instead of the translation, "All Scripture is given by inspiration of God, and is profitable," etc. the alternative rendering is preferred: "Every Scripture inspired of God is also profitable," etc. The R.V. margin, however, retains: "Every Scripture is inspired of God, and profitable," etc. On this it is to be remarked that, whichever form is adopted, the sense is not essentially altered. The form "Every Scripture inspired of God is also profitable" may be a broader, but it is certain that it is not intended to be a *narrower,* form of statement than the other. The apostle assuredly does not mean to draw a distinction between a Scripture which is inspired, and a Scripture which is not inspired, or to suggest that any of the "sacred writings" of the previous verse fall into the latter category.[5] Such an idea is totally foreign to his thought. What he plainly means is that "every Scripture," as being inspired (*theopneustos*), is also profitable.

3. That for which inspired Scripture is "profitable" is thus described: "For teaching, for reproof, for correction, for instruction in righteousness; that the man of God may be complete, furnished completely unto every good work."

The doctrine of the passage, then, may be thus briefly summed up:—

(1) There is a collection of "sacred writings" which Timothy had known from his childhood. These are, it need hardly be said, the Old Testament Scriptures.

(2) The contents of these books were able to make wise unto salvation through faith in Jesus Christ. To Him they pointed; in Him they were fulfilled; in the light of His appearance and salvation they were now read.

(3) The Scriptures included in this collection were "God-inspired" —more broadly, "every Scripture," which *may* include a Gospel like Luke's (cf. I Tim. 5:18), or even Paul's own Epistles (cf. II Peter 3:15).

(4) As having this character, the Scriptures were profitable for teaching, etc., and had as their end "that the man of God may be complete, furnished completely unto every good work." There is no want of the spiritual life which they did not meet.

Paul, it will be observed, does not give any description of the *nature* or *degree* of the inspiration he attributes to the Old Testament (or other) Scriptures. He does not, e.g., say that it secured verbal inerrancy in ordinary historical, geographical, chronological, or scientific matters. But (1) it seems at least clearly implied that there was no error which could interfere with or nullify the utility of Scripture for the ends specified; and (2) the qualities which inspiration is said to impart to Scripture, rendering it profitable in so great and rich a degree, make it clear that the inspiration itself was of a high and exceptional kind.

IV. Inspiration and the Record

A. The Person

With these general determinations in view, we now proceed to an examination of the *fact* of inspiration as that meets us in the actual phenomena of Scripture. The chief question which invites attention here is the *general relation to inspiration of its record*. The nature of this relation has already been indicated in speaking of the record of revelation as made, either by the original recipients of the revelation, or by those who stood within the circle of revelation, and were possessed in a special degree of its Spirit. The subject must now be more closely investigated.

A first question arises as to the relation of the *inspired person* to the record. Scripture is spoken of as "God-inspired"; but it is important to notice that inspiration belongs primarily to the *person,* and to the *book* only as it is the product of the inspired person. There is no inspiration inhering literally in the paper, ink, or type, of the sacred volume. The inspiration was in the soul of the writer; the qualities that are communicated to the writing had their seat first in the mind or heart of the man who wrote. It is on the mind, heart, faculties of the *man* that the Spirit works: the work is inspired as coming from his thought and pen, and as having the power of quick-ening and awakening a like glow of soul in those who read. This is seen very clearly in considering the inspiration of *genius,* as it appears, e.g., in the works of a Shakespeare, a Milton, or a Goethe. The in-spiration in these cases is in the souls of the men, and only deriva-tively in their writings.

B. Materials of the Record

A more difficult question arises with respect to the relation of in-spiration to the *materials* of the record. It is not uncommon to hear inspiration spoken of as if it rendered the subject of it superior to ordinary sources of information, or at least was at hand to supply supernaturally all gaps or deficiencies in that information. The records of the Bible have only to be studied as they lie before us to show that this is an entire mistake. It was said above that it is reasonable to expect that, if God has given a revelation, He will provide for the knowledge of that revelation being preserved, and handed down in its purity. The facts warrant us in saying that this has been actu-ally done. But this, as has likewise been pointed out, and as the most conservative writers will admit, is the work of *providence* rather than of inspiration. Inspiration does not in any case create the fact-ma-terials it works with. It works with the materials it has received. Its presence reveals itself in the use it makes of the materials, and in the insight it shows into their meaning. This will be seen by looking more carefully at the nature of these materials.

1. In *historical* matters it is evident that inspiration is dependent for its knowledge of facts on the ordinary channels of information— on older documents, on oral tradition, on public registers, on genea-logical lists, etc. No sober-minded defender of inspiration would now think of denying this proposition. One has only to look into the Biblical books to discover the abundant proof of it. The claim made is that the sources of information are *good,* trustworthy, not that inspiration lifts the writer above the need of dependence on them. In the Old Testament, for instance, reference is constantly made to older or contemporary writings as authorities for the information given as to the acts of the various kings. Thus, for the history of David, reference is made to three works—the Book of Samuel the Seer, the Book of Nathan the Prophet, the Book of Gad the Seer.[6] For numerous reigns extracts are given from "the Book of the Chron-icles of the Kings of Israel"[7] (or "of the Kings of Judah," or "of the Kings of Israel and Judah"). The Books of Ezra and Nehemiah em-body genealogies (thus also Chronicles), letters of Persian kings, and other documents.[8] The Gospel of Luke, in the New Testament, explains distinctly the manner in which that book was composed, viz., by accurate research into those things which had been delivered to the Church by first-hand witnesses. "Forasmuch," says the evangelist,

"as many have taken in hand to draw up a narrative concerning those matters which have been fulfilled among us, even as they delivered them unto us, who from the beginning were eyewitnesses and ministers of the word, it seemed good to me also, having traced the course of all things accurately from the first, to write unto thee in order, most excellent Theophilus, that thou mightest know the certainty concerning the things wherein thou wast instructed."[9] Where sources of information fail, or where, as may sometimes happen, there are *lacunae,* or blots, or misreadings of names, or errors of transciption, such as are incidental to the transmission of all MSS., it is not to be supposed that supernatural information is granted to supply the lack.[10] Where this is frankly acknowledged, inspiration is cleared from a great many of the difficulties which misapprehension has attached to it.

2. This principle applies not only to historic, but to *prehistoric* times, where written records altogether fail. It does not follow that a sound tradition in essential things may not have been preserved from the beginning. On the Biblical representation of man's origin and relation to God, and of a line of blessing from the earliest age, it may be presumed that it would be. But that tradition will necessarily differ in character from the tradition of historical times, when language, arts, and letters are in some degree developed. It will be couched in part in the forms of thought and speech characteristic of the childhood of the world. As the hieroglyphic precedes alphabetic writing, so the media of transmission of the knowledge of events will be of necessity poetical, symbolical, pictorial, imaginative. This is to be distinguished from "myth," which is a pure creation of the imagination, and not the medium of the knowledge of an actual transaction. The example in Scripture is the early chapters of Genesis. The theory at present prevailing, that these chapters—the story of creation and paradise, antediluvian lists, flood, etc.—are based on Babylonian myths, appropriated and purified by the spirit of revelation in Israel, falls below the mark of dignity in the narratives. It is truer to regard them as the embodiments of the earliest and most precious traditions of the race, in the purer form in which they descended through the ancestors of the Hebrew people. They may, however, be ancient, and yet bear traces of transmission in a more or less allegorical or symbolical form. Few, e.g., will be disposed to take literally the account of the making of Eve out of the rib taken from Adam's side while he slept.[11] The story of the Fall, again, may well be the account of an actual historical catastrophe in the commencement of the race, in its cradle in the region of the Tigris and Euphrates.[12] Truths of eternal moment may be enshrined, it is believed are, in its simple narrative. Yet, with many of the most devout expounders of the story, we can hardly err in seeing symbolical elements, or an allegorical dress, in the features of the serpent, the

trees, the cherubim. The cherubim, throughout Scripture, are *ideal* figures.[13] While, again, remarkable longevity may have been, and probably was, characteristic of the oldest race of men, there is, even in the most conservative circles, a growing consensus of opinion that the early genealogies cannot be interpreted with modern literality—that chronology demands an extensive lengthening of the pre-Abrahamic period, and that the names given in the lists stand rather for representatives of tribes, or clans, or for heads of families, than for individuals.[14] The genealogies also are obviously reduced to a technical scheme in which many links may be omitted. These chapters, nevertheless, embody valuable ancient material, picturing the earliest age of humanity, and conveying profound truths, which inspiration can appropriate, and utilise for its own ends.

The words of Herder on these early chapters of Genesis may here be recalled. "This is a wonder," he says, "to which the worshippers of reason have not yet given a name—the story of the fall of the first man. Is it allegory—history—fable? And yet there it stands, following the account of the Creation, one of the pillars of Hercules, beyond which there is nothing—the point from which all succeeding history starts. . . . And yet, ye dear, most ancient and undying traditions of my race—ye are the very kernel and germ of its most hidden history. Without you, mankind would be, what so many other things are—a book without a title, without the first leaves and introduction. With you our race receives a foundation, a stem and root, even in God and in father Adam."[15]

This principle applies, finally, to the relations of inspiration to *scientific* knowledge. The Bible is not, nor was ever intended to be, an anticipative text-book of science. This is evident on the face of it. Where natural phenomena are described, it is as they appear to the natural observer. There is no pretence of acquaintance with our modern astronomy, geology, physics, or biology; or with modern scientific classifications of plants and animals. The standpoint is religious—the creation of the world by God, its dependence on Him, His universal activity in it and providence over it. These conceptions stand on a distinct footing from details of science. They have their origin in no source lower than revelation, and carry in them already the outlines of a cosmogony such as we have in the opening chapter of Genesis. If there is so little real conflict—one would rather say so remarkable a harmony—between the Biblical representations and science, it is because the Bible, at the outset, has got the right *standpoint* for the contemplation and interpretation of nature—the true key for the unlocking of its riddle. Without seeking a visional or other special origin for the narrative in Genesis, this at least may be asserted: that the sublimity, freedom from mythology, monotheism, and general agreement with scientific truth of the Genesis account puts it on a totally different plane from all heathen cosmogonies. It is related to the Babylonian myth by contrast rather than by resemblance.

C. Literary Form of the Record

A last question relates to the relation of inspiration to *the literary form* of the record. The chief point to be laid stress on here, in opposition to mechanical views of inspiration—now, however, seldom entertained—is, that inspiration does not annul any power or faculty of the human soul, but raises all powers to their highest activity, and stimulates them to their freest exercise. It is not an influence acting on the soul as a passive instrument, as a player might draw music from a harp, but a life imparted to the soul which quickens it to its finest issues. It follows that there is no form of literature capable of being employed by the genius of man which inspiration cannot employ as its medium. Every one recognises this to some extent in the variety of styles and forms of composition in the Bible. We have in its pages historical narrative and biography; poetry in psalm, hymn, song; gnomic wisdom in proverbs; didactic and doctrinal composition in the epistles; hortatory discourses and appeals; parable and allegory; apocalyptic vision. Each writer in these departments has his own style and idiosyncrasies of thought and treatment. His genius is enkindled, not suppressed, by the power of the Holy Spirit inspiring him.

This principle of the free use by the Spirit of every form of literature will, in the main, be accepted by all; and hesitation need not be felt in carrying out the principle to its fullest extent. Some have scrupled to admit this.

1. There is the form of *drama*. Job, e.g., is a great dramatic poem; one of the grandest in literature. It turns, on the human side, on the possibility of disinterested piety; on the divine side, on the vindication of the divine righteousness and goodness in the permission of the sufferings of the righteous. Its plan is carried through in a prologue, setting forth the theme of the Book; in dialogues between Job and his friends, in the noblest style of poetry; and in an epilogue, restoring the union of virtue and happiness in the return of Job's prosperity. Inspiration could not have found a nobler medium for the inculcation of its lesson; yet some have shrunk from admitting the dramatic form of the work, lest it should detract from the truthfulness of its contents. One has only to ask—How could an accurate report of these long, sustained discourses be obtained or preserved? to see the untenableness of the opposite supposition.

2. There is, again, the form of composition which consists in presenting a theme in *the dress of a speech or treatise* of some person of repute. Few, probably, will dispute that this is a legitimate mode of composition, if used simply as a literary form, without attempt

to deceive. As such it is often employed in ordinary literature. No one, e.g., objects to such a work as Landor's *Imaginary Conversations*. Where, on the other hand, there is a deliberate attempt to deceive by passing off one man's work as the production of another, as in Macpherson's *Ossian,* the practice is condemned. It is "forgery." The same principle must be applied in judging of Holy Scripture. If a writing is intended to deceive, there is psuedonymity in the bad sense, and this, one cannot but judge, the Spirit of inspiration must exclude. Simply as a form of literary composition no legitimate exception can be taken to it. Critics as conservative in tendency as Hengstenberg and Keil, e.g., admit this to be the character of the Book of Ecclesiastes. The Book is a didactic work composed in the name of Solomon. Most modern critics regard the Book of Deuteronomy as either a free literary composition of this kind, or at least a free reproduction of speeches traditionally attributed to Moses. Many things, however, have to be taken into account before this can, to the extent claimed, be conceded: the testimony of the Book itself, the archaic character of its content, the circumstances of its discovery, its unequivocal acceptance as a Book of Moses in the age of Josiah.[16] Many who take this view frankly stamp the Book as a pseudograph. This would, on the principle here stated, be fatal to its inspiration. It is sounder to argue that the manifest inspiration of the Book affords warrant for the rejection of the theory of its fraudulent character.[17]

3. Under this principle of dramatic representation may be brought the *didactic expansions* of speeches, as in the Books of Chronicles—the speech of Abijah,[18] for example—where the homiletic aim of the book has to be considered. In modern preaching on the characters and events of the Bible the same thing is continually witnessed. Scenes are depicted; and the thoughts, feelings, and supposed actions of the persons are dramatically exhibited.[19] The genius of the Hebrew language in using direct speech ("He said," "Then answered they," etc.), where a modern would use the indirect form (*oratio obliqua*), not professing to give the exact words, contributed to this form of composition. Especially is this dramatic form of narration inevitable in matters handed down by oral tradition, and acquiring a particular form by repeated telling. There is no more charming idyll than the story of the meeting of Abraham's servant with Rebekah in Gen. 24. But certainly there was no stenographer at the wellmouth or in Laban's house to take down *verbatim* reports of the conversations between the parties. This does not militate against the exquisite literary form, or essential truth, of the narrative, but it means that the form in which it reached the narrator was that which it had acquired in long-preserved tradition. Still less can it be claimed that *verbatim* reports are preserved of conversations in Eden, or from days before the Flood. The *substance* belongs to antiquity; the form is that assumed in traditional transmission.

4. Another literary form frequently used in Scripture—pre-eminently in the discourses of Jesus—is *parable,* and, as before seen, commentators are not a little exercised as to whether some of the descriptions in the prophets—e.g., Hos. 1.—given in the form of narrative, are not really parabolic or visionary. Many modern interpreters maintain that the Book of Jonah, with its story of "the great fish," is really, and in design, a parabolic work. Without questioning that parable is, for prophetic purposes, an admissible form of teaching, one would like to feel surer that the application of the principle in this case is not simply a way of escaping from a felt difficulty in the contents of the Book. The Book of Jonah teaches certainly the loving regard of God for the heathen, but it is in no way clear that the Book is intended as a parable to teach this lesson; still less that the fish incident is an allegory of the swallowing up of Israel by heathenism, etc. Chap. 2 apart, the Book—entirely different in cast from the Jewish "Haggada"—reads like a piece of serious history, and is, so far as one can see, meant to be so accepted. There is a verisimilitude in the account of Jonah's preaching in Ninevah which forbids its rejection off-hand as fiction. Chap. 1:17; 2:10 has a different character, and *may* be emblematic of some deliverance, the exact nature of which was not known, but the memory of which is preserved in the verses of the psalm (2:1-9). But many will feel that they could accept even the difficulty of the "fish" more readily than they could reject the historicity of the entire book. Emblem or history, the incident appears in the New Testament as the foreshadowing of a greater event than itself—a "sign."[20]

5. A more delicate point arises when it is asked how far *legend* may be employed by inspiration as a vehicle of instruction. Here again there is room for distinction. Legend in itself is a legitimate form of literature, and few preachers or orators would hesitate to introduce a beautiful or appropriate legend to adorn their speech or convey a moral. What is open to the preacher now in proclaiming the word of God can hardly be thought of as inadmissible to the divine Spirit in preparing a Scripture for the world. There is, however, a very clear difference between the use of legend for ornament, or for purely literary purposes, and the passing off of legend as a substitute for historic truth. A literary use of legend may be permissible;[21] it may be not unlawful, even, to use narratives into which legendary elements have crept, provided the substance of the narrative is true, and the truth to be conveyed remains unaffected. It is a very different matter when, as in some theories, practically the whole history is converted into legend, and the foundation-facts on which revelation rests are assailed, or converted into fictions, inventions, and imaginations of men. This happens, e.g., when the whole patriarchal history, and the larger part even of the Mosaic history, are converted into legend; or when, in the New Testament, the inci-

dents in the life of Jesus, including His miracles and resurrection, are resolved into myth, or Babylonian fable. Against such tendencies strong protest must be entered. The spirit of the Bible is *truth,* and history is a thing sacred in its eyes. The Bible is jealous of its historical truthfulness, and few books have stood the most rigorous tests applied to their statements, even in regard to the remotest times, better than the Bible has done.

INSPIRATION—RESULTS FOR DOCTRINE OF HOLY SCRIPTURE

It is now time to gather up results, and ask whether a doctrine of inspiration is attainable which shall at once be true to the facts of the record and true to the claims of Scripture itself on this important subject. In the answer to this question is involved the answer to another—Is there for the Church of to-day a tenable doctrine of Holy Scripture?

I. Revelation and Inspiration—Their Relations

1. It will have been seen that it is sought in the preceding pages to approach the subject of inspiration through that of *revelation.* This seems the right method to pursue. The doctrine of inspiration grows out of that of revelation, and can only be made intelligible through the latter. The older method was to prove first the inspiration (by historical evidence, miracles, claims of writers), then through that establish the revelation. This view still finds an echo in the note sometimes heard—"If the inspiration of the Bible (commonly some *theory* of inspiration) be given up, what have we left to hold by?" It is urged, e.g., that unless we can demonstrate what is called the "inerrancy" of the Biblical record, down even to its minutest details, the whole edifice of belief in revealed religion falls to the ground. This, on the face of it, is a most suicidal position for any defender of revelation to take up. It is certainly a much easier matter to prove the reality of a divine revelation in the history of Israel, or in Christ, than it is to prove the inerrant inspiration of every part of the record through which that revelation has come to us. Grant the Gospels to be only ordinary historical documents—trustworthy records of the life of Christ, apart from any special inspiration in their authors—we should still, one may contend, be shut up as much as ever to the belief that the Person whose words and works they narrate was One who made superhuman claims, and whose character, words, and deeds attested the truth of these claims.[22] It is assuredly easier to believe that Jesus spoke and acted in the way the Gospels declare Him to have done, than to prove that Mark and Luke possessed an exceptional inspiration in the composition of their writings—though, as

has been already stated, there is the best reason for believing that they did.

2. The same remark applies to the tendency to make "inerrancy" —i.e., hard and fast literality in minute matters of historical, geographical, and scientific detail—a point in the *essence* of the doctrine of inspiration. The subject will come up later, but at present it may be observed that, at best, such "inerrancy" can never be demonstrated with a cogency which entitles it to rank as the foundation of a belief in inspiration. It must remain to those who hold it a doctrine of faith; a deduction from what they deem to be implied in an inspiration established independently of it; not a ground of belief in the inspiration.[23] It is, as before, easier to establish the fact of the reality and all-pervading presence of an inspiration adequate to the ends of revelation than to demonstrate this particular aspect of it.

3. But now another fact has to be taken into account. If, on the one hand, it has been seen that, in the order of inquiry, revelation precedes inspiration, it has become not less clearly evident that over a large area, in the fact itself, revelation and inspiration are *closely and inseparably united*. Internal revelation, e.g., such as we have in prophecy, or in the "revelation of Jesus Christ" claimed for himself by Paul, is not conceivable save as accompanied by an inspired state of soul. Inspiration is involved in the very reception of such a revelation; it is a necessary condition of the revelation being apprehended, possessed, and communicated to others. In the very acknowledgement, therefore, of revelation as an element pervading the Bible and giving unity to its parts, there is implied an acknowledgement of inspiration. Just as, on the other side, there can be no degree of inspiration, however humble, which does not imply some measure of revelation.

4. Revelation and inspiration thus go together, and conjointly give to the written word *a quality* which distinguishes it from any product of ordinary human wisdom. Inspiration, Paul says, confers on Scripture the properties of being "profitable for teaching, for reproof, for correction, for instruction which is in righteousness"—of being able "to make wise unto salvation through faith which is in Christ Jesus."[24] Of similar nature are the qualities ascribed in the psalms to the law of God—"restoring the soul," "making wise the simple," "rejoicing the heart," "enlightening the eyes,"[25] etc. As Jesus says of His own words, that they "are spirit and are life,"[26] so of the word of God in general it is declared that it "is living and active, and sharper than any two-edged sword, and piercing even to the dividing of soul and spirit, of both joint and marrow, and quick to discern the thoughts and intents of the heart."[27] The last passage is the more significant that, in the context, the writer has been identifying words from the Book of Genesis and the Psalms with words of God and of the Holy Spirit.[28] Paul and John likewise declare that to the spiritual man (and *only* to him) belongs the discernment of the word of God.[29]

II. Witness of the Spirit to Inspiration

1. On this undeniable, self-attesting spiritual quality of Scripture some would lay the whole weight of the proof of inspiration. It is the *testimonium Spiritus Sancti*—the witness of the Holy Spirit—on which Calvin, some of the Reformed Confessions, and a writer like John Owen, would rest almost exclusively the certainty of the divine origin and authority of Scripture.[30] The aim is to obtain a ground for assured faith in God's Word independently of Church and tradition. The Westminster Confession—somewhat broader in its outlook—states the matter in this way: "We may be moved and induced by the testimony of the Church to an high and reverent esteem of the Holy Scripture, and the heavenliness of the matter, the efficacy of the doctrine, the majesty of the style, the consent of all the parts, the scope of the whole (which is to give all glory to God), the full discovery it makes of the only way of man's salvation, the many other incomparable excellences and the entire perfection thereof, are arguments whereby it doth abundantly evidence itself to be the word of God; yet, notwithstanding, our full persuasion and assurance of the infallible truth, and divine authority thereof, is from the inward work of the Holy Spirit, bearing witness by and with the word in our hearts."[31]

2. The principle here enunciated has undoubtedly wide scope, and may be applied with effect to sustain belief in the inspiration of *parts of Scripture* which do not of themselves directly make such claim—the Psalms, e.g., or certain Epistles, or the Gospels. The New Testament Epistles have only to be compared with the productions of the post-apostolic age,[32] or the canonical with the apocryphal Gospels, to see how immense—in the case of the Gospels how incredibly great—is the descent. It is not simply that the Gospels, as embodying the words of Jesus, and narrating His acts, have a divineness that goes beyond any dignity that inspiration could impart; but the record itself, in its simplicity, manifest fidelity, self-effacement of the human author, pervasive sense of the divine greatness of One, to the significance for the world of whose appearance the wise men of the age were so utterly blind, compels the acknowledgement that more than human care and skill were involved in its production—that the finger of God is there! If the other internal evidences are added,[33] a strong argument may be built up, not only for the reality of revelation in Scripture, but for an inspiration in the books in which that revelation is conveyed.

3. It must still be confessed that the principle here employed may be *pushed too far,* and made to sustain conclusions which cannot in justice be rested on it. How, e.g., can it legitimately be employed, taken by itself, to sustain the canonicity, not to say the inspiration, of books like the Song of Solomon, Esther, or Ecclesiastes, which be-

long, in the opinion of some, to the lowest grade of inspiration; or, still further, to establish a perfectly "errorless" record?[34] The principle, in fact, may be, and often has been, applied in a quite opposite direction, viz., to warrant the rejection of all parts of Scripture which do not appeal to the individual mind, or, as Coleridge says, "find" it. One recalls here Luther's rejection of the Epistle of James as "an epistle of straw," because he did not find in it Paul's doctrine of justification. Richard Baxter, one of the saintliest of men, thus wrote: "I confess, for my part, I could never boast of any such testimony or light of the Spirit or reason; neither of which, without human testimony or tradition, would have made me believe that the book of Canticles is canonical and written by Solomon, and the book of Wisdom apocryphal and written by Philo, as some think, or that Paul's Epistle to the Laodiceans and others is apocryphal, and the second and third Epistle of John canonical. Nor could I ever have known all or any historical books, such as Joshua, Judges, Ruth, Samuel, Kings, Chronicles, Ezra, Nehemiah, to be written by divine inspiration, but by tradition," etc.[35] This may be felt to carry objection too far on the other side; but the fact that a man like the author of *The Saints' Everlasting Rest* could write in this strain shows the precariousness of the principle as one on which to rest the whole Biblical case for inspiration. Many evidences converge to sustain inspiration—internal witness, testimony of the books, use by other Scriptures, witness of Christ and His apostles, effects and fruits in experience and history—and all are to be welcomed.

4. The inspiration which gives its distinctive quality to Scripture, as claimed for its writings by Jesus, by prophets and apostles, and often by the books themselves, is not of a kind that can properly be paralleled by human *genius,* or even by the ordinary illumination of Christians. It is sometimes said: "Isaiah was inspired as Shakespeare, Burns, Scott, or Carlyle was; Paul was inspired as Luther or Mazzini was." But could any of these gifted men have prefaced their utterances, as the prophets did, with a "Thus saith the Lord"; could it be said of the greatest of them what is said of New Testament apostles and prophets, that a church was founded on their witness? "Built upon the foundations of the apostles and prophets. . . . The mystery of Christ, which in other generations was not made known unto the sons of men, as it hath now been revealed unto His holy apostles and prophets in the Spirit."[36] The Spirit is given to all Christians, but in diversity of measures, and with specific gifts. And what ordinary Christian will feel that he could use language about himself like the above!

III. Inspiration in History

1. For further light on the nature of inspiration one turns naturally to *history,* to inquire what views on the subject have been entertained,

inside the Church and out of it, at different periods. Ideas of both revelation and inspiration, as before seen, are not wanting in heathenism. Analogies drawn from these foreign sources, however, are apt to mislead oftener than to help. No heathen religion possesses that which is the fundamental presupposition of Biblical inspiration—a living God, and a community within which the Holy Spirit of God is continuously active. The sporadic oracles of heathenism—pythonic responses and the like—assuming these to be as genuine as they were generally spurious, had nothing in common with this continuous, growing form of revelation through chosen, inspired organs. Neither is the analogy required furnished by the "sacred books" of other religions. The "Rishis" of the Vedas do not claim for themselves more than a poetical inspiration. Buddha's "enlightenment" was no inspiration from above, for his system had in it no place for either God or Holy Spirit. The Gathas or hymns which form the oldest parts of the Zend-Avesta are put into the mouth of Zoroaster. They contain invocations and prayers for enlightenment, and Ahura answers; but this is probably not more than literary form. The Confucian classics make no claim to inspiration. Mohammed, of course, claims that the messages combined in the Koran were communicated to him by direct revelation, and his claim must be treated on its merits; but few, treating it impartially, will be disposed to concede it. The Bible makes no claim for the origin of its books such as is made for the Koran—that their parts came down in external revelation from heaven,—and the claim if made, could not be entertained.

2. Philo and Josephus sufficiently attest the belief in the inspiration of the Scriptures among the Jews. The early Rabbis held the same doctrine.[37] Josephus connects inspiration with the prophetic gift; Philo, the earlier of the two, borrows from heathen mantic the idea of ecstasy, in which the individuality of the inspired man is wholly suppressed, and his soul reduced to pure passivity. This, it has been seen, is far from the conception of inspiration in the Bible itself. It is a position now universally recognised by writers on the subject that inspiration does not suppress individual genius, but heightens and develops it. All the powers that lie in a man's natural endowment, the gains of his training, the results of his experience, are laid hold of, and fused into a new unity round the central point of the new revelation that is given to him. Self-consciousness, the power of self-control, are not lost. "The spirits of the prophets are subject to the prophets."[38] This, too, in the main, is the doctrine of the early Church. That the early Fathers, in the most emphatic way, maintained the complete inspiration of the Holy Scriptures, Old Testament and New, no one acquainted with their writings will deny;[39] and if the favourite illustration of the lyre and plectrum may appear to lean to a view akin to Philo's of the suppression of the human consciousness, the general trend of their teaching will show that this is by no

means the intention.[40] Montanism, which took this view, was rejected. Origen, in particular, contends strongly against the comparison of Jewish prophecy to the frenzied utterances of the Pythian prophetess.[41] He holds for himself the strictest doctrine of inspiration, getting over the contradictions and other difficulties which he allows to exist (really, and not merely, as some say, "apparently") in the historical and prophetic parts by the aid of his allegorical method of interpretation.[42]

The opinions of the Reformers on inspiration have frequently been discussed. There is a singular breadth and modernness in Calvin's exegesis; but his faith in the entire inspiration of the Scriptures is profound and uncompromising. The ultimate guarantee of inspiration, as already seen, is found by him in the internal witness of the Holy Spirit.[43] The creeds of the Reformed Church embodied the same conceptions. Occasionally divines carried them to extremes that never obtained general sanction.[44] Luther's views, as his ordinary teaching and use of Scripture show, were scarcely less high; but, applying a subjective standard, his judgments on certain books, as the Epistle of James, Revelation, Esther, even the Epistle to the Hebrews, were rash and arbitrary.[45] These judgments affected canonicity rather than inspiration. Sometimes Luther is misjudged, as, e.g., when Dr. F. Watson states: "He described the argument St. Paul derived from Hagar and Sarah in the Galatians as too weak to hold."[46] This is a mistaken statement, as any one will see who reads what Luther really wrote on what he calls "this goodly allegory," "a wonderful allegory," praising the apostle for his use of it. What he does say is: "For if Paul had not proved the righteousness of faith against the righteousness of works by strong and pithy arguments, he should have little prevailed by this allegory. But, because he had fortified his cause before with invincible arguments . . . now, in the end of his disputations, he addeth an allegory, to give beauty to all the rest. For it is a seemly thing sometimes to add an allegory," etc.[47] There is no suggestion of any feebleness in Paul's inspiration.

Later views came gradually to prevail, especially through Arminian influence, and modern opinions have already been adverted to. Disputes turn largely in recent times on what is named "verbal" inspiration, and on the degree to which "inerrancy," or complete freedom from error or contradiction in matters not directly involved in the substance of the inspired teaching, is implied in inspiration.

IV. "Verbal Inspiration"

1. The phrase "verbal inspiration" is one to which so great ambiguity attaches that it is now very commonly avoided by careful writers.[48] There is, indeed, a sense in which the phrase expresses a true and important idea. It opposes the theory that revelation and inspira-

tion have regard only to thoughts and ideas, while the language in which these ideas are clothed is left to the unaided faculties of the sacred penman. This is a defective view. Thought of necessity takes shape and is expressed in words. If there is inspiration at all, it must penetrate words as well as thought, must mould the expression, and make the language employed the living medium of the idea to be conveyed.[49] The Scripture lays stress upon the *words*—often on the very form of the expression. "We speak," says Paul, "not in words which man's wisdom teacheth, but which the Holy Spirit teacheth."[50]

2. "Verbal inspiration," however, is often taken to mean much more than this. It is apt to suggest a *mechanical* theory of inspiration, akin to dictation, which all intelligent upholders of inspiration now agree in repudiating. In the result it may be held to imply a *literality* in narratives, quotations, or reports of discourses, which the facts, as we know them, do not warrant.

(1) A very evident illustration of the untenableness of this theory is in the *reports of the Lord's own sayings* in the Gospels. It is well known that in the reports of Christ's words in the Synoptic Gospels there is often a very considerable variation in expression—a difference in phraseology—while yet the *idea* conveyed in all the forms is the same. At most one side or another of the truth is brought out with slightly different emphasis. In illustration, let the version of the Lord's sayings in the Sermon on the Mount in Matthew be compared with that in Luke,[51] and the wide divergence in expression, with identity in idea, will at once be seen. Here the advocates of verbal inspiration are themselves compelled to recognise that absolute literality is not of the essence of inspiration—that the end is gained if the *meaning* of the saying is preserved, though the precise form of words varies. There may be compression, combination, change of construction—even (as in John) interpretation; but the truth is purely given.

(2) Another palpable illustration of this freedom in regard to the letter, while the sense is accurately conveyed, is found in the New Testament *quotations* from the Old Testament. In these, it is again well known, great variety in the method of quotation prevails. Sometimes, where the end is better served, the quotation is taken directly from the Hebrew (e.g., Matt. 2:15); occasionally the translation is free (Matt. 2:6); ordinarily the quotation is made with more or less exactness from the Greek version—this even where the Hebrew is somewhat widely departed from (Matt. 12:17-21; Rom. 9:33; I Peter 2:6; Heb. 10:5-7, etc.). Inspiration here again must be held compatible with a want of literality in the words.[52]

3. In view of these facts, it is felt by many that, to express the idea of an inspiration which pervades all the parts of the record, the word *plenary* is more suitable than "verbal." This term, while doing justice to the freedom of the sacred writer in his use of language, argument, and illustration, in the employment of his facul-

ties in research, and in his methods of using his material, avoids the mistake into which others fall of speaking as if *parts* of the record were inspired, and *parts* uninspired. The passages usually quoted in support of this view are Paul's words in I Cor. 7:10, 12, 25: "Unto the married I give charge, yet not I, but the Lord. . . . But to the rest say I, not the Lord. . . . Concerning virgins I have no commandment of the Lord, but I give my judgment." These verses, however, are not valid to establish any such distinction as is alleged. What Paul means to say is only that he had no direct "command" from the Lord for what he said—no word of Jesus spoken while on earth—such as he had in the case of marriage. Yet Paul claimed that he had "the Spirit of God" in giving his judgment on the cases before him;[53] nay, goes so far as to declare: "If any man thinketh himself to be a prophet, or spiritual, let him acknowledge of the things which I write unto you, that they are the commandments of the Lord."[54]

V. "Inerrancy" of the Record

While, by most of the older writers, the inspiration of the entire record in the Bible is strenuously affirmed, great diversity of view prevails as to the *mode* of the action of the divine influence by which this result is secured. Theories of dictation of historical matter, or of communication of facts that could be ascertained by ordinary methods, are now universally surrendered;[55] the distinction of "revelation" and "inspiration" is better recognised; but whereas some would lay chief stress on the exaltation of the human faculties, and conscious direction and "suggestion," others are content to resolve inspiration into a divine "superintendence," often unconscious, leaving everything else—and this the greater part—in the production of an "errorless" record to "providence."[56] The question which here arises is—Does the Bible itself claim, or inspiration necessitate, such an "errorless" record, in matters of minor detail? The discussion may close with a few words on this subject of "inerrancy."

1. Very commonly it is argued by upholders of this doctrine that "inerrancy" in every minute particular is involved *in the very idea* of a book given by inspiration of God. This might be held to be true on a theory of verbal dictation, but it can scarcely be maintained on a just view of the actual historical genesis of the Bible. One may plead, indeed, for "a supernatural providential guidance" which has for its aim to exclude all, even the least, error or discrepancy in statement, even such as may inhere in the sources from which the information is obtained, or may arise from corruption of anterior documents. But this is a violent assumption which there is nothing in the Bible really to support. It is perilous, therefore, to seek to pin down faith to it as a matter of vital moment. Inspiration, in sanctioning the incorporation of an old genealogy, or of an historic docu-

ment in some respects defective, no more makes itself responsible for these defects than it does for the speeches of Job's friends in the Book of Job, or for the sentiments of many parts of the Book of Ecclesiastes, or for the imperfect translation of Old Testament passages in quotations from the Septuagint.

2. Even on the assumption of a "verbal" inspiration, it has been seen in how wide a sense *literal accuracy* in the Biblical records has to be interpreted. The theory may be stretched, moreover, by qualifications, admissions, and explanations, till there is *practically* little difference between the opposite views. Thus, writing on the New Testament quotations, with reference to the objection of Dr. S. Davidson that, on the theory of verbal inspiration, the New Testament writers should have adhered to the *ipsissima verba* of the Holy Spirit in the Old Testament, seeing these were best, the able defenders of an "errorless" record already repeatedly cited remark: "Here, however, a false view of inspiration is presupposed, and also a false view of the nature and laws of quotation. Inspiration does not suppose that the words and phrases written under its influence are the best possible to express the truth, but only that they are an adequate expression of the truth. Other words and phrases might be equally adequate: —might furnish a clearer, more exact, and therefore better expression, especially of those truths which were subordinate or incidental for the original purpose of the writings."[57] It would be difficult, however, to show that this superiority always belongs to the LXX. renderings adopted. More generally, we have such wide acknowledgments as the following: "It is not claimed that the Scriptures any more than their authors are omniscient. The information they convey is in the forms of human thought, and limited on all sides. They were not designed to teach philosophy, science, or human history as such. They were not designed to furnish an infallible system of speculative theology. They are written in human languages, whose words, inflections, constructions, and idioms bear everywhere indelible traces of human error. The record itself furnishes evidence that the writers were in large measure dependent for their knowledge upon sources and methods in themselves fallible, and that their personal knowledge and judgments were in many matters hesitating and defective, or even wrong." So much being admitted, it hardly seems worth while to deny the compatibility of inspiration with the possibility of minor errors also in the *matter* of the record. Yet "the *ipsissima verba* of the original autographs" are held to be free from the slightest taint of such error.

3. These things have in justice to be said on the one side. On the other side, one finds himself in substantial harmony with the defenders of this view in affirming that *the sweeping assertions* of error and discrepancy in the Bible often made cannot be substantiated. Ascribe it to "providence," to "superintendence," to "suggestion," or what one will,—and inspiration is probably more subtle and all-pervading

than any of these things,—it remains the fact that the Bible, impartially interpreted and judged, is free from demonstrable error in its statements, and harmonious in its teachings, to a degree that of itself creates an irresistible impression of a supernatural factor in its origin. It is of little profit to discuss such a subject as "inerrancy" in the abstract. When the objector descends from generalities to details, one knows where to find him; and here, in cases without number, it has been shown by the progress of knowledge that it is *he*, not the Bible, that is wrong. Many of the alleged discrepancies are such only in appearance, or are readily explained by difference in point of view or aim, or from technicalities of structure, as in genealogies, or from methods of grouping and generalising, where precise detail is not aimed at. Some are due to corruption in the texts—this frequently in names and numbers—either in the existing texts, or possibly in the MSS. sources used by the sacred writer himself. Archaeology has brought confirmation to the statements of the Bible, even in its oldest parts, in a multitude of particulars in which its accuracy had been confidently challenged. Illustration of these assertions has been furnished in abundance elsewhere.[58] When, in smaller matters, discrepancy is urged, as, e.g., in the various reports of the titles of the Cross, it is time for the discussion to stop.

4. On this broad, general ground the advocates of "inerrancy" may always feel that they have *a strong position*, whatever assaults may be made on them in matters of lesser detail. They stand undeniably, in their main contention, in the line of apostolic belief, and of the general faith of the Church,[59] regarding Holy Scripture. The most searching inquiry still leaves them with a Scripture, supernaturally inspired to be an infallible guide in the great matters for which it was given—the knowledge of the will of God for their salvation in Christ Jesus, instruction in the way of holiness, and the "hope of eternal life, which God, who cannot lie, promised before times eternal."[60]

VI. Conclusion

This leads, in closing, to the remark that, in the last resort, the proof of the inspiration of the Bible—not, indeed, in every particular, but in its essential message—is to be found in the life-giving effects which that message has produced, wherever its word of truth has gone.[61] This is the truth in the argument for the inspiration based on the witness of the Holy Spirit. The Bible has the qualities claimed for it as an inspired book. These qualities, on the other hand, nothing but inspiration could impart. It leads to God and to Christ; it gives light on the deepest problems of life, death, and eternity; it discovers the way of deliverance from sin; it makes men new creatures; it furnishes the man of God completely for every good work.[62] That it possesses these qualities history and experience through all the centuries have attested; its saving, sanctifying, and civilising effects among all races of men in the world attest it still. The word of God is a "pure word."[63] It is a true and "tried" word;[64] a word never found wanting by those who rest themselves upon it. The Bible that embodies this word will retain its distinction as *the Book of Inspiration* till the end of time!

Notes

[1]Exod. 12:26, 27; Deut. 6:7, 20 ff.; Ps. 78:3, 4; Luke 1:1, 2, etc.; Gen. 18:19.

[2]See above.

[3]I Cor. 10:11; II Peter 1:20-21.

[4]Eph. 1:17.

[5]Cf. Sanday, *Inspiration,* pp. 88, 89.

[6]I Chron. 29:20; cf. on Solomon, II Chron. 9:29; on Rehoboam, II Chron. 12:15, etc.

[7]The quotations from this large work, under one or other of its titles, occur more than thirty times in the Books of Kings (e.g., I Kings 14:19, 16:20). Also repeatedly in the Books of Chronicles (II Chron. 20:34, 27:7, etc.).

[8]Ezra 2:22, 4:8-22, 8:1, etc., Neh. 7:5, 64, etc.

[9]Luke 1:1-4.

[10]See further below.

[11]Gen. 2:21-5.

[12]Gen. 2:8-15.

[13]On the cherubim, cf., as an older writer, Dr. P. Fairbairn, *Typology of Scripture,* 1. pp. 222 ff.

[14]Cf., e.g., Dr. A. A. Hodge, *Outlines of Theology* (1879), p. 297; Dr. W. H. Green, *Bib. Sacra,* April 1890; Dr. J. D. Davis, in his *Dict. of Bible,* art. "Chronology."

[15]*Aelteste Urkunde des Menschengeschlechts* (quoted by Auberlen, *Div. Revelation,* p. 188, which also consult on this subject).

[16]Cf. *Problem of the O.T.,* chap. VIII.

[17]The same remark may apply to the Second Epistle of Peter.

[18]II Chron. 13:1-12.

[19]The late D. L. Moody was an expert at this dramatic form of Biblical story-telling.

[20]Matt. 12:39-41.

[21]E.g., legendary allusions seem to be found in the Epistle of Jude (vers. 3, 14, are drawn from Apocryphal sources).

[22]This has often been put as strongly as it can be by the stoutest defenders of the infallibility of Scripture. Cf., e.g., Bannerman, *Inspiration: the Infallible Truth and Divine Authority of the Holy Scriptures,* pp. 18 ff. Drs. Hodge and Warfield, arguing for an "errorless Scripture," write: "Nor should we ever allow it to be believed that the truth of Christianity depends upon any doctrine of inspiration whatever. Revelation came in large part before the record of it, and the Christian Church before the New Testament Scriptures. Inspiration can have no meaning if Christianity is not true, but Christianity would be true and divine, and being so, would stand, even if God had not been pleased to give us, in addition to his revelation of saving truth, an infallible record of that revelation absolutely errorless by means of inspiration" (*Presby. Rev.,* April 1881, p. 227).

[23]Bannerman says: "The unintentional errors which may be and are found in writings marked by perfect historical veracity, cannot be taken account of as affecting the force or conclusiveness of this argument. Making any allowance that can reasonably be demanded for the possibility of such errors, and subtracting from the sacred text what might by any chance be set to that account, there remains enough for the purpose which the friends of inspiration have in view," etc. (*op. cit.,* p. 284).

[24]II Tim. 3:15-17.

[25]Ps. 19:7-9; 119, etc.

[26]John 6:63.

[27]Heb. 4:12.

[28]Heb. 3:7—4:11.

[29]I Cor. 2:14, 16; I John 4:1-3.

[30]Calvin, *Instit.* I. 7.4, 5; Helvet. and French Confessions; Owen, *Div. Orig. of Script.,* chaps. 11. iv.

[31]Chap. 1:5.

[32]The Early Fathers, as will be seen, were fully conscious of this difference.

[33]In his (posthumous) work on *Inspiration,* Dr. F. Watson, of Cambridge, justly lays stress on the evidence from the Biblical Doctrine of Sin (chap. vii), the Harmony of the Teaching (viii), the Purity of the Teaching (ix), the Abidingness of the Teaching (x), etc.

[34]Cf. Bannerman, *op. cit.,* pp. 270-1, who points out this weakness. In the view of the present writer, the Book of Esther, which Dr. Sanday puts lowest, gets scant justice from some of its critics. It is a wonderful record of God's providence. The permission given to the Jews to defend themselves (Esth. 8:11; 9:1, 2) is not to be confounded with the decree

to massacre issued earlier at the instance of Haman (3:13). Cf. Dr. Sanday's note, *op. cit.,* pp. 222-3.

[35]Preface to Second Part of *Saints' Rest.*

[36]Eph. 2:20; 3:4, 5. Cf. Dr. Sanday on "Modern Prophets," *op. cit.,* pp. 166-7.

[37]See in detail on the teaching of Philo and Josephus in the works on inspiration by Sanday, Lee, Bannerman, Watson, etc. On the Rabbinical views, cf. Sanday, pp. 80-2, 90: "What might be thought somewhat strange, the disputed books (Eccles., Song, Esther) seem to be used quite as freely as the rest."

[38]I Cor. 14:32.

[39]The testimony of the Early Church is very fully exhibited in Westcott's *Introd. to the Study of the Gospels,* Appendix B. A long catena of passages is given in Lee, Appendix G. Clement of Rome says: "The blessed Paul at the beginning of the Gospel in very truth wrote by inspiration" to the Corinthians. Ignatius says: "I do not give you injunctions as Peter and Paul; they were apostles, I a condemned man."

[40]Athenagoras is an exception. He speaks of the prophets as "entranced and deprived of their natural powers of reason."

[41]*Contra Celsum,* vii. 4.

[42]*De Princip.* iv. 1; *Contra Cels.* iv. 48.

[43]*Instit.* I. 7. 4, 5.

[44]E.g. The younger Buxtorf (followed by the "Formula Consensus Helvetica") affirmed the inspiration of the Hebrew vowel points.

[45]"He was as thoroughly convinced of the inspiration and authority of the Word of God as the most orthodox divine can be, but he had free views on the mode of inspiration and the extent of the traditional canon" (Schaff, *Creeds of Christendom,* i. 215).

[46]*Inspiration,* pp. 232-3.

[47]*Com. on Gal.* iv. 24, etc.

[48]E.g., by Lee, Bannerman, etc. The former prefers "plenary," the latter "dynamical." Hodge and Warfield defend the word "verbal," but with careful explanation. "There is the more excuse," they say, "for this misapprehension because of the extremely mechanical conceptions of inspiration maintained by many former advocates of this term 'verbal.' This view, however, we repudiate as earnestly as any of those who object to the language in question" (*op. cit.,* p. 233).

[49]"The slightest consideration," says Dr. Westcott, "will show that words are as essential to intellectual processes as they are to mutual intercourse. . . . Thoughts are wedded to words as necessarily as soul is to body" (*Study of Gospels,* p. 14).

[50]I Cor. 2:13.

[51]Matt. 5—7; Luke 6:20-40.

[52]See further on this point, *The Bible under Trial,* pp. 268 ff.

[53]Ver. 40.

[54]I Cor. 14:37.

[55]The slight qualifications of this which Dr. Lee (p. 147) and others make, e.g., in the supernatural communication to Paul of the institution of the Lord's Supper (Bannerman, p. 189), rest on a misunderstanding. Paul undoubtedly "received" the Lord's words at the Supper from the apostles or general tradition.

Hodge and Warfield lay stress on this human side. "Each drew from the stores of his own original information, from the contributions of other men, and from all other natural sources. Each sought knowledge, like all other authors, from the use of his own natural faculties of thought and feeling," etc. (p. 299).

[56]This is the thesis, elaborated with much fulness, of Hodge and Warfield. "We intentionally," they say, "avoid applying to this inspiration the predicate 'influence.' It summoned, on occasion, a great variety of influences, but its essence was superintendence. This superintendence attended the entire process of the genesis of Scripture, and particularly the final composition of the record. . . . The Scriptures were generated through sixteen centuries of this divinely regulated concurrence of God and man, of the natural and supernatural, of reason and revelation, of providence and grace. . . . The natural knowledge came from all sources, as traditions, documents, testimonies, personal observations, and recollections, . . . yet all were alike under the general direction of God's providence. The supernatural knowledge became confluent with the natural in a manner which violated no law of reason or of freedom. And throughout the whole of His work the Holy Spirit was present, causing His energies to flow into the spontaneous exercises of the writer's faculties, elevating and directing where need be, and everywhere securing the errorless expression in language of the thought designed by God. This last element we call inspiration" (pp. 226, 229, 231).

[57]Hodge and Warfield, *op. cit.,* p. 256.

[58]See, in illustration, *Prob. of O. T.,* chap. xi; *The Bible under Trial,* chaps. vi., xi.

[59]This is shown, as respects the Early Church, in the copious extracts compiled by Dr. Westcott and by Archdeacon Lee in their appendices to their works formerly referred to.

[60]Titus 1:2.

[61]Col. 1:5, 6.

[62]II Tim. 3:17.

[63]Ps. 1:6; 19:8; 119:140, etc.

[64]Ps. 12:6; 18:30.

The Authority of the Bible

17

Bernard Ramm

The Principle and Pattern of Authority in Christianity

The Problem

The key-problem in religious authority is to find the central principle of authority and the pattern through which it expresses itself concretely and practically. Principles of religious authority founded on a bare monistic principle soon founder. Most treaties on religious authority assert that God is the final authority in religion, but this bare assertion does not make its way. Unless the assertion is expressed in a more concrete fashion it becomes mere platitude. A principle of religious authority, along with its pattern designed for its practical and concrete expression and execution, should incorporate all the necessary elements associated with such a complex notion as religious authority. The authority of God, of Jesus Christ, of Sacred Scripture, and of truth must be properly related, as well as proper regard given for human personality and freedom. The result will be a mosaic of authority, with the central piece being the principle of authority. Properly understood, one could even speak of a chain of authority

From Bernard Ramm, *The Pattern of Religious Authority*. Grand Rapids: Wm. B. Eerdmans Publishing Company, 1959. Used by permission.

with the principle of authority being the first and most important link.

From another perspective the problem of religious authority is to steer a wise course between subjectivism and authoritarianism. If the truth is merely that which appeals to the individual (no matter how carefully this be disguised to appear as something else), then it is impossible to differentiate the true from the false, delusion from reality. In subjectivism each man is his own authority, and if each man is his own authority there is neither truth nor authority. Subjectivism in authority is subjectivism in truth, and subjectivism in truth implies the radical relativity of knowledge. The subjectivistic interpretation of religious authority founders on the rocks of a radical relativity of religious truth which it implies.

Authoritarianism (defined here as the sheer appeal to authority, or the excessive claims of an authority) is also indigestible. Authoritarianism as the sheer appeal to authority is artificially separated from necessary considerations of veracious authority. To separate imperial authority from any reckoning with veracious authority is to stultify the intellect, whether it be operating in religion or politics. Any principle which does not properly relate itself to veracious authority will eventually prove itself to be demonic, or oppressive, or arbitrary.

As previously noted, most books on religious authority state that God is the final authority in religion. Here is where the discussion must begin, and it begins with this question: *How does God express His authority?*[1] Does He express it through the Roman Catholic Church? or through the ecumenical councils of the Eastern Church? or through religious intuition? or through man's best thoughts about God?

The creative genius of the mind of Augustine wrestled with this problem as with others. Step by step and line by line Augustine was led by the momentum of his own inward experience and thought to see that *revelation and authority* were correlates. The answer to his question, How does God express His authority? is precisely this: *By divine self-revelation.*

Augustine found that his soul was clouded by sin, beset by weaknesses and uncertainties, and therefore in need of a divine Word.[2] That divine Word was mediated by revelation and received by faith. Faith was the acceptance of the witness of God in the divine Word. Thus the ground for the appeal to a divine Word, and hence an authoritative Word, was based on rational considerations. Augustine did not desert reason, but he was pushed on by reason to see the true grounds of religious authority. His stand on authority was not a call for the sacrifice of his intellect; to the contrary, it was the *demand* of his intellect.

Revelation is the key to religious authority. How is this so? In science the object of science controls the hypotheses. The data are given to the scientist. If he is a physical anthropologist, the human body prescribes the data. If he is a chemist, he must submit his theories to the phenomena of the chemicals. If he is a sociologist, his theories must tune themselves to the data of sociological description. Subjective wish cannot play the role of object in science. Science would cease to exist if subjective wish replaced the authority of the object.

The Object of religion is God. Religion should be no more determined by subjective wish than chemistry. If a religion is true, it is true because in some manner its theses are prescribed for it by its Object. The objects of science convey their properties to the scientists in a number of ways, but in religion the knowledge of the Object is conveyed to the subject of religion by revelation. Revelation is but the Religious Object determining the character and truth of religion to the subjects of religion. Forsyth accurately described this when he wrote: "In religion the fundamental movement of knowledge is in the reverse direction from that of science. In science we move to the object of knowledge; in religion it moves to us. . . . Religion is only possible by Revelation."[3]

The next step which should be undertaken is an investigation of all the claimants to a revelation from God and by some appropriate methodology discover if any of them is a valid revelation. But this is the more ambitious task of apologetics, and since the present effort is basically a delineation of the pattern of authority, that step—as important as it is—must be omitted. If the authority of God is expressed by means of revelation, then the central thesis may be formulated as follows: *In Christianity the authority-principle is the Triune God in self-revelation.* This is the central piece of the mosaic of authority, and the first and most impressive link in the chain of authority.

This is the Object of religion declaring Himself to men, and in this declaration there is not only the imperial authority of God ("hallowed be thy name") but the truth from God about God. Upon inspection of this authority-principle certain merits of this principle are evident:

(1) Such a principle is free from *subjectivism*. This principle of authority finds its locus outside the individual. It is a frank recognition that the final authority in religion is God Himself. There are not as many authorities as there are individuals, and there are not as many religious truths as there are religious thinkers. There is only one authority—God; and only one truth—divine revelation.

(2) Such a principle avoids the resident evils of *authoritarianism* (as defined within this book). Authoritarianism is a principle of authority which is top-heavy. God's revelation is a revelation of grace and truth (John 1:17). As Warfield states it: "God's authoritative revelation is His gracious revelation; God's redemptive revelation is His supernatural revelation."[4] God's saving action in the world and in

the human heart is an action of grace. God's imperial authority is graciously expressed. When God binds His authority upon man, it is an act of grace. In God's supreme revelation, Jesus Christ, exists the epitome of God's authority—grace and truth (John 1:17). There is no impersonal force in grace, and God's authority is sealed by grace, not by impersonal force. Bound to God by love and grace, the believer's mind is free from all traces of imposed authoritarianism or forced obedience.

Further, in that God's revelation is a revelation of truth, His authority is not only veracious but just. Justice is veracity in the ethical realm. God is sovereign and gracious; He is gracious and just; He is just and veracious.

God's imperial authority ("hallowed be thy name") is eternally conjoined to His veracity, His love, and His justice. When God appears stern in His action and causes His wrath to fall upon man, it is a wrath based on the veracity of the facts, and governed by impeccable justice. Without the sterner voice of God in Scripture, the Scripture would contain less of God, not more of God. The Scriptures *never* sentimentalize God.

Repeatedly the divine Word is followed by the expression: "I am the Lord." Because God is sovereign, and just, and veracious, the only signature necessary for a word to be authoritative to man is the name of the Lord.

In Biblical religion it is *ex hypothesi* impossible to have a separation of veracity and justice from the imperial voice of God. The expression, "I am the Lord," eternally unites them.

The New Testament emphasis on veracity is most pronounced. It asserts that God is the true God, or the God of truth (John 3:33; 17:3; Rom. 3:4; I Thess. 1:9); that His judgments are veracious and just (Rom. 2:2; 3:7; Rev. 16:7; 15:3); that a knowledge of God is a knowledge of the truth (Rom. 1:18, 25). It asserts that Christ is the true light (John 1:9), the true bread (John 6:32), and the true vine (John 15:1). Christ bears a true witness (John 8:14; Rev. 3:14); His judgments are true (John 8:16); He is a minister of the truth of God (Rom. 15:8); He is full of truth (John 1:14); He is personally the truth (John 14:6; Rev. 3:7; 19:11). Further, He speaks the truth of God (John 8:40-47). The Holy Spirit is repeatedly called the Spirit of truth (I John 5:7; John 14:17; 15:26; 15:13). His ministry is to guide into truth (John 16:13). The gospel, or Christian faith, is called the word of truth (II Cor. 6:7; Eph. 1:13; Col. 1:5; II Tim. 2:15; James 1:18). It is called the truth of Christ (II Cor. 11:10) and the way of truth (II Peter 2:2). The Christians are said to have found the truth, and the heretic or unbeliever to have missed the truth (I John 2:27; II Thess. 2:13; Eph. 5:9; I John 3:19). The Church is called the pillar and ground of the truth (I Tim. 3:15).

Some writers on religious authority would eliminate imperial authority from religion altogether. But if God is the *Object* of religion, how can the imperial authority of God be out of place in religion? There is either the direct affirmation or the subtle innuendo that the imperial authority of God expressed in revelation and then in Scripture creates an unrelievable tension between truth and Christianity.

It is true that man in his pride will discover that Christianity calls for intellectual humility and repentance as well as moral humility and repentance. Paul does state that Christians are to cast down "reasonings" and every high thing that is exalted against the knowledge of God, bringing every thought into captivity to the obedience of Christ (II Cor. 10:5). Paul does not scout reason (*logos*), but specious reasoning (*logismous*), as the scope of the passage clearly indicates. Because man is a sinner, much of his thinking about religion will involve specious reasoning, and this specious reasoning needs to be corrected by the true knowledge of God and brought into obedience to Christ.

But the call to intellectual humility and repentance is not a call to the separation of truth from God, of reality from Christianity. It is but the clear recognition that the sinner who is defective in moral powers is also defective in rational powers, and especially so when those powers are directed toward the knowledge of God.

God's revelation is a revelation of *Truth,* and therefore the authority of God can never call for the stultification of the intelligence. The humility of all finite minds before God—*yes;* the divorce of veracity from God's imperial authority—*no.*

If God is the Object of religion and is known only as He reveals Himself, there can be no rational objection to the authority of a divine revelation. If God's revelation is God's truth, it cannot be scouted. Only in the principle of the living God in a revelation of grace and truth is the tension between truth and authority resolved.

Certainly the modern scientist does not feel restricted because nature is determined. Although a strict deterministic program in science is now in question (owing to the implication of Heisenberg's principle, and the statistical character of many physical laws), the orderliness and uniformity of nature is still a major premise of the scientists. The goal of the scientists is to bring as much phenomena of the universe as possible under general laws. The scientist should not, therefore, be surprised to find that the domain of spirit is structured for him by divine revelation. Rather than the spirit-world being a chaos of cults, a Babel of religious confusion, or a quaking jelly of subjectivism, it is structured by a certain and true knowledge of God.

(3) This principle avoids the problem of an exclusively written authority. If it is affirmed that the Bible is the *exclusive* authority in

religion, then a difficulty which is insurmountable is created: wherever there is no written word, there is no religious authority.[5] There was one period of sacred history when no written authority existed—from Adam to Moses. There was a second period when Christianity existed only as the remembered word and Person in the minds of the Apostles. True, the Church had the Old Testament, but the authority of the words of Jesus Christ was transmitted orally till fixed by inscripturation. The principle of authority must recognize this fact. The authority to Abraham was the living God in self-revelation, and the authority of Jesus Christ to the early Church was the remembered divine word which came from the lips of Jesus Christ.

John the Baptist received the Word of God (Luke 3:2) and therefore preached with the authority of God, as our Lord Himself recognized (Matt. 21:23-27). Our Lord taught with authority before a word of His was written (Matt. 7:29), and claimed to have spoken the veritable word of God in His oral ministry (John 17:14). Our Lord promised a special power and authority to His apostles (John 16:12-15; Matt. 28:18-20). Before the first word of the New Testament was written, the Apostles and the early Church were under the authority of the remembered oral word of Jesus Christ. Hence the specifically Christian authority to the infant Church (for they had the Old Testament) *was the self-revelation of God in Jesus Christ.*

(4) *Such a principle avoids the finite's sitting in the place of the Infinite.* The voice of man must not be substituted for the voice of God. In all those instances in which man mistakenly speaks for God, the finite sits in the place of the Infinite. The Object of religion must be allowed to speak for Himself. Any other voice that poses as an authority in religion is the voice of man and not of God.

Every subjectivistic principle of religious authority is finally man sitting in the place of the Infinite. A subjectivistic principle is one which expressly rejects an oral or written propositional revelation from God, and which identifies religious experience with the speaking of God (although admitting the identity is imperfect). The subjectivistic principle is not only the end of authority, but the end of truth.

The Roman Catholic Church in teaching that the authority of the divine revelation has rubbed off onto it is another instance of the finite sitting in the place of the Infinite. In that the Catholic Church claims a measure of delegated imperial authority, it has presumed to sit where God sits. That this interpretation of religious authority fails in theory and fact will be a matter for later discussion.

The Protestant thus judges that both religious liberalism's subjectivism and Catholicism's ecclesiastical authoritarianism (as extreme as they are with regard to each other) are instances of the finite sitting in the place of the Infinite. However, if the self-revelation of God is the proper principle of religious authority, and if all other religious authorities are strictly delegated and never imperial, then the finite never sits in the place of the Infinite. Accordingly the voice of man will never be confused with the voice of God (even though God uses man's voice through inspiration to speak His truth).

(5) This is *personal authority*. Imperial authority is the authority of the station or dignity or rank of a person or group. Veracious authority is directly or indirectly the authority of a person. This authority is God in self-revelation; therefore it is personal. God as God occupies the highest conceivable personal station, and possesses all the authority which derives from that station. The supreme majesty of God's person is indicated by the words, "hallowed be thy name" (Matt. 6:9); and His supreme right to govern as such is argued by Paul in Romans 9:14-23. Because God is truth He possesses full veracious authority. This is argued by Paul in Romans 3:4. In both instances He is the personal God. In subjection of this authority the Christian is subject to a Person—a person absolutely reliable, absolutely true, and absolutely love. Here thankfully and doxologically ends the quest for a credible religious authority.

Notes

[1]Rees is correct in stating that this is the crux of the entire problem of religious authority. "Authority in Religion," ISBE, I, 334.

[2]Cf. B. B. Warfield, "Augustine's Doctrine of Knowledge and Authority," *Studies in Tertullian and Augustine*. E. C. Rich, in his work on religious authority (*Spiritual Authority in the Church of England*), concurs that revelation and authority are correlates, and therefore the authority of Christianity is that it professes to be a divine revelation (p. 79).

[3]*The Principle of Authority*, pp. 150-151. Cf. similar sentiments by Lecerf (*An Introduction to Reformed Dogmatics*, pp. 370-371).

[4]*The Inspiration and Authority of the Bible*, p. 100.

[5]Clearly pointed out by Kuyper, *Principles of Sacred Theology*, p. 399. Heppe notes that the older theologians made a distinction between the Word of God and Holy Scripture, to account for the unwritten period of revelation. The Word of God to them was the sum total of divine actions about revelation at first orally transmitted, then subsequently written down. Cf. *Reformed Dogmatics*, p. 15.

18

Charles H. Dodd

The Bible as "The Word of God"

We started from the position that authority in the absolute sense resides in the truth alone, or, in religious language, in the mind and will of God. In so far as the Bible possesses authority in religion, it can be only as mediating the truth, or as "the Word of God."[1] Our enquiry has indicated certain ways in which it does in fact mediate truth: first, through the "inspiration" of individual genius, conferring not inerrancy but a certain cogent persuasiveness;[2] next through the appropriation of "inspired" ideas by a whole community, whose experience through many generations tests, confirms and revises them;[3] and finally through the life of One in whom His followers found so decisive an answer to their needs that they hailed Him as the Wisdom of God incarnate.[4] We further saw that these three stages form a continuous history in which as a whole, even more clearly than in its several parts, a divine process of revelation can be discerned.[5] All through our study it has been clear that anything we can say about revelation is relative to the minds that receive it. Nowhere is the truth given in such purely "objective" form that we can find a self-subsistent external authority. Even where it might appear that if

---

From Charles H. Dodd, *The Authority of the Bible*. London: James Nisbet and Company, Ltd., 1928. Used by permission.

Christian belief is true we should have such absolute authority, name-ly, in the words of Jesus Christ, we have been forced to conclude that we must still accept responsibility for our judgments. For the report of His teaching is not inerrant, and the criticism of it calls for spiri-tual insight in the last resort; and further, even supposing we had before us His own undoubted words, they would need "translation" out of their historical setting before they could be directly applied to our own case, and that again calls for spiritual insight. Nor again does the impressive evidence of history attain to complete objectivity, since for its interpretation we must assume a certain estimate of the end towards which its development tends. Thus in every way we are brought back to the importance of the "subjective" factor. Granted that religious authority somehow resides in the Bible, how does it become authoritative *for me?*

If the Bible as a whole is a revelation of God, and the crown of this revelation is the life and teaching of Jesus Christ, then we may start by asking, How did Jesus reveal God? He seems to have made very few general theological propositions, and those of the simplest, as that there is none good but One, that is God,[6] that all things are possible to God,[7] that He is kind to the unthankful and the evil.[8] Nor does He appear to have imparted ineffable secrets concerning God and the spiritual world, in the manner of the apocalyptists or of Greek mystagogues.[9] Some of His followers, indeed, mistook His parables for allegorical mystifications; but when they had done their worst with them the parables still conveyed their own meaning to simple sincerity. The parables in fact, as we have seen, are pictures of life as it is, and in telling them Jesus challenged men to find God in life. That is characteristic of His method. In a sense we might say that Jesus never told men anything about God but what they could see for themselves—when He had brought them into the right attitude for seeing Him—and this He did, not only by what He said, but by what He was and did, and most conclusively through His death and resurrection.

As we have said, the ability to see and to speak of the things of God is not an extraordinary faculty communicated apart from what a man is, but a function of the personality reconciled to God. The work of Jesus was primarily this of reconciliation. He released men from falsehoods and perversions of affection and will which obscured their view of God—and then they began to know God. Jesus is Saviour and Reconciler even before He is Revealer. The first disciples clearly failed to understand much of what their Master said. But His words lodged in their minds, and after they had been completely re-orientated to life through the experience of His death and resurrection, they saw for themselves the truth to which He had pointed.

We may study the process most clearly in Paul and the anonymous author of the Fourth Gospel.

Paul was a man of religious genius and shows in all his work the originality of genius. Like all prophets, he is conscious of being directly guided by the divine Spirit. Yet he is also aware that this guidance has been made possible for him by Jesus Christ. It is not that he habitually quotes Jesus as an "authority." He does indeed so quote Him explicitly two or three times,[10] and in his writings there are more reminiscences of the teaching of Jesus than the casual reader observes. But Christ had "apprehended" him, and given him a new relation to God and to life. Christ had "saved," had "reconciled" him. He speaks of his own experience when he says, "If any man be in Christ, he is a new creation."[11] The phrase "in Christ" is a profoundly theological one, and we must not water down its significance. Yet it means, among other things, that through contact with Jesus he had found a new centre from which to contemplate life and the world. Looking from that new centre he found that God revealed Himself in all experience in new and surprising ways.

John speaks of the way in which Jesus revealed God partly in more intellectual terms. He starts from the highly philosophical idea of the Logos or "uttered Thought" of God: and identifies Christ with the Logos in that He has "declared" the invisible God. But this intellectualism is not the deepest thing in his teaching. He is fully aware of personal and moral conditions which must be present before one can receive a revelation of God. He has faced the question, How can I know that Christ speaks of God with authority? He replies, "He who is willing to do God's will can recognize whether the teaching (of Jesus) is from God or not."[12] That is, a personal reconciliation to God is the condition of knowledge of God; even the authority of the Logos is not independent of that. Further, when he comes to tell what Christ actually does for men, he makes it clear that He does something more than speak to us about God with authority. What would be the use of showing a light to a blind man? His eyes must first be opened. This Christ does for us. He does not ask us to believe on His authority; He puts us in a condition to see for ourselves. To John this is prior to any decision about the Person of Christ: "Whether He is a sinner or not, I do not know; I only know that whereas I was blind, now I see." Then follows the inference, "If this man were not from God, He could do nothing."[13] The divine authority of Christ is inferred from His power to enable men to see God. Now John accepts in the fullest way the mystic's presupposition that "like is known by like,"[14] so that there is no knowledge of God apart from a measure of participation in the life of God. What Christ does for us is to communicate to us the life of God. Through Christ we are "born anew" into a divine life.[15] This may fairly be described as mysticism: yet it is not so far removed after all from experience such as the non-mystic may have. For "God is love: and he who abides in love abides in God."[16] The discourses of the

Upper Room set us in the midst of a circle of "friends" of Christ;[17] and we shall not be wrong in concluding that the author had learnt in the company of friends of Christ that way of living by love that He communicated, and through it had found unity with God. When once he had found that, then the demand his soul had been making all his life—"Show us the Father"—was satisfied. "He who has seen Me has seen the Father."[18]

If we are to follow the leading of this evangelist, even to see God in Christ is not the first step in the Christian revelation. That "God is like Christ" is often commended to us to-day as an entirely non-dogmatic statement which anyone might accept as a starting-point. As a matter of fact it is a colossal assumption, for anyone who has not first accepted Christ's attitude to life. We may more modestly and more sincerely start by recognizing, as people aware of disharmony within ourselves, of non-adaptation to our environment, and of estrangement from God, that Christ stands for a thoroughgoing reconciliation, and offers such reconciliation to us. When we accept His way, then we come into a position in which we can begin to see the truth of God in our own experience as interpreted by what He said and what He was.

From what the New Testament shows us of the manner in which Jesus revealed God to men, we may learn something about the way in which the Bible as a whole may become the "Word of God" to us. Jesus was primarily concerned not with delivering "doctrine," but with making men anew, so that they could receive the revelation of Himself which God is always seeking to communicate. Similarly, the most important thing we find in the Bible is not "doctrine" but something that helps us into a new attitude to God and to life. Of course, no mere reading of books could make anyone good or religious, if he did not wish to be such. There are indeed many cases on record where the casual reading of a portion of Scripture awakened a desire for God which seemed to be completely dormant. Perhaps, if fuller *data* were available, it would be found to have been more awake than the subject himself realized. In general we may take it that if the Bible is to do its work it makes certain demands upon its readers at the outset. In the same way Jesus Himself could not save men without their own goodwill. There was a village where "He could not do any deed of power, and He was astonished at their lack of faith."[19] Still less can the Bible do anything for a reader who does not satisfy such minimum requirements, which may be summed up as sincerity, openness of mind, and that fundamental reverence that is a willingness to be commanded. To ask how a man who is radically insincere can become sincere is to raise ultimate questions about personality which cannot here be discussed. No one is born insincere, and probably no one is without his moments of sincerity.

For those who approach the Bible in this spirit (which Jesus described as that of a child), it is capable of awakening and redirecting the powers of mind, heart and will, so that a man's whole attitude and relation to the last realities is shaped anew. It can do this because it is the sincere utterance of men who were themselves mightily certain of God in their own experience, individual and corporate.

The written word is the medium through which we reach the personality and its experience. It is never a perfect medium,

> For words, like nature, half reveal
> And half conceal the soul within.

But it is the best we have. In almost all parts of the Bible we can feel ourselves in touch with religious personalities, some of them displaying exceptional inspiration, all of them men of insight and sincerity. They write out of their experience of God in the soul, or of God's dealings in what happened to them and their people. Because they were "men of God," their experience is a valid representation of divine reality. It profits us as we "live ourselves into it."[20] As we have seen, the range of experience reflected in the Bible is amazingly wide, and to share it by yielding ourselves to the guidance of its writers is to expose our souls on all sides to the divine action.

The Bible has suffered from being treated too much as a source of information. The traditional theory valued it as giving authoritative information, in the form of dogma, upon matters known only by special revelation. The critical method has too often issued in treating it as a collection of information for the antiquary. Its place as a whole is rather with the masterpieces of poetry, drama and philosophy, that is, the literature which does not so much impart information but stirs the deeper levels of personality. "Tragedy," said Aristotle, "effects through pity and fear the purgation of such passions."[21] The dramatist has experienced life in terms of the suffering that besets it and the spirit that triumphs over the suffering. The compassion and awe that the experience arouses in him he succeeds in conveying to his audience or his readers. Through identifying themselves with his personages in their pitiful and terrible experiences, they undergo an emotional awakening and cleansing. Thus *King Lear* or *Tess of the D'Urbervilles* does not instruct us in a theory of life, but makes us sharers in an experience of life more intense and profound than our normal level. We are greater men, potentially, for reading such works.

It is here that we find the best analogy to that which the reading of the Bible should do for us. Its writers are men who had an experience of life both deep and intense. They felt with sincerity, and express what they felt with strong conviction. As we identify ourselves with them in our reading, we too may come to a deeper and more intense experience of life. And as God touches us in all great literature, wherein is "the precious life-blood of a master-spirit," so

He touches us supremely in the literature of the Bible, because of the intrinsic sublimity of its writings and because the experience they transmit is so organically related to history and to the divine Incarnation in Christ, in which we recognize the supreme act of God in history. The criterion lies within ourselves, in the response of our own spirit to the Spirit that utters itself in the Scriptures. The Reformation theologians, who appealed from the authority of the Church to the authority of the Scriptures, sought confirmation for the latter in the "interior witness of the Holy Spirit." This is in effect the "subjective" criterion of which we are speaking.[22]

Thus the religious authority of the Bible comes home to us primarily in inducing in us a religious attitude and outlook. The use that may be made of the Bible as a source of doctrine is secondary to this. It is, however, by no means unimportant. The reaction against the old dogmatic use of the Scriptures has in some quarters gone too far. Anyone, of course, can find in the Bible materials for a "history of dogma." As we have said, the first question we must ask in our study is, What did this writer actually say and what did he mean by it? It is the conscientious putting of that question that has so greatly advanced our knowledge of the actual contents of the Scriptures during the period of critical study. But anyone who takes the matter with full seriousness will not be content to stop there. When he has discovered what the writer actually said and meant, he wants to ask further, Is this what I am to believe about God? Is it *true?* Probably no one who reads this book will think that this question has the self-evident answer, Of course it is true, *because* it is in the Bible. We must take responsibility for our beliefs. But supposing we have found that by approaching the Bible in that "child-like" spirit of openness and sincerity our outlook on life has been altered, our experience deepened, and our sense of God made stronger, then the beliefs enunciated by the writers to whom we owe this will carry weight with us. We shall not lightly dismiss any theological propositions they may put forth. And after all there are some very dogmatic beliefs indeed which stand out boldly from the pages of the Bible, as for instance the prophetic maxim that there is one God and He is good, and the New Testament definition, "God is love." Neither is at once self-evident, or always easy of belief. Both are challenged today, as they have been in the past, on grounds which no serious person can treat with contempt. In our best moments, it may be, we see that the world of our experience as a whole will not make sense on any other hypothesis. But there are times, it may well be, when doubts are stronger than our faith. It would not be honest at such times simply to silence our questionings with a text. Nevertheless we may well turn away from the narrow scene of individual experience at the moment, to the spacious prospect we command in the Bible.[23] Here we meet with men whom we must acknowledge as experts in life, and find them asserting with the firmest conviction that God is of such a nature. Here also we trace the long history of a community which through good fortune and ill tested their belief in God, and experimented too in varieties of belief, with the result that the "logic of facts" drove deeper and deeper the conviction that while some ways of thinking of God are definitely closed, this way lies open and leads on and on. We can go forward if we will till we come to the great *denouement* of the story in the evangelical facts of the life and death of Jesus Christ and the emergence of the redeemed society. When we have "lived ourselves into" all that, we may well see our doubts and difficulties in a different perspective; and so belief raises itself afresh upon a deeper and wider basis. The impressive witness of religious genius and of history has not indeed overborne our individual judgment, but it has delivered us from the tyranny of proximate impressions, made us free of a larger experience, and helped us to a true objectivity of judgment. Such is the "authority" of the Bible in its true and legitimate sense.

The appeal to biblical authority in this sense does not lay Christian thought under the dead hand of the past. Its effect is to associate the Christian mind of to-day with a tradition of life and experience rather than of dogma, of religion rather than of theology. To refuse such an association is to deny something which belongs to the genius of Christianity itself, for an irresponsible individualism in religion is not Christian; and when once the corporate factor in Christian experience is admitted, the factor of historical tradition cannot be excluded. But one element in the life and tradition so transmitted is progressive movement. The attempt to find a static finality in religion, as for instance in the fixing of the Torah, never succeeded.[24] In the New Testament it is the witness to the evangelical facts, as experienced in history by the first believers, that is regarded as constant and unchanging. Their interpretation is subject to development.[25] The last of the great prophetic writers in the canon, the author of the Fourth Gospel, makes Christ take leave of His followers with the words, "I have much still to say to you, but at present you cannot bear the weight of it. When however He comes, who is the Breath of the Truth, he will lead you into the whole truth."[26] We need not confine that leading to the New Testament period. It is not in the nature of an historical religion to be static, and the "faith once delivered to the saints"[27] has actually grown and developed as any faith which encounters life and experience in a changing world must develop. Catholic Christianity has its organs for recording and formulating such development, in spite of its traditional conservatism. On the other hand, it was a representative of a type of Protestantism most rigorous in its appeal to the Scripture who declared, "The Lord hath more light and truth yet to break forth out of His holy word."[28] If the Bible is indeed "the Word of God," it is so not as the "last word" on all religious questions, but as the "seminal word" out of which fresh apprehension of truth springs in the mind of man.

Notes

[1]Chap. I, pp. 16-17.

[2]Part I.

[3]Part II.

[4]Part III.

[5]Part IV.

[6]Mark 10:18.

[7]Mark 10:27; 14:36.

[8]Luke 6:35 (Matt. 5:45)

[9]Those who would maintain that He did so must refer to apocalyptic passages; these contain statements (among others) which in their plain meaning are not true (see p. 233). Either therefore the tradition is at fault, or such revelations were not inerrant, or their interpretation remains an open question. Apart from these, it is only possible to refer to a supposed esoteric tradition for which there is no historical evidence.

[10]In I Cor. 7:10; 9:14, and perhaps in other less unambiguous places.

[11]II Cor. 5:17: the whole context is illuminating.

[12]John 7:17.

[13]John 9:24-33. Whatever historical event may or may not lie behind the narrative, the evangelist is telling, in his own intention, the story of the illumination of the spiritually blind.

[14]*Corpus Hermeticum* (ed Scott), XI. ii. 20b.

[15]John 3:5-8.

[16]I John 4:16.

[17]John 15:14-15.

[18]John 14:8-9.

[19]Mark 6:5-6.

[20]If we may borrow from the Germans their expressive phrase *"sich hineinleben."*

[21]*Poetics,* 1449[b.] 27.

[22]In a sense this may be said to involve a *circulus in probando:* we look to the Bible for guidance towards religious truth; we recognize this truth by reference to our own sincere religious standards. It is in some sense parallel to Aristotle's attempt to define moral good. After all his attempts

to find an "objective" or quantitative standard for virtue he has to fall back upon the test ὡς ἂν ὁ φρόνιμος ὁρίσειε —virtue is that which the man of moral insight judges to be such (*Eth. Nic.* 1107ᵃ). In morals and religion no purely objective evidence is obtainable. But Christianity recognizes a "somewhat not ourselves" in the most inward form of experience: that is the *testimonium Spiritus Sancti internum*. The ultimate "fact" is the unity of experience in which "subjective" and "objective" are one. See H. Wheeler Robinson, *The Christian Experience of the Holy Spirit*, pp. 95-96.

[23]"Though it is morally certain that we are wiser than our fathers, it is doubtful whether we are more profound than all the ages" (Keith Feiling in *The Times*, Feb. 9th, 1928).

[24]After the Torah was completed, the Mishna was created to bring it up to date, and the Gemara of the Talmud to bring the Mishna up to date!

[25]I Cor. 15:1-11; 3:10-11.

[26]John 16:13.

[27]Jude 3.

[28]John Robinson to the "Pilgrim Fathers."

The Dependability of the Bible

19

Benjamin B. Warfield

The Real Problem of Inspiration

Immense Weight of Evidence for the Biblical Doctrine

It is only to turn another face of the proposition with which we are dealing towards us, to emphasize next the important fact, that, the state of the case being such as we have found it, the evidence for the truth of the doctrine of the plenary inspiration of Scripture is just the whole body of evidence which goes to show that the apostles are trustworthy teachers of doctrine.

Language is sometimes made use of which would seem to imply that the amount or weight of the evidence offered for the truth of the doctrine that the Scriptures are the Word of God in such a sense that their words deliver the truth of God without error, is small. It is on the contrary just the whole body of evidence which goes to prove the writers of the New Testament to be trustworthy as deliverers of doctrine. It is just the same evidence in amount and weight which is

From Benjamin B. Warfield, *The Inspiration and Authority of the Bible*. Philadelphia: Presbyterian and Reformed Pub. Co., 1964. Used by permission.

adduced in favor of any other Biblical doctrine. It is the same weight and amount of evidence precisely which is adducible for the truth of the doctrines of the Incarnation, of the Trinity, of the Divinity of Christ, of Justification by Faith, of Regeneration by the Holy Spirit, of the Resurrection of the Body, of Life Everlasting. It is, of course, not absurdly intended that every Biblical doctrine is taught in the Scriptures with equal clearness, with equal explicitness, with equal frequency. Some doctrines are stated with an explicit precision that leaves little to systematic theology in its efforts to define the truth on all sides, except to repeat the words which the Biblical writers have used to teach it—as for example the doctrine of Justification by Faith. Others are not formulated in Scripture at all, but are taught only in their elements, which the systematician must collect and combine and so arrive finally at the doctrine—as for example the doctrine of the Trinity. Some are adverted to so frequently as to form the whole warp and woof of Scripture—as for example the doctrine of redemption in the blood of Christ. Others are barely alluded to here and there, in connections where the stress is really on other matters—as for example the doctrine of the fall of the angels. But however explicitly or incidentally, however frequently or rarely, however emphatically or allusively, they may be taught, when exegesis has once done its work and shown that they are taught by the Biblical writers all these doctrines stand as supported by the same weight and amount of evidence—the evidence of the trustworthiness of the Biblical writers as teachers of doctrine. We cannot say that we will believe these writers when they assert a doctrine a hundred times and we will not believe them if they assert it only ten times or only once; that we will believe them in the doctrines they make the main subjects of discourse, but not in those which they advert to incidentally; that we will believe them in those that they teach as conclusions of formal arguments, but not in those which they use as premises wherewith to reach those conclusions; that we will believe them in those they explicitly formulate and dogmatically teach, but not in those which they teach only in their separate parts and elements. The question is not *how* they teach a doctrine, but *do* they teach it; and when that question is once settled affirmatively, the weight of evidence that commends this doctrine to us as true is the same in every case; and that is the whole body of evidence which goes to show that the Biblical writers are trustworthy as teachers of doctrine. The Biblical doctrine of inspiration, therefore, has in its favor just this whole weight and amount of evidence. It follows on the one hand that it cannot rationally be rejected save on the ground of evidence which will outweigh the whole body of evidence which goes to authenticate the Biblical writers as trustworthy witnesses to and teachers of doctrine. And it follows, on the other hand, that if the Biblical doctrine of inspiration is rejected, our freedom from its trammels is bought logically at the somewhat serious cost of discrediting the evidence which goes to show that the Biblical writers are trustworthy as teachers of doctrine. In this sense, the fortunes of distinctive Christianity are bound up with those of the Biblical doctrine of inspiration.

Let it not be said that thus we found the whole Christian system upon the doctrine of plenary inspiration. We found the whole Christian system on the doctrine of plenary inspiration as little as we found it upon the doctrine of angelic existences. Were there no such thing as inspiration, Christianity would be true, and all its essential doctrines would be credibly witnessed to us in the generally trustworthy reports of the teaching of our Lord and of His authoritative agents in founding the Church, preserved in the writings of the apostles and their first followers, and in the historical witness of the living Church. Inspiration is not the most fundamental of Christian doctrines, nor even the first thing we prove about the Scriptures. It is the last and crowning fact as to the Scriptures. These we first prove authentic, historically credible, generally trustworthy, before we prove them inspired. And the proof of their authenticity, credibility, general trustworthiness would give us a firm basis for Christianity prior to any knowledge on our part of their inspiration, and apart indeed from the existence of inspiration. The present writer, in order to prevent all misunderstanding, desires to repeat here what he has said on every proper occasion—that he is far from contending that without inspiration there could be no Christianity. "Without any inspiration," he added, when making this affirmation on his induction into the work of teaching the Bible[1]—"without any inspiration we could have had Christianity; yea, and men could still have heard the truth and through it been awakened, and justified, and sanctified, and glorified. The verities of our faith would remain historically proven to us—so bountiful has God been in His fostering care—even had we no Bible; and through those verities, salvation." We are in entire harmony in this matter with what we conceive to be the very true statement recently made by Dr. George P. Fisher, that "if the authors of the Bible were credible reporters of revelations of God, whether in the form of historical transactions of which they were witnesses, or of divine mysteries that were unveiled to their minds, their testimony would be entitled to belief, even if they were shut up to their unaided faculties in communicating what they had thus received."[2] We are in entire sympathy in this matter, therefore, with the protest which Dr. Marcus Dods raised in his famous address at the meeting of the Alliance of the Reformed Churches at London, against representing that "the infallibility of the Bible is the ground of the whole Christian faith."[3] We judge with him that it is very important indeed that such a misapprehension, if it is anywhere current, should be corrected. What we are at present arguing is something entirely different from such an overstrained view of the importance of inspiration to the very existence of Christian faith, and something which has no connection with it. We do not think that the doctrine of plenary inspiration is the ground of Christian faith, but if it was held and taught by the New Testament writers, we think it an element in the Christian faith; a very important and valuable element;[4] an element that appeals to our acceptance on precisely the same ground as every other element of the faith, viz., on the ground of our recognition of the writers of the New Testament as trustworthy witnesses to doctrine; an element of the Christian faith, therefore, which cannot be rejected without logically undermining our trust in all the other elements of distinctive Christianity by undermining the evidence on which this trust rests. We must indeed prove the authenticity, credibility and general trustworthiness of the New Testament writings before we prove their inspiration; and even were they not inspired this proof would remain valid and we should give them accordant trust. But just because this proof is valid, we must trust these writings in their witness to their inspiration, if they give such witness; and if we refuse to trust them here, we have in principle refused them trust everywhere. In such circumstances their inspiration is bound up inseparably with their trustworthiness, and therefore with all else that we receive on trust from them.

On the other hand, we need to remind ourselves that to say that the amount and weight of the evidence of the truth of the Biblical doctrine of inspiration is measured by the amount and weight of the evidence for the general credibility and trustworthiness of the New Testament writers as witnesses to doctrine, is an understatement rather than an overstatement of the matter. For if we trust them at all we will trust them in the account they give of the person and in the report they give of the teaching of Christ; whereupon, as they report Him as teaching the same doctrine of Scripture that they teach, we are brought face to face with divine testimony to this doctrine of inspiration. The argument, then, takes the form given it by Bishop Wordsworth: "The New Testament canonizes the Old; the INCARNATE WORD sets His seal on the WRITTEN WORD. The Incarnate Word is God; therefore, the inspiration of the Old Testament is authenticated by God Himself."[5] And, again, the general trustworthiness of the writers of the New Testament gives us the right and imposes on us the duty of accepting their witness to the relation the Holy Ghost bears to their teaching, as, for example, when Paul tells us that the things which they uttered they uttered "not in words taught by human wisdom, but in those taught by the Spirit; joining Spirit-given things with Spirit-given things" (I Cor. 2:13), and Peter asserts that the Gospel was preached by them "in the Holy Spirit" (I Peter 1:12); and this relation asserted to exist between the Holy Ghost and their teaching, whether oral or written (I Cor. 14:37; II Thess. 2:15; 3:6-14), gives the sanction of the Holy Ghost to their doctrine of

Holy Scripture, whatever that is found to be. So that, even though we begin on the lowest ground, we may find ourselves compelled to say, as Bishop Wilberforce found himself compelled to say: "In brief, my belief is this: The whole Bible comes to us as 'the Word of God' under the sanction of God, the Holy Ghost."[6] The weight of the testimony to the Biblical doctrine of inspiration, in a word, is no less than the weight to be attached to the testimony of God—God the Son and God the Spirit.

But our present purpose is not to draw out the full value of the testimony, but simply to emphasize the fact that on the emergence of the exegetical fact that the Scriptures of the New Testament teach this doctrine, the amount and weight of evidence for its truth must be allowed to be the whole amount and weight of the evidence that the writers of the New Testament are trustworthy as teachers of doctrine. It is not on some shadowy and doubtful evidence that the doctrine is based—not on an *a priori* conception of what inspiration ought to be, not on a "tradition" of doctrine in the Church, though all the *a priori* considerations and the whole tradition of doctrine in the Church are also thrown in the scale for and not in that against this doctrine; but first on the confidence which we have in the writers of the New Testament as doctrinal guides, and ultimately on whatever evidence of whatever kind and force exists to justify that confidence. In this sense, we repeat, the cause of distinctive Christianity is bound up with the cause of the Biblical doctrine of inspiration. We accept Christianity in all its distinctive doctrines on no other ground than the credibility and trustworthiness of the Bible as a guide to truth; and on this same ground we must equally accept its doctrine of inspiration. "If we may not accept its account of itself," asks Dr. Purves, pointedly, "why should we care to ascertain its account of other things?"[7]

Immense Presumption Against Alleged Facts Contradictory of the Biblical Doctrine

We are again making no new affirmation but only looking from a slightly different angle upon the same proposition with which we have been dealing from the first, when we emphasize next the fact, that the state of the case being as we have found it, we approach the study of the so-called "phenomena" of the Scriptures with a very strong presumption that these Scriptures contain no errors, and that any "phenomena" apparently inconsistent with their inerrancy are so in appearance only: a presumption the measure of which is just the whole amount and weight of evidence that the New Testament writers are trustworthy as teachers of doctrine.

It seems to be often tacitly assumed that the Biblical doctrine of inspiration cannot be confidently ascertained until all the facts concerning the contents and structure and characteristics of Scripture are fully determined and allowed for. This is obviously fallacious. What Paul, for example, believed as to the nature of Scripture is obviously an easily separable question from what the nature of Scripture really is. On the other hand, the assumption that we cannot confidently accept the Biblical doctrine of inspiration as true until criticism and exegesis have said their last word upon the structure, the text, and the characteristics of Scripture, even to the most minute fact, is more plausible. But it is far from obviously true. Something depends upon our estimate of the force of the mass of evidence which goes to show the trustworthiness of the apostles as teachers of truth, and of the clearness with which they announce their teaching as to inspiration. It is conceivable, for example, that the force of the evidence of their trustworthiness may be so great that we should be fully justified in yielding implicit confidence to their teaching, even though many and serious difficulties should stand in the way of accepting it. This, indeed, is exactly what we do in our ordinary use of Scripture as a source of doctrine. Who doubts that the doctrines of the Trinity and of the Incarnation present difficulties to rational construction? Who doubts that the doctrines of native demerit and total depravity, inability and eternal punishment raise objections in the natural heart? We accept these doctrines and others which ought to be much harder to credit, such as the Biblical teaching that God so loved sinful man as to give His only-begotten Son to die for him, not because their acceptance is not attended with difficulties, but because our confidence in the New Testament as a doctrinal guide is so grounded in unassailable and compelling evidence, that we believe its teachings despite the difficulties which they raise. We do not and we cannot wait until all these difficulties are fully explained before we yield to the teaching of the New Testament the fullest confidence of our minds and hearts. How then can it be true that we are to wait until all difficulties are removed before we can accept with confidence the Biblical doctrine of inspiration? In relation to this doctrine alone, are we to assume the position that we will not yield faith in response to due and compelling evidence of the trustworthiness of the teacher, until all difficulties are explained to our satisfaction—that we must fully understand and comprehend before we will believe? Or is the point this—that we can suppose ourselves possibly mistaken in everything else except our determination of the characteristics and structure of Scripture and the facts stated therein? Surely if we do not need to wait until we understand how God can be both one and three, how Christ can be both human and divine, how man can be both unable and responsible, how an act can be both free and certain, how man can be both a sinner and righteous in God's sight, before we accept, on the authority of the teaching of Scripture, the doctrines of the Trinity, of the Incarnation, of man's state as a sinner, of God's eternal predestination of the acts of free agents, and of acceptance on the ground of Christ's righteousness, because of the weight of the evidence which goes to prove that Scripture trustworthy as a teacher of divine truth; we may on the same compelling evidence accept, in full confidence, the teaching of the same Scripture as to the nature of its own inspiration, prior to a full understanding of how all the phenomena of Scripture are to be adjusted to it.

No doubt it is perfectly true and is to be kept in mind that the claim of a writing to be infallible may be mistaken or false. Such a claim has been put forth in behalf of and by other writings besides the Bible, and has been found utterly inconsistent with the observed characteristics of those writings. An *a priori* possibility may be asserted to exist in the case of the Bible, that a comparison of its phenomena with its doctrine may bring out a glaring inconsistency. The test of the truth of the claims of the Bible to be inspired of God through comparison with its contents, characteristics and phenomena, the Bible cannot expect to escape; and the lovers of the Bible will be the last to deny the validity of it. By all means let the doctrine of the Bible be tested by the facts and let the test be made all the more, not the less, stringent and penetrating because of the great issues that hang upon it. If the facts are inconsistent with the doctrine, let us all know it, and know it so clearly that the matter is put beyond doubt. But let us not conceal from ourselves the greatness of the issues involved in the test, lest we approach the test in too light a spirit, and make shipwreck of faith in the trustworthiness of the apostles as teachers of doctrine, with the easy indifference of a man who corrects the incidental errors of a piece of gossip. Nor is this appeal to the seriousness of the issues involved in any sense an appeal to deal deceitfully with the facts concerning or stated in the Bible, through fear of disturbing our confidence in a comfortable doctrine of its infallibility. It is simply an appeal to common sense. If you are told that a malicious lie has been uttered by some unknown person you may easily yield the report a languid provisional assent; such things are not impossible, unfortunately in this sinful world not unexampled. But if it is told you of your loved and trusted friend, you will probably demand the most stringent proof at the point of your walking stick. So far as this, Robert Browning has missed neither nature nor right reason, when he makes his Ferishtah point out how much more evidence we require in proof of a fact which brings us loss than what is sufficient to command.

> The easy acquiescence of mankind
> In matters nowise worth dispute.

If it is right to test most carefully the claim of every settled and accepted faith by every fact asserted in rebuttal of it, it must be equally right, nay incumbent, to scrutinize most closely the evidence for an asserted fact, which, if genuine, wounds in its vitals some important interest. If it would be a crime to refuse to consider most carefully and candidly any phenomena of Scripture asserted to be inconsistent with its inerrancy, it would be equally a crime to accept the asserted reality of phenomena of Scripture, which, if real, strike at the trustworthiness of the apostolic witness to doctrine, on any evidence of less than demonstrative weight.

But we approach the consideration of these phenomena alleged to be inconsistent with the Biblical doctrine of inspiration not only thus with what may be called, though in a high sense, a sentimental presumption against their reality. The presumption is an eminently rational one, and is capable of somewhat exact estimation. We do not adopt the doctrine of the plenary inspiration of Scripture on sentimental grounds, nor even, as we have already had occasion to remark on *a priori* or general grounds of whatever kind. We adopt it specifically because it is taught us as truth by Christ and His apostles, in the Scriptural record of their teaching, and the evidence for its truth is, therefore, as we have also already pointed out, precisely that evidence, in weight and amount, which vindicates for us the trustworthiness of Christ and His apostles as teachers of doctrine. Of course, this evidence is not in the strict logical sense "demonstrative"; it is "probable" evidence. It therefore leaves open the metaphysical possibility of its being mistaken. But it may be contended that it is about as great in amount and weight as "probable" evidence can be made, and that the strength of conviction which it is adapted to produce may be and should be practically equal to that produced by demonstration itself. But whatever weight it has, and whatever strength of conviction it is adapted to produce, it is with this weight of evidence behind us and with this strength of conviction as to the unreality of any alleged phenomena contradictory of the Biblical doctrine of inspiration, that we approach the study of the characteristics, the structure, and the detailed statements of the Bible. Their study is not to be neglected; we have not attained through "probable" evidence apodeictic certainty of the Bible's infallibility. But neither is the reality of the alleged phenomena inconsistent with the Bible's doctrine, to be allowed without sufficient evidence. Their reality cannot be logically or rationally recognized unless the evidence for it be greater in amount and weight than the whole mass of evidence for the trustworthiness of the Biblical writers as teachers of doctrine.

It is not to be thought that this amounts to a recommendation of strained exegesis in order to rid the Bible of phenomena adverse to the truth of the Biblical doctrine of inspiration. It amounts to a recommendation of great care in the exegetical determination of these alleged phenomena; it amounts to a recommendation to allow that our exegesis determining these phenomena is not infallible. But it is far from recommending either strained or artificial exegesis of any kind. We are not bound to harmonize the alleged phenomena with the Bible doctrine; and if we cannot harmonize them save by strained or artificial exegesis they would be better left unharmonized. We are not bound, however, on the other hand, to believe that they are unharmonizable, because we cannot harmonize them save by strained exegesis. Our individual fertility in exegetical expedients, our individual insight into exegetical truth, our individual capacity of understanding are not the measure of truth. If we cannot harmonize without straining, let us leave unharmonized. It is not necessary for us to see the harmony that it should exist or even be recognized by us as existing. But it is necessary for us to believe the harmony to be possible and real, provided that we are not prepared to say that we clearly see that on any conceivable hypothesis (conceivable to us or conceivable to any other intelligent beings) the harmony is impossible—if the trustworthiness of the Biblical writers who teach us the doctrine of plenary inspiration is really safeguarded to us on evidence which we cannot disbelieve. In that case every unharmonized passage remains a case of difficult harmony and does not pass into the category of objections to plenary inspiration. It can pass into the category of objections only if we are prepared to affirm that we clearly see that it is, on any conceivable hypothesis of its meaning, clearly inconsistent with the Biblical doctrine of inspiration. In that case we would no doubt need to give up the Biblical doctrine of inspiration; but with it we must also give up our confidence in the Biblical writers as teachers of doctrine. And if we cannot reasonably give up this latter, neither can we reasonably allow that the phenomena apparently inconsistent with the former are real, or really inconsistent with it. And this is but to say that we approach the study of these phenomena with a presumption against their being such as will disprove the Biblical doctrine of inspiration—or, we may add (for this is but the same thing in different words), correct or modify the Biblical doctrine of inspiration—which is measured precisely by the amount and weight of the evidence which goes to show that the Bible is a trustworthy guide to doctrine.

The importance of emphasizing these, as it would seem, very obvious principles, does not arise out of need for a very great presumption in order to overcome the difficulties arising from the "phenomena" of Scripture, as over against its doctrine of inspiration. Such difficulties are not specially numerous or intractable. Dr. Charles Hodge justly characterizes those that have been adduced by disbelievers in the plenary inspiration of the Scriptures, as "for the most part trivial," "only apparent," and marvelously few "of any real importance." They bear, he adds, about the same relation to the whole that a speck of sandstone detected here and there in the marble of the Parthenon would bear to that building.[8] They do not for the most part require explaining away, but only to be fairly understood in order to void them. They constitute no real strain upon faith, but when approached in a candid spirit one is left continually marveling at the excessive fewness of those which do not, like ghosts, melt away from vision as soon as faced. Moreover, as every student of the history of exegesis and criticism knows, they are a progressively vanishing quantity. Those which seemed most obvious and intractable a generation or two ago, remain today as only too readily forgotten warnings against the ineradicable and inordinate dogmatism of the opponents of the inerrancy of the Bible, who over-ride continually every canon of historical and critical caution in their eager violence against the doctrine that they assail. What scorn they expressed of "apologists" who doubted whether Luke was certainly in error in assigning a "proconsul" to Cyprus, whether he was in error in making Lysanias a contemporary tetrarch with the Herodian rulers, and the like. How easily that scorn is forgotten as the progress of discovery has one by one vindicated the assertions of the Biblical historians. The matter has come to such a pass, indeed, in the progress of discovery, that there is a sense in which it may be said that the doctrine of the inerrancy of the Bible can now be based, with considerable confidence, on its observed "phenomena." What marvelous accuracy is characteristic of its historians! Dr. Fisher, in a paper already referred to, invites his readers to read Archibald Forbes' article in the *Nineteenth Century* for March, 1892, on "Napoleon the Third at Sedan," that they may gain some idea of how the truth of history as to the salient facts may be preserved amid "hopeless and bewildering discrepancies in regard to details," in the reports of the most trustworthy eye-witnesses. The article is instructive in this regard. And it is instructive in another regard also. What a contrast exists between this mass of "hopeless and bewildering discrepancies in regard to details," among the accounts of a single important transaction, written by careful and watchful eye-witnesses, who were on the ground for the precise purpose of gathering the facts for report, and who were seeking to give an exact and honest account of the events which they witnessed, and the marvelous accuracy of the Biblical writers! If these "hopeless and bewildering discrepancies" are consistent with the honesty and truthfulness and general trustworthiness of the uninspired writers, may it not be argued that the so much greater accuracy attained by the Biblical writers when describing not one event but the history of ages—and a history filled with pitfalls for the unwary—has something more than honesty and truthfulness behind it, and warrants the attribution to them of something more than general trustworthiness? And if in the midst of this marvel of general accuracy there remain here and there a few difficulties as yet not fully explained in harmony with it, or if in the course of the historical vindication of it in general a rare difficulty (as in the case of some of the statements of Daniel) seems to increase in sharpness, are we to throw ourselves with desperate persistency into these "last ditches" and strive by our increased insistence upon the impregnability of *them* to conceal from men that the main army has been beaten from the field? Is it not more reasonable to suppose that these difficulties, too, will receive their explanation with advancing knowledge? And is it not the height of the unreasonable to treat them like the Sibylline books as of ever-increasing importance in proportion to their decreasing number? The importance of keeping in mind that there is a presumption against the reality of these "inconsistent phenomena," and that the presumption is of a weight measurable only by the weight of evidence which vindicates the general trustworthiness of the Bible as a teacher of doctrine, does not arise from the need of so great a presumption in order to overcome the weight of the alleged opposing facts. Those facts are not specially numerous, important or intractable, and they are, in the progress of research, a vanishing quantity.

The importance of keeping in mind the principle in question arises rather from the importance of preserving a correct logical method. There are two ways of approaching the study of the inspiration of the Bible. One proceeds by obtaining first the doctrine of inspiration taught by the Bible as applicable to itself, and then testing this doctrine by the facts as to the Bible as ascertained by Biblical criticism and exegesis. This is good logical procedure; and in the presence of a vast mass of evidence for the general trustworthiness of the Biblical writings as witnesses of doctrine, and for the appointment of their writers as teachers of divine truth to men, and for the presence of the Holy Spirit with and in them aiding them in their teaching (in whatever degree and with whatever effect)—it would seem to be the only logical and proper mode of approaching the question. The other method proceeds by seeking the doctrine of inspiration in the first instance through a comprehensive induction from the facts as to the structure and contents of the Bible, as ascertained by critical and exegetical processes, treating all these facts as co-factors of the same rank for the induction. If in this process the facts of structure and the facts embedded in the record of Scripture—which are called, one-sidedly indeed but commonly, by the class of writers who adopt this procedure, "the phenomena" of Scripture—alone are considered, it would be difficult to arrive at a precise doctrine of inspiration, at the best: though, as we have already pointed out, a degree and kind of accuracy might be vindicated for the Scriptures which might lead us to suspect and to formulate as the best account of it, some divine assistance to the writers' memory, mental processes and expression. If the Biblical facts and teaching are taken as co-factors in the induction, the procedure (as we have already pointed out) is liable to the danger of modifying the teaching by the facts without clear recognition of what is being done; the result of which would be the loss from observation of one main fact of errancy, viz., the inaccuracy of the teaching of the Scriptures as to their own inspiration. This would vitiate the whole result: and this vitiation of the result can be avoided only by ascertaining separately the teaching of Scripture as to its own inspiration, and by accounting the results of this ascertainment one of the facts of the induction. Then we are in a position to judge by the comparison of this fact with the other facts, whether this fact of teaching is in accord or in disaccord with those facts of performance. If it is in disaccord, then of course this disaccord is the main factor in the case: the writers are convicted of false teaching. If it is in accord, then, if the teaching is not proved by the accord, it is at least left credible, and may be believed with whatever confidence may be justified by the evidence which goes to show that these writers are trustworthy as deliverers of doctrine. And if nice and difficult questions arise in the comparison of the fact of teaching with the facts of performance, it is inevitable that the relative weight of the evidence for the trustworthiness of the two sets of facts should be the deciding factor in determining the truth. This is as much as to say that the asserted facts as to performance must give way before the fact as to teaching, unless the evidence on which they are based as facts outweighs the evidence on which the teaching may be accredited as true. But this correction of the second method of procedure, by which alone it can be made logical in form or valid in result, amounts to nothing less than setting it aside altogether and reverting to the first method, according to which the teaching of Scripture is first to be determined, and then this teaching to be tested by the facts of performance.

The importance of proceeding according to the true logical method may be illustrated by the observation that the conclusions actually arrived at by students of the subject seem practically to depend on the logical method adopted. In fact, the difference here seems mainly a difference in point of view. If we start from the Scripture doctrine of inspiration, we approach the phenomena with the question whether they will negate this doctrine, and we find none able to stand against it, commended to us as true, as it is, by the vast mass of evidence available to prove the trustworthiness of the Scriptural writers as teachers of doctrine. But if we start simply with a collection of the phenomena, classifying and reasoning from them, whether alone or in conjunction with the Scriptural statements, it may easily happen with us, as it happened with certain of old, that meeting with some things hard to be understood, we may be ignorant and unstable enough to wrest them to our own intellectual destruction, and so approach the Biblical doctrine of inspiration set upon explaining it away. The value of having the Scripture doctrine as a clue in our hands, is thus fairly illustrated by the ineradicable inability of the whole negative school to distinguish between *difficulties* and *proved errors*. If then we ask what we are to do with the numerous phenomena of Scripture inconsistent with verbal inspiration, which, so it is alleged, "criticism" has brought to light, we must reply: Challenge them in the name of the New Testament doctrine, and ask for their credentials. They have no credentials that can stand before that challenge. No single error has as yet been demonstrated to occur in the Scriptures as given by God to His Church. And every critical student knows, as already pointed out, that the progress of investigation has been a continuous process of removing difficulties, until scarcely a shred of the old list of "Biblical Errors" remains to hide the nakedness of this moribund contention. To say that we do not wish to make claims "for which we have only this to urge, that they cannot be absolutely disproved," is not to the point; what is to the point is to say, that we cannot set aside the presumption arising from the general trustworthiness of Scripture, that its doctrine of inspiration is true, by any array of contradictory facts, each one of which is fairly disputable. We must have indisputable errors—which are not forthcoming.

The real problem brought before the Churches by the present debate ought now to be sufficiently plain. In its deepest essence it is whether we can still trust the Bible as a guide in doctrine, as a teacher of truth. It is not simply whether we can explain away the Biblical doctrine of inspiration so as to allow us to take a different view from what has been common of the structure and characteristics of the Bible. Nor, on the other hand, is it simply whether we may easily explain the facts, established as facts, embedded in Scripture, consistently with the teaching of Scripture as to the nature, extent and effects of inspiration. It is specifically whether the results proclaimed by a special school of Biblical criticism—which are of such a character, as is now admitted by all, as to necessitate, if adopted, a new view of the Bible and of its inspiration—rest on a basis of evidence strong enough to meet and overcome the weight of evidence, whatever that may be in kind and amount, which goes to show that the Biblical writers are trustworthy as teachers of doctrine. If we answer this question in the affirmative, then no doubt we shall have not only a new view of the Bible and of its inspiration but also a whole new theology, because we must seek a new basis for doctrine. But if we answer it in the negative, we may possess our souls in patience and be assured that the Scriptures are as trustworthy witnesses to truth when they declare a doctrine of Inspiration as when they declare a doctrine of Incarnation or of Redemption, even though in the one case as in the other difficulties may remain, the full explanation of which is not yet clear to us. The real question, in a word, is not a new question but the perennial old question, whether the basis of our doctrine is to be what the Bible teaches, or what men teach. And this is a question which is to be settled on the old method, viz., on our estimate of the weight and value of the evidence which places the Bible in our hands as a teacher of doctrine.

Notes

[1]"Discourses Occasioned by the Inauguration of Benj. B. Warfield, D.D., to the Chair of New Testament Exegesis and Literature in the Western Theological Seminary, April 25, 1880." Pittsburgh, 1880. P. 46. Cf. "Inspiration." By Prof. A. A. Hodge and Prof. B. B. Warfield. Philadelphia: Presbyterian Board of Publication, 1881. Pp. 7, 8 (also in *The Presbyterian Review* for April, 1881). Also "The Inspiration of the Scriptures." By Francis L. Patton, D.D. Philadelphia: Presbyterian Board of Publication, 1869. Pp. 22, 23, 54.

[2]*The Congregationalist,* Nov. 3, 1892; *The Magazine of Christian Literature,* Dec., 1892, p. 236, first column. This whole column should be read; its statement and illustration are alike admirable.

[3]This address may be most conveniently consulted in *The Expositor* for October, 1888, pp. 301, 302. In expressing our concurrence with portions of this address and of Dr. Fisher's papers just quoted, we are not to be understood, of course, as concurring with their whole contents.

[4]How important and valuable this element of the Christian faith is, it is not the purpose of this paper to point out. Let it suffice here to say briefly that it is (1) the element which gives detailed certitude to the delivery of doctrine in the New Testament, and (2) the element by which the individual Christian is brought into immediate relation to God in the revelation of truth through the prophets and apostles. The importance of these factors in the Christian life could not be overstated. The importance of the recognition of plenary inspiration to the preservation of sound doctrine is negatively illustrated by the progress of Rationalism, as thus outlined briefly by Dr. Charles Hodge ("Syst. Theol.," iii. p. 195): "Those who admitted the divine origin of the Scriptures got rid of its distinctive doctrines by the adoption of a low theory of inspiration and by the application of arbitrary principles of interpretation. Inspiration was in the first instance confined to the religious teachings of the Bible, then to the ideas or truths, but not to the form in which they were presented, nor to the arguments by which they were supported. . . . In this way a wet sponge was passed over all the doctrines of redemption and their outlines obliterated." It looks as if the Church were extremely slow in reading the most obvious lessons of history.

[5]Wordsworth, "On the Canon," p. 51, Am. Ed.

[6]"Life of the Rt. Rev. S. Wilberforce, D.D.," Vol. III. p. 149.

[7]"St. Paul and Inspiration." Inaugural Address, etc. A. D. F. Randolph & Co., 1892. P. 52. *Presbyterian and Reformed Review,* January, 1893, p. 21.

[8]"Systematic Theology," i. pp. 169, 170: We have purposely adduced this passage here to enable us to protest against the misuse of it, which, in the exigencies of the present controversy, has been made, as if Dr. Hodge was in this passage admitting the reality of the alleged errors. The passage occurs in the reply to objections to the doctrine, not in the de-

velopment of the doctrine itself, and is of the nature of an *argumentum ad hominem*. How far Dr. Hodge was from admitting the reality of error in the original Biblical text may be estimated from the frequency with which he asserts its freedom from error in the immediately preceding context —pp. 152, 155, 163 (no less than three times on this page), 165, 166, 169 (no less than five times).

20

Dewey Beegle

Inerrancy and the
Phenomena of Scripture

The discussion thus far has dealt with Biblical teachings and data that are instructive with respect to the autographs, manuscript transmission, and translations. This evidence, when viewed inductively, seems to indicate that the Bible makes no essential distinction between the three categories of Scripture. All three are considered as trustworthy and authoritative because they derive ultimately from God. However, the Biblical writers did not express themselves on many technical aspects related to the doctrine of inspiration; therefore there is the genuine problem of trying to determine just how far implications and areas of silence can be elaborated and still be true to the intent of the writers. Those who approach the issue deductively with the assumption that God, if he were truly God, had to reveal himself inerrantly are inclined to see this teaching as a clear implication of the Biblical passages.

Both approaches are sincere, but both can hardly be correct in the areas where they come to opposite conclusions. In the interests of

From Dewey Beegle, *The Inspiration of Scripture*. Philadelphia: Westminster Press, 1963. Used by permission.

truth, there needs to be some careful consideration of the phenomena or data of Scripture that have relevance for the concept of inerrancy. Let it be said at the outset, however, that it is not the writer's intention to parade the difficulties of Scripture. Those to be considered have been known for many years, but additional information warrants a new discussion of the issues.

Jude 14

Jude says in v. 14 of his one-chapter letter, "It was of these also that Enoch in the seventh generation from Adam prophesied, saying," and then follows a quotation that is found in I Enoch 1:9. The latter is one of a series of Jewish books not included within the Old Testament canon. These were written, for the most part, in the period between the Old and New Testament. The general term for these non-canonical books is the Greek word *apocrypha* (meaning "hidden," either because they were thought to be too difficult for the common person to understand, or they were considered spurious). But the book of Enoch is usually classified among the *pseudepigrapha* (literally, "false writings") because the author, employing a fictitious name, gives the impression that the work comes from a Biblical character.

The specific problem concerning us here is not, however, the quotation from an apocryphal or pseudepigraphic book. The difficulty lies in Jude's qualifying statement "seventh from Adam." Every known manuscript of Jude has this qualification, so there is good reason to believe that it came from Jude himself. But what did Jude mean by inserting this additional phrase? Some have interpreted the insertion as a literary device identifying the source of Jude's quotation in terms commonly accepted by his readers. According to this view, then, the insertion would not express Jude's actual thoughts as to the ultimate source of the quotation. In brief, "seventh from Adam" is taken as the claim in the book of Enoch: for example, Enoch is reported as saying, "I was born the seventh in the first week, while judgment and righteousness still endured" (I Enoch 93:3), and Noah, the grandson of Enoch, purports to mention "the garden where the elect and righteous dwell, where my grandfather was taken up, the seventh from Adam, the first man whom the Lord of Spirits created" (I Enoch 60:8). These references to "seventh" stem from the genealogical table found in Gen. 5.

On the other hand, Jude quotes I Enoch 1:9 as a *prophecy* which is being fulfilled in his day. Would he have done so had he thought the book and the passage originated during the period between the Testaments? Does not the cruciality of the quotation indicate, rather, that Jude thought the authority of his source derived from Enoch, the pre-Flood patriarch, who was taken up by God when he was 365 years old? At least for many centuries this was the traditional interpretation of Jude's intent. When the book of Enoch came to light, tradition generally solved the problem by claiming that Jude's source was oral tradition and that Enoch was a later book which copied from Jude.

This attempt at solving the difficulty has proved to be baseless, however. Portions of various copies of Enoch have been found among the Dead Sea (Qumran) scrolls. These date mainly from the first century B.C., so without question Jude got his quotation from a copy of the book of Enoch. There is good evidence (for example, the defence of a solar calendar) to show that the Enoch literature originated within the Qumran (Essene) tradition. Mainstream Judaism, on the contrary, followed a lunar calendar, consequently the book of Enoch was considered heretical. Even though the book was not incorporated in the Septuagint, the early Christians (with many affinities to the Qumran group) accepted it. This is quite evident because the New Testament is influenced more directly by the book of Enoch than by any other noncanonical book. Jude clearly alludes to the book in v. 6 and he quotes it in vs. 14-15, but his apparent conviction that the quotation derived from Enoch the Patriarch is untenable. As Edward Carnell observes, "Of course, orthodoxy can always say that Jude knew by inspiration that the seventh from Adam spoke the words that now appear in the book of Enoch; but the explanation sounds suspiciously affected."[1]

If one is to contend that the book of Enoch represents an oral tradition stemming from the Patriarch, one should also account in similar fashion for the mass of literature that appears in the inter-testament period under the names of various Old Testament characters. It is exceedingly strange that not one reference is made in the Old Testament to any such literature. One reads of the book of Jashar but never the book of Enoch. Is it possible that Abraham, Isaac, Jacob, and the Israelites knew of this oral tradition and yet failed to mention it? Hardly. It is equally difficult to show that God preserved the material by an oral tradition distinct from Abraham and the people of promise.

The facts at hand would seem to indicate that Jude did not realize the origin of his source. However, this view is criticized by some because it is made on partial evidence. Maybe further information would vindicate Jude, so it is reasoned. But an *argument from silence* is recognized by all to be quite weak. It implies that one must have almost total evidence before demonstration is possible. If this is the case, one could argue just as cogently that there may have been airplanes in the time of Christ. By this period, man had conceived of the idea of human flight and he knew how to work metals, etc., so why not airplanes? While this proposition sounds fantastic, it would be difficult to produce sufficient data to disprove the claim in the mind of the proponent. He could always say that someday the evidence would be forthcoming to prove his point. Likewise, in the case of Jude's quotation from Enoch, absolute proof will probably never be accessible, but is this justification enough for the fond hope of having the problem resolved in favor of Jude?

There is, of course, a place for the argument from silence, but it should not be used unless the available evidence permits a *genuine probability*, not a theoretical possibility, that the proposition is true. In far too many cases the argument from silence is resorted to only when the facts are on the side of one's opponents. On the contrary, it is amazing how little evidence it usually takes to convince a person of a point when it agrees with his presuppositions. To some extent every human being is guilty of wishful thinking, but there must come a time when the facts become determinative, and in the case of inerrancy Jude 14 is as good a place to start as any.

Either the quotation originated with Enoch the Patriarch or it did not. Aside from Jude's claim, all the evidence indicates that it did not. Jude did not intend to deceive or falsify the issue. His error was an innocent one which he made in common with his fellow Jews and Christians. But sincerity of motive did not eliminate the mistake. Moreover, the Holy Spirit did not override the human concept of Jude. How, then, does this accord with the dogma that the Holy Spirit "bore" the writers along, guiding them inerrantly in all that they wrote? The seriousness of the problem is also indicated by the fear of many even to recognize the dfficulty; for example, commentaries by evangelicals seldom discuss the problem.

Jude 9

The little book of Jude is a warning against false brethren who have infiltrated the Christian ranks and undermined "the faith which was once for all delivered to the saints" (v. 3). Jude reminds his readers that God will punish such sinners, and as proof he cites three examples: the unbelieving Israelites who died in the wilderness (v. 5), the fallen angels chained in nether gloom (v. 6), and the immoral residents of Sodom and Gomorrah who perished by fire (v. 7). The first and last examples are described in the Pentateuch and without question the author considered them as historical events in God's dealing with mankind. Apparently Jude considered God's condemnation of the fallen angels (described in an expansion of Gen. 6:1-4 found in the book of Enoch) as an actual happening in the past.

In contrast to the revilings of the false brethren, "loud-mouthed boasters" (v. 16) who "boldly carouse" (v. 12) at love feasts, Jude cites in v. 9 the example of the archangel Michael: "But when the archangel Michael, contending with the devil, disputed about the body of Moses, he did not presume to pronounce a reviling judgment upon him, but said, 'the Lord rebuke you.' "

The event to which Jude alludes is not recorded in the canonical

Old Testament. His source was another apocryphal book, The Assumption of Moses, which is usually dated early in the first century A.D. After the death of Moses, according to this account, the archangel Michael had to contend with Satan for the body. Satan claimed the body because Moses had been a murderer (Exod. 2:11). This blasphemous charge was intolerable to Michael, but rather than accuse Satan of blasphemy he simply said, "The Lord rebuke you."

While some have interpreted Jude's allusion to the apocryphal book as an argument *ad hominem* in which he cites the passage because the book was respected by his opponents, one gets the impression, just as in v. 6, that Jude believed the incident was an actual fact and thus a valid basis for refuting his adversaries.

But Jude 9 (which was also a part of the autograph of Jude) is, according to the traditional view, just as much inspired as John 3:16. If it is inspired, then why be hesitant about discussing the implications? Either the archangel Michael contended with the devil for the body of Moses or he did not. Joshua and the prophets never refer to any such struggle, so there is no Biblical reason, aside from Jude's allusion, for believing in the actuality of the story. On the other hand, does not the authoritative function of Jude's illustration show the importance that he attached to it? If, as the evidence seems to indicate, Jude accepted the current tradition with respect to the body of Moses, what becomes of the doctrine of inerrancy?

The Reign of Pekah

According to II Kings 15:27, "in the fifty-second year of Azariah king of Judah Pekah the son of Remaliah began to reign over Israel in Samaria, and reigned twenty years." For some years now, the figure 20 has been known to be wrong. James Orr, speaking of the cross references or synchronisms in the books of Kings, said, "Pekah's twenty years in II Kings 15:27 . . . is shown by the Assyrian synchronisms to be a mistake."[2] He did not explain further, and nothing was generally accessible to the layman until Edwin R. Thiele's *The Mysterious Numbers of the Hebrew Kings* appeared in 1951.

The chronology of the kings of Israel and Judah is one of the most complex problems in all the Bible, but Thiele has given sufficient evidence to clinch the matter concerning Pekah's twenty years. In the ancient world there were two systems for reckoning the years of a king's reign, the difference between the two being a matter of one year. Since Israel followed one system and Judah the other during part of their histories, there is often a difference of one year in the records. To simplify the discussion, both of Pekah's reign and of Hezekiah's reign (which is to follow), a single date will be used in each case, although technically the actual date may be a year off one way or the other. Furthermore, unless indicated otherwise, all references in the two sections will be from II Kings.

The verse in question (15:27) says Pekah began to reign in the fifty-second year of Azariah (another name for Uzziah). Azariah's death, coming in the fifty-second year of his reign, occurred about 739 B.C., and therefore Pekah's reign began then. This was also the year in which Isaiah the prophet "saw the Lord . . . high and lifted up" (Isa. 6:1). If Pekah is given his twenty years, then he finished in 719. The Biblical record says Hoshea, the last king of Israel, followed Pekah and reigned for nine years. This would mean that Samaria, the capital of Israel, fell in 710. However, archaeological evidence has confirmed beyond doubt that Samaria submitted to the Assyrians in 722. It is impossible, then, to give Pekah his twenty years after 739 B.C.

Accordingly, some early commentators figured back twenty years from 731, the end of Pekah's reign and the beginning of Hoshea's. But this reconstruction is equally impossible. Pekah was preceded by Pekahiah (two years) and Menahem (ten years). If Pekah's reign began in 751, then Menahem reigned from 763-753. Yet ch. 15:19 informs us, "Pul the king of Assyria came against the land; and Menahem gave Pul a thousand talents of silver, that he might help him to confirm his hold of the royal power." "Pul" was the Babylonian nickname for the great Assyrian king Tiglath-pileser III, whose dates 745-727) have also been settled beyond question. The annals of Tiglath-pileser refer to this same event, mentioning Menahem by name. Since the payment of tribute was made in 743 or later, Menahem could not have reigned 763-753. If Menahem cannot be moved Pekahiah's reign must remain, 741-739, with Pekah's rule beginning in 739. Inasmuch as his reign closed in 731, the twenty years ascribed to him shrink to eight.

Some scholars have accounted for Pekah's twenty years by assuming that he began reigning as a rival king in Israel at the same time Menahem did. He may have played a small part in the revolt during which Shallum was slain and Menahem set up his new dynasty (15:14), but he was in no sense a king because he was a *shalish* "captain, official" under Menahem's son, Pekahiah, the man he slew in order to gain power (15:25). Thiele is most likely correct in suggesting that Pekah took credit to himself for the twelve years that Menahem and Pekahiah had ruled.[3] Evidently Pekah, the usurper, wanted to blot out the memory of the Menahem dynasty so he had the records changed to show that the Pekah dynasty began in 751. It is virtually certain, therefore, that the notation of a twenty-year reign for Pekah originated in the court records of Israel.

Most scholars recognize that the twenty years assigned to Pekah are in error, but some are still inclined to account for it as a scribal error in transmission of the text of 15:27. This argument fails to reckon, however, with two synchronisms in 15:32 and 16:1. The text of 15:32 notes that Jotham began to reign in "the second year of

Pekah." Jotham began to reign as a coregent with his father Uzziah (who was a leper, II Chron. 26:21) about 750. If this date was considered the second year of Pekah, then his first year would have been 751. In other words, the scribe who compiled this section had assigned 751-731 as the time of Pekah's reign. The most plausible explanation for the scribe's action is that his records also attributed a twenty-year reign to Pekah. He was working up his synchronisms between the kings of Israel and of Judah about 125 to 150 years after the fall of Samaria, and so he had no way to check the accuracy of the data that had come from the Northern Kingdom. In making his comparative chart, he gave Pekah twenty years, not realizing that it was impossible (as we have noted) to put Menahem's reign 763-753 and Pekahiah's 753-751. This slip may appear a bit foolish, but the scribe of Judah knew nothing of B.C. or A.D. and the specific numbers we are using as dates. He did not have an absolute time scale (with Tiglath-pileser's dates, for example) to warn him that he could not actually give Pekah twenty years.

In 16:1 the scribe notes that Ahaz began to reign in "the seventeenth year of Pekah." This synchronism is obviously based on the assumption that Pekah reigned twenty years. But the interesting fact is that once we grant the original error of twenty years instead of eight, the dates which this relative chart gives for Jotham (750) and Ahaz (735) prove to be amazingly accurate. On the other hand, if the original text of II Kings had been inerrant (that is, in accord with the actual reigns of Menahem, 751-741, and of Pekah, 739-731), the scribe would have had Jotham beginning in "the second year of Menahem" and Ahaz starting in "the fifth year of Pekah."

Some of those who contend for the doctrine of an inerrant original text take the next logical step by suggesting that the synchronisms are later scribal insertions that did not appear in the original text of II Kings. But again the suggestion is fruitless. Chapter 15:33 begins, "He was twenty-five years old when he began to reign, and he reigned sixteen years in Jerusalem." If 15:32 is dropped, then "he" refers back to Pekah, who is discussed in 15:31. This is impossible, however, so there is no other way out but to admit that the erroneous details of 15:27, 32; 16:1 were in the original compilation of II Kings.

The Reign of Hezekiah

Another difficult chronological problem has to do with the dates of Hezekiah's reign. Chapter 18:1 states, "In the third year of Hoshea son of Elah, king of Israel, Hezekiah the son of Ahaz, king of Judah, began to reign." Hoshea began reigning in 731, when he slew Pekah (15:30). According to 18:1, then, Hezekiah began to reign about 728. But 18:13 notes that Sennacherib invaded Judah in "the fourteenth year of King Hezekiah." Since Sennacherib's campaign against Judah and Jerusalem was in 701, Hezekiah began his reign in 715.

He ruled for twenty-nine years (18:2), that is, down to 686. This conclusion is also in line with the inference from 20:6 that after Hezekiah's illness (which occurred about the time of Sennacherib's campaign) God spared his life fifteen years. Practically all scholars are agreed now that Hezekiah reigned 715-686. Then what is to be done with 18:1, which seems to begin Hezekiah's reign in 728?

In discussing this problem, Thiele writes, "Long after the original records of the kings had been set in order and when the true arrangement of the reigns had been forgotten—certain synchronisms in II Kings 17 and 18, were introduced by some late hand strangely out of harmony with the original pattern of reigns."[4] In Thiele's opinion, some scribe gave Pekah his twenty years, but this time the reign was started at 739 and pushed down twenty years. Thus Hoshea's reign was 719-710. On the basis of this chart, the scribe noted that it was in the third year of Hoshea, about 716, that Hezekiah began to reign. With this interpretation both 18:1 and 18:13 indicate the same time (716-715) for the start of Hezekiah's reign.

Chapter 17:1 indicates that Hoshea began to reign in "the twelfth year of Ahaz." Ahaz' reign of sixteen years (16:2) began in 731, therefore his twelfth year was 719, the year (according to the scribe's chart) that Hoshea began to rule. The scribe went farther and noted in 18:9-10 that the siege of Samaria began in Hezekiah's fourth year and ended in his sixth. Thus, in Thiele's judgment, the synchronisms in 17:1; 18:1, 9-10 are erroneous because the scribe allotted Pekah twenty years, 739-719.

In the joint article, "Chronology of the Old Testament," pages 212-223, in *The New Bible Dictionary,* K. A. Kitchen and T. C. Mitchell state that Thiele's interpretation of the four synchronisms is invalid. They feel that "the twelfth year" noted in 17:1 refers to Ahaz' last year of a twelve-year coregency with Jotham, rather than to the twelfth year of his sole reign. Hoshea began in 731, so according to this assumption Ahaz became a coregent with his father Jotham in 743. Chapter 16:2 ascribes to Ahaz a sixteen-year reign (undoubtedly the period 731-715), but the previous verse (16:1) tells us that his reign began in 735. Mitchell and Kitchen interpret htis to mean that Ahaz became a "senior partner" at that time. It is even more probable that the pro-Assyrian group in Judah forced Jotham (who, like his father Uzziah, was anti-Assyrian) to relinquish the rule to his son Ahaz. The policy of Ahaz was decidedly pro-Assyrian (II Chron. 28:16) and it was he, not Jotham, who was the active king when Rezin and Pekah came up (about 734) against Jerusalem (Isa. 7:1). Ahaz was twenty when he began to reign (16:2), but the text does not make it clear which beginning (735 or 731) was intended. If the former date was meant, then Ahaz was twelve years old in 743; otherwise he was eight. In 751, when he began his twelve-year coregency with Uzziah, Jotham was twenty-five (15:33). The question is whether in fact Ahaz began a twelve-year coregency in 743 when he was only twelve (or possibly eight) and when Jotham, his father, was himself technically a coregent (because Uzziah did not die until 739).

To account for 18:1, 9-10, Kitchen and Mitchell have also to postulate a twelve-year coregency for Hezekiah (beginning about 728, when he was thirteen years old). In other words, their solution necessitates twelve-year coregencies for three successive kings: Jotham, Ahaz, and Hezekiah. This coincidence does not rule out the possibility, but it raises some doubt. Clearly, the interpretation of the synchronisms in II Kings 17 and 1, hinges on the number 12. Did Ahaz and Hezekiah, like Jotham, have twelve-year coregencies (making the synchronisms technically accurate) or was Pekah given twelve years beyond his actual reign (thus resulting in erroneous synchronisms)? It is difficult to prove which view is correct, but in any case the final solution does not alter the fact of erroneous details in II Kings 15:27, 32; 16:1.

In discussing the problem of inerrant autographs—the "infallible Bible-X," as he puts it—Emil Brunner comments: "Thus an otherwise absolutely honorable orthodox view of the authority of the Bible was forced to descend to apologetic artifices of this kind. As a result the theology of the church became, and rightly, the butt of scientific criticism. In the long run this solution was untenable. At present it only continues to drag out an unhappy existence in certain Fundamentalist circles."[5] This often-quoted criticism has been characterized by many as unfounded and disrespectful of God's Word. Admittedly, Brunner overstated his case in the last sentence, not realizing how widely the view of inerrancy was held in the United States. But the main thrust of the criticism is that the doctrine of inerrancy has not faced up squarely to all the facts, and as a result it has become "the butt of scientific criticism." To be sure, scientific criticism is not inerrant, but, on the other hand, should we not earnestly reexamine our interpretation of the evidence to see whether or not Brunner's comment has some validity? We would do well to have the attitude of mind and spirit described in the following statement by Everett F. Harrison: "It would seem that the only healthy attitude for conservatives is to welcome criticism and be willing to join in it. No view of Scripture can indefinitely be sustained if it runs counter to the facts. That the Bible claims inspiration is patent. The problem is to define the nature of that inspiration in the light of the phenomena contained therein."[6]

Genesis 5

Chapter 5 in Genesis contains the genealogy of man from Adam on through the three sons of Noah: Shem, Ham, and Japheth. The interpretation of the chapter varies from individual to individual; but regardless of this, the pattern of the writer is clear. He gives the age of a man at the birth of his son, how much longer he lived after that, and finally his age at death. On the strength of this and other genealogies in the Old Testament the Jewish and Christian communities reckoned the date of creation.

Since the numbers in the Hebrew and Septuagint texts vary, the two systems vary as well. The year 1963, being the year 5723 in Jewish tradition, puts the creation in 3760 B.C. On the other hand, many Christians have accepted the date 4004 B.C., determined by Archbishop James Ussher (1581-1656).

It was not until the nineteenth century that enough evidence was available to disprove the 4004 date as the beginning of the world, and even today many Bibles still carry the old chronology. During the latter part of the nineteenth century, however, some evangelical scholars became aware of the problem and attempted to reckon with it. The genealogies of Genesis, according to these studies, were to be considered trustworthy only for the purpose which the Biblical compiler had in mind. This issue hinged, therefore, on one's interpretation of the compiler's intent.

We do not know who worked up the material as it is in our Bible. Whether it was Moses or someone else, he certainly did so on the basis of ancient records or oral tradition. If he intended the genealogy merely as a survey highlighting the main men in the long history of the pre-Flood world, why did he retain, evidently from his sources, the three precise numbers of years (age at birth of son, years lived afterward, and age at death) for each of the men named? True, the ancient Orientals were selective in their genealogies at times, but when doing so, they did not pay such close attention to exact figures as in Gen. 5. A selective list may have been the intent at the beginning of the oral tradition that transmitted the information, but it is hard to reconcile this intent with the specific figures which are an integral part of the present list. When the writer claims that Adam lived 130 years and then begat Seth, and that he lived 800 years afterward, making his total age 930 years, it is apparent that the writer intended the figures literally.

Until geological information disproved the 4004 date, most Jews and Christians (including many alert, even brilliant, persons) thought the genealogy in Gen. 5, was intended to show the consecutive history of man. Inasmuch as some evangelicals in the nineteenth century felt the force of the new geological information, they were inclined to stretch the genealogy enough to provide gaps for the scientific data. But how did this relate to the intent of the author? If the geological and other scientific data known today had not been made available to us, would we have doubted that Gen. 5, was intended to be chronological? Not likely. The Biblical evidence is too explicit at this point. It is our scientific knowledge that causes us to ignore the clear meaning of the passage. Obviously, then, the intent of the Biblical writer can hardly be accommodated to the scientific facts made available from generation to generation.

Acts 7:4

Stephen's speech before the council, which appears in Acts 7:2-53, begins with the details of Abraham's call. In v. 4, Stephen states: "Then he departed from the land of the Chaldeans, and lived in Haran. And after his father died, God removed him from there into this land in which you are now living." According to Gen. 11:26, Terah was 70 at the birth of Abraham, and he died in Haran at the age of 205 (11:32). Abraham, therefore, was 135 at the death of his father. However, Abraham left Canaan when he was 75 (12:4), sixty years before the death of his father. On what grounds, then, does Stephen declare that Abraham left for Canaan "after his father died"? Neither the Hebrew nor the Septuagint supports this claim.

This same idea is found in the writings of Philo, the Jewish scholar at Alexandria. Apparently Stephen and Philo were drawing from some kind of oral tradition that was alive in Judaism and the early church. Most likely Stephen's Jewish audience did not pick any flaws in his historical survey because they shared the same interpretation of history from the factual point of view.

It is difficult to determine why Philo, a student of the Pentateuch, believed that Abraham left Haran after his father died, because neither the Hebrew nor the Greek texts (as we have them now) would support such an interpretation. Possibly he had access to a Greek text that had Terah dying at 145 instead of 205. In any event there is strong evidence to show that it formed a part of an oral tradition.

Further support for this conclusion is found in Acts 7:23, where Stephen says Moses was forty years old when he felt he should visit his own people. This too is found in Philo, not in the Old Testament. Moreover, Stephen added in v. 25, "He supposed that his brethren understood that God was giving them deliverance by his hand, but they did not understand." This concept is not based on any Old Testament passage, and so it may well be another bit of the traditional interpretation of that day.

Stephen, after all, was speaking with his very life at stake. He had no scrolls to consult. He spoke out of the fullness of his heart and the store of information in his mind. He thought he was portraying a correct historical picture, and evidently his audience did too, but again honesty of intent does not rectify the difficulty. There is hardly any way out but to admit that Stephen, even while under the inspiration of the Holy Spirit, probably made a mistake in declaring that Abraham left Haran after Terah died.

Acts 7:15-16

Another statement in Stephen's speech demands attention also. In vs. 15-16 we read, "And he [Jacob] died, himself and our fathers, and they were carried back to Shechem and laid in the tomb that Abraham had bought for a sum of silver from the sons of Hamor in Shechem." Jacob was buried at Hebron (Mamre) in the field of Machpelah (Gen. 50:13), which Abraham had purchased from Ephron the Hittite (Gen. 23:16-18). Joseph, on the other hand, was buried at Shechem in the plot of ground which Jacob had purchased from the sons of Hamor (Josh. 24:32). According to Josephus (*Antiquities* II, 8, 2), all the sons of Jacob, except Joseph, were buried at Hebron.

This is the Old Testament and traditional evidence. What can we make of Stephen's statement? One of the most popular explanations of the older commentators was that of Daniel Whitby, which Matthew Henry quotes in his commentary: *"Jacob went down into Egypt and died, he and our fathers;* and *(our fathers) were carried over into Sychem; and he,* that is, *Jacob,* was laid *in the sepulchre that Abraham bought for a sum of money,* Gen. xxiii 16. (Or, they laid there, that is, Abraham, Isaac, and Jacob.) And *they,* namely, the other patriarchs, were *buried in the sepulchre bought of the sons of Emmor, the father of Sychem."*[7] Thus, Whitby splits the verse up and supplies words to make Stephen mean what Genesis and Joshua say.

Others solve the difficulty by regarding the name "Abraham" as a scribal error for "Jacob," supposedly the original wording of the text. This conjecture, however, is without any textual basis. Still others, recognizing the weight of the textual evidence, suggest the possibility that Jacob bought again at a later time a field previously purchased by Abraham. The better part of wisdom is to accept the evidence we have, and frankly admit, as F. F. Bruce does, "The two purchases of land are telescoped here in much the same way as two separate calls of Abraham are telescoped in v. 2 and two separate Pentateuchal quotations in v. 7."[8]

Some commentators readily acknowledge that Stephen was mistaken, but they claim inerrancy for the autograph of The Acts in that Luke accurately copied Stephen's words, mistakes and all. However, this easy answer ignores the clear Biblical statement that Stephen spoke under the influence of the Holy Spirit. The difficulty, as Bruce implies, may well have arisen with Luke when he condensed Stephen's sermon. But with respect to the doctrine of inerrant autographs it makes no essential difference whether the telescoping occurred in Stephen's original speech or in Luke's condensation.

Galatians 3:17

In Gal. 3:16-17 of his letter to the churches of Galatia, Paul writes: "Now the promises were made to Abraham and to his offspring. It does not say, 'And to offsprings,' referring to many; but, referring to one, 'And to your offspring,' which is Christ. This is what I mean: the law, which came four hundred and thirty years afterward, does not annul a covenant previously ratified by God, so as to make the promise void." All the Greek manuscripts have 430, so in all likelihood Paul's original letter had it as well. There is a problem with this figure, however. Abraham was 75 when he went to Canaan (Gen. 12:4), he was 100 when Isaac was born (21:5), Isaac was 60 when Jacob was born (25:26), and Jacob was 130 when he went to Egypt (47:9). Adding together 25, 60, and 130 gives 215 years in Canaan. The Hebrew text of Exod. 12:40 notes, "The time that the people of Israel dwelt in Egypt was four hundred and thirty years." Therefore, the time from the promise to Abraham to the giving of the law was 645 years (215+430). Did Paul get his information from another source, or did he mean something else when he wrote the number 430?

The Septuagint of Exod. 12:40 reads, "The time that the people of Israel dwelt in Egypt and in the land of Canaan was four hundred and thirty years." Thus, the Greek translation allots 215 years to Canaan and 215 to Egypt. It is quite possible, therefore, that Paul was following the LXX figure.

Another concern is the question whether the Hebrew or the LXX is correct. While the genealogies indicate only four generations from Levi through Moses, the preponderance of evidence which archaeology offers at the present time favors the 430-year stay in Egypt as noted in the Hebrew text.

Paul's reference to "the promise" is, according to one interpretation, a reference to the entire patriarchal period down to Jacob's descent into Egypt. Similarly "the law" is taken to mean the period beginning with Moses and the exodus. Granting this interpretation of the passage, Paul was correct and in accord with the Hebrew text of Exod. 12:40.

But Paul's argument in Gal. 3:16-17 hinges not on periods of time but on events in Israel's history. At first he relates the promises both to Abraham and to his descendents, but later he makes his intention clear by referring to "a covenant . . . ratified by God." What else could this have meant to Paul's readers except the personal covenant that God made with Abraham, ratifying his previous promises? This dramatic event is described in Gen. 15. After the details are noted, v. 18 summarizes, "On that day the Lord made a covenant with Abram." The sign of the covenant, circumcision, came later (Gen. 17:10). Inasmuch as these historic episodes took place within twenty-four years after Abraham arrived in Canaan, the span of time between it and the giving of the law on Mt. Sinai would logically include the 215 years of Canaan and the 430 in Egypt.

What justification is there, then, for interpreting Paul to mean 430 years after the patriarchal period closed (that is, when Jacob went to Egypt)? Had he wanted to say this, would he not have expressed himself more explicitly? As noted previously, Paul used the Septuagint a great deal, so why should one doubt its use here? In fact, because most of his readers probably read the Septuagint, the reference to 430 years would agree with their understanding of history and not distract their minds, therefore, from his main point. Evidently it seemed good to the Holy Spirit to let Paul use the traditional 430 years without informing him that he was technically wrong and should be using 645 years as found in the Hebrew.

Mark 14:30, 72

In Mark 14:30 Jesus says to Peter, "Truly, I say to you, this very night, before the cock crows twice, you will deny me three times." In v. 72 of the same chapter we read: "And immediately the cock crowed a second time. And Peter remembered how Jesus had said to him, 'Before the cock crows twice, you will deny me three times.' "

This same pattern (prediction by Jesus, occurrence of the event, and Peter's remembrance of the prediction) is also found in Matthew (26:34, 74-75) and Luke (22:34, 60-61). However, both of these accounts omit the words "twice," "second time," and "twice." In short, they report that Jesus said, "Before the cock crows, you will deny me three times."

In explaining the difference in detail in Mark's report of the denial episode, some evangelical scholars suggest that Matthew and Luke generalized the cock's crowing twice to mean "shall not have finished crowing." But why generalize if they knew the cock crowed twice?

Another explanation is the claim that the difficult reading is due to a scribal error. True, the Sinaiticus manuscript of the Greek New Testament omits the words "twice" and "second." In some other manuscripts the word "twice" or "second" is omitted in one or two cases, but never in all three occurrences. Moreover, the majority of the high quality manuscripts of Mark have "twice" or "second" in all three places.

Furthermore, there is no evidence to suggest that the words "twice" and "second" crept into the text on the basis of some later tradition. How is it that this supposed tradition spread through practically all the Greek manuscripts of Mark and yet had no influence in Matthew and Luke? What basis would there be for any scribe's attempt to insert the words into the text? There is plenty of reason, on the other hand, why a scribe would want to omit the words from Mark and thus harmonize it with the other two Gospels. Mark makes good sense as it is. The source of the scribal activity was most likely Mark himself as he took down bits of information from Peter's lips. The strong probability is that the words "twice" and "second" were in the autograph of Mark.

But what essential difference is there if the other Gospel writers,

Matthew and Luke, follow the general tradition of the cock's crowing just once? All three Gospels contain the historical features necessary to convey the truth of the matter: the prediction of denial and Peter's boast, the fulfillment of the prediction, and Peter's remorse on remembering Jesus' words.

I Corinthians 3:19

Paul, in writing to the church at Corinth, said: "For the wisdom of this world is folly with God. For it is written, 'He catches the wise in their craftiness' " (3:19). The source of the quotation is Job 5:13, which is part of the first speech of Eliphaz the Temanite. Traditionally speaking, Eliphaz has never been considered as inspired. Job, so it is claimed, was the inspired one and he recorded the addresses of Eliphaz and his friends, errors and all.

Certain evangelicals more or less equate the expressions "It is written" and "God says." It cannot mean this in I Cor. 3:19 if Eliphaz is uninspired. Apparently Paul did not care who said it, nor whether he was inspired. The statement was true as far as he was concerned and so he used it in his argument. This illustration does not involve an error as such, but it does show how Biblical evidence is often at variance with some of the more precise formulations of inspiration. As Carnell observes, "Whether orthodoxy realized it or not, it was really saying that inspiration, at times, ensures no more than an infallible account of error."[9]

Inerrancy and Consistency

While the specific problems considered thus far in this chapter by no means exhaust the difficulties that Biblical phenomena present to Christians, they are sufficiently varied and precise to show the seriousness of the issue. The question is, What are we to make of these findings? The evidence can be viewed from three possible points of view: (1) Scripture teaches the doctrine of inerrancy, but the phenomena of Scripture disprove this claim; (2) Scripture teaches the doctrine of inerrancy, therefore any contradictions or errors are in appearance only; and (3) Scripture does not teach the doctrine of inerrancy, therefore the phenomena of Scripture are to be accepted as an important factor in determining a Biblical view of inspiration.

The first point of view frankly acknowledges that Scripture is not consistent in all the evidence relevant to the doctrine of inspiration. While some within the church accept this conclusion, the majority of Christians take either the second or third of the possible interpretations. The basic premise of this latter views is that God, being the author of all truth, was consistent in his revelation.

The determinative factor for the second point of view is the assurance that Scripture teaches the doctrine of inerrancy. The probability of some errors in the autographs is intolerable, therefore, because a perfect God would never have allowed such a thing to happen. As a result, the usual mood is one of caution with respect to the interpretation of the phenomena. Problems are recognized, but there is little inclination to resolve them on the basis of the evidence at hand. Let us not be hasty, so the argument goes, because we do not have all the information. Maybe future discoveries will resolve these apparent contradictions. But is such a fond hope justified? A number of scholars who hold to inerrancy recognize that some of the Biblical phenomena cannot be harmonized without employing strained or forced methods. This intellectual honesty is to be commended, but this series of suspended judgments indicates that the totality of Biblical evidence does not prove the doctrine of inerrancy to be a fact. It is still a theory that must be accepted by faith.

This conclusion is also supported by the kind of apologetic that is usually employed to parry the thrusts of the phenomena. The chief refutation is a negative one which concentrates on some glaring examples of error that the liberals have made. A favorite target is the German critic Anton F. Hartmann, who said that Moses could not have written the Pentateuch because the Hebrews did not start writing until the period of the Judges. Now we know that the Hebrews were literate and capable of writing from Abraham on down. Another example is early liberalism's verdict that Isa. 20:1 was erroneous in mentioning Sargon, a king otherwise unknown. Since that time a mass of information about Sargon, including his annals, has been discovered.

Of course, the idea back of such an argument is that in numerous instances liberalism has been proved wrong and in due time it will be proved wrong everywhere. But will this suggestion stand up under close scrutiny? The most extreme liberals today recognize the folly of these early statements. In many instances it has been the liberal camp itself that has corrected its earlier excesses. Many of the so-called "assured results" of higher criticism have proved to be "assumed results," but the evidence does not warrant the conclusion that this will happen to *all* of the liberal findings. In some instances, the so-called "assured results" of *tradition* are in reality "assumed results."

Truth is like a two-way street or a double-edged sword. Although facts confirm the Biblical record in many instances, they also disprove it in other cases. In the last analysis we must let the truth cut both ways. If we try to hold to the teaching of Scripture in preference to the phenomena, are we not saying in effect, "Determine the Biblical writers' doctrine of inspiration from what they say, not what they do"? The true Biblical view of inspiration must account for all the evidence of Scripture. The peril of the view of inerrancy is its rigidity and all-or-nothing character. If only one of the illustrations discussed in this chapter is correct, the doctrine is invalidated.

Notes

[1]Carnell, *The Case for Orthodox Theology,* pp. 98-99.

[2]Orr, *Revelation and Inspiration,* p. 180.

[3]Thiele, *The Mysterious Numbers of the Hebrew Kings,* p. 114.

[4]*Ibid.,* p. 268.

[5]Brunner, *Revelation and Reason,* p. 275.

[6]Harrison, "The Phenomena of Scripture," *Revelation and the Bible,* p. 239.

[7]Henry, *Commentary on the Whole Bible,* Vol. VI, p. 80.

[8]Bruce, *Commentary on the Book of Acts, The New International Commentary on the New Testament,* p. 149, note 39.

[9]Carnell, *op. cit.,* pp. 102-103.

21

Everett F. Harrison

Criteria of Bible Inerrancy

Inerrancy is not a formally stated claim made by the Scriptures on their own behalf. It is rather an inference that devout students of the Word have made from the teaching of the Bible about its own inspiration.

If the Spirit of God has really wrought in the production of this Book from start to finish, it is hard to conceive of error save such as may have crept into the text in the course of its transmission.

What of Original Texts?

The appeal to the original texts of the Old and New Testaments has indeed often been ridiculed as an unworthy refuge. Who has seen the so-called infallible originals? so the query goes. No one in our time, certainly. No one in possession of the facts would argue that the text of Scripture has come down to us unchanged from the beginning. The Scriptures contain no promise of the supernatural overshadowing of the transmitters of the Word such as is claimed for the writers. The variations are numerous, though mostly unimpor-

From Everett F. Harrison, *Christianity Today,* Jan. 20, 1958, pp. 16-17.
Copyright © 1958, *Christianity Today.* Used by permission.

tant in relation to the message of Scripture. But we have no reason to conclude from the data of textual criticism that the writers of Scripture were so left to their own devices that error should be expected in the autographs.

If the Bible were of such a nature that it was composed by men and only subsequently was adopted by God and breathed into by the Holy Spirit, then it might conceivably be allowed that God was so concerned with the spiritual message that he tolerated a measure of error in the factual material. But this is not the Scriptural doctrine of its own origin. Rather, it is insisted that the Spirit was active and controlling in the very production of the Word in its entirety.

Granted that the spiritual message is intrinsically more important than the historical minutiae of the narrative framework, yet the Scripture gives no hint of distinction as far as trustworthiness is concerned. This is understandable since the historical element is itself the unfolding of God's providential and saving activity. Herein lies the fallacy of the kernel-husk solution to the problem we are considering. The history of biblical interpretation shows that the abandonment of the inerrancy of Scripture in nondoctrinal items has a tendency to make criticism of the doctrinal data much easier.

Consequently, it is not wholly satisfactory to rest in the solution that the Bible is "the only infallible rule of faith and practice" and be indifferent to the question of its infallibility in areas that do not directly relate to faith and practice. Evidence is lacking in the statements of Scripture for the notion that the Word is the product of a division of labor, God working with the writers on doctrinal matters and leaving them their own wisdom on historical matters.

Approaching inerrancy then as a corollary of the biblical exposition of its own origin, there seems to be every reason to insist upon it. But when the data of Scripture are examined, many problems present themselves, problems that seem to make the retention of inerrancy difficult if not impossible. Parallel accounts appear to contradict one another, and quotations from the Old Testament do not always agree with the Old Testament text we have or even with the text of the Septuagint as we have it. So if the fact of inerrancy is to be derived from Scripture deductively, the form that our view of inerrancy ought to take is to be derived inductively from the data of the text.

Some Excessive Criteria

It may be helpful to start with the negative approach. Certain criteria of inerrancy ought not to be applied. One is the insistence that there should be verbal agreement in multiple accounts of the same event. Such agreement would involve mechanical control over the writers of Scripture such as is not suggested by the liberty given to them to utilize their own vocabulary and style of writing. Or, on the supposition that they consulted one another's work, it would make them echoes and rubber stamps of one another. Identity of language in such instances could even suggest the distinct possibility of collusion, which would tend to destroy confidence in the record. It is widely recognized, especially in courts of law, that witnesses may diverge from one another in details and even in perspective without being chargeable with untruth.

This should be kept in mind when one is wrestling with the problems of the Resurrection narratives in the Gospels. Again, in the account of Jesus' baptism, Mark reports the voice from heaven saying, "Thou art my beloved Son." Matthew puts it in the third person, "This is my beloved Son." It is disingenuous to insist that the voice can only have spoken in one way, so that one of the reports must be erroneous. Mark gives the words in the form of direct address as they are found in Psalm 2. Matthew puts the words in the third person, possibly to emphasize that the baptism was properly witnessed, and by no less a witness than God himself. Testimony to the divine sonship is equally clear in both accounts.

Another criterion to be avoided is that there should be the same degree of completeness and finality in the statements of Scripture at all periods. There is such a thing as progress in the Word of God, and that progress is discernible both in the area of revelation and in the area of reception and response. The early chapters of Genesis have a primitive, almost naive, character about them that befits the record of events in the distant past. Only when the Son of God was revealed could the knowledge of God be at all fully communicated or a fully adequate response by men be expected.

The claim of inerrancy should not be made dependent upon verbal exactness in quotation. It is anachronistic to apply the standards of our own time to the Scripture. With our wealth of printed books and other materials, all so easy of access, we can justly demand that quotations be verbally accurate. But such was not the standard of antiquity when written materials could be consulted only under great difficulties. Quotation from memory was common.

We ought not to expect scientifically precise statements of natural phenomena. The very thought that the biblical writers should be required to anticipate the discoveries and the terminology of modern times is altogether incongruous. As we might expect, their descriptions of nature are popular and not technical. What is more, we can still use the language of Scripture touching scientific matters without being counted antiquarian or incorrect. Even the scientists do it in ordinary conversation.

Finally, difficulties ought not to be prejudged as errors. The folly of this has been demonstrated many times over. One of the best known examples is the case of Sargon, mentioned in Isaiah 20:1 but unknown otherwise. Hostile criticism did not hesitate to pronounce the Scripture inaccurate. But now Sargon's palace has been excavated and his royal records uncovered. Some items in the Word of God remain to be confirmed, such as the enrolment under Cyrenius (Luke 2:2). Some may never be confirmed. But lack of confirmation is no basis for repudiation.

Having cleared the ground somewhat, it is well to ask ourselves, What then are the proper criteria of inerrancy? Three, at least, are worthy of special consideration.

Cultural Milieu Important

First, the Bible must be evaluated in terms of its cultural milieu. If the soul of Scripture is universal and eternal, its body remains Oriental. It was written by men who had patterns of thought that differ from ours at many points. The more one can steep himself in these the better will be his position as translator or interpreter. With us, for example, the word "son" has one commonly accepted meaning. But in Scripture it sometimes means descendant. It may also connote the possession of certain characteristics, as in the phrase "sons of darkness" or "sons of disobedience." Still other nuances of thought are conveyed by this word. The symbolic use of numbers, to take another example, is more congenial to the ancients than to our mental climate. Only occasionally does one get the impression that numbers in Scripture are given with great precision. Those who know most about the East tell us that the Bible is eminently true to the life and setting of the Orient as it persists today.

Second, diversity in Scripture statements is not incompatible with the unity of truth they represent. It was recognized in the early Church that differences existed in the Gospel accounts, but the prevailing attitude was that this did not disturb the unity of presentation, which was guaranteed by the operation of the sovereign Spirit upon the writers. This is the testimony of the canon of Muratori (ca. A.D. 170) and of Irenaeus a few years later. Doubtless these men were therefore not sympathetic to the idea of presenting the Gospel narrative in one continuous account so as to relieve the story of apparent contradictions, the very thing which was done by Tatian in his *Diatessaron* at about the same period. The apostle Paul had advanced the thought, in dealing with spiritual gifts, that there are diversities of operation but it is the one Spirit who works through them all. Our western way of thinking, patterned closely after the Greek, inclines to demand uniformity. We tend to associate diversity with deviation and so with error. Apart from the question as to which outlook is correct, we ought not to sit in judgment on Scripture as untrustworthy because of a variety of presentation of the same basic material. It is a well-known fact that our Lord accepted the Old Testament of his day as the Word of God which could not be broken. In that Old Testament are many duplicate narratives, such as the accounts in Kings and Chronicles of the reigns of the kings of Judah. Evidently the compiler of Chronicles made use of Kings as source material, having also the records of certain prophets to draw upon. Even where the same event is being described, it is not always told in the same way, certainly not in the same words. All we are concerned to point out here is the fact that our Lord, familiar as he was with both portions, apparently accepted both as equally the Word of God. The bearing of this on the Synoptic problem is quite obvious.

Faithfulness to Purpose

Third, Scripture must be judged in terms of faithfulness to the purpose in view. A change in readers often necessitates a change of statement in order to achieve communication. In the account of the Triumphal Entry, Matthew and Mark have the words "Hosanna in the highest." Luke has instead, "Glory in the highest." "Hosanna," being a Semitic word, would be unintelligible to Luke's Gentile readers. One of our greatest authorities on the language of the Gospels, Gustaf Dalman, says, "It cannot be doubted that *hosanna* was understood to be a cry of homage in the sense of *glory* or *hail to the Son of David*." The change was imperative, but it was made without falsification.

One of the knottiest problems in the New Testament is the evaluation to be put upon the discourses in John's Gospel. They are quite different from anything to be found in the Synoptics. Did the Lord actually speak them? Are they authentic reproductions of what he said? It is no doubt an oversimplification to quote Jesus' prediction about the Spirit bringing to the remembrance of his disciples whatever he had said to them. The Saviour also predicted that the Spirit would lead his followers into all truth. We need a combination of these two sayings to explain the discourses in John. That they rest upon Jesus' utterances we have no doubt. That they constitute in part an interpretation of those utterances under the tutelage of the Spirit we have no doubt also.

Too Little or Too Much

Our conception of inerrancy ought not to require us to adopt an a priori position about verbatim reporting. Our concern ought to be to learn with all humility as much as we can of the methodology that God the Spirit has chosen to use in giving us the Word of God. Those who are hostile to the claim of the veracity of Scripture commonly expect too little of the Bible. Its friends, on the other hand, may err in expecting too much.

Part Three

What God Is Like

Editor's Introduction

With this section we come to actual consideration of who God is and what He is like. It is an area of renewed concern, for as we saw in earlier portions of this work, we can no longer take the traditional doctrines for granted, not even a doctrine as basic as the doctrine of God. There was a time when the disputed problems lay in the peripheral areas of doctrine, or involved only very conservative positions on the issues. In recent years, however, such a central conception as the meaningfulness and reality of the doctrine of God has been called into question. Consequently, a thorough restudy of the doctrine is forced upon us.

The article by John A. T. Robinson proposes a radical revision of the understanding of God. The traditional view was that God is a

Being, the supreme being, distinct from all other beings. In earlier days He was understood spatially, as a God "up there" above a flat earth. With the passing of this conception of the earth, the idea of God was revised, to a God "out there." Even this, however, is rejected by Robinson. What he proposes, following Tillich, is a radical shift in the understanding of God as the depth within reality. He is to be found within the rest of reality, rather than something detached. He is known in the experiences of love which we have in the universe.

In a more traditional understanding of God, Louis Berkhof discusses the characteristics of God's nature, or as they are often termed, His attributes. These are the qualities which He has revealed regarding Himself. Different classifications of these have been employed by different theologians. Berkhof works with a distinction between communicable and incommunicable attributes. The communicable attributes are those to which there is some parallel or corresponding quality in man; the incommunicable attributes are those which are unique to God. Various theologians have often suggested that one particular attribute is the supreme or distinct divine attribute, some naming love, others holiness. Berkhof does not single out any one attribute as supreme.

A pair of articles follows, emphasizing opposite sides of the issue of divine immanence versus transcendence. Immanence means God is present within nature, history, and man. Bowne, a personal idealist, represents the emphasis prominent in religious liberalism upon the immanence of God. According to Bowne, the causal activity of God and the laws of nature are not in competition; they are different ways of describing the same fact. Nature is not the ultimate cause; it is merely the proximate cause. Behind it is intelligence, upon which it depends for its origin and implications. God is the ever-present agent in the on-going of the world. He is not simply to be identified with nature; nature does not exhaust the reality of God. Yet He does work through it, and He works in regular, orderly fashion, which may even be referred to as "laws."

A sharply different conception emerges in the selection by Martin Heinecken, which is from a book expounding the ideas of the Danish philosopher and theologian, Soren Kierkegaard. Kierkegaard argued that man does not have a spark of the divine within him. God is not merely like the good qualities within man, magnified to a greater degree. Rather, there is a sharp difference between them, an "infinite qualitative distinction." This means that one cannot get from man to God by any process of extrapolation. No new quality can emerge from quantitative additions or subtractions of a given quality.

There are a number of reasons why Kierkegaard felt this issue to be so important, as did Karl Barth, who picked up this motif and reiterated it so emphatically. The advocates of immanence claimed that unless there were within man some similarity to God, it would be impossible for man to know God. This, says Heinecken, overlooks the Christian epistemological doctrine, that knowledge comes by a supernatural enlightenment by the Holy Spirit. As such, it can never be man's accomplishment. He never obtains a hold upon God. He must always depend upon God's grace for the knowledge of God. There is also here an emphatic rejection of any type of idolatry. When liberalism stressed divine immanence, it identified God with almost all that transpired. Thus, German Christians in many cases identified the war policies of Kaiser Wilhelm as the movement of God in history, and similarly with respect to Naziism in the 1930s. What is being advocated here is a transcendence of "dimensional beyondness," in which God is everywhere, yet never to be identified with any part of the creation. He comes to us, in some mysterious way, from another realm of existence. He "stands clear of entanglement with the created world," is the way Heinecken puts it.

The immanence/transcendence continuum, it seems, must be a matter of both-and, not either-or. The two concepts are two facets of one tenet, and must be clung to together. The temptation to ease the tension by abandoning either of the concepts must be resisted. When one of these is emphasized to the neglect of the other, a distortion takes place. So, immanence pressed to its logical extreme becomes pantheism. Conversely, transcendence developed apart from immanence becomes a type of deism.

The form which a doctrine takes varies with different periods. In the contemporary scene, the issue seems to be joined with respect to the sacred-secular question. An emphasis upon the transcendence of God leads to a more sacral view and practice. God is largely "apart from" man and the world, and religion consists of various types of devotional actions, based upon sacred Scriptures, and conducted within the context of a religious society, or "church." God accomplishes His purposes through those who have identified themselves as His people, and He works in direct or supernatural fashion.

Where immanence is stressed, a more secular or "worldly" religion emerges. Here God is not merely found in the church, but is active everywhere in the world. Some who do not actually believe in Him or acknowledge Him may be His agents. Religion is less a matter of withdrawing from the world into worship within a sanctuary, than it is involvement with actual needs of people within this world. The Christian holding this view could well be involved in and participate in the activity of organizations which are not explicitly Christian, for these may also be God's means of accomplishing His purposes.

Here, also, it seems, it is essential that the church keep its sense of balance. If in the past the church has erred in the direction of separatism because it thought of God as too exclusively transcendent, it is also in danger of erring toward too close a connection with the world and a consequent neglect of the devotional and worshipful because it overemphasizes the immanence of God in the world. And it should be reemphasized that the style of life should be governed by the understanding of God, and not vice versa.

We have noted that there are some rather recent challenges to the traditional ways of thinking of God. One of the most far-ranging of these, process theology, is based upon a completely revised understanding of the nature of reality itself. The Biblical understanding of God stresses His permanence and everlasting nature. This seemed to accord quite well with the Greek substance philosophy of permanent essences. Pittenger's thesis, however, is that reality is not static, but dynamic, and that consequently God should be thought of this way as well.

God, then, is not the unmoved mover of Aristotle, nor the impassive one of classical thought. He is the chief causative influence in all that is. Conversely, however, He is also what Pittenger terms the "supreme affect," experiencing the process. God is not simply a permanent, fixed being, whose nature remains unchanged for all time. Rather, He is growing, developing, even maturing. Process theology generally supports this assertion by appealing to two types of considerations: (1) Every living thing develops and changes. This seems to be part of the very nature of life itself. If God is really alive, He must reflect a similar process. (2) Since God in a sense participates within the whole of reality, He of necessity must display process. He is therefore not so much the God who *is,* as the God who *will be.*

Carl Henry does not share this enthusiasm for a process conception of God's nature. Working from an assumption of the authority of Biblical revelation, Henry offers two major criticisms: its God is less than the Biblical conception of God, in several important respects; and it is internally inconsistent. While it is at least encouraging because it represents an attempt to rejuvenate metaphysics, it is not a satisfactory option, particularly for the evangelical. Not a return to the Greek concepts, but rather to the Biblical picture of God, is what Henry prescribes as the solution to the problem.

The doctrine of the trinity concerns us next. The doctrine is not explicitly affirmed in the Bible, but rather is an inference from two types of Biblical data: the assertions that God is one; the seeming attribution of deity to three—the Father, Son and Holy Spirit. The attempt to relate these two apparently contradictory considerations in some intellectually adequate and spiritually satisfying fashion has occupied the greatest theological minds of the Christian church over the years. Some of the formulations were in ancient metaphysical categories which are no longer viable or even intelligible to us. All of the analogies which have been suggested as aids to understanding this difficult concept display evident imperfections.

Two selections dealing with the doctrine of the trinity are included, one general and one specific. Charles Lowry gives us a survey of the doctrine particularly in relation to Christian devotion, and some of the historical attempts to formulate the doctrine. He concludes with a brief construction of his own view. A study of this work, titled *The Social Analogy of the Trinity in Four Twentieth Century Anglican Theologians,* was made by April Oursler Armstrong in an unpublished Ph.D. thesis, Fordham University.

Augustine formulated one of the classic statements of the trinity. He began with the Biblical teaching that man is created in the image of God. If this is true, and if God is triune, then man must be made in the image of the triune God. The best place to look for an analogy to use in understanding the trinity, therefore, is not in physical nature, but rather in the personal realm of man's makeup.

As a transition from what God is like to what He has done and is doing come two articles dealing with the decrees of God. If God acts, then presumably His actions are a result of His decisions or plan. But just what is the basis of such a plan? Two broad conceptions of these decrees are represented by the two articles reprinted here. These have been known since the seventeenth century as Calvinism and Arminianism. The Calvinist, represented here by the selection from Charles Hodge, holds that everything that occurs, including the acts of men, is the result of the unconditional will or decree of God. The Arminian, such as Wakefield, draws a distinction between absolute and conditional decrees. The absolute decrees are not in any sense dependent upon the free actions of moral creatures. These will come to pass irrespective of any contingent events. The conditional decrees, on the other hand, are dependent upon the free actions of men. God foresees what man will do, and bases His decree upon this foreknowledge. The major difference that results is the extent of God's guidance of what occurs. In the Calvinistic scheme everything is what it is because God has willed so. For the Arminian, in certain areas God wills because it is going to happen.

This leads us to a consideration of the acts or works of God. There is a logical progression in the study of the doctrine of God. Because of what God is like, He has willed or decreed in a certain fashion. Then, on the basis of what He has willed, He has acted to carry out His plan.

Basic to all of the considerations is the doctrine of creation: the belief that everything that has come into being has derived from the action of God. Harold Kuhn discusses the meaning of the Christian affirmation, both in terms of its basic content, and in contrast to non-Christian systems. He relates it to some of the common objections. He observes that the Bible does not discuss the "how" of creation, preferring to dwell upon the fact that God has brought all things into being.

The doctrine of creation seems to have growing significance for our day. A correct understanding here goes far toward a man's proper regard for himself and for other men. It puts nature in its proper perspective, giving a sound basis for ecology. It is a doctrine which needs reemphasis and is beginning to get it.

The activity of God in relation to His world did not cease with His work of creation, however. His continued care for the world and man is referred to as divine providence. This often is thought of under two general classifications. God maintains in existence what He has brought into being. This is called preservation. Further, He guides and directs the creation to His appointed purposes. This is often denominated government, or providence proper.

G. C. Berkouwer, a leading contemporary Dutch conservative, discusses providence as government in the selection before us. He relates it to such contemporary issues as the nature and status of the state, and the role of angels and demons. It is apparent that the doctrine of providence, correctly understood, has real practical significance for our personal lives.

The Qualities of God

22

John A. T. Robinson

The Ground of Our Being

A Depth at the Centre of Life

The break with traditional thinking to which I believe we are now summoned is considerably more radical than that which enabled Christian theology to detach itself from a literal belief in a localized heaven. The translation from the God "up there" to the God "out there," though of liberating psychological significance, represented, as I have said, no more than a change of direction in spatial symbolism. Both conceptions presuppose fundamentally the same relationship between "God" on the one hand and "the world" on the other: God is a Being existing in his own right to whom the world is related in the sort of way the earth is to the sun. Whether the sun is "above" a flat earth or "beyond" a round one does not fundamentally affect the picture. But suppose there is no Being out there at all? Suppose, to use our analogy, the skies are empty?

Now it would again be possible to present the transposition with which we are concerned as simply a change in spatial metaphor. I

From *Honest to God*, by John A. T. Robinson. Published in the U.S.A., 1963, by The Westminster Press, Philadelphia. © SCM Press, Ltd., London, 1963. Used by permission.

quoted earlier the passage from Tillich in which he proposes replacing the images of "height" by those of "depth" in order to express the truth of God. And there is no doubt that this simple substitution can make much religious language suddenly appear more relevant. For we are familiar today with depth psychology, and with the idea that ultimate truth is deep or profound. Moreover, while "spiritual wickedness in high places," and all the mythology of angelic powers which the Biblical writers associate with it, seems to the modern man a fantastic phantasmagoria, similar, equally mythological, language when used by Freud of conflicts in the unconscious appears perfectly acceptable.

And the change of symbolism has real and not merely apparent psychological significance. For the category of "depth" has richer associations than that of height. As Tillich points out:

> "Deep" in its spiritual use has two meanings: it means either the opposite of "shallow," or the opposite of "high." Truth is deep and not shallow; suffering is depth and not height. Both the light of truth and the darkness of suffering are deep. There is a depth in God, and there is a depth out of which the psalmist cries to God.[1]

And this double meaning may explain why "depth" seems to speak to us of concern while "height" so often signifies unconcern. The Epicurean gods, serene in their empyrean above the cares and distractions of this world, are the epitome of "sublime" indifference. And Browning's supreme affirmation of optimism, "God's in his heaven: all's right with the world," strikes the modern man somewhat more cynically. For if God is "above it all" he cannot really be involved.

Yet we are not here dealing simply with a change of symbolism, important as that may be. This is not just the old system in reverse, with a God "down under" for a God "up there." When Tillich speaks of God in "depth," he is not speaking of another Being *at all*. He is speaking of "the infinite and inexhaustible depth and ground of all being," of our ultimate concern, of what we take seriously without reservation. And after the passage I quoted earlier[2] he goes on to make the same point in relation not only to the depths of our personal life but to the deepest springs of our social and historical existence:

> The name of this infinite and inexhaustible ground of history is *God*. That is what the word means, and it is that to which the words *Kingdom of God* and *Divine Providence* point. And if these words do not have much meaning for you, translate them, and speak of the depth of history, of the ground and aim of our social life, and of what you take seriously without reservation in your moral and political activities. Perhaps you should call this depth *hope,* simply hope. For if you find hope in the ground of history, you are united with the great prophets who were able

to look into the depth of their times, who tried to escape it, because they could not stand the horror of their visions, and who yet had the strength to look to an even deeper level and there to discover hope.[3]

What Tillich is meaning by God is the exact opposite of any *deus ex machina,* a supernatural Being to whom one can turn away from the world and who can be relied upon to intervene from without. God is not "out there." He is in Bonhoeffer's words "the 'beyond' in the midst of our life," a depth of reality reached "not on the borders of life but at its centre,"[4] not by any flight of the alone to the alone, but, in Kierkegaard's fine phrase, by "a deeper immersion in existence." For the word "God" denotes the ultimate depth of all our being, the creative ground and meaning of all our existence.

So conditioned for us is the word "God" by associations with a Being out there that Tillich warns us that to make the necessary transposition, "you must forget everything traditional that you have learned about God, perhaps even that word itself."[5] Indeed, the line between those who believe in God and those who do not bears little relation to their profession of the existence or non-existence of such a Being. It is a question, rather, of their openness to the holy, the sacred, in the unfathomable depths of even the most secular relationship. As Martin Buber puts it of the person who professedly denies God,

> When he, too, who abhors the name, and believes himself to be godless, gives his whole being to addressing the *Thou* of his life, as a *Thou* that cannot be limited by another, he addresses God.[6]

For in the conditioned he has seen and responded to the unconditional. He has touched the hem of the eternal.

The difference between the two ways of thought can perhaps best be expressed by asking what is meant by speaking of a *personal* God. Theism, as the term was understood earlier, understands by this a supreme Person, a self-existent subject of infinite goodness and power, who enters into a relationship with us comparable with that of one human personality with another. The theist is concerned to argue the existence of such a Being as the creator and most sufficient explanation of the world as we know it. Without a Person "out there," the skies would be empty, the heavens as brass, and the world without hope or compassion.

But the way of thinking we are seeking to expound is not concerned to posit, nor, like the antitheists, to depose, such a Being at all. In fact it would not naturally use the phrase "*a* personal God"; for this in itself belongs to an understanding of theology and of what theological statements are about which is alien to it. For this way of thinking, to say that "God is personal" is to say that "reality at its very deepest level is personal," that personality is of *ultimate* significance in the constitution of the universe, that in personal relationships we touch the final meaning of existence as nowhere else. "To predicate personality of God," says Feuerbach, "is nothing else than to declare personality as the absolute essence."[7] To believe in God as love means to believe that in pure personal relationships we encounter, not merely what ought to be, but what is, the deepest, veriest truth about the structure of reality. This, in face of all the evidence, is a tremendous act of faith. But it is not the feat of persuading oneself of the existence of a super-Being beyond this world endowed with personal qualities. Belief in God is the trust, the well-nigh incredible trust, that to give ourselves to the uttermost in love is not to be confounded but to be "accepted," that Love is the ground of our being, to which ultimately we "come home."

If this is true, then theological statements are not a description of "the highest Being" but an analysis of the depths of personal relationships—or, rather, an analysis of the depths of *all* experience "interpreted by love." Theology, as Tillich insists, is about "that which concerns us ultimately."[8] A statement is "theological" not because it relates to a particular Being called "God," but because it asks *ultimate* questions about the meaning of existence: it asks what, at the level of *theos,* at the level of its deepest mystery, is the reality and significance of our life. A view of the world which affirms this reality and significance in personal categories is *ipso facto* making an affirmation about the ultimacy of personal relationships: it is saying that *God,* the final truth and reality of "deep down things," *is* love. And the specifically Christian view of the world is asserting that the final definition of this reality, from which "nothing can separate us," since it is the very ground of our being, is "the love of God in Christ Jesus our Lord."[9]

Man and God

If statements about God are statements about the "ultimacy" of personal relationships, then we must agree that in a real sense Feuerbach was right in wanting to translate "theology" into "anthropology." He was concerned to restore the divine attributes from heaven to earth, whence, he believed, they had been filched and projected on to a perfect Being, an imaginary Subject before whom impoverished man falls in worship. Feuerbach believed that true religion consists in acknowledging the divinity of the attributes, not in transferring them to an illegitimate subject (dubbed by his Marxist disciple Bakunin "the mirage of God"). "The true atheist," he wrote, "is not the man who denies God, the subject; it is the man for whom the attributes of divinity, such as love, wisdom and justice, are nothing. And denial of the subject is by no means necessarily denial of the attributes."[10] This is, of course, very near to the position we have been taking; and Bultmann, in answer to a challenge from Karl Barth, says, "I would heartily agree: I *am* trying to substitute anthropology for theology, for I am interpreting theological affirmations as assertions about human life."[11]

Yet it is also clear that we are here on very dangerous ground. For, to Feuerbach, to say that "theology is nothing else than anthropology" means that "the knowledge of God is nothing else than a knowledge of man."[12] And his system runs out into the deification of man, taken to its logical conclusion in the Superman of Nietzsche and Auguste Comte's Religion of Humanity.

The same ambiguity is to be found in the deeply Christian humanism of Professor John Macmurray, whose thought follows similar lines. At the beginning of his Gifford Lectures he says, "The conception of a deity is the conception of a personal ground of all that we experience,"[13] and he concludes them with a chapter, "The Personal Universe,"[14] which argues a position close to that for which we have been contending. But both in these lectures and even more in his earlier book, *The Structure of Religious Experience,* he makes statements which leave one wondering whether there is anything distinctive about religion at all. For instance, "Religion is about fellowship and community,"[15] and, "The task of religion is the maintenance and extension of human community."[16] The question inevitably arises, if theology is translated into anthropology, why do we any longer need the category of God? Is it not "semantically superfluous"? Is not the result of destroying "supranaturalism" simply to end up with naturalism, as the atheists asserted?

The dilemma can be stated in another passage of Macmurray. The question of God is the question of transcendence. It is precisely this that the location of God "up there" or "out there" was to express and safeguard and which its denial appears to imperil. But for Macmurray transcendence is a category that applies equally to humanity:

> We are both transcendent of experience and immanent in it. This union of transcendence and immanence is . . . the full fact about human personality. . . . We are accustomed to find it applied in theology to God, and it is usually assumed to be a peculiar and distinguishing attribute of Deity. We see now that this is a mistake. The union of immanence and transcendence is a peculiar and defining characteristic of all personality, human or divine; but it is primarily a natural, empirical fact of common human experience. Religious reflection applies it to God as a defining characteristic of universal personality because it finds it in experience as a given fact of all finite personal experience.[17]

Macmurray here denies that transcendence is distinctively an attribute of God: he asserts it as a feature of all our experience. I believe that he is wrong in what he denies, but right in what he asserts. Contrary to what he says, our experience of God *is* distinctively and characteristically an awareness of the transcendent, the numinous, the unconditional. Yet that is a feature of *all* our experience—*in depth.* Statements about God are acknowledgements of the transcendent, unconditional element in all our relationships, and supremely in our relationships with other persons. Theological statements are indeed affirmations about human existence—but they are affirmations about the ultimate ground and depth of that existence. It is not enough to say that "religion is about human fellowship and community," any more than one can simply reverse the Biblical statement and say that "love *is* God." And that, significantly, is what Feuerbach thought St. John should have said.[18] But it is what the apostle rather carefully refuses to do. He is clear that *apart from* the relationship of love there is no knowledge of God: "He who does not love does not know God; for God is love."[19] And conversely: "He who abides in love abides in God, and God abides in him."[20] But the premise of this last sentence is not, as we might logically expect, "Love is God," but, "God is love."[21] The most he will say the other way round is that "love is *of* God."[22] It is *ek theou:* it has God as its source and ground. For it is precisely his thesis[23] that our convictions about love and its ultimacy are not projections from human love; rather, our sense of the sacredness of love derives from the fact that in this relationship as nowhere else there is disclosed and laid bare the divine Ground of all our being. And this revelation for St. John finds its focus and final vindication in the fact of Jesus Christ—"the humanity of God"[24]—rather than in the divinity of Man.

To assert that *"God* is love" is to believe that in love one comes into touch with the most fundamental reality in the universe, that Being itself ultimately has this character. It is to say, with Buber, that "Every particular *Thou* is a glimpse through to the eternal *Thou,*"[25] that it is "between man and man"[26] that we meet God, not, with Feuerbach, that "man with man—the unity of *I* and *Thou*—is God."[27] Nevertheless, as Bonhoeffer insists, "God is the 'beyond' *in the midst,*"[28] "The transcendent is not infinitely remote but close at hand."[29] For the eternal *Thou* is met only *in, with and under* the finite *Thou,* whether in the encounter with other persons or in the response to the natural order.

Yet the eternal *Thou* is not to be equated with the finite *Thou,* nor God with man or nature. That is the position of naturalism, whether pantheistic or humanistic. And, Tillich insists, it is necessary to push "beyond naturalism and supranaturalism."[30] The naturalist critique of supranaturalism is valid. It has torn down an idol and Christianity must not be found clinging to it. But equally Christianity must challenge the assumption of naturalism that God is merely a redundant name for nature or for humanity. John Wren-Lewis observes that the naturalist critique of supranaturalism itself points to depths, divine depths, in experience for which it fails to account. He claims that Freud's own analysis of religion indicates as much:

> For it is an integral part of his argument that fantasies about spiritual forces in the occult world are really "projections" or "displacements" of elements in our experience of personal relationships which we seek to avoid recognizing, but it is hard to see why the common projections made by the human race should have a numinous, transcendental character *unless there is something numinous and transcendental in the experience of personal relationships themselves.*[31]

The necessity for the name "God" lies in the fact that our being has depths which naturalism, whether evolutionary, mechanistic, dialectical or humanistic, cannot or will not recognize. And the nemesis which has overtaken naturalism in our day has revealed the peril of trying to suppress them. As Tillich puts it,

> Our period has decided for a *secular* world. That was a great and much-needed decision. . . . It gave consecration and holiness to our daily life and work. Yet it excluded those deep things for which religion stands: the feeling for the inexhaustible mystery of life, the grip of an ultimate meaning of existence, and the invincible power of an unconditional devotion. These things *cannot* be excluded. If we try to expel them in their divine images, they re-emerge in daemonic images. Now, in the old age of our secular world, we have seen the most horrible manifestations of these daemonic images; we have looked more deeply into the mystery of evil than most generations before us; we have seen the unconditional devotion of millions to a satanic image; we feel our period's sickness unto death.[32]

There are depths of revelation, intimations of eternity, judgment of the holy and the sacred, awarenesses of the unconditional, the numinous and the ecstatic, which cannot be explained in purely naturalistic categories without being reduced to something else. There is the "Thus saith the Lord" heard by prophet, apostle and martyr for which naturalism cannot account. But neither can it discount it merely by pointing to the fact that "the Lord" is portrayed in the Bible in highly mythological terms, as one who "inhabits eternity" or "walks in the garden in the cool of the evening." The question of God is the question *whether this depth of being is a reality or an illusion,* not whether *a* Being exists beyond the bright blue sky, or anywhere else. Belief in God is a matter of "what you take seriously without any reservation," of what for you is *ultimate* reality.

The man who acknowledges the transcendence of God is the man who *in* the conditioned relationships of life recognizes the unconditional and responds to it in unconditional personal relationship. In Tillich's words again,

> To call God transcendent in this sense does not mean that one must establish a "superworld" of divine objects. It does mean that, within itself, the finite world points beyond itself. In other words, it is self-transcendent.[33]

This, I believe, is Tillich's great contribution to theology—the reinterpretation of transcendence in a way which preserves its reality while detaching it from the projection of supranaturalism. "The Divine, as he sees it, does not inhabit a transcendent world *above nature;* it is found in the 'ecstatic' character of *this* world, as its transcendent Depth and Ground."[34] Indeed, as a recent commentator has observed, supranaturalism for Tillich actually represents "a loss of transcendence":

> It is the attempt to understand and express God's relation to the world by a literalization of this-worldly categories. . . . The result is a God who *exists* as *a* being, *above* the world. . . . Thus God is described as an entity within the subject-object structures of the spatial-temporal world.[35]

Or, as Tillich puts it himself:

> To criticise such a conditioning of the unconditional, even if it leads to atheistic consequences, is more religious, because it is more aware of the unconditional character of the divine, than a theism that bans God into the supranatural realm.[36]

Nevertheless, the abandonment of any idea of a God "out there" will inevitably appear a denial of his "otherness" and the negation of much in the Biblical assertion of what Kierkegaard called "the infinite qualitative difference between God and man." It will be valuable therefore to look again at what the Bible is saying about the nature of God and see how it can retain, and indeed regain, its deepest significance in the light of this reinterpretation.

God in the Bible

One of the most searching meditations in all literature on the meaning and presence of God is to be found in Psalm 139. Here, if anywhere, there is a sense of the utterly inescapable and surpassing wonder of God *in every direction*—above, beneath, behind and before. This Psalm is a *locus classicus* for the doctrine of the omnipotence and omniscience of God. It is from this source as much as from any other that traditional theology has constructed its picture of an all-powerful Being out there beyond us, who can do everything, who knows everything, and who watches all with unsleeping eye—a sort of celestial Big Brother. It is therefore instructive to see how a theologian of Tillich's views reinterprets such a passage.

He makes the point first of all, though it may be difficult to avoid such concepts of a super-Being in religious thought and education, "they are at least as dangerous as they are useful." For

> in making God an object besides other objects, the existence and nature of which are matters of argument, theology supports the escape to atheism. It encourages those who are interested in denying the threatening Witness of their existence. The first step to atheism is always a theology which drags God down to the level of doubtful things. The game of the atheist is then very easy. For he is perfectly justified in destroying such a phantom and all its ghostly qualities. And because the theoretical atheist is just in his destruction, the practical atheists (all of us) are willing to use his argument to support our own attempt to flee God.[37]

He then continues his profound meditation on this Psalm with the words:

> Let us therefore forget these concepts, as concepts, and try to find their genuine meaning within our own experience. We all know that we cannot separate ourselves at any time from the world to which we belong. There is no ultimate privacy or final isolation. We are always held and comprehended by something that is greater than we are, that has a claim upon us, and that demands response from us. The most intimate motions within the depths of our souls are not completely our own. For they belong also to our friends, to mankind, to the universe, and to the Ground of all being, the aim of our life. Nothing can be hidden ultimately. It is always reflected in the mirror in which nothing can be concealed. Does anybody really believe that his most secret thoughts and desires are not manifest in the whole of being, or that the events within the darkness of his subconscious or in the isolation of his consciousness do not produce eternal repercussions? Does anybody really believe that he can escape from the responsibility for what he has done and thought in secret? Omniscience means that our mystery is manifest. Omnipresence means that our privacy is public. The centre of our whole being is involved in the centre of all being; and the centre of all being rests in the centre of our being. I do not believe that any serious man can deny that experience, no matter how he may express it. And if he has had the experience, he has also met something within him that makes him desire to escape the consequence of it. For man is not equal to his own experience; he attempts to forget it; and he knows that he *cannot* forget it.[38]

And yet the Psalmist goes on to recognize that that which he is trying to escape is nothing alien to him.

> The God whom he cannot flee is the Ground of his being. And this being, his nature, soul, and body, is a work of infinite wisdom, awful and wonderful. The admiration of the Divine Wisdom overcomes the horror of the Divine Presence in this passage. It points to the friendly presence of an infinitely creative wisdom. . . . There is a grace in life. Otherwise we could not live.[39]

God as the ground, source and goal of our being cannot but be represented at one and the same time as removed from the shallow, sinful surface of our lives by infinite distance and depth, and yet as nearer to us than our own selves. This is the significance of the traditional categories of transcendence and immanence.

The same paradoxical relationship of our lives to the deepest ground of our being is presented in the New Testament by St. Paul's language about the Spirit of God and our spirits. "Spirit"—as opposed to "flesh," which is life in its shallowness and superficiality—speaks of that level of being and perception where the divine depths are to be known.

> The Spirit searches everything, even the depths of God. For what person knows a man's thoughts except the spirit of the man which is in him? So also no one comprehends the thoughts of God except the Spirit of God.[40]

But St. Paul continues, it is precisely this level of comprehension which is open to Christians:

> We have received not the spirit of the world, but the Spirit which is from God, that we might understand the gifts bestowed on us by God. . . . The unspiritual man does not receive the gifts of the Spirit of God, for they are folly to him, and he is not able to understand them because they are spiritually discerned. But we have the mind of Christ.[41]

And that this "Spirit of God" is nothing alien to us but the very ground of our own true being is brought out in a further passage, for whose proper sense it is necessary to turn to the New English Bible:

> In the same way the Spirit comes to the aid of our weakness. We do not even know how we ought to pray, but through our inarticulate groans the Spirit himself is pleading for us, and God who searches our inmost being knows what the Spirit means, because he pleads for God's own people in God's own way; and in everything, as we know, he cooperates for good with those who love God and are called according to his purpose.[42]

In other words, the deepest groans of suffering of which the Apostle has been speaking,[43] so far from separating us from the source of our being in the love of God are in fact pointers to it, inarticulate sighs too deep for words, which the Spirit can take up and translate into prayer, because "the Spirit" represents the link between the depths of our individual being (however shallow) and the unfathomable abyss of all being in God. God is not outside us, yet he is profoundly transcendent.

But for the Bible "the deep things of God" cannot be plumbed, the transcendence of God cannot be understood, simply by searching the depths of the individual soul. God, since he is Love, is encountered in his fullness only *"between* man and man." And this is the burden of the whole Prophetic tradition—that it is only in response and obedience to the neighbour that the claims of God can be met and known. This message is focused in a passage to which I constantly find myself returning in the book of Jeremiah, where the prophet is addressing Jehoiakim, the son of Josiah:

> Did not your father eat and drink and do justice and righteousness? Then it was well with him. He judged the cause of the poor and needy; then it was well. *Is not this to know me? says the Lord.*[44]

God, the unconditional, is to be found only in, with, *and under* the conditioned relationship of this life: for he *is* their depth and ultimate significance.

And this receives specifically Christian expression in the profoundly simple "parable" of the Sheep and the Goats.[45] The only way in which Christ can be met, whether in acceptance or rejection, is through "the least of his brethren." The Son of Man can be known only in unconditional relationship to the son of man, to the one whose sole claim upon us is his common humanity. Whether one has "known" God is tested by one question only, "How deeply have you loved?"—for "He who does not love does not know God; for God is love."[46]

Now this links up with what Bonhoeffer was saying about a "non-religious" understanding of God. For this ultimate and most searching question has nothing to do with "religion." It rests our eternal salvation upon nothing peculiarly religious. Encounter with the Son of Man is spelt out in terms of an entirely "secular" concern for food, water supplies, housing, hospitals and prisons, just as Jeremiah had earlier defined the knowledge of God in terms of doing justice for the poor and needy. Indeed, in Macmurray's words, "the great contribution of the Hebrew to religion was that he did away with it."[47] A right relationship to God depended on nothing religious: in fact religion could be the greatest barrier to it.[48]

The Way of the Irreligious

Our contention has been that God is to be met not only by a "religious" turning away from the world but in unconditional concern for "the other" *seen through to its ultimate depths,* that God is, to quote Macmurray again, the "personal ground of all that we experience."[49] But this means, as he says, a denial that encounter with him "rests upon some special and extraordinary type of experience apart from which it could not arise."[50] That there are veridical experiences of the type usually called "mystical" or "religious" no one would be so foolish as to deny, and a man may thank God for them as St. Paul did for his visions. But the capacity for religious or mystical awareness, as for aesthetic or psychic awareness, is largely a question of natural endowment. Women, for instance, appear to be naturally more religious—and more psychic—than men. To make the knowledge of God depend upon such experiences is like making it depend on an ear for music. There are those who are tone-deaf, and there are those who would not claim to have any clearly distinguishable "religious" experiences: Oliver Chase Quick was one of them, and he wrote one of the outstanding books on Christian doctrine of our generation.[51]

That God is the "depth" of common non-religious experience is a point upon which John Wren-Lewis also fastens in the account of his conversion. Belief in a personal God came to him, he says, through the experience of discovering in a community "the creative and 'numinous' power" inherent in *ordinary* personal relationships. And this awareness, he believes, is open to anyone.

> It is indeed one of my strongest convictions, which I insist upon as the foundation for any apologetic work I set out to do, that experience of this type is common to all human beings. . . . Prayer and mystical vision are real and important, but they cannot be the primary basis for religious conviction; this must come from *common* experience, and special experiences like prayer are only meaningful, in my view, insofar as they refer back to common experience. But it is one thing to say that religious propositions can be referred to the common experience of the creative character of personal relationships: it would be quite another to say that people commonly *recognize* their experience of personal relationship for what it is—an encounter with the Transcendent. Clearly they do not, or there would be no need for religious apologetics—and what was special about the group of people I met through this Anglican clergyman was that he had led them to be aware of the full religious significance of their relations with one another.[52]

In fact it began to dawn upon him what he had encountered

was actually an entirely different mode of living-in-relationship from anything known in the world, a *redeemed* mode of relationship in which the special energy Blake called "mutual forgiveness" operated in a way that made the professional "permissiveness" of the psychotherapist's consulting-room seem a pale shadow in comparison.[53]

It was, of course, a specifically *Christian* community, manifesting what Tillich describes as the power of "the *new* being." But it was not for that reason any the more *religious,* based upon some new kind of esoteric or pietistic experience. It was pointing through to God as the ground of all personal relationship and all being, but insisting that a man can only know that Love as the fount and goal of his own life in so far as the alienation from the ground of his being is overcome "in Christ." In traditional theological terms, it was declaring that the way to "the Father"—to acknowledgement of the "ultimacy" of pure personal relationship—is only "by the Son"— through the love of him in whom the human is completely open to the divine—and "in the Spirit"—within the reconciling fellowship of the new community.

And this leads us directly into the reassessment, in this whole context, of the person and work of Christ.

Notes

[1]*The Shaking of the Foundations,* p. 60.

[2]*Op. cit.,* pp. 63 f.

[3]*Op. cit.,* pp. 65 f.

[4]*Op. cit.,* p. 124.

[5]*Op. cit.,* p. 64.

[6]*I and Thou* (1937), p. 76; cf. Tillich, *The Protestant Era* (1951), p. 65.

[7]*The Essence of Christianity* (Eng. tr. 1854, from the second ed. of 1843), p. 97.

[8]*Systematic Theology,* vol. i, p. 15.

[9]Rom. 8:39.

[10]*Op. cit.,* p. 21. I have preferred, for this quotation, the translation in H. de Lubac, *op. cit.,* p. 11.

[11]*Kerygma and Myth,* vol. i, p. 107.

[12]*Op. cit.,* p. 206.

[13]*The Self as Agent* (1957), p. 17.

[14]*Persons in Relation* (1961), Ch. X.

[15]*The Structure of Religious Experience* (1936), p. 30 f.

[16]*Op. cit.*, p. 43.

[17]*Op. cit.*, pp. 27 f.

[18]*Op. cit.*, p. 261; cf. p. 47: "Love is God himself, and apart from it there is no God."

[19]I John 4:8.

[20]I John 4:16.

[21]*Ibid.*

[22]I John 4:7.

[23]I John 4:10, 19.

[24]The title of Karl Barth's book (1961) and of the central lecture in it (pp. 37-65). Feuerbach interestingly enough also uses the phrase "the human nature of God" (*op. cit.*, p. 49), but as always with a subtly different twist.

[25]*I and Thou*, p. 75.

[26]*Between Man and Man* (1947), pp. 30, 203-5; cf. *I and Thou*, p. 39.

[27]*Philosophie der Zukunft*, p. 62.

[28]*Op. cit.*, p. 124 (italics mine).

[29]*Op. cit.*, p. 175.

[30]*Systematic Theology*, vol. ii, p. 5.

[31]"The Decline of Magic in Art and Politics," *The Critical Quarterly*, Spring 1960, p. 18. I should add that there is much in Wren-Lewis's writings (for instance, in his subsequent elaboration of this last sentence or in his article "Modern Philosophy and the Doctrine of the Trinity" in *The Philosophical Quarterly*, vol. v (1955), pp. 214-24, which makes me doubt whether in the last analysis he himself is not expounding the thesis "love is God." At any rate he certainly does not guard himself adequately against this interpretation.

[32]*The Shaking of the Foundations*, p. 181.

[33]*Systematic Theology*, vol. ii, p. 8.

[34]W. M. Horton, "Tillich's Role in Contemporary Theology" in *The Theology of Paul Tillich* (ed. C. W. Kegley and R. W. Bretall, 1952, p. 37). In his "Reply to Interpretation and Criticism" in the same volume, Tillich describes his own position as "self-transcending or ecstatic naturalism" (p. 341).

[35]E. Farley, *The Transcendence of God* (1962), p. 77.

[36]*The Protestant Era*, p. 92.

[37]*The Shaking of the Foundations,* pp. 52 f.

[38]*Op. cit.,* pp. 53 f.

[39]*Op. cit.,* pp. 54 f.

[40]I Cor. 2:10 f.

[41]I Cor. 2:12-16.

[42]Rom. 8:26-8.

[43]Rom. 8:18-23.

[44]Jer. 22:15 f.

[45]Matt. 25:31-46.

[46]I John 4:8.

[47]Quoted by G. Macleod, *Only One Way Left,* p. 67; cf. J. Macmurray, *The Clue to History* (1938), Ch. II.

[48]E.g., Amos 5:21-5.

[49]*The Self as Agent,* p. 17.

[50]*Op. cit.,* p. 18.

[51]*Doctrines of the Creed* (1938).

[52]*They Become Anglicans,* pp. 175 f.

[53]*Op. cit.,* pp. 176 f.

23

Louis Berkhof

The Attributes of God

The Incommunicable Attributes

God as the Absolute Being

It has been quite common in theology to speak of God as the absolute Being. At the same time the term "absolute" is more characteristic of philosophy than it is of theology. In metaphysics the term "the Absolute" is a designation of the ultimate ground of all existence; and because the theist also speaks of God as the ultimate ground of all existence, it is sometimes thought that the Absolute of philosophy and the God of theism are one and the same. But that is not necessarily so. In fact the usual conception of the Absolute renders it impossible to equate it with the God of the Bible and of Christian theology. The term "Absolute" is derived from the Latin *absolutus,* a compound of *ab* (from) and *solvere* (to loosen), and thus means free as to condition, or free from limitation or restraint. This fundamental thought was worked out in various ways, so that the Absolute was regarded as that which is free from all conditions (the Unconditioned or Self-Existent), from all relations (the Unrelated), from all imper-

From Louis Berkhof, *Systematic Theology*. Grand Rapids: Wm. B. Eerdmans Publishing Company, 1939. Used by permission.

fections (the Perfect), or free from all phenomenal differences or distinctions, such as matter and spirit, being and attributes, subject and object, appearance and reality (the Real, or Ultimate Reality).

The answer to the question, whether the Absolute of philosophy can be identified with the God of theology, depends on the conception one has of the Absolute. If Spinoza conceives of the Absolute as the one Self-subsistent Being of which all particular things are but transient modes, thus identifying God and the world, we cannot share his view of this Absolute as God. When Hegel views the Absolute as the unity of thought and being, as the totality of all things, which includes all relations, and in which all the discords of the present are resolved in perfect unity, we again find it impossible to follow him in regarding this Absolute as God. And when Bradley says that his Absolute is related to nothing, and that there cannot be any practical relation between it and the finite will, we agree with him that his Absolute cannot be the God of the Christian religion, for this God does enter into relations with finite creatures. Bradley cannot conceive of the God of religion as other than a finite God. But when the Absolute is defined as the First Cause of all existing things, or as the ultimate ground of all reality, or as the one self-existent Being, it can be considered as identical with the God of theology. He is the Infinite One, who does not exist in any *necessary* relations, because He is self-sufficient, but at the same time can *freely* enter into various relations with His creation as a whole and with His creatures. While the incommunicable attributes emphasize the absolute Being of God, the communicable attributes stress the fact that He enters into various relations with His creatures. In the present chapter the following perfections of God come into consideration.

A. *The Self-Existence of God*

God is self-existent, that is, He has the ground of His existence in Himself. This idea is sometimes expressed by saying that He is *causa sui* (His own cause), but this expression is hardly accurate, since God is the uncaused, who exists by the necessity of His own Being, and therefore necessarily. Man, on the other hand, does not exist necessarily, and has the cause of his existence outside of himself. The idea of God's self-existence was generally expressed by the term *aseitas,* meaning *self-originated,* but Reformed theologians quite generally substituted for it the word *independentia* (independence), as expressing, not merely that God is independent in His Being, but also that He is independent in everything else: in His virtues, decrees, works, and so on. It may be said that there is a faint trace of this perfection in the creature, but this can only mean that the creature, though absolutely dependent, yet has its own distinct existence. But, of course, this falls far short of being self-existent. This attribute of God is generally recognized, and is implied in heathen religions and in the Absolute of philosophy. When the Absolute is conceived of as the self-existent and as the ultimate ground of all things, which voluntarily enters into various relations with other beings, it can be identified with the God of theology. As the self-existent God, He is not only independent in Himself, but also causes everything to depend on Him. This self-existence of God finds expression in the name Jehovah. It is only as the self-existent and independent One that God can give the assurance that He will remain eternally the same in relation to His people. Additional indications of it are found in the assertion in John 5:26, "For as the Father hath life in Himself, even so gave He to the Son also to have life in Himself"; in the declaration that He is independent of all things and that all things exist only through Him, Ps. 94:8 ff.; Isa. 40:18 ff.; Acts 7:25; and in statements implying that He is independent in His thought, Rom. 11:33, 34, and in His will, Dan. 4:35; Rom. 9:19; Eph. 1:5; Rev. 4:11, in His power, Ps. 115:3, and in His counsel, Ps. 33:11.

B. The Immutability of God

The Immutability of God is a necessary concomitant of His aseity. It is that perfection of God by which He is devoid of all change, not only in His Being, but also in His perfections, and in His purposes and promises. In virtue of this attribute He is exalted above all becoming, and is free from all accession or diminution and from all growth or decay in His Being or perfections. His knowledge and plans, His moral principles and volitions remain forever the same. Even reason teaches us that no change is possible in God, since a change is either for better or for worse. But in God, as the absolute Perfection, improvement and deterioration are both equally impossible. This immutability of God is clearly taught in such passages of Scripture as Exod. 3:14; Ps. 102:26-28; Isa. 41:4; 48:12; Mal. 3:6; Rom. 1:23; Heb. 1:11, 12; James 1:17. At the same time there are many passages of Scripture which seem to ascribe change to God. Did not He who dwelleth in eternity pass on to the creation of the world, become incarnate in Christ, and in the Holy Spirit take up His abode in the Church? Is He not represented as revealing and hiding Himself, as coming and going, as repenting and changing His intention, and as dealing differently with man before and after conversion? Cf. Exod. 32:10-14; Jonah 3:10; Prov. 11:20; 12:22; Ps. 18:26, 27. The objection here implied is based to a certain extent on misunderstanding. The divine immutability should not be understood as implying *immobility,* as if there were no movement in God. It is even customary in theology to speak of God as *actus purus,* a God who is always in action. The Bible teaches us that God enters into manifold relations with man and, as it were, lives their life with them. There is change round about Him, change in the relations of men to Him, but there is no change in His Being, His attributes,

His purpose, His motives of action, or His promises. The purpose to create was eternal with Him, and there was no change in Him when this purpose was realized by a single eternal act of His will. The incarnation brought no change in the Being or perfections of God, nor in His purpose, for it was His eternal good pleasure to send the Son of His love into the world. And if Scripture speaks of His repenting, changing His intention, and altering His relation to sinners when they repent, we should remember that this is only an anthropopathic way of speaking. In reality the change is not in God, but in man and in man's relations to God. It is important to maintain the immutability of God over against the Pelagian and Arminian doctrine that God is subject to change, not indeed in His Being, but in His knowledge and will, so that His decisions are to a great extent dependent on the actions of man; over against the pantheistic notion that God is an eternal becoming rather than an absolute Being, and that the unconscious Absolute is gradually developing into conscious personality in man; and over against the present tendency of some to speak of a finite, struggling, and gradually growing God.

C. The Infinity of God

The infinity of God is that perfection of God by which He is free from all limitations. In ascribing it to God we deny that there are or can be any limitations to the divine Being or attributes. It implies that He is in no way limited by the universe, by this time-space world, or confined to the universe. It does not involve His identity with the sum-total of existing things, nor does it exclude the co-existence of derived and finite things, to which He bears relation. The infinity of God must be conceived as intensive rather than extensive, and should not be confused with boundless extension, as if God were spread out through the entire universe, one part being here and another there, for God has no body and therefore no extension. Neither should it be regarded as a merely negative concept, though it is perfectly true that we cannot form a positive idea of it. It is a reality in God fully comprehended only by Him. We distinguish various aspects of God's infinity.

1. His Absolute Perfection. This is the infinity of the Divine Being considered in itself. It should not be understood in a quantitative, but in a qualitative sense; it qualifies all the communicable attributes of God. Infinite power is not an absolute quantum, but an exhaustless potency of power; and infinite holiness is not a boundless quantum of holiness, but a holiness which is qualitatively free from all limitation or defect. The same may be said of infinite knowledge and wisdom, and of infinite love and righteousness. Says Dr. Orr: "Perhaps we can say that infinity in God is ultimately: (a) internally and qualitatively, absence of all limitation and defect; (b) boundless potentiality."[1] In this sense of the word the infinity of God is simply identical with the perfection of His Divine Being. Scripture proof for it is found in Job 11:7-10; Ps. 145:3; Matt. 5:48.

2. His Eternity. The infinity of God in relation to time is called His eternity. The form in which the Bible represents God's eternity is simply that of duration through endless ages, Ps. 90:2; 102:12; Eph. 3:21. We should remember, however, that in speaking as it does the Bible uses popular language, and not the language of philosophy. We generally think of God's eternity in the same way, namely, as duration infinitely prolonged both backwards and forwards. But this is only a popular and symbolical way of representing that which in reality transcends time and differs from it essentially. Eternity in the strict sense of the word is ascribed to that which transcends all temporal limitations. That it applies to God in that sense is at least intimated in II Peter 3:8. "Time," says Dr. Orr, "strictly has relation to the world of objects existing in succession. God fills time; is in every part of it; but His eternity still is not really this being in time. It is rather that to which time forms a contrast."[2] Our existence is marked off by days and weeks and months and years; not so the existence of God. Our life is divided into a past, present and future, but there is no such division in the life of God. He is the eternal "I am." His eternity may be defined as *that perfection of God whereby He is elevated above all temporal limits and all succession of moments, and possesses the whole of His existence in one indivisible present.* The relation of eternity to time constitutes one of the most difficult problems in philosophy and theology, perhaps incapable of solution in our present condition.

3. His Immensity. The infinity of God may also be viewed with reference to space, and is then called His immensity. It may be defined as *that perfection of the Divine Being by which He transcends all spatial limitations, and yet is present in every point of space with His whole Being.* It has a negative and a positive side, denying all limitations of space to the Divine Being, and asserting that God is above space and fills every part of it *with His whole Being.* The last words are added, in order to ward off the idea that God is diffused through space, so that one part of His Being is present in one place, and another part in some other place. We distinguish three modes of presence in space. Bodies are in space circumscriptively, because they are bounded by it; finite spirits are in space definitively, since they are not everywhere, but only in a certain definite place; and in distinction from both of these God is in space repletively, because He fills all space. He is not absent from any part of it, nor more present in one part than in another.

In a certain sense the terms "immensity" and "omnipresence," as applied to God, denote the same thing, and can therefore be regarded as synonymous. Yet there is a point of difference that should be carefully noted. "Immensity" points to the fact that God transcends all space and is not subject to its limitations, while "omnipresence" denotes that He nevertheless fills every part of space with His entire Being. The former emphasizes the transcendence, and the latter, the immanence of God. God is immanent in all His creatures, in His entire creation, but is in no way bounded by it. In connection with God's relation to the world we must avoid, on the one hand, the error of Pantheism, so characteristic of a great deal of present day thinking, with its denial of the transcendence of God and its assumption that the Being of God is really the substance of all things; and, on the other hand, the Deistic conception that God is indeed present in creation *per potentiam* (with His power), but not *per essentiam et naturam* (with His very Being and nature), and acts upon the world from a distance. Though God is distinct from the world and may not be identified with it, He is yet present in every part of His creation, not only *per potentiam,* but also *per essentiam.* This does not mean, however, that He is equally present and present in the same sense in all His creatures. The nature of His indwelling is in harmony with that of His creatures. He does not dwell on earth as He does in heaven, in animals as He does in man, in the inorganic as He does in the organic creation, in the wicked as He does in the pious, nor in the Church as He does in Christ. There is an endless variety in the manner in which He is immanent in His creatures, and in the measure in which they reveal God to those who have eyes to see. The omnipresence of God is clearly revealed in Scripture. Heaven and earth cannot contain Him, I Kings 8:27; Isa. 66:1; Acts 7:48-49; and at the same time He fills both and is a God at hand, Ps. 139:7-10; Jer. 23:23-24; Acts 17:27-28.

D. The Unity of God

A distinction is made between the *unitas singularitatis* and the *unitas simplicitatis.*

1. The Unitas Singularitatis. This attribute stresses both the oneness and the unicity of God, the fact that He is numerically one and that as such He is unique. It implies that there is but one Divine Being, that from the nature of the case there can be but one, and that all other beings exist of and through and unto Him. The Bible teaches us in several passages that there is but one true God. Solomon pleaded with God to maintain the cause of His people, "that all the peoples of the earth may know that Jehovah, He is God; there is none else," I Kings 8:60. And Paul writes to the Corinthians, "But to us there is but one God, the Father, of whom are all things, and we in Him; and one Lord Jesus Christ, by whom are all things, and we in Him," I Cor. 8:6. Similarly he writes to Timothy, "For there is one God, and one Mediator between God and men, the man Christ Jesus," I Tim. 2:5. Other passages do not stress the numerical unity of God as much as they do His uniqueness. This is the case in the well known words of Deut. 6:4, "Hear, O Israel; Jehovah our God is one Jehovah." The Hebrew word *'echad,* translated by "one" may also be rendered "an only," the equivalent of the German "einig" and the Dutch "eenig." And this would seem to be a better translation. Keil stresses that fact that this passage does not teach the numerical unity of God, but rather that Jehovah is the only God that is entitled to the name Jehovah. This is also the meaning of the term in Zech. 14:9. The same idea is beautifully expressed in the rhetorical question of Exod. 15:11, "Who is like unto thee, O Jehovah, among the gods? Who is like thee, glorious in holiness, fearful in praises, doing wonders?" This excludes all polytheistic conceptions of God.

2. *The Unitas Simplicitatis.* While the unity discussed in the preceding sets God apart from other beings, the perfection now under consideration is expressive of the inner and qualitative unity of the Divine Being. When we speak of the simplicity of God, we use the term to describe the state or quality of being simple, the condition of being free from division into parts, and therefore from compositeness. It means that God is not composite and is not susceptible of division in any sense of the word. This implies among other things that the three Persons in the Godhead are not so many parts of which the Divine essence is composed, that God's essence and perfections are not distinct, and that the attributes are not superadded to His essence. Since the two are one, the Bible can speak of God as light and life, as righteousness and love, thus identifying Him with His perfections. The simplicity of God follows from some of His other perfections; from His Self-existence, which excludes the idea that something preceded Him, as in the case of compounds; and from His immutability, which could not be predicated of His nature, if it were made up of parts. This perfection was disputed during the Middle Ages, and was denied by Socinians and Arminians. Scripture does not explicitly assert it, but implies it where it speaks of God as righteousness, truth, wisdom, light, life, love, and so on, and thus indicates that each of these properties, because of their absolute perfection, is identical with His Being. In recent works on theology the simplicity of God is seldom mentioned. Many theologians positively deny it, either because it is regarded as a purely metaphysical abstraction, or because, in their estimation, it conflicts with the doctrine of the Trinity. Dabney believes that there is no composition in the substance of God, but denies that in Him substance and attributes are one and the same. He claims that God is no more simple in that respect than finite spirits.[3]

The Communicable Attributes

God as a Personal Spirit

If the attributes discussed in the previous chapter stressed the

absolute Being of God, those that remain to be considered emphasize His personal nature. It is in the communicable attributes that
God stands out as a conscious, intelligent, free, and moral Being, as
a Being that is personal in the highest sense of the word. The question has long engaged the attention of philosophers, and is still a
subject of debate, whether personal existence is consistent with the
idea of absoluteness. The answer to that question depends to a great
extent on the meaning one ascribes to the word "absolute." The word
has been used in three different senses in philosophy, which may be
denominated as the agnostic, the logical, and the causal sense. For
the agnostic the Absolute is the unrelated, of which nothing can be
known, since things are known only in their relations. And if nothing
can be known of it, personality cannot be ascribed to it. Moreover,
since personality is unthinkable apart from relations, it cannot be
identified with an Absolute which is in its very essence the unrelated.
In the logical Absolute the individual is subordinated to the universal,
and the highest universal is ultimate reality. Such is the absolute substance of Spinoza, and the absolute spirit of Hegel. It may express
itself in and through the finite, but nothing that is finite can express
its essential nature. To ascribe personality to it would be to limit
it to one mode of being, and would destroy its absoluteness. In fact,
such an absolute or ultimate is a mere abstract and empty concept,
that is barren of all content. The causal view of the Absolute represents it as the ultimate ground of all things. It is not dependent on
anything outside of itself, but causes all things to depend on it.
Moreover, it is not necessarily completely unrelated, but can enter
into various relations with finite creatures. Such a conception of the
Absolute is not inconsistent with the idea of personality. Moreover,
we should bear in mind that in their argumentation philosophers were
always operating with the idea of personality as it is realized in man,
and lost sight of the fact that personality in God might be something
infinitely more perfect. As a matter of fact, perfect personality is
found only in God, and what we see in man is only a finite copy of
the original. Still more, there is a tri-personality in God, of which
no analogy is found in human beings.

Several natural proofs, quite similar to those adduced for the existence of God, have been urged to prove the personality of God. (1)
Human personality demands a personal God for its explanation. Man
is not a self-existent and eternal, but a finite being that has a beginning and an end. The cause assumed must be sufficient to account for
the whole of the effect. Since man is a personal product, the power
originating him must also be personal. Otherwise there is something
in the effect which is superior to anything that is found in the cause;
and this would be quite impossible. (2) The world in general bears
witness to the personality of God. In its whole fabric and constitution
it reveals the clearest traces of an infinite intelligence, of the deepest,

highest and tenderest emotions, and of a will that is all-powerful. Consequently, we are constrained to mount from the world to the world's Maker as a Being of intelligence, sensibility, and will, that is, as a person. (3) The moral and religious nature of man also points to the personality of God. His moral nature imposes on him a sense of obligation to do that which is right, and this necessarily implies the existence of a supreme Lawgiver. Moreover, his religious nature constantly prompts him to seek personal communion with some higher Being; and all the elements and activities of religion demand a personal God as their object and final end. Even so-called pantheistic religions often testify unconsciously to belief in a personal God. The fact is that all such things as penitence, faith and obedience, fellowship and love, loyalty in service and sacrifice, trust in life and death, are meaningless unless they find their appropriate object in a personal God.

But while all these considerations are true and have some value as *testimonia,* they are not the proofs on which theology depends in its doctrine of the personality of God. It turns for proof to God's Self-revelation in Scripture. The term "person" is not applied to God in the Bible, though there are words, such as the Hebrew *panim* and the Greek *prosopon,* that come very close to expressing the idea. At the same time Scripture testifies to the personality of God in more than one way. The presence of God, as described by Old and New Testament writers, is clearly a personal presence. And the anthropomorphic and anthropopathic representations of God in Scripture, while they must be interpreted so as not to militate against the pure spirituality and holiness of God, can hardly be justified, except on the assumption that the Being to whom they apply is a real person, with personal attributes, even though it be without human limitations. God is represented throughout as a personal God, with whom men can and may converse, whom they can trust, who sustains them in their trials, and fills their hearts with the joy of deliverance and victory. And, finally, the highest revelation of God to which the Bible testifies is a personal revelation. Jesus Christ reveals the Father in such a perfect way that He could say to Philip, "He who hath seen me hath seen the Father," John 14:9. More detailed proofs will appear in the discussion of the communicable attributes.

A. The Spirituality of God

The Bible does not give us a definition of God. The nearest approach to anything like it is found in the word of Christ to the Samaritan woman, "God is Spirit," John 4:24. This is at least a statement purporting to tell us in a single word what God is. The Lord does not merely say that God is *a* spirit, but that He is Spirit. And because of this clear statement it is but fitting that we should discuss first of all the spirituality of God. By teaching the spirituality of

God theology stresses the fact that God has a substantial Being all His own and distinct from the world, and that this substantial Being is immaterial, invisible, and without composition or extension. It includes the thought that all the essential qualities which belong to the perfect idea of Spirit are found in Him: that He is a self-conscious and self-determining Being. Since He is Spirit in the most absolute, and in the purest sense of the word, there is in Him no composition of parts. The idea of spirituality of necessity excludes the ascription of anything like corporeity to God, and thus condemns the fancies of some of the early Gnostics and medieval Mystics, and of all those sectarians of our own day who ascribe a body to God. It is true that the Bible speaks of the hands and feet, the eyes and ears, the mouth and nose of God, but in doing this it is speaking anthropomorphically or figuratively of Him who far transcends our human knowledge, and of whom we can only speak in a stammering fashion after the manner of men. By ascribing spirituality to God we also affirm that He has none of the properties belonging to matter, and that He cannot be discerned by the bodily senses. Paul speaks of Him as "the King eternal, immortal, invisible" (I Tim. 1:17), and again as "the King of kings, and Lord of lords, who only hath immortality, dwelling in light unapproachable; whom no man hath seen, nor can see: to whom be honor and power eternal," I Tim. 6:15, 16.

B. *Intellectual Attributes*

God is represented in Scripture as Light, and therefore as perfect in His intellectual life. This category comprises two of the divine perfections, namely, the knowledge and the wisdom of God.

1. *The Knowledge of God.* The knowledge of God may be defined as *that perfection of God whereby He, in an entirely unique manner, knows Himself and all things possible and actual in one eternal and most simple act.* The Bible testifies to the knowledge of God abundantly, as, for instance, in I Sam. 2:3; Job 12:13; Ps. 94:9; 147:4; Isa. 29:15; 40:27, 28. In connection with the knowledge of God several points call for consideration.

a. *Its nature.* The knowledge of God differs in some important points from that of men. It is *archetypal,* which means that He knows the universe as it exists in His own eternal idea previous to its existence as a finite reality in time and space; and that His knowledge is not, like ours, obtained from without. It is a knowledge that is characterized by *absolute perfection.* As such it is *intuitive* rather than demonstrative or discursive. It is *innate and immediate,* and does not result from observation or from a process of reasoning. Being perfect, it is also *simultaneous* and not successive, so that He sees things at once in their totality, and not piecemeal one after another. Furthermore, it is *complete and fully conscious,* while man's knowledge is always partial, frequently indistinct, and often fails to rise into the clear light of consciousness. A distinction is made between the *necessary* and *free* knowledge of God. The former is the knowledge which God has of Himself and of all things possible, a knowledge resting on the consciousness of His omnipotence. It is called *necessary knowledge,* because it is not determined by an action of the divine will. It is also known as *the knowledge of simple intelligence,* in view of the fact that it is purely an act of the divine intellect, without any concurrent action of the divine will. *The free knowledge of God* is the knowledge which He has of all things actual, that is, of things that existed in the past, that exist in the present, or that will exist in the future. It is founded on God's infinite knowledge of His own all-comprehensive and unchangeable eternal purposes, and is called free knowledge, because it is determined by a concurrent act of the will. It is also called *scientia visionis,* knowledge of vision.

b. Its extent. The knowledge of God is not only perfect in kind, but also in its inclusiveness. It is called *omniscience,* because it is all-comprehensive. In order to promote a proper estimate of it, we may particularize as follows: God knows Himself and in Himself all things that come from Him (internal knowledge). He knows all things as they actually come to pass, past, present and future, and knows them in their real relations. He knows the hidden essence of all things, to which the knowledge of man cannot penetrate. He sees not as man sees, who observes only the outward manifestations of life, but penetrates to the depths of the human heart. Moreover, He knows what is possible as well as what is actual; all things that might occur under certain circumstances are present to His mind. The omniscience of God is clearly taught in several passages of Scripture. He is perfect in knowledge, Job 37:16, looketh not on outward appearance but on the heart, I Sam. 16:7; I Chron. 28:9, 17; Ps. 139:1-4; Jer. 17:10, observes the ways of men, Deut. 2:7; Job 23:10; 24:23; 31:4; Ps. 1:6; 119:168, knows the place of their habitation, Ps. 33:13, and the days of their life, Ps. 37:18. This doctrine of the knowledge of God must be maintained over against all pantheistic tendencies to represent God as the unconscious ground of the phenomenal world, and of those who, like Marcion, Socinus and all who believe in a finite God, ascribe to Him only a limited knowledge.

There is one question, however, that calls for special discussion. It concerns God's foreknowledge of the free actions of men, and therefore of conditional events. We can understand how God can foreknow where necessity rules, but find it difficult to conceive of a previous knowledge of actions which man freely originates. The difficulty of this problem led some to deny the foreknowledge of free actions, and others to deny human freedom. It is perfectly evident that Scripture teaches the divine foreknowledge of contingent events. I Sam. 23:10, 13; II Kings 13:19; Ps. 81:14, 15; Isa. 42:9; 48:18;

Jer. 2:2, 3; 38:17-20; Ezek. 3:6; Matt. 11:21. Moreover, it does not leave us in doubt as to the freedom of man. It certainly does not permit the denial of either one of the terms of the problem. We are up against a problem here which we cannot fully solve, though it is possible to make an approach to a solution. God has decreed all things, and has decreed them with their causes and conditions in the exact order in which they come to pass; and His foreknowledge of future things and also of contingent events rests on His decree. This solves the problem as far as the foreknowledge of God is concerned.

But now the question arises, Is the predetermination of things consistent with the free will of man? And the answer is that it certainly is not, if the freedom of the will be regarded as *indifferentia* (arbitrariness), but this is an unwarranted conception of the freedom of man. The will of man is not something altogether indeterminate, something hanging in the air that can be swung arbitrarily in either direction. It is rather something rooted in our very nature, connected with our deepest instincts and emotions, and determined by our intellectual considerations and by our very character. And if we conceive of our human freedom as *lubentia rationalis* (reasonable self-determination), then we have no sufficient warrant for saying that it is inconsistent with divine foreknowledge. Says Dr. Orr: "A solution of this problem there is, though our minds fail to grasp it. In part it probably lies, not in denying freedom, but in a revised conception of freedom. For freedom, after all, is not arbitrariness. There is in all rational action a *why* for acting—a reason which decides action. The truly free man is not the uncertain, incalculable man, but the man who is *reliable*. In short, freedom has its laws—spiritual laws—and the omniscient Mind knows what these are. But an element of mystery, it must be acknowledged, still remains."[4]

Jesuit, Lutheran, and Arminian theologians suggested the so-called *scientia media* as a solution of the problem. The name is indicative of the fact that it occupies a middle ground between the necessary and the free knowledge of God. It differs from the former in that its *object* is not all possible things, *but a special class of things actually future;* and from the latter in that its *ground* is not the eternal purpose of God, *but the free action of the creature as simply foreseen.*[5] It is called *mediate,* says Dabney, "because they suppose God arrives at it, not directly by knowing His own purpose to effect it, but indirectly by His infinite insight into the manner in which the contingent second cause will act, under given outward circumstances, foreseen or produced by God."[6] But this is no solution of the problem at all. It is an attempt to reconcile two things which logically exclude each other, namely, freedom of action in the Pelagian sense and a *certain* foreknowledge of that action. Actions that are in no way determined by God, directly or indirectly, but are wholly dependent on the arbitrary will of man, can hardly be the object of divine foreknowledge. Moreover, it is objectionable, because it makes the divine knowledge dependent on the choice of man, virtually annuls the certainty of the knowledge of future events, and thus implicitly denies the omniscience of God. It is also contrary to such passages of Scripture as Acts 2:23; Rom. 9:16; Eph. 1:11; Phil. 2:13.

2. *The Wisdom of God.* The wisdom of God may be regarded as a particular aspect of His knowledge. It is quite evident that knowledge and wisdom are not the same, though they are closely related. They do not always accompany each other. An uneducated man may be superior to a scholar in wisdom. Knowledge is acquired by study, but wisdom results from an intuitive insight into things. The former is theoretical, while the latter is practical, making knowledge subservient to some specific purpose. Both are imperfect in man, but in God they are characterized by absolute perfection. God's wisdom is His intelligence as manifested in the adaptation of means to ends. It points to the fact that He always strives for the best possible ends, and chooses the best means for the realization of His purposes. H. B. Smith defines the divine wisdom as "that attribute of God whereby He produces the best possible results with the best possible means." We may be a little more specific and call it *that perfection of God whereby He applies His knowledge to the attainment of His ends in a way which glorifies Him most.* It implies a final end to which all secondary ends are subordinate; and according to Scripture this final end is the glory of God, Rom. 11:33; 14:7, 8; Eph. 1:11, 12; Col. 1:16. Scripture refers to the wisdom of God in many passages, and even represents it as personified in Proverbs 8. The wisdom of God is seen particularly in creation, Ps. 19:1-7; 104:1-34; in providence, Ps. 33:10, 11; Rom. 8:28; and in redemption, Rom. 11:33; I Cor. 2:7; Eph. 3:10.

3. *The Veracity of God.* Scripture uses several words to express the veracity of God: in the Old Testament *'emeth, 'amunah,* and *'amen,* and in the New Testament *alethes (aletheia), alethinos,* and *pistis.* This already points to the fact that it includes several ideas, such as truth, truthfulness, and faithfulness. When God is called the truth, this is to be understood in its most comprehensive sense. He is the truth first of all in a metaphysical sense, that is, in Him the idea of the Godhead is perfectly realized; He is all that He as God should be, and as such is distinguished from all so-called gods, which are called vanity and lies, Ps. 96:5; 97:7; 115:4-8; Isa. 44:9, 10. He is also the truth in an *ethical* sense, and as such reveals Himself as He really is, so that His revelation is absolutely reliable, Num. 23:19; Rom. 3:4; Heb. 6:18. Finally, He is also the truth in a *logical* sense, and in virtue of this He knows things as they really are, and has so constituted the mind of man that the latter can know, not merely the appearance, but also the reality, of things. Thus the truth of God

is the foundation of all knowledge. It should be borne in mind, moreover, that these three are but different aspects of the truth, which is one in God. In view of the preceding we may define the veracity or truth of God as *that perfection of His Being by virtue of which He fully answers to the idea of the Godhead, is perfectly reliable in His revelation, and sees things as they really are.* It is because of this perfection that He is the source of all truth, not only in the sphere of morals and religion, but also in every field of scientific endeavor. Scripture is very emphatic in its references to God as the truth, Exod. 34:6; Num. 23:19; Deut. 32:4; Ps. 25:10; 31:6; Isa. 65:16; Jer. 10:8, 10, 11; John 14:6; 17:3; Titus 1:2; Heb. 6:18; I John 5:20, 21. There is still another aspect of this divine perfection, and one that is always regarded as of the greatest importance. It is generally called His *faithfulness,* in virtue of which He is ever mindful of His covenant and fulfils all the promises which He has made to His people. This faithfulness of God is of the utmost practical significance to the people of God. It is the ground of their confidence, the foundation of their hope, and the cause of their rejoicing. It saves them from the despair to which their own unfaithfulness might easily lead, gives them courage to carry on in spite of their failures, and fills their hearts with joyful anticipations, even when they are deeply conscious of the fact that they have forfeited all the blessings of God. Num. 23:19; Deut. 7:9; Ps. 89:33; Isa. 49:7; I Cor. 1:9; II Tim. 2:13; Heb. 6:17, 18; 10:23.

C. Moral Attributes

The moral attributes of God are generally regarded as the most glorious of the divine perfections. Not that one attribute of God is in itself more perfect and glorious than another, but relatively to man the moral perfections of God shine with a splendor all their own. They are generally discussed under three heads: (1) the goodness of God; (2) the holiness of God; and (3) the righteousness of God.

1. The Goodness of God. This is generally treated as a generic conception, including several varieties, which are distinguished according to their objects. The goodness of God should not be confused with His kindness, which is a more restricted concept. We speak of something as good, when it answers in all parts to the ideal. Hence in our ascription of goodness to God the fundamental idea is that He is in every way all that He as God should be, and therefore answers perfectly to the ideal expressed in the word "God." He is good in the metaphysical sense of the word, absolute perfection and perfect bliss in Himself. It is in this sense that Jesus said to the young ruler: "None is good save one, even God," Mark 10:18. But since God is good in Himself, He is also good for His creatures, and may therefore be called the *fons omnium bonorum.* He is the fountain of all good, and is so represented in a variety of ways throughout the Bible. The poet sings: "For with thee is the fountain of life; in thy light shall we see light," Ps. 36:9. All the good things which the creatures enjoy in the present and expect in the future, flow to them out of this inexhaustible fountain. And not only that, but God is also the *summum bonum,* the highest good, for all His creatures, though in different degrees and according to the measure in which they answer to the purpose of their existence. In the present connection we naturally stress the ethical goodness of God and the different aspects of it, as these are determined by the nature of its objects.

a. The goodness of God towards His creatures in general. This may be defined as *that perfection of God which prompts Him to deal bountifully and kindly with all His creatures.* It is the affection which the Creator feels towards His sentient creatures as such. The Psalmist sings of it in the well known words: "Jehovah is good to all; and His tender mercies are over all His works. . . . The eyes of all wait for thee; and thou givest them their food in due season. Thou openest thy hand, and satisfiest the desire of every living thing," Ps. 145:9, 15, 16. This benevolent interest of God is revealed in His care for the creature's welfare, and is suited to the nature and the circumstances of the creature. It naturally varies in degree according to the capacity of the objects to receive it. And while it is not restricted to believers, they only manifest a proper appreciation of its blessings, desire to use them in the service of their God, and thus enjoy them in a richer and fuller measure. The Bible refers to this goodness of God in many passages, such as Ps. 36:6; 104:21; Matt. 5:45; 6:26; Luke 6:35; Acts 14:17.

b. The love of God. When the goodness of God is exercised towards His rational creatures, it assumes the higher character of love, and this love may again be distinguished according to the objects on which it terminates. In distinction from the goodness of God in general, it may be defined as *that perfection of God by which He is eternally moved to self-communication.* Since God is absolutely good in Himself, His love cannot find complete satisfaction in any object that falls short of absolute perfection. He loves His rational creatures for His own sake, or, to express it otherwise, He loves in them Himself, His virtues, His work, and His gifts. He does not even withdraw His love completely from the sinner in his present sinful state, though the latter's sin is an abomination to Him, since He recognizes even in the sinner His image-bearer, John 3:16; Matt. 5:44-45. At the same time He loves believers with a special love, since He contemplates them as His spiritual children in Christ. It is to them that He communicates Himself in the fullest and richest sense, with all the fulness of His grace and mercy, John 16:27; Rom. 5:8; I John 3:1.

c. The grace of God. The significant word "grace" is a translation of the Hebrew *chanan* and of the Greek *charis.* According to

Scripture it is manifested not only by God, but also by men, and then denotes the favor which one man shows another, Gen. 33:8, 10, 18; 39:4; 47:25; Ruth 2:2; I Sam. 1:18; 16:22. In such cases it is not necessarily implied that the favor is undeserved. In general it can be said, however, that grace is the free bestowal of kindness on one who has no claim to it. This is particularly the case where the grace referred to is the grace of God. His love to man is always unmerited, and when shown to sinners, is even forfeited. The Bible generally uses the word to denote *the unmerited goodness or love of God to those who have forfeited it, and are by nature under a sentence of condemnation.* The grace of God is the source of all spiritual blessings that are bestowed upon sinners. As such we read of it in Eph. 1:6, 7; 2:7-9; Titus 2:11; 3:4-7. While the Bible often speaks of the grace of God as saving grace, it also makes mention of it in a broader sense, as in Isa. 26:10; Jer. 16:13. The grace of God is of the greatest practical significance for sinful men. It was by grace that the way of redemption was opened for them, Rom. 3:24; II Cor. 8:9, and that the message of redemption went out into the world, Acts 14:3. By grace sinners receive the gift of God in Jesus Christ, Acts 18:27; Eph. 2:8. By grace they are justified, Rom. 3:24; 4:16; Titus 3:7, they are enriched with spiritual blessings, John 1:16; II Cor. 8:9; II Thess. 2:16, and they finally inherit salvation, Eph. 2:8; Titus 2:11. Seeing they have absolutely no merits of their own, they are altogether dependent on the grace of God in Christ. In modern theology, with its belief in the inherent goodness of man and his ability to help himself, the doctrine of salvation by grace has practically become a "lost chord," and even the word "grace" was emptied of all spiritual meaning and vanished from religious discourses. It was retained only in the sense of "graciousness," something that is quite external. Happily, there are some evidences of a renewed emphasis on sin, and of a newly awakened consciousness of the need of divine grace.

    d. The mercy of God. Another important aspect of the goodness and love of God is His mercy or tender compassion. The Hebrew word most generally used for this is *chesed.* There is another word, however, which expresses a deep and tender compassion, namely, the word *racham,* which is beautifully rendered by "tender mercy" in our English Bible. The Septuagint and the New Testament employ the Greek word *eleos* to designate the mercy of God. If the grace of God contemplates man as guilty before God, and therefore in need of forgiveness, the mercy of God contemplates him as one who is bearing the consequences of sin, who is in a pitiable condition, and who therefore needs divine help. It may be defined as *the goodness or love of God shown to those who are in misery or distress, irrespective of their deserts.* In His mercy God reveals Himself as a compassionate God, who pities those who are in misery and is ever ready to relieve their distress. This mercy is bountiful, Deut. 5:10; Ps. 57:10; 86:5, and the poets of Israel delighted to sing of it as enduring forever, I Chron. 16:34; II Chron. 7:6; Ps. 136; Ezra 3:11. In the New Testament it is often mentioned alongside of the grace of God, especially in salutations, I Tim. 1:2; II Tim. 1:1; Titus 1:4. We are told repeatedly that it is shown to them that fear God, Exod. 20:2; Deut. 7:9; Ps. 86:5; Luke 1:50. This does not mean, however, that it is limited to them, though they enjoy it in a special measure. God's tender mercies are over all His works, Ps. 145:9, and even those who do not fear Him share in them, Ezek. 18:23, 32; 33:11; Luke 6:35, 36. The mercy of God may not be represented as opposed to His justice. It is exercised only in harmony with the strictest justice of God, in view of the merits of Jesus Christ. Other terms used for it in the Bible are "pity," "compassion," and "lovingkindness."

e. *The longsuffering of God.* The longsuffering of God is still another aspect of His great goodness or love. The Hebrew uses the expression *'erek 'aph,* which means literally "long of face," and then also "slow to anger," while the Greek expresses the same idea by the word *makrothumia.* It is *that aspect of the goodness or love of God in virtue of which He bears with the froward and evil in spite of their long continued disobedience.* In the exercise of this attribute the sinner is contemplated as continuing in sin, notwithstanding the admonitions and warnings that come to him. It reveals itself in the postponement of the merited judgment. Scripture speaks of it in Exod. 34:6; Ps. 86:15; Rom. 2:4; 9:22; I Peter 3:20; II Peter 3:15. A synonymous term of a slightly different connotation is the word "forbearance."

2. *The Holiness of God.* The Hebrew word for "to be holy," *quadash,* is derived from the root *qad,* which means to cut or to separate. It is one of the most prominent religious words of the Old Testament, and is applied primarily to God. The same idea is conveyed by the New Testament words *hagiazo* and *hagios.* From this it already appears that it is not correct to think of holiness primarily as a moral or religious quality, as is generally done. Its fundamental idea is that of a *position* or *relationship* existing between God and some person or thing.

a. *Its nature.* The Scriptural idea of the holiness of God is twofold. In its original sense it denotes that He is absolutely distinct from all His creatures, and is exalted above them in infinite majesty. So understood, the holiness of God is one of His transcendental attributes, and is sometimes spoken of as His central and supreme perfection. It does not seem proper to speak of one attribute of God as being more central and fundamental than another; but if this were permissible, the Scriptural emphasis on the holiness of God would seem to justify its selection. It is quite evident, however, that holiness in this sense of the word is not really a *moral* attribute, which can be co-ordinated with the others, such as love, grace and mercy, but is rather something that is co-extensive with, and applicable to, everything that can be predicated of God. He is holy in everything that reveals Him, in His goodness and grace as well as in His justice and wrath. It may be called the "majesty-holiness" of God and is referred to in such passages as Exod. 15:11; I Sam. 2:2; Isa. 57:15; Hos. 11:9. It is this holiness of God which Otto, in his important work on *Das Heilige,*[7] regards as that which is most essential in God, and which he designates as "the *numinous.*" He regards it as part of the non-rational in God, which cannot be thought of conceptually, and which includes such ideas as "absolute unapproachability" and "absolute overpoweringness" or "awful majesty." It awakens in man a sense of absolute nothingness, a "creature-consciousness" or "creature-feeling," leading to absolute self-abasement.

But the holiness of God also has a specifically ethical aspect in Scripture, and it is with this aspect of it that we are more directly concerned in this connection. The ethical idea of the divine holiness may not be dissociated from the idea of God's majesty-holiness. The former developed out of the latter. The fundamental idea of the ethical holiness of God is also that of separation, but in this case it is a separation from moral evil or sin. In virtue of His holiness God can have no communion with sin, Job 34:10; Hab. 1:13. Used in this sense, the word "holiness" points to God's majestic purity, or ethical majesty. But the idea of ethical holiness is not merely negative (separation from sin); it also has a positive content, namely, that of moral excellence, or ethical perfection. If man reacts to God's majestic-holiness with a feeling of utter insignificance and awe, his reaction to the ethical holiness reveals itself in a sense of impurity, a consciousness of sin, Isa. 6:5. Otto also recognizes this element in the holiness of God, though he stresses the other, and says of the response to it: "Mere awe, mere need of shelter from the 'tremendum,' has here been elevated to the feeling that man in his 'profaneness' is not *worthy* to stand in the presence of the Holy One, and that his entire personal unworthiness might defile even holiness itself."[8] This ethical holiness of God may be defined as *that perfection of God, in virtue of which He eternally wills and maintains His own moral excellence, abhors sin, and demands purity in His moral creatures.*

b. *Its manifestation.* The holiness of God is revealed in the moral law, implanted in man's heart, and speaking through the conscience, and more particularly in God's special revelation. It stood out prominently in the law given to Israel. That law in all its aspects was calculated to impress upon Israel the idea of the holiness of God, and to urge upon the people the necessity of leading a holy life. This was the purpose served by such symbols and types as the holy nation, the holy land, the holy city, the holy place, and the holy priesthood. Moreover, it was revealed in the manner in which God rewarded the keeping of the law, and visited transgressors with dire punishments. The highest revelation of it was given in Jesus Christ, who is called "the Holy and Righteous One," Acts 3:14. He reflected in His life the perfect holiness of God. Finally, the holiness of God is also revealed in the Church as the body of Christ. It is a striking fact, to which attention is often called, that holiness is ascribed to God with far greater frequency in the Old Testament than in the New, though it is done occasionally in the New Testament, John 17:11; I Peter 1:16; Rev. 4:8; 6:10. This is probably due to the fact that the New Testament appropriates the term more particularly to qualify the third Person of the Holy Trinity as the One whose special task it is, in the economy of redemption, to communicate holiness to His people.

3. *The Righteousness of God.* This attribute is closely related to the holiness of God. Shedd speaks of the justice of God as "a mode of His holiness"; and Strong calls it simply "transitive holiness." However, these terms apply only to what is generally called the *relative,* in distinction from the *absolute,* justice of God.

a. *The fundamental idea of righteousness.* The fundamental idea of righteousness is that of strict adherence to the law. Among men it presupposes that there is a law to which they must conform. It is sometimes said that we cannot speak of righteousness in God, because there is no law to which He is subject. But though there is no law above God, there is certainly a law in the very nature of God, and this is the highest possible standard, by which all other laws are judged. A distinction is generally made between the absolute and the relative justice of God. The former is *that rectitude of the divine nature, in virtue of which God is infinitely righteous in Himself,* while the latter is *that perfection of God by which He maintains Himself over against every violation of His holiness, and shows in every respect that He is the Holy One.* It is to this righteousness that the term "justice" more particularly applies. Justice manifests itself especially in giving every man his due, in treating him according to his deserts. The inherent righteousness of God is naturally basic to the righteousness which He reveals in dealing with His creatures, but it is especially the latter, also called the justice of God, that calls for special consideration here. The Hebrew terms for "righteous" and "righteousness" are *tsaddik, tsedhek,* and *tsedhakah,* and the corresponding Greek terms, *dikaios* and *dikaiosune,* all of which contain the idea of conformity to a standard. This perfection is repeatedly ascribed to God in Scripture, Ezra 9:15; Neh. 9:8; Ps. 119:137; 145:17; Jer. 12:1; Lam. 1:18; Dan. 9:14; John 17:25; II Tim. 4:8; I John 2:29; 3:7; Rev. 16:5.

b. *Distinctions applied to the justice of God.* There is first of all a *rectoral justice* of God. This justice, as the very name implies, is the rectitude which God manifests as the Ruler of both the good and the evil. In virtue of it He has instituted a moral government in the world, and imposed a just law upon man, with promises of reward for the obedient, and threats of punishment for the transgressor. God stands out prominently in the Old Testament as the Lawgiver of Israel, Isa. 33:22, and of people in general, James 4:12, and His laws are righteous laws, Deut. 4:8. The Bible refers to this rectoral work of God also in Ps. 99:4 and Rom. 1:32.

Closely connected with the rectoral is the *distributive justice* of God. This term usually serves to designate God's rectitude in the execution of the law, and relates to the distribution of rewards and punishments, Isa. 3:10, 11; Rom. 2:6; I Peter 1:17. It is of two kinds: (1) *Remunerative justice,* which manifests itself in the distribution of rewards to both men and angels, Deut. 7:9, 12, 13; II Chron. 6:15; Ps. 58:11; Micah 7:20; Matt. 25:21, 34; Rom. 2:7; Heb. 11:26. It is really an expression of the divine love, dealing out its bounties, not on the basis of strict merit, for the creature can establish no absolute merit before the Creator, but according to promise and agreement, Luke 17:10; I Cor. 4:7. God's rewards are gracious and spring from a covenant relation which He has established. (2) *Retributive justice,* which relates to the infliction of penalties. It is an expression of the divine wrath. While in a sinless world there would be no place for its exercise, it necessarily holds a very prominent place in a world full of sin. On the whole the Bible stresses the reward of the righteous more than the punishment of the wicked; but even the latter is sufficiently prominent, Rom. 1:32; 2:9; 12:19; II Thess. 1:8, and many other passages. It should be noted that, while man does not merit the reward which he receives, he does merit the punishment which is meted out to him. Divine justice is originally and necessarily obliged to punish evil, but not to reward good, Luke 17:10; I Cor. 4:7; Job 41:11. Many deny the strict punitive justice of God and claim that God punishes the sinner to reform him, or to deter others from sin; but these positions are not tenable. The primary purpose of the punishment of sin is the maintenance of right and justice. Of course, it may incidentally serve, and may even, secondarily, be intended, to reform the sinner and to deter others from sin.

D. Attributes of Sovereignty

The sovereignty of God is strongly emphasized in Scripture. He is represented as the Creator, and His will as the cause of all things. In virtue of His creative work heaven and earth and all that they contain belong to Him. He is clothed with absolute authority over the hosts of heaven and the inhabitants of the earth. He upholds all things with His almighty power, and determines the ends which they are destined to serve. He rules as King in the most absolute sense of the word, and all things are dependent on Him and subservient to Him. There is a wealth of Scripture evidence for the sovereignty of God, but we limit our references here to a few of the most significant passages: Gen. 14:19; Exod. 18:11; Deut. 10:14, 17; I Chron. 29:11, 12; II Chron. 20:6; Neh. 9:6; Ps. 22:28; 47:2, 3, 7, 8; 50:10-12; 95:3-5; 115:3; 135:5, 6; 145:11-13; Jer. 27:5; Luke 1:53; Acts 17:24-26; Rev. 19:6. Two attributes call for discussion under this head, namely (1) the sovereign will of God, and (2) the sovereign power of God.

1. The Sovereign Will of God

a. The will of God in general. The Bible employs several words to denote the will of God, namely the Hebrew words *chaphets, tsebhu* and *ratson* and the Greek words *boule* and *thelema*. The importance of the divine will appears in many ways in Scripture. It is represented as the final cause of all things. Everything is derived from it; creation and preservation, Ps. 135:6; Jer. 18:6; Rev. 4:11, government, Prov. 21:1; Dan. 4:35, election and reprobation, Rom. 9:15, 16; Eph. 1:11, the sufferings of Christ, Luke 22:42; Acts 2:23, regeneration, James 1:18, sanctification, Phil. 2:13, the sufferings of believers, I Peter 3:17, man's life and destiny, Acts 18:21; Rom. 15:32; James 4:15, and even the smallest things of life, Matt. 10:29. Hence Christian theology has always recognized the will of God as the ultimate cause of all things, though philosophy has sometimes shown an inclination to seek a deeper cause in the very Being of the Absolute. However, the attempt to ground everything in the very Being of God generally results in Pantheism.

The word "will" as applied to God does not always have the same connotation in Scripture. It may denote (1) the whole moral nature of God, including such attributes as love, holiness, righteousness, etc.; (2) the faculty of self-determination, i.e., the power to determine self to a course of action or to form a plan; (3) the product of this activity, that is, the predetermined plan or purpose; (4) the power to execute this plan and to realize this purpose (the will in action or omnipotence); and (5) the rule of life laid down for rational creatures. It is primarily the will of God as the faculty of self-determination with which we are concerned at present. It may be defined as *that perfection of His Being whereby He, in a most simple act, goes out towards Himself as the highest good (i.e., delights in Himself as such) and towards His creatures for His own name's sake, and is thus the ground of their being and continued existence.* With reference to the universe and all the creatures which it contains this naturally includes the idea of causation.

b. Distinctions applied to the will of God. Several distinctions have been applied to the will of God. Some of these found little favor in Reformed theology, such as the distinction between an *antecedent* and a *consequent* will of God, and that between an *absolute* and a *con-*

ditional will. These distinctions were not only liable to misunderstanding, but were actually interpreted in objectionable ways. Others, however, were found useful, and were therefore more generally accepted. They may be stated as follows: (1) *The decretive and the preceptive will of God.* The former is that will of God by which He purposes or decrees whatever shall come to pass, whether He wills to accomplish it effectively (causatively), or to permit it to occur through the unrestrained agency of His rational creatures. The latter is the rule of life which God has laid down for His moral creatures, indicating the duties which He enjoins upon them. The former is always accomplished, while the latter is often disobeyed. (2) *The will of eudokia and the will of eurestia.* This division was made, not so much in connection with the purpose to do, as with respect to the pleasure in doing, or the desire to see something done. It corresponds with the preceding, however, in the fact that the will of *eudokia,* like that of the decree, comprises what shall certainly be accomplished, while the will of *eurestia,* like that of the precept, embraces simply what God is pleased to have His creatures do. The word *eudokia* should not mislead us to think that the will of *eudokia* has reference only to good, and not to evil, cf. Matt. 11:26. It is hardly correct to say that the element of complacency or delight is always present in it. (3) *The will of the beneplacitum and the will of the signum.* The former again denotes the will of God as embodied in His hidden counsel, until He makes it known by some revelation, or by the event itself. Any will that is so revealed becomes a *signum.* This distinction is meant to correspond to that between the decretive and the preceptive will of God, but can hardly be said to do this. The good pleasure of God also finds expression in His preceptive will; and the decretive will sometimes also comes to our knowledge by a signum. (4) *The secret and the revealed will of God.* This is the most common distinction. The former is the will of God's decree, which is largely hidden in God, while the latter is the will of the precept, which is revealed in the law and in the gospel. The distinction is based on Deut. 29:29. The secret will of God is mentioned in Ps. 115:3; Dan. 4:17, 25, 32, 35; Rom. 9:18, 19; 11:33, 34; Eph. 1:5, 9, 11; and His revealed will, in Matt. 7:21; 12:50; John 4:34; 7:17; Rom. 12:2. The latter is accessible to all and is not far from us, Deut. 30:14; Rom. 10:8. The secret will of God pertains to all things which He wills either to effect or to permit, and which are therefore absolutely fixed. The revealed will prescribes the duties of man, and represents the way in which he can enjoy the blessings of God.

c. The freedom of God's will. The question is frequently debated whether God, in the exercise of His will, acts necessarily or freely. The answer to this question requires careful discrimination. Just as there is a *scientia necessaria* and a *scientia libera,* there is also a *voluntas necessaria* (necessary will) and a *voluntas libera* (free will) in God. God Himself is the object of the former. He *necessarily* wills Himself, His holy nature, and the personal distinctions in the Godhead. This means that He necessarily loves Himself and takes delight in the contemplation of His own perfections. Yet He is under no compulsion, but acts according to the law of His Being; and this, while necessary, is also the highest freedom. It is quite evident that the idea of causation is absent here, and that the thought of complacency or self-approval is in the foreground. God's creatures, however, are the objects of His *voluntas libera.* God determines *voluntarily* what and whom He will create, and the times, places, and circumstances, of their lives. He marks out the path of all His rational creatures, determines their destiny, and uses them for His purposes. And though He endows them with freedom, yet His will controls their actions. The Bible speaks of this freedom of God's will in the most absolute terms, Job 11:10; 33:13; Ps. 115:3; Prov. 21:1; Isa. 10:15; 29:16; 45:9; Matt. 20:15; Rom. 9:15-18, 20, 21; I Cor. 12:11; Rev. 4:11. The Church always defended this freedom, but also emphasized the fact that it may not be regarded as absolute indifference. Duns Scotus applied the idea of a will in no sense determined to God; but this idea of a blind will, acting with perfect indifference, was rejected by the Church. The freedom of God is not pure indifference, but rational self-determination. God has reasons for willing as He does, which induce Him to choose one end rather than another, and one set of means to accomplish one end in preference to others. There is in each case a prevailing motive, which makes the end chosen and the means selected the most pleasing to Him, though we may not be able to determine what this motive is. In general it may be said that God cannot will anything that is contrary to His nature, to His wisdom or love, to His righteousness or holiness. Dr. Bavinck points out that we can seldom discern why God willed one thing rather than another, and that it is not possible nor even permissible for us to look for some deeper ground of things than the will of God, because all such attempts result in seeking a ground for the creature in the very Being of God, in robbing it of its contingent character, and in making it necessary, eternal, divine.[9]

d. God's will in relation to sin. The doctrine of the will of God often gives rise to serious questions. Problems arise here which have never yet been solved and which are probably incapable of solution by man.

(1) It is said that if the decretive will of God also determined the entrance of sin into the world, God thereby becomes the author of sin and really wills something that is contrary to His moral perfections. Arminians, to escape the difficulty, make the will of God to permit sin dependent on His foreknowledge of the course which man would choose. Reformed theologians, while maintaining on the basis of such passages as Acts 2:23; 3:8; etc., that God's decretive

will also includes the sinful deeds of man, are always careful to point out that this must be conceived in such a way that God does not become the author of sin. They frankly admit that they cannot solve the difficulty, but at the same time make some valuable distinctions that prove helpful. Most of them insist on it that God's will with respect to sin is simply a will to permit sin and not a will to effectuate it, as He does the moral good. This terminology is certainly permissible, provided it is understood correctly. It should be borne in mind that God's will to permit sin carries certainty with it. Others call attention to the fact that, while the terms "will" or "to will" may include the idea of complacency or delight, they sometimes point to a simple determination of the will; and that therefore the will of God to permit sin need not imply that He takes delight or pleasure in sin.

(2) Again, it is said that the decretive and preceptive will of God are often contradictory. His decretive will includes many things which He forbids in His preceptive will, and excludes many things which He commands in His preceptive will, cf. Gen. 22; Exod. 4:21-23; II Kings 20:1-7; Acts 2:23. Yet it is of great importance to maintain both the decretive and the preceptive will, but with the definite understanding that, while they appear to us as distinct, they are yet fundamentally one in God. Though a perfectly satisfactory solution of the difficulty is out of the question for the present, it is possible to make some approaches to a solution. When we speak of the decretive and the preceptive will of God, we use the word "will" in two different senses. By the former God has determined what He will do or what shall come to pass; in the latter He reveals to us what we are in duty bound to do.[10] At the same time we should remember that the moral law, the rule of our life, is also in a sense the embodiment of the will of God. It is an expression of His holy nature and of what this naturally requires of all moral creatures. Hence another remark must be added to the preceding. The decretive and preceptive will of God do not conflict in the sense that in the former He does, and according to the latter He does not, take pleasure in sin; nor in the sense that according to the former He does not, and according to the latter He does, will the salvation of every individual *with a positive volition*. Even according to the decretive will God takes no pleasure in sin; and even according to the preceptive will He does not will the salvation of every individual *with a positive volition*.

2. *The Sovereign Power of God.* The sovereignty of God finds expression, not only in the divine will, but also in the omnipotence of God or the power to execute His will. Power in God may be called the effective energy of His nature, or *that perfection of His Being by which He is the absolute and highest causality*. It is customary to distinguish between a *potentia Dei absoluta* (absolute power of God) and a *potentia Dei ordinata* (ordered power of God). However, Re-

formed theology rejects this distinction in the sense in which it was understood by the Scholastics, who claimed that God by virtue of His absolute power could effect contradictions, and could even sin and annihilate Himself. At the same time it adopts the distinction as expressing a real truth, though it does not always represent it in the same way. According to Hodge and Shedd absolute power is the divine efficiency, as exercised without the intervention of second causes; while ordinate power is the efficiency of God, as exercised by the ordered operation of second causes.[11] The more general view is stated by Charnock as follows: "Absolute, is that power whereby God is able to do that which He will not do, but is possible to be done; ordinate, is that power whereby God doth that which He hath decreed to do, that is, which He hath ordained or appointed to be exercised; which are not distinct powers, but one and the same power. His ordinate power is a part of His absolute; for if He had not power to do everything that He could will, He might not have the power to do everything that He doth will."[12] *The potentia ordinata* can be defined as *that perfection of God whereby He, through the mere exercise of His will, can realize whatsoever is present in His will or counsel.* The power of God in actual exercise limits itself to that which is comprehended in His eternal decree. But the actual exercise of God's power does not represent its limits. God could do more than that, if He were so minded. In that sense we can speak of the *potentia absoluta,* or absolute power, of God. This position must be maintained over against those who, like Schleiermacher and Strauss, hold that God's power is limited to that which He actually accomplishes. But in our assertion of the absolute power of God it is necessary to guard against misconceptions. The Bible teaches us on the one hand that the power of God extends beyond that which is actually realized, Gen. 18:14; Jer. 32:27; Zech. 8:6; Matt. 3:9; 26:53. We cannot say, therefore, that what God does not bring to realization, is not possible for Him. But on the other hand it also indicates that there are many things which God cannot do. He can neither lie, sin, change, nor deny Himself, Num. 23:19; I Sam. 15:29; II Tim. 2:13; Heb. 6:18; James 1:13, 17. There is no absolute power in Him that is divorced from His perfections, and in virtue of which He can do all kinds of things which are inherently contradictory. The idea of God's omnipotence is expressed in the name *'El-Shaddai;* and the Bible speaks of it in no uncertain terms, Job 9:12; Ps. 115:3; Jer. 32:17; Matt. 19:26; Luke 1:37; Rom. 1:20; Eph. 1:19. God manifests His power in creation, Rom. 4:17; Isa. 44:24; in the works of providence, Heb. 1:3, and in the redemption of sinners, I Cor. 1:24; Rom. 1:16.

Notes

[1]*Side-Lights on Christian Doctrine*, p. 26.

[2]*Ibid.*, p. 26.

[3]*Syst. and Polem. Theol.*, p. 43 f.

[4]*Side-Lights on Chr. Doct.*, p. 30.

[5]A. A. Hodge, *Outlines of Theol.*, p. 147.

[6]*Syst. and Polem. Theol.*, p. 156.

[7]Eng. tr. *The Idea of the Holy*.

[8]*The Idea of the Holy*, p. 56.

[9]*Geref. Dogm.* II, p. 241.

[10]Cf. Bavinck, *Geref. Dogm.* II, pp. 246 ff.; Dabney, *Syst. and Polem. Theol.*, p. 162.

[11]Shedd, *Dogm. Theol.* I, pp. 361 f.; Hodge, *Syst. Theol.* I, pp. 410 f.

[12]*Existence and Attributes of God* II, p. 12. Cf. also Bavinck, *Geref. Dogm.* II, p. 252; Kuyper, *Dict. Dogm., De Deo* I, pp. 412 f.

The Immanence and Transcendence of God

24

Borden P. Bowne

The Immanence of God

Introduction

The progress of thought is slow, but there is progress nevertheless. In every field of life men have had painfully to find their way. In religion man has always had some sense, more or less dim, of an alliance with the unseen and the eternal, but it has taken ages to organize and clarify it and bring it to clear apprehension and rational expression. As men begin on the plane of the senses, this unseen existence has been mainly conceived in sense terms, and hence has always been exposed to destructive criticism from the side of philosophy. The crude anthropomorphism of early thought invited and compelled the criticism. Again, this vague sense of the unseen has always been confronted by the apparent realities and finalities of the outer world; and in comparison with them it has often seemed unreal and fictitious. Matter we know and things we know; but God and spirit, what and where are they? When thus skeptically accosted by the senses, they sometimes fade away. Hence religious faith has always had a double difficulty to combat, arising from its alliance with sense

From Borden P. Bowne, *The Immanence of God*. Boston: Houghton-Mifflin, 1905.

forms, on the one hand, and from sense dogmatism, on the other. The alliance was perpetually plunging religion into destructive anthropomorphism; and the sense dogmatism led to a frequent rejection of religion as baseless, because spiritual realities lie beyond seeing and hearing. But we are slowly outgrowing this. Religious thought is gradually casting off its coarse anthropomorphism; and philosophic criticism is fast discrediting the shallow dogmatism of sense thinking, with its implication of mechanical and materialistic naturalism. Thus religious thought is progressing; and the result to which all lines of reflection are fast converging is the ancient word of inspiration, that in God we live and move and have our being. This is at once the clear indication of thought and the assured conviction of faith. In this conclusion, moreover, both religion and philosophy find their only sure foundation.

This doctrine we call the divine immanence; by which we mean that God is the omnipresent ground of all finite existence and activity. The world, alike of things and of spirits, is nothing existing and acting on its own account, while God is away in some extra-sidereal region, but it continually depends upon and is ever upheld by the ever-living, ever-present, ever-working God.

This divine immanence has important bearings on both speculative and religious problems, and contains the solution of many traditional difficulties. To trace this doctrine into its implications is the aim of the discussion. The thought will centre on four leading points—God and Nature, God and History, God and the Bible, and God and Religion. On each of these points naturalistic and deistic dogmatism has long wrought confusion and mischief.

God and Nature

There is a scholastic maxim that truth emerges sooner from error than from confusion. Allied to this is Goethe's remark, that the gods themselves can do nothing with stupidity. One is often reminded of both these truths in reading popular discussions of the supernatural, whether from the religious or the irreligious standpoint. Their most prominent feature is confusion. Out of such a state of things nothing but babble and Babel can result. Our first duty in this matter is to clear up our thought so as to know what we really mean and desire.

And first we must find out what we mean by nature. A great deal of bad metaphysics is commonly concealed under this term, and it is the unsuspected source of many of our woes. What, then, is nature?

Popular thought is based on a crude sense realism. There is a system of material things, it holds, about us in space and producing a great variety of changes in time. The immediate agent in the case is matter, which by its inherent forces and laws initiates and maintains the cosmic processes and produces their manifold results. This system of things and laws we call nature; and all events arising in this system and in accordance with its laws we call natural.

This view seems to be an undeniable fact of experience. Things and their forces are manifestly there, and nothing else is in sight. Whatever else may be doubtful, there can be no question about the reality and activity of nature. God and spirit are hypotheses, but matter is a solid and substantial fact.

This type of thought has always had a strong tendency to atheism. Nature is made into a self-running system, at least for the present. Within the system all things seem to be accounted for by the system; and as the beginning disappears in the infinite past, and horizons vanish in infinite space, the thought is not far away that perhaps nature has always been there in self-equality and self-sufficiency. Thus "Nature" in such a scheme is always on the point of setting up for itself. In any case, a division of labor is made between the work of God and that of nature. Whatever can be referred to nature is supposed to be sufficiently explained without further reference. If there be any mind at all in connection with nature, it is needed only to explain the outstanding facts which are not yet accounted for by the natural order. Thus God is at best only a provisional hypothesis, and becomes less and less necessary the more the reign of natural law is extended. Atheism is the limit of this way of thinking. As Comte once said, science will finally conduct God to the frontier, and bow him out with thanks for his provisional services. When law becomes all-embracing, God will be a needless hypothesis. How general this way of thinking has been is familiar to all who are acquainted with the naturalistic literature of the last generation.

Our present discussion is not with the atheist, but with the theist who too often holds the same conception of nature as the atheist. He is openly or tacitly afraid of nature, and naturalism is with him a term of dislike or reproach. He is suspicious of the reign of law, and is quite depressed when some outstanding irregularity is at last reduced to order. He looks rather anxiously for breaks in the natural order, insists especially on the things that "science cannot explain," and carefully treasures reports of miracles as things without which religion would vanish, but with which we may hope to put to flight all the armies of the aliens. And it must be admitted that historically there has been much to excuse, if not to justify, this attitude. Naturalism often has been an atheistic doctrine. Nature and mind have been set up in mutual exclusion; and the theist with a shallow sense philosophy has seen no relief but in decrying naturalism and natural law and "science falsely so called," and insisting on breaks and miracles and things "science cannot explain." Matter might possibly explain the solar system and even all inorganic processes and products, but it could not explain life, it was said, with the tacit admission, which sometimes became explicit, that spontaneous generation, if it should be established, would be the final overthrow of theism. Meanwhile, neither theist nor atheist suspected that perhaps matter cannot explain anything whatever, and as an ontological fact does not even exist.

For the sake of the "natural realist," to whom this will seem manifest error, if not raving, a word must be interpolated here respecting the phenomenality and non-substantiality of the apparent world. Let us begin by admitting the most realistic doctrine of things. This table on which I am writing is of course real, that is, it is no dream or illusion. But when we begin to reflect upon the nature of its reality, puzzles soon emerge. The physicist tells us of molecules and atoms which compose the table, and when we ask concerning them, we hear of vortex rings and centres of force and various other mysteries. When these questions are thought out, we see that the things about us are only phenomenal, and that the true causality is behind them. Thus physics itself speedily leads us away from the common-sense notion of substantial things about us with various inherent forces which do the work of the world, and brings us to the conception of one supreme causality behind phenomena, on which they all depend and from which they all proceed. From this point of view, the theist need not be in the least disturbed if so-called spontaneous generation were established as a fact; for it would only show that the supreme cause has more than one way of working. Theism is concerned with causality, not with method.

But apart from this metaphysical suggestion, the theist's horror of naturalism is logically inconsequent in any case. It rests on the tacit fancy that nature is a blind mechanical system which does a great many unintended things on its own account. These represent no plan or purpose of any kind, but are just blind happenings for which nature alone is responsible. Whatever comes about in accordance with the natural order expresses no purpose; it is simply natural. For purpose we must have "interpositions," "interferences," "special providences," and that sort of thing. Wherever law can be traced we are forbidden to think of any purposive interpretation, whether in the individual life or in the larger field of history.

How shallow this is, is plain upon inspection. If nature be dependent on intelligence for its origin, it is equally dependent on intelligence for all its implications. Mechanism of itself can never make any new departures, or reach anything not implied in it from the beginning. If, then, we suppose that God created a system of nature which was intended to unfold according to inherent laws, we must say that the creative act implied and carried with it to the minutest details all that should ever arrive in the unfolding of the system. There is no way by which things or events could slip in which were not provided for in the primal arrangement. And if we suppose the Creator to have known what he was doing, we must suppose him to have intended the implications. But this is all that theism cares to assert. If an event represents a divine purpose, or is part of a divine plan, it is truly purposeful when realized through natural processes as it would be if produced by fiat. But we miss the reality of the purpose from the fancy that the natural system can do a lot of things to which it was not determined by the creative act, and which therefore are mere mechanical occurrences without any further significance. And when we allow the purpose, we practically cancel it by overlooking the relativity of our temporal judgments and placing the purpose so far away in time that we think it must have faded out of the divine thought and interest altogether. The things we planned years ago we have forgotten or they have lost all value for us, and we suppose it must be so with God. Of a faithful purpose moving across the ages and forever keeping tryst with foreseen need, we have no conception.

But this is superficial to the last degree. Long and short are relative terms at best, and have no significance for the Eternal. Metaphysics, too, adds its suggestion, which nullifies all these traditional intimidations drawn from the measureless age of the world, that time itself is only a relation in self-consciousness and has no such meaning for the Infinite as it has for us. In that case, time is merely the shadow of our finitude and not a supreme law of all existence. We need not, then, give up the belief in purpose because of law, or because of the age of things. To be sure, we are often unable to discern any special significance in events; but that only means that the underlying purpose is not always evident. But that the event is natural, in the sense of occurring in an order of law, is absolutely unrelated to the question of purpose; and this is the only question of importance for the theist.

The theist, then, is guilty of bad logic when he makes the order of law a reason for denying purpose. The way in which events occur in an order of law is one thing; the meaning of such events in a scheme of purpose is forever another. Hence we might maintain the naturalness of all events, in the sense defined, and at the same time might include all events in a purposive interpretation. Man's control of nature is realized through mechanical processes in accordance with natural law, but it is informed with purpose, nevertheless. If some lunar scientist, well versed in physics and chemistry but ignorant of human personality, should visit our planet, he could rule out human purpose in nature with the same logic with which we rule out divine purpose. The same fact of law applies to both, and is equally compatible or incompatible with both. This false antithesis of law and purpose is one of the great superficialities of popular thought, and rests upon an untenable philosophy.

But both theists and atheists are alike guilty of bad metaphysics when they erect the system of nature into an ontological reality in any case. The progress of philosophical criticism has shown nature in this sense to be only an idol of the dogmatic den. There is no substantial or ontological nature, but only natural events; and a natural event is one which occurs in an order of law, or one which we can connect with other events according to rule. But this order has no causality in it. In the causal sense it explains nothing, being really only a rule according to which some power beyond it proceeds. Respecting the natural order two quite distinct questions may be asked. These concern, first, the uniformities of coexistence and sequence which constitute the order; and, second, the underlying causality and purpose of the order. Things exist and events happen in certain ways. To discover, describe, and register these ways of being and happening is the function of science. But when this is done, we further need to form some conception of the causality at work, and of the purpose which may underlie the whole. This is the field of philosophy. These two questions, as said, are quite distinct and the answer to both is necessary to the full satisfaction of the mind. As a result of this distinction, which is fast making its way in the higher speculative circles, the antithesis of natural and supernatural is taking on another form, and one from which many scandals that infest the traditional view disappear.

In the new conception the supernatural is nothing foreign to nature and making occasional raids into nature in order to reveal itself, but so far as nature as a whole is concerned, the supernatural is the everpresent ground and administrator of nature; and nature is simply the form under which the Supreme Reason and Will manifest themselves. This is the doctrine of the divine immanence to which philosophy is coming in its search after the cosmic causality. We come down, not to a world of lumps, nor to any impersonal principle, but to a Living Will which worketh hitherto, and which worketh forevermore. And nature being but the fixed form of the divine causality, we must say that events in general are at once natural in the mode of their occurrence, in that they come about according to rule, and supernatural in their causation, in that they all alike abut on that Living Will by which all things stand and from which they forever proceed. The commonest event, say the fall of a leaf, is as supernatural in its causation as any miracle would be; for in both alike God would be equally implicated.

This division of labor between science and philosophy has brought about a better understanding than formerly existed. Both parties are seen to have important interests to guard, and each party has inalienable rights in its own field. They can collide only through confusion. Science as such explains nothing, for it only classifies and coordinates facts according to rule; and philosophy as such is empty until experience furnishes the facts. When, then, we are told that science must never have recourse to supernatural explanations, on the one hand, or that "science cannot explain" this, that, or the other thing, on the other, we know that confusion lieth at the door, and that a distinction is in order. In the scientific sense, explanation consists in exhibiting the fact as a case or implication of an empirically discovered rule; and in this sense we must never have recourse to supernatural explanations. If the fact cannot be reduced to rule of any sort, science can only let it alone and wait for light. But in the causal sense science explains nothing. Here the alternative is supernatural explanation or none. Metaphysics shows that mechanical explanation must lose itself in barren tautologies and the infinite regress, and must even disperse existence itself into nothingness through the infinite divisibility of space and time. But these two types of explanation, the scientific and the causal, in no way conflict. If we admit that things hang together in certain ways, the causality and purpose are not revealed thereby; and if we affirm a supernatural causality, the form and contents of its working remain an open question.

The failure to make this distinction is well illustrated by a recent discussion in the London "Times." Lord Kelvin, who is well known as one of the greatest leaders of physical science, said, in a letter to the "Times": "Scientific thought is compelled to accept the idea of Creative Power. Forty years ago, I asked Liebig, walking somewhere in the country, if he believed that the grass and the flowers which he saw around us grew by mere chemical forces. He answered, 'No, no more than I could believe that the books of botany describing them could grow by mere chemical forces.' Every action of human free will is a miracle to physical and chemical and mathematical science."

This letter called out considerable correspondence and comment. Lord Kelvin himself seemed to think that "mere chemical forces" would explain much, but were not equal to the explanation of life. This laid him open to obvious reply. If "mere" natural forces could do so much, who can tell where the "mereness" becomes inadequate? But neither Lord Kelvin nor his critics, some of whom were inclined to view his utterance as an outbreak of Scotch orthodoxy, had any clear idea of what they meant by explanation, and hence came to no conclusion. If by explanation we mean a view which will enable the mind to interpret the facts in all their aspects, Lord Kelvin was right; but if by explanation we mean simply a classification of the facts under empirical rules, his critics were right. For such explanation the idea of God is as little needed in science as it is in shoemaking, and is equally irrelevant in both; but at the same time, such explanation remains on the surface and does not touch the deeper questions of thought at all.

The same is true of explanations by evolution, natural selection, etc. They simply describe an order for which they do not account, and hence, so far as any real insight is concerned, we get no help from them. For real insight we need to know what the power is which is at work, why it works as it does, why the arrivals and survivals are such that their net result is to produce an orderly and progressive system; and to these inquiries mechanical naturalism has no answer. The distinction between evolution as a description of method and evolution as a doctrine of causality has reduced this doctrine to a very subordinate significance, and has deprived it entirely of all those fearsome implications which it had for superficial thought. As a mode of procedure, it is as good as any other; as a doctrine of mechanical causality and progress, it is altogether impossible.

We cannot, then, too carefully distinguish between the description and formulation which science gives and the causal and purposive interpretation for which philosophy seeks. The notion that science is gradually enabling us to dispense with God is superficial almost to illiteracy; and the opposite notion that would confuse scientific descriptions, classifications, and formulations by irrelevant theistic suggestions is equally so. Imagine a theologian who should interrupt a geographer in his surveys and measurements to ask what geography says about God; and then imagine a geographer who, because God is not needed in surveying and map-making, should conclude that God is a "needless hypothesis." Each would be worthy of the other. According to Mrs. Carlyle, "the mixing of things is the great bad;" and there certainly never was a greater "bad," in its way, than the "mixing" of the question of scientific description and formulation with that of philosophic interpretation, the sure result being a "conflict of science and religion," or some other unprofitable aberration.

The instructed theist, then, sets aside the self-running nature and the absentee God. For him there is no nature which does at least the bulk of the world's work, while God is reserved for interpositions. For him God is the ever-present agent in the on-going of the world, and nature is but the form and product of his ceaseless activity. The theist, therefore, is not afraid of naturalism; for the naturalism of atheistic thought he knows to be an illusion, while naturalism in theistic thought is merely the search for God's familiar and orderly methods in all his works. The theist knows that he is in God's world, and that the ultimate reason why anything is, or changes, or comes to pass, must be sought not in any mechanical necessity, nor in any natural antecedents, nor in any impersonal agency of any kind, but in the will and purpose of that God in whom all things live and move and have their being. Every system of whatever sort must come down at last to some fact, or system of facts, of which no more can be said than that it is. This fact, to which all else is referred, and from which all else takes its rise, is, for theism, the will and purpose of the Eternal.

At the same time the instructed theist recognizes that the divine causality proceeds in orderly ways, so that events do not happen at random but according to rule. To discover the modes of being and happening is the function of inductive science; and practical wisdom depends on this knowledge. When we know how things hang together in the order of law, we can adjust ourselves thereto, and to a very considerable extent can subordinate nature to our purposes. In the fact and knowledge of this system of law we have the condition of science and practical living. In the insight that this system is no self-sufficient fact, but simply the form of a divine causality, we have the supreme condition of religion.

Thus we have to correct the false conception of nature and the natural which underlies popular thought. Nature is supposed, for the present at least, to run itself, and is set up as a rival of God; so that God is needed only to explain the outstanding facts which as yet have found no natural explanation. With this conception naturalism could not fail to be looked upon as hostile to religion, and it became a synonym for infidelity. And there was a great deal of naturalism of this sort, which promised to dispense with God altogether after a while. This was "bald naturalism," and it was met by an equally "bald" supernaturalism, a thing of portents, prodigies, and interpositions, spooking about among the laws of nature, breaking one now and then, but having no vital connection with the orderly movement of the world.

Both views were bald, and they were especially bald inside. A better metaphysics, however, enables us to set aside with all conviction both sorts of baldness. The cosmic order is no rival of God, but is simply the continuous manifestation and product of the divine activity. There is no longer any reason for being afraid of naturalism, for naturalism is now merely a tracing of the order in which the divine causality proceeds. It is description, not explanation. It classifies events under familiar heads, but for the causal explanation and purpose of all events we must fall back on God; and that not on a God that was, but on a God that is, and whose activity did not cease with the end of creation's week, but continues forevermore.

We are, then, in God's world, and all things continuously depend on him. We have not to attempt an impossible division between God's work and that of nature, for there is no such division; we have rather to study the method and contents of God's work which we call nature, and in which God is forever immanent. Thus the naturalistic and deistic banishment of God from the real world is recalled, and the doctrine of the divine immanence is put in its place; yet not an immanence of disorder and arbitrariness, but an immanence of goodness and wisdom and law.

This general conception of the divine immanence has only imperfectly passed from philosophical thought into theological and religious thinking. It has, however, important religious bearings which need to be pointed out; for too often we mistake our sense dogmatism for science, and our misunderstandings for religion.

In a recent number of the "Sunday School Times" a story is told of an Eastern king which illustrates at once our delusion respecting natural processes, and also God's work and presence in them. The king was seated in a garden, and one of his counselors was speaking of the wonderful works of God. "Show me a sign," said the king, "and I will believe." "Here are four acorns," said the counselor; "will your majesty plant them in the ground, and then stoop down for a moment and look into this clear pool of water?" The king did so. "Now," said the other, "look up." The king looked up and saw four oak-trees where he had planted the acorns. "Wonderful!" he exclaimed; "this is indeed the work of God." "How long were you looking into the water?" asked the counselor. "Only a second," said the king. "Eighty years have passed as a second," said the other. The king looked at his garments; they were threadbare. He looked at his reflection in the water; he had become an old man. "There is no miracle here, then," he said angrily. "Yes," said the other; "it is God's work, whether he do it in one second or in eighty years."

Comte held that human thought begins in the theological stage, where all phenomena are referred to arbitrary wills in them or beyond them. It then passes to the metaphysical stage, where phenomena are explained by abstract notions of cause, etc. These abstractions are only the ghosts of the theological personalities of the earlier stage; and when they are seen as such, thought passes into the third and last stage of development, the positive stage. Here we content ourselves with simply studying the orders of coexistence and sequence among things and events, and abandon all metaphysical inquiry as fruitless and hopeless. In this Comte was partly right and partly wrong. His limitation of science to the study of the uniformities of coexistence and sequence among phenomena, and the exclusion therefrom of all causal inquiry, was a stroke of genius. His rejection of abstract metaphysics as only a spectral shadow of the earlier personal explanations was equally profound and important and just. Later philosophic criticism has shown that the categories of abstract metaphysics are only the abstract forms of the self-conscious life, and that apart from that life they are empty or self-contradictory. But Comte was mistaken in ruling out all metaphysics. The human mind was never more prolific of metaphysical constructions than it has been since Comte put metaphysics under the ban. It only remains that we give our metaphysics a tenable form, that of personality. Personalism is the only metaphysics that does not dissolve away into self-canceling abstractions. Thus in a way thought returns to the theological stage again, but with a difference. We return, not to a rabble of arbitrary and capricious wills behind nature, but to a Supreme Rational Will, which forever founds and administers the order of the world.

Back of the loaf is the snowy flour,
    Back of the flour the mill;
Back of the mill is the wheat and the shower
    And the sun and the Father's will.

The Father's will is not back of these things at some awful distance
of time and space, but is their present living source; and they in turn
are but the form in which that will expresses and realizes itself. For
in him we live and move and have our being.

25

Martin Heinecken

The Qualitative Difference

A good many years have passed now since Karl Barth shocked the complacent liberalism of his day by restating Kierkegaard's insistence upon the absolute qualitative difference between God and man.

> But as between God and a human being . . . there is an absolute difference. In man's absolute relationship to God this absolute difference must therefore come to expression, and any attempt to express an immediate likeness becomes impertinence, frivolity, effrontery, and the like. . . . Precisely because there is an absolute difference between God and man, man will express his own nature most adequately when he expresses this difference absolutely. *Worship* is the maximum expression for the God-relationship of a human being, and hence also for his likeness with God, because the qualities are absolutely different. But the significance of worship is, that God is absolutely all for the worshipper; and the worshipper is again one who makes the absolute distinction.[1]

Since then the anxious defenders of the citadel of reason have had

---

From Martin Heinecken, *The Moment before God* (Philadelphia: Muhlenberg Press, 1956). Used by permission.

time to rally and to call out the shock troops. They believe they have saved the day—once more man can, so to speak, hob-nob with God as an equal. Barth's extreme statement of absolute difference may have been effective by way of hyperbole as a temporary corrective against the pantheism of Hegel and the ultimate outcome of this Hegelianism in the deification of the state under the Nazis. But they feel that an absolute difference between God and man is difficult to take seriously, especially when it leads to the denial that man since the fall is in possession of the image of God and to the ruling out of "general" revelation and any point of contact whatsoever between the natural man and God's approach to him in the gospel. Moreover, if the difference between man and God is *absolute*, then it becomes conclusively impossible for man ever to know anything whatsoever about God. None of the words we use about God would be meaningful and we could not speak of God as ruler, judge, father, or shepherd. All the anthropomorphisms would have to be ruled out which alone make God meaningful to us as a living God: his wrath, his love, his eyes turned upon us, his ears attentive to our prayers, his everlasting arms stretched out to help. How ridiculous of Kierkegaard and Barth and others to say that God is absolutely other and then to write volume after volume about him! If God really were the absolutely other, our only recourse would be absolute silence based upon absolute and irremediable ignorance. A *relative* difference must be allowed, they say, because an absolute difference is as senseless as an absolute paradox.

Such objections are based upon a misunderstanding of what is involved. The fundamental difference which forms the basis for every other possible difference that we can establish is the difference between creator and creature, between the eternal, unchanging, yet ever living and active God, and the existing individual, not only in his finitude but in his sinfulness. This absolute difference is basic to the recognition of the paradox as the category which expresses the relationship between an existing cognitive spirit and the eternal truth. There cannot possibly be any conclusive miracle or mystery in the world except on the basis of this initial recognition. There can be no true awe before God and no genuine worship except on this basis. Neither can the pitfall be avoided of substituting a top-of-the-head, intellectual relationship for a personal encounter with the living God which involves a transformation of the total man in his existence, while God still remains "unknown" (i.e., "hidden"—not reduced to a simple idea) even in this most intimate union.

Kierkegaard does not deny what has come to be called "a point of contact" with the natural man. He acknowledges this in his recognition of aesthetic, ethical, and universally humane religiosity. Each of these stages is to be corrected and fulfilled in that transformation of existence which alone is specifically Christian. Luther also maintained, *"Der Mensch hat immer entweder Gott oder Abgott,"* i.e., every man always worships either the true God or an idol. The gods of natural man are one and all idols, who must be supplanted by the true God, made "known" only in Jesus Christ. This making known is the miracle of revelation. If there is a denial of general revelation it depends upon the definition of "general." A general revelation would be a contradiction in terms if "general" means universal concepts accessible to the mind of man, such as, e.g., a first cause; and if revelation is understood as the personal encounter and self-impartation of God. To reduce the *creator* God—who meets man at a time and a place in the "masks" of creation—to a first cause is to lose the living God. It is precisely because of God's qualitative otherness that he cannot be reduced to a universal concept such as a first cause. There may in this sense, therefore, be a denial of a general revelation without the denial of a point of contact. There may also be the assertion of a qualitative otherness without denying the image of God in man. The difference is as between an existing human being, caught up in the limitations of time and space and that God who does not "exist" but is the ground of all existence, who *is* eternally, without, however, being reduced to a static, lifeless idea. He remains the eternally active God, Lord of all space and time. This is the conclusive mystery of the qualitatively other, living God who is eternal and changeless and yet is active.

The Epistemological Problem

The attack of the "philosophers of religion" who presume to sit in judgment upon the theologians from outside the theological circle, i.e., from outside revelation itself, is made at the point of episte-mology, the question of "How do we know God?"[2] The answer of the Christian tradition is that God is "known" only through the enlightenment of the Holy Spirit who proceeds from the Father and the Son and whose coming is a part of the revelation of God in Christ, so that there is no revelation except as the sending of the Spirit is included as a part of the revelatory event.

The obvious neglect of the festival of Pentecost in the Christian church tells a significant story. Christmas and Easter have been adopted by the non-Christian world. Once this has happened there is, of course, no use for Pentecost. If the significance of Christmas and Easter can be grasped by natural, unregenerate man without his being transformed in his existence, then there is no need for any excitement over Pentecostal fires and a speaking with "new tongues." Christmas becomes the festival that celebrates the birth of the greatest founder of the best religion whose teachings about God and man make their appeal to every thinking person if only he will take the trouble to examine them. In this setting it is obvious what to do with Pentecost. The celebration of Christmas will differ only in degree, not absolutely and qualitatively, from the celebration of such a coming to knowledge as when Archimedes in his bathtub discovered the law of floating bodies and in all his native, naked splendor ran shouting, "Eureka." This would be indistinguishable from the shout of the disciples, "We have found him who is the consolation of Israel" or of the shepherds who at the angelic voice said, "Let us go unto Bethlehem and see this thing which has come to pass."

It is the same with Easter. Pentecost is unnecessary if this is merely to celebrate the fact of every man's immortality and the insight, as Plato suggests, that a dead soul is a contradiction in terms and that therefore we must welcome the release of the soul from its prison in the body. Every thinking man could come to this conclusion. Pentecost is not necessary if this day is to celebrate only the recurrence of the roses, to give assurance that after every winter there will be another spring, and to encourage men never to lose heart for the morrow. This kind of defiantly despairing hope springs eternal in the human breast and nowhere have men resigned themselves with equanimity to the fact of their extinction once the last breath has been exhaled. To every man, with all his love of life, there comes the poignant realization that he could also *not* be. He is stabbed to the quick with the realization that the life within him can be extinguished as easily and decisively as the flickering flame of a candle. It is in defiance of this dread of the unknown and of nothingness that man's uncertain hopes of immortality are born. If this is what Easter celebrates, then, of course, Pentecost is unnecessary.

It must be clear to any observant reader of the New Testament that there is no witness to the resurrection of the Lord of life which is not post-Pentecost. This is not just the witness that a man who was really dead and laid into the grave once more walked upon the earth, although that too is included. The Easter witness is the witness to One who is himself the Lord of life and the victor over death and the grave. The witnesses to this "fact" are chosen witnesses. "God raised him on the third day and made him manifest; not to all people but to us who were chosen by God as witnesses, who ate and drank with him after he rose from the dead."[3] "No one can say that Jesus is Lord, except by the Holy Ghost."[4]

For this reason any critic of the epistemology of the Christian religion ought to be silenced by the fact of Pentecost. It would be a denial of revelation itself to say that it would be impossible for God to reveal himself to man if there were not something in man which would enable him to recognize the revelation when he is confronted with it. This is just the meaning of revelation—God himself must do the revealing and must make *himself* known. The assertion that there must be some kind of kinship between God and man which makes of man something more than an animal dare not belittle by one iota the absolute miracle of revelation. Any other God, except the one whom God himself causes you to behold in Jesus Christ, is still an idol, as any honest examination of all the various "conceptions" of God (a conserver of values, a power that makes for righteousness, an unmoved mover, an ideal of beauty, truth and goodness, etc.) will reveal. The coming to "faith," therefore, is itself a miracle and as absolute a paradox as the Incarnation. Therefore, the criticism that if God is absolutely different there could be no knowledge of him at all will not greatly impress the one who has celebrated Pentecost and knows that he has come to a knowledge of God—even though he "knows" this in a different way than he "knows" that two times two is four or that Caesar crossed the Rubicon. Neither of these items of "fact" is comparable to the knowledge I have that "Jesus is Lord and that he died on the cross for my sins and that by that act I am redeemed from the guilt and anxiety of my predicament in existence." This I know in the contemporaneity of faith and in no other way.

God is absolutely other from the existing individual but he has revealed himself and therefore I "know" him in this revelation. But he still remains the subject. The moment I make him the object I lose the living God and clasp an idol of my own creation. God as he is in and for himself, apart from his revelation to me, is still the God who dwells in a light unapproachable, whom no man has ever seen or can see, who is the utterly hidden God, an impenetrable, opaque mystery. But this God has *manifested* himself and we can behold his glory. In Jesus Christ he has revealed his heart, his true disposition to us. This I may affirm and yet insist upon an absolute qualitative otherness, for it is one thing to be creator; it is absolutely qualitatively different to be a creature. It is one thing to be a self grounded in your own being; it is an absolutely qualitatively different thing to be a self grounded in another self. Between these two there is an unbridgeable chasm, the strictest kind of either-or; I must be one or the other. Either I have life in and out of myself and can stand on my own feet or else I have life only as I receive it as the free gift of that God who is the author and fountain of all life, and every attempt of mine to stand on my own feet is a defiant despair. *Tertium non datur.*[5]

Qualitative Not Quantitative

This is a difference of kind and not just of degree. Differences of degree must necessarily be relative, even though the degrees soar into infinity. Man is finite, God is infinite. This is like saying that man is six feet tall, but God reaches to infinity in height and width and depth, since he fills all space. It is like saying that man knows a few things, and his knowledge is increasing progressively. Now he has split the atom and can fly sixteen hundred miles per hour and some-day he may be able to fly ten thousand miles per hour. But God knows everything there is to know and he can outdo even the angels for speed, since he is everywhere present at all times. Here you see a sort of progressive increase of speed. According to the old angelologies the angels are supposed to possess definite ubiety, not being like God everywhere present, but bound to one spot at a time, so that they have to be sent out by God to be his messengers. But to compensate for this definite ubiety they are possessed of "marvelous agility" so that in their journeyings they can hop from the distant heavens to the earth almost instantaneously. The same quantitative difference in degree between man, angels, and God appears in the speculations about how many angels could stand on the head of a pin. Since angels occupy no space and yet are possessed of definite ubiety the head of a pin (any imaginary point of no extension whatsoever) could, of course, accommodate an infinite number of angels. This is how the angels are superior to man. But God is superior to the angels by being able to be totally present everywhere and not just partially, as though you could traverse across his body from the soles of his feet to his crown, the mountains being his footstool and the flowing clouds the waves of his silvery hair, with the valley of death his giant navel. This is what happens when you speak of quantitative differences.

It is clear that such quantitative differences, even if you would try to refine them so as to eliminate their ridiculousness would still not get you anything but an anthropomorphic God made in the image of man. It is the old formula of eminence, negation, and causation.[6] You apply to God all the human qualities to an eminent or infinite degree. But you must strip him also of whatever is not worthy of your conception of God. Wherever your capacities fail you in the way of finding an explanation, you must ring in God as the cause. This is the quantitatively constructed God, and obviously he comes under the condemnation of the ancient Democritus who said that if a pig could think, his God would be an infinite pig with all the glories of infinite "pigness," minus whatever is unworthy of "pigness."

A new quality cannot be arrived at by quantitative increments. It is like piling up quantities of the same stuff higher and higher and supposing that in this way it is possible to leap over suddenly into a new quality. To use a simple analogy—no matter how much you would refine and spin out cotton you could never get it to have the quality of silk, for silk is of a different origin, a different quality. Somewhere there must be this break into the different quality. When this break occurs the difference is absolute.

This is a primary consideration in the discussion of difference. One could say that every difference, if it is discernible, is a qualitative difference and is, therefore, absolute and not just one of degree. This would take us back to the paradoxes of Zeno when he speaks of the dropping of the single grains of wheat. Dropping one grain makes no audible sound, therefore the swishing spilling of a bushel of wheat can make no sound either for you cannot get something out of nothing. The transition from no sound at all to sound, however slight, is not a quantitative difference but a qualitative one and, therefore *absolute*, coming into being not by degrees but by a leap. One grain makes no sound. Five grains make no sound, but at the sixth or seventh something rises over the threshold of consciousness. Perhaps it *is* this quantitative increase that accounts for the awareness of the difference and perhaps with finer and more delicate organs of hearing, such as in a dog, other sound waves may be apprehended. But whenever the sound emerges it is perceived as a new quality. There is thus an absolute transition from nothing to something. It is an absolute qualitative difference. The same would apply also to every subsequent discernible difference, or in the discernible differences between musical instruments, however true it may be that the sounds of the reed instruments resemble each other much more than the sound of the brass instruments. Yet it is quite meaningful to assert that every discernible difference, even between clarinet and oboe, is an absolute one or it is not a difference at all. It is the same with colors. We are apt to say that shades of yellow are relatively more similar than those colors at the opposite end of the spectrum. The primary colors differ more from each other than do the various shades produced by the mixtures. But what answer is there to the one who says that even here every difference that is discerned must be absolutely, qualitatively different or it is not discerned? This takes the fire out of the assertions of the philosophers who say that it is meaningless to speak of an absolute qualitative difference between two beings who, after all, have so much in common. It is a necessary exercise in semantics to call attention to the need for a careful definition of terms before one dismisses one of the most astute thinkers our world has seen as an irrationalist.

No Visible Representation

Certainly it should be granted that God is absolutely different as far as any visible representation of him is concerned. We can form absolutely no conception of what God looks like, and it doesn't help any to say that he is spiritual and nonspatial. This is only the confession of our ignorance which we must take seriously, not just making him a more gaseous replica of ourselves. The absolute difference must be taken quite seriously. Of the absolutely different we can form no kind of picture. As Kierkegaard points out in *Philosophical Fragments*,[7] the mere idea of difference will suggest the monstrous, the ludicrous, etc., and the imagination will have free play. This is the mistake of paganism. "On this point paganism has been sufficiently prolific in fantastic inventions."[8] The idols of the pagan are different all right, monstrous and ludicrous combinations of everything under the sun, so that no such prodigy surely ever existed. This may merely reflect the pagan's pantheistic notions as he incorporates into his picture of God a little bit of everything. On the other hand it may be his groping to give expression to "the other," the unknown and unseen "x," with which he feels himself confronted. But he forgets one thing. His idols are different all right, but they are not *absolutely* different, and "deepest down in the heart of piety lurks the mad caprice which knows that it has itself produced its God."[9] Hence the prohibition against the making of images in the Old Testament has its good reasons. In the Holy of Holies there is no representation of the unseen and unseeable God. There is either complete emptiness, so that the Creator of heaven and earth should by no means be confused with the creature, or, at best, there is the ark of the covenant which this God has made with his people. There is thus the evidence of his relationship and of how he feels toward man, but God himself remains unseen. No wonder then that the intruding pagans were struck dumb with awe when they blasphemously intruded upon the Holy of Holies and found *nothing*— emptiness and silence. It is only in emptiness and silence that we apprehend the presence of the holy.

Nowhere in the so-called theophanies of the Old Testament does God "appear." Nowhere in the visions of God, neither that of Isaiah in the temple, of Ezekiel at the river Chebar or of Moses on the mount, nor anywhere else, is there any description of God himself. Isaiah, burdened by the thought of the sinful forgetfulness of God's people, has a vision of one seated upon a throne, high and lifted up, but he does not describe that vision. Ezekiel, lonely in his exile, tortured by thoughts that God has forgotten, has a vision of omniscience and omnipresence, wheels that move pervasively through all space and eyes that see all, but the best he can say of the God this vision brings near is, ". . . the likeness as the appearance of a man." Moses, not knowing whether God is able to deliver his people in bondage or whether, being able, he cares, sees a bush that is not consumed. But he does not see God, and even when the covenant has been established and the most extravagant and fervent promises have been given, it is only from a cleft in the rock, with God's hand shielding him, that he glimpses the back of the God of his deliverance. There are many symbols indicating watchfulness, faithfulness, omnipresence, omniscience, quick readiness to help, and so on, but there is no attempt whatsoever to indicate the looks of this God. "God dwelleth in a light whereunto no man can approach. . . . No man hath seen God at any time. . . . No man can see God and live."

All this seems elementary, and yet it seems not to be taken seriously enough, when some people talk as though Jesus' divinity were discernible in the look of his eyes or the pressure of his hands. There is no mark by which divinity can be recognized directly. God does not "appear" objectively for all to see with their eyes. God does not take "on the figure of a very rare and tremendously large green bird, with a red beak, sitting in a tree on the mound, and perhaps even whistling in an unheard of manner" so that the captain of the hunt riding by can see him and recognize him and shout out the news.[10] Any such direct visibility is paganism. Though objectively present God is discerned only in inwardness.

> All paganism consists in this, that God is related to man directly, as the obviously extraordinary to the astonished observer. But the spiritual relationship to God in the truth, i.e., in inwardness, is conditioned by a prior irruption of inwardness, which corresponds to the divine elusiveness that God has absolutely nothing obvious about Him, that God is so far from being obvious that He is invisible. It cannot immediately occur to anyone that He exists, although His invisibility is again His omnipresence.[11]

God's omnipresence is, therefore, inseparable from his absolute otherness. A village policeman or the town "snoop" may get around and be constantly showing up at the most unlikely and unwanted places, but such ubiquity is far from omnipresence.

> An omnipresent person is one that is everywhere to be seen, like a policeman, for example: how deceptive then, that an omnipresent being should be recognizable precisely by being invisible, only and alone recognizable by this trait, since his visibility would annul his omnipresence. The relationship between omnipresence and invisibility is like the relationship between mystery and revelation. The mystery is the expression for the fact that the revelation is a revelation in the stricter sense, so that the mystery is the only trait by which it is known; for otherwise a revelation would be something very like a policeman's omnipresence.[12]

The Hiddenness of God

Taking seriously the absolute qualitative difference between God and man and not allowing any direct discernibility of God sets the stage for the way in which God reveals himself. This is never done directly but always—to use John Baillie's phrase—in a "mediated immediacy," or in accordance with Luther's much misunderstood formula, "in, with, and under" an earthly medium. God is *immediately* present, but never directly discernible, always employing a medium which effectually "hides" his presence. He is never to be identified with the medium (pantheism, transubstantiation), nor is he ever to be removed from the medium (paganism). The medium is not a sort of basket in which he is contained (e.g., impanation with respect to the sacrament). It is not something that merely happens to run parallel to and accompany his presence (consubstantiation). The medium is always the "creature" never to be identified with the "creator," yet "charged with" the presence of the "creator." The encounter with the creature is, therefore, the God-encounter. This is as immediate and direct an encounter with the living God as man can have. The medium does not destroy the immediacy and if anyone hopes to make "closer" contact by evading the medium in some kind of direct intuition or vision, he will substitute an "idol" for the true God.

This hiddenness of God is true also of what has been, rather unfortunately, called "general revelation." God is present, as Luther says, in the "masks" of creation. This is not a "general" revelation at all, in the sense that God is accessible to man's thought processes in the grasping of universal ideas, but it, too, is an actual confrontation with an "unknown" other at a time and place. It is precisely because it is this kind of specific confrontation with "an unknown other" that the confusions and the idolatry occur. Here lies the temptation to pantheism and other forms of idolatry as the creature is bowed down to rather than the creator.

Psalm 104 admirably illustrates the encounter with the living God in the masks of creation. For all the anthropomorphisms he employs, the psalmist does not confuse creator and creature. For him God is really the Lord of the creation upon whom man is absolutely dependent, and the proper awe before God is preserved. "O Lord my God, . . . thou art clothed with honour and majesty who coverest thyself with light as with a garment: who stretchest out the heavens like a curtain, who layeth the beams of his chambers in the waters: who maketh the clouds his chariot: who walketh upon the wings of the wind." The psalmist sees only the goodness of this sovereign Lord, who "causeth the grass to grow for the cattle, and herb for the service of man: that he may bring forth food out of the earth; and wine that maketh glad the heart of man, and oil to make his face to shine, and bread which strengtheneth man's heart. . . . These wait all upon thee; that thou mayest give them their meat in due season . . . thou openest thine hand, they are filled with good. Thou hidest thy face, they are troubled; thou takest away their breath, they die, and return to the dust. Thou sendest forth thy spirit, they are created: and thou renewest the face of the earth." When this whole psalm is read for the full impact, the God who is here felt to be so close, so human, so made in the image of man, will nevertheless be felt to be separated from his created world by an impassable gulf.

To this testimony of faith there must be added the testimony of the one who is offended by the facts of the created world and does not behold in it the workings of a good God. Where does the providence and care so plaintively and appealingly sung by the psalmist disappear to when contradicted a million times over by starving, clawing, battling beasts, by parched throats, and bleached bones in the desert? For every bird that sings its carefree song a thousand perish miserably. There are animals so cunningly devised to trap and torture their prey that you would swear that only a fiend could be responsible for such deviltry. So, for example, a peculiarly sensitive Oriental writes:

> At evening the gold and blood of sunset, the long muzzled, gray-backed, golden-bellied otters of cloud, swift-gathered for a kill, a terrible death behind the implacable sullen hills. How cruel God who made his creatures so beautiful that they may prey upon each other, spirit and limb and life. God who made the mantis, slim jade murderess with the razor jaws, and the oriole with the liquid golden voice, and the civet cat, and the sparrow hawk swift-pouncing, and the bamboo snake, and the sea eagle sky-suspended; hair and feather and scale, claw and dart and beak, each a miracle, that they may end as this sun has done today, in terror and torn flesh and spilt blood and agony. We must accept it and tolerate it, though it is intolerable. . . . And then the night wind, filling the world and the darkness.[13]

Thus we see how this God of providence is not directly discerned, but is beheld only by the eyes of faith. He is not proved from his works, but those who believe in him defy all the evidence because of their prior faith in him. So the *absolutely other* God remains hidden in the masks of his creation behind a welter of contradictory evidence.

Unlikeness Revealed in Likeness

This absolute unlikeness, hidden behind the masks of creation, is revealed in the absolute likeness of the Incarnation. "No man hath seen God at any time, the only begotten Son he hath declared him." Only in this way is groveling before God avoided—as the slave grovels before the ostentatious display of his tyrant master. Only in this way can men be prevented from climbing aboard this magnificent God and tearing him to pieces for the fulfilment of their desires, using him for their satisfaction. When there is an actual historical revelation at a time and place, this is the only way to keep the actual contemporaries in time from having the advantage because of their direct view of the glory there revealed.

Kierkegaard's analogy of the king who loved the humble maiden must be read in this context. The king did not want to overwhelm her with his glory but rather to establish the real equality of love.

> Would she be happy in the life at his side? Would she be able to summon confidence enough never to remember what the king wished only to forget, that he was king and she had been a

humble maiden? For if this memory were to waken in her soul, and like a favored lover sometimes steal her thoughts away from the king, luring her reflections into the seclusion of a secret grief; or if this memory sometimes passed through her soul like the shadow of death over the grave: where would then be the glory of their love? Then she would have been happier had she remained in her obscurity, loved by an equal, content in her humble cottage; but confident in her love, and cheerful early and late. What a rich abundance of grief is here laid bare, like ripened grain bent under the weight of its fruitfulness, merely waiting the time of the harvest, when the thought of the king will thresh out all its seed of sorrow! For even if the maiden would be content to become as nothing, this could not satisfy the king, precisely because he loved her, and because it was harder for him to be her benefactor than to lose her. And suppose she could not even understand him? For while we are thus speaking foolishly of human relationships, we may suppose a difference of mind between them such as to render an understanding impossible. What a depth of grief slumbers not in this unhappy love, who dares to rouse it![14]

The king in the analogy can do nothing to establish the equality of his love but actually to give up his throne and become a commoner, though he could never undo his royal lineage. So it is also with God when he chose to reveal himself. He had no choice but to become man's equal and to take on human flesh, truly and in reality, though he could not at the same time shake off, so to speak, the fact of his eternal godhead.[15] There is not a mere incognito or a perfect disguise. There is to be no docetism.

Since we found that the union could not be brought about by an elevation it must be attempted by a descent. Let the learner be x. In this x we must include the lowliest; for if even Socrates refused to establish a false fellowship with the clever, how can we suppose that God would make a distinction! In order that the union may be brought about, God must therefore become the equal of such an one, and so he will appear in the likeness of the humblest. But the humblest is one who must serve others, and God will therefore appear in the form of a *servant*. But this servant-form is no mere outer garment, like the king's beggar-cloak, which therefore flutters loosely about him and betrays the king; it is not like the filmy summer-cloak of Socrates, which though woven of nothing yet both conceals and reveals. It is his true form and figure. For this is the unfathomable nature of love, that it desires equality with the beloved, not in jest merely, but in earnest and truth. And it is the omnipotence of the love which is so resolved that it is able to accomplish its purpose, which neither Socrates nor the king could do, whence their assumed figures constituted after all a kind of deceit.[16]

There is no way of penetrating the disguise. The absolute unlikeness has become absolute likeness and only the eyes of God-given faith can make this known.

Otherness as Dimensional Beyondness

The question will inevitably arise as to *where* God is to be found. A further consideration of God's otherness in terms of *dimensional beyondness* does not seem out of place although it must be clear that this was not Kierkegaard's primary concern. It has already been indicated that, even in a time when there was the tripartite cosmology which put the abode of God spatially above the curtain of the sky, there was among the pious Israelites a profound awareness of the absolute difference between creator and creature. Now that the heavens above the curtain of the sky have disappeared, the question of the abode of God will naturally arise for the unsophisticated mind. The mere answer that God is spirit does not seem enough. If one begins using philosophical terms and speaks in terms of transcendence, this must be explained as certainly not meaning a spatial transcendence—that God is way off somewhere outside of this world of space and time. This word "outside" is itself a spatial term. "Transcendence" means that God is not at all spatial and temporal. It means that God is without beginning and end, neither confined to time and place nor spread out in it. He is other than all this. Yet his "otherness" does not consist, as should already have been clear from the above, merely in his "transcendence." Otherness means not only transcendence, but is means *transcendence plus immanence*. It is precisely this that constitutes the mystery. God is immanent in everything, yet he is by no means to be identified with it. What this means can be apprehended in part by speaking of a "dimensional beyondness." God is in a different dimension from ours.[17]

In our world of space the horizontal dimension must be distinguished as absolutely different from the vertical. For something that is spread out in only one dimension on a horizontal plane this would mean certain absolute limitations. A creature living on such a plane could have no awareness of height or depth and such phenomena would not even be conceivable to it. Yet the moment you add a second or third dimension these dimensions interpenetrate. The vertical dimension crosses the horizontal at every point and is yet not to be identified with it. The multiple-dimensional creature, moreover, has a greater flexibility and has access to more than one dimension. It includes the realm of the one-dimensional creature, while the poor one-dimensional creature has no access to what so absolutely "transcends" it. The same would be true of the difference between the so-called inanimate, the merely extended in time and space, and that to which there is added the other dimension of spirit, not confined to time and space.

The law of contradiction applies quite literally. A stone cannot be present in two places at the same time. A human being, however, with his powers of the imagination is not so confined. While the body is confined, the spirit roams. This would, of course, seem quite impossible to the stone, and by the laws of logic it would have to deny that anything could actually be in two places at once, for it has no access to this other dimension. For the stone this is a paradox which is resolved by the human being, for he says he is in one place in his body while he is elsewhere in his thoughts that transcend both space and time.

Now what is wrong, without in the least reducing the mystery, in saying God occupies a different dimension to which I have no access and which is as closed to me as is my dimension to a stone, or the dimension of space to one who is limited to that of time?

The God of this other dimension could not then be confused with the electro-chemical energy that pervades our universe, but he would be its ground. This God in his eternity could not be confused with endlessly drawn out time. Even if eternity is described by saying that there is a diamond mountain higher than Mt. Everest against which a hummingbird lightly brushes a silken thread once every million years and that when the mountain has been worn away by this process then one second of eternity shall have passed, such an eternity still involves change. There will come a time when the diamond mountain will be no more. For us time and change go together, but God is changeless and not subject to the ravages of time. There will never be a time when he is not. Nevertheless this God is not to be confused with the static changelessness of ideas completely outside of the realm of space and time. This lord is the living lord, ever active, changing all things, though he himself remains unchanged. How he can be living and yet unchanging is for us, therefore, precisely the mystery. Life for us is change and if we beheld no change we would behold no life. A static world is a dead world. God, therefore, is not just nonspatial and nontemporal, but in his dimension he is the lord of all space and time, he encloses it and enfolds it as an ocean does an island. He is the infinity that limits the infinity of the world that is itself infinite in both space and time, for we can set no limits to either space or time.

Such a dimensional beyondness may at least preserve the Christian proclamation from the charge of being antiscientific and anti-intellectual. Nor would this be confusing the gospel with a world view and prevailing scientific notions. It would only be addressing the situation today in terms which it can understand so as not to draw the battle line at the wrong place and demand faith in the wrong kind of mystery. I am not asked to have faith that there is some kind of other dimension, but I am to have faith in that God who comes to me out of that dimension of the unknown and reveals to me his true heart of love and how he really feels toward me. I am not to get hung up with difficulties which arise out of a twentieth-century cosmology and to suppose that I am asked to violate my intellectual integrity by forcing myself to believe in a God who lives above the familiar curtain of the sky. A merely "supernatural" God, therefore, must be replaced by a God who really stands clear of entanglement with the created world and who is really Lord and not just a superman. If this is understood then the "offense" will not be a pseudo offense occurring at the wrong place. Rather the offense will arise when a man is asked to humble himself utterly before this God who deigns to approach man out of his dimension and to declare his love for man.

Notes

[1]*Concluding Unscientific Postscript*, p. 369.

[2]See Weiman (sic) and Meland, *American Philosophies of Religion* (New York: Willett, Clark and Co., 1936), p. 16, where the theologian is compared to the cook who makes the food palatable while the philosopher is the dietician.

[3]Acts 10:40-41.

[4]I Corinthians 12:3.

[5]There is no third possibility.

[6]*Via eminentiae, via negationis*, and *via causalitatis*.

[7]p. 35.

[8]*Ibid.*, p. 36.

[9]*Ibid.*, pp. 35-36.

[10]*Concluding Unscientific Postscript*, p. 219.

[11]*Ibid.*

[12]*Ibid.*, pp. 219-20.

[13]Han Suyin, *A Many-Splendored Thing* (Boston: Little, Brown, 1952), pp. 328-29.

[14]*Philosophical Fragments*, pp. 20-21.

[15]As in the doctrine of the kenosis, which tries to make God empty himself only of certain of the prerogatives of divinity while retaining his actual divinity.

[16]*Philosophical Fragments*, pp. 24-25.

[17]This is dealt with by Karl Heim in his *God Transcendent*. This brief indication of what is involved is included here because it is believed relevant to an understanding of a "qualitative otherness."

God's Nature as Changing
or Permanent

26

Norman Pittenger

The Attributes of God
in the Light of Process-Thought

We have been reminded by Peter Baelz, in his recent study of metaphysics and theology, of an aphorism of H. H. Price: that theism is the metaphysics of love. One can think of varieties of theism which might more appropriately be styled the metaphysics of absolute power, or changeless essence, or unyielding will; but it is certainly true that the kind of theism with which Christians are concerned has *intended* to be characterized by love. And I should claim that Christian *theology*, despite much in it which seems contradictory, ought to be a theology of love. By this I mean that whatever else may be said in that theology, its dominant motif should be love, love of the quality disclosed in the historical events which we call by the name of Jesus Christ.

Christian faith, as Whitehead saw, finds the disclosure of "God's nature and His agency in the world" in the Man of Nazareth, with what went before to prepare for Him, what took place in the response

From Norman Pittenger, "The Attributes of God in the Light of Process-Thought." *The Expository Times*, Edinburgh, T. and T. Clark, October, 1969. Used by permission.

made to Him, and what happened in consequence of His impact upon history. Here, Christians claim, we see "revealed in act" what Plato "discerned in theory"—and others besides Plato, too. What was thus "revealed"? The answer, surely, is that the revelation shows what Whitehead called "persuasion," rather than coercive power. This is deepest in things; it is the nature of God and the means by which God works in the world. The "Galilean vision"—again in Whitehead's phrase—is taken in Christian faith as the *important* moment in history, bringing into focus "what is going on" in the world and in history and human experience and providing us with a clue, *the* clue, to that "going on."

This insight, known through response to Jesus Christ, led the writer of I John to give us his magnificent fourth chapter, where we read how "God is love," how we know this because "he sent his Son," how "dwelling in love" means "dwelling in God," and how the human response to all this is "love of the brethren." Not that the love about which the writer speaks is some vague sentiment, some generalized good-will; on the contrary, it is given content, defined, specified for what it is by Jesus Christ, Who taught and lived and acted and died in such a manner that those who did respond were enabled to say that love *like* that, indeed that very love itself, was present and at work not only there in that moment in history but also everywhere in creation. God is love and God always and everywhere acts lovingly; He does not and cannot contradict Himself.

The contemporary Christian theologians who work with the conceptuality offered by "process thought" are concerned to develop a metaphysics which will permit this insight to be central and determinative; and the theology which they seek to work out is likewise concerned to make that insight decisive for everything that is said about God, about God's way in the world, about the world itself, and about the end or destiny of the creation. Such thinkers are prepared to say, *against* Pascal, that "the God of Abraham, of Isaac, and of Jacob," the God of faith, *is* "the God of the philosophers," for they cannot reject the metaphysical inquiry. *But* the sort of metaphysics they envisage is not the construction of a grandiose and all-inclusive scheme in which God becomes essentially and exclusively the conclusion of an argument, and is described as *esse a se subsistens*, "being itself," "unmoved mover." It is a series of generalizations drawn from lived experience and adequate to give meaning to that experience, generalizations to be verified by continuing reference back to experience in its widest sense and never supposed to be above or beyond all such experiential reference.

The concept of God, reached in this manner, is a concept of God related to and active in the creative advance which we know and experience. God is the chief, although not the only, causal principle and He is also the "supreme affect," participant in what goes on in the world and profoundly influenced by that going on. Yet He remains always God, the supremely worshipful One, unsurpassable (as Professor Hartshorne has said) by anything other than Himself, yet enriched in His own experience *as* God, able to use what has happened in the world; and He is faithfully and triumphantly love, the lover, Who moves and acts lovingly by lure, attraction, solicitation, invitation, to bring the creation to its ever-fuller realization of "initial aims" supplied by Him and hence to the fulfilment of itself which is at the same time conformity to God's own purpose or aim.

In the conventional theological scheme, we find that the divine attributes are usually listed under three headings: the metaphysical, the relational, and the moral. In this scheme, God's "root attribute" is not taken to be love, although Christian theologians would not deny that He *is* indeed loving; the "root attribute" is said to be God's *aseity*: His self-existence and self-containedness apart from relationships and without reference to His moral qualities.

Thus, in the conventional scheme, *aseity* is analysed to give the so-called "metaphysical attributes." These are commonly listed as: infinity, eternity, immensity, and incomprehensibility. To be self-existent means to be beyond all creaturely limitations or contingencies —hence "infinite." It means to be unrestricted by temporal succession—hence "eternal;" and it means to be beyond all spatial and creaturely boundaries—hence "immense." It also means to be utterly beyond all finite descriptions, in the mystery of sheer transcendence, and hence "incomprehensible."

Such a concept of God is so remote that the conventional scheme does not stop there. It goes on to the "relational attributes," derived from its insistence that this God who *is,* apart from the creation and unrelated to it, is *also* with His creation and in some sense related to it. Although He is transcendent and hence incomprehensible, He is also immanent and hence present in and to the world. He is omnipotent in relation to the creation, the source and possessor of all power. He is omniscient in relation to His creation, knowing past, present, and future, both things actual and things potential; and He is omnipresent in the creation, since at every point or moment it is dependent upon Him for its existence and dependent upon Him too for sustaining it in existence.

Finally, the conventional scheme speaks of the "moral attributes" of God—and these are styled, or were when I was taught the scheme, adjectival to the substantival attributes found in the first two classes ("metaphysical" and "relational"). God is possessed of wisdom, knowing all things in instantaneous intuition; He is possessed of justice, apportioning its due to everything, although He is also good and so seeks the *best* apportioning of that which is due. Above all, He is characterized by love, which means that He is both able and willing to care for and even to give Himself to the creation.

Such is the conventional scheme. What shall we say about it, if we prefer to begin our theologizing with the "Galilean vision" of love or persuasion as central, rather than with some abstract notion of *aseity*? Is this kind of division sound? Is it genuinely Christian? For myself I must say that it is not sound and that I think that it cannot be called truly Christian. I should wish to begin at another point and proceed in another way. Let me explain what I mean.

First, I believe that this procedure is tied up with a sort of metaphysics which is abstract and theoretical, rather than with the sort which follows the lines to which I have referred earlier. Professor D. D. Williams, in his recent *The Spirit and the Forms of Love*, has made this point effectively: "Metaphysics is not a search for being beyond all existence and experience. It is not a speculation about remote causes. It is as Whitehead has said 'a description of the generalities which apply to all the details of practice. . . . The inquiry is difficult and it does lead us into the ultimate mysteries. But what we are doing is to inquire about what it means to grow, to love, to create, to remember, to become, to hope, to die, and in short, to be. . . .' Much contemporary thought is trying to get rid of 'metaphysics,' meaning by that trying to get rid of timeless, static being. But why not get rid of 'timeless metaphysics' by exploring a temporalistic doctrine of being? . . . Process philosophy wants to show that our categories must reflect the creative being which is exhibited in the world. God as the ground and source of the world's life really participates in that life and history. . . . To say what love *is* in the Christian way means to say what we believe about God and man as known in Jesus Christ. Love is not an idea which we add to our beliefs about God and His self-revelation. . . . The new metaphysics of social relationship can help to set free the theological insight which the Bible sustains" (pp. 9-12, *passim*). To which I should add that this approach makes possible a meaningful if modest use of analogy.

I cannot explore here the many issues which this quotation raises. It will suffice to say that if Williams' point is taken, what is required in our treatment of the divine attributes is a re-ordering of them, a different view of them, with love, *as relationship,* central in the pattern.

For process theology, I have said, God is the chief causative principle, although there are other creaturely causes; He is also the "supreme affect," influenced by what goes on in the creation and in what Whitehead styled His "consequent nature" participant in the world's suffering as in its joy, receiving into Himself the good achieved in that world, making the evil which has occurred into an occasion for new good, rejecting such evil as cannot thus be "used"—and acting always for the establishment of greater good in more ways, despite the setbacks, the recalcitrance, the selfish decisions, and the sin which must be taken seriously into account.

Now if this be true, we must look at the divine attributes in a somewhat different way. To talk about them in abstraction from the concrete reality of God as Love, God as cosmic Lover, is to see them as *so* abstract that they make little sense. But to see them as pointers to what God is, in His creative action, is to find them very illuminating indeed. They are not abstract "things" which characterize the divine substance; they are modes of God's energizing, hence concrete and rich.

Thus we can say that God as love in act is utterly faithful to Himself as lover; *eternally* He is and He acts in love. There are no limits to His love, whatever may happen by creaturely decision; God is *infinitely* loving, under any and every conceivable circumstance. His love is inclusive of all that occurs, without respect to its place or time; it is, in the theological phrase, "unmeasured" or *immense*. Certainly it is of a quality and depth beyond creaturely comprehension and thus is to us *"incomprehensible."*

Furthermore, while the divine Charity, God Himself as Love, is active in all times and places and hence immanent, it is inexhaustible, indefatigable, and utterly indefeasible—so it is *transcendent* to all creaturely occasions although it is present and operative in them all. In each situation the divine Love sees things *as they are,* both in their actual present and with their potentialities, knowing the routing which brought them to where they now are and the variety of decisions which are open to them; thus God is both supremely *wise* and in His wisdom *omniscient.*

In any and every occasion, the divine Love is present, operative, working to provide both the "initial aims" and the environing pressures, as well as the lure of future possibility of self-fulfilment; it is *omnipresent*. And love, such as God really *is,* is in the strongest of all powers, the only truly strong power, yet never contradicting itself but unfailingly acting in love and for love's aims; so God is *omnipotent,* but with a subtle difference from that sort of omnipotence which would think in terms of coercion or externally imposed controls.

Evaluating each occasion as it is, with its history and its possible future, God sees and appraises it in such a way that the inexorability of His love is unshaken and His judgment is *right;* hence God is *"just."* But His justice is expressed in His loving care, as "the fellow-sufferer who understands." As supremely *good,* He wills to share His goodness and to receive the response of His creatures as they achieve whatever goods are open to them by their free decision. He does not hug His goodness to Himself; He *gives* it, here and there, in this and that particular moment, so that the relationship which is established between Him and His world is a mutuality, a "togetherness," making it possible for His creatures to become what they have it in them to be, not by imposition from outside but by responsive goodness from within. God unfailingly *acts* lovingly, precisely because unfailingly He *is* love, the Lover.

I have only suggested here a way of speaking of the divine attributes; I have not developed as I should wish the implications of what I have suggested. But I make two closing comments.

First, I believe that some such approach will correct the tendency to think of God as *really* what Whitehead called the three erroneous ideas that have plagued Christian theology: "the unmoved mover" who is in no sense *acted upon;* the "ruling Caesar," who controls (as it were from outside) a creation which He shoves about with no respect for its own specific decisions and its freedom to make them; and the "ruthless moralist," who imposes laws which bear little relationship to the created occasions, above all to the human persons, who are supposed to obey them. This approach, I should claim, *does* take with utmost seriousness the "Galilean vision" which, in Whitehead's words, "dwells upon the tender elements in the world, which slowly and in quietness operate by love." For my part, I cannot see how a *Christian* theologian can do otherwise. I regard it as the great apostasy of much Christian theology that it has *tried* to do otherwise, for reasons that are understandable yet regrettable, and in consequence has often appeared to deny *in word* what Christian faith and Christian experience must affirm *in fact*.

Second, and finally, I am convinced that it is possible to work out an "open-ended" theology in which this insight of Christian faith and this deliverance of Christian experience are given their rightful place. Whatever else may be wrong about those of us who are called "process theologians," our purpose is to attempt just this task. A theology of love, set in the context of a metaphysics of love such as theism might be, is our goal. At its very heart is the abiding Christian affirmation that in the event which is named when we say "Jesus Christ," there is a disclosure of human love *and* what I have ventured to style cosmic love. This affirmation may very well be, as A. E. Taylor remarked, "undemonstrated and indemonstrable"; yet surely it is not unreasonable. In any event, to be a Christian *is* to say, not only with one's lips but in one's heart and by one's life, that the love poured out in Jesus is the very reflection in act of "the Love that moves the sun and the other stars."

27

Carl F. H. Henry

A Critique of Process-Theology

Part One

Influences governing religious thought in the mid-twentieth century have dealt rather scurrilously with theological metaphysics.

For quite different reasons, both recent Continental theology and English positivism have repudiated philosophical theology. While the one, the dialectical-existential school, has espoused personal non-propositional decision over against external revelation and objective reason, the other, logical positivism, has dismissed metaphysical assertions as meaningless nonsense because unverifiable by empirical scientific method.

All the while evangelical Protestant theologians have been busying themselves largely with matters other than the metaphysical implications of biblical belief. And the few significant contributions that have appeared in evangelical circles have been overlooked in ecumenical theological dialogue.

Under these circumstances, the task of descriptive metaphysics

From Carl F. H. Henry, "The Reality and Identity of God." *Christianity Today*, March 14 and 28, 1969. Copyright © 1969, *Christianity Today*. Used by permission.

has gone by default, as it were, to the neo-Thomists and to the Marxists.

Indications are growing, however, that both English positivists and Continental existentialists have failed to clamp a permanent "veto" on metaphysics; their influence in contemporary theology seems to be waning.

Process-metaphysicians already are aggressively jockeying for position in the philosophical race; a number of American liberal theologians energetically support process-theory as the framework for expounding Christian beliefs. At the same time, Jurgen Moltmann and Wolfhart Pannenberg in Germany, by their breakaway from the dialectical-existential repudiation of external divine revelation in nature and history, suggest fresh promise for theistic metaphysics. And a number of evangelical Protestant scholars who think process-theology unnecessarily dilutes supernatural theism are showing new interest in the metaphysical implications of rational revelational theism.

In this conflict over metaphysical perspective, Marxists and neo-Thomists, as already suggested, are vocal spokesmen for so-called organizational philosophies. Protestant ecumenism, on the other hand, has no "officially approved" metaphysical theory; its theological vision is quickly dissipated in the chaotic diversity of contemporary philosophy. It might be said that the neo-Thomists are trying to revive a dead horse, and the Marxists to mechanize a live one. As for process-theologians, they may be trying to rejuvenate and rerun a previous loser. Evangelical Christians, on the other hand, are demanding a steed of biblically heritaged form, fitness and fettle.

Evangelical Christian theology is metaphysically affirmative. For that reason, when process-metaphysics re-emerges as a serious contemporary inquiry into the nature of God, it confronts a climate of theological discussion within which the Living God of the Bible is seen to be a very real alternative and challenge. Karl Barth's "theology of the Word of God" expounded the self-revealing God in the context of immediate personal revelation as over against that of universally valid propositions of objective reason. Process theologians appeal to experience and logical coherence rather than to miraculous divine disclosure as the source of truths about God. Evangelical theologians tend to consider modern movements of religious thought as concessive reactions and therefore short-lived; the separation of revelation and reason they regard as a costly misadventure. In the mounting debate over who and what God is, they simultaneously champion revelational truths and rational coherence. Over against the process-metaphysicians they stand with Barth, therefore, on the side of revelation. But together with the process-metaphysicians they stand against Barth on the side of coherence. Moreover, evangelical theologians stand against both Barth and process-metaphysicians in emphasizing the intelligible content and universal validity of divine revelation.

What do these theological differences imply for the reality and identity of God? Does this intellectual controversy promise new significance for reason and revelation in defining the knowledge of God and the life of the spirit? No more critical issue than this confronts the scientific culture of our late twentieth century, and no responsible theologian will sidestep engagement in it.

Process-metaphysics is not a new nor even a modern theory, though its recent form has distinctively fresh features. In its post-Christian format, it tries to correlate the evolutionary view of a growing universe with that of a religious reality which, though directly and necessarily involved in time and space, somehow transcends and guides the process of which it is a part. Unlike traditional Christian theism, process-metaphysics does not totally differentiate God from the universe, but neither does it, like pantheism, identify God with the whole of reality. On the basis of evolutionary theory, process-philosophy assimilates God to the universe more immanently than Christian orthodoxy allows; in fact, it repudiates God's absolute transendence by making creation inevitable if not necessary to his being. Process philosophers emphasize the temporal flow of all reality; time, as they see it, is an ingredient of Being itself.

Even in its post-Christian statement, process-metaphysics has taken a number of forms. All of them depart from orthodox Christian theology by importing part of the creative process into the inner reality of God; they differ, however, in how they distinguish the universe, or aspects of it, from divine being.

Late in the nineteenth century, process-philosophy found a prophet in the French philosopher Henri Bergson (*Creative Evolution, 1911*), and early in this century, in England, it gained quasi-naturalistic statement by Samuel Alexander (*Space, Time and Deity, 1927*), and quasi-pantheistic statement by C. Lloyd Morgan (*Emergent Evolution, 1926*). (For an evangelical critique see C. F. H. Henry, *Remaking the Modern Mind*, Eerdmans, 1948.) Both Bergson and Alexander had influenced Alfred North Whitehead before he left Cambridge for Harvard. Whitehead's subsequent *Process and Reality (1929)* attracted such attention that he is now widely credited as the seminal mind and formative influence in later definitive statements of process-metaphysics. The so-called Lotze-Bowne tradition of "personalism," which A. S. Knudson and E. S. Brightman influentially expounded in America, was somewhat competitive; its premise was that while the physical world is a part of God (is God's externalized thought), human selves are divine creations other than God. (The influence of this tradition on an American evangelical theologian is sketched in C. F. H. Henry, *Strong's Theology and Personal Idealism*, Van Kampen, 1951.) In Whitehead's view, however, the structure of all being is the eternal order in the mind of God, and all reality (God included) manifests a real history of actual events.

Whatever attention process-metaphysicians commanded in England and the United States was largely eclipsed in the mid-thirties by the impact of Barthian theology which stressed divine transcendence and the impropriety of depicting Christianity in terms of evolutionary immanence, and by the rise of logical positivism, which was more interested in physics than in biological process. But even through this period American interest in the process-concept of deity was maintained somewhat through the exposition and development of Whitehead's thought by Charles Hartshorne (*Man's Vision of God*, 1941; *The Divine Relativity*, 1948).

Through the breakdown of the logical positivist indictment of metaphysics, and the faltering of dialectical-existential theory, supporters of process-metaphysics gained a propitious opportunity to reassert their view, just at a time when interest in metaphysics was beginning to revive. Since then, the significant development in process-metaphysics has been its growing support by a number of American Protestant theologians as the preferred vehicle for expounding Christian theology. Among them are Bernard Meland, *The Realities of Faith* (1962); John Cobb, Jr., *Towards a Christian Natural Theology* (1965); Schubert M. Ogden, *The Reality of God* (1967); W. Norman Pittenger, *Process Thought and Christian Faith* (1968); and Daniel Day Williams, *The Spirit and the Forms of Love* (1968). In England process thought has waned since the twenties and thirties, when at Cambridge J. F. Bethune-Baker, Canon C. E. Raven, and H. C. Bouquet showed some interest, though Pittenger has recently retired to King's College, his alma mater, and is promoting process-theory. Also at Cambridge, a Trinity College research scholar, Peter Hamilton, wrote a volume entitled *The Living God and the Modern World* (1967); in it he proposes a Christian theology based on Whitehead's thought. A number of Roman Catholic writers— among them Teilhard de Chardin, Peter Schoonenberg, and Leslie Dewart—express a similar trend. It is necessary, therefore, to recognize process-theology for what it is: a movement trying aggressively to articulate metaphysics on a presumably Christian basis in order to overcome the recent dearth of metaphysical theology.

What is its theological methodology? What is its view of God and the world? Is process-metaphysics authentically biblical?

Daniel Day Williams has given the fullest schematic statement by a process-theologian of the theory's implications for the Christian view of God. His basic premise in *The Spirit and the Forms of Love* (Harper & Row, 1968) is that the structures of human existence reflect the being of God or Divine Love. God is mirrored, he contends, in the categorical structures of human love, including the conditions of historical existence, limitation of freedom by another's freedom, suffering, and risk.

Foundational to Williams's experiential appeal is a skeptical view ✗ of the reliability of the Gospels and a relativistic view of truth. Jesus' words are said to be so qualified and reinterpreted that we cannot be sure what he said and did (*The Spirit and the Forms of Love*, p. 157). Quite apart from the miracles, however, Jesus is the Incarnate Logos, "the Truth acted out in love." Creative Divine . Love is the metaphysical ground of everything else.

But both love and intellectuality have a history (*ibid.*, p. 294). Williams concurs with the dogma of scientific evolutionary philosophy that "the structures which reason abstracts are set in the concreteness of process," and so considers all rational formulations to be tentative (p. 286). His doctrine of Divine Love as creative becoming therefore relativizes both revelation and reason. Possibly, despite Williams's intentions, even love may not escape this fate. For it is difficult to see how Williams can exempt his own view from the premise he invokes to discredit all earlier views: "In a creative history where God opens up new possibilities of understanding it is an error to confine the meaning of reason to the historical forms of certain cultural presuppositions and values" (p. 297). What's more, if this assertion is an epistemological absolute, it is self-refuting; if it is not, it still breaks down. In either event, the premise dooms all truth—the truth of Christianity included—to cultural relativity, and ultimately overtakes and judges Williams's view as well. Williams, in fact, cautiously contends, not that his view is superior or impervious, but that other views are outmoded (p. 294). Perhaps, we might add, it would be safer merely to insist that one's own view is not yet passé. For all pretensions to enduring truths are twice relativized in a creative process in which God is assertedly changing and growing, and in which man's knowledge is assertedly culture-bound.

Instead of appealing to intelligible divine self-revelation, which is the strength of traditional Christian theism, Williams's theological method relies on the analogy of being, and in a highly selective way. The central realities of our self-understanding, the categorical conditions of human life—namely, time, freedom, self-limitation by another's freedom, historical existence, action and causality, suffering, risk—have metaphysical consequences, says Williams, for the analysis of God's love, and hence of his very being. The analogy, he claims, explodes the doctrine of God's absolute simplicity, unchangeableness, impassability, and preferential election-love, and requires instead the view that God is neither absolutely transcendent nor completely perfect, but is creatively relational and temporal (p. 123). The necessary result is said to be a reconception of the being of God that involves the divine nature both in time and in becoming. The relation of love to suffering in human experience is said to imply similar consequences for God in his historical involvement (p. 91). In reconceiving the Creator-Redeemer of the Bible as creative being, Williams uses the human analogy of love's "dealing with broken relationships and the consequent suffering" to restate the incarnation and atonement of Christ (pp. 40 f.) in a way that accommodates "the fully social relationship of God and man" (p. 55).

The difficulty of metaphysical theology built on an appeal to analogy, Williams concedes, "is to carry through the analogy of being with full justice both to the structures of experience and to the transmutation of structures as they apply to the being of God" (p. 124). And in extrapolating *agape* from human experience, Williams faces a greater problem than he seems to recognize. For the christological foundation of ethics turns on whether *agape* is divinely derived or present in the experience of sinful man. Williams wavers: on the one hand he refuses to identify the form of any human life with *agape* (p. 204), but on the other he thinks *agape* may be present even in humanitarian concern (pp. 260 ff.).

What Williams actually does is to invoke analogy inconsistently without disclosing that this selectivity rests upon convictions about God previously held and otherwise derived. Indeed, even the premise that "love is the key to being" reflects this selective approach, for human experience entails far more than love. And human love falls at times into disorder and perversity, features that Greek mythology readily attributed even to the gods.

Williams concedes that there are undeniable differences between the divine and human: "There is indeed a dimension in the love of God which differs from human love" (p. 139). It is hard to see, however, just how Williams derives such information from an analysis of human existence. He says: "God as a reality which is necessary to all being cannot sustain exactly the same relationship to time, space and change, which the creatures exhibit. . . . God does not come to be or pass away" (p. 124). This apparent acknowledgment of God's qualitatively different being, whose relation to the universe does not involve God's own becoming, nor experiences that constitute his essential reality in a new way—such acknowledgment in principle demolishes the argument that temporality, mutability, and suffering must be posited of God analogically of man's experience, for what structures man's relationships need not then structure God's. Indeed, Williams is impelled to concede that "there is that in God which does not suffer at all," for his relationship to the world's suffering does not involve finite limitations (p. 128), and he also protests any attempt to "fit Jesus' experience to our limited understanding" because "we cannot delimit another's experience by our own" (p. 162).

But these commendable observations—which would require a higher principle than the analogy of being to define the nature of God—are set aside to give metaphysical speculation the right of way.

We are told that analysis of the structures of human experience, as illuminating the ultimate world, constitutes "the sole justification of metaphysical thought" (p. 129), and that "whatever is present in the inescapable structures of human experience" must be present in "being-itself." "It is the essence of God to move the world toward new possibilities, and his being is 'complete' only as an infinite series of creative acts, each of which enriches, modifies, and shapes the whole society of being" (p. 139). God's love for others is said to involve suffering that alters his experience (p. 127).

(margin note: MUTAB-ILITY)

To the degree that Williams exempts the nature of God from structures found in finite, changing experience, he holds a view of God that is not derived from analogy predicated on human relationships but is in secret debt, rather, to revelational theism, at least insofar as his attributions agree with the Living God of the Bible. To the extent that he limits the nature of God to human structures, to that extent he objectionably compromises the God of Judeo-Christian revelation. How, on the basis of analogical argument, can Williams speak of "that in God which does not suffer at all" if, as he contends, love inherently involves suffering—unless, contrary to what he contends elsewhere, God's being is not wholly identical with love?

According to the Scriptures, fallen man loves neither God nor neighbor as he ought. The gulf between divine, and human love might seem therefore to require the non-analogy of being, without thereby necessarily denying to man the fractured remnants of the divine image. May it not be the height of human presumption, rather than the mark of a meritorious theology, to project divine love from within an experience of human love that needs always to be not only fulfilled but also redeemed? The fact and nature of God's love, if deducible at all, are deducible only from some higher principle than human analogy, indeed, from intelligible divine self-revelation alone.

Why do process-theologians object to the evangelical view of God? Basically, they read into the historic Christian view that God is supernatural, absolute, timeless and immutable the outlines of the immovable static Being of Greek philosophy; in this interpretation, time and man are sacrificed to God's eternity. They propose, instead, a God of temporality and becoming.

This tendency of process-theology to identify the God of classical Christian theism with the static Being of Greek philosophy actually overlooks several important considerations: (1) Classic Greek philosophy itself wrestled with the problem of eternity and time and tried, however unsuccessfully, to save significance for the temporal; (2) ever since its New Testament beginnings, evangelical Christianity has affirmed a supernatural Creator who is active and personally involved in history; by emphasizing God's election-love and the incarnation, atonement, and resurrection of the Logos, it espoused a divine relationship to the universe irreconcilable with Greek notions of a "self-contained static God"; (3) the Protestant Reformers repudiated the medieval scholastic attempt to expound the God of the Bible in Greek philosophical motifs; (4) neither the Church Fathers, the Protestant Reformers, nor recent evangelical theologians have found in the biblical view of God's relation to the world any need to repudiate the absoluteness, non-temporality, and immutability of God.

In view of these observations, it appears that process-theology's proposal to redefine the nature of the Divine as creative becoming does not rest on evangelical and biblical motivations. It issues, rather, from attempts to fuse modern evolutionary theory with arbitrarily selected elements of the scriptural heritage. And therefore it substitutes a modern speculative abstraction for the God of the Bible.

Part Two

A brief outline of the biblical view of God may help to clarify the main departures of process-theology.

The God of the Bible is first and foremost known as the sovereign One, the Monarch of all. Unlike the gods of pagan polytheism, who struggled to survive in a battle against fate, the biblical God from the very first towers as Creator and Lord of all things by his own word and will. The objects of pagan worship—sun, moon, and stars, beasts and creeping things—in the Bible are mere creations of the God of the universe. He it was, the sovereign Lord of All, who assigned man to have dominion over the earth and its creatures in moral obedience to his spiritual purposes. Contemporary moralists tend to deny any necessary connection between divine command and human morality and destiny; no less than Alfred North Whitehead conceded, however, that Christian belief in the rational, inexhaustible Logos as the source of a creative and dependable order was an indispensable element in the rise of modern science. The one God, sole sovereign of the universe, is at the heart of biblical religion.

The God of the Bible is known as the sovereign Lord through the fact of his self-revelation: as personal mind and will, he makes himself known in thought, word, and deed. In this emphasis on personality in God, the Bible contrasts both with Greek philosophy and with Greek popular religion. The classic philosophers spiritualized the polytheistic god-figures. Using such general concepts as the Divine, cosmic reason, and abstract Being, they postulated the ultimately real in terms of impersonal principle. The religious poets not only espoused polytheism but also ascribed to their multiplied gods all features and actions of human existence. The Bible, to be sure, depicts God as personal, speaks of his relation to human beings in concrete personal terms, and uses metaphors of human relationships, including the intimate terminology of love. But, as Daniel Day

Williams notes, a striking difference distinguishes the biblical from polytheistic religion: "Never are the erotic and the emotional satisfactions of human life asserted to be the key to the relationship of God and man. The Bible . . . never makes the ecstatic or emotional fulfillment of familial or sexual experience the key to the experience of God" (*The Spirit and the Forms of Love*, 1968, p. 20). From the very outset the Bible uses generic terms for deity in conjunction with proper names for God; Yahweh, as the distinctive Old Testament name for God, highlights the fact that the sovereign One has introduced himself by name and made his purposes known. By making man the unique bearer of the divine image for intelligible spiritual relationships, God manifests his personal being. In intelligible, purposive communication to his chosen prophets, in the covenant with Israel with its mighty promises, in his saving acts in behalf of his people, he reinforces his redemptive relationship to Israel, depicting it in terms of highest intimacy: "You only have I known of all the nations of the earth" (Amos 3:2); "For your Maker is your husband, the LORD of hosts is his name" (Isa. 54:5). In and through incarnation he reveals finally the inner secret of his personal life; the Son assumes human nature to mirror his perfect fellowship with the Father, and to accomplish atonement for alienated mankind. The Spirit who is given, moreover, indwells and renews the community of faith in the divine image. What is already hinted at in the creation narratives, and now and again throughout the Old Testament revelation, is thus articulated in the New Testament revelation, namely, that there exists even in the personal life of the sovereign One a divine social relationship.

The God of the Bible is not only the one sovereign personal God: he is also the Living God, an assertion frequently made in the biblical revelation. As Paul Tillich pointed out, "few things about God are more emphasized in the Bible, especially in the Old Testament, than the truth that God is a living God" (*Systematic Theology*, 1951, I, 268). By this truth of the Living God, the biblical writers do not mean simply that God is alive, in contrast to God-is-dead attitudes ("The fool hath said in his heart, There is no God"—Ps. 14:1). Nor do they merely contrast him in this regard with the ultimately non-existent pagan divinities (Jer. 2:11; Isa. 6:3, 41:4, 42:8, 43:10 ff., 45:36, 48:11), let alone suggest only that he is at least as much alive as animate creatures. No; for the biblical writers, God as God "has life in himself" and exists eternally; he is the "I AM" (Exod. 3:14). All being and structures therefore have their ground of being and existence in him who is subject to no determination but self-determination. He is the ground of the being of the universe, and the source of man's creation-life, redemption-life, and resurrection-life.

The God of the Bible is not only the one sovereign personal, living God: he is also supernatural Creator and transcendent judge, the metaphysical ground of the Good and the True, the foundation of rationality and morality and order, the ultimate source of all the forms and structures of existence, and of the coherence of experience and life. He is, moreover, the immanent preserver of men and things who works out his comprehensive purposes in history and nature, to be consummated in a new heaven and earth. He is independent of the universe, however; man and the world are in no sense necessary to his being or perfection, for he is not subject to variation, to increase or diminution of being or perfection. The supernatural Creator is transcendent ontologically, ethically and epistemologically. The Good is what God wills, the Truth is what God thinks and says. The Greek gods were strangers to such independence of the cosmos, since they presupposed no doctrine of creation and were circumscribed in their activities by a cosmos that included them as well as all other beings. The pagan gods were not other-worldly, and hence could sustain no comprehensive relationship to the world.

The God of the Bible is the God of election-love, known as such in his self-revelation as the sovereign eternal Spirit, the God of holy love, who works out his redemptive purpose in a created and fallen world. As Norman Snaith put it: "Either we must accept this idea of choice on the part of God with its necessary accompaniment of exclusiveness, or we have to hold a doctrine of the love of God other than that which is biblical" (*The Distinctive Ideas of the Old Testament*, 1944, p. 139). God is the God of holy love. Himself fulfilling all the claims of righteousness, he provides free redemption for sinners unable to rescue themselves from the entrapments of sin. By the incarnation, atonement, and resurrection of the Logos, he lifts the lost to everlasting life. In brief, God reveals his love especially in his saving action and prophetic word in behalf of Israel, and in the gift of his promised Son to provide redemption and reconciliation for repentant sinners.

Over against this background, how does process-theology alter the biblical doctrine of God?

1) Process-metaphysicians compromise the sovereignty of God. God, says Whitehead, is "Co-creator of the universe" (a phrase attributed by Lucien Price in *Dialogues of Alfred North Whitehead*, 1956, p. 297). God's creation is said to be a continuing evolutionary process, a co-existence of order and freedom in which man takes part in determining the future. The divine-human relationship is viewed solely in terms of divine persuasion. Williams notes "large coercive aspects in the divine governance of the world" (in *Process and Divinity*, E. Freeman, ed., 1964, p. 177), and Charles Hartshorne remarks that God's influence may approach compulsion during our unconscious experiences of him (*The Divine Relativity*, 1948, p. 141). Divine love is defined in such a way, however, as to require

the rejection of any concept of a sovereign Monarch who predetermines the course of events. To be sure, Peter Hamilton remarks that "process philosophy *requires* the existence of the living God, who supplies to every entity its 'initial conceptual aim' " (*The Living God and the Modern World*, 1967, p. 250). The reference is, of course, to Whitehead's statement that "each temporal entity . . . derives from God its basic conceptual aim, relevant to its actual world, yet with indeterminations awaiting its own decisions" (*Process and Reality*, 1929, p. 317); this idea, Hamilton asserts, "closely corresponds to the Christian doctrine of the 'prevenience' of God" (*op. cit.*, pp. 159 f.). W. A. Christian holds that "the concept of God in Whitehead's philosophy is categorically contingent, systematically necessary, and existentially contingent" (in *Process and Divinity*, p. 195). In any event, can one possibly reconcile God's prevenience, as biblically stated, with Whitehead's notion that "God and the world interact upon and affect each other; the initial aim which God offers to successive entities is continually adjusted to allow for environmental changes, so as to aim for maximum intensity of experience according to the circumstance of the moment" (*Dialogues*, p. 160)? One may be tempted to read the biblical view of God's purpose in creation and redemption into Whitehead's assertion: "Apart from the intervention of God, there could be nothing new in the world, and no order in the world. The course of creation would be a dead level of ineffectiveness with all balance and intensity progressively excluded by the cross currents of incompatibility." But if one follows the thought to its conclusion one soon discovers the central thrust: "The novel hybrid feelings derived from God . . . are the foundations of progress" (*ibid.*, p. 349). Accordingly, Hamilton is only too happy to discard the physical resurrection of Christ; an empty tomb followed by corporeal appearances would have constituted divine compulsion overwhelming "the disciples' free will," whereas in Hamilton's view "neither human free will nor the normal processes of nature are subjected to, or interrupted by, divine compulsion" (*op. cit.*, p. 226). Williams's systematic exposition of process-theology contains no section on eschatology; he merely asserts that God "never refuses to love" (*The Spirit and the Forms of Love*, p. 127) and suggests that the doctrine of universal salvation be probed (p. 97).

Although process-theology depicts God as personal, it tends to reduce the Divine to a principal aspect of the whole of things. Paul Tillich had explicitly rejected divine personality; he used the term "personal" only symbolically of God, conceived impersonally as Being-itself (*op. cit.* I, 270 f.). But Whitehead viewed God as "an actual entity" or perhaps as a succession of entities with personal order, and Hartshorne went a step further by defining God as "living person." This emphasis Hamilton develops to the point of justifying prayer to "the great companion—the fellow-sufferer who understands" (*op. cit.*, pp. 240 ff.). No one was more aware than Hartshorne, however, that process-metaphysics shifts the case for divine personality to philosophical considerations of its own. "It may be said," he wrote of Whitehead's theory, "that this is one of the first philosophies which has any intellectual right to speak of divine personality. . . . We doubt if anyone can really, or other than verbally, mean by a 'person' more than what Whitehead means by a 'personally ordered' sequence of experiences within certain defining characteristics or personality traits" (in *Philosophers Speak of God*, Hartshorne and Reese, eds., 1953, p. 274). And Williams says that "process metaphysics proposes analogies in which the Creator-Redeemer God of the Bible is really conceived as creative being" (*op. cit.*, p. 125, n. 14); he is quite aware that Whitehead's imprecision about how God acts on the world jeopardizes the being of God as "a fully actual, effective subject." This weakness Williams first proposed to overcome by stressing "the disclosure of the divine initiative in religious experience" (in *The Relevance of Whitehead*, I. Leclerc, ed., 1961, p. 370). But not even Williams's later emphasis on love as the structure of reality guarantees the personality of God, whatever may be his intentions. This fact becomes fully evident in our subsequent discussion of the process-theory's transformation of the concept of divine love. Here we note only that the loss of intelligible divine self-communication reduces the reality of God in fact to an unsure inference from experience, whereas the more God is postulated in personal categories, the more decisive becomes the question of his cognitive disclosure. Although process-theologians retain the vocabulary of revelation, they abandon its biblical sense. In the Bible, revelation is a mental concept, and involves God's disclosure of truths about himself and his purposes; the God of the Bible does not wait for speculative philosophers to postulate his nature on the basis of analogies from human experience. The personal God of revealed religion speaks and acts for himself, and declares his purposes intelligibly.

Process-theologians take seriously the reality of a divine life and insist that the living God has an existence that must be differentiated from mere cosmic process. They disagree with Tillich's assertion that "we must speak of God as living in symbolic terms" (*op. cit.*, I, 268). Tillich earlier had held that God has actual being as the ground of all being, as Being-itself; God is the structure of all being, and these structural elements "make him a living God, a God who can be man's concrete concern" (I, 264). In later statements Tillich considered merely symbolical even the assertion that God is the structure or ground of being (II, 10). The statement that God is what concerns man ultimately and unconditionally (I, 17) thus became detached from any objective cognitive reality whatever; those who insisted that atheism might equally well be one's ultimate concern saw in Tillich's view a transition to death-of-God speculation. But process-metaphysicians insist upon creative being as the objective reality of Tillich's "ultimate concern"; emphasis on God as the ground and structure of all being they coordinate with a theory of God's function in the world as an active being who enters into relationships, and who may thus be distinguished conceptually from the universe of which he is the depth, ground, or structure. Yet such coordination in fact hardly requires much advance over the view of Henry Nelson Wieman, who saw no need to carry Whiteheadean metaphysics beyond the emphasis that "deity" is the impersonal value-producing frontier of evolutionary process (*The Source of Human Good*, 1946); here the term God, when identified with creative good, seems merely complimentary. More than one critic of Whitehead's theory has suggested that God is quite a dispensable appendage to his metaphysics and reflects more of cultural heritage than of integral logical necessity. The newer process-theologians seek to give their theory of God biblical overtones. Nonetheless creation becomes evolution, redemption becomes relationship, and resurrection becomes renewal; the supernatural is abandoned, miracles vanish, and the Living God of the Bible is submerged in immanental motifs.

Process-metaphysics, while affirming the transcendence of God, repudiates his supernaturalness and absolute transcendence. It rejects the pantheistic identification of God with the whole of reality, but insists that God is an aspect of all reality. Whitehead held that not God alone, but every actual entity, transcends the rest of actuality; "the transcendence of God is not peculiar to him" (*op. cit.*, p. 130). Hartshorne formulates the process-doctrine of divine transcendence by saying: "God literally contains the universe." Yet he would add, God is both the cosmos and something independent of it (*The Divine Relativity*, p. 90). Because Hartshorne's literal inclusion of creatures within God jeopardizes their independence, W. A. Christian argues that God neither is the cosmos nor includes the cosmos. While, he says, the cosmos does not determine God's activity, it always conditions it (*An Interpretation of Whitehead's Metaphysics*, 1959, p. 407). In either case, the world is necessary to God, and God's absolute transcendence is therefore compromised both through his necessity for the world and through a reciprocity of influence.

Process-theology subverts the love of God into a principle of universal causality which it dignifies with personal categories. This is evident, first and foremost, from its dismissal of the biblical motif of preferential election-love. In the Old Testament the election-love of God focuses exclusively upon Israel, and in the New Testament upon called-out believers who constitute the Church. On the basis of the divine creation of mankind viewed as an act of love, Williams gratuitously extends God's election-love for Israel to all nations, and universalizes God's election-love in the New Testament by first concentrating it in Jesus Christ as the Elect Man and then extending it through him to all mankind. Williams concedes that "perhaps there is nothing in scripture which explicitly identifies God's act of creation as an act of love" (*op. cit.*, p. 27). The Old Testament passages which he thinks suggest "that God's care for all nations is the same character as that for Israel" (*ibid.*)—particularly Amos 9:7; Ruth; Isaiah 19:19-25; 42:1-6; 49:6—surely cannot be read in terms of divine covenant with a chosen people. The underlying motivation for rejecting God's preferential-love is clearly speculative: Williams contends that it is sinful to withhold love from some (p. 142) and not to bestow the same love on all (pp. 121 f.). The latter premise would turn human matrimony into a shambles, and both premises would discredit preferential divine love as immoral. Williams nowhere discusses the implications of his premise for the Father's unique love for the Son. That the Son is uniquely the object of the Father's love is a truth fundamental to New Testament Christology (cf. John 5:20). Are we to demand the divine extension of this love to all persons as the precondition of divine moral integrity? And if so, what becomes of divine grace? A second way in which process-theology tends to dilute the love of God, even when it expounds God as Divine Love, is by eroding the miraculous in the interest of evolutionary process and scientific uniformity. Despite the process emphasis on God as a social being, the matter of personal immortality is left in doubt through the eclipse of Christ's bodily resurrection. Whitehead declared his theory "entirely neutral on the question of immortality" (*Religion in the Making*, 1926, p. 111); Hartshorne is disposed to reject the concept of personal immortality (*Philosophers Speak of God*, Hartshorne and Reese, eds., p. 285). Contemporary process-theologians, on the other hand, are somewhat more conditioned by biblical expectations. Williams treats Christ's resurrection as incidental to the incarnation, rather than as an external physical miracle; he emphasizes "a new situation in human existence" (*op. cit.*, p. 168), reconciliation involving our "hope for eternal communion with God" (p. 169; cf. p. 188). W. Norman Pittenger seems to consider man permanently valuable to God and perhaps indispensable; one is tempted to ask how God managed so well before man was created. Says Pittenger: "Precisely because God is love and precisely because the achievement of greater good, especially through the activity of such personalized occasions as man may be said to be, is in itself a good, may not the achieved good include the agency *by which it was achieved?* (*Process Thought and Christian Faith*, 1968, p. 81. But he adds that "there never has been . . . any strict logical demonstration of what the Christian is talking about . . . when he declares his faith in 'resurrection,'" a term Pittenger translates into "some sort of persistence of the creaturely agent" (pp. 81 f.). Hamilton settles for Whitehead's view that what survives death is not our personality but God's as inclusive of our concrete experiences (*op. cit.*, p. 141).

In discussing God's relation to man, the process-theologians so strip away the distinctive biblical manifestations of divine personality —intelligible revelation, election-love, promise and fulfillment, and miracle—and so completely assimilate it to experiential routines that one can only ask: Is this idea of a personal God in process-metaphysics merely an emotional overtone or a bit of religious coloring added to cosmic theory? If, as Hamilton states, "the existence of a transcendent God is not intellectually essential" (*ibid.*, p. 166), the existence of a non-transcendent God would seem even more dispensable on process-presuppositions. Indeed, Whitehead himself acknowledged that he had never fully worked out his doctrine of God, and Dorothy Emmet, in the preface to the second edition of her work on *Whitehead's Philosophy of Organism* (Macmillan, 1966), expressed uncertainty as to whether the reality of God is integral to Whitehead's view of the world.

Let us assume, however, that process-theology does indeed seriously postulate divine personality on its own premises. We would still ask whether its view of God as a person is logically coherent. As I see it, process-theorists involve their God in a split personality. For all the criticism non-evangelical theologians level at Chalcedonian Christology, charging that the concept of two natures in one person destroys the integrity of the self, this problem is not only duplicated but escalated to the point of logical contradiction in the process-theory exposition of God. In brief, process-theology sacrifices God's simplicity and unity as well as his supernaturalness.

What process-metaphics emphasizes is that God in his nature is temporal and socially related; independent of the actual world in his abstract identity without being wholly external to it, he nonetheless includes the actual world in his concrete existence; at the same time the world is completely contingent and radically dependent upon him as its sole necessary ground.

When process-theologians depict the nature of God as at once eternal and unchanging and yet temporal and changing, as perfect and yet growing, their dialectical ambivalence becomes quite apparent. As Schubert Ogden puts it:

> If God is the immanently temporal and changing One, to whose time and change there can be neither beginning nor end, then he must be just as surely the One who is also eternal and unchanging . . . the immutable ground of change as such both his own and all others. . . . That God is not utterly immaterial . . . but, on the contrary, is the *eminently* incarnate One establishes a qualitative difference between his being and everything else. . . . His only environment is wholly internal, which means that he can never be localized in any particular space and time but is omnipresent.

> Hence, just because God is the eminently relative One, there is
> also a sense in which he is strictly absolute . . . the absolute
> ground of any and all real relationships, whether his own, or
> those of his creatures [*The Reality of God*, London: SCM Press,
> 1967, pp. 59 f.].

To top it all off, Ogden assures us that a God who is growing is "infinitely more perfect" than a God who wholly actualizes all possibilities of being and value (p. 60, n. 97).

We might say, with tongue in cheek, that this theory is so intricate and complex that God would and could have disclosed himself only to twentieth-century metaphysicians to make his existence intelligible. What's worse, however, is the theory's questionable logical coherence. While Ogden insists that "it is clear at least in principle" that process-theology surpasses traditional Christian theism in "theoretical coherence" (*ibid.*, p. 65), he offers no convincing demonstration. He condemns classical Christian theism for its so-called contradictory emphasis on the absolute and relative attributes of God. But then he proceeds to justify the dipolar nature of God in process-theology as expressing an authentically Protestant theology of "difference and identity" grounded in divine love (pp. 68 f.).

Far more is needed than verbal assurance to validate the statement that process-theory can "show how maximum temporality entails strict eternity; maximum capacity for change, unsurpassable immutability; and maximum passivity to the actions of others, the greatest possible activity in all their numberless processes of self-creation" (*ibid.*, p. 65). One is tempted to call this a colossal fiction or to suspect that God has acquired a Dr. Jekyll and Mr. Hyde ambivalence from his exposure to process-metaphysicians. At best, after the high promise of a coherent view, the process-theologians seem to offer us only a theology of squiggle. The dilemma of process-thought comes from trying both to maximize and to minimize the differences between the Superself and the human self, from trying to preserve and yet to prune such metaphysical attributes of God as eternity, immutability, and immateriality. Process-theology therefore not only loses the coherence of evangelical theism, but also substitutes for the biblical perfections of the self-revealed God merely abstract philosophical projections of the nature of deity.

Whatever else may be said about process-theology as a contemporary conceptuality of a theory of God, its deity is certainly not the God of the Bible, nor is the "new theism" demonstrably as coherent as evangelical Christianity. If the new conceptuality becomes an influential modern option, it will be only because contemporary man has taken to trading even his gods for periodically new models, or because those who know the true, abiding God have gone into hiding. If, at its crossroads of confusion, ecumenical theology now turns hopefully to process-metaphysics, it will finish the twentieth century no less disillusioned than when it tracked the trails of modernism, neo-orthodoxy, and existentialism.

God as Three-in-One

28

Charles W. Lowry

What Is the Doctrine
of the Trinity?

The Christian religion is, in the first instance, a story or epic. It is
the narrative of the acts and words of God to men, performed and
uttered with a view to disclosing His Divine nature and will and to
rescuing and putting back on the right track the special object of
His love—the race of men. The Bible is the record of God's self-
revelation—as Creator, Ruler of the Nations, Giver of law, Tutor
and Disciplinarian of humanity; as Redeemer, Lover of men, Provider
of sacrifice for sin, Seeker of reconciliation, Forgiver of transgressions,
Physician of souls; and as Sanctifier, Convicter of the world "in
respect of sin, and of righteousness, and of judgment,"[1] Inspirer of
holiness, truth, and beauty, Giver, Preserver, and Increaser of
Spiritual life.

The Bible was written by inspired men, who yet remained men
and therefore weak and fallible. It is not sheer miracle; it is not comparable to transcription from a Divinely arranged and loaded dicta-
phone. It is in a real sense a single, unified work; yet it is in two

From Charles W. Lowry, *The Trinity and Christian Devotion*. New York:
Harper and Brothers, 1946. Used by permission.

main divisions that are discontinuous as well as continuous. Each division or Testament, furthermore, is made up of numerous individual compositions or compilations, written at different times and containing the impress of varied interests and points of view. In the case of the Old Testament we have to do with a literary work that resembles nothing so much as an infinitely complex geological formation. The layers or strata are all there, but there has been such a crisscrossing of faults at points that it is next to impossible to unscramble and rearrange them in chronological order. Then the parts, although all have a definite contribution to make, are not of equal value. Discrimination and sound judgment in "dividing the Word of truth"[2] are not an option but a necessity. Even the Canon is a problem as well as a fact. The omission of certain Apocryphal Books is from the Christian standpoint, as many of the ablest Christian Fathers saw, unjustifiable and a serious loss.

All this means that in the Bible we have to do with a human process, which may be and should be approached and studied from a scientific point of view. It means, further, that pure Biblicism is unsound. The Scriptures need as an auxiliary of understanding and interpretation the tradition of the Church. Here the *Articles of Religion*, weaving their way deftly if cumbersomely between the Scylla of extreme Protestantism and the Charybdis of unmitigated Catholicism, are fundamentally sound. Article xx could hardly be improved on. Article viii could bring out more clearly than it does the fact that the Creeds, by the grace of the Holy Ghost, have a contribution of their own to bring to the right use and understanding of Holy Scripture.

Yet the Bible remains, when all is said and done, the greatest miracle of all time. It is in actuality the Word of God, since it is only through its witness, record, and interpretation that we confront and are confronted by the deeds and the speech of the living God. In it is set down once and for all the epic story which is the Gospel of God, the Father, the Son, and the Holy Spirit.

Christianity, in the second place, is doctrine. It is a body of doctrines.[3] A doctrine . . . is a view of reality in some aspect. It is a formulation of a more or less general truth, required by a certain body of facts. It is an inference from cogent and definitely implicative evidence. A Christian doctrine is a statement of some truth either given with the Gospel or implied by the Gospel, taken in connection with all possible relevant facts. Among the Christian doctrines are the Creation, the Incarnation, the Atonement, the Holy Spirit, and the Trinity. These, together with Church and Sacraments, which are closely related to the Holy Spirit; Grace, which includes or rather intersects them all; and Eternal Life, the great Consequent emerging ineradicably from all, constitute the primary Christian doctrines.

The doctrine of the Trinity is the most comprehensive and the most nearly all-inclusive formulation of the truth of Christianity. It is in and of itself a not inadequate summation of the principal teachings of the Christian religion. This doctrine is the view that the Father, the Son, and the Holy Spirit of Scripture and the Creeds and the universal continuing consciousness of the Christian Church, ever to be worshiped and glorified as distinct, individual, personal determinations and centers of Godhead, are nevertheless one God—one single, unified Divine essence or being. In phraseology suggested in part by the ancient Catechism of the Church of England, the doctrine of the Trinity is the teaching that God, who as the Father hath made me and all the world, who as the Son hath redeemed me and all mankind, and who as the Holy Ghost sanctifieth me and all the people of God, is within the unity and perfection of His eternal being Three as well as One, and that the Divine Three are mutually and personally related to One Another.

There are various other ways of stating the doctrine or dogma of the Trinity. One of the simplest of all classical statements, which yet seems to be a rock of stumbling to most people, perhaps because of its calculated severity of paradox and economy of speculative admixture—is the declaration of the so-called Athanasian Creed:[4]

> So the Father is God, the Son is God: and the Holy Ghost is God. And yet they are not three gods: but one God. So likewise the Father is Lord, the Son Lord: and the Holy Ghost Lord. And yet not three Lords: but one Lord. For like as we are compelled by the Christian verity: to acknowledge every person by himself to be God and Lord;
> So are we forbidden by the Catholick Religion: to say, There be three Gods, or three Lords.

This formulation of the Trinity is really a bald transcript of the salient ideas of the Nicene Creed (of which it may have been originally an exposition or commentary: hence the name "Athanasian"), under the influence of the Trinitarian theology of St. Augustine. It accents the mystery of the Divine Trinity, the necessity of accepting it on authority, and—at the same time—the absolute equality of the three Persons.

Another fine statement, minimal in content of thought yet careful in hewing to the line of perfect orthodoxy, and flawless in distinction of style, is that of Article I, the title of which, very significantly, is simply: "Of Faith in the Holy Trinity." It reads:

> There is but one living and true God, everlasting, without body, parts, or passions; of infinite power, wisdom, and goodness; the Maker, and Preserver of all things both visible and invisible. And in unity of this Godhead there be three Persons, of one

substance, power, and eternity; the Father, the Son, and the Holy Ghost.

This formulary incorporates the technical Trinitarian terms long established in the usage of the Latin West, namely "substance" from *substantia* (= concrete being: including both the sum of attributes and the unique principle of individuality) and "person" from *persona* (= a permanent, individual mode or manner of Divine existence). It is a useful introduction to the greatest and weightiest short statement of the doctrine of the Trinity on record—that of the Eastern Bishops and Doctors assembled in Constantinople in A.D. 382 (the year after what we now know as the Second General Council). This statement occurs as part of a Synodal Letter addressed to Damasus, Ambrosius, and the rest of the Bishops "assembled in the great city of Rome." After speaking of the many sufferings undergone "for the sake of the Evangelical faith, ratified by the three hundred and eighteen fathers at Nicaea in Bithynia," "the orthodox bishops" proceed:

> This is the faith which ought to be sufficient for you, for us, for all who wrest not the word of the true faith; for it is the ancient faith; it is the faith of our Baptism; it is the faith that teaches us to believe in the name of the Father, of the Son, and of the Holy Ghost. According to this faith there is one Godhead, Power and Being (ousía) of the Father and of the Son and of the Holy Ghost; the dignity being equal, and the majesty being equal in three perfect hypostases, i.e., three perfect persons.

Several things in this formulation of the doctrine of the Trinity are noteworthy. First, there is the emphasis upon the Evangelical (referring of course to the Gospel) character of the Nicene Creed and a kindred stress upon the relation between Baptism and the faith of the Trinity. (Let the reader recall here what we said about the Matthean Baptismal Formula. . . .) Second, it is a dogmatic, not a speculative or philosophical statement. No attempt is made to explain or clarify or illuminate the conception of a God who is both One and Three. Third, technical terms are used—the Greek word for "being," of which "substance" (see above) is a common translation; "hypostasis," a transliteration of a Greek word meaning "that which stands under" and hence that which supports in being various attributes or a concrete individual determination of being; and the Greek word for "person," this being equated with hypostasis and recalled to Trinitarian use for the first time since Sabellius. Fourth, a perfect equality of the Three persons is asserted. Here, as in the revival of the word "person," East and West may be seen as drawing together, after a long period of sharp divergence in thought as well as confusion in language. We have, in fact, in the declaration of the Synod of Constantinople a clear indication that the Church in respect of its Trinitarian consciousness has come of age. Henceforth there is general agreement that the God of Christian faith is "one Being in three Hypostases" or "one Substance in three Persons."

Or, finally, apart from technical terms, we may perhaps say that the Christian doctrine of the Trinity is the doctrine that the one, living, and true God, who has manifested Himself as Father, as Son, and as Holy Spirit, is within Himself also, in a real and concrete manner, three. He is a Trinity of persons within a fundamental and absolute unity of being, consciousness, and will.

Christian worship affords numerous specific illustrations. Worship is directed to God as Trinity and as Unity. Sometimes the accent falls on one aspect, sometimes on the other. With us who are creatures, and who are reaching out in trust and adoration to that which is infinitely great and therefore beyond the best efforts of our thought and imagination to understand and picture, such an alternation of emphasis is as proper as it is inevitable. What is important intellectually is that a balance be maintained.

Take, for example, Reginald Heber's Trinitarian hymn—to the writer the premier hymn in the English language. The first and last stanzas stress in the context of the strikingly symbolic *Trisagion*— "Holy, Holy, Holy"—the Divine Trinity. The first stanza ends, and the hymn ends, with the line:

God in three persons, blessed Trinity.

This is the overshadowing impression conveyed by the hymn: that God in His eternal praiseworthiness, in His impenetrable yet not unillumined mysteriousness and in His unconcealed glory, is a Trinity. Yet if the hymn be studied carefully, one will see that it is "the Lord God Almighty," "perfect in power, in love, and purity," of whom the singular personal pronouns "Thee," "Thou," and "Thy" are used consistently, who is the "blessed Trinity."

A second, very obvious illustration is the *Gloria Patri* ("Glory be to the Father, and to the Son, and to the Holy Ghost; as it was in the beginning, is now, and ever shall be, world without end"). This *Gloria* is probably used more often in Episcopalian (or Anglican) worship than it is in the regular services of any other Christian Church. (Monastic offices may be an exception.) It contains no direct reference, even by implication, to the unity of God. In this it is like the New Testament, where the foreground is dominated by God's revelation of Himself in word and act and distributive personal manifestation as Father, as Son, and as Holy Spirit. The monotheism of Israel is there; there is no thought of denying it or calling it into question; but it remains in the background. The primary object of concern in each case is God the Father, God the Son, and God the Holy Spirit.

For everyday use in Christian worship this is sufficient. Yet it is good to have an occasional variation even in the Liturgy, which drives home the point that the great central theologians in the ancient Catholic Church, Irenaeus, Tertullian, Athanasius, and Augustine, found themselves obliged to defend with might and main, namely, that Christians believe in and worship one God. Such a variation is found in the amplified conclusion of a number of classical collects: "through Jesus Christ our Lord, who liveth and reigneth with thee and the Holy Ghost, one God, world without end." Even more striking and more nearly perfect as an expression of the paradox of the Christian doctrine of God, is the special doxology found in the present American Book of Common Prayer as the close of the *Benedicite*, commonly sung since 1549 in Lent instead of the *Te Deum*. It reads:

> Let us bless the Father, and the Son, and the Holy Ghost: praise *him*, and magnify *him* forever.[5]

Other illustrations, among almost any number that could be cited, are the fourth invocation of the opening section of the English Litany as composed by Archbishop Cranmer just over four hundred years ago, and the Collect for Trinity Sunday. In the Litany as Cranmer composed it, one prays, after invoking severally and individually the three Persons of the Trinity:

> O holy, blessed, and glorious Trinity, three Persons and one God: have mercy upon us miserable sinners.

In the American Book of Common Prayer as revised in 1928 in line with the old Sarum Litany, this invocation was cut down drastically and was divided between Minister and People instead of being repeated in full. It now reads:

> O holy, blessed, and glorious Trinity, one God; *Have mercy upon us.*

In this form the accent is more on the oneness of God. The Trinity Collect, as contained without alteration in all "Anglican" Prayer Books, states in perfect balance the Christian doctrine of Trinity in Unity:

> Almighty and everlasting God, who has given unto thy servants grace, by the confession of a true faith, to acknowledge the glory of the eternal Trinity, and in the power of the Divine Majesty to worship the Unity; we beseech thee that thou wouldst keep us stedfast in this faith, and evermore defend us from all adversities, who livest and reignest, one God, world without end.

This prayer is equally useful both as a plain man's guide and as a theologian's compass needle in thinking about and in blessing and adoring that Divine Trinity which is the one only and eternal God, the Lord of all being and the Maker and Preserver of all things, visible and invisible.

Such is the doctrine or dogma of the Trinity. Such is the Christian religion as doctrine in at least its major and most inclusive single formulation. . . . if we keep in mind the vital connection between this religion as epic or Gospel and as doctrine, we shall feel and respect the significance of such unelaborated and unadorned statements of the doctrine of the Trinity as those just noted and presented. They are utterly necessary as a preliminary intellectual and moral and liturgical or devotional step. They are required by the Christian facts, and they illuminate, in turn, and vivify and throw into clear focus, alike for the faithful and for the inquiring, the mighty acts and the adorable being of the blessed God.

Yet this type of formulation, indispensable as it is, is not a final goal. It represents, at best, a halfway house for the mind and also for the heart—for the affections and the will. By and for itself it is bound to prove unsatisfactory. This is the reaction of ordinary people to the doctrine of the Trinity, baldly stated, and to other doctrines as well. Theologians have nearly always shared this reaction and have tried to carry further the work of Christian thought. They have tried to think through, so far as possible, the implications of the various doctrines of the Christian faith and then to relate them to the world viewed as a whole, taking into account the knowledge made available at any given period by science, psychology, and philosophy. This gives us the key to Christianity in its third phase or stage. *Christianity is, thirdly, a philosophy.* It is a world view. It is a systematic map of the real, drawn up in the light of the self-revelation of God in Jesus Christ.

Evidently, in such a structure the keystone of the main arch is the doctrine of God. This statement applies to every positive philosophy if instead of the word "God" we read "Ultimate" or "Supreme Real." It applies to materialism, Platonism, Stoicism, Spinozism, idealism, positivism, Marxism, and National Socialism, as much as to Christianity.

The God of Christianity is a Trinitarian God. The Christian Ultimate is a superpersonal union of three Divine persons—the Father, the Son, and the Holy Spirit. Yet this union is not something impersonal. It is not an abstract common nature such as our minds discern when they compare the members of a species, as, for example, tigers or men. The universal (the technical name for tigerhood or manhood or justice or liberty) is in some sense real, as Aristotle saw, over and above its existence *post rem* (after the thing) in the perceiving and analyzing mind. But this reality, whatever it is—whether simply in individuals (*in re*) or as an idea first in the mind of God (*ante rem*) —is an impersonal abstraction.

Or, again, the union of the Divine Three is more than the unity of spirit that may exist between two people bound together closely in love or friendship. This mystical unity is likewise real; it may seem to be a new creation, and incapable of ever ceasing to be. Perhaps in God there is a possibility of perpetuity for high human relationships. Yet the most exalted human unities do not achieve, so far as we know, a hypostatic (from hypostasis—see above) or personal condition. And experience teaches us that they partake deeply, also, of man's transitoriness and variability. They may, and not infrequently do, pass into a virtual nothingness.

Then there is the union of members of a group—a family, a clan, a school, a race, or a nation. These names denote real entities. Such entities seem to be capable of generating a certain group spirit, which may be an extremely powerful thing, able to absorb into itself for the time being the individual spirits that make up the group. We are today vividly aware of this possibility and of the threat inherent in it to individual, scientific, and even religious integrity. But its metaphysics, if not its psychology, remains obscure. It is a testimony to the social and finite character of man and to the fact of his creation for community. There is, however, no evidence that the spirit of a group is real in the persistent, concrete sense in which a horse is real or a man is real. We do outgrow in America some stages at least of "school spirit," and in Great Britain some transcendence of the "school tie" is not unknown even in conservative circles. When a Napoleon or a Hitler is overthrown, and with him both the myth of invincibility and the power of the communal spirit engendered by his personal magnetism and mastery of the word, individual followers remain to experience disillusionment and often to react in hate.

There is in fact no human analogy that is more than weakly partial or faintly suggestive when we come to the Unity of the Trinitarian God. The Christian doctrine is not one of three Gods or Lords, however sublimated the polytheism proposed—however closely united in concord, fraternity, affinity, and a common purpose the Divine Three are held to be. It is the doctrine of one God—one ultimate Divine being, life, mind, will, and consciousness. This God is Himself a "Thou" or a "He." The Trinity as a whole is to be identified with the Jehovah of the Old Testament, as St. Augustine clearly saw. We can speak of "they" or even "the Three" only relatively—in relation to the fact of One God. Here the Athanasian Creed has an importance all its own, which has not been outgrown.

So the question arises and is insistent, How can this be? How can the human mind grasp and make real to its thought or in its imagination this stupendous but baffling conception of the Trinity in Unity and the Unity in Trinity?

From an early time Christian thinkers have faced and wrestled with the problem thus set them. At first the solution did not seem so difficult. The analogy widely used, following St. John's Prologue and Philo, was that of the Word—uttering thought or expressing ideas. This is in a sense a psychological approach to the problem. Psychology was, however, much less important to the first Christian theologians, who were as a whole conspicuously Greek-minded, than cosmology (= science of the world) and transcendental theology (a God so perfect metaphysically that He cannot be in direct touch with the world). The Logos or Word had, therefore, a double value: He explained the rationality of the world (its being a cosmos), and He connected the world with the transcendent Father. His being Himself a secondary or subordinate deity—a god "in the second rank" (Justin Martyr) or "intermediate between the nature of the Uncreated and that of created things" (Origen)—fitted in perfectly with the numerous utterances of our Lord and His interpreters in the New Testament that seemed to teach a subordination of the Son. The fallacy in this, as mature theology pointed out in time, was a failure to distinguish between the pre-existent, eternal God-head of the Son and His Incarnate condition—His living a human life and having a human will and consciousness. Furthermore, such a Christology (= science of Christ) could never do justice to the heart of New Testament Christianity, namely, that God was verily in Christ and that the Divine love expressing itself in His sacrifice was of the very nature of Absolute Deity.

A second attempt at solving the problem presented by the Trinity was made early in the third century. It was made in Rome by a man named Sabellius. His proposal was startling in its originality and simplicity. He advocated, in a word, untying the Gordian knot by cutting it in two. God is one; He is the Divine monad. This is the clear teaching of the Scriptures. It is equally clear that God appeared to men and made Himself known as Father, as Son, and as Holy Spirit. Both things being true, the obvious solution is that the Trinity is one of manifestation. God is like an actor on the Greek stage; He is able to take different parts at different times by putting on a new mask or face. (This is the literal and original meaning of the Greek word for person, Prósópon, which was applied by Sabellius to the roles of Father, Son, and Spirit.) He was influenced, I believe, at this point by noting (a) that in the Old Testament God patently appears in diverse ways, and (b) that according to the Fourth Gospel the Holy Spirit does not come until the Son is glorified.[6]

The Sabellian interpretation of the Trinity is tenable only if we allow such an exposition of "one place of Scripture, that it be repugnant to another" (Article xx). It does irreparable violence to the Christian facts. It is, further, a highly sophisticated and a too cleverly simple view. Yet it had two strong points, which have left a permanent impress upon subsequent Trinitarian theology. It taught that the Persons of the Trinity were entirely equal and that Christ was fully God. Neither point was ever forgotten in Western teaching, and both were ultimately accepted, with only the slightest modification in respect of the first, by Greek or Eastern theology.

It is unnecessary to say anything more about the contribution of St. Athanasius to thought regarding the Trinity. His work was to assert the Trinitarian character of Christianity as a religion. He put great emphasis, too, upon the unity of God. An Oxford lecturer in theology used to say in his classroom, with pardonable exaggeration, that "Athanasius was the only man in the fourth century who was more afraid of polytheism than of unitarianism." But he elected to stay out of the deeper waters of speculation and analogical research with a view to greater understanding. In this respect he resembles a great Christian and Bishop of the late second century, St. Irenaeus of Lyons in Gaul.

The first real theologians of the Trinity, after the Council of Nicaea and the long-drawn-out but decisive and final repulse of Arianism, were the so-called Cappadocian Fathers, Basil of Caesarea, Gregory of Nyssa, and Gregory of Nazianzus. These are the men behind the formula of Constantinople in A.D. 382, cited and emphasized above. They were typical Easterners, university men, trained in logic and philosophy. They were for a time under Semi-Arian influence (the most conservative school of Arianism which was willing to say that Christ was of *like* but not *the same* substance as the Father—*homoiousion* not *homoousion*—and thus gave Gibbon and Carlyle the chance to invent neat epigrams on the theme that the fate of the world hung on an iota or i). They used in their earlier thinking the analogy of three men and a common manhood. They were prepared, even as mature theologians, to see the Christian doctrine of the Trinity as a *via media* between Judaism and Paganism. They set out instinctively from the reality of the Trinity, conceived as given with Christianity itself, and then sought to reconcile the threeness of God with His unity.

The solution which the Cappadocians reached was something like this. Each Divine person (hypostasis was their preferred term—see definition above) was entirely and perfectly God. He partook without addition or subtraction of the Divine essence or being. He had every attribute of Godhead. He differed from the other two Persons only in having a distinct subsistence (= absolute existence, such as only God has). The idea of generation (compare the Nicene Creed: "begotten, not made") was carefully separated from its human and finite associations and pared down to mean a permanent, eternally distinct mode of Divine existence (trópos hurádzeos). No more could be said of the distinct existence of the Father except that He was logically prior to the Son. Of the distinct person of the Spirit, likewise, no further specific definition could be given. This is the basis for the unconsciously dry remark of the Greek Summit or Summarizer of doctrine, John of Damascus, in the eighth century:

> The Holy Spirit is from the Father, not by generation, but by procession; that there is a difference between the two we have been taught, but wherein they differ we know not.

It would be easy to gain from a bare summary of this kind the impression that the Cappadocian Fathers were dry-as-dust logicians and no more. This would be to do them a grave injustice. There is in their writings, especially perhaps those of Gregory of Nazianzus, a spirit of devotion and a sense of rapt adoration in the very thought of the Blessed Trinity that are not unworthy of comparison with anything in the history of Christian literature. Here is a sample from the Gregory just mentioned:

> Adoring Father, Son, and Holy Ghost; knowing the Father in the Son, and the Son in the Holy Ghost—into whose names we were baptized, in which we have believed; under whose banner we have been enlisted; dividing Them before we combine Them, and combining before we divide; not receiving the Three as one Person (for they are not impersonal or names of one Person, as though our wealth lay in names alone and not in facts), but the three as one Thing for they are One, not in Person but in Godhead, Unity adored in Trinity, and Trinity summed up in Unity; all adorable, all royal, of one throne and one glory; above the world, above time, uncreated, invisible, impalpable, uncircumscript; in Its relation to Itself known only to Itself but to us equally venerable and adorable; alone dwelling in the Holiest, and leaving all creatures outside and shut off.

This passage brings out a special quality of Cappadocian Trinitarianism. No theologians have ever been more convinced than these Fathers of the reality of the Trinity or more resolute in their faith. For them God is first and foremost the Father, the Son, and the Holy Spirit. They reveal no disposition to explain away the Divine Threeness, in an ultimately Sabellian manner, as a necessity of our thought arising out of the division and plurality native to us. At the same time it must be confessed that the Cappadocians tended to solve the problem in terms of logical abstractions and to be satisfied with the result. They evince no interest in psychology or the social nature of man as affording possibly an analogical purchase for vaulting into the empyrean of high speculation. It is here that St. Augustine comes into the picture.

In Augustine's work on the Trinity all previous major influences converge. In some cases they are pruned of excess and always they are reforged in the crucible of his own mind, but they are there. The essentially psychological analogy of the rational Word is present. The Sabellian note of an absolute equality of the three Persons is present. So is the strongly monotheistic and Biblical slant on the Divine unity that was characteristic of Athanasius; and also the "modal" interpretation of the three Persons, with each identically God from the standpoint of being or all concrete qualities. Finally, Augustine introduces into Trinitarian thought an appeal to the Johannine dictum, "God is Love," and in his analysis of it utilizes necessarily the analogy of human love and friendship. This was not a totally new idea. The great Gnostic Valentinus, in the second century, had a not dissimilar idea. (See the quotation at the head of this chapter.) Presumably it was the excess of the Gnostic mythology that brought into disrepute this approach. Also, as has happened several times since, Christianity gave reason a new lease on life. It was rational categories that attracted the Greek Christian Fathers. With the analogy of love Augustine combined the notion of the Spirit as the union or communion of the Father and the Son. This common bond is love, in distinction from lover and object of love. From this combination of conceptions is derived the thought that the Holy Spirit is in a special sense Love.

Such was the inheritance of St. Augustine as he undertook, not wholly willingly, the task of endeavoring to understand more clearly the mystery of the Trinity. In some ways it was an embarrassment of riches. Also Augustine was a true Christian in having a sense of intellectual as well as personal humility. He was keenly aware of the limitations of the human mind. In his long and repetitious work *On the Trinity*, he is constantly urging his inability to get far in his chosen task. The mystery of light is too great. It blinds. (This must be the present writer's defense, too, if in the end the reader feels a sense of disappointment in the answer given to the question which is the title of this chapter.)

Still Augustine did pursue, with energy and persistence, his aim. Briefly, these are the conclusions which he reached. The Scriptures teach that the one God, who is Creator of the world, is a Trinity. They speak not only of a Father who is God, but of an only begotten Son Jesus Christ, who is God made man, and of a Holy Spirit, who is likewise God. The Son, as His name implies, is generated or begotten. This is best understood by examining our own minds and their power of knowledge. The Son of God is eternally generated as the object of the Divine self-knowledge. With God, however, such a relation is subsistent and personal. It is the Divine substance or Godhead in a distinct mode of existence, and is absolutely equal to the Father. There is no subordination.

Augustine then carries his psychological analogy a step further. As there is generated within the mind of God a perfect object, so there proceeds an accompanying motion of His will, which is Love. This Love, which is of the Son or Divine *alter ego*, is likewise a personal relation. It is the Godhead in a distinct mode of existence. The third Person, also, is on an absolute equality with the other two, and is equal to the entire Trinity. Both as Spirit (John 4:24) and as Love (I John 4:8, 16), He is in a special manner the content of Deity or, as Augustine liked to say, the vinculum or bond uniting the Father and the Son.

Is this Trinity social or not? Is the eternal Divine love to be conceived in line with the analogy of human affection or in terms of self-love? This is a problem on which I have pondered a long time. No certain answer, I presume, can be given. Augustine starts out, after opening up the analysis of the proposition "God is Love," on a social tack. Then he gets cold feet and spends most of his remaining space on analogies derived from individual human personality. But now and again he is drawn back to the first idea. He was, it would seem, powerfully attracted to the idea of a communion of Father and Son within the unity of the Holy Spirit, whose special name is Love. But he was unable to see the compatibility of genuine sociality in God with the Divine unity, which he conceived, in company with all rational philosophers and theologians of antiquity, mathematically and rigidly, not as an organic manifold—at once single and plural.

In any case it was the image of the solitary thinker and solitary lover that became the standard rationale of the Trinity for the next fifteen hundred years. There is, I believe, no evidence (here Dean Rashdall was right) that St. Thomas Aquinas entertained any notion of a Divine sociality. Indeed he appears to wish it to be understood explicitly that alterity in a social sense is not required by the concept of infinite or perfect goodness.[7] There are sporadic appeals to Augustine's *dicta* on Love, and occasionally a writer, like Richard of St. Victor (d. A.D. 1173) sets forth boldly a social doctrine of the Trinity. Bishop George Bull in the late seventeenth century, in responding to the request of an English lord for an explanation of the Trinity, put forward a social construction with a eudaemonistic tinge. Since God must be thought of as having "self-sufficiency and most perfect bliss and happiness in himself alone, before and without all created things . . . it plainly appears, that himself alone is a most perfect and blessed society, the Father, the Son, and the Spirit eternally conversing with and enjoying one another."

Broadly speaking, however, the psychological analogy of St. Augustine commanded the field until Hegel. (The Reformers eschewed rational speculation as much as possible, but this renunciation included also any social analogy.) The parallel between the influence of the *City of God* of Augustine and that of his *On the Trinity* is very close. As it was Hegel who put forward a new philosophy of history in terms not of two opposing cities corresponding to opposing loves but of the self-evolution of one Absolute Spirit, so it was he who revived the Philonic and Greek Christian speculation that the generation of the Son was the creation of the world. Following Augustine, however, and at the same time altering him, Hegel made the Spirit the focus of Divine unity, or, in his terminology, the final and absolute moment in the process of the Divine self-consciousness. For Hegel the world ultimately is God, and God is the innermost, true reality of the world.

The second major development in nineteenth century Trinitarianism was a very widespread conscious turning to a social doctrine of God. By the end of the century this trend had assumed the proportions of a landslip[8] on a continental scale. Undoubtedly it was in part a reflection in theology of the instinct manifest in social reform, socialism, the social Gospel so-called, social psychology, and the various social sciences. From literally scores of possible illustrations of the new emphasis, we select a few sentences from a volume published in 1903 by an eminent American divine, born in Scotland, George A. Gordon. Gordon went to Harvard College after he had finished a theological seminary, and became a serious student of Greek philosophy. It is said that he was accustomed to read the works of Aristotle in the original for his winter reading, and the dialogues of Plato for his summer reading. On one occasion he remarked of these two thinkers, "Everything is in them."

For Gordon the truth behind the symbol of the Trinity is "the essentially social nature of God; the faith that he is in his innermost being an eternal family." "Love in man is passion for another; its existence depends upon the society in which man is placed. Love in God must mean passion for another; its reality depends upon the society in the Godhead." "The Christian doctrine of the Trinity is the full statement of the truth at which Greek mythology aimed. . . . Put into the Godhead some reality answering to the words, the Father and the Son and the Holy Spirit, and one is able to conceive of God's existence as ineffably blessed, and as containing in itself the ground of human society."

Such a view, at first largely accepted, ran in time into heavy opposition. In one of his first published works, *The Nature of Personality*, the late Archbishop William Temple (then a young philosophy don at Oxford) wrote, "We are not . . . called upon to handle riddles such as, How can God be Love if there is no object for His love? For there is the whole Universe for such object." Professor Pringle-Pattison directed to this version of the Trinity the most withering criticism of which as an idealist philosopher he was capable. Dean Rashdall spent much time in his later years exposing its fallacy. Dr. F. R. Tennant of the University of Cambridge, one of the greatest philosophical theologians so far produced in this century, holds that there is no point of view intermediate between Monarchianism (or Sabellianism) and Tritheism that can claim empirical or logical standing ground. He has put forward as a possible solution of the problem an ethicised Christian Tritheism, without committing himself personally to this speculation. Where are we today with respect to some kind of ultimate construction and understanding of the doctrine of the Trinity? The issues are perhaps in clearer and sharper focus than for a good while.

They involve a choice between three alternative interpretations or theories of the Trinity. The first is Sabellianism. It might be better to say essential Sabellianism. The time is by when any good purpose is served through muddying the stream of clear thinking by technical evasions of the charge of Sabellianism. It is easily possible to do this in the case of lines of thought that convey much that is meaningful and true about the nature of God but that refrain from asserting a Trinity of persons, since the main trend of the Sabellian fragments in our possession indicates a temporal succession in the manifesting of the "persons" of the Father, the Son, and the Spirit. The heart of the Sabellian view is, however, not the side issue of time and God, but the fundamental thesis that the Trinity is one of appearance or experience, not of the being of God.

The second possibility is a "modal" construction of the Trinity. (The word "modal" I coin so as to distinguish the view in question from "modalism," a synonym in the textbooks for "Sabellianism.") This is the doctrine to which the Cappadocians finally came and which is the main trunk of developed Eastern Trinitarian theory. It was transmitted to the West, perhaps as a modification of Sabellianism, and has existed in Trinitarian thought since Augustine as one among several elements of a less static and a more dynamic but more subtle and difficult conception.

A useful illustration of the modal notion is the standard tradition of Byzantine art with respect to the depiction of the Blessed Trinity. In marked contrast to the use of artists in the medieval West, marked by a simple fidelity to the Bible, this tradition calls for three identical human figures, mature in countenance rather than old, with the middle figure identified by a cross. Gregory of Nazianzus uses the metaphor of "one mingling of light, as it were of three suns joined together." The point that these illustrations are meant to bring out is that there is one identical Divine being in point of internal content, but that this Being, God Himself, exists really and objectively in a threefold manner—as Father, as Son, and as Holy Spirit. Or, in the words of an eminent professor of the University of Cambridge, the late Dr. J. F. Bethune-Baker, the "Catholic interpretation" of the Trinity is that of "one God existing permanently and eternally in three spheres of consciousness and activity, three modes, three forms, three persons: in the inner relations of the divine life as well as in the outer relations of the Godhead to the world and to men."

There is much to be said for the modal view of the Trinity. It avoids both Sabellianism and Tritheism. It says clearly that the Trinity is not merely a matter of revelation as registered in our experience, but is of the nature of God. Further, the three Persons can rightly be seen as having particular and distinctive functions alike in creation and in redemption. They can be intelligibly thought of as the object of Christian worship and faith. For long I was persuaded that this construction of the doctrine of the Trinity was not only the one most decisively indicated by Christian tradition viewed as a whole, but also the wisest and soundest solution of the intellectual problem presented by this doctrine.

It now seems to me that this conclusion is of doubtful validity. The modal view has numerous strong features, but it has two grave and possibly fatal defects:

1. It has no clear analogy in human experience. Man is a personality; he is the self-conscious union of feeling, intellect, and will; he is a being who desires and reasons. Here is a possible analogy to the being of God, especially if man be regarded, as by Christianity, as created in the image of God. Or, man is a social being. Personality is a social product, and lives and thrives only in a context of social relations. The human being may be egocentric to an extreme degree, but even at the moment of his most intense egoism he is the subject of other-regarding thoughts and desires. Here, too, is a clear-cut analogy to the being of God, who has thus created man. But of a God who is in some manner plural, who is in His essence a Trinity of persons, and who yet has within Himself no analogue of love, friendship, communion of souls, we have no analogy, no hint, in things human. This is perhaps the reason for the popularity, from the days of the Christian Fathers down to the generality of sermons preached on last Trinity Sunday, of impersonal and material analogies such as the sun, its ray, and a sunbeam; a fountain, a river, and a rivulet; water, ice, and vapor; and all the complicated diagrams of traditional Trinitarian symbolism.

2. The modal view leans too heavily on the relation of God to the world or creation (and redemption as a process set within it). It contains nothing within it that is intrinsically self-explanatory and intellectually satisfying from the standpoint of God-in-Himself. It is of course possible that creation is eternal and that there is no reason to posit a beginning (or presumably an end) of the world. This was the view of Aristotle and of Origen. St. Thomas Aquinas may have been prevented from espousing it only by the authority of the Catholic Church. It was revived by idealism in the nineteenth century. Modern Anglican theologians like Temple and W. R. Matthews have advocated it. The question is highly speculative. But there is much evidence adduced by modern scientific experiment and theory that is against an eternal creation . . . compare Sir James Jeans' *The Mysterious*

Universe and Sir Arthur Eddington's *The Nature of the Physical World*). Christian orthodoxy, influenced no doubt mainly by the Bible, is against it. And in any case the Christian doctrine of creation is decisive in asserting that God is independent of creation and in no way organic to it. If this be true, no one can dismiss the question of the nature of God-in-Himself, of the eternal and timeless essence and life of Godhead, as meaningless or irrelevant or futile. It is the most important question there is.

The third alternative in thought about the Trinity is the admission of the analogy of personal society, intercourse, and fellowship. It is the view that God within the unity of His Divine life experiences and comprehends communication, mutuality, love, and shared beatitude. It is the conception set forth by St. Augustine in expounding St. John's assertion that "God is Love," but from which he shrank back, feeling, as it were, an excess of light, as he tried thus to think of God. Here he is wiser than many expositors of a social God in the late nineteenth and early twentieth centuries. We shall do well, if we embrace the third alternative, as I am persuaded we must to be truly and fully Christian in our thinking about God, to imitate the candor and theological modesty of the great Doctor and Bishop of Hippo.

In accepting and trying to state in terms that are valid for the Being of God the social analogy, great care must be taken to safeguard and to emphasize the ultimate and absolute unity of God. On this Christian tradition, following Holy Scripture, is adamant in firmness and unmistakable in clarity. There is, however, nothing in the Christian revelation that requires a unity conceived in terms of a mathematical abstraction. It so happened that classical theology was dominated by Greek modes of thought, which had been elaborated when mathematics was the supreme science. The analogy of a complex organism, animated by a single organizing principle or center but constituted out of diverse elements, is just as valid so far as the idea of unity is concerned, and is required if any sense is to be made of the conception of three Persons in one God. Professor Hodgson has advanced Trinitarian thought by insisting on this in his recent book, already cited.

In addition, and finally, we shall be helped, and a certain break, not with the orthodox dogma of the Trinity, but with the standard elaborations of it by the majority of classical theologians, will be cushioned if we keep in mind the position . . . that it is more reasonable to face and accept the fact that every resort to analogy in trying to think about God ends in symbolic and mythopoeic representation, than it is to pretend that pure reason yields valid and satisfactory conclusions in theology. Christianity stands at this point midway between the rationalism of Western philosophy in its main line and the self-conscious ideologism of Marxist thought and of the prevailing contemporary mentality. Applied to the doctrine of the Trinity, this means that the Christian facts, plus the logic of the highest and most satisfactory analogy which human experience yields, demand a realistic, dramatic, and mythological interpretation of the being and the relations of Father, Son, and Holy Spirit.

It remains to attempt a very simple statement of the doctrine of the Trinity. Taking our lead from Holy Scripture and from many passages in the ancient Fathers, we shall make this statement as concrete as possible. We shall give it the form of a description of the being of God as Trinity and Unity. Such a description will necessarily be in part a picture. And since God has given us only one portrait of Himself, and that in a mode adapted to our vision and understanding, namely, human flesh, our attempt at portraiture of Eternal Divinity will have to be done with the aid of imagination. But we have also and must use reason, working on the basis of (a) the Christian facts and (b) the principles and ideas worked out and tested through centuries of exact and exacting thought by Christian Doctors and philosophers.

In the beginning God, called at divers time and with differing meanings "Father," created the heavens and the earth. But in this work of making worlds God the Father was not alone. With Him was the Logos (Word), and the Logos was God. Through the Logos, in whom dwelt perfectly as in an identical image the whole mind of God, were all things made (John 1:1-3).

With God, also, was His Spirit, identical with Him in knowledge, the searcher of "all things, yea, the deep things of God" (I Cor. 2:10), yet ever proceeding from Him and at the same time abiding with Him. Through the Spirit, also, were all things made. His it was to brood over the face of ancient waters and to give both energy to matter and breath to living things (Gen. 1:2).

In the beginning, then, was God the Father, and with Him His Word or only begotten Son and the uncreated Divine Spirit. Not with the creation did this Trinity come into being; rather from before all beginnings and apart from all succession, timelessly and eternally, God was a Triune God. He was both One and Three. He was alone —the only, awful, invisible, unapproachable, inconceivable ground of all things and abyss of all being. Yet He was not alone—not blank existence, not an immovable, everlasting fixture, not a lifeless absolute or an impersonal structure of universal order. In Him, of His very essence as God, was life, motion, self-knowledge, self-communication, self-giving, love, bliss, beatitude. How could it be otherwise when, as the writer says, "At thy right hand there is pleasure forevermore"?[9]

Whence arose these qualities, and how is it that God is within Himself not sheer unity but a complex and manifold being, the union and communion of three Divine persons? Such a question is very difficult. The answer, as Plato said long ago of the problem of the creation and generation of the world, is hard to come at and indeed can only be given in the form of a likely story. Or, we might say, a fitting picture or representation. We have, however, with regard to the question of the eternal Trinity a long tradition of reflection and imaginative thought by men who worshiped and prayed to the God of whose nature and being they desired to form the best and truest conception that was possible.

As these men have taught us, and looking also ourselves at the Scriptures as well as using to the best of our ability our own minds, we may speak in this wise of the origin and nature of the Divine Trinity. God is in Himself thought and energy, knowledge and will, reason and love. But in Him these qualities exist not as attributes now active and then passive, as with us. They exist in Him in the fullness of perfect actuality, and this actuality gives rise to a plurality of persons within the being of the One God (or in the technical language of classical Trinitarianism—a multiplicity of concrete individual determinations of the Divine essence or substance). God as personal, conscious subject knows Himself as object. This knowledge involves a bringing into existence or generation, from all eternity, of an other—a perfect or identical image of the Father, in which the Father sees Himself, His own mind, and all truth, all beauty, and all goodness. Yet this other is living and substantial. It is a real Divine *alter ego*. Or, to put it another way, God, in knowing Himself, utters or projects or begets Himself as a distinct Divine person. This self-utterance of God is the eternal Word or Son.

But God is also love. In Him, if we know what we are saying, there is infinite desire, infinitely and perfectly satisfied. (For the benefit of any theologians who may read this book, such a statement is not incompatible with the essential and distilled truth of the idea of the impassibility of God—an idea designed to bring out the contrast between the conditions of Divine life and the changes, chances, sufferings, and passions of mortal human life.) So in the uttering of the Word, from which act we must try to think away time and becoming as we know them, we are not dealing with pure intellectual contemplation. Thinker and thought there must be, but that the thought must be personal and substantive, we do not know. The generation of the Son occurs, therefore, because it is the nature of God as Love to communicate Himself. Simultaneously with this generation there goes forth or proceeds from the same Divine subject a burning and yet never to be consumed fire of love. This Godly *dilectio*, this Primal energy of spirit and motion of will, is likewise not transient and a mere quality, as with us, but is a subsistent Person—the eternal Spirit.

Such is the Holy Trinity, so far as we can apprehend and make real to our minds this Three-Personal God of Christian worship and faith. Within the unity of one God there are three real and distinct

Persons, three centers of consciousness, will, and activity. Each is a personal agent, fully God. Yet each partakes of and has His being in the same identical Godhead, and is constituted internally by the same attributes and a common Divine consciousness. Thus there is a real sharing, a genuine communion, an authentic love. But the diversity is within a unity which in intensity and completeness surpasses all human thought and imagination.

This means that the action of one Divine person is His own and at the same time the work of the undivided Trinity. The climax of this is seen in the Incarnation, which is of the Word and hence is in a special sense a deed of the only Son of God. Yet it is also an act of the whole Trinity. The same applies to the sovereignty of the Father in history, the immanence of the Spirit in the Church, and the presence of Christ in the Holy Eucharist. St. Thomas Aquinas is right in the invocation of his Eucharistic hymn:

> O Saving Victim, opening wide
> The gate of heaven to man below.

He is equally right in passing at once to the praise of the undivided and eternal Trinity.

> All praise and thanks to thee ascend
> For evermore, blest One in Three.

We have to do at every point with the love of the blessed Trinity—love in action, love manifested to us—but love first of being, love that eternally is, and love in which there is a true participation and fellowship of three Divine persons, the Father, the Son, and the Holy Spirit.

Notes

[1]John 16:8.

[2]II Tim. 2:15.

[3]The word "dogmas" could be used equally well, if with less precision. The number of Christian dogmas, if we stick to a rigid definition and use the term to mean an enacted and authoritatively set forth view or teaching, is small. The General Councils were pretty well occupied with two subjects, the Trinity and the Incarnation. Yet who would question that there is a Christian dogma, or doctrine carrying weight or authority, of the Atonement, of the Eucharist, of man, etc.?

[4]Included in all English Books of Common Prayer beginning with 1549 and including the "Deposited" Book of 1928; omitted in all American Books beginning with the first "proposed" Book, which was never approved by a General Convention.

[5]Italics mine. This doxology was introduced into the Revised American Prayer Book of 1928. It is evidently taken from the Roman Breviary, where it forms a part of the special doxology that follows the *Benedicite* in the service of *Lauds.* This doxology is said to have been composed by Pope Damascus (A.D. 306?-384).

[6]John 7:39.

[7]*Summa Theologica, Treatise on the Trinity,* Qu. 32, Art. 1 (*ad secundum*).

[8]Or, landslide.

[9]Ps. 16:12.

29

Augustine

The Trinity

We are indeed seeking a trinity, but not any trinity at all, but that Trinity which is God, and the true, the supreme, and the only God. Keep waiting, therefore, whoever you are, who hear these words. For we are still seeking, and no one rightly blames him for engaging in such a search, provided only that he remain firmly-rooted in the faith, while he seeks that which it is so difficult to know or to express.

But he who sees or teaches better, may quickly and justly find fault with him who speaks positively concerning it. "Seek God," he says, "and your soul shall live."[1] And that no one might rashly rejoice as though he had apprehended Him, he declared: "Seek his face evermore."[2] And the Apostle states: "If anyone thinks that he knows anything, he does not yet know as he ought to know. But if anyone loves God, the same is known by him."[3] He certainly did not express it in this way: "He knew Him," for that would be a dangerous presumption, but "he is known by him." In another place, too, when he had spoken as follows: "But now you know God," he immediately corrected himself: "or rather you are known by God."[4] And above all in that passage: "Brethren," he said, "I do not con-

From Augustinus Aurelius, *The Trinity*, Book Nine, Chs. 1-12. Washington: Catholic University of America Press, 1963.

sider that I myself have laid hold of this. But one thing I do: forgetting what is behind, I strain forward to what is before. I press on in purpose towards the goal of God's heavenly call in Christ Jesus. Let us then, as many as are perfect, be of this mind."[5]

He says that perfection in this life is to forget what is behind, and to press forward in purpose towards the goal that lies before us. For the safest purpose for him who seeks is to continue seeking until he has laid hold of that towards which we tend and for which we are striving. But the right purpose is that which proceeds from faith. For a certain faith is in some way the beginning of knowledge, but a certain knowledge will only be perfected after this life when we shall see face to face.[6] Let us then be of this mind: so as to know that the inclination to seek the truth is safer than the presumption which regards unknown things as known. Let us, therefore, so seek as if we were about to find, and so find as if we were about to seek. For "when a man has done, then he begins."[7]

Let us not doubt with unbelief about things to be believed, and let us affirm without rashness about things to be understood; in the former case, authority is to be upheld; in the latter, the truth is to be sought. With regard to the question at hand, therefore, let us believe that the Father, the Son, and the Holy Spirit are one God, the Creator, and the ruler of the whole creature; that the Father is not the Son, nor is the Holy Spirit the Father or the Son, but that there is a trinity of inter-related persons, and the unity of an equal substance.

But let us seek to understand this, imploring the help of Him whom we wish to understand; and in the measure that He shall grant, desiring to explain what we understand, with such pious care and solicitude, that even if we should say one thing for another, we may yet say nothing that is unworthy of Him. For example, if we say something of the Father, which in the strict sense is not suitable to the Father, that it may at least be suitable to the Son, or to the Holy Spirit, or to the Trinity itself; and if we say anything of the Son, which does not properly belong to the Son, that it may at least belong to the Father, or to the Holy Spirit, or to the Trinity; and likewise if we say anything about the Holy Spirit, which may not be fittingly called a property of His, that it may, nevertheless, not be alien from the Father, or the Son, or from the one God, the Trinity itself.

We are now eager to see whether that most excellent love is proper to the Holy Spirit, and if it is not so, whether the Father, or the Son, or the Holy Trinity itself is love, since we cannot contradict the most certain faith and the most weighty authority of Scripture which says: "God is love."[8] Nevertheless, we should not be guilty of the sacrilegious error of attributing to the Trinity that which does not belong to the Creator, but rather to the creature, or is imagined by mere empty thought.

Since this is the case, let us fix our attention on these three things which we seem to have discovered. We are not yet speaking of heavenly things, not yet of God the Father, the Son, and the Holy Spirit, but of this imperfect image, which is an image nevertheless, that is, of man. For the weakness of our mind perhaps gazes upon the image more familiarly and more easily.

Behold, when I, who conduct this inquiry, love something, then three things are found: I, what I love, and the love itself. For I do not love love, except I love a lover, for there is no love where nothing is loved. There are, therefore, three: the lover, the beloved, and the love. But what if I love only myself? In that case will there be only two, what I love and the love? For the lover and the beloved are one and the same when one loves himself, as to love and to be loved are in like manner one and the same when anyone loves himself. For the same thing is said twice when it is said, he loves himself, and he is loved by himself. For here to love is not one thing, and to be loved another thing, just as the lover is not one person and the beloved another person. But yet even so, the love and the beloved are two. For there is no love when anyone loves himself, except when the love itself is loved. But it is one thing to love oneself and another thing to love one's love. For love is not loved unless as already loving something; for where nothing is loved, there is no love. Hence, when anyone loves himself there are two: the love and what is loved, for here the lover and the beloved are one.

It does not seem to follow, therefore, that wherever there is love, three things must be understood. For let us not consider in this inquiry the many other things of which man is composed; and that we may clearly discover what we are now seeking, insofar as we can discover anything at all in these questions, let us confine the discussion to the mind alone.[9]

When the mind, then, loves itself it makes known two things: the mind and the love. But what does to love oneself mean, other than to desire to help oneself to enjoy oneself. And when anyone wishes himself to be just as much as he is, then the will is equal to the mind, and the love is equal to the lover. And if love is a substance, it is certainly not body but spirit; the mind is not body but spirit. Yet love and mind are not two spirits, but one spirit; not two essences, but one essence; and still the two are one, the lover and the love, or, so to say, the beloved and the love. And these two are truly said to be mutually related. The lover is referred to the love and the love to the lover. For the lover loves with some love, and love is of someone who loves.

But mind and spirit are not spoken of relatively, but denote essence. For mind and spirit do not exist, therefore, because mind and spirit exist in some particular man. Even if we take away the body from that which is man, which he is called with the addition of the body, the mind and the spirit still remain; but if you take away the lover, there is no love; and if you take away the love, there is no lover. Insofar, therefore, as they are mutually related, they are two; but when they are spoken of in respect to themselves, each is spirit, and both together are one spirit; and each is mind and both together are one mind. Where, then, is the Trinity? Let us concentrate as much as we can, and call upon the everlasting light to enlighten our darkness, so that we may see the image of God in ourselves, insofar as we are permitted.

The mind cannot love itself unless it also knows itself, for how can it love what it does not know? Or if anyone says that the mind by a general or special knowledge believes that it is such, as he knows from experience that others are, he is speaking in a very foolish manner. For whence does a mind know another mind if it does not know itself? For not as the eye of the body sees other eyes and does not see itself, so does the mind know other minds and does not know itself. For we see bodies through the eyes of the body, because we cannot refract the rays which shine through them and touch whatever we see, and reflect them back into the eyes themselves, except when we are looking into a mirror. But this is a subject that is discussed very subtly and very obscurely, until it can be clearly shown whether it is actually so, or whether it is not so.

But whatever may be the nature of the power by which we see through the eyes, we certainly do not see the power itself, whether it be rays or anything else, with the eyes, but we seek it in the mind; and if it is possible, we also comprehend it in the mind. As the mind itself, therefore, gathers the knowledge of corporeal things through the bodily senses, so it gains the knowledge of incorporeal things through itself, since it is incorporeal. For if it does not know itself, it does not love itself.

But just as there are two things, the mind and its love, when it loves itself, so there are two things, the mind and its knowledge, when it knows itself. Therefore, the mind itself, its love and its knowledge are a kind of trinity; these three are one, and when they are perfect they are equal. For if anyone loves himself less than he is —if, for example, the mind of man loves itself as much as the body of man is to be loved, whereas the mind is more than the body—he is guilty of sin and his love is not perfect. Similarly, if he loves himself more than he is—if, for example, he loves himself as much as God is to be loved, whereas he is incomparably less than God—he also sins by excess and does not have a perfect love of himself. But he sins with greater perversity and malice when he loves the body as much as God is to be loved.

His knowledge, likewise, is not perfect if it is less than the object known, when this is fully knowable. But if it is greater, then the nature which knows is superior to that which is known, just as the knowledge of the body is greater than the body itself which is known by that knowledge. For knowledge is a kind of life in the understanding of one who knows; but the body is not life. And any life is greater than the body, not in bulk but in power. But when the mind knows itself, its knowledge does not surpass it, because itself knows and itself is known. When the mind, therefore, knows itself fully and nothing else with itself, then its knowledge is equal to it, because its knowledge is not from another nature when it knows itself. And when it perceives itself fully and nothing more, then its knowledge is neither less nor greater than itself. We have, therefore, rightly said that when these three are perfect, they are necessarily equal.

We are also reminded at the same time, if we can in any way visualize it, that these [knowledge and love] exist in the soul; they are, so to speak, so folded within it that, when unfolded, they are perceived to be numbered substantially, or, what is the same thing, essentially. They are not in the soul as in a subject, as color, or shape, or any other quality or quantity are in the body. For anything of this kind [i.e., an accident] does not extend beyond the subject in which it is. Thus the color or the shape of this body cannot be the color or the shape of another body. But the mind can also love something else besides itself by the same love by which it loves itself.

Similarly, the mind does not know itself alone, but also many other things. Therefore, love and knowledge are not in the mind as in a subject, but they are also there substantially as the mind itself is. For even though they are spoken of as mutually related, yet each is there in its own substance. Nor is the relationship that we predicate of them the same as that of color and a colored subject. For color is in a colored subject, but does not have its own proper substance in itself, for the colored body is the substance, but the color is in the substance; the relationship is rather that of two friends, who are also men, which are substances; since they are not said to be men relatively, but friends relatively.

Moreover, although the one who loves or knows is a substance, and love is a substance, and knowledge is a substance, but the lover and the love, or the knower and the knowledge, are spoken of in relation to each other as are friends; yet mind or spirit are not relative terms, as men are not; in spite of this, the lover and the love, and the knower and the knowledge, cannot be separated from each other as men can be who are friends. Although it seems that friends can also be separated from each other in body, but not in mind, inasmuch as they are friends; but it can happen that a friend begins to hate a friend, and thereby ceases to be a friend, while the other does not know this and still loves him.

But if the love by which the mind loves itself ceases to be, then the mind will also cease to love at the same time; likewise, if the knowledge by which the mind knows itself ceases to be, the mind will also cease to know at the same time. Just as the head of anything having a head is certainly a head, and they are spoken of in relation to each other, although they are also substances; for the head is a body, as well as that which has a head; and if there is no head, neither will there be that which has a head. But these can be separated from each other by a simple cutting off; those cannot.

Even if there are some bodies which cannot be separated or divided at all, yet unless they were composed of their own parts they would not be bodies. It is called a part, therefore, in relation to the whole, because every part is a part of some whole, and the whole is a whole by having all of its parts. But since the part as well as the whole is a body, they not only express a relationship, but also possess their own being as substances. Perhaps the mind, therefore, is a whole, and its parts are as it were the love by which it loves itself, and the knowledge by which it knows itself, and from these two parts that whole is composed. Or are there three equal parts which complete that one whole? But no part embraces the whole of which it is a part; but when the mind knows itself as a whole, that is, knows itself perfectly, its knowledge extends through the whole of it; and when it loves itself perfectly, it loves itself as a whole, and its love diffuses itself through the whole of it. Or is it, therefore, that as one drink is made up of wine, water, and honey, each of which is found throughout the whole, and yet there are three (for there is no part of the drink which does not contain these three; they are not joined as if they were water and oil, but are mingled throughout and all are substances, and that whole liquid is one substance composed of three substances); so we are to consider these three, mind, love, and knowledge, as being together in some such way? But the water, the wine, and the honey are not of one substance, although the one substance of the drink is brought about by mixing them together.

But I do not see how these three are not of the same substance, since the mind loves itself and knows itself, and these three so exist that the mind is neither loved by nor known to any other thing. These three, therefore, must necessarily be of one and the same substance, and consequently, if they were mingled together as it were in a confused mass, then they would in no way be three, nor could they be mutually related. It is just as if you were to make three similar rings from one and the same gold; although they are connected with one another, yet they are related to one another in that they are similar, for everything similar is similar to something. In this case you have a trinity of rings and one gold. But if they are melted together, and the gold is spread thoughout the whole of its own mass, then that trinity will perish and will cease altogether; and not only will it be called one gold, as it was called in the example of the three rings, but now it will not be called a golden trinity.

But in these three, when the mind knows itself and loves itself, a trinity remains: the mind, love, and knowledge; and there is no confusion through any commingling, although each is a substance in itself, and all are found mutually in all, whether each one in each two, or each two in each one. Consequently, all are in all. For the mind is certainly in itself, since it is called a mind in respect to itself, although in relation to its knowledge it is spoken of as knowing, as being known, or as knowable; and when referring to the love by which it loves itself, it is also spoken of as loving, as being loved, or as lovable. And knowledge, although it is referred to a mind that either knows or is known, yet in respect to itself it is also spoken of both as known and as knowing, for the knowledge by which the mind itself knows itself is not unknown to itself. And love, although it is referred to the mind that loves, of which it is the love, yet it is likewise love in respect to itself, so that it also exists in itself. For love is also loved, nor can it be loved with anything else except with love, that is, with itself. And so each exists in itself. But they are mutually in each other in such a way that the mind that loves is in the love, and love is in the knowledge of him that loves, and knowledge is in the mind that knows.

And so each one is in each two, because the mind that knows and loves itself is in its own love and knowledge; and the love of the mind that knows and loves itself is in the mind and in its knowledge; and the knowledge of the mind that knows and loves itself is in the mind and in its love; because it loves itself as knowing and knows itself as loving. And for this reason each two are also in each one, because the mind that knows and loves itself is in the love with its knowledge, and in the knowledge with its love, since the love itself and the knowledge are also together in the mind that loves and knows itself. But we have shown above, how all are in all, since the mind loves itself as a whole, and knows itself as a whole, and knows all its love, and loves all its knowledge, when these three are perfect in respect to themselves. These three, therefore, are in a marvelous manner inseparable from one another; and yet each of them is a substance, and all together are one substance or essence, while the terms themselves express a mutual relationship.

When the human mind, however, knows itself and loves itself, it does not know and love something immutable; each individual man, attentive to what is going on within him, speaks in one way when he expresses his own mind, but defines the human mind in a different way by a special and general knowledge. Therefore, when anyone speaks to me about his own mind, as to whether he understands or does not understand this or that, and whether he wishes or does not wish this or that, I believe what he says; but when he speaks the truth about the human mind, either specially or generally, I recognize it and approve.

It is, therefore, obvious that what a person sees in himself is one thing, for another does not see this but believes what the speaker tells him; but what he sees in the truth itself is another thing, for another can also behold the same thing; the former is changeable in time, while the latter remains steadfast in its unchangeable eternity. For it is not by seeing many minds with our bodily eyes that we gather, by way of analogy, a general or special knowledge of the human mind; but we contemplate the inviolable truth, whence we can as perfectly as possible define, not what each man's mind is, but what it ought to be in the light of the eternal types.

Whence the images of corporeal things also, which we draw in through the bodily sense and which flow in some way into the memory, and from which things that have not been seen are also presented to the mind under a fancied image, whether it contradicts the reality or by chance agrees with it, are approved or disapproved within ourselves by rules that are wholly different, which remain unchangeably above our mind when we rightly approve or disapprove of anything. Thus, when I call to mind the walls of Carthage which I have seen, and form an image of those of Alexandria which I have not seen, and prefer some of these imaginary forms to others, I prefer them for a good reason; the judgment of the truth from above is strong and clear, and remains steadfast by the most incorruptible rules of its own right; and even if it is concealed by bodily images, as by a kind of cloud, still it is not hidden nor confused.

But it does make a difference, whether, while I am under or in that darkness, I am shut off as it were from the clear heavens or, as usually happens on the highest mountains, whether I behold the most dazzling light above and the most dense clouds below, while enjoying the free air between both. For whence is the flame of brotherly love enkindled in me, when I hear of any man who has suffered bitter torments in defense of the beauty and the strength of the faith? And if this man himself is pointed out to me with the finger, I am eager to be united with him, to make myself known to him, and to bind him to myself in friendship. Therefore, if given the opportunity, I approach him, address him, engage him in conversation, express my affection for him in whatever words I can; and in turn I wish that the same affection should be brought about in him and expressed towards me; and since I cannot discern so quickly and investigate his innermost heart thoroughly, I strive after a spiritual embrace in the way of faith. Therefore, I love a faithful and strong man with a chaste and genuine love.

If in the course of our talk, however, he were to confess to me, or in an unguarded moment were somehow to let it be known that he either believes absurd things concerning God, and is even seeking for some carnal good in Him, and has endured those torments in defense of such an error, or from the desire of money for which he hoped, or else from an excessive eagerness for human praise, that love by which I was borne towards him is at once offended, and as it were rejected. But, although my love is withdrawn from that unworthy man, yet it remains in that form, according to which I had loved him when I believed him to be such. Unless perhaps I now love him for this purpose, that he may be such, when I had ascertained that he was not such.

But nothing has been changed in that man; yet he can be changed and can become what I had once believed him to be. But the estimation itself, which I formerly had of him in my mind, is not the same as that which I now have, and it certainly has undergone a change. And the same love has likewise been turned from the purpose of finding pleasure to the purpose of providing help, by virtue of the unchangeable justice commanding me from above. Nevertheless, the form of the unshaken and abiding truth itself, wherein I should have found enjoyment in that man when I believed him to be good, and wherein I counsel him to be good, sheds in its imperturbable eternity the same light of the incorruptible and most sound reason upon the glance of my mind, as well as upon the cloud of images which I discern from above, when I again think of this same man whom I have seen.

Something similar takes place when I recall a beautifully and symmetrically intorted arch which I have seen, for example, in Carthage. In this case a certain reality, which was made known to my mind through the eyes and transferred to my memory, produces an imaginary view. But in my mind I behold something else, according to which that work pleases me; whence also, I should correct it if it displeased me. Therefore, we pass judgment upon these particular things according to that form of the eternal truth, and we perceive that form through the eye of the rational mind. But these particular things we touch, if present, with the bodily sense, or recall them, if absent, through the image fixed in our memory, or form images of things that are similar to them, such as we ourselves would also endeavor to construct, if we wished and were able. For we form images of bodies in our mind or see bodies through the body in one way, but we comprehend in a different way the types and the ineffably beautiful art of such forms, as are above the eye of the mind, by simple intelligence.

With the eye of the mind, therefore, we perceive in that eternal truth, from which all temporal things have been made, the form according to which we are, and by which we effect something either in ourselves or in bodies with a true and right reason. The true knowledge of things, thence conceived, we bear with us as a word, and beget by speaking from within; nor does it depart from us by being born. But in conversing with others we add the service of our voice or of some bodily sign to the word that remains within, in order to produce in the mind of the listener, by a kind of sensible remembrance, something similar to that which does not depart from the mind of the speaker. Thus there is nothing that we do through the members of our body, in our words and actions, by which the conduct of men is approved or disapproved, that is not preceded by the word that has been brought forth within us. For no one willingly does anything which he has not spoken previously in his heart.

This word is conceived in love, whether it be the word of the creature or the word of the Creator, that is, of a changeable nature or of the unchangeable truth. Therefore, it is conceived either by desire [*cupiditis*], or love [*caritas*]: not that the creature ought not to be loved, but if that love for him is referred to the Creator, it will no longer be desire but love. For desire is then present when the creature is loved on account of himself. Then it does not help him who uses it, but corrupts him who enjoys it. Since the creature, therefore, is either equal or inferior to us, we must use the inferior for God and enjoy the equal, but in God. For just as you ought to enjoy yourself, but not in yourself but in Him who made you, so you ought also to enjoy him whom you love as yourself. And, therefore, let us enjoy ourselves and our brethren in the Lord, and not dare to return from there to ourselves, and, as it were, to let ourselves slip downwards. But the word is born when that which is thought pleases us, either for the purpose of committing sin or of acting rightly. Love, therefore, as a means, joins our word with the mind from which it is born; and as a third it binds itself with them in an incorporeal embrace, without any confusion.

The word that has been conceived and born is one and the same when the will rests in the knowledge of itself; this happens in the love of spiritual things. For example, he who knows justice perfectly and loves it perfectly is already just, even though the necessity does not exist for acting outwardly according to it through the members of his body. But in the love of carnal and temporal things, as in the offspring of animals, the conception of the word is one thing and the birth another thing. In such cases, what is conceived by desiring is born by attaining. For it does not suffice for avarice to know and love gold, unless it also possesses it; nor does it suffice to know and love to eat and to lie together, unless these actions are also performed; nor does it suffice to know and love honors and power, unless they are obtained. But all of these things do not suffice, even when they are acquired. "For he who shall drink of this water," He said, "shall thirst again."[10] And, therefore, it is also said in the Psalm: "He conceived sorrow and brought forth iniquity."[11] He says that sorrow or labor is conceived when those things are conceived which it does not suffice to know and to desire, and when the mind yearns for and grows sick for the want of them, until it arrives at them and as it were begets them. And for this reason *parta* [brought forth] is elegantly used in Latin for *reperta* [found] and *comperta* [discovered]; and these words sound as if they are derived from *partus* [bringing forth]. For "when conscupiscence has conceived, it brings forth sin."[12] Wherefore the Lord cries out: 'Come to me, all you who labor and are burdened,'[13] and in another place: 'Woe to those who are with child or have infants at the breast in those days.' "[14] Since he referred all things, whether rightly done or sins, to the bringing forth of the word He said: "For by thy mouth thou wilt be justified, and by thy mouth thou wilt be condemned."[15] He wanted mouth to be understood not in the sense of this visible mouth, but of that which is invisible and within, of the thought and the heart.

The question, then, is rightly raised, whether all knowledge is a word, or only knowledge that is loved. For we also know those things which we hate; but those that displease us cannot be said to be either conceived or brought forth in the mind. For not all things which touch it in any way are conceived; some things are only known, but may not be called words, as those we are now discussing. For we use the term "word" in one sense, when we speak of words which fill a determined space of time with their syllables, whether they are spoken or simply thought; in a different sense, when everything that is known is called a word impressed on our mind, as long as it can be brought forth from our memory and defined, even though the thing itself displeases us; and in still another sense when that which is conceived by the mind pleases us. What the Apostle says is to be understood according to this last kind of "word": "No one says, 'Lord Jesus,' except in the Holy Spirit";[16] while they also say the same thing according to another meaning of "word," of whom the Lord Himself declares: "Not everyone who says to me, 'Lord, Lord,' shall enter into the kingdom of heaven."[17]

But when we are rightly displeased with, and rightly disapprove of those things which we also hate, our disapproval of them is approved, is pleasing to us, and is a word. Neither does the knowledge of vices displease us, but the vices themselves. For I am pleased at being able to know and define what intemperance is, and this is its word. Just as there are known faults in art, and the knowledge of them is rightly approved when an expert discerns the species and the lack of excellence, so as to affirm and to deny that it is and that it is not; still to be lacking in excellence and to be guilty of a fault is blameworthy. To define intemperance and to express its word belongs to the science of ethics, but to be intemperate belongs to what is branded as a fault by this science. To know and define what a solecism is belongs to the art of speaking, but to be guilty of such is a defect which this same art blames. The word, therefore, which we now wish to discern and study is knowledge with love. Hence, when the mind knows and loves itself, its word is joined to it by love. And because the mind loves its knowledge and knows its love, then the word is in the love and love in the word, and both are in him who loves and who speaks.

But all knowledge according to the species is similar to that which it knows. For there is, in addition, a knowledge according to privation, which we express when we disapprove of anything. And this disapproval of privation praises the species, and, therefore, is approved. The mind, therefore, possesses a certain likeness of the species known to it, whether we are pleased with the species or displeased with its privation.

Wherefore, we are like God inasmuch as we know Him, but we are not like Him to the extent of being His equal, because we do not know Him as He Himself knows Himself. And as, when we learn of bodies through our bodily sense, some likeness of them arises in our mind, and is a phantasm of the memory (for the bodies themselves are by no means in our mind when we think of them, but only their likenesses. Were we, therefore, to approve of the object for the image, we would be in error, for the approval of one thing for another is an error. Yet the image of the body in the mind is better than that bodily species, insofar as it is in a better nature, that is, in a living substance, such as the mind is); so, when we know God, although we become better than we were before we knew Him, and especially when this knowledge also pleases us, and worthily loved, is a word, and thereby produces some similarity to God, yet that knowledge is less than He, because it is in a lower nature; for the mind is creature, but God is Creator.

We conclude from this that, when the mind knows itself and approves what it knows, this same knowledge is in such way its word, that it is wholly and entirely on a par with it, is equal to, and is identical with it, because it is not the knowledge of a lower essence, such as the body, nor of a higher essence such as God. And since knowledge has a likeness to that thing which it knows, namely, that of which it is the knowledge, then in this case it has a perfect and equal likeness, because the mind itself, which knows, is known. And, therefore, knowledge is both its image and its word, because it is an expression of that mind and is equalled to it by knowing, and because what is begotten is equal to its begetter.

What, then, is love? Will it not be an image? Will it not be a word? Will it not be begotten? For why should the mind beget its knowledge when its knows itself, and not beget its love when it loves itself? For if the cause of its knowing is, therefore, that it is knowable, then the cause of its loving is also that it is lovable. That being so, it is difficult to say why it has not begotten both. And this same question also arises in regard to the most exalted Trinity itself, the most omnipotent God the Creator, to whose image man has been made, and it is wont to disturb men, whom the truth of God invites to the faith through human language. Why, they ask, is not the Holy Spirit also believed or understood to be begotten by God the Father, so that He Himself may likewise be called the Son?

We are now endeavoring in one way or another to investigate this question in the human mind; and after the inferior image has responded as it were to our interrogation in language, with which our human nature itself is more familiar, we may be able to direct a better-trained mental vision from the illuminated creature to the unchangeable light; we pre-suppose, however, that the truth itself has persuaded us that, as no Christian doubts, the Son is the Word of God, so the Holy Spirit is love. Let us return, therefore, to that image which the creature is, that is, to the rational soul for a more careful questioning and consideration of this matter. The knowledge of some things that exist in time which were not there previously, and the love of some things which were not loved previously, opens the way for us to explain more clearly what we have to say, because it is easier to explain the things which are comprehended in the order of time, to speech itself which must also be sent forth in time.

To begin with, it is, therefore, clear that something can be knowable, that is, it can be the object of knowledge, and yet it may not be known; but it is impossible for something to be known that is not knowable. Therefore, we must obviously hold fast to this principle that everything which we know begets the knowledge of itself within us at the same time. For knowledge is born from both, from the one who knows and the object that is known. When the mind, therefore, knows itself, it alone is the parent of its own knowledge, for it is itself both the object known and the one that knows. It was, however, knowable to itself, even before it knew itself; but the knowledge of itself was not in it, since it had not yet known itself. Hence, when it knows itself, it begets a knowledge of itself, that is equal to itself. For it does not know itself as less than it is, nor is its knowledge that of another essence, not only because it is itself that which knows, but also because it knows itself, as we have said above.

What, then, are we to say about love? When the mind loves itself, does it not also seem to have begotten the love of itself? For it was lovable to itself even before it loved itself, because it could love itself, just as it was knowable to itself even before it knew itself, because it could know itself. For if it were not knowable to itself, it would never have been able to know itself; so, if it were not lovable to itself, it would never have been able to love itself. Why do we not say, therefore, that it has begotten its own love, as we say that by knowing itself it has begotten its own knowledge? Is it, perhaps, to indicate clearly that this is the principle of love from which it proceeds—for it proceeds from the mind itself that is lovable to itself before it loves itself, and so is the principle of its own love by which it loves itself—but that it is, therefore, not rightly said to be begotten by the mind, as is the knowedge of itself by which it knows itself, because that has already been found through knowledge which is called born or discovered [*partum vel repertum*], and is usually preceded by a search which will come to rest in knowledge as its goal?

For inquiry is a desire to find, which is the same as saying, to discover. But things that are discovered are as it were brought forth. Hence, they are similar to an offspring; but how else are they born, except through knowledge itself? For they are as it were uttered there and formed. For even though the things already were which we find by seeking, yet the knowledge itself did not exist which we regard as an offspring that is born. Further, that desire, which is latent in seeking, proceeds from one who seeks, remains as it were in suspense, and only comes to rest in the goal towards which it is directed, when that which is sought has been found and is united with him who seeks. Although this desire, that is, this seeking does not seem to be love, by which that which is known is loved, for we are still striving to know, yet it is something of the same kind.

For it can already be called will, since everyone who seeks wishes to find; and if what he seeks belongs to the order of knowledge, then everyone who seeks wishes to know. And if he wishes it ardently and earnestly, he is said to study, a term we generally use for those who pursue and acquire any branch of learning. A kind of desire, therefore, precedes the birth in the mind, and by means of it, that is, by our seeking and finding what we wish to know, an offspring, namely, knowledge itself is born. Therefore, that desire by which knowledge is conceived and born cannot be rightly called a birth and offspring; and this same desire by which one yearns for the knowing of the thing becomes love of the thing when known, while it holds and embraces the beloved offspring, that is, knowledge, and unites it to its begetter.

And so there is a certain image of the Trinity: the mind itself, its knowledge, which is its offspring, and love as a third; these three are one and one substance. The offspring is not less, while the mind knows itself as much as it is; nor is the love less, while the mind loves itself as much as it knows and as much as it is.

Notes

[1] Cf. Ps. 68:33.

[2] Ps. 104:4.

[3] I Cor. 8:2-3.

[4] Gal. 4:9.

[5] Cf. Phil. 3:13-15.

[6] I Cor. 13:12.

[7] Ecclus. 18:6.

[8] I John 4:16.

[9] By "mind," St. Augustine means the "intellectual soul."

[10] John 4:13.

[11] Cf. Ps. 7:15.

[12] Cf. James 1:15.

[13] Matt. 11:28.

[14] Matt. 24:19.

[15] Cf. Matt. 12:37.

[16] I Cor. 12:3.

[17] Matt. 7:21.

God Plans

30

Charles Hodge

The Decrees of God

The Nature of the Decrees

It must be remembered that theology is not philosophy. It does not assume to discover truth, or to reconcile what it teaches as true with all other truths. Its province is simply to state what God has revealed in His Word, and to vindicate those statements as far as possible from misconceptions and objections. This limited and humble office of theology it is especially necessary to bear in mind, when we come to speak of the acts and purposes of God. "The things of God knoweth no man; but the Spirit of God" (I Cor. 2:11). In treating, therefore, of the decrees of God, all that is proposed is simply to state what the Spirit has seen fit to reveal on that subject.

"The decrees of God are his eternal purpose, according to the counsel of his will, whereby for his own glory He hath foreordained whatsoever comes to pass."[1] Agreeably to this statement: (1) The end or final cause contemplated in all God's decrees, is His own glory. (2) They are all reducible to one eternal purpose. (3) They are free and sovereign, determined by the counsel of His own will. (4) They comprehend all events.

From Charles Hodge, *Systematic Theology*, Grand Rapids: Wm. B. Eerdmans Pub. Co., 1952.

The Glory of God the Final Cause of All His Decrees

The final cause of all God's purposes is His own glory. This is frequently declared to be the end of all things. "Thou art worthy," say the heavenly worshippers, "O Lord, to receive glory, and honour, and power: for thou hast created all things, and for thy pleasure they were created" (Rev. 4:11). All things are said to be not only of God and through Him, but for Him. He is the beginning and the end. The heavens declare His glory; that is the purpose for which they were made. God frequently announces His determination to make His glory known. "As truly as I live, all the earth shall be filled with the glory of the Lord" (Num. 14:21). This is said to be the end of all the dispensations of His providence, whether beneficent or punitive. "For mine own sake, even for mine own sake, will I do it; for how should my name be polluted? and I will not give my glory unto another" (Isa. 48:11). "I wrought for my name's sake, that it should not be polluted before the heathen" (Ezek. 20:9). In like manner the whole plan of redemption and the dispensations of His grace, are declared to be designed to reveal the glory of God (I Cor. 1:26-31; Eph. 2:8-10). This is the end which our Lord proposed to Himself. He did everything for the glory of God; and for this end all His followers are required to live and act. As God is infinite, and all creatures are as nothing in comparison with Him, it is plain that the revelation of His nature and perfections must be the highest conceivable end of all things, and the most conducive to secure all other good subordinate ends. Order and truth, however, depend on things being put in their right relations. If we make the good of the creature the ultimate object of all God's works, then we subordinate God to the creature, and endless confusion and unavoidable error are the consequence. It is characteristic of the Bible that it places God first, and the good of the creation second. This also is the characteristic feature of Augustinianism as distinguished from all other forms of doctrine. And when the Protestants were divided at the time of the Reformation, it was mainly on this point. The Lutheran and Reformed churches are distinguished in all that characterizes their theological systems, by the fact that the latter allow the supremacy and sovereignty of God in the workings of His providence and grace to determine everything for His own glory, while the former lean more or less to the error of restraining God's liberty of action by the assumed powers and prerogatives of man. The Bible, Augustine, and the Reformed, give one answer to all such questions as the following: Why did God create the world? Why did He permit the occurrence of sin? Why was salvation provided for men and not for angels? Why was the knowledge of that salvation so long confined to one people? Why among those who hear the gospel, do some receive and others reject it? To all these, and similar questions, the answer is not because the happiness of creatures would be secured in a higher degree by the admission of sin and misery, than by their entire exclusion; some men are saved and others perish not because some of their own will believe and others do not believe, but simply because, Thus it seemed good in the eyes of God. Whatever He does or permits to be done, is done or permitted for the more perfect revelation of His nature and perfections. As the knowledge of God is the ground and sum of all good, it of course follows that the more perfectly God is known, the more fully the highest good (not merely nor necessarily the highest happiness) of the intelligent universe is promoted. But this is a subordinate effect, and not the chief end. It is therefore in accordance with the whole spirit and teachings of the Bible, and with the essential character of Augustinianism, that our standards make the glory of God the end of all His decrees.

The Decrees Reducible to One Purpose

The second point included in this doctrine is, that the decrees of God are all reducible to one purpose. By this is meant that from the indefinite number of systems, or series of possible events, present to the divine mind, God determined on the futurition or actual occurrence of the existing order of things, with all its changes, minute as well as great, from the beginning of time to all eternity. The reason, therefore, why any event occurs, or, that it passes from the category of the possible into that of the actual, is that God has so decreed. The decrees of God, therefore, are not many, but one purpose. They are not successively formed as the emergency arises, but are all parts of one all-comprehending plan. This view of the subject is rendered necessary by the nature of an infinitely perfect Being. It is inconsistent with the idea of absolute perfection, that the purposes of God are successive, or that He ever purposes what He did not originally intend; or that one part of His plan is independent of other parts. It is one scheme, and therefore one purpose. As, however, this one purpose includes an indefinite number of events, and as those events are mutually related, we therefore speak of the decrees of God as many, and as having a certain order. The Scriptures consequently speak of the judgments, counsels, or purposes of God, in the plural number, and also of His determining one event because of another. When we look at an extensive building, or a complicated machine, we perceive at once the multiplicity of their parts, and their mutual relations. Our conception of the building or of the machine is one, and yet it comprehends many distinct perceptions, and the apprehension of their relations. So also in the mind of the architect or mechanist, the whole is one idea, though he intends many things, and one in reference to another. We can, therefore, in a measure, understand how the vast scheme of creation, providence, and redemption, lies in the divine mind as one simple purpose, although including an infinite multiplicity of causes and effects.

The Decrees of God Are Eternal

That the decrees of God are eternal, necessarily follows from the perfection of the divine Being. He cannot be supposed to have at one time plans or purposes which He had not at another. He sees the end from the beginning; the distinctions of time have no reference to Him who inhabits eternity. The Scriptures therefore always speak of events in time as revelations of a purpose formed in eternity. The salvation of men, for example, is said to be "according to the eternal purpose which he purposed in Christ Jesus" (Eph. 3:11). What is revealed in time was hidden for ages, i.e., from eternity in the mind of God (Eph. 3:9). Believers were chosen in Christ before the foundation of the world (Eph. 1:4). "Who hath saved us, and called us . . . according to his own purpose and grace, which was given us in Christ Jesus, before eternal ages" (II Tim. 1:9). Christ as a sacrifice was "foreordained before the foundation of the world, but was manifest in these last times for you, who by him do believe in God" (I Peter 1:20, 21; Rom. 11:33-36; Acts 2:23). This is the constant representation of Scripture. History in all its details, even the most minute, is but the evolution of the eternal purposes of God. It is no objection to this doctrine that the Scriptures often represent one purpose of God as consequent upon another, or that they speak of His purposes as determined by the conduct of men. The language of Scripture is founded on apparent truth; they speak, as men always do, as things appear, not as they themselves know or believe them to be. We speak of the concave heavens, or the firm foundation of the heavens, although we know that it is not concave, and that it does not rest on any foundation. So the Bible speaks of the decrees of God as they appear to us in their successive revelation and in their mutual relations, and not as they exist from eternity in the divine mind. Neither is there any force in the objection that the agent must be before his acts. The sun is not before his brightness, nor the mind before thought, nor life before consciousness, nor God before his purposes. These objections are founded on the assumption that God is subject to the limitations of time. To Him there is neither past nor future, neither before nor after.

The Decrees of God Are Immutable

Change of purpose arises either from the want of wisdom or from the want of power. As God is infinite in wisdom and power, there can be with Him no unforeseen emergency and no inadequacy of means, and nothing can resist the execution of His original intention. To Him, therefore, the causes of change have no existence. With God there is, as the Scriptures teach, "no variableness, neither shadow of turning" (James 1:17). "The counsel of the Lord standeth for ever, the thoughts of his heart to all generations" (Ps. 33:11). "The Lord of hosts hath sworn, saying, Surely as I have thought, so shall it come to pass; and as I have purposed, so shall it stand" (Isa. 14:24). "I am God . . . declaring the end from the beginning, and from ancient times the things that are not yet done, saying, My counsel shall stand, and I will do all my pleasure" (Isa. 46:9, 10). The uniformity of the laws of nature is a constant revelation of the immutability of God. They are now what they were at the beginning of time, and they are the same in every part of the universe. No less stable are the laws which regulate the operations of the reason and conscience. The whole government of God, as the God of nature and as moral governor, rests on the immutability of his counsels.

The Decrees of God Are Free

This includes three ideas—

1. They are rational determinations, founded on sufficient reasons. This is opposed to the doctrine of necessity, which assumes that God acts by a mere necessity of nature, and that all that occurs is due to the law of development or of self-manifestation of the divine being. This reduces God to a mere *natura naturans*, or *vis formativa*, which acts without design. The true doctrine is opposed also to the idea that the only cause of events is an intellectual force analogous to the instincts of irrational animals. The acts performed under the guidance of instinct are not free acts, for liberty is a *libentia rationalis*, spontaneity determined by reason. It is therefore involved in the idea of God as a rational and personal being that His decrees are free. He was free to create or not to create; to create such a world as now is, or one entirely different. He is free to act or not act, and when He purposes, it is not from any blind necessity, but according to the counsel of His own will.

2. Our purposes are free, even when formed under the influence of other minds. We may be argued or persuaded into certain courses of action, or induced to form our designs out of regard to the wishes or interests of others. God is infinitely exalted above all *ab extra* influence. "Who hath known the mind of the Lord? or who hath been his counsellor?" (Rom. 11:34). "Behold, God exalteth by his power: who teacheth like him? Who hath enjoined him his way?" (Job 36:22, 23). "Who hath directed the Spirit of the Lord? or being his counsellor hath taught him? With whom took he counsel, and who instructed him, and taught him in the path of judgment?" (Isa. 40:13, 14). "Who hath known the mind of the Lord, that he may instruct him?" (I Cor. 2:16). God adopted the plan of the universe on the ground of His own good pleasure, for His own glory, and every subordinate part of it in reference to the whole. His decrees are free, therefore, in a far higher sense than that in which the ordinary purposes of men are free. They were formed purely on the counsel of His own will. He purposes and does what seemeth good in His sight.

3. The decrees of God are free in the sense of being absolute or

sovereign. The meaning of this proposition is expressed negatively by saying that the decrees of God are in no case conditional. The event decreed is suspended on a condition, but the purpose of God is not. It is inconsistent with the nature of God to assume suspense or indecision on His part. If He has not absolutely determined on what is to occur, but waits until an undetermined condition is or is not fulfilled, then His decrees can neither be eternal or immutable. He purposes one thing if the condition be fulfilled, and another if it be not fulfilled, and thus everything must be uncertain not only in the divine mind, but also in the event. The Scriptures, therefore, teach that He doeth whatsoever He pleaseth (Ps. 11:3). He doeth His pleasure in the army of heaven, and among the inhabitants of the earth (Dan. 4:35; Ps. 135:6). Of Him, and through Him, and to Him are all things (Rom. 11:36). It is expressly taught that the purposes of God, even as to the future destiny of men, are founded on His own good pleasure. As all have sinned and come short of the glory of God, He has mercy upon whom He will have mercy. It is not according to our works, but of His grace that He saves us. It is of Him that we are in Christ Jesus, that those who glory should glory in the Lord (Matt. 11:26; Rom. 8:29, 30; 9:15-18; Eph. 1:5; etc.).

The Decrees of God Are Certainly Efficacious

The decrees of God are certainly efficacious, that is, they render certain the occurrence of what He decrees. Whatever God fore-ordains, must certainly come to pass. The distinction between the efficient (or efficacious) and the permissive decrees of God, although important, has no relation to the certainty of events. All events embraced in the purpose of God are equally certain, whether He has determined to bring them to pass by His own power, or simply to permit their occurrence through the agency of His creatures. It was no less certain from eternity that Satan would tempt our first parents, and that they would fall, than that God would send His Son to die for sinners. The distinction in question has reference only to the relation which events bear to the efficiency of God. Some things He purposes to do, others He decrees to permit to be done. He effects good, He permits evil. He is the author of the one, but not of the other. With this explanation, the proposition that the decrees of God are certainly efficacious, or render certain all events to which they refer, stands good. This is proved,—

1. From the perfection of God, which forbids the ascription to Him of purposes uncertain as to their accomplishment. No man fails to execute what he purposes, except through the want of wisdom or power to secure the end proposed or through some vacillation in his own mind. It would be to reduce God to the level of His creatures, to assume that what He decrees, should fail to come to pass.

2. From the unity of God's plan. If that plan comprehends all

events, all events stand in mutual relation and dependence. If one part fails, the whole may fail or be thrown into confusion.

3. From the evident concatenation of events in the progress of history, which proves that all things are intimately connected, the most important events often depending on the most trivial, which shows that all must be comprehended in the plan of God.

4. From the providential and moral government of God. There could be no certainty in either if the decrees of God were not efficacious. There could be no assurance that any divine prophecy, promise, or threatening, would be accomplished. All ground of confidence in God would thus be lost, and chance and not God would become the arbiter of all events. The Scriptures variously and constantly teach this doctrine, (a) By all those passages which assert the immutability and sovereignty of the divine decrees. (b) By those which affirm that He fixes the bounds of our habitations, that our days are all numbered, and that even a hair from our heads cannot perish without His notice. (c) By those which declare that nothing can counteract His designs. "The Lord of hosts," says the prophet, "hath purposed, who shall disannul it? And his hand is stretched out, and who shall turn it back" (Isa. 14:27). "I will work, and who shall let it?" (43:13). (d) By those which teach doctrines that necessarily assume the certainty of all God's decrees. The whole plan of redemption rests on that foundation. It is inconceivable that God should devise such a scheme, and not secure its execution, and that He should send His Son into the world, and leave the consequences of that infinite condescension undetermined. It is therefore, the doctrine of reason as well as of Scripture, that God has a plan or end for which the universe was created, that the execution of that plan is not left contingent, and that whatever is embraced in the decrees of God must certainly come to pass.

The Decrees of God Relate to All Events

God foreordains whatsoever comes to pass. Some events are necessary, that is, are brought about by the action of necessary causes; others are contingent or free, or are acts of free agents; some are morally good, others are sinful. The doctrine of the Bible is, that all events, whether necessary or contingent, good or sinful, are included in the purpose of God, and that their futurition or actual occurrence is rendered absolutely certain. This is evident,—

1. From the unity of the divine purposes. That unity supposes that the whole scheme of creation, providence, and redemption was fixed by the divine decree. It was formed from ages in the divine mind, and is gradually unfolded by the course of events. It is therefore inconsistent with this sublime and Scriptural representation, to suppose that any class of actual events, and especially that class which is most influential and important, should be omitted from the divine

purpose. He who purposes a machine, purposes all its parts. The general who plans a campaign, includes all the movements of every corps, division, and brigade in his army, and if his foresight were perfect, and his control of events absolute, his foreordination would extend to every act of every soldier. Whatever is wanting in his fore-ordination is due to the limitation of human power. As God is infinite in knowledge and resources, His purpose must include all events.

2. It is therefore inconsistent with the perfection of God to suppose either that He could not form a plan comprehending all events, or that He could not carry it into execution, without doing violence to the nature of His creatures.

3. The universality of the decree follows from the universal dominion of God. Whatever He does, He certainly purposed to do. Whatever He permits to occur, He certainly purposed to permit. Nothing can occur that was not foreseen, and if foreseen it must have been intended. As the Scriptures teach that the providential control of God extends to all events, even the most minute, they do thereby teach that His decrees are equally comprehensive.

4. Another argument is derived from the certainty of the divine government. As all events are more or less intimately connected, and as God works by means, if God does not determine the means as well as the event, all certainty as to the event itself would be destroyed. In determining the redemption of man, He thereby determined on the mission, incarnation, sufferings, death, and resurrection of His Son, on the gift of the Spirit, upon the faith, repentance, and perseverance of all His people. The prediction of future events, which often depend on the most fortuitous occurrences, or which include those that appear to us of no account, proves that the certainty of the divine administration rests on the foreordination of God extending to all events both great and small.

The Scriptures in various ways teach that God foreordains whatever comes to pass.

1. They teach that God works all things according to the counsel of His will. There is nothing to limit the words "all things," and therefore they must be taken in the fullest extent.

2. It is expressly declared that fortuitous events, that is, events which depend on causes so subtle and so rapid in their operation as to elude our observation, are predetermined; as the falling of the lot, the flight of an arrow, the falling of a sparrow, the number of the hairs of our heads.

Free Acts Are Foreordained

3. The Bible especially declares that the free acts of men are decreed beforehand. This is involved in the doctrine of prophecy, which assumes that events involving the free acts of a multitude of men are foreseen and foreordained. God promises to give faith, a new

heart, to write His law upon the minds of His people, to work in them to will and to do, to convert the Gentiles, to fill the world with the true worshippers of Christ, to whom every knee is gladly to bow. If God has promised these things, He must of course purpose them, but they all involve the free acts of men.

4. The Scriptures teach that sinful acts, as well as such as are holy, are foreordained. In Acts 2:23, it is said, "Him, being delivered by the determinate counsel and foreknowledge of God, ye have taken, and by wicked hands have crucified and slain;" 5:27, "For of a truth against thy holy child Jesus, whom thou hast anointed, both Herod and Pontius Pilate, with the Gentiles and the people of Israel were gathered together, for to do whatsoever thy hand and thy counsel determined before to be done." "Truly the Son of Man goeth as it was determined; but woe unto that man by whom he is betrayed" (Luke 22:22). It was foreordained that He should be betrayed; but woe to him who fulfilled the decree. Here foreordination and responsibility are by our Lord Himself declared to coexist and to be consistent. In Rev. 17:17, it is said, "God hath put in their hearts to fulfil his will, and to agree, and give their kingdom unto the beast, until the words of God shall be fulfilled." The crucifixion of Christ was beyond doubt foreordained of God. It was, however, the greatest crime ever committed. It is therefore beyond all doubt the doctrine of the Bible that sin is foreordained.

5. Besides this, the conquests of Nebuchadnezzar, the destruction of Jerusalem, and many other similar events, were predicted, and therefore predetermined, but they included the commission of innumerable sins, without which the predictions, and consequently the revealed purposes of God, could not have been accomplished.

6. The whole course of history is represented as the development of the plan and purposes of God; and yet human history is little else than the history of sin. No one can read the simple narrative concerning Joseph, as given in the book of Genesis, without seeing that everything in his history occurred in execution of a preconceived purpose of God. The envy of his brethren, their selling him into Egypt, and his unjust imprisonment, were all embraced in God's plan. "God," as Joseph himself said to his brethren, "sent me before you, to preserve you a posterity in the earth, and to save your lives by a great deliverance. So now it was not you that sent me hither, but God" (Gen. 45: 7, 8). This is but an illustration. What is true of the history of Joseph, is true of all history. It is the development of the plan of God. God is in history, and although we cannot trace His path step by step, yet it is plain in the general survey of events, through long periods, that they are ordered by God to the accomplishment of His divine purposes. This is obvious enough in the history of the Jewish nation, as recorded in the Scripture, but it is no less true in regard to all history. The acts of the wicked in

persecuting the early Church, were ordained of God as the means for the wider and more speedy proclamation of the Gospel. The sufferings of the martyrs were the means not only of extending but of purifying the Church. The apostasy of the man of sin being predicted, was predetermined. The destruction of the Huguenots in France, the persecution of the Puritans in England, laid the foundation for the planting of North America with a race of godly and energetic men, who were to make this land the land of refuge for the nations, the home of liberty, civil and religious. It would destroy the confidence of God's people could they be persuaded that God does not foreordain whatsoever comes to pass. It is because the Lord reigns, and doeth His pleasure in heaven and on earth, that they repose in perfect security under His guidance and protection.

Objections to the Doctrine of Divine Decrees

Foreordination Inconsistent with Free Agency

It is urged that the foreordination of all events in inconsistent with the free agency of man. The force of this objection depends on what is meant by a free act. To decide whether two things are inconsistent, the nature of each must be determined. By the decrees of God are to be understood the purpose of God rendering certain the occurrence of future events. By a free act is meant an act of rational self-determination by an intelligent person. If such an act is from its very nature contingent, or uncertain, then it is clear that foreordination is inconsistent with free agency. This theory of liberty has been adopted by a large body of philosophers and theologians, and is for them an insuperable objection to the doctrine of the divine decrees. In answer to the objection, it may be remarked, (1) That it bears with equal force against foreknowledge. What is foreknown must be certain, as much as what is foreordained. If the one, therefore, be inconsistent with liberty, so also is the other. This is sometimes candidly admitted. Socinus argues that the knowledge of God embraces all that is knowable. Future free actions being uncertain, are not the objects of knowledge, and therefore it is no impeachment of the divine omniscience to say that they cannot be known. But then they cannot be predicted. We find, however, that the Scriptures are filled with such predictions. It is, therefore, evident that the sacred writers fully believed that free acts are foreknown by the divine mind, and therefore are certain as to their occurrence. Besides, if God cannot foreknow how free agents will act, He must be ignorant of the future, and be constantly increasing in knowledge. This is so incompatible with all proper ideas of the infinite mind, that it has been almost universally rejected, both by philosophers and by Christian theologians. A still weaker evasion is that proposed by some Arminian writers, who admit that God's knowledge is not limited by anything out of Himself, but hold that it may be limited by His own will. In creating free agents, He willed not to foreknow how they would act, in order to leave their freedom unimpaired. But this is to suppose that God wills not to be God; that the Infinite wills to be finite. Knowledge with God is not founded on His will, except so far as the knowledge of vision is concerned, i.e., His knowledge of His own purposes, or of what He has decreed shall come to pass. If not founded on His will, it cannot be limited by it. Infinite knowledge must know all things, actual or possible. It may, however, be said that there is a difference between foreknowledge and foreordination, in so far that the former merely assumes the certainty of future events, whereas the latter causes their futurition. But as the certainty of occurrence is the same in both cases, it makes no difference as to the matter in hand. The decree only renders the event certain; and therefore if certainty be not inconsistent with liberty, then foreordination is not. That an event may be free and yet certain, may be easily proved. (1) It is a matter of consciousness. We are often absolutely certain how we shall act, so far as we are free to act at all, and conscious that we act freely. A parent may be certain that he will succor a child in distress, and be conscious that his free agency is not thereby impaired. The more certain, in many cases, the more perfectly are we self-controlled. (2) Free acts have been predicted, and therefore their occurrence was certain. (3) Nothing was more certain than that our Lord would continue holy, harmless, and undefiled, yet His acts were all free. (4) It is certain that the people of God will repent, believe, and persevere in holiness forever in heaven, yet they do not cease to be free agents. The decrees of God, therefore, which only secure the certainty of events, are not inconsistent with liberty as to the mode of their occurrence. Although His purpose comprehends all things, and is immutable, yet thereby "no violence is offered to the will of the creatures, nor is the liberty or contingency of second causes taken away, but rather established."

Foreordination of Sin Inconsistent with Holiness

It is further objected that it is inconsistent with the holiness of God that He should foreordain sin. There are two methods of dealing with this and all similar objections. The one may be called the Scriptural method, as it is the one often adopted by the sacred writers. It consists in showing that the objection bears against the plain declarations of Scripture, or against the facts of experience. In either case, it is for us sufficiently answered. It is vain to argue that a holy and benevolent God cannot permit sin and misery, if sin and misery actually exist. It is vain to say that His impartiality forbids that there should be any diversity in the endowments, advantages, or happiness of His rational creatures. It is vain to insist that a holy God cannot permit children to suffer for the sins of their parents, when we constantly see that they do thus suffer. So it is utterly irrational to contend that God cannot foreordain sin, if He foreordained (as no Christian doubts) the crucifixion of Christ. The occurrence of sin in the plan adopted by God, is a palpable fact; the consistency, therefore, of foreordination with the holiness of God cannot rationally be denied. The second method of dealing with such objections is to show that the principle on which they are founded is unsound. The principle on which the objection under consideration rests, is that an agent is responsible for all the necessary or certain consequences of his acts. The objection is, that a holy God cannot decree the occurrence of sin, because His decree renders that occurrence certain. That is, an agent is responsible for whatever his act renders certain. That principle, however, is utterly untenable. A righteous judge, in pronouncing sentence on a criminal, may be sure that he will cause wicked and bitter feelings in the criminal's mind, or in the hearts of his friends, and yet the judge be guiltless. A father, in excluding a reprobate son from his family, may see that the inevitable consequence of such exclusion will be his greater wickedness, and yet the father may do right. It is the certain consequence of God's leaving the fallen angels and the finally impenitent to themselves, that they will continue in sin, and yet the holiness of God remain untarnished. The Bible clearly teaches that God judicially abandons men to their sins, giving them up to a reprobate mind, and He therein is most just and holy. It is not true, therefore, that an agent is responsible for all the certain consequences of his acts. It may be, and doubtless is, infinitely wise and just in God to permit the occurrence of sin, and to adopt a plan of which sin is a certain consequence or element; yet as He neither causes sin, nor tempts men to its commission, He is neither its author nor approver. He sees and knows that higher ends will be accomplished by its admission than by its exclusion, that a perfect exhibition of His infinite perfections will be thereby effected and therefore for the highest reason decrees that it shall occur through the free choice of responsible agents. Our great ground of confidence, however, is the assurance that the judge of all the earth must do right. Sin is, and God is; therefore the occurrence of sin must be consistent with His nature; and as its occurrence cannot have been unforeseen or undesigned, God's purpose or decree that it should occur must be consistent with His holiness.

The Doctrine of Decrees Destroys All Motive to Exertion

A third objection is, that the doctrine of foreordination, which supposes the certainty of all events, tends to the neglect of all use of means. If everything will happen just as God has predetermined, we need give ourselves no concern, and need make no effort. (1) This objection supposes that God has determined the end without reference to the means. The reverse, however, is true. The event is determined in connection with the means. If the latter fail, so will the former. God has decreed that men shall live by food. If any man refuses to eat, he will die. He has ordained that men shall be saved through faith. If a man refuses to believe, he will perish. If God has purposed that a man shall live, He has also purposed to preserve him from the suicidal folly of refusing to eat. (2) There is another fallacy included in this objection. It supposes that the certainty that an event will happen, acts as a motive to neglect the means of its attainment. This is not according to reason or experience. The stronger the hope of success, the greater the motive to exertion. If sure of success in the use of the appropriate means, the incentive to effort becomes as strong as it can be. On the other hand, the less hope, the less disposition there is to exert ourselves; and where there is no hope, there will be no exertion. The rational and Scriptural foundation for the use of means, and the proper motives to avail ourselves of them, are, (1) The command of God. (2) Their adaptation to produce the effect. (3) The divine ordination which makes the means necessary to the attainment of the end. And (4) The promise of God to give His blessing to those who obediently avail themselves of the means of His appointment.

It Is Fatalism

It is objected, in the fourth place, that the doctrine of decrees amounts to the heathen doctrine of fate. There is only one point of agreement between these doctrines. They both assume absolute certainty in the sequence of all events. They differ, however, not only as to the ground of that certainty, the nature of the influence by which it is secured, and the ends therein contemplated, but also in their natural effects on the reason and conscience of men.

The word Fatalism has been applied to different systems, some of which admit, while others deny or ignore the existence of a supreme intelligence. But in common usage it designates the doctrine that all events come to pass under the operation of a blind necessity. This system differs from the Scriptural doctrine of foreordination, (1) In that it excludes the idea of final causes. There is no end to which all things tend, and for the accomplishment of which they exist. According to the Scriptural doctrine, all things are ordained and controlled to accomplish the highest conceivable of possible good. (2) In that according to Fatalism the sequence of events is determined by an unintelligent concatenation of causes and effects. According to the doctrine of decrees, that sequence is determined by infinite wisdom and goodness. (3) Fatalism admits of no distinction between necessary and free causes. The acts of rational agents are as much determined by a necessity out of themselves as the operations of nature. According to the Scriptures, the freedom and responsibility of man are fully preserved. The two systems differ, therefore, as much as a machine differs from a man; or as the actions of infinite intelligence, power, and love differ from the law of gravitation. (4) The one system, therefore, leads to the denial of all moral distinctions, and to stolid insensibility or despair. The other to a sedulous regard to the will of an infinitely wise and good ruler, all whose acts are determined by a sufficient reason; and to filial confidence and submission.

Notes

[1]*Westminster Shorter Catechism*, 7.

31

Samuel Wakefield

The Decrees of God

We have hitherto considered God with regard to his existence, his nature and attributes, and the manner of his subsisting in a Trinity of Persons; but we will now proceed to contemplate him in his *acts* or *efficiency*.

The *acts* of God are, in theological language, either *internal* or *external*. His *internal* acts are either those which belong to himself alone, as the generation of the Son, and the procession of the Holy Ghost; or those which take place in himself with respect to external objects. Such are his *decrees* "which he hath purposed in himself." Eph. 1:9.

The *external* acts of God are those exertions of his power which terminate upon his creatures. These are comprehended in his works of *creation* and *providence*.

As it is reasonable to believe that God does nothing without previous deliberation, and thence resolving upon what his infinite wisdom perceives to be best, which resolves have obtained among divines the name of *decrees*, it will be proper, before we consider his external acts, to present a scriptural view of these decrees; and to this subject

From Samuel Wakefield, *Complete System of Christian Theology*, New York: Eaton and Mains, 1869.

our attention will be directed in the present chapter. We will *first* prove their existence, and *secondly*, inquire into their nature and properties.

The Existence of the Divine Decrees

No one who believes God to be an intelligent being, and who considers what intelligence implies, will deny that there are Divine decrees. As God knew all things that his power could accomplish, there were undoubtedly reasons which determined him to do certain things in preference to others, and his choice, which was founded upon those reasons, was his purpose or decree.

It will certainly be admitted, that God intended to create the world before he actually created it; that he intended to make man before he fashioned his body, and breathed into him the breath of life; and that he intended to govern the world according to certain laws. It will be admitted also, that when he resolved to create the world, to make man, and to establish laws physical and moral, he had some ultimate object in view. Having constructed a machine and set it in motion, he knew what would be the result; and this result was the true reason or the final cause why the machine was constructed. This intention of God is, therefore, his decree.

To this general idea of the Divine decrees it would be unreasonable to object, because it is as necessarily forced upon our mind as the idea of a purpose in the mind of a wise man previous to his entering upon any important enterprise; and with this idea the teachings of the holy Scriptures are in perfect harmony. They speak of the purpose of God, his will, his good pleasure, his determinate counsel, and his predestination. "All things work together for good to them that love God, to them who are called according to his *purpose*." Rom. 8:28. "Paul, an apostle of Jesus Christ by the *will* of God." II Cor. 1:1. "Having made known unto us the mystery of his will, according to his *good pleasure* which he hath *purposed* in himself." Eph. 1:9. "Him being delivered by the *determinate counsel* and foreknowledge of God, ye have taken," etc. Acts 2:23. "Having *predestinated* us unto the adoption of children by Jesus Christ to himself." Eph. 1:5. But it is unnecessary to multiply quotations. These Scriptures clearly prove, as do many others, that the operations of God are not the effects of necessity, but of *counsel* and *design*.

The Nature and Properties of the Divine Decrees

The decrees of God may be defined to be, *his purposes or determinations respecting his creatures*. For this reason they are sometimes called the *counsel*, and sometimes the *will* of God; terms which are never applied to necessary things, but only to the determinations of free agents.

When the Scriptures represent the decrees of God as his *counsel*, the word is not to be taken in its common acceptation, as implying consultation with others; nor is it to be understood as denoting reflection, comparison, and the establishment of a conclusion by logical deduction. But the decisions of an infinite mind are instantaneous; and they are called *counsel*, to signify that they are consummately wise.

Nor are we to conclude, because the decrees of God are denominated his *will*, that they are arbitrary decisions; but merely, that in making them he was under no control, but acted according to his own sovereignty. When a man's own will is the rule of his conduct, it is in many instances capricious and unreasonable; but *wisdom* is always associated with *will* in the Divine proceedings. Accordingly, the decrees of God are said to be "the counsel of his will."

But in considering more particularly the nature and properties of the Divine decrees, it may be remarked,

1. *That they are eternal.*—This is virtually taught by the apostle when he says, "Known unto God are all his works from the beginning of the world." Acts 15:18. The passage clearly imports, that at the commencement of time the plan was arranged according to which the works of God were to be executed. To suppose any of the Divine decrees to be made in time, is to suppose that the knowledge of God is limited; that he receives accessions to it in the progress of time, and that he forms new resolutions as new occasions require. Surely no one who believes that the Divine understanding is infinite, comprehending the past, the present and the future, will ever assent to the doctrine of temporal decrees. If God has any plan at all, it must be eternal; and hence St. Paul speaks of "the *eternal purpose* which he purposed in Christ Jesus our Lord." Eph. 3:11.

2. *The decrees of God are free.*—By this we are to understand, that his determinations were not necessitated by any external cause, that he was at liberty to decree or not to decree, and to decree one thing and not another. This liberty we must ascribe to Him who is supreme, independent, and sovereign in all his dispensations. "Who hath directed the Spirit of the Lord, or being his counselor hath taught him? With whom took he counsel, and who instructed him, and taught him in the path of judgment, and taught him knowledge, and showed to him the way of understanding?" Isa. 40:13, 14.

To deny the *freedom* of the Divine decrees is the same as to assert that they could not have been different from what they are. But are we prepared to adopt this sentiment? As well might we affirm that God could not have performed the work of creation sooner or later than he did; that he could not have made the world in any respect different from what it is; that he could not have placed man in a higher or lower degree in the scale of being; and that, when he had fallen, he could not have done otherwise than to redeem him by the death of his Son. Such a view of necessity, however, in regard either to the operations or the purposes of God, is both contrary to Scripture, and injurious to the feelings of piety, and must, therefore, be rejected.

We assert, then, that the decrees of God are *free*. No necessity can be supposed to influence the procedure of a self-existent and independent Being, except the necessity arising from his own perfections, of always acting in a manner worthy of himself. To his infinite understanding there must have appeared more than one way of doing this; and though there were doubtless reasons for the choice which he made, it would be boldness, not to be vindicated from the charge of impiety, to say that he could not have made a different choice.

3. *The decrees of God are immutable.*—This characteristic of the Divine decrees results from the infinite perfection and immutability of God; for if the least change should take place in his plans and determinations, it would be an instance of imperfection. The mutability of human purposes is owing to the uncertainty and defectiveness of human knowledge; but God knows with absolute certainty all things that ever were, now are, or ever shall be, and his purposes must therefore continue the same, amid all the changes of created things. "He is of one mind, and who can turn him?" Job 23:13. "The counsel of the Lord standeth forever; the thoughts of his heart to all generations." Psalm 33:11. He declares, "My counsel shall stand, and I will do all my pleasure." Isa. 46:10.

To the immutability of the Divine decrees it has been objected that the Scriptures represent God, in some cases at least, as changing his purpose. For instance, he said to King Hezekiah, "Set thine house in order; for thou shalt die and not live." But afterward he said to him, "I will add unto thy days fifteen years." II Kings 20:1, 6. Again, God commanded Jonah to say to the people of Nineveh, "Yet forty days, and Nineveh shall be overthrown." But when he saw that "they turned from their evil way," he "repented of the evil that he had said that he would do unto them; and he did it not." Jonah 3:10.

To meet the objection, and to reconcile these and all similar cases with the immutability of God's purposes, it is only necessary to observe, *first*, that the objector confounds two things which are essentially different, the Divine *purpose*, and the Divine *administration*. The former is nothing more than the *plan* according to which God operates as the Creator and Governor of the world; while the latter consists in his *actual operation* in accordance with this plan. *Secondly*, that man is a free moral agent, and is, therefore, governed by laws and motives adapted to his moral constitution; and that the purpose of God extends to the whole duration of his existence, and not merely to some particular period of it. Hence it is easy to conceive, in view of the conditionality of God's moral government and of the mutability of man, that the Divine administration respecting him may at one time be very different from what it is at another;

while in both cases it accords with the immutability of the Divine decrees.

For the sake of illustration, we may remark that the law which at one time protects a man in the possession of civil liberty may, at a subsequent period, condemn him to death. Would this imply a change in the law? By no means. The *law would continue the same—* the only change would be in the *subject* who should incur its penalty. When man was created he was placed under a law, in obedience to which he enjoyed life in its highest sense; but under the operation of that same law he became liable to death spiritual, temporal, and eternal. Did the law change? No; but man changed by disobeying it, and thus subjected himself to its curse. If, then, it is consistent with the immutability of God's *law* that the same moral agent should at one time be acquitted and at another time condemned, it may be equally consistent with the immutability of his *decrees;* for of these his revealed will is only the formal declaration.

When, therefore, we meet with passages of Scripture in which a change of the Divine purpose seems to be indicated, as in the case of Hezekiah, or in which God is said to repent, as it is asserted of him in regard to the inhabitants of Nineveh, we must understand them to imply a change of the Divine *administration,* but not of the Divine purpose. It is to be remembered that in many of the most positive declarations of Scripture there are implied conditions. Thus, when God said to the Jewish king, "Thou shalt die, and not live," it was only the announcement of what must have been the inevitable consequence of his sickness had it not been divinely prevented. But as Hezekiah did not believe the sentence to be unconditional, he "prayed unto the Lord" and "wept sore"; and God regarded his supplications, removed his disease, and added to his "days fifteen years." So also in the case of the Ninevites the threatening was conditional, as the event clearly proves; consequently, when they "turned from their evil way" they escaped the threatened judgment.

4. *The decrees of God have been considered by theologians as either Absolute or Conditional.*

(1) *Absolute* decrees are such as relate to those events in the Divine administration which have no dependence upon the free actions of moral creatures. These decrees are not called absolute, however, because they were made in the exercise of mere arbitrary power; but because, though made in view of wise and good reasons, the execution of them is not suspended upon any condition that may or may not be performed by moral creatures, but is to be ascribed to Divine agency. Thus, the purpose of God to create the world, to send his Son to redeem it, to bestow Gospel privileges upon one people and to deny them to another, and all his determinations of this nature, are called *absolute decrees.*

(2) *Conditional* decrees are those in making which God had

respect to the free actions of his moral creatures. Of this class are the purposes of God respecting the eternal welfare of men. They are founded upon that foreknowledge of men's moral actions which we are compelled to ascribe to God, and are never absolute, but always conditional. We must not conclude, however, as some have done, that conditional decrees are necessarily uncertain and mutable. They no more involve the idea of mutability than do those that are absolute. To the mind of God the end is as certain in one case as in the other, the only difference being in the means by which it is brought about. In *absolute* decrees God has respect to his own agency alone; in those that are *conditional,* to the agency of his free moral subjects; but in neither case can uncertainty or mutability be justly ascribed to them. God foresaw from eternity how every man would act, and whether he would comply with the conditions under which the designs of God concerning him would take effect or would reject them; and upon this perfect foreknowledge were his decrees founded. It is on this account, therefore, and this alone, that they are denominated *conditional.*

It is maintained by some that the foreknowledge of God is dependent upon his decrees. "If we allow the attribute of *prescience,*" says Mr. Buck, "the idea of a decree must certainly be allowed also; for how can an action that is really to come to pass be foreseen if it be not determined? God knew everything from the beginning; but this he could not know if he had not so determined it." This notion, though advocated by high authority, we must regard as both absurd in itself and contrary to Scripture. It is absurd in itself, because it makes an essential attribute of God depend upon his efficiency. "God could not have known everything from the beginning if he had not so determined it. Thus the Divine prescience is brought into existence by an exercise of the Divine mind, in decreeing "whatsoever comes to pass." Again, if "God foresees nothing but what he has decreed, and his decree precedes his knowledge," as Piscator tells us, then it follows that, as the cause cannot be dependent on the effect, God must have made his decrees and contrived his plans independent of his knowledge, which only had an existence as the effect of these decrees. But if these conclusions are absurd, so must that doctrine be also of which they are the legitimate consequences.

This notion is, moreover, contrary to Scripture. St. Paul says, Rom. 8:29, "For whom he did *foreknow,* he also did *predestinate* to be conformed to the image of his Son"; and St. Peter, in addressing believers, calls them "elect *according to the foreknowledge* of God the Father." I Peter 1:2. In these passages the decree of predestination or election is clearly founded on the foreknowledge of God. He foreknew in order to predestinate, but he did not predestinate in order to foreknow. Now as St. Paul tells the Christians at Rome that they were predestinated according to Divine foreknowledge, and St.

Peter informs those in Asia Minor that they were elected in the same way, it follows either that all the elect are thus chosen, or that God pursued one plan in electing the Christians of Rome and Lesser Asia, and a different one for the rest of the world. But as the latter cannot be true, the former must be admitted. It is therefore evident that, in the order of cause and effect, the *exercise* of the Divine attributes is consequent upon their *existence;* that the plan of the Almighty is the result of his infinite knowledge; and that the decrees of his throne flow forth from the eternal fountain of his wisdom.

The conditionality of the Divine decrees, so far as they relate to the eternal destiny of men, may be argued, *first,* from the manner in which God actually saves sinners. Does he effect their salvation *unconditionally?* We answer, that he never would have saved men had not Christ died for them. This, then, is a *condition* of human salvation, the grand event on account of which God forgives sin. But does God actually save sinners without any condition *on their part?* The Bible furnishes the answer: "Except ye repent, ye shall all likewise perish." Luke 13:3. "He that believeth and is baptized shall be saved; but he that believeth not shall be damned." Mark 16:16. "If thou wilt enter into life, keep the commandments." Matt. 19:17. The conditions, then, of eternal life are repentance, faith, and obedience. These conditions, it is true, are of a different nature from the atonement; but they are equally necessary. Hence we come to the conclusion, that, as the actual salvation of men is *conditional,* the decrees of God respecting it are *conditional* also.

It must be admitted, that the manner in which God will distribute happiness and misery in the future world is the precise mode which he eternally intended to pursue. If, then, it can be made to appear that he certainly will reward men according to their works, it will follow that he eternally purposed to do so. But the Scriptures do most explicitly declare that God "will render to every man according to his deeds"; that every man shall "receive the things done in his body, according to that he hath done, whether it be good or bad"; and that "whatsoever a man soweth, that shall he also reap." Therefore, as it is certain that God will, in the world to come, treat men according to their moral conduct here, it follows that he always intended to do so; and if the decrees of God relative to men's future destiny were thus based upon their foreseen voluntary actions, they may be properly denominated *conditional.*

Secondly, the view which we have taken of this subject is further confirmed by what we know of the *character of God.* The Scriptures declare that "God is love"; that He "is good to all, and his tender mercies are over all his works"; and that he has "no pleasure in the death of him that dieth." How, then, could he have decreed to consign millions of the human family to endless perdition regardless of their conduct? Or, how could he place men under circumstances in which they must inevitably continue in sin, and then punish them in hell for ever for not exercising that repentance and faith which he determined never to give them? The Scriptures assert that God is "long-suffering to usward, not willing that any should perish, but that all should come to repentance." But how could his bearing with the non-elect be properly an act of long-suffering, if he had determined to withhold forever from them that special grace by which alone they could repent, however long he might wait with them? How could the inspired apostle say that God is "not willing that any should perish," if from all eternity he had doomed, unconditionally, a large portion of the human family to endless misery? How could he assert the willingness of God "that *all* should come to repentance," if he had unconditionally determined to leave millions of our race in that moral condition in which true repentance is impossible?

Moreover, what *sincerity* could there be in the proclamation of the "Gospel to every creature," if God had determined by an absolute decree the eternal destiny of all men? The Gospel would offer a free and full salvation to those for whom no provision had been made in the redeeming plan, and life eternal to those who had been ordained to eternal death. And how can we reconcile with the *justice* and *impartiality* of God the opinion, that while he calls men into existence with a fallen and depraved nature, he should, irrespective of their conduct, elect some to everlasting life and consign others to hell? "God is no respecter of persons; but in every nation he that feareth him, and worketh righteousness, is accepted with him." How could this be said if God had made among his creatures a distinction of such incalculable magnitude and eternal duration as would be implied in the unconditional salvation of some, and unavoidable damnation of others?

The conclusion, then, of the whole matter is this: that though we ascribe to God decrees which are absolute and unconditional, yet, so far as they relate to the eternal destiny of men, they were formed in full view of men's free moral actions, and are, therefore, *conditional*. Properly speaking, however, these decrees cannot be said to depend on any thing but God himself, who perfectly knew from the beginning what would be the nature and consequences of every future occurrence.

We will close this chapter by a brief notice of the distinction which some theologians make between the revealed will of God, and what they are pleased to call his *secret* will. If this distinction were based upon the opinion, that God has plans and purposes which he has not fully revealed to mankind, it might very readily be allowed; for the Scriptures declare that "secret things belong unto the Lord our God; but those things which are revealed belong to us and to our children." Deut. 29:29. It is generally assumed, however, by the advocates of this distinction, that the *secret* will of God is, in many cases, directly contrary to what he has revealed in his word. For instance, God "will have all men to be saved, and to come unto the knowledge of the truth." I Tim. 2:4. This is acknowledged to be his *revealed* will; but it is nevertheless contended that his *secret* will is, that many of the human race should *not* "be saved," or "come to the knowledge of the truth," but perish forever.

To this view of the secret will of God we object, for several reasons: 1. It is wholly gratuitous. There is not a single passage of Scripture which, when fairly interpreted, teaches the doctrine that the *will* of God as in any case contrary to his *word*. 2. It is absurd in itself. We can become acquainted with the purposes of God only so far as they are revealed. Of his secret or unrevealed will we can know nothing. If, therefore, we assume, in any given case, that the *secret* will of God is contrary to what he has revealed, we virtually assume that we know, by some means or other, what the secret will of God is, and consequently that it is both secret and revealed at the same time, which is a contradiction. But, 3. This opinion is dishonorable to the Divine character. It represents God as having two wills, which are in many cases contrary to one another, as declaring in the most solemn manner that he has "no pleasure in the death of him that dieth," while it is according to his *secret will* that multiplied thousands should die eternally. We conclude, therefore, that this theory is untenable, and that we can only judge of the will of God by what he has revealed.

God Makes

32

Harold Kuhn

Creation

Among the basic affirmations of the Christian faith is that "God the Father Almighty" is "Maker of heaven and earth." This affirmation answers to a deep requirement and a deep questioning upon the part of the human mind. The doctrine has a profound significance for the entire structure of Christian thought, and specifically for our understanding concerning His freedom, His self-sufficiency, and His uniqueness as an eternal Existent. As F. R. Tennant points out, the existence of a "general order of Nature" forces upon the human mind the conviction that the universe is the outcome of intelligent design. It will not do to dismiss this as a lingering echo of eighteenth-century rationalism. This generalization is as well established and as widely recognized as any generalization of science.[1]

Non-Christian Systems

These have tended to view "creation" in one of the following ways: they have regarded the universe as being the result of self-origination; they have imagined it to be some sort of unfolding or emanation of a

From *Basic Christian Doctrines* edited by Carl F. H. Henry. Copyright © 1962 by Carl F. H. Henry. Reprinted by permission of Holt, Rinehart and Winston, Inc.

divine being; they have posited some form of eternally existing chaos, which an intermediate "creator" fashioned into a cosmos; or they have regarded the visible universe as an illusion. These find a common denominator of sorts in the belief in the eternity of matter or of "pre-matter." Ancient paganism could rise no higher than this. Its systems proved to be unstable, particularly in their attempt to defend the belief that the universe contained two eternals, two absolutes, two infinites. Slowly, the human mind came to perceive the metaphysical impossibility of such a position.

Historically, the Christian assertion of an absolute creation by a transcendent God was not only a scandal to the pagan mind (for example, the Graeco-Roman mind), but it represented as well a threat to the entire thought world of ancient civilization. As Galen, of the second century after Christ, says: "Moses' opinion greatly differs from our own and from that of Plato and all the others who among the Greeks have rightly handled the investigation into nature. To Moses, it seems enough that God willed to create a cosmos, and presently it was created; for he believes that for God everything is possible. . . . We however do not hold such an opinion; for we maintain, on the contrary, that certain things are impossible by nature, and these God would not even attempt to do. . . ."[2]

This we quote to point out that opposition to the biblical account of an absolute origination of the universe by God is by no means contemporary. True, some contemporary alternatives are based upon slightly other grounds. At the same time, opposition has been in the name of a form or type of world view which seemed to be threatened by the Christian teaching at this point.

The Christian Affirmation

With reference to the origination of the universe, the basic Christian affirmation is that God is the Author of the whole cosmos. This is found in the Old Testament and in the Judaism which emerged from Old Testament times. It is continued in the Christian system. The basic elements of the Christian teaching concerning creation are the following: that the universe has its beginning and end in God's spontaneous will; that the universe is in no sense independent of Him, but that its maintenance represents a continuing exertion of His creative power and ability; and that God made the universe not out of some type of pre-existent "stuff" but out of nothing. This assumes that prior to the "moment" of creation, God existed in self-sufficient and majestic aloneness. It is just here that the Christian understanding of God differs profoundly from that of classical paganism, which assumed, at best, the co-existence of God and the material universe (or its proto-elements); or from radical forms of moral dualism, which assumed that evil (or the factors which make for it) were co-eternal with God.

The Christian understanding of God involves the conviction that while God is One, He is not for that reason *one thing*. Within the fundamental unity of His Godhead there exists a Trinity of Persons; He contains within Himself three centers of personal activity, each capable of being denoted by personal pronouns. This means that there is an incomprehensible richness in the inner life of God, and that creation is one of the expressions of this inner richness of self-determination. Karl Barth summarily suggests that the doctrine of creation assumes the tri-unity of God's being.[3] In any case, God's eternal self-existence and self-sufficiency do not imply a precreation life of motionlessness upon His part. They do assert that God is in no sense dependent upon His world and in no sense under compulsion to create, except as a spontaneous manifestation of His love.

The Christian understanding of creation implies, we repeat, that prior to the "moment" of creation, God existed in sovereign self-sufficiency. It suggests also that there came a "point" in the divine life in which He determined to project into being that which was not Himself and yet which was dependent upon Him for its continuing being and existence. This *projection* represents an absolute origination, that is, it implies a beginning and bringing out of nothing (*ex nihilo*) and not any mere fashioning of some pre-existent matter or pre-matter. The accent falls here upon His freedom, upon His sovereign intelligence. The consequent universe is real; it is no illusion. Its reality is a *conferred* reality, which is always relative to His upholding Word. The universe is distinct from God; it is not, properly speaking, continuous with Him. That is, in creation, God set over against Himself in the realm of being that which was *not Himself*.

At this point it must be noted that the biblical account of creation has two aspects: there is the aspect of absolute origination in the initial creation, indicated by the words, "In the beginning God created the heavens and the earth." This denotes the calling into being, in the dateless past, of the basic "finite" which is our universe. Then, there is the second and detailed aspect, sketched in the first two chapters of Genesis in terms of six successive creative days,[4] and specialized in the account of human origins.[5]

Objections

It should be noted here that the Christian affirmation has been challenged upon several grounds. Some have felt that it represents a too-narrow monotheism. We have given brief attention to this objection earlier in this study. Others suggest that the "Let it be" or fiat of creation is too simple, that it describes in a few words what was in reality most complex. It must be recalled in this connection that the account of Genesis is designedly simple. The New Testament does, however, show an increased awareness of the issues for human thought which the teaching concerning creation implies and involves.

Others object to what they consider to be the "childishness" of the Old Testament account, which divides creation, rather creative activity, into six successive days. This objection loses much of its force in the light of two things. First, the creative sequence indicates progress in the formation of the world, progress which upon closer study may not be, after all, illogical. Second, it is recognized in nearly all evangelical circles that in Hebrew the term "day" is used to denote more than one quantity of time. In some contexts, the term "day" denotes an era or an epoch. This may be illuminated by the words, "These are the generations of the heavens and of the earth" in Genesis 2:4. Reverent scholars allow for the possibility that the "days" of Genesis 1 may be generic periods.

There have been objections to the Christian doctrine of creation upon more directly philosophical grounds. Some have asserted in more "modern" form the view of Greek paganism, to the effect that prior to and behind the cosmos existed some primordial "world-stuff," variously understood as Prime Matter or as "the receptacle"— a formless precondition of all reality. Jakob Boehme,[6] regarded as the first writing philosopher in the German language, has offered on this point a Germanic version of the general view of ancient Greek thought (that is, Platonic thought). He suggests: "We understand that without [outside of] nature there is an eternal stillness and rest, viz., the Nothing, and then we understand that an eternal will arises in the nothing, to introduce the nothing into something, that the will might find, feel, and behold itself."[7]

This quotation is significant in that it is a prototype of more modern views raised in objection to the historic Christian view of creation. These more modern opinions are, in general, directed at the objective of absolving God from responsibility for the existence of evil in the world. Now, no one will pretend that the existence of evil in the universe is something to be shrugged off. No division of the question (as, for example, into terms of "natural" and "moral" evil) will eliminate the problem. But the Christian can scarcely content himself with such an explanation as is advanced by Nicholas Berdyaev, who, in the general tone of Boehme, suggests that prior to and outside of God there existed a primal *Ungrund*, which accounts for the irrational "freedom" which in turn accounts for evil and which exists in God as a "tragic conflict" within His nature.[8] Nor can the Christian content himself with the view, advanced in our country by Edgar S. Brightman, that within the being of God, there exists a "Given" which is irrational and disorderly and which is an ever-present internal obstacle to the realization of His purposes.

The Christian understanding of God cannot divorce freedom from God, nor can it locate evil with God's being. The doctrine of creation presupposes God's sovereign self-determination. Any proper solution to the "problem of evil" must be found elsewhere than in a limitation of God's sovereignty. In the last analysis, any light cast upon this tragic problem must be found in the self-giving of the divine Son upon the cross.

God's Free Will

In reality, the heart of the Christian world view is revealed in this aspect of the Christian understanding of creation. The biblical record is clear at the point of ascribing to God the ultimate and sole *will* in the matter of creation. Creation reflects and represents His own freedom in action.

It needs to be noted that modern objections to the Christian understanding of creation have been raised at the point of the relation of creation to time. If we reject the classic pagan view of the eternity of matter, we must yet consider the question of whether creation was, after all, eternal. If we reply that the biblical doctrine implies an *origination*, a beginning of the universe, we answer this question in the negative. The question then arises: did creation occur in time? Christian thought has, in general, suggested that we know too little of the matter of sequence in the career of God to offer a final answer at this point. Some early thinkers (Origen, for example) felt that God's self-determination to create must have been eternal. Others held that creation was an act which did not fall within the categories of time and space as we understand them. Augustine held that the universe was not created in time, but that time was created along with the universe. This means that time (as we know it) was something which became manifest at the point at which the universe was projected. Perhaps this is the best available answer.

Conclusion

We have noted seriatim some of the alternatives which have been proposed to the Christian affirmation of creation, the basic content of the Christian teaching, some of the objections raised to it, and something of the larger bearings of the doctrine. We need to note, finally, that the doctrine creates no new mysteries. The mysteries are already present and confront the thoughtful with a perennial challenge. Nor does the Christian doctrine suggest that the concept of absolute creation is an easy one. It is ultimately an article of faith, based upon the acceptance of divine revelation. However, as the reverent mind ponders the alternatives, it finds nothing comparably satisfying to the answer given by the Christian faith.

The Christian Scriptures do not attempt to describe the "how" of creation. They do assure us that the entire Trinity was active in the production of the universe. While it is God the Father Who is, in the broad sense, Creator of heaven and earth, it was through the agency of the Word, the eternal Son, that all things were made. During the creative process, it was the Holy Spirit who moved upon "the face of the waters," bringing order out of the formless and empty chaos.

At the core of the doctrine of creation stands the mighty assertion that the universe is the product of the release of creative energies of an infinitely free and completely holy God, utterly self-sufficient in His being and infinite in His ability to perform that which His heart of love dictates. And in the person of the eternal Son, the activities of creation and redemption meet and conjoin.

Notes

[1] F. R. Tennant. *Philosophical Theology,* Volume II, pp. 79 f.

[2] Galen. *De Usu Partium Corporis Humani,* XII, p. 14.

[3] K. Barth. *Church Dogmatics,* III, 1, pp. 46 ff.

[4] Gen. 1.

[5] Gen. 2.

[6] Jakob Boehme, 1575-1624.

[7] J. Boehme. *Signatura Rerum,* p. 14.

[8] N. Berdyaev. *The Destiny of Man,* p. 177.

God Is in Charge

33

G. C. Berkouwer

Providence as Government

We have remarked that sustenance and government should not be isolated from each other, but must be seen as two aspects of the one almighty and omnipresent act of God. In thinking of Providence as government, we accent the purpose that God proposes and achieves in His holy activity. The sustaining of the world, as we have noted, is also related to His purpose for the future. The only difference is that in the government of God we deal with the purposefulness more explicitly.

This rule has neither spatial nor temporal boundaries. It proceeds from generation to generation. No less than the doctrine of sustenance, God's government reveals His grandeur and incomprehensibility. Earthly analogies are common to us; we know governments, kings, and other authorities. But it is not possible to fathom the rule of God. Who can trace the paths where His foot treads? "For my thoughts are not your thoughts, neither are your ways my ways, saith Jehovah" (Isa. 55:8). His ways are beyond those estranged from Him; but neither can those who know His fellowship comprehend Him. Inspired Israel sings in Psalm 77 of God's ways, His ways in the

From G. C. Berkouwer, *The Providence of God*, Grand Rapids, Michigan: Wm. B. Eerdmans Pub. Co., 1952. Used by permission.

sanctuary: "Who is a great god like unto God?" (Ps. 77:13).

Recalling the miracle of the exodus excites delight and inspires reverence in Israel. "Thy way was in the sea, And thy paths in the great waters, And thy footsteps were not known" (Ps. 77:19). The unfathomableness of God's works, however, forms no obstacle to Israel's trust in His salvation. Psalm 77 ends with the writer, while impressed by the unsearchableness of God's activity, contemplating His salvation: "Thou leddest thy people like a flock, By the hand of Moses and Aaron" (Ps. 77:20). The enigmatic methods of God's government do not inhibit worship. Paul concludes his chapter on the mystery of God's work in the fall and rejection of Israel and the accepting of the Gentiles by exclaiming: "For who hath known the mind of the Lord? or who hath been his counsellor? O the depth of the riches both of the wisdom and the knowledge of God! how unsearchable are his judgments, and his ways past tracing out!" (Rom. 11:33, 34).

As God's rule is incomprehensible, so is it invincible. His throne is not moved. He breaks through all resistance, and makes the universe servant to the coming of His kingdom. "Thy throne is established of old: Thou art from everlasting. The floods have lifted up, O Jehovah, The floods have lifted up their voice; The floods lift up their waves. Above the voices of many waters, The mighty breakers of the sea, Jehovah on high is mighty" (Ps. 93:2-4).

The invincibility of God's purposeful ruling cannot be measured with human standards, nor exhausted by analogies of human might and power. But that the rule of God is invincible is certain. He is invincible in a Divine way; his method is strange to human techniques. He is the Lord of Hosts, but His conquest is best revealed in the shame and forsakenness of the cross of His Son. He conquers, but He stoops to darkness and distress. Yet, one day the Divine victory shall rise as a sun to everlasting morning.

The rule of God is the gladness of His people: "Say among the nations, Jehovah reigneth" (Ps. 96:10). He rules from age to age: He is the King of Eternity (I Tim. 6:15). The Scriptures do not teach this in systematic outline. They reveal it in the dynamic movement of history, in God's leading, guiding, and compelling of races and individuals. It is the living God of history who bends and breaks His challengers, who makes an end to wars and directs the wars of the Lord, and who as the Holy One is active in all the world, spanning the length and breadth of it. In no phase of the world's history is the rule of God in danger. "Jehovah will reign for ever, Thy God, O Zion, unto all generations" (Ps. 146:10). This rule is no abstract, immobile potency. It is the acting of the God of Israel in Israel's history. Nothing is too wonderful for Israel's God, the Almighty of Jacob. In the face of His invincible power—in which the people share through faith—all threats from hostile powers are neutralized. He is aways the All Highest; He who dwells in His refuge abides in the shadow of the Almighty (Ps. 91:1). "A thousand shall fall at thy side, And ten thousand at thy right hand; But it shall not come nigh thee" (Ps. 91:7).

He, in grace, is the Protector of Israel, His mountains are about Jerusalem (Ps. 125:2). He slumbers not nor sleeps, and guards the goings and comings of His people forever (Ps. 121:8). "He is my refuge and my fortress" (Ps. 91:2). The future is His future; the so-called powers of fate lie in His hands. "My times are in thy hand" (Ps. 31:15). "And which of you by being anxious can add one cubit unto the measure of his life?" (Matt. 6:27). There is no sphere in which dread need possess the believer's existence. For the spheres that He spans are wider than those that encircle man. The believer is never the victim of the powers of nature or fate. Chance is eliminated. "He humbled thee and suffered thee to hunger . . ." (Deut. 8:3). In the judgment of their sins, too, Israel rediscovers the presence of God, when He has consumed their days "in vanity, And their years in terror" (Ps. 78:33). He destroyed their vines and their cattle with hail (Ps. 78:47, 48), and "spared not their soul from death" (Ps. 78:50).

Israel's relation to Him is not like that of the heathen to a nature-god, static and unchanging. He is the God of salvation and judgment. His acts are judgments when the people forget His favors (Ps. 78:11) and fail to remember that their whole existence rests upon His election. He cleaves the rocks in the wilderness and causes water to run down like rivers (Ps. 78:15, 16). And in the distress of judgment Israel rediscovers God.

God's purposes are in all His activity. When He seems most distant, even concealed, He is often near in judgment. But in the judgment He never loses sight of His purpose. He compels Israel to ask again for His comforting presence. (Isa. 63:15 ff.). God sells Israel to Jabin of Canaan as judgment on her sins, but in turn brings Jabin to account (Judg. 4:23). When Israel again honors His holy name, He again draws near in blessing: feeds her people with manna, leads them against their enemies, guides them with the cloud and the fire. The people learn the limitlessness of His rule; they learn that all life from conception to death lies open to Him as a book. Israel offers a paean to His greatness: "For thou didst form my inwards parts: Thou didst cover me in my mother's womb. I will give thanks unto thee; for I am fearfully and wonderfully made: Wonderful are thy works; And that my soul knoweth right well. My frame was not hidden from thee, When I was made in secret, And curiously wrought in the lowest parts of the earth. Thine eyes did see mine unformed substance; And in thy book they were all written, Even the days that were ordained for me, When as yet there was none of them" (Ps. 139:13-16). Then, having recognized God's knowledge of the beginning, Israel looks to the future: "Lead me in the way everlasting" (Ps. 139:24).

Past, present, future. In unshaken certainty, Israel is led through life in His hands. He imparts strength and courage to go on.

Earthly and human factors play their part, but the problem of first and second causes is not experienced as a real difficulty in the light of the overshadowing power of God. "Remember, I beseech thee, that thou hast fashioned me as clay. . . . Hast thou not poured me out as milk, And curdled me like cheese? Thou hast clothed me with skin and flesh, And knit me together with bones and sinews" (Job 10:9-11). Thou! Thou! It sounds all the time—through birth, nature, and history.

In modern times "enlightened" human thought grants nature independence from God. Thunder and lightning, rain and clouds, conception and birth, historical events and their consequences—these are tracked down to their natural causes and endowed by human thought with their own immanent force. They form an independent power, which the Divine activity seems able only to limit and curtail.

Not so with Israel in her fear of God.

Israel, too, knows of conception and birth, of streams that go to the sea, and of the cycle of nature. But this knowledge does not stifle her "Thou, O Lord." In her knowledge, she still looks to the living God, the Unchangeable. This is no primitive religious naivete that later is sloughed off with increase of intelligence. "The voice of Jehovah cleaveth the flames of fire. The voice of Jehovah shaketh the wilderness; . . . the voice of Jehovah maketh the hinds to calve" (Ps. 29:7-9). This is Israel's understanding of natural events. For Israel's eyes are trained on Him.

The might of the Lord is not seen as a consuming energy that rules out all human activity. But neither does His use of human means limit the scope of His activity. "I was cast upon thee from the womb; Thou art my God since my mother bare me. Be not far from me; for trouble is near; For there is none to help" (Ps. 22:10, 11). This direct relation to God embraces the whole span of life. He is Israel's expectation even from her youth (Ps. 71:17). Scripture stands, thus, in polar opposition to every form of deism which isolates God from the affairs of the world. His immanent leading spans all the ways of man and reaches into the intents of the heart: "A man's heart deviseth his way; But Jehovah directeth his steps" (Prov. 16:9). The heart of the king is in the hand of the Lord as the watercourses. He leads it wherever He pleases (Prov. 21:1). The poet, moved by the marvels of His activity, writes: "There is no wisdom nor understanding nor counsel against Jehovah" (Prov. 21:30).

Now He impresses us with His guidance of the great, then with

His leading of the small; now with the universal, then with the particular. It has been suggested that the notion of God's rule over individuals was a later phenomenon in Israel's religious history. Eichrodt, for instance, says, "Gradually, as the people gained faith in Providence, the destiny of the individual was included in its scope."[1] But Eichrodt himself would agree that personal trust in God's guidance is revealed very early. Joseph in Egypt already expresses it: "And as for you, ye meant evil against me; but God meant it for good, to save much people alive" (Gen. 50:20). God includes the people in His view, but Joseph knows that God also encircles his individual life. This is the way with Abraham and Sarah, with the marriage of Isaac, and with the life of Jacob. All facets of life are embraced in God's rule.

The plurality of life is brought under one perspective. It is not that there is a confusion of countless atomistic events in all of which God's activity is manifest. There is a pivot, a centrum, which unifies the diversity of His activity. The unity includes the progress of events from His promise at the time of the fall to the completion of the formation of His holy people. It is not surprising that Israel, when reflecting about God's activity, always looks back to the old days. The intervention of God in the exodus always remains a searing reminder of her dependence on God. In the history following the exodus it is made clear that the Lord has interfered in the life of Pharaoh and stretched His arms out against the Egyptians (Exod. 9:5). Moses and the children of Israel sing of the intervening hand of God: "Who is like unto thee, O Jehovah, among the gods? Who is like thee, glorious in holiness, Fearful in praises, doing wonders?" (Exod. 15:11). His right hand brings the decision (Exod. 15:12). It is directed against Pharaoh, but means leading and redemption for His people (Exod. 15:13). The entire 15th chapter is a song to His wrath (Exod. 15:7), His gentle leading (Exod. 15:13), the strength of His arms (Exod. 15:16). "Jehovah shall reign for ever and ever" (Exod. 15:18).

God's works must be seen as His immanent activity—works not confined to Israel, though defined by His purpose for and in her. These acts of God are reviewed for Israel through the generations. Israel's entire history is controlled by Jehovah, just as her formation was conceived by Him. "When Old Testament piety is reminded of the power of God, it thinks of God's deed at the Red Sea, the act that completed the exodus."[2] If Israel is estranged from God's gracious leading, the prophets remind her of the power and grace of God. "For I brought thee up out of the land of Egypt, and redeemed thee out of the house of bondage; and I sent before thee Moses, Aaron, and Miriam" (Mic. 6:4). It was His path in the sea. He led the people (Ps. 77:19, 20). "I am Jehovah, your Holy One, the Creator of Israel, your King. Thus saith Jehovah, who maketh a

way in the sea, and a path in the mighty waters; who bringeth forth
the chariot and horse, the army and the mighty man . . ." (Isa.
43:15-17).

Not only the exodus manifests the ruling of God. Israel is reminded
of the consul of Balak, and of how Balaam the son of Beor answered
him (Mic. 6:5). Israel sings of God's paths and works in the desert:
His sending of manna (Ps. 105:40), His cleaving of the rock (Ps.
105:41). They remember His judgments when they tempted Him
(Ps. 106:14), His wrath at their images (Ps. 106:29). These are
not incidental acts, but cohesive elements in His continuous guidance.
Israel is expected to know that her God is He who rules all things.
He, the Holy One of Israel, is Redeemer God of the whole earth
(Isa. 54:5). The Old Testament is not the history of the Eastern
peoples. They do, however, stand in the shadow of Israel's election,
through which, as was promised, all the peoples of the earth were to
be blessed. God goes *through* Israel to the lost world. His grace and
judgment is directed to the future, His salvation for the world.

To explain away this purposeful activity of God evolutionistically
or subjectively is to miss the deepest secret of Israel's history. The
secret is buried in the sovereign rule of God that leads to His full
salvation and to the redemption of the world. Though the rule of God
goes uncomprehended by us, His paths are lighted up in various
ways by the Scriptures. We see Him working in the historical matrix
of human counsels, plans, and deeds. Stauffer has quite rightly spoken
of the trend often observed in Divine government as "a law of
deflection." "The more the adversary opposes, so much the richer
becomes the revelation of the infinite superiority of God."[3] This is
because God's rule is executed and manifested in and through human
activity. There are not two powers working apart from and parallel
to each other, the Divine and the human, each limiting the other.
Yet, we see men performing extraordinarily important rules in sacred
history.

Joseph's brothers devise and execute their plans; aroused by
jealousy they gradually commit themselves irrevocably to their
chosen course. The plan to kill Joseph is frustrated, but the historical
reason even for this falls within the orbit of human devices. Reuben
comes between. Thus the story of Joseph is a tale of human initiative
from his sale to the Midianites to his arrival in Egypt. It is first in
Genesis 39 that a new element enters the story: we are told, "And
Jehovah was with Joseph." Then the "deflection" takes place as the
plot of the brothers runs itself out. The activity of God is revealed,
not as a *deus ex machina*, but *in* the action of the brothers. Their
evil plan achieves historical realization, but the historical events are
products of the Divine activity. God's good intents follow the mis-
chievous path of the brothers or, rather, the brothers unwittingly

follow the path that God has blazed. They work in His service. The purpose of God lights up the horizon of evil, jealous, malicious activity. The dispute in Jacob's house turns into an important link in the way of God with His people. Joseph, with his background of experiences in Egypt, understands something of this, and later explains it to his brothers—for their consolation.

God's hand *in* history!

This does not mean that the work of God is always evident in the interlacing of Divine and human activity. We cannot set Divine action under any one common denominator. He does not, for instance, always allow human plans to be consummated. He often frustrates their execution by an interference from outside. He thwarts Pharaoh in his fury against Israel. There is an intervention from without history as well as a "deflection" from within, a thwarting as well as a bending. God can allow the heathen aggressor to reach his goal, using the pagan triumph as a judgment on and humbling of His people. But, on the other hand, He can also resist Sennacherib's attack on Jerusalem and thwart all his plans. He can hear Hezekiah's prayer in a concrete situation and open His eyes to the danger (Isa. 37:17). He can hear the reproach of Rabshakeh. "Therefore thus saith Jehovah concerning the king of Assyria, He shall not come unto this city, nor shoot an arrow there, neither shall he come before it with shield, nor cast up a mound against it. . . . For I will defend this city . . ." (Isa. 37:33, 35). "And the angel of Jehovah went forth, and smote in the camp of the Assyrians a hundred and fourscore and five thousand" (Isa. 37:36).

Yet it is striking to observe how often the purpose of God is reached without radical intervention. On the surface there may be nothing to see except human activity creating and defining history on a horizontal level. But in revelation the final sense of the historical events is unveiled. We could illustrate this historical activity from scores of Biblical examples. We shall mention only a few.

In Judges we read of a conflict between the citizens of Shechem and Abimelech. The dispute arises from the treachery of the men of Shechem, which treachery seems to be the determining factor in the story. The conflict actually executes a judgment on both Abimelech and the Shechemites. God sends an evil spirit between Abimelech and the citizens of Shechem so that the crime committed by Abimelech against the seventy sons of Jerubbaal is turned on both Abimelech and the Shechemites who had aided him (Judg. 9:24). God's activity is *in* the conflict. "The uprising of the Schechemites was not undertaken to expiate a crime of which they themselves were also guilty. They did not know themselves what they were doing. They were instruments of God."[4]

Or, observe Saul's battle against Amalek. A purely horizontal perspective cannot explain this war, but revelation shows that it executes judgment against the Amalekites for what they did against Israel in the then almost forgotten days right after the exodus (I Sam. 15:2). Saul's attack on the Amalekites is not inconsistent with his sparing of the Canaanites, since they, unlike the Amalekites, were friendly to the Israelites in their migration (I Sam. 15:6). God's leading spans the centuries, and in His leading the action of man is taken up as instrument in His service. Man's activity falls, as the smaller of two concentric circles, completely within the greater circle of God's purpose.

The nature of God's activity is seen uniquely in the establishment of the monarchy in Israel. Here, too, there is an interweaving of Divine and human acts. The installation of the monarchy is closely related to Israel's sin of rejecting, in principle, the Lordship of God. God Himself describes their action thus, sees it as evil, and commands Samuel to warn the people before announcing the decision to give them their king. Human disloyalty to God, then, seems to have created the monarchy. We can imagine similar developments in other nations. But in the setting up and historical development of Israel's monarchy the free and overruling activity of God is revealed. Through the disloyal rejection of His Lordship and the establishment of the monarchy comes the messianic future.

We encounter similar lines in the rupture of the kingdom, born out of sin, but revelatory, nonetheless, of God's activity. The split is the fruit of Rehoboam's sin. Yet, God says, "This thing is of me" (I Kings 12:24). This becomes clearer when the rendering of I Kings 12 is viewed against the background of I Kings 11:29 ff., where Jeroboam and Ahijah meet alone in the field, and where Jeroboam hears that the Lord has said: "Behold, I will rend the kingdom out of the hand of Solomon, and will give ten tribes to thee" (I Kings 11:31). God works in Rehoboam's sin so that Rehoboam actualizes the word that He has spoken through Ahijah. God's wisdom triumphs in Rehoboam's foolishness. In every "deflection" it becomes clear that God's activity is not limited by man's sin. He is conqueror even *in* man's sin. This is the light that shines through Israel's entire history.

God's "thinking it for good" makes His enemies accessories to the salvation of His people. We see this also in the threatened judgments which gather as dark thunder clouds over the people. The exile, for example, is as mere human activity historically unaccountable. Jeremiah in his vision sees the historical factors leading to the fall of his people as a nation: a seething cauldron with its face toward the north (Jer. 1:13). From the north shall come evil against the inhabitants of the land. This, it would seem, is still human activity exclusively. But another perspective lies in the threat: "For, lo, I will call all the families of the kingdoms of the north, saith Jehovah; and they shall come, and . . . I will utter my judgments against them touching all their wickedness, in that they have forsaken me . . ." (Jer. 1:15, 16). Once again, the revelation of the judgment of God *in* history.

The activity of God is revealed again in the return from the exile, even though the human, historical factors seem to predominate in the event. Cyrus, the Prince of Persia, arises on the horizon but, on his way to greatness, becomes another instrument of God. He becomes the liberator of God's people. Another exodus! There is always perspective in God's activity, always a pivot on which everything turns, a purpose to which everything is servant. From this center the lines of God's rule are drawn around the foreigner Cyrus. He is aroused to march from the east against Babylon. Nations are sacrificed to this heathen so that nothing may hinder his triumphal march. "Who hath wrought and done it, calling the generations from the beginning? I, Jehovah, the first, and with the last, I am he" (Isa. 41:4). Of Cyrus, He says, "He is my shepherd, and shall perform all my pleasure, even saying of Jerusalem, She shall be built; and of the temple, Thy foundation shall be laid" (Isa. 44:28). Cyrus is the anointed, the messiah of the Lord (Isa. 45:1). For the sake of His people, God enlists Cyrus though he did not know Him (Isa. 45:4). The affair with Cyrus is summarized thus: "I am Jehovah, and there is none else; besides me there is no God . . . I form the light, and create darkness; I am Jehovah, that doeth all these things" (Isa. 45:5, 7). Cyrus liberates God's people, builds God's city, and lets His people go, "not for ransom nor for gifts," so that, in and through Cyrus, the Divine rule is raised above doubt.

And, as with Babylon and Cyrus, so is it with Assur. Assur is the rod with which God disciplines His people. In his deceit, the fire of judgment flames. God rouses Assur to lead the Assyrians to attack (Isa. 10:5-13). That these events are prearranged comes out more clearly in that, at the same time, a double woe is spoken over Assur. The Assyrian Assur, servant to God's purposes, oppresses Jerusalem; but then God saves Jerusalem by oppressing Assur. When Assur boasts over his achievements, Isaiah says to him, "Shall the axe boast itself against him that heweth therewith? shall the saw magnify itself against him that wieldeth it?" (Isa. 10:15).

We encounter similar relationships in the New Testament. When Stauffer spoke of the "law of deflection," he mentioned the suffering of Christ as well as the history of Joseph. The interweaving of Divine and human action can, indeed, be observed in the life of Jesus Christ, not only in His suffering, but beginning already at His birth. The story of the nativity begins in Luke 2 with human activity. The general order for the registration of the people comes from the man Caesar. The path of Joseph and Mary, too, falls within the circle of human sovereignty, and, as consequence of this human act, they find themselves in Bethlehem. The course of human events climaxes at the city spoken of in Micah's messianic prophecy. Again, there is a deflecting toward God's proposed purpose. (On the other hand, it is true that the more immediate method is used in the intervention in Herod's plans by means of a dream revelation to Joseph.)

The interlacing of Divine and human activity is revealed pre-eminently in the history of Christ's suffering. Satan and men act out their part. The disciples of Jesus play their role, too, through their denial, disloyalty, and desertion. Their action brings Christ into total loneliness, and in this loneliness God executes His judgment. Christ experiences Divine abandonment in the crucible created by human enterprise—in the opposition against Him and the delivering of Him to the death of the cross. God acts *in* men's acts: in Pilate's sentence, in Judas's betrayal, yea, in everything that men do with Christ. God's activity embraces all these and leads them along His mysterious way.

The New Testament sees human actions as being nonetheless fully responsible. Christ was nailed to the cross by unrighteous, responsible men. You, says Peter, have killed the Prince of life (Acts 3:15). You, and Herod, and Pilate, you were in league with the Romans and the Jews against God's holy child Jesus, *but*—"to do whatsoever thy [God's] hand and thy counsel foreordained to come to pass" (Acts 4:28). From our perspective it becomes evident that the tramping of human paths paves the way of God, that all these things work together toward the achievement of God's purpose. He is delivered up by the determinate counsel and foreknowledge of God (Acts 2:23). There is no accident on Christ's journey into suffering. It is a Divine must, as Christ Himself says to the Emmaus travelers: "Behooved it not the Christ to suffer these things, and to enter into his glory?" (Luke 24:26).

The relation between Divine and human activity is illuminated also in the role played by Caiaphas (John 11:47-53). In the confusion and indecision of the high priests and pharisees, Caiaphas hits upon a suggestive idea, a broad hint at a solution: "Ye know nothing at all, nor do ye take account that it is expedient for you that one man should die for the people, and that the whole nation perish not" (John 11:49, 50). This is the stimulus to reorganization of the opposition forces. From this day on they deliberate as to how they shall kill him. Caiaphas's suggestion is the turning point in Christ's path of suffering; but God acts in this human act too. John makes this explicit by way of a two-verse parenthesis (John 11:51, 52). Caiaphas does not speak merely out of his free thoughts as a man, but officially as high priest and prophet. In Caiaphas's extremist opposition to Jesus, God's revelation of the meaning of Christ's suffering and death becomes more clear. He unintentionally gives a definition of substitutionary suffering. This is not a matter of Caiaphas's cunning or guileful ingenuity, but a revelation of the profound congruity between God's and man's actions. Schilder remarks pointedly, "When Caiaphas formulated his answer thus, *one must die for all,* he ended the last sacrifice-hungry priestly discourse with the same conclusion, the same aphorism that was written before all time in the Book of God as the principle and ultimate rationale of the covenant of peace: *one for all, one for all.*"5

In all this we can observe the overruling power of God. He is the Holy One, the Incomparable who fulfills His purposes in the actions of the sinners of all generations. To place God and man in one line as comparable powers is to fail to understand this activity of God. He who listens to the preaching of Scripture knows that God works thus for good. God is no blind force or foreign "will" who plays His incomprehensible game to confound us. He who does these things is the God of salvation, the God of Abraham, Isaac, and Jacob. And who has withstood His will? God does not give the initiative for His work over to the Devil, though He allows sinners to serve Him. In the light of revelation, God's own initiative is disclosed in its invincibility, mysteriously disclosed even in the acts of His enemies.

Paul—to conclude this array of examples—observes with profound respect this activity of God in the transition of salvation from Israel to the Gentiles. Israel's unbelief bothers him to the extent that he prefers himself rejected if his rejection could save his brothers (Rom. 9:3), but he sees the work of God in Israel's unbelief: ". . . by their fall salvation is come unto the Gentiles, to provoke them to jealousy. Now if their fall is the riches of the world, and their loss the riches of the Gentiles; how much more their fulness?" (Rom. 11:11, 12).

Every word of Paul's interpretation is teleologically directed. "For if the casting away of them is the reconciling of the world, what shall the receiving of them be, but life from the dead?" (Rom. 11:15). In this way—through Israel's fall and unbelief—the original Divine plan is executed, and the purpose is achieved: the redemption of the world. This is the way of God, which Paul in another place summarizes by saying: God was in Christ reconciling the world unto Himself. Thus the words about the fruitful significance of Israel's fall can be recorded without minimizing its seriousness. And when Paul ends his discussion with: "O the depth of the riches . . ." he is not moved by an inscrutable, arbitrary force that puts the finger over one's lips. It is the fullness of God's love and wisdom that inspires Paul to exultation.

It is said that there are accents in Paul which the Church has hesitated to assume. Where the Church has thus hesitated she has impoverished herself and blurred her outlook on God's activity. Hesitation where Paul was bold has caused the Church often to make only a problem of God's rule and man's responsibility. She thus undermines either the providence of God or human responsibility. They do not exist together in the Scriptures as something problematic. They both reveal the greatness of Divine activity, in that it does not exclude human activity and responsibility but embraces them and in them manifests God on the way to the accomplishment of His purposes.

God's purpose, while involving *all* His activity, is peculiarly coupled with the mystery of reconciliation, from the standpoint of which faith finds her rest in God's universal rule. How could anyone oppose *this* purpose and this ruling power? He who waits on Him learns to know His loveliness, though it be in the tempest through which His course sometimes leads us.

This God of grace and judgment is, in the revelation of His power, disclosed to faith as the Merciful and Trustworthy. He is the shepherd of His people: "He will feed his flock like a shepherd, he will gather the lambs in his arm, and carry them in his bosom, and will gently lead those that have their young" (Isa. 40:11). Israel's way is not hidden from Him (Isa. 40:27). He gives strength to the tired. The richness and abundance of His mercy sustains His people on their way into the future (Isa. 63:7). He takes them up and carries them as in the days of old (Isa. 63:9).

In His sovereign rule God brings in His Kingdom and prepares the coming of the Messiah for the redemption of the world. God comes into history; His coming is foretold in the earliest moments of salvation's history as the blessing which is to come for all the generations of the earth (Gen. 12; 26:4; 28:14). God Himself shall bring in the future, and He is Himself surety for the fulfillment of His promises. "The sceptre shall not depart from Judah, Nor the ruler's staff from between his feet until Shiloh come . . ." (Gen. 49:10). The heathen Balaam calls out: "A sceptre shall rise out of Israel" (Num. 24:17). And though at that point in the history of revelation the Messiah was not completely and clearly delineated by this scepter it is in the light of further revelation to be understood only as messianic. The revelation of God's messianic activity is given only in gradual augmentation. It is never impeded by Israel's sin. Contrariwise, their sin often occasions a new step in the revelation. It receives in David its typological epitome. After that, the coming of the messianic King is inseparably bound to the house of David. The prophet says this in plain language to David himself: "When thy days are fulfilled, and thou shalt sleep with thy fathers, I will set up thy seed after thee, that shall proceed out of thy bowels, and I will establish his kingdom. He shall build a house for my name, and I will establish the throne of his kingdom for ever" (II Sam. 7:12-13). This, in contrast to the kingship of Saul: "but my lovingkindness shall not depart from him, as I took it from Saul, whom I put away before thee. And thy house and thy kingdom shall be made sure for ever before thee: thy throne shall be established for ever" (II Sam. 7:15, 16).

David speaks in his dying words about his certainty regarding the future: "There shall be one that ruleth over men righteously, That ruleth in the fear of God" (II Sam. 23:3).

This special course of the history of revelation and of God's salvation in the world does not abridge the Divine sovereignty over all things and all peoples. On the contrary, the whole world lies within the sphere of God's purposeful activity and, in her universal development, stands beneath His scepter. We do see, nevertheless, the concentration of His redemptive activity in His particular line of sacred revelation—in Israel and, more particularly, in David. We hear that God shall raise up for David a righteous scion, who shall reign as king, caring for justice and righteousness in the land, and who shall be called the Lord our Righteousness (Jer. 23:5). This King from the house of David shall, through redemption, bring His people into service for God (Jer. 30:9), so that "David shall never want a man to sit upon the throne of the house of Israel" (Jer. 33:17). And, just as God's covenant of the seasons will not be forgotten, so God's covenant with David His servant will never be broken. As numerous as are the stars of the night, as countless as the sands of the sea, so many shall be the seed of David (Jer. 33:21, 22). God shall never reject the seed of Jacob and David, for He will cause their captivity to return and have mercy on them (Jer. 33:26). David's house, though fallen, shall always rise again (Amos 9:11).

Isaiah, too, points to Him who shall wear the government upon His shoulders and to the magnitude of the government, to its peace which shall have no end, and to the throne of David which shall strengthen and confirm His kingdom through eternity. The zeal of the Lord of Hosts shall perform it (Isa. 9:5-7). The King shall come with justice and salvation (cf. Zech. 9:9), and, in the King, God's plan of salvation for the world will be fully revealed. His shall not be an imperious force but a unique ruling authority, singular for that this King shall be at once King and Priest. In Him peace shall prevail between the priesthood and the kingship. This is why salvation and forgiveness both shall come from His kingship. In Isaiah's prophecy we receive light on the question of how God shall rule over the world.

The Messianic expectation has too often been explained apart from the reality of God's promise. The eschatological outlook of Israel is often accounted for on the basis of the foreign influence of other religions, and the kingdom expectation out of purely human and earthly motivations. The source of Israel's eschatology is construed to be the disaster situation in which the people become involved and in which they satisfy their desire for relief by projecting their future glorious redemption. This type of construction stubbornly ignores many pre-exilic texts. Israel's eschatological anticipation does not arise out of a psychological need occasioned by national emergency.

It is found in prosperous times as well as in crises. It is a trusting response to the prophetic word regarding the coming King. God Himself shall in the course of history establish His eternal kingdom. Though the eschatological expectation becomes keenest in times of crisis, it is clear that it has its root, not in wish projections, but in the promise of God.

This is perhaps most apparent in the emphatic manner in which Scripture speaks about the remnant. The Bible revelation of God's ominous judgment on the sins of His people always has as its correlative the comforting word about the remnant. The idea of survivors has its origin in the saving activity of God. The light of the remnant promise shines in the darkness of the grimmest judgment. The remnant and the coming kingdom are eschatalogical correlatives. "And I will make that which was lame a remnant, and that which was cast far off a strong nation: and Jehovah will reign over them in mount Zion from henceforth even for ever" (Mic. 4:7). On the other side of judgment lies the mercy of God on behalf of the remnant. The possibility of this remnant lies outside Israel's sin. Her sin, viewed alone, gives sense only to totality of judgment. "Except Jehovah of hosts had left unto us a very small remnant, we should have been as Sodom, we should have been like unto Gomorrah" (Isa. 1:9). The remnant, plucked as a brand from the burning, stands as a monument of God's miraculous grace. God acts in judgment and grace—and through the grimness of judgment it is revealed that His deliverance is Divine deliverance, mighty and holy, giving mercy from generation to generation (Luke 1).

The prophecy of Daniel also adds illumination to the coming of the kingdom, God's definitive work with this world. Here the coming kingdom is preached to Israel in calamity as a reminder that God is still working. Daniel sees in his visions the glory and invincibility of God's rule, especially in relation to and in contrast to the kingdoms of this world. Nebuchadnezzar's dream, too, reveals the events of the future (Dan. 2:29). He sees a huge and brilliant image, and then a stone—hewn by no human hands—that hits and shatters the image (Dan. 2:34 ff.). Daniel, explaining the dream, points out first that the God of heaven has given Nebuchadnezzar his kingdom and made him ruler over men, but that another kingdom should come after Nebuchadnezzar's kingdom and those of others have been destroyed. Against this kingdom, all others are impotent. It is the kingdom of God, in which He, through the Messiah, shall reign forever in invincible might.

This is enough to indicate that the entire Old Testament is full of prophetic expectation of the kingdom of God. The gist is that God Himself shall establish His kingdom in justice and mercy.

There can exist no doubt as to whether the New Testament contains, in the revelation of the kingdom in Jesus Christ, the inceptive fulfillment of this prophecy and anticipation. Jesus is the King who, through redemption, puts His claim on all things. He is the Son of David (Matt. 22:42, et. al.), and is in this sense King entirely in His own right. (Cf. prophecy of Zechariah.) His kingdom is not of this world, which is to say, it does not arise from this world's power but is, nevertheless, an actual kingdom to be established on this earth. John the Baptist, as forerunner of Christ, proclaimed the approach of the kingdom. Christ's power comes out in the victory over the demons, as expressed by Christ Himself: "But if I by the Spirit of God cast out demons, then is the kingdom of God come unto you" (Matt. 12:28). This is a revelation of the authority of God. In Christ, the kingdom becomes actual in the present world of time and history.

The coming of the kingdom is sometimes called a "breakthrough," an invasion. This gives something of the picture. Powers are unthroned; "possessed" territories liberated. Christ was tempted in the wilderness to take possession of the kingdoms of this earth and thus forsake His true calling, and in His loyalty to His calling, the kingdom begins to reveal itself. The strong become weak before Him (Matt. 8:28-34). The decisive difference is in Christ's revelation as a fundamental reconstruction of the times, as the breakthrough of Divine salvation, as the overthrow of the rulers of this world. In the might revealed in Christ the disciples whom he called were conscripted, and given this commission: ". . . heal the sick that are therein, and say unto them, The kingdom of God is come nigh unto you" (Luke 10:9). And when the seventy return exuberant that the devils were subject to them, Christ said: "I beheld Satan fall as lightning from heaven" (Luke 10:18). Then they received power, that is to say, authority, to tread on snakes and scorpions, and over all the power of the enemy.

The entire New Testament witnesses irrefutably to the kingship of Christ, and from this witness we can learn something as to its nature. It is no rule of terror and brute power. Men derided Him in His suffering because of the strange nature of His kingdom. It remained in its true nature hidden to those who watched Him on His way to death. "Art thou a king then?" asked Pilate (John 18:37). In His affirmation, Jesus gave a hint to the nature of His kingship: "To this end have I been born, and to this end am I come into the world, that I should bear witness unto the truth" (John 18:37). But it remains a riddle to Pilate the sceptic. "What is truth?" he asks (John 18:38). For the Jews, too, His royal pretensions were an offense. They testify against Him that He claimed to be Christ, the King (Luke 23:2). And in His kingship He is jeered: "Hail, King of the Jews!" (Matt. 27:29). They can only sceptically inquire and shamefully mock as they measure His strange kingship according to earthly patterns and fail to see the revelation of royalty within His utter humiliation, as the prophecy of Zechariah is fulfilled in this King without troops, in His transition from suffering to glory. But he who can see the light of revelation falling upon this poverty, sympathetically understands the prayer of the murderer who turns to the middle cross and discovers there a King.

What does this kingship mean, this kingship which was "today" fulfilled in their ears (Luke 4:21)? What means this victory in the midst of death? What does this kingship mean as Christ rises from the dead and ascends to heaven, there to sit at the right hand of God? What means this kingdom of God's beloved Son in which we too have been made citizens (Col. 1:13)? Is it relevant to God's Providence? Or is its place, dogmatically, in the study of christology when we discuss His kingly office? Is there a sharp distinction between the kingship of Christ—His lordship and authority over all things (Matt. 28:18)—and the royal rule of God over all things? Or is there such a profound congruity between them that we must discuss the kingship of Christ in our reflection here upon the government of God?

This question sets us immediately in the midst of many discussions which now again occupy the center of theological interest. We refer to the discussions about *the*ocracy and *christ*ocracy, and about the kingdom of Christ and the kingdoms of this world. The relationship between Christ's kingdom and the kingdom of God is too important for us to avoid. The Heidelberg Catechism has a statement that has immediate relevance to these discussions. The article "sitting at the right hand of God" is explained in the 19th Lord's Day thus: "Because Christ ascended into heaven for this end, that he might there appear as Head of his Church, by whom the Father governs all things." The Catechism does not merely state generally that the Father rules all things. His ruling is indicated as a ruling through Christ. What must, then, be understood by the Father's ruling through Christ?

This question is currently raised in the discussion of the so-called christological basis of the state. We are not concerned here with a particular theory of the state, but we cannot avoid the question altogether since it touches on the nature of God's ruling. The Heidelberg Catechism, too, in saying that God rules all things through Christ, urges us to further reflection.

That the relation between God's government and the kingship of Christ is of such interest is easily understandable considering the manner in which the New Testament speaks of the power of Christ. Paul talks in Ephesians 1:22, 23 about the overwhelmingly great power of God, according to the working of the strength of His might which He has wrought in Christ to awaken Him from the dead and to set Him on His own right hand. Jesus is now set above all governments and powers and authorities. God has put all things under His feet and has given Him to His body, the Church, as Head of all that is. Christ, then, is given to His Church as Authority over all. Other passages, too, attract our attention in the same way. Christ's own words, for example: "All authority hath been given unto me in heaven and on earth" (Matt. 28:18). Again, "the Lamb shall overcome them, for he is Lord of lords, and King of kings" (Rev. 17:14). And *this* name is "written on His robe and on His thigh." We read in Psalm 2 that God has annointed the Messiah as King over Zion, and hence urges: "Be wise, O ye kings: Be instructed, ye judges of the earth. Serve Jehovah with fear, And rejoice with trembling. Kiss the son, lest he be angry, and ye perish in the way . . ." (Ps. 2:10-12). These references suggest that the kingdom of Christ rises out of His redemptive work. Has He not received His authority through His cross and resurrection? Has He not been promoted to the highest place; and has He not received a Name above all names? Has He not disarmed the governments and powers of the world, publicly triumphing over them? Reading these Scriptural passages one may perhaps wonder how it is possible that there could be such intense debate around them.

In answer we may say that the problem does not arise as to whether or not there is a kingdom of Christ; this is denied in the discussion by no one. The problem lies in the relationship between this, Christ's kingdom, and the kingdom of God, and also in the relationship of both to the governments of this world. We may phrase the question thus: Does earthly government stand in a special relationship to Christ through the fact of His resurrection and His receiving of power over all things? Or does human government exist through the grace of the triune God, quite apart from Christ's resurrection and ascension?

This is where a rather profound difference of opinion currently arises. Generally, it is in circles where Barth's theology has been most influential that the christological basis of the state has found most support. Barth posed the question when he wrote in 1938 that the current interest in the relation between the kingdom of Christ and the kingdom of God begins where the Reformation confessions leave off. The reformers confessed the validity and authority of governments as emphatically as they confessed the justification of the sinner, but the relation between the two never became too clear. Government, in the mind of the reformers, lay in the sphere of general Providence. It was established because of sin. Calvin, it is true, when discussing government brought in Psalm 2 and spoke about the "Christian state." But Barth asks, "Christian in what respect? What has Christ to do with government, we ask, and are left with the question essentially unanswered, as though a special rule of a general, to an extent anonymous, Providence has the last word here."[6] Our fathers reveal, according to Barth, an hiatus basic in the matter of the christological basis of state and government. Did they base political power *in* the power of Christ, or did they indicate another basis for it? And did they, Barth asks, perhaps speak of God, but not of the Father of Jesus Christ?

This is not a question in which the dialectical theologians have exclusive interest. The problem of whether governments rule as subject to God the Father or as subject to Christ as crowned by the Father has been subject to debate in nondialectical Reformed circles. We may best understand the modern discussions by first reviewing the contribution of Kuyper[7], who pioneered in the problem of christocracy or the problem of whether earthly governments rule by the grace of Christ rather than by the grace of God—a problem which he called "extremely difficult and complex." Kuyper was afraid that men would view the rule of Christ as a competitor to the rule of God. To avoid this he made a distinction between the essential rule and the temporary rule of grace (*regnum essentiale* and *regnum oeconomiam*). The essential rule is grounded in original creation, in the exercise of the sovereignty of God as Creator. This kingdom is permanent, and to it belong the governors of the world. They are immediate instruments through which God exercises His sovereignty on earth. The governments of the world, then, belong to what Kuyper calls the essential rule of God, the creation order. They do not belong to the temporary rule of grace. The rule of grace—also called the special rule—has only a mediating character, having as its purpose the reconstruction of the essential rule which has been temporarily disrupted by sin. This mediating kingdom shall some day disappear, leaving the essential rule forever remaining, after the fashion of I Cor. 15.

The point of contact between these two kingdoms, according to Kuyper, lies in the person of the Mediator, who is King in the rule of grace and, at the same time, second person of the Trinity. This personal connection between the two kingdoms is suggested in the Scriptures by the expression "sitting at the right hand of God." Kuyper sees a sort of duality between the essential and the special rules. He misses this duality in the Heidelberg Catechism which says, ambiguously, according to Kuyper, only that it is Christ "through whom the Father rules all things." There is, says Kuyper, a *special* relation between Christ and earthly governments, *besides* that relation which exists in virtue of Christ's being a member of the Trinity and thereby sharer in the essential rule of God over governments. This *special* relation is subservient to the essential, but it is nevertheless real in itself.

Governments rule by the grace of God and possess their origin, not in Jesus Christ the Mediator, but in the triune God. The Scriptures say that Christ has power over all things, but this would be unthinkable, Kuyper says, "if He were not at the same time, as Second Person of the Trinity, the Mediator of creation." Kuyper is opposed to construing the matter "as though the Father, having given all things over to His Son—let it be said with respect—retired into the background for the time, abdicating as God and becoming temporarily unemployed." For this reason he opposes the so-called christocracy and points to the confessions which, when dealing with Providence, do not discuss the rule of Christ, but "the work of God exclusively."

This protest against what Kuyper calls the abdication of God is quite justified. It is not as though, after Jesus' ascension "the Providential rule of God Triune is suspended temporarily and given over to the Mediator. . . ." The majesty of the Mediator is never shoved into the place belonging to the majesty of the Divine Being. Besides, recalls Kuyper, when Christ was questioned about God's Providence, He always pointed to the Father, not to Himself.

All this, though true, does not solve the problem; and Kuyper had no illusions that it did. He writes: "Still, we would not conceal the fact that with this we have not yet reached a clear insight into the relationship with which we are here concerned." In the rejection of the abdication idea, Kuyper creates the opportunity of giving the really quite unambiguous word of the Heidelberg Catechism in Lord's Day 19 its full say. For in the light of the Scriptures, there can be no exercise of power by Christ which is, though for an instant, abstracted from the government of God. The Scriptures, too, should be allowed to speak about the unique significance of the glorification of Christ. *In* the ruling of Christ we encounter "God *in* Christ." There is no dilemma here between Christ's and God's rule. It is not, as is sometimes said, that God's rule is something abstract, while Christ's kingship is historical. God rules *in* Christ. Though rejecting any sort of abdication theory which views God as retiring in the face of Christ's ascension to the throne, Kuyper was nevertheless profoundly impressed by the universality of Christ's kingly authority, and without reservation named Him as King over all things. Christ rules, but this does not mean that God has abdicated. In this connection, Kuyper points to the modification in the Divine government that took place with Christ's ascension: God's rule then receiving a mediating character through Christ's sitting at His right hand. In this way Kuyper intended to do justice to the historical aspect of God's ruling. A change occurred only in the *mode* of God's rule. After Christ ascended, the same activity that was formerly immediate became mediate through Him who sits on God's right hand.

At this point, Kuyper's view links up with the discussions of the present day, which, in great measure, are concerned with the kingship of Christ, and particularly with the christological basis of the state.

What is really meant by the christological foundation of the state? Brunner calls the idea of a derivation of the institutions of law and state from the rule of Christ fantastic and impossible. On the other hand, he fully recognizes that state and church both stand under the lordship of Christ.[8] Cullmann interprets Brunner's statement as allowing for a christological basis for the state. He then goes on to say that when the New Testament speaks of Christ's rule over all things, it means a rule that is distinct from His rule over the Church.[9]

According to this view, the universal kingship became effective with Christ's ascension, while its basis was secured in His death and resurrection. It had an historical beginning, then, and will have an historical end—with Christ's return. Christ's kingdom is "redemptive-historical." Angels and authorities, together with all other things, are now subject to Him, as to the King of kings and Lord of lords. He is Lord of all creation, and, thus, of the state. For this reason, says Cullmann, we may speak in the state's christological basis. But the question still remains as to the real import of this aspect of Christ's rule. For, in Cullmann's view, the kingdom of Christ is not only distinguished from the Church, but both are distinguished from the kingdom of God. The kingdom of God is future, while that of Christ is historically present.

The rule of God, then, seems separated from the rule of Christ. But certainly the Scriptural speech is never this absolute in its distinctions. It sometimes even combines the rules, for example, as the "kingdom of Christ and God" (Eph. 5:5). The kingdom of Jesus Christ is at the same time the kingdom of God.

We would be doing injustice to the New Testament by abstracting the authority of Christ from the government of God. An antithesis between theocracy and christocracy is the fruit only of speculative thinking. The New Testament sees the ascension as historically unique, but at the same time it shows us that *God* rules the world in Christ. This rule in Christ is a particular mode of the Divine government. Our inability to plummet God's method of ruling should not lead us to close our eyes to the irrefutable givens of Scripture; the mystery of the Divine rule *in* Christ is inseparable from the mystery of the Word become flesh and, like it, shall never be fathomed by us. This is why we may not lightly yield to the notion of a christological basis of the state, which can lead only to attenuation of the trinitarian activity of our God. We can, quite responsibly, say with the Belgic Confession (Art. 36) that God has established governments and that, after the ascension, the more specific relations between Christ, the second person of the Trinity, and governments come to the fore. Barth is incorrect when he says that a hiatus exists in the evangelical confession in regard to government. Nor does such a hiatus exist in Calvin, who speaks of the second Psalm, a Messianic Psalm, in this connection and still does not give the state a so-called christological basis. There is no polarity in his scriptural and historical thought, as there is in that of Barth.

He who consistently maintains the christological basis of human government faces the question of what the basis of the state was before Christ's death and resurrection. The answer, typified in Cullmann, is that even then it was "established in subjection to Jesus Christ." But then he weakens his argument of the historically unique significance of the ascension. And he, in turn, fails to do justice to the scriptural significance of Christ's being placed at God's right hand. We must not and cannot divorce *this* hand of God from the hand with which He rules the world and all things in it. The placing of all powers beneath Christ—the fruit of His suffering and death—limits neither the working of God nor His authority, while it does allow for the unique significance of the ascension in the progression of the one work of the triune God. The scriptures speak quite emphatically about this. Christ has received dominion over all things (Matt. 28:18) and a name above every name, that at His Name every knee should bow and every tongue confess that He is Lord, to the glory of God the Father (Phil. 2:10-11). This position of strength is revealed always in a universal and unbounded perspective.

These words must not be emasculated by saying that they mean only that nothing, neither governments nor "powers," can prevail against Christ and His kingdom. The Heidelberg Catechism in Lord's Day 19 speaks concisely of God's ruling through Christ, while the Belgic Confession in Article 36 says that God rules through governments. The discussion should, then, center about the *nature* of God's rule through Christ. It is here that we observe the interdependence of the so-called christological foundation of the state and a distinct view of the connection between government and angelic "powers." This is seen in Barth and Cullmann, among others, and, since it controls their concept of Christ's authority, we should discuss it a bit further.

The new exegesis of the "powers" of the New Testament[10] proposes that the New Testament reveals a double attitude toward the state. First, there is the positive attitude revealed in Romans 13:1-7. The question is asked how Paul, in view of the total situation, comes by this "remarkably positive statement" regarding the state. It must be remembered, we are told, that Paul sees a connection between government and angelic powers, so that when he speaks of government, the idea of angels always lurks in the background. This notion is derived from the fact that Paul uses the same names, *exousia* and *arche,* for both angelic powers and earthly governments. Paul, it is said, really has angelic powers in mind in Romans 13, and this is the explanation of his respect for the state. He sees something sacred in the angelic powers that stand behind government and he says that it is to them that we must subject ourselves. The angels, after all, are God's creatures, "God's extended arm." They have their origin in God and are His servants.

But this is only one aspect. We cannot limit ourselves to the positive attitude of Romans 13, Barth says, lest we transform the living dynamic of Biblical thought to dead staticism. There is, in the second place, also a marked aloofness, a distance, indeed a critical attitude, in the New Testament over against the state. We begin to grasp this second line of thought when we recall that angels can fall. They are, it is true, created in Christ and have Him as their head, but they can also, as angelic powers, become God's enemies. As fallen demons, they can possess governments. The government of Romans 13 can become the government of Revelation 13—the beast out of the abyss. Thus, because of the nature of these powers, their relationship to the state must be dialectical, and this is revealed in the dialectic of New Testament thought ordained of God—possibility of fall. In government we may be dealing with fallen angels. They are, through Christ's victory, rendered impotent in principle, but they still, nonetheless, exert their influence and must be withstood.

Barth formerly, in an extraordinary exegesis, interpreted Romans 13 negatively. In his commentary on Romans (date 1922) he explained this chapter as being a prohibition of all revolution, since revolution merely exchanges one form of existence for another and does not bring existence itself under judgment. Since then he has modified his interpretation to that which we have presented above. He says that when the New Testament Church thinks about the state she has before her eyes "the image of . . . active angelic powers." In this way he supposes to explain the "apparent opposition to the state that we find in the New Testament."

A relevant question is: concretely, how can we bring the connection between angelic powers and government into bearing on the kingdom of Christ?

According to Barth, Christ has in His resurrection triumphed over all powers. The state, which originally belonged to Christ, can be demonized, but even when it is under the sway of demons, it has not fully escaped from the rule of Christ. Every rebellion can end only in "the form of unwilling service to the kingdom of Christ." Emancipation or escape from this original arrangement is impossible during the time between Christ's resurrection and His return. The empirical state-power becomes the executive agent of the angelic powers. But the angelic powers must not be construed exclusively as evil. The Gnostics looked on them so and for that reason their great antagonist, Ireneaus, opposed the interpretation of *powers* in Scripture as being angelic powers. If angelic powers were evil powers and nothing else, Paul would not have called us to be in subjection to them. There is no such ultimate dualism in the New Testament. Having been subjected to Christ, these powers have lost their evil character, according to Barth, and now stand under His authority, though this holds only so long as they "remain under Him and do not seek emancipation from their status of servitude." Even now they have a certain limited freedom, and it is within this freedom that they can manifest a tendency toward self-emancipation. In this possibility of breaking away lies the possibility of the demonization of the state. Hence, Barth argues, the Church may not always view the state as under Divine rule. It is a question as to how, in Barth's view, the state can still elicit respect as a positive institution of God. The powers are placed in the service of the kingdom of Christ and are thus deserving of respect. But, on the other hand, it is admitted that they can from time to time escape from their servitude and reveal their demonic character. In its origin the state is not Divine; it receives its respected functions only since it is bound under the kingly authority of Christ. One can, then, hold to a christological founding of the state and still be kept from a truly positive respect for government— at least from such respect for government that we find in the Old Testament: "By me kings reign, And princes decree justice. By me princes rule, And nobles, even all the judges of the earth" (Prov. 8: 15, 16). Barth and the other dialectical theologians can see in such a verse only an "earmarking" for future subjection to Jesus Christ, who in the time of the Old Testament had not achieved His present royal position. Only after being bound do the demonic powers receive authority in Christ's kingdom.

It need not surprise us that this exegesis of Romans 13 has been attacked from many sides. It is clearly not in harmony with the positive statements of Scripture. What is the real meaning of *powers* in this chapter? Out of the approximately ninety times that *power* (*exousia*) appears in the Scripture, it refers in at least eighty of these to the power that someone actually possesses. In this, the constructive element of the angelic power theory becomes clear. The powers to whom "every soul" (Rom. 13:1) must be subject are obviously human governmental powers, which possess their authority as a result of their being instituted by God. We find this not only in Paul but also in Peter when he writes: "Be subject to every ordinance of man for the Lord's sake: whether to the king, as supreme; or unto governors, as sent by him for vengeance on evil-doers and for praise to them that do well" (I Peter 2:13, 14). There is a positive respect for government in this passage, in which authorities are concretely specified just as in vs. 17 of the same chapter, in which Peter exhorts us to honor the king (cf. also I Tim. 2:1 ff. and Titus 3:1).

That Peter calls them human institutions does not mean that they carry any less Divine authority. We must, in fact, subject ourselves to them for the Lord's sake, though they remain, nevertheless, purely human institutions, real and concrete powers on the human level; there, visible and demonstrable. The word human indicates the matrix in which the institution operates. It does not denote its origin. The fault of the Barthian exegesis is that it brings the angelic powers into an *essential* connection with government, and sees the grounds for our subjection to government not in its institution by God, but in the conquest of the evil angelic powers by Christ and their servitude in His rule. Actually, according to this concept, the demonized state is the only state, and the state accordingly merits precious little respect. Positive respect is directed to the overpowering by Christ's kingdom, but not to the state itself.

We certainly do not mean to deny that earthly government as a human institution cannot come into league with fallen angels. Scripture, indeed, does speak of this possibility and directs our attention therewith to the background of national life. Consider the human-angels of the Old Testament, of which we read, for example, in Daniel 10:13: "But the prince of the kingdom of Persia withstood me one and twenty days; but, lo, Michael, one of the chief princes, came to help me. . . ." This "prince" is generally construed to mean a spiritual power who stood antithetically opposed to Michael and, through him, to the people of God. There are evidently definite evil spirits who exercise influence on the activity of peoples. It is certain that these spiritual disruptive and corruptive influences also go out to earthly powers and governments. We recall also Isaiah 24:21, in this connection, where we read of Jehovah's judgment over "the host of the high ones on high, and the kings of the earth upon the earth." Over against these evil spirits and their influence stands Michael, who "standeth for the children of thy people" (Dan. 12:1). Thus, a close relationship between governments and demons is possible. Kuyper suggested this, too, when he wrote that the influence of fallen angels reaches out over all of life, and not least over governments.

The aims of this kingdom of darkness are the thwarting of God's purpose and the disruption of God's order on earth. God's preservation of life and order with an eye to His kingdom in Jesus Christ is certainly high on the fallen angels' list of targets. The longsuffering revealed in the disposition that God makes of earthly governments is seized as an opportunity to frustrate the use to which God would put government. These demonic powers still have time and power. Revelation 13 can stand along with Romans 13 in the same New Testament. This is not because there is an original and essential relation between demons and governments, but because government is sovereignly instituted by God, inherently analogous to the kingdom of God, and, because of this, an object of Satanic opposition. Satan's opposition to and seduction of government forms a new invasive element in governmental life as instituted by God. It involves a possibility of fall, if government forsakes her Divine calling to service or oversteps the limits of her authority. The new exegesis of angelic powers arises from an awareness of the dangers of the demonized state which tyrannizes life rather than serves it. But this exegesis cannot really stimulate resistance to the totalitarian state. It can only weaken the concept of the positive Divine institution of earthly rule and order. It fails to see where the dangers really lie. The dangers lie in the despising and violating of Divine sovereignty which expresses itself in governmental authority.

This suggests, in turn, that obedience to government also has its limits. These limits become evident whenever the Divine authority that rests on human shoulders is misused. (This danger exists not only for government, but also for other bearers of authority, such as parents. Parental authority can also be demonized. Parents can misunderstand their calling and forget that theirs is a given and responsible authority.) The government can throw off its responsibility and become a power without service, a tyranny denying its own boundaries, boundaries to which Paul so clearly points in Romans 13 (cf. vs. 4). This defiance is certainly inspired by demonic influence, but, on the human level, it in itself progresses to an exaggerated tension with and opposition to the economy of God.

This Divine economy, since Christ's ascension to the right hand of God, is subject to the power of Jesus Christ, the glorified Lord. Through Him, the Father rules all things. His ascension, then, is of decisive historical significance. Though the establishment of the state is not christological but trinitarian, the victory of Christ becomes a crisis for the state—and an intensification of the call to service. The kingdom of God has come with decision, and in this decision and the authority of Christ implied in it, all attempts by the "powers" to gain autonomy are revealed as senseless. Nothing can triumph over this kingdom; neither the presumptive powers of the earth, who refuse to acknowledge their limitations, nor the powers "of the air"—powers concentrated in one power, in the power that fell as lightning from heaven when the kingdom of heaven triumphantly approached (Luke 10:18). The decision still falls in government decisions for or against service to God.

This is not to say that only a Christian government is a valid government. When the cause of the Christian state is pleaded, it is not meant that only Christian government constitutes true government, nor that the Church should involve herself in government, but simply that, in the light of the Gospel, the state should be understood as servant, and that it should recognize and operate within its Divinely imposed limits. In the service of justice, which is continually menaced by human sin and by demons, the state makes the path of the kingdom of Christ through the world a path through an ordered world. The state is not to be despised as being of trifling and external significance in the rule of God. To despise the state is to despise the Noahic covenant, is to underestimate the cross which restores and reestablishes God's justice and law in the redemption of the world.

A shyness to accept this bond between Christ and government has often been prompted by a fear that that which ought to be kept distinct may be confused and that Christ's kingdom would devaluate the laws and punishments of the state. This fear is, indeed, historically understandable for men have not seldom, out of conviction of Divinely forgiven sin, protested against earthly judgment, punishment, and armed might. Men arguing the law of love have given themselves to chaos and lawlessness, passivity and nihilism. These excesses resulted from a misunderstanding of love, from the fallacious idea that only the love of God, and not His justice, could be associated with the kingdom of Christ. His kingdom, however, is rooted in the cross, and allows for no tension between love and justice. In the cross love and justice have been inseparably united (Rom. 3:25). This is why Christ's kingdom can extend over all of life, government included, and why, through Him, the Father can rule all things. There is a Divinely ordained place on earth, then, for government; it is meant to serve the kingdom of Christ in the specific function which it has received by Divine commission. Government takes up its service, its liturgy (Rom. 13:6: *leitourgia*) and in it becomes something comparable to the angels in their liturgical (Heb. 1:14: *leitourgika*) service.

The liturgy of government is—true enough—offered on this earth; it serves in an area of danger, danger of apostasy and demonization. The greater, then, is its responsibility now that the kingdom of Christ has been established and the One Name rules all things. If it is true that the term "liturgy" connotes something of ceremony for Paul, then it becomes even more evident that the government is not glorified and given "sacred" untouchableness, but that the respect owed to government derives from the service it is meant to perform and from the fact that "God through Christ is the recipient of its services."

It is clear that the laws and the service of government cannot operate in a dialectical or antinomian tension with the kingdom of Christ. However, these laws and this service stand in danger of sin and demons. The government cannot through apostasy become an independent power with independent significance, free from the royal lordship of Christ (Rom. 8:38-39), though, within this lordship, government, in apostasy, can severely distress life and, thus, the Church as well. However, even in apostasy, the powers are bound to serve the kingdom of Christ and will finally be stripped of their evil influence (I Cor. 15:24). The "prince of the powers of the air" still works "in the sons of disobedience" (Eph. 2:2) but every time he trespass his limits he only underscores the limitlessness of Christ's kingdom. Whenever the image of the state found in Revelation 13 becomes actualized, the believers shall know that this power is no worthy rival of the power of Christ but has already been defeated by Him. The reality of the evil powers avails nothing against Him. The perseverance of the saints is, nevertheless, still necessary (Rev. 13:10) —the saints, who keep the commands of God through faith in Jesus (Rev. 14:12). (It is noteworthy that the perseverance of the saints appears in Revelation 13—the chapter of the beast.)

Meanwhile, believers are called upon to pray for "kings and all that are in high place" (I Tim. 2:2). Paul indicates by his repetition of synonyms how important he considers this duty: "supplications, prayers, intercessions, thanksgivings." We are to pray and supplicate before the face of God for His blessing on earthly government in her service in the world "that we may lead a tranquil and quiet life in all godliness and gravity." We are to ask God that He, through government, will bless our lives and spread His justice through the world so that life may have opportunity to expand in service to Him. The course of the kingdom of God is not in our hands: He charts the course. The Heidelberg Catechism is relevant to this when it says: in prosperity, thankfulness and in adversity, patience. Faith in God's rule through Christ may be tried when we are faced by the powers of the world and when we hear many, who had laughed at the idea of real demons, again talking seriously about the demonization of life. Only the light of the Gospel can dispel this confusion and hold our eyes open for Christ's kingdom.

When the new idea of government and angelic-power relationship was first discussed, the Providence of God was also brought into consideration. It has been said, for example, that the Providence doctrine cannot be understood apart from the angelic powers or demons. Without accepting the new exegesis, we must agree that dogmatics runs the danger of considering the confession of God's ruling too abstractly. Faith in what the Scriptures say about angels and demons was attacked at its root long before the crisis of the Providence doctrine of this century. Biblical acceptance of the influence of angels and demons was considered as a concession to or conditioning by the unenlightenment of the times. In our informed era, we were told, such supernatural nonsense must be sifted out of the New Testament. The elimination of demonization played a role in the "genial providence" notion of the eighteenth century, and the theology of the nineteenth century also assumed that this part of the New Testament could be disregarded. Kuyper, in the nineteenth century, said that a rejection of evil spirits and the Devil ends with a denial of the existence of angels in any form. And we observe that, outside of theological circles, to the present day angels do not receive the recognition that they do in the New Testament. If they are not consciously denied, they are relegated to a vague sentimental recollection of their appearances in sacred history or to the hymn singers in the field of Ephratha on Christmas eve. In fact, the Church by and large today is probably more conscious of demons than of angels.

Modern theology, however, prompted by the tensions in and devilishness of the modern state, is again earnestly discussing angels. The danger of this sudden revival of interest in angelology is that the nature and function of angels shall be defined by the cultural phenomena of a certain time. This is certainly at present the case. As previously first demons and then angels were rejected, so now, via the demons, angels have returned to the attention of theology. The tension of the times has led to an unacceptable notion of the relationship of angels to government, but this should not hold us back from further reflection on God's ruling through Christ to Whom all angelic powers are subject. And since demonization is currently on the agenda of dogmatic study, it is not impossible that, precisely in this time, Scripture may be listened to more attentively than before as it speaks about the angels of God. The tension of the times can lead to new insights.

Currently the problem of demonization is posed in connection with the terror of the totalitarian state and with the dehumanization to which our century, in spite of its background of development, has been witness. This could lead us to a better appreciation of what the Scriptures teach us about angels, their service (Heb. 1:14), their worship (Isa. 6; Luke 2:14), and their joys (Luke 15:7, 10). The understanding of the service of angels must involve, in addition to seeing it as an example of the fulfillment of the will of God, an appreciation of their work under God's rule in Christ whose kingdom they are permitted to serve. Should not the teaching about the relation between the service of the angels and our salvation keep us from attenuating our thinking on this subject? And should not the scriptural teaching about angels have existential significance now that the problem of the state is unprecedentedly acute, and when study of demonology marks the demise of the last remnant of nineteenth century theology?

It may be that the offence of the words of Scripture is still too strong. It may be that subjective bias still prejudges the idea of angels. But it may also be that with demonology in the center of theological interest the "depopulated heaven" may be felt to be an impoverishment. Within the convulsed life of the peoples, threatened by the dangers always implicit in the service of the government, the Church must become concrete in praying for the salutary service of angels. Angels are not in the center of the stage where there is room only for the Lord Himself, but they do service in the wings; and this service is directly connected with the main performance—the coming of the kingdom. Our doctrine of angels must never become anything like Roman Catholic mariology. But neither must we ever think, as did the nineteenth century theologians, that no angels or demons stand between us and God.

He who sees the kingdom of Christ revealed, according to the

Scriptures, in the irresistibleness of His justice and love, may well be praying earnestly in the near future, not *to* the angels, but *for* their service. The angels *serve* in the kingdom that has come, comes, and is yet to come. There is no place here for speculation. The Church must be warned away from all abstract thought in her Providence doctrine. This may now mean that we realistically anticipate the service of the angels in the kingdom of Christ.

Notes

[1]W. Eichrodt, *Theologie des Alten Testaments*, II, 1933, p. 91.

[2]Kittel, *Theologische Wörterbuch zum N. T.*, Vol. II, 1940, p. 293.

[3]E. Stauffer, *Theologie des Neuen Testaments*, 1948, p. 186.

[4]Kittel, Theologische Wörterbuch zum N.T., IV, 1942, p. 711.

[5]K. Schilder, *Christus in Zign lijden*, 2nd ed., I, 1949, p. 60.

[6]Barth, *Rechtfertigung und Recht*, 1938, p. 5.

[7]For the discussion of Kuyper's views presented here, cf. *Dictaten Dogmatiek*, Locus V, pp. 186, 209 and *Gemeene Gratie*, III, pp. 124, 278-280.

[8]Cf. E. Brunner, *Gerechtigkeit*, 1943, p. 321.

[9]O. Cullmann, *Königsherrschaft Christi und Kirche in N.T.*, 1941, pp. 7, 8, 11 ff.

[10]Cf. Barth, *Rechtfertigung und Recht*, 1938; Cullmann, *Christus und die Zeit*, 1946, p. 169 ff.; also, W. Aalders, *Cultuur en Sacrament*, 1948, p. 63 f. For a criticism of this exegesis, see G. Kittle, *Christus and Imperator*, 1939, p. 48 f.

4050